THE LIFE AND TIMES OF
George McGovern

THE RISE OF A
PRAIRIE STATESMAN

Thomas J. Knock

PRINCETON UNIVERSITY PRESS
Princeton and Oxford

Copyright © 2016 by Princeton University Press

Published by Princeton University Press, 41 William Street, Princeton, New Jersey 08540

In the United Kingdom: Princeton University Press, 6 Oxford Street, Woodstock, Oxfordshire OX20 1TR

press.princeton.edu

Jacket photograph: George McGovern, 1956, courtesy of Dakota Wesleyan University Archive

Library of Congress Cataloging-in-Publication Data

The rise of a prairie statesman : the life and times of George McGovern / Thomas J. Knock.
pages cm.—(Politics and society in twentieth-century America)
Includes bibliographical references and index.
ISBN 978-0-691-14299-9 (hardcover : alk. paper) 1. McGovern, George S. (George Stanley), 1922–2012. 2. Legislators—United States—Biography. 3. Presidential candidates—United States—Biography. 4. United States. Congress. Senate—Biography. 5. United States—Politics and government—1945–1989. 6. United States—Politics and government—1989–I. Title.
E840.8.M34K58 2016
973.923092—dc23
[B]
2015019637

British Library Cataloging-in-Publication Data is available

This book has been composed in Palatino and Franklin Gothic

Printed on acid-free paper. ∞

Printed in the United States of America

10 9 8 7 6 5 4 3 2 1

For Betty Jane Mori and George D. Sellers

CONTENTS

PROLOGUE

On an evening during the twilight summer of his administration, President Bill Clinton for the last time presided over an annual White House event he had always found gratifying. Into the East Room he and First Lady Hillary Rodham Clinton welcomed some two hundred guests to recall the achievements of fourteen special Americans who were about to receive the nation's highest civilian honor, the Medal of Freedom. The fourteen included Daniel Patrick Moynihan, retiring senator from New York and presidential adviser since the Kennedy era; Mathilde Krim, pioneering AIDS activist and researcher; Jesse Jackson, the dynamic civil rights leader; John Kenneth Galbraith, one the twentieth century's most influential economists; Marian Wright Edelman, indefatigable champion of underprivileged children; General Wesley Clarke, lately commander of United Nations forces in the Kosovo conflict; and George McGovern.

"Day in and day out," Mrs. Clinton said, the individuals being celebrated "have widened our horizons and opened our minds and hearts." The president added that he and his wife had played a role in the selections: "Some of them reflect, now that we've been . . . involved in public life for nearly three decades, a lot of personal experiences that we have had, and we've had a lot of good times talking about who should be here today."[1] Clinton no doubt was thinking of the former Democratic standard bearer in whose presidential campaign he and the First Lady had worked twenty-eight years earlier. But memories of 1972 were not the real reason that the current ambassador to the UN Food and Agricultural Organization was among those being honored that night in August 2000. "War hero, Senator, diplomat, George McGovern embodies national service," the Medal of Freedom citation read. It also acknowledged the Distinguished Flying Cross that his brave exploits had earned him during World War II, his "stalwart voice for peace in Vietnam," and his unwavering "commitment to bring food to the hungry." Invoking the telling phrase, "the power of his example, the courage of his convictions," the commendation concluded: "George McGovern is one of the greatest humanitarians of our time, and the world will benefit from his legacy for generations to come."[2] In all respects, the words were fitting and unexaggerated. But, of course, no formal tribute, no matter how felicitous, could adequately convey the fullness or assess the legacy of a career of the historical significance of George McGovern's.

This is the first of a two-volume study of the life and times of George McGovern. My aim is to tell a story that, as yet, has gone untold—about a politician and statesman who never became president of the United States, but whose life and career nonetheless remain as compelling and enlightening as those of any Cold War president. Indeed, Bill Clinton ventured in October 2006, at the dedication of the George and Eleanor McGovern Library at Dakota Wesleyan University, in Mitchell, South Dakota: "In the storied history of American politics, I believe that no other presidential candidate ever had such enduring impact in defeat." Clinton was right on the mark for several reasons—for the candidate's principled stand against the Vietnam War and, more broadly, for his wide-ranging critique of Cold War foreign policy; and for the role he played in the course of postwar American liberalism and the history of the Democratic Party.[3]

Just after winning the presidential nomination, McGovern received a letter from Ray Allen Billington, one of his PhD mentors at Northwestern University and one of the great historians of the American frontier. "You are, to me, a new FDR, a new Adlai Stevenson," Billington wrote. "Men with such vision come along only once each generation, and find their places in history, as they deserve to."[4] His identification of his former student with Roosevelt and Stevenson is instructive, for McGovern was steeped in the progressive tradition that they personified and was an unusually courageous politician as well. Whereas his candidacy owed to his opposition to the Vietnam War, his position constituted an all-embracing rethinking of American internationalism—a critical treatise on the original notion of the "American Century" itself. Unlike any other Democratic presidential aspirant before or since, George

McGovern actually asked his fellow citizens to think critically about their country—in particular, about American military and economic interventionism in the Third World in the name of anticommunism and about the amassing of a nuclear arsenal of such size as to threaten human existence. Yet he was no less interested in domestic affairs than he was in foreign policy, and he always stressed the connections between the two. Thus McGovern's critique held implications for the political economy and perhaps also for the soul of the United States. While millions of Americans did not have enough to eat or a decent place to live, the Cold War, he argued, had squandered untold treasure that might have been far better spent on programs for education and social reform. The historic potentiality of the United States was indivisible; it could not fulfill its promise around the globe if it did not fulfill its promise at home.

Many factors of biography, naturally, shaped McGovern's outlook on the world: a spare boyhood in the prairie town of Mitchell during the Great Depression and his upbringing in his father's religious household; his participation in the parapolitical activity of high school and college debate; his incredible experiences flying thirty-five combat missions as a B-24 bomber pilot during World War II; his graduate studies in American history, at Northwestern, under the tutelage of two of the nation's great historians; his controversial involvement in the 1948 presidential campaign of Henry Wallace at the dawn of the Cold War and McCarthyism; and his astonishing success in bringing the Democratic Party of South Dakota back to life, notwithstanding the state's conservative Republicanism, and then winning election to Congress in 1956 and 1958.

McGovern's first endeavor in high-level foreign policy came as director of Food for Peace for President Kennedy. In this capacity, he traveled constantly for almost two years to underdeveloped countries, overseeing the allotment of millions of tons of surplus American food and fiber in order to engineer, among other projects, a vast expansion of the overseas school lunch program. By the end of his directorship, Food for Peace, with its emphasis on humanitarian goals, had become the most successful foreign aid program since the Marshall Plan. Thereon, the things that McGovern saw firsthand exerted a profound influence on his thinking about the role the United States could play in world affairs. Then, in 1962, he achieved a long-standing ambition when he won a seat in the US Senate. His first speech in that chamber, "Our Castro Fixation vs. the Alliance for Progress," signaled the critical perspective for which he would become famous. History might honor Fidel, the senator submitted audaciously, because his revolution at least had "forced every government of the hemisphere to take a new and more searching look at the crying needs of the great masses of human beings."[5]

In the face of the perils of the Cold War, McGovern believed that the United States must have a defense force second to none, yet he voiced serious concerns about runaway defense budgets and the dangers of the arms race that the administration seemed to have embarked upon. Even before Kennedy's assassination, McGovern began to worry about the country's deepening involvement in Vietnam. American resources were being used "to suppress the very liberties we went in to defend," he said in September 1963. "The trap we have fallen into there will haunt us in every corner of the globe." (Decades later Senator Bob Dole would remark, "I guess George knew something the rest of us didn't.") From 1965 onward, McGovern would stand out as one of the two or three most important leaders of the antiwar movement within the liberal establishment, which had conceived the war. By 1966–67, he was warning that, if the fighting in Southeast Asia did not soon abate, the "dreams of a Great Society and a peaceful world will turn to ashes." At that point, he could not have predicted the Tet Offensive in Vietnam and Lyndon Johnson's demise; the murders of Martin Luther King and his dear friend, Robert F. Kennedy; and certainly not the subsequent "Draft McGovern" movement that would thrust him into the vortex of the political upheaval of 1968—setting in motion his dramatic first bid for the leadership of his party and his emergence from the Chicago convention as a major force in American politics and one of the three most likely Democratic nominees in 1972.[6]

These, then, are but a few of the highlights that this first volume explores. It ends with the election of 1968, the turning point in the history of both the Vietnam War and contemporary American politics as well as in McGovern's career. (He was reelected to the Senate that year by a near-landslide.) Already his life had composed, as none other than Lyndon Johnson once allowed, "a dramatic and inspiring story of what America is," not to mention a compelling alternative understanding of the American Century.[7] In most respects he was then well along in establishing his historical legacy—a legacy that, perhaps to some, is still unclaimed. Nonetheless, it is there, in its intrinsic and tangible qualities alike, as we shall see herein.

THE RISE OF A PRAIRIE STATESMAN

1   YOURS, FOR FIXING UP THIS WORLD

Although their grandson would grow up to become a United States senator and run for president, Thomas Henry McGovern and Mary Love McGovern lived on the edge of poverty practically all their lives. In 1849, when he was five, Thomas and his parents had immigrated to America from Ireland, fleeing the Great Potato Famine that would force more than a million others to leave their homeland as well. The McGoverns were farm people. They made their way to Illinois and eventually settled in Knox County. Their small farm never prospered. In 1865, shortly after his father's death, Thomas enlisted in the Union Army and served as a bugler. Upon mustering out he resolved to quit farming and went to work in a slaughterhouse. The following year he met and married Mary Love, whose own family had emigrated from Scotland. Mary would bear six children within twelve years. Joseph, their first and the father of the future Democratic standard-bearer, was born in April 1868, during the time of president Andrew Johnson's impeachment trial.[1]

Meanwhile the McGoverns had moved to Pennsylvania and back again to Illinois so Thomas could take jobs mining coal, a trade that was hardly more healthful or profitable than the one he had left. Indeed, for most people who sold their labor in order to live, the decades between the Civil War and the turn of the century were arguably the worst of times in American history. Although the United States grew into the mightiest agricultural and industrial machine on earth during that era, chronic downturns and "panics" plagued the economy, climaxing in the country's first great depression, in 1893. Throughout the West and the South, farmers were in revolt over plummeting commodity prices and ruinous transportation costs. Drastic wage cuts and massive unemployment sparked hundreds of strikes and widespread violence. Moreover, apart from everything else, the United States was then far and away the most dangerous workplace in the world. In the final two decades of the nineteenth century, for the lack of safety regulations, 700,000 workers were killed in on-the-job accidents, while literally millions suffered serious injury. Thomas McGovern was among the latter. Mishaps in the mines laid him up with broken legs, cracked ribs, and shattered ankles, throwing him out of work for months at a time and making the family's lot all the more desperate.[2]

Even when he was able-bodied Thomas rarely made more than $500 a year—not nearly enough to feed, let alone clothe, a family of five, then seven, then eight. It was essential, therefore, that the eldest son be taken out of school to go to work. And so, Joseph McGovern, at the age of nine years, began his career as a "breaker boy." At dawn, Joseph often had to be carried to the mines, asleep in his father's arms. He would then trudge into the breaker with his fellows, tying on a bandana to cover his mouth and nose. Inside the breaker, a kind of processing plant, the coal rumbled down through long chutes; beside them sat the boys, their small, bare hands plucking out jagged pieces of rock and other debris mixed in with the coal. Here the twelve-hour day held for all, regardless of age. The scene was not uncommon. From the sweatshop to the factory, one in five of America's children thus contributed to the nation's industrial achievements.[3]

"Their faces are peculiarly aged in expression," a contemporary journalist once observed of the youngsters of Pittsburgh's steel mills, "and their eyes gleam with premature knowledge, which is the result of daily struggle not for life, but for existence."[4] The reporter might well have been describing Joe McGovern. But it was not the toil in the breaker alone that so transformed the boy's mien. When he was thirteen, his mother died, less than a year after giving birth to his youngest sibling, George, after whom he would name his own first son. Mary's death at the age of thirty-five threw the family into dire crisis. Thomas did not know what to do. He began to drink heavily, and Joe had to take on the additional responsibility for looking after his brothers and sisters. The three youngest—Tommy, Anna, and the baby—were sent to live in Des Moines with their aunt, Kate McGovern King. Tommy and Anna's stay was temporary. Little George would remain, although his father would never allow Mrs. King to adopt him formally.[5]

For Joe, having to give up his baby brother was a source of enduring sadness; he was determined to keep the rest of the family intact. To that end, within a couple of years, he discovered an unexpected way of breadwinning. Now and then on Sundays and after work in summer, Joe played sandlot baseball, the recreation of choice among late nineteenth-century working-class youth. Football, in contrast, was then the province of the wealthy eastern elite—those whose credo was "the survival of the fittest," and the more violent the competition, the better to demonstrate their superiority. The sons of immigrants, however, defied hardship and peril every day and felt no need to build "character" through athletic rites that sporadically proved fatal. For them, baseball's tamer form of mayhem was far more appealing. And Joe McGovern, his friends told him all the time, was really good at it. The constant physical exertions and dangers inside the breaker had nurtured a powerful body and a keen eye, and they enhanced his natural talent for the game. Almost miraculously, the sport lifted him out of the mines and into a paying job at second base on a minor league team in Des Moines, which eventually became a farm team for the St. Louis Cardinals.[6]

Throughout his late teens and early twenties, Joe traveled all over Iowa and the Middle West with his teammates and continued to send money home. Family oral history posits that he also became something of an archetypal hell-raiser, indulging in off-the-field enticements generally associated with itinerant, young bush leaguers. But whatever the extent of Joe's companionship with those other professionals—hard-drinking gamblers, fast women, and the like—his quest to break into the majors came to an end. Sometime in 1891 or 1892, he forswore the glory and temptations of the diamond to seek the grace of God (not entirely unlike his famous contemporary, Billy Sunday, who also had played professional baseball and raised lots of hell before heeding the call).[7]

Joe's religious conversion owed mainly to a young female acquaintance, Anna Faulds, of Pilot Rock, Iowa. The exact circumstances of their meeting remain unclear, but Anna apparently convinced her rough-hewn friend that he might lead a better life by following the compass of the Good Book. Before long they were married and, together, Joe and Anna aimed to propagate the word of one of the eighteenth century's leading religious lights, John Wesley. Their means of ascent lay eastward. In the fall of 1893, they enrolled at Houghton Wesleyan Methodist Seminary, in the village of Houghton, New York, nestled in the Genesee River valley south of Rochester.[8]

3

The founder of the institution, Willard J. Houghton, was a visionary lay preacher. In 1851 he had been "reclaimed" during a Methodist revival meeting at the local schoolhouse. That year, a 120-mile-long spur channel of the Erie Canal, running parallel along the unnavigable Genesee, reached Houghton Creek. Although the waterway to Rochester became the tiny hamlet's lifeline, it was attended by horse racing, saloons, and other "evils of this world," as Houghton called them. To counter such elements, he began to organize Sunday schools all up and down the valley. Then, one day in 1882, he was seized by the idea of building a seminary to train and send forth into the valley and beyond "young men and young ladies in whose minds are instilled the principles of sobriety and morality." In fulfilling his mission, the Reverend became famous throughout the region—as an inspirational speaker, as a fund raiser so scrupulous in his record keeping that he entered into the ledger donations as small as five cents, and as an indefatigable letter writer who signed his correspondence, "Yours, for fixing up this world."[9]

Everything about Houghton Seminary befitted Joe and Anna's motivations, not the least the Methodist precepts of living, especially as they pertained to the influences that once had caused the breaker-boy-turned-athlete to go astray. In the preceding century, the followers of John Wesley had resolved to govern their personal and religious lives by strict "rule and method" (hence the name, "methodist," a term of derision aimed at Wesley's original adherents at Oxford University). Over the decades, the list of forbidden social activities was extended to dancing, drinking, gambling, smoking, attending the theater (later, the movies), and (as in many respectable communities back in Iowa) the frequenting of pool halls. The McGoverns did not find any of these proscriptions unreasonable.

As for intellection, although Houghton was by today's standards more of a high school than a college in the early years, its ten faculty members offered a sound curriculum. Anna and Joe started off with the basics of "classical preparatory"—arithmetic, botany, grammar, history, and spelling—to make up for certain deficiencies in their education. Their religious studies included courses titled "Bible Training," "Discipline," "Evidences of Christianity," "Holiness," "Natural Theology," and "Plan of Salvation." The fee for the preparatory year was twelve dollars; for the commercial and business program, eighteen dollars; tuition for Bible classes was free to those who pledged to enter Christian service.[10]

The ultimate goal of most of the eighty or so students who enrolled in the seminary each year was to equip themselves for field preaching and other kinds of evangelistic endeavor. When Houghton was established, the concept of individual responsibility and repentance in seeking God's grace—with some assistance from circuit-riding preachers—had long since become commonplace. Near the end of 1895, Joseph was ordained a minister of the faith, and he and Anna were ready to carry on the Wesleyan tradition of helping plain-speaking, everyday folks open their hearts to Jesus. Like all aspiring pilgrims, the most important decision the couple now faced was where they should go to undertake their life's work. The majority of Willard Houghton's spiritual offspring tended to favor posts east of the Alleghenies. A few stalwarts, however, shipped out to distant provinces—to Africa, India, South America, or the Philippines.[11] The McGoverns fixed upon a destination across the inland ocean, one they well knew would present hardships only slightly less daunting than those they might have encountered overseas.

"Tell me the landscape in which you live," José Ortega y Gasset once observed, "and I will tell you who you are."[12] If Ortega had had in mind that vast expanse of plains and prairie bestriding the Missouri River valley that once was called Dakota Territory, then never was a philosopher's insight into the relationship between geography and human experience more applicable. If nothing else, there was the fact of the river, "a great vein running through the heart of the Dakotas," as a contemporary writer put it.[13] Although surveyors would carve the territory horizontally into two states in 1889, the more apt halving (according to inhabitants then and now) would have been roughly vertical, following the Missouri's southeasterly course as it meanders down from northern Montana. As John Steinbeck wrote in *Travels with Charlie*, "Here is where the map should fold. Here is the boundary between east and west." For on the river's near side lay "eastern landscape, eastern grass, with the look and smell of eastern America"; across the other, it was "pure west with brown grass and water scorings and small outcrops."[14] Indeed, East River, as it is known, is pretty much an extension of Iowa and Minnesota's tall-grass plains and prairie hills; they surround South Dakota's richest farmland—the Dakota Basin, 250 miles long and fifty to seventy-five miles wide and amply watered by not only the Missouri but also the James, "the longest unnavigable river in the world," according to a historical marker. West River embraces the northern reaches of the Great Plains, an area tedious in its flatness and infinite, treeless ranges of buffalo grass. Here, cattle grazing predominates. Excepting the Black Hills, semiarid West River receives barely sixteen inches of rain annually, whereas East River averages twenty-four. John Steinbeck may have exaggerated when he said, "The two sides of the river might well be a thousand miles apart," but, for most people, the differences determined a fundamental reality: Depending on which side of the river one lived, it was said, one either herded or plowed.[15]

Yet in the early days it was precious metal that drew the first wave of white migration—up to twenty thousand prospectors, with pan and pickax in their gear, who, in the Black Hills Gold Rush of 1875–77, braved the elements and the wrath of the Sioux whose domain they transgressed. Until then, agrarian settlers had yet to venture farther than forty miles beyond the Minnesota border. But the discovery of gold precipitated a series of events that changed everything—the final phase of the Plains Indian Wars, the reduction the buffalo herds, and the coming of railroads. From Chicago, Minneapolis, and St. Paul, three companies now began to construct their steel-ribbon highways far into the territory and set in motion another kind of rush. By 1885, 1,500 miles of track were enough, along with the self-binding reaper, to have helped the population surge to 248,000 (up from 81,000 just five years before) in the southern half of East River alone. Thus the Great Dakota Land Boom had begun. By 1890, an additional thousand miles of rails had been laid, and land entries, through the Homestead Act and purchases, totaled over twenty-four million acres, while the US Census put the population at 328,000 for the entire state (with 182,000 for North Dakota).[16]

A good portion of this influx emanated from the Old World—mainly Germany, Russia, and Scandinavia. These immigrants often left their homelands in groups, as distinct ethnic colonies; they would make a lasting impact on the social character of the counties they occupied. They were the last true pioneer generation, whose collective flight and struggles would be immortalized in the novels of O. E. Rolvaag and Willa Cather. Most of the newcomers, however, were like Joe and Anna McGovern—native born, and the majority of them from the surrounding states.[17] Nevertheless, a common experience bound all Dakota settlers together in their search for a new beginning: a life inexorably ruled by the conditions of the countryside and the dome above it.

There were, for example, practically no trees when they arrived to stake their claims. Hence—for lumber, windbreaks, and beautification alike—they became devoted arborists. During a single week in May 1885, a dealer in central East River sold 200,000 small trees for planting. Meanwhile, a tent or wagon sufficed for shelter until a family could rive strips of prairie to build a sod house, itself a temporary dwelling. After that, the main task was to break open the earth with plow and ox and put in wheat, East River's first big cash crop.

Their ordeal did not end there. Settlers of the northern plains and prairie had to contend with a disheartening variety of natural calamities, most of them relating to the region's extremes in climate, with temperatures varying as much as 140 degrees in the same year. In general, winter was more so the rancher's bane than the farmer's. Massive snows destroyed whole herds of cattle on the open range in the late nineteenth century. (They would do so in modern times as well. In January 1949, four days of intense snowfall kept hundreds of families isolated for weeks and killed thousands of cattle.) In "the hard winter" of 1880–81, accumulations exceeded eleven feet, blockading the eastern portion of South Dakota from the outside world from October to March. The spring thaw only compounded the disaster when unprecedented flooding carried away town after town perched along the banks of the Big Sioux and the Missouri. Five years later cattlemen again lost upwards of 90 percent of their stock in unrelenting subzero temperatures. The Blizzard State's most infamous weather disaster, however, occurred on January 12, 1888, and Joe and Anna McGovern heard the story over and over from survivors. It was called forlornly the "schoolchildren's storm." It struck without warning in the middle of the afternoon and, though most of the teachers and students rode it out in their rickety schoolhouses, too many children had tried to get home on foot and ended up freezing in the wind-driven snow. In all, more than five hundred Dakotans froze to death on that day.[18]

For the farmers, who would become the Reverend McGovern's main constituency, spring and summer visited yet the greatest scourges, and these often approached biblical proportions. Gigantic swarms of locusts, for instance, descended upon South Dakota, usually at harvest time, throughout the 1870s and continued to do so intermittently into the 1930s, until the introduction of pesticides. Overspreading the horizon in immense dark clouds that concealed the sun, millions of hoppers would cascade down upon the fields of wheat and corn. Sometimes they might feast for days, leaving behind but a fraction of an entire year's crop. But there were other reasons why Dakotans lived by the words, "Never turn your back on the sky." For hail, too, could blow in from out of nowhere and, like innumerable miniature wrecking balls, flatten miles of ripening grain within minutes. (On occasion the stones were not so small; in one hailstorm, in July 1892, they measured six inches in diameter and put out the eyes of sixteen horses.) Finally, as if the plagues of Egypt were not enough, there were prairie fires. Fed by drought, dry grass, and high winds, a blaze could turn into a terrifying conflagration, sweeping over the countryside and consuming everything in its path—barns and farmhouses along with crops and grasslands. The worst of them, in 1889, 1909, and 1947, covered enormous stretches, over 400 square miles (a quarter of a million acres) before burning out.[19]

If any people needed reassurance that God was on their side, then, it was surely these folks, and, in the wake of the land boom and statehood, missionaries flocked in to minister to them. A dozen denominations already had set up churches when, in the spring of 1896, Joe and Anna McGovern entrained westward from New York. After stop-offs in Iowa to visit family, they proceeded by horse-drawn wagon to their objective, Richland, an obscure settlement of some thirty souls in South Dakota's southeast corner. As they surveyed the emptiness of the landscape around them, Joe and Anna must have had thoughts akin to those of a Methodist minister who, in a later era, found himself unloading his belongings in Faith, South Dakota. "I can see where it got its name," he sighed. "You would have to have faith to settle here." And so, not far from a site where Lewis and Clark once encamped nine decades earlier, the young couple from Houghton Seminary erected their first house of worship.[20]

Richland Wesleyan Methodist Church was a modest, wooden-frame structure, two stories high and replete with a steeple that could be seen for a mile or so rising out of the prairie. To communities of so few people, so isolated and deprived of so many things, such a gathering place was an indispensable comfort. To them, missionaries like the McGoverns seemed to have alighted from Heaven. But Joe and Anna's lives were no less precarious, or less subject to random adversity meted out by the elements, than those who worked the land upon which they all depended. The relationship was reciprocal: the parson and his wife tended to the farmers' spiritual welfare while the farmers requited with offerings from their harvests, a welcome supplement to the meager stipend from the Methodist missionary fund.[21]

The couple did not remain at Richland for the long haul. Joseph became what in those days was called "a building minister." His assignment was literally to build churches and then move on to another such project after a while, and he was highly successful at it. His was not a flamboyant personality, but he possessed a certain kind of motivational charisma. Granite-like in his conviction in the work that he was about, he was able to get people to contribute money, material, and their labor; because of his own frugality and willingness to put his own broad back to the job of raising a church, his parishioners tended to redouble their exertions. The McGoverns would found several such ministries, none of them ever larger than fifteen to twenty families.[22]

Then, early in the new century, life improved somewhat. Joe and Anna were able to put down roots when they graduated to a choicer post far to the north, in Aberdeen, a metropolis by Middle Border standards and one large enough to boast of a public library and a visit by William Jennings Bryan during the campaign of 1896. For Joe, this assignment was fortuitous for another reason: it allayed the recurring sadness he still felt over the abandonment of Little George so many years ago. For by now George McGovern King Jr. (he had taken his aunt and uncle's name) had grown to manhood, married, and had three children. He had also established a flourishing lightning rod and X-ray machine company in Des Moines, with branches in Winnipeg and, auspiciously, Aberdeen. George's frequent business trips there rekindled the fraternal bond, and Joe took great pride in his brother's success. Occasionally George would bring his children along to see their uncle and hear a sermon. These reunions meant a lot to Joe, partly because Anna was unable to bear children, and he enjoyed involving George's in prayer meetings. George and Joe also managed to make their peace with their father, who had since remarried, sired seven more children before being widowed again, and now resided at a soldier's home in Milwaukee.[23] Joseph McGovern, it seemed, had finally achieved a measure of contentment.

It did not stay long. In March 1913, the old man expired. Then, in June, George, thirty-two years old, suddenly collapsed during a fishing trip and slipped into a diabetic coma. He died within the week. Losing his brother twice—this time to premature death—was something Joe had never counted on, and he did not accept it easily. Yet an even greater blow was near at hand. In 1916, Anna was diagnosed with cancer and died the following winter. She was the woman who had turned his life around and who, for a quarter of a century, had withstood all the trials of a preacher's wife on the Plains and lived by Willard J. Houghton's injunction about "fixing up this world." What would have happened to him, Joe wondered many times, what sort of blighted life might he have led if he had never met her? Now, at the age of forty-nine, Joseph McGovern suddenly found himself alone, widowed, and childless, in Aberdeen, South Dakota. For months afterward, he often could be seen kneeling in prayer at Anna's gravesite in the churchyard. No one could understand better than he the meaning of the passage from the Bible he was often obliged to quote to console others, "The Lord giveth and the Lord taketh away."

2   A BOY NEVER GETS OVER HIS BOYHOOD

But the Lord did giveth again. One Sunday, a year or so after Anna's death, the Reverend McGovern noticed a woman sitting in a forward pew of Aberdeen Wesleyan Methodist as he delivered his sermon. Frances McLean had recently arrived from Calgary, Canada, to visit her sister, who had herself made the thousand-mile journey to Aberdeen to keep house for their two bachelor uncles. A statuesque figure peaked with flowing auburn hair, Frances was beautiful, and Joseph was immediately drawn to her. Twenty-seven and single, she had already decided to stay on and help look after her uncles. The next Sunday she returned to church and made the pastor's acquaintance. Presently she joined the choir as a soloist. Before long Joseph made opportunities to see her outside of church, and parishioners noticed he was emerging from his bereavement. The courtship was mainly the object of cheerful tidings. They were married in 1918.

Frances and Joseph had four children. Olive, their first, was born in Aberdeen. During Frances's second pregnancy, they were reassigned to the Methodist parsonage in Avon (population 600), not far from Richland; there, on July 19, 1922, a son was born. In honor of Joseph's brother, the infant was christened George Stanley McGovern. Two-and-a-half years later Frances gave birth to a girl, Mildred, and, in another two years, to a boy, Lawrence. Three years later the family relocated to Mitchell, a community in the southeastern quadrant, seventy miles west of Sioux Falls and destined to become the family's permanent home.[1]

Although much of it remained constant, the pattern of Joseph McGovern's life had taken a radical turn for a man advancing past middle age. Frances was twenty-two years his junior, and he was almost sixty by the time all the children were born. A difference in age of this sort is not necessarily a decisive factor in spousal and parental relationships, but it was in their case. When he remarried, Joseph had already lived virtually a lifetime marked by seemingly unrelieved adversity. And there was the correlative depressive impact of his environment—of years of isolation in remote frontier settlements, of interminable winters, hard times, and heartbreak—which one authority on South Dakota has referred to as "the numbing effects thereof on the primitive prairie psychology." All of these circumstances had made of Joseph McGovern a man the camera rarely caught smiling. As he set about to build his last and most substantial church and to provide for his brood, he was tired out. To his children, he was as much grandfather as father, and hardly the kind who played on the floor with them. He was, rather, a disciplinarian, and he expected them to set the standard of behavior for others. Except in the case of Larry (the youngest, mischievous, and Joseph's favorite), punishments for breaches of conduct could be harsh and unjust. Once, when Larry took his brother's collection of Indian-head pennies to buy some candy, it was George his father chastised for not having kept the prized coins out of reach. In another incident, a joke that George made about a neighbor's apple pie earned him a severe whipping for which Joseph felt deep remorse. A certain formality would always characterize his relationship with his children.[2]

This much could be said of his relationship with Frances as well. Never did the kids hear their parents address each other by their first names; instead, it was "Mr. McGovern" and "Mrs. McGovern." Joseph looked upon her as a kind of mother-child who had to be taken care of, and he was master of the household and its superintendent. He made all the financial decisions, did the bill paying and the grocery shopping, and often prepared the meals. For her part, Frances was the devoted caretaker of the children. She made a fair amount of their clothes, taught them all to read before they reached school age, and saw to it that they learned to play the piano. Her children adored her. "I was always proud," McGovern once wrote, "to have my friends know that this elegant woman was my mother."[3]

As for the children, they divided up as pairs—Olive and George as one, Mildred and Larry as the other. All of them, except Larry, tended toward the quiet and shy side. As a little boy, George was downright bashful, a handicap he would not overcome until he was in his teens. Yet at every stage of his development, he evinced a maturity beyond his years, which siblings and playmates apparently discerned. He and Olive were best friends. Of the two, she was more outgoing, the more gifted pianist, and the slightly better student. Olive also possessed a strong-willed personality, which manifested in various family situations, and she attended to her younger brother's education almost like a third parent (as many big sisters are inclined to do). For George, she was a protector and an important early role model he readily looked up to. At the same time, he would become her guide and instructor, too. For instance, when they were nine or ten, he overheard Olive taunting another girl who was overweight and severely chided her for the unkindness. The reprimand forever impressed her. As he began to show other signs of character, she became his greatest patron and fiercest defender.[4]

George and Mildred were close also. The shyest of the four, Mildred was struck with her brother's concern for others and his passion for knowledge. His standing among peers was such that, as she explained, "if he thought something was right, the rest of us thought it was, too." Her regard for him knew no bounds. One day as the two of them were doing homework, their mother asked what they wanted to be when they grew up. Thirteen at the time, George said he "wanted to learn as much as he could about as many subjects as he could, and that he wanted to get into some work where he could help the largest number of people." Mildred recalled "thinking then that maybe someday he would be president."[5]

Olive would grow up to become a high school music teacher, while Mildred would become a highly skilled registered nurse. That both girls would go on to college and have careers outside the home was not the norm for women of their generation. Yet neither considered it extraordinary. In part owing to the obstacles he had faced in getting an education, Joseph McGovern was determined that his sons and daughters alike would attend college. "It was just one more step," according to Mildred. "We almost grew up thinking that was just something you did—just like cod liver oil at some stages of your life."[6]

For George, starting school was far worse than cod liver oil. Indeed, because he was so painfully shy, the first grade was a nightmare. Even though he was already a good reader, he refused to take part in oral reading exercises. All he wanted was "to go unnoticed and to remain silent." His teacher began to interpret his reticence and stammering as a lack of intelligence. By year's end she had doubts about promoting him. Frances occasionally visited his classroom and realized there was a problem. But she also knew that her little boy read well at home. Although she shrank from confrontation of any sort, she could not help pressing his case with the teacher, who agreed to promote him "on condition."

In the second grade George had a more sensitive instructor who persuaded him to read aloud for her after school. In the third grade, he encountered Grace Cooley. A dedicated traveler who enthralled students with stories of her summer journeys to foreign lands, she was the first person outside of home to have a real influence on his life. Miss Cooley detected the brightness in George and knew how to use positive reinforcement to draw him out. He, in turn, wanted to please her. Fortified by her praise for his love of books and budding writing skills, he began to develop self-confidence. Never again would he have serious problems in school. Indeed, thereafter his teachers seemed drawn to him and frequently singled him out for special attention—according to his daughter Susan, not only because he was among the smartest in the class, but because he was such a handsome boy as well.[7]

By the time he moved on to Mitchell's middle school, he had become a voracious reader. The town's Carnegie Library, a two-story Greco-Roman building crowned by a modest dome and constructed of tan and purple quartzite from Sioux Falls in 1909, fascinated George. The rotunda inside featured an octagonal balcony with ornamental wrought iron railings and fluted supporting columns and a distinctive staircase all lavishly made of honey-blond oak, as were the outsized window frames and reading tables. Here George first encountered the works of Zane Grey and Mark Twain as well as those of Willa Cather, Hamlin Garland, and O. E. Rolvaag, the three greatest chroniclers of the Middle Border. George was a fixture in the reading room, and he carried books home every week. Often he would read all through the night, until day broke through his bedroom curtains.[8]

Had they known about it, Frances and Joseph would have only mildly scolded their son for such zeal, for they were teachers at heart. But whereas both parents assisted in the children's academic pursuits, Joseph mainly saw to their religious education. Every morning before they packed off to school, for example, he led them in the reading of Scripture. "It only lasted five or ten minutes," Mildred remembered, "but of course it seemed like five or ten hours to us." Sundays were filled with formal worship and religious instruction. In all of this, the children came to appreciate at least one side to their father's disposition. Despite the sternness and the emphasis on the struggle between good and evil, he was a little more liberal than most conservative ministers. Seldom did he inveigh about Hell's fire to his parishioners, and he eschewed a literal interpretation of the Bible. His sermons leaned instead toward the dignified lecture on the meaning of character and faith and on the importance of service and Christian values in one's daily life. To one degree or another, all four of the children absorbed the lessons. George himself would never fully embrace the conservatism of Wesleyan Methodism. Its prohibitions—against activities like dancing and moviegoing in which his friends partook—made no sense to him. Yet he esteemed his father's philosophical approach to religion (and his restrained style), and a lot of the spiritual curriculum would stay with him. As a politician, he would quote readily from hundreds of favorite passages from Scripture when they were germane to a debate. And he would keep framed in his study the quotation from St. Mark that his father always kept framed in his: "For whosoever will save his life shall lose it; but whosoever shall lose his life for my sake and the gospel's, the same shall save it."[9]

In their home at the corner of Fifth and Sanborn, a few blocks from the Methodist church, the McGoverns' day-to-day life was more somber than most. Yet lightness, even merriment, gained entry. Olive and George showed talent for the piano, and Frances regularly led everyone in song. Joseph sang around the house, with or without accompaniment. For entertainment, the children played records, and they all listened to popular radio programs on WNAX Yankton. Happy Jack and His Old Timers and the young Dakota bandleader, Lawrence Welk, were favorites, whereas baseball broadcasts seemed to transport Joseph to another world. (Since he never encouraged the boys to go out for athletics, the Reverend's enthusiasm for the play-by-plays mystified the children.)[10]

The lot of the preacher's family yielded other forms of amusement. Every summer, for instance, the local Methodist community set aside routine and shuttled up to the Holiness Campgrounds located on the heights above the James River outside of town. For two weeks they stayed in tents on wooden platforms and welcomed diverse traveling evangelists and musicians and quartets. Frequently, the intensity of the revivals frightened some folks into stepping to the altar to be "saved," but the holy rolling just as often took on a vaudevillian temper. The well-treed environs of the campgrounds, not incidentally, also afforded the older girls and boys (including George) chances for romantic dalliances.

But George's most memorable experience at Holiness Camp, at the age of twelve, involved a startling revelation about his father. One day George and some friends were tossing a baseball when they noticed a field mouse crouching beside one of the tents several yards away. Just then, Joseph happened by and whispered, "Let me see that ball." Suddenly, as the boys looked on, the sixty-six-year-old assumed the stance of a seasoned athlete, did a wind-up, and let the ball fly, scoring a dead hit on the hapless rodent from ten yards. "How'd you do it, Dad?" George asked as his pals went running to spread word of the feat. Joseph knew the time for confession had come. Thus the son at last learned about the father's checkered history—that he once was but a step away from playing for the St. Louis Cardinals and probably only a step away from moral ruination. That was why—despite his love of the major league radio broadcasts, he explained—he had always discouraged his sons from getting caught up in sports. He did not want them to fall prey to the temptations that had polluted his own youth. Far better, he went on, to cultivate an appreciation for literature and music, to read, to study, to excel at academics or debate—although in a couple of years he would allow George to join the high school track team.[11]

The disclosure did not alter their relationship fundamentally, but it was an important little moment of truth. For Joseph, it was an opportunity to unburden himself, and to justify to George at least some of his behavior. (Perhaps he even savored his son's admiration for his proficiency; the boy could not help boasting to his friends, "My Dad used to be a professional baseball player!") As for George, he was sensitive enough to realize it was not easy for the man he so deeply respected to admit to weakness, let alone that he used to gamble, drink, and maybe even cavort with women unlike his mother. Indeed, he was far better able to accept the Reverend's flaws than the latter was. And so George discovered that his father was a more interesting person than he had ever given him credit for. Even so, because intimate moments like this were rare and Joseph demanded so much of his eldest son (though not of Larry), he and George would never be truly close.

Yet the future presidential candidate's early years were not unhappy. To be sure, he grew up in a troubled era and the family lived frugally.

Cash income from the church averaged about $100 a month, and they could not have made do without the bushels of potatoes and the occasional chicken that parishioners brought by, or without the money from the Reverend's sideline enterprise of buying and repairing broken-down houses to turn around at a profit. Groceries were bought on the basis of what was on sale, Larry's and Mildred's wardrobe consisted mainly of the clothing George and Olive had outgrown, and the furniture never changed through the years. Still the McGoverns never went hungry and they had electricity when two-thirds of the state's population did not; their two-story, whitewashed house was large enough so that George could have his own room. Far more important in the face of the worst depression in history, his mother and father provided him and his siblings with a sense of security and the example of their character. As McGovern once wrote, "I never doubted the essential integrity and sincerity of my parents—a priceless parental gift to a child."[12]

George was a comparatively happy boy owing to Mitchell, too. In this community of farmers, small factory workers, and independent merchants and business owners, folks appreciated what God had given them; notwithstanding the regional emphasis on individualism, they lived by the philosophy that one of McGovern's future campaign workers would expound in a famous book many decades later, "It takes a village." And for him this village was a wonderful place. Mitchell was a small, insular town, yet it was among South Dakota's major railheads and the site of a liberal arts college. In context, with a population exceeding 10,000, it was really a compact city of sufficient resources to give youngsters like George some idea of the outside world. For instance, it was big enough to support three movie theaters. These included the Paramount, an air-conditioned art deco palace with seating for nine hundred, and the smaller Roxy, boasting a ten-story spire capped by a beacon, whose owner sometimes put caged monkeys and a lion on display to attract patrons. Practically every feature that played New York City in time played Mitchell during Hollywood's "golden era." On Saturdays, when the typical farm family made the trip to town to buy groceries and shop at Penney's, all three theaters filled up noon to midnight. Movies were high on the list of Methodist prohibitions but they formed an integral part of George's introduction to life beyond the prairie, and he would become a devoted filmgoer in adulthood. His initiation occurred one afternoon when a friend persuaded him to spend ten cents to see the story of Aladdin's magic lamp. By the age of twelve he was hooked. Hardly a week passed that he did not sneak off to a matinee, as his siblings also did. If Joseph and Frances ever caught drift of it, they were discreet enough not to intrude into this corner of their children's secret world.[13]

Mitchellites not only could behold on the screen the likes of Clark Gable, Claudette Colbert, Gary Cooper, and Ingrid Berman, they also could meet celebrities in person, in the town's most exotic work of architecture, the Corn Palace. Conceived by real estate developers to promote an annual agricultural exposition and street festival, "The World's Only Corn Palace" occupies a block on Main Street. Since 1892, the entire structure's exterior has been covered with mosaics and large panels contrived of corncobs, halved laterally, and tufts of wheat. The rendering of cowboys and Indians on horseback and wagon trains—the scenes are changed every two years—requires up to 3,000 bushels of corn in ten different hues and forty tons of other grains. (Some locals call it "the world's largest birdfeeder.") The effect is all the more stunning for the building's Moorish turrets, minarets, and tapering domes, all of them painted in outlandish colors—"the sort of place that must be seen to be believed," as South Dakota historian Linda Hasselstrom has written. Over the years, it has functioned as both hippodrome and civic hall, hosting popular cultural icons from John Philip Sousa to Duke Ellington to Peter, Paul, and Mary. During the depression and World War II, young and old alike were comforted to know that for a few days almost every month they could sing along with Roy Rogers and Dale Evans, swing to Harry James and Betty Grable, or have their burdens dispelled by Jack Benny or the Three Stooges. The list of politicians who courted them at the Corn Palace included William Jennings Bryan, William Howard Taft, Franklin Roosevelt, Wendell Willkie, Adlai Stevenson, John F. Kennedy, Richard Nixon, and George McGovern himself.[14]

Along with such metropolitan allures, Mitchell offered up the surrounding prairie and rolling countryside, Firesteel Creek, Lake Mitchell, and a sizable tributary to the Missouri. In the summer, George earned fifteen to twenty-five cents an hour by mowing lawns around town, but he also indulged in the joys of the "Jim" River—the finest in swimming, fishing, and exploration, not to mention a strategically situated elm, near the stone water gate, for diving. Even more breathtaking was the cliff rising above the river near the Holiness Campgrounds; George exultantly scaled it over and over again, both for the challenge and the view of the channel below. He and his pals also built a huge tree house and dug a cave twelve feet deep in a vacant lot.[15]

Then there were the "rubber gun wars," a phenomenon possibly unique to Mitchell. These peculiar conflicts were fought by adolescents armed with a genus of sling-shot made of wood and handcrafted to resemble a small rifle. Its trigger was a clothespin, which clasped a rubber band, of sorts, some three-quarters of an inch wide and two feet long, cut from old inner tubes, and stretched to the end of the "gun barrel." The weapon could fire its projectile thirty feet and raise a bad welt on a person's chest or leg. Battles took place in "Hobo Jungle," as the stockyards were known; they could draw as many as fifty boys choosing sides based on what part of town they lived in. Some thought it odd that the preacher's son was an avid combatant in these skirmishes, but, for his competitiveness and prowess, George gained both notoriety and esteem.[16]

Woodrow Wilson once remarked, "A boy never gets over his boyhood, and can never change those subtle influences which have become a part of him." Like Wilson (a minister's son), McGovern's upbringing in a religious household was undoubtedly the central influence on his early development. The Great Depression ran a close second. It is an important fact that George McGovern experienced, at an impressionable age, the effects of that calamity—and in the Dakotas, where the agricultural economy, the climate, and the landscape made its repercussions all the more pronounced. Whereas the industrial output of the United States had fallen 50 percent and one out of four workers was unemployed by the end of Herbert Hoover's presidency, farm state economies had collapsed before the Depression had engulfed the rest of the country. Overproduction, due to the demand for foodstuffs stimulated by World War I and the quadrupling tractors during the postwar decade, had driven commodity prices to all-time lows. From 1919's high of $2.10 and $1.50 a bushel, the price of wheat and corn had slumped to half those amounts by 1929; in 1933 the two cash crops were fetching 39 cents and 33 cents. Across the nation, net farm income had dropped by two-thirds, while foreclosures, including 35,000 of South Dakota's 83,000 farms, had reached epidemic proportions as Franklin Roosevelt entered the White House. Seventy percent of the state's banks had failed, and 40 percent of its population was on relief.[17]

Then, in mid-decade, the economic cycle collided with Mother Nature and years of inadequate conservation practices. "I shall never forget the grasshopper invasions that stripped the fields clean," McGovern said years afterward, or "the anxious faces of farmers scanning the sky for rain that did not come." From Lubbock to Lincoln the topsoil turned to powder, and millions of tons were blown to the four corners of the Plains. To Bill Timmins, one of George's chums, it seemed that "all the dust from Texas came up to South Dakota." For the children of this region, the Depression was rendered into an overpowering spectacle, as frightening as any nightmare. Schools seldom closed in Mitchell on account of snow, but dust storms were another thing, as the masses of billowing particles appeared in the sky and the teacher told them to run home. The students did not tarry. They knew how easy it was to become lost in a dust storm that moved in at fifty miles an hour, turning midday darker than midnight and making the air nearly impossible to breathe. Once it passed, everyone would come out to see what had happened this time. Often crops were ruined, livestock lay suffocated, and the whole town had to be swept clean of inches and tons of fine dirt.[18]

Of course, youngsters more routinely suffered privations and witnessed tragedies wrought by forces other than Nature—and these sometimes were accompanied by disturbing discoveries. For example, at the age of ten, McGovern learned that grown men could cry. The incident occurred when he and his father called on Art Kendall, a member of the congregation and a hardworking farmer. Mr. Kendall was generally unflappable and something of a prankster. From time to time in the autumn, he and Reverend McGovern would take their sons pheasant hunting, a favorite regional pursuit done for both sport and sustenance. When George and his father drove up to the Kendall farm this time, their friend sat sobbing on the back porch steps. "Art, what is the matter?" Joseph asked. In his hand Kendall held a check for his entire year's production of hogs. The amount did not even cover the cost of shipping them to market. George was as shaken by the reality that a strong man wept as he was baffled by the circumstance. He knew that great numbers of Americans were out of work and that many went to bed hungry each night. Rarely did a week go by that his parents did not invite a penniless stranger into the house for supper. (Such acts of charity were the norm in Mitchell. "Mom never turned away a hobo," Bill Timmins recollected.) Yet Art Kendall's situation puzzled George. Whether harvests were meager or plentiful, farmers still struggled just to eke out an existence. It did not add up. The ravages of the Depression remained a constant fact of life; he would see many times over how farmers strained and sweated and then received literally nothing for all the effort. This encounter planted the first seeds of political consciousness.[19]

George's sensitivity to the things that went on around him was also manifest in his strivings as a student. By the time he entered Mitchell High he was captivated by American history. He read about his region's statesmen—Robert La Follette of Wisconsin, George Norris of Nebraska, and South Dakota's own Peter Norbeck—whom he grew to admire for their achievements on behalf of farmers and laborers. All three were US senators, Republicans, and, more significantly, political progressives.[20] That Norbeck was both a Republican and a progressive would not have struck George as remarkable. South Dakota was Republican at birth, which stood to reason. The GOP was, after all, the party of Lincoln, of "Free Soil," and of the Homestead Act. But early South Dakota politics were also tinged with a kind of radicalism, in part because statehood roughly coincided with the depression of 1893. Like the one of George's youth, its miseries had befallen farmers several years before. In this instance the agrarian response was much different. Plunging commodity prices in tandem with dear money based on gold, exorbitant transportation costs, and a general feeling of isolation from the mainstream fueled a national farmers' revolt, leading to the formation of the Populist Party in 1892—the first major challenge to the two-party system in modern times. Then, in 1896, Nebraska's William Jennings Bryan captured the Democratic presidential nomination and appropriated most of the agrarian platform. The Populists declared Bryan their standard-bearer, too, and he went on to carry most of the West, including South Dakota, which also elected a Populist governor and congressional delegation.[21]

Although his defeat at the hands of William McKinley hastened the demise of the Populist Party, the cause was not ill served. For the movement had helped to rejuvenate a dormant idea that it was democratic government's bounden duty always to take steps to promote the general welfare and thereby secure the blessings of liberty for all. This reform impulse began to overtake most of the farm states and, within a few years, segments of both major parties throughout the country. More and more Americans—in particular, well-educated middle-class groups in urban centers like Chicago and New York—now not only worried about the farmer's decline, they also feared dire consequences, possibly even revolution, if the giant corporations that coldly ruled the economy continued to go unchecked while the laboring classes lived on the verge of poverty, toiling under conditions that had barely improved since Joseph McGovern's days as a breaker boy.[22]

When Theodore Roosevelt became president in 1901, the Progressive movement had found its first great champion. The country's most electrifying politician, Roosevelt believed that the captains of industry ("the criminal rich," he often called them) did not know what was best for themselves or the country, and that their exercise of irresponsible power and their indifference to the plight of working people courted social upheaval. Like other progressives, he was convinced that, in order to avert disaster, government must take on a new and more assertive role and serve as the mediator between the public interest and the private. Woodrow Wilson came to the same conclusion. "Modern industrial organization has so distorted competition . . . as to enable the rich and strong to combine against the poor and weak," he had written. "In such circumstances, must not government lay aside all timid scruple and boldly make itself an agency of social reform as well as political control?" As if to declare, "the era of Big Government has begun," the Republican Roosevelt proceeded to bust up several flagrantly abusive "trusts," to steer the Meat Inspection and Pure Food and Drug Acts toward passage, and to intervene in serious labor disputes on the side of unions; with the Hepburn Act, he established the precedent for federal regulation of the railroads. This, then, was TR's "Square Deal," and American politics would never be the same.[23]

Meanwhile, in South Dakota, the progressive wing of the GOP had wrested control from the conservatives. Responding to their constituency, these prairie reformers outlawed monopolies within the state, set maximum rates the railroads could charge, doubled taxes on corporations, provided free textbooks in the public schools, and established a direct primary to counterbalance machine politics. South Dakota progressivism would come into full flower when Peter Norbeck was elected governor in 1916. Somewhat resembling Theodore Roosevelt physically, Norbeck lived by TR's political philosophy as well: "When the water gets too high, let a little of it over the dam," he would say when opponents accused him of advocating socialism. Accordingly, he made government the instrument for creating "works of public necessity." During two terms in Pierre, he pushed through pioneering legislation to establish a state-owned cement plant, grain elevators, hail insurance, rural credits, and workmen's compensation.[24]

In the 1920s, Norbeck's party turned onto a more conservative path upon the advent of Harding and Coolidge. And so, for the first time, South Dakotans chose a Democrat for governor, reelected him, and then sent him to the US Senate. For a decade, the party of Bryan, Wilson, and now Franklin Roosevelt managed either to dominate or to maintain a balance of power against the Republicans. As for Norbeck, voters split their tickets and rewarded him with a seat in the US Senate in 1920 and twice again thereafter. For sixteen years, he kept the progressive faith, rising to national prominence for his investigations of the stock market and the banking industry, until cancer of the esophagus claimed his life in 1936. The passing of "undoubtedly the most liberal Governor and Senator" the state had ever produced signaled the end of one era and the start of another. Commencing with the midterm elections of 1938, with its progressive elements having all but expired, South Dakota Republicanism would thrive in antagonism toward the policies and legacy of Franklin Roosevelt.[25]

Until he decided to run for a third term in 1940, most South Dakotans seemed to admire FDR almost as much as they had done his distant cousin Theodore. They recognized that the New Deal and the Square Deal were grounded in closely related principles that had suffused their own civic culture for forty years. More crucially, despite their ingrained sense of fatalism and "rugged individualism," South Dakotans understood that, in the face of omnipresent human distress, the cost of doing nothing—of voting Republican—was too great. In 1932, while electing by a landslide a Democratic governor (and again in 1934), they gave Roosevelt a 65 percent margin of victory over Hoover and a somewhat less handsome one against Alf Landon in 1936.[26]

George McGovern did not know for sure if his mother and father were among that majority. Although Joseph and Frances were Republicans at least nominally, they tended to "vote for the man rather than the party," as others often did. Hence, George's own sense of partisanship was somewhat perfunctory. Occasionally he might hear someone scoff about the make-work nature of the Works Progress Administration. Yet like everyone else in Mitchell, he knew that for many families, those temporary jobs made all the difference in the world. (The WPA employed 67,000 South Dakotans when Roosevelt ran for reelection.) George also saw that the New Deal's farm programs, with roots in the Populist movement and designed by secretary of agriculture Henry Agard Wallace of Iowa, kept afloat other friends such as Art Kendall. In fact, no other state depended on federal assistance for its survival more than South Dakota did. Then, too, never at home did George hear criticism of the New Deal or its architect. His parents listened eagerly to FDR's fireside chats and regarded him as a good man and a strong leader. Joseph even took his eldest son to see the president when he came through Aberdeen on a campaign swing in 1936.[27] And when a prosperous parishioner might complain about Roosevelt and taxes, the Reverend would say, "Now, Brother Smith, the man is doing the best he knows how," or, "Sister Jones, if you're paying higher taxes, that means you're making a lot of money. Praise the Lord."[28] And so, if George considered himself a Republican, his convictions did not run in a conservative direction. His own life experiences, his parents' disposition, and the fact that the region's most significant politicians were steeped in the Populist-Progressive tradition—all of these influences mitigated against any other outcome.

George's political education proceeded apace at Mitchell High School. Among the student body of six hundred, he distinguished himself especially in history. (Throughout his four years he earned nothing but solid As in English, music, and social studies.) But it was in his sophomore year that he really found his métier. His discovery was yet another illustration of why "it takes a village." Of all the blessings Mitchell bestowed upon its own, none was more consequential than the public school system, endowed as it was with a large number of educators who felt his or her vocation in the blood and bone. There was, for example, Rose Hopfner, the school's librarian and finest English teacher. Miss Hopfner instilled in her students appreciation for literature and analytical writing. In her English composition class, students learned to expect a taskmistress who gave out weekly essay assignments and sent them up to the blackboard to diagram sentences. She was kind, but not above friendly needling, and she could be funny. "My," she might say to prod a student and make him laugh, "your *sister* was certainly smart." At the same time, she could offer lavish praise, as she frequently did with George.[29]

Miss Hopfner's fondness for the boy was mixed with concern. Whereas she admired his intelligence and work habits and the "sweetness" of his personality, she was also mindful of his shyness and worried that it could prevent him from reaching his fullest potential. One day she sat him down for a talk. She told him he possessed a talent for clear expression. But, she went on, it would do him good to break from routine and seek out a worthwhile extracurricular activity. He might want to discuss it with Bob Pearson, the history teacher who coached debate, she said. George would always remember the conversation; Rose Hopfner had given him the most important piece of advice he would ever receive.[30]

No teacher at Mitchell High was more venerated by students than Bob Pearson. A bachelor and a younger instructor, he was favored with charisma and a capacity to inspire. Sixty and seventy years later, students could call up anecdotes about how Mr. Pearson had changed their lives. His success rested on his impartial attentiveness to them as well as on his personal qualities. For, in addition to the academically stronger students, he also took under his wing those such as the "outlaws," as George's friend, Dean Tanner, referred to himself, Bill Timmins, and a few other boys on the basketball team. As a devout Episcopalian, Pearson was dedicated to both the spiritual and intellectual welfare of his charges. To get the basketball players into church, for example, he would drive around on Sunday mornings and roust them out of bed. After services, he would treat them all to hamburgers and rhubarb pie downtown at the Lawler Café—a generous dispensation, given his ninety-dollar-a-month teacher's salary, as the boys knew. "He made Christians out of all of us," Bill Timmins reckoned.[31]

Out of others Pearson made debaters. "No other person did more to strengthen my confidence and draw out my latent powers of expression," McGovern later said. "Competitive high school debate literally transformed my personality and my approach to life." He did not exaggerate. And it did not take long for everyone to see the change. George threw himself into the activity. He became an indefatigable researcher, practically living in the Carnegie Library. He learned how to organize his research and turn facts into the building blocks of effective argument. (Conversely, he would develop a knack for exposing weaknesses in his opponent's evidence and logic.) In advance of a tournament he and his main debate partner, Eddie Mizel, examined every facet of a prospective proposition and practiced their presentations over and over again, privately and for Coach Pearson, alternating back and forth between the affirmative and the negative. Thus he also learned how to speak, extemporaneously and from a prepared text. Whereas he had undeniable presence, his style resembled his father's—restrained. His standing as a debater would owe less to how he sounded than to what he said; the judges and the audiences were impressed by his unaffected eloquence and the persuasiveness of his arguments.

As mere sophomores, the team of McGovern and Mizel started bringing home trophies. By their senior year, they had established a formidable reputation throughout the eastern half of South Dakota, a state that took the forensic arts almost as seriously as Texas took football. "Back then," as Bill Timmins observed, "a debater was looked up to as well as a person on an athletic team." But if high school debate became the chief means of George's social ascent, more importantly it gave him his first taste of political discourse. As anyone who has ever competed knows, formal debate thrusts participants into the study of history and contemporary affairs simultaneously; it promotes unaccustomed ways of thinking about questions of public policy and often impels disputants to advocate positions they otherwise might have considered radical. For example, during the 1939–40 school year, George found himself arguing, in the affirmative, on a wide array of controversial propositions, including the desirability of government ownership of the railroads and of a permanent alliance between the United States and Great Britain. (He won in the first instance, but lost in the second.)[32] Then, too, there was the influence of Bob Pearson himself, who was George's American history teacher. Pearson believed in "old-fashioned Jeffersonian democracy" and leaned a bit right of center on many issues of the day. But he welcomed contrary views and encouraged students to sort things out for themselves. His passion for history was infectious, and he made it both dramatically engaging and intellectually stimulating. Moreover, from time to time, as his students listened spellbound, he would philosophize on the meaning of life and the rewards of service to others. Just being around Pearson was an exhilarating experience.

By the end of his sophomore year, George was inching toward a major crossroads. Joseph and Frances were not necessarily set on their son becoming a minister of the faith, the most obvious path. They wanted him to be prosperous, respected, and useful to society, but neither tried to sway him one way or the other. When Dakota Wesleyan University offered him a scholarship on the basis of his achievements in debate, it seemed destiny confirmed what he already knew. He would become a history teacher, like Mr. Pearson.[33]

The shy little boy whose first grade teacher had been reluctant to advance him to the second had traveled some distance by the time he graduated from Mitchell High School in the spring of 1940. Academically, he ranked third from the top of his class of 140. Throughout the regional commonwealth of high schools he was famous. And under his photograph the editors of the yearbook recorded, "For a debater, he's a nice kid." (Even as a bona fide member of the adolescent elite, he was still a fellow "that you just went up to and said, 'Hi,'" said Bill Timmins, because, as he put it, "George was George.") Everyone in the village who had had a hand in his upbringing was very proud of him—of the person he already was and the one that he might become—and none more so than Frances who had had to plead for his promotion to the second grade. As she sat with the hundreds of other parents, Graduation Day took on a poignancy that only two people there could appreciate fully. At the end of the ceremony George was called to the stage to receive Mitchell High's most coveted award. Around his neck the principal hung a band of ribbon suspending a bronze medal. The inscription read, "Most Representative Senior Boy." The audience applauded warmly, and for a few seconds mother and son exchanged glances as their thoughts ran back to the seventeen-year-old's uncertain beginnings.[34]

Notwithstanding certain privations of small-town life and coming of age during the Depression in a strictly managed religious household, George had, indeed, been fortunate to have had a stable home and a community and school in which he could flourish, not to mention the advantage of always knowing that college was in his future. Yet not long into his launching time, he suffered a traumatic jolt involving the girlfriend of a good pal of his that could have undone him. George had no sweetheart in his life despite dating throughout high school. He had naturally experienced some petting sessions but he had never gone beyond that; he knew of couples who had, however, including his friends Arthur and Laura, who had graduated the year before.

An unlucky incident was set in motion toward the end of George's first semester at college after Arthur took a job out of state and Laura stayed behind. One evening in January, she and George attended a social event together. Afterward they drove out to Lake Mitchell and there, in what he later described as "an unplanned, somewhat frenzied episode," they had sexual intercourse (his first time). It was over in a few moments; they regretted their impulsiveness almost instantly. They decided not to see each other socially again. Then, on a Sunday evening weeks later, Laura asked George to walk her home from church. When she told him she was pregnant he was seized by remorse and shame. What troubles had he caused Laura and the betrayed Arthur? What terrible scandal was in the offing for the Reverend McGovern's family?

For the next few days George endured paralyzing anxiety, the worse for not being able to unburden himself to his parents, though Laura and

Arthur confided in theirs. Many years later, in an unpublished portion of his memoir, he wrote, "Laura was calm and remarkably strong." She resolved within a week or so to go to live with her older sister and brother-in-law in Indiana and give birth there. Her long visit proved fortuitous; her sister and brother-in-law had never been able to conceive and they desperately wanted to adopt the baby, a girl, to which Laura consented. About a year later she and Arthur were married. On one thing Laura insisted: Neither she nor George should ever intrude into their daughter's life—so that she might grow up comparatively normally, believing her aunt and uncle were her parents—though in middle age decades later they would each meet her. The story was very sad in many ways, yet things *seemed* to work out all right for all concerned.

For George, the more immediate crisis passed within two or three months. Potential scandal would stay contained. Psychologically he found a way to put it behind him. The "circumstances that confronted two teenagers on that winter night," he rationalized not unreasonably, "could have happened to nearly everyone I have known." The impending intervention of World War II into everyone's existence and the arc of his pursuits thereafter helped him to gain perspective as well. Still, he would keep the incident to himself for thirty-five years. In the meantime, as the shock of it gradually receded, he resumed the life of an active college student. And before the school year was out he would fall quite seriously in love.[35]

3 A CLASPING OF HANDS MEANT EVERYTHING

Lyndon Johnson once commented about his boyhood in the Texas Hill Country, "Poverty was so common we didn't know it had a name." Johnson no doubt spoke for many young people across America who came of age between the world wars. For example, it never occurred to the daughters of Earl and Marion Stegeberg that their family was in fact poor. When they were little girls, Eleanor, Ila, and Phyllis longed to have mail-order dolls from the Sears catalog, but they had to content themselves with dressing milk bottles in bits of cloth and making paper dolls out of pictures cut from magazines. An ice cream cone was a luxury. Their home had no running water, electricity, or central heating. Coal was expensive and wood was scarce. The family often burned corncobs in the furnace during the bitter South Dakota winters, though a glass of water left on the nightstand could still freeze by morning. The frame house itself—an eight-room, two-story structure with broad front porches upstairs and down and surrounded by several sizable trees—was a source of pride. Their 320-acre spread, located eight miles from a hamlet called Woonsocket in the heart of the Dakota grain belt, yielded up the essentials—garden vegetables, apples from a small orchard, and several feed grains (most importantly, corn, for the hogs, the family's main source of cash income, along with egg money).[1]

From the time they were eight or nine, Eleanor and Ila, who were identical twins, had assigned chores—turning eggs in the hen house, feeding the hogs, milking the cows, cranking the cream separator. They were each responsible as well for procuring a bushel of fuel a day—either wood or cobs from the hogs' pen once the corn had been eaten off. The girls found the livestock they tended almost as appealing as Laddie, their collie, who met them every day on the country road at the halfway point on their mile-long walk home from school. Eleanor perceived personalities in all the animals, even in the cattle. Some of them, it seemed, were by nature amiable and others irritable. If most of them were endearingly stupid, a couple showed qualities of leadership. And there was a cow she was partial to—the peaked-looking one that brought up the rear when she fetched the small herd home from the west pasture at sundown. Sometimes, as she walked along, she would lean her head against the swaying side of this particular bovine, its hide at once coarse and silky to the touch and smelling of salt and clover. These were moments of contemplation, of sensing an elemental connection to the cycle of nature, and of spiritual appraisement of her surroundings. Eleanor liked to see far, and where she lived the horizon was far away. Toward the prairie and the sky she came to feel a reverence. The rustic life, despite its deprivations and drudgery, was not all toil. As she remembered in an evocative autobiography:

> Like most farm children we slid down haystacks and played hide-and-seek in the fragrant alfalfa and sweet clover fields. North of the barn was a grove of shade trees where Mother sometimes took us on picnics. . . . Every day, every hour, as she hugged us and talked to us and sang to us, . . . [s]he let us know by every action that it was her joy to care not only *for* us but *about* us, that we were as essential to her as she was to us.[2]

If the girls harbored any childhood fears, the worst of them were borne by Nature—the fear of losing cattle to disease, of getting caught out in the open during a dust storm, of losing a year's crop to hail, or of battling dreaded swarms of locusts (for which their father paid them a penny for every twenty-five they could catch). Otherwise, they felt protected during these tender years, because of their parents' demonstrative love for each of them as well as for each other.

Earl Stegeberg and Marion Payne's families had arrived in the Dakotas in the 1880s, from Norway and New England, respectively. Theirs was the story of Romeo and Juliet on the prairie, with neither the romantic nor the tragic qualities diminished for the setting. While they were still children they had fallen deeply in love. As with the Capulets and Montagues, both families disapproved. Earl grew into a handsome, if withdrawn, young man not particularly suited to the life to which he was bound on the two adjoining homestead sections the Stegebergs owned. After high school, he enrolled in an engineering program in Milwaukee. Meanwhile, the delicate, beautiful Marion went on to Normal School in Aberdeen to earn a teaching certificate. But they were miserable apart. Earl lasted only a few months in Milwaukee, then came back to the farm to work and wait for Marion to finish her degree. Upon her return, Marion taught in a one-room country schoolhouse outside of Woonsocket. No one was really surprised when, after a year, she gave it up to marry her adoring Earl and raise a family. Ila and Eleanor came first, in November 1921, then Phyllis seven years later. Childbirth had been difficult for Marion, and she suffered from recurring pain. When the twins were eleven, she at last submitted to surgery to relieve it. But something went wrong during the operation. Earl rushed home to fetch the children. Before they could return to the hospital, Marion's heart stopped beating. She was thirty-four. Her last words, spoken to her mother, were, "Take care of my boy and my babies."[3]

Until the day he died twenty years later, Earl continued to blame the doctors and himself for Marion's death. For months after the funeral he was unable to cope, and everyone worried about him to such an extent that they seemed to overlook the painful time the children were going through. For a year he went off to work at a New Deal conservation camp near Watertown while the girls took turns staying with the two sets of grandparents. Once he came home, the twins, now nearing their teens, shared responsibilities of housekeeping and mothering Phyllis and of trying to assuage their father's grief. To Eleanor, he seemed more than ever out of place on the farm as he worked the fields in silence.[4]

Meanwhile, Earl had found refuge in a new-sprung preoccupation with books. In seeking answers to some of life's mysteries, he turned himself into a comparatively learned man, as do many farmers without a formal education. He was drawn to philosophy and history. Hour after hour at the Carnegie Library in Woonsocket he would pore over the works of Hegel, Spinoza, and Swedenborg. And for just as many hours at home, he would read aloud to Eleanor and Ila or launch into discourses about those philosophers. Swedenborg, a pioneer in the study of psychology who claimed to have communicated with angelic spirits, mesmerized Earl partly because of his inability to let go of Marion. The treatises of Spinoza and Hegel—on political rationality, religion, and human motivation and the nature of the historical process—heightened his interest in politics and the Hobbesean notion of the social contract.

The latter were long-standing interests. In his monologues, Earl's message to his daughters was humanitarian and political. Especially in times such as theirs, people had a responsibility to look out not only for themselves but for the welfare of their fellow human beings, too. It was an idea not unfamiliar to the girls. They heard it expounded every Sunday after church, when the families on both sides gathered to talk about farm policy, Roosevelt's latest fireside chat, or unemployment—a custom that harkened back to the days of Marion's grandfather's campaign for the state senate as a Populist in 1896. During these sessions, Earl seemed like a different person to the girls—animated, impassioned, and often quite partisan. (Some years later, he would be elected Democratic county chairman.) Retrospectively, Eleanor thought it astonishing that her dad and all four grandparents espoused views as liberal as they did, given their conservative social milieu. But the Paynes and the Stegebergs were products of the Populist-Progressive tradition and unapologetic Democrats. By their mid-teens, Eleanor and Ila had come to understand why this was so and also to appreciate both FDR and the New Deal in their ongoing political education.[5]

In many ways—having lost their mother at an early age and having to contend with a perpetually grieving father—the Stegeberg twins were reared in unenviable circumstances. Then, too, the effects of the Depression were everywhere. Yet the girls never pitied themselves; instead, their situation made them strong and accepting of hardship. "We'd grown up with it and didn't even know it was hardship," Eleanor once remarked, not unlike LBJ. Neither did they find adolescence painful. Month by month, they were maturing into conspicuously attractive young women, graceful and petite like their mother—perhaps even more so than she had been, it was said. Their twinship was a constant comfort, and they would always be each other's best friend. They were also excellent students. Earl took them to the library on most Saturdays; they became insatiable readers and felt fortunate to be able to go on to high school after the eighth grade. Eleanor and Ila were always busy; their grandmother used to tell them they had "working hands." Each morning, they awakened at dawn to help Earl with the milking, fixed breakfast for the family and got little Phyllis ready for school, and then drove the eight miles to Woonsocket High. In addition, one or the other usually had a part-time job. Still they managed to attend basketball games and even to be chosen as cheerleaders. Their social status, however, rested as much on their academic achievements as on other attributes. The years of listening to their father and the Sunday political discussions made Eleanor and Ila naturals when it came to reasoned argumentation. And though only two other girls before them had entered upon the activity at Woonsocket High, it was almost a matter of course that they would go out for debate.[6]

In organized competition, the best practice recommends the pairing of teammates with contrasting personalities. But their coach could see that the twins bolstered each other's confidence, and he allowed them to be partners. "We must have been a sight," reminisced Eleanor, "two eager farm girls, not quite five feet tall, carbon copies of each other, echoing our arguments with double zeal." Occasionally, preparing for tournaments got in the way of obligations at home as they scoured the stacks of the libraries in Woonsocket and Mitchell, amassing card files by the shoebox. But Earl rarely complained. Eleanor and Ila became the stars of the varsity squad.[7]

At length, debate would alter Eleanor's life fundamentally. During their senior year, when Woonsocket met Mitchell High, she and Ila found themselves pitted against East River's most acclaimed polemicist, George McGovern, and his formidable partner for this match, Matt Smith. The proposition was controversial in 1940—"Resolved, that Great Britain and the United States should form a permanent alliance." Drawing the affirmative, McGovern and Smith staked out the "internationalist" position, making the case that such "a preponderance of power" offered the better chance of keeping the United States from being pulled into yet another European war. But Eleanor and Ila underscored the United States' historic aversion to "entangling alliances." They also held that the special relationship between the Americans and the British amounted to a potent union already and obviated the need for a binding treaty. The boys were stunned when the judges awarded their opponents the victory. "I can't believe it. I can't believe it," Matt Smith kept muttering to himself as they all shook hands. The girls were later annoyed to hear a rumor that the boys thought they had flirted with the judges. But Eleanor and George had nonetheless made a decidedly favorable first impression on each other, though months would go by before either would know it was mutual.[8]

Meanwhile, graduation approached and Eleanor was named class salutatorian. Her thoughts and Ila's were focused on where they might go to college, which would not be easy to manage in any case. Earl had been able to put aside a hundred dollars for each of them—a start, but barely enough for one semester's expenses. When a recruiter from Dakota Wesleyan University promised them secretarial jobs at twenty-five cents an hour, their decision was made. Ila would work for the university's business manager and Eleanor would assist the college dean, Dr. Matthew Smith Sr., the father of young Matt, who had had such a hard time accepting defeat at the hands of the Stegeberg twins. Although they would come home on weekends, the girls still felt guilty about leaving their father and eleven-year-old Phyllis. Earl was worried, too, though not only because their absence would radically alter his day-to-day life. He could see that they were excited about college, but, as he carried their suitcases into the dormitory and surveyed the campus, he could not help thinking about Marion and wondering whether he had done enough to prepare their daughters, now that the time had come for them to take flight.[9]

In the spring of 1883, a little band of Wesleyan pioneers acquired a twenty-acre tract of rising grassland on the southern end of Mitchell. Upon it, as the story goes, they "built a college of stone while living in houses of sod." Within just two years they had erected Merrill Hall—four stories sheathed in Sioux Falls quartzite and the school's sole building—which housed forty students, classrooms, and the president's quarters. It was the era of the "university movement" in America and, by the late nineteenth century, the Methodists were excelling the Baptists and Presbyterians as builders of denominational schools to accompany migrating settlers into the West.[10] Like many small prairie colleges, Dakota Wesleyan University had a rocky beginning. In 1888, a fire destroyed Merrill Hall and killed two students and injured a dozen others. Then came the depression of 1893. By then, just seven students had earned degrees in the regular college curriculum and thirty had completed the Normal School program (comparable to a high school degree, the new standard for teachers).

Somehow the institution survived. In the early 1900s, it began to prosper. Dakota Wesleyan now had several storied buildings of fine red granite and lanes of maturing trees. At its center stood College Hall, an impressive Victorian structure with an imposing bell tower rising eighty feet above the ground to call students to chapel. The curriculum was expanding, too; in response to the Progressive movement, courses in pragmatism and scientific method flourished alongside classical studies. By the 1920s, in addition to Latin, mathematics, and philosophy, the university emphasized history, modern languages, science, and sociology, and offered a major in music as well. Enrollment reached three hundred. Among the twenty-eight faculty members, seven held PhDs and eighteen held master's degrees. By the time McGovern and the Stegebergs arrived, over twenty thousand students had matriculated at Dakota Wesleyan.[11]

Still the school struggled. The Depression forced big cuts in the budget. Only 60 percent of the faculty could be guaranteed cash salaries, while the rest had to get by with a kind of scrip that local merchants agreed to honor. President Earl Roadman devised an emergency barter system for student fees. Three cows or 300 bushels of wheat could be traded for a year's tuition. The college was likewise awash in chickens, corn, and hogs. As Roadman said with pride, "we accepted everything that would make it possible for students to come to school."[12]

Hard times did not dampen the vibrancy of campus life. Except for the ban on dancing and fraternities and sororities, the Methodist administration continued to allow all manner of student activities. Choirs, drama clubs, intramural athletics, and literary societies abounded. As a wellspring for both social and religious enterprise, the YMCA chapter gave expression to Dakota Wesleyan's motto, "Sacrifice or Service," while budding journalists found their opportunity on the *Phreno Cosmian*, the college newspaper. Basketball (played at the Corn Palace) was the signature sport, and the "Blue and White" made it to eight national tournaments in ten years. There was a fair amount of horseplay, too. University annals tell of a group of freshmen boys who overpowered several sophomores, clipped their captives' hair down to the scalp, iodine-stained their foreheads, and left them tied to telephone poles along the highway. Then there was the cow that wound up in one of the literary societies' nicely furnished clubrooms. The means employed remain a mystery, but late one Friday night the cow was conducted up to the third floor of College Hall. Having been fed and watered in advance, it created a scene of unspeakable infamy by Monday morning. The perpetrators never identified themselves.[13]

Of all its institutional memories and accomplishments, none made the school prouder than its record in the forensic arts. For, as Violet Miller Goering, one of the university's chroniclers, has observed, "Mastery of the spoken word became the hallmark of the prairie college." At Dakota Wesleyan, that distinction could be traced back to the formation of McKinley and Bryan clubs in 1896. Debate and oratory were so much admired back then that students chartered trains to travel to their classmates' contests and cheer them on. Returning conquerors were welcomed back by a brass band and hundreds of Mitchellites and transported to campus in a carriage drawn by thirty undergraduate "footmen." During the Progressive Era and the 1920s, the university cemented its position as a powerhouse, proving, as Mrs. Goering put it, "that no one could outtalk the Methodists." In 1918, Francis Case, the future US senator, took the crown in a nationwide peace oratory contest; by 1924 Dakota Wesleyan could boast of thirty-nine first- or second-place awards in the forty-five state meets its teams had entered. Over the next two decades, despite average enrollments of only 450, it captured twenty-one state or regional championships and three national first-place titles in women's "old line."[14]

Dakota Wesleyan offered a perfect setting for the higher education of such as George McGovern and the Stegeberg twins. No student would add more luster to the university's reputation than Mitchell High's "Most Representative Senior Boy" of 1940. Almost from the moment he first walked the commons that autumn, George began his rise as the archetypal "Big Man on Campus." Few of his peers would have guessed that he had ever had a problem with shyness; as in high school, he continued to excel at all levels of collegiate forensic competition. In his freshman and sophomore years at Dakota Wesleyan, for instance, he placed first in a local speech contest. In the Red River Valley Tournament, a major conference attracting hundreds of participants from throughout the Middle West, he ranked among the top ten in the category of extemporaneous speaking; in a statewide event, he won first prize for a speech titled "My Brother's Keeper." The Intercollegiate Peace Association of the National Council of Churches selected the manuscript as one of the twelve best in the nation.[15]

George also held office in several clubs and honorary societies. He became a popular toastmaster, and the *Phreno Cosmian* dubbed him "the polished Mr. McGovern." He wrote a regular opinion column for that publication and once or twice acted on the stage as well. He also began to show signs of political ambition: He won election as president of his sophomore class and, in the next electoral cycle, as vice president of the student body. Annual campus-wide balloting conferred upon him as well the title, "Glamour Boy" of 1942. Yet the accolades that meant the most to him remained those he earned through debate. During the following winter, for instance, he undertook his second foray into the Red River Valley competition. Both George and Matt Smith returned from that tournament covered in glory. Against thirty-two teams, they copped first place in men's debate, while the judges also rated them, respectively, first and second in the category of outstanding individual speaker.[16]

On one level, there was nothing unique about his collegiate triumphs. Thousands of students across America engaged in the same kind of parapolitical activities—debate, journalism, student government —as their counterparts do today. Yet whereas their numbers are always relatively small, as a social class they exert a disproportionate influence in their immediate communities; for many, their activities constitute the formative experiences that often spur distinguished careers in public service, among other fields. And so, McGovern's college years were of far more than routine consequence. At Mitchell High School, competitive debate had not only given him confidence and social status; it had also sharpened his insights about the ends that government might serve, especially in times of economic depression. His endeavors at Dakota Wesleyan were rendered all the more significant, however, by the fact that grave apprehensions over foreign policy now were rapidly eclipsing concerns about the nation's economic woes.

On September 1, 1939, Adolf Hitler sent his armies into Poland. Two days later, Britain and France declared war on Germany. That evening, the McGovern family, like millions of others, gathered around the radio to hear Franklin Roosevelt's most momentous fireside chat. "This nation must remain a neutral nation," he averred, much as Woodrow Wilson had done in August 1914; unlike Wilson, the president also said, "I cannot ask that every American remain neutral in thought as well." Most of his listeners caught his meaning, but by no means were all citizens of the Great Plains and Middle West comforted by it. Since 1935 and 1936, after Italy invaded Ethiopia and the Spanish Civil War broke out, Congress had enacted a series of so-called neutrality laws as insulation against the deepening crisis. Supported by the entire South Dakota delegation, this legislation prohibited loans and the sale of munitions to any country at war—the aggressor and the victim alike. (The measures reflected revisionist thinking about how the nation had been pulled into World War I—by becoming an Allied supply base, provoking Germany into unrestricted submarine warfare.) Later generations would characterize World War II as "the good war," the necessary war. Even so, it was not until the conflict was well into its third year that Americans at last would resolve to take up arms against the threat of fascism. The outbreak of war—in particular, the fall of France in the spring of 1940—set in motion the most profound foreign policy debate in American history.

It was mainly Republicans who questioned whether Nazi Germany actually constituted a mortal danger to American security. To many of them, the graver menace lay in going to war "to save the British Empire" and in the impact that such action might have on democratic institutions at home—that, in the process of girding on the sword to vanquish fascism, America might itself become a fascist state. Merely by fortifying the defenses of the Western Hemisphere, these anti-interventionists, or "isolationists," argued, the United States could avoid "yet another European war" and preserve its institutions. Public opinion polls showed that a majority of Americans initially agreed. But Roosevelt maintained that the key to forestalling direct involvement was to extend to the Allies "all aid short of war." The United States must become "the great arsenal of democracy." His partisan critics interpreted such watchwords as part of a deliberate plan for intervention. Nonetheless, in 1940, after the fall of France, the president was able to persuade Congress to revise the neutrality laws so that Britain now could purchase arms and supplies on a "cash-and-carry" basis. At his behest, the Congress also instituted the first peacetime draft in American history and increased military appropriations dramatically. Then, in response to a plea from Winston Churchill, Roosevelt transferred fifty World War I–vintage destroyers to the British in exchange for several of their naval bases in the West Indies, just as he set out on his quest for a third term. Around these initiatives swirled the campaign of 1940, the great debate between the interventionists and the anti-interventionists.[17]

These were heady times to be in college, especially for young debaters and journalists like George McGovern whose activities conferred a certain expertise and capacity for reasoned opinions about foreign affairs and the country's future. Not until the Vietnam War would another generation of students feel such a personal stake in the events of their times. At Dakota Wesleyan, the *Phreno Cosmian* sustained what came to be known as the "isolationist" position, which reflected the views of the state's congressional delegation. For example, in December 1940, it resuscitated the Ludlow Amendment—a constitutional amendment voted down by Congress in 1938—which would require a national referendum before war could be declared. Linking that proposal to democracy, education, and the cause of peace, the student editors opined that, "when war must be declared by a plebiscite of all its citizens, there will be no war because not even the thickest of people would be naturally inclined to leave their home and family to kill." Three months later, in March 1941, Congress enacted Lend-Lease, an enormous $7 billion appropriation to manufacture vast amounts of war materiel to convoy to Hitler's beleaguered foes—the British and the French and, within the year, the Russians as well. A number of prominent Republicans, including Wendell Willkie, their nominee for president in 1940, endorsed this unneutral act. The "America First Committee," the nation's leading anti-interventionist organization, opposed the legislation, as did Charles Lindbergh and Senator Taft of Ohio. In May the *Phreno Cosmian* praised Colonel Lindbergh for his opposition—the aviator would soon fall from grace for making anti-Semitic remarks—because the editors feared it was only a matter of time before Lend-Lease would "throw the world's last great democracy totally and unconditionally into the maelstrom of foreign war."[18]

Although Dakota Wesleyan was a thousand miles from any ocean, the war was a constant in the extracurricular life of George McGovern because of national collegiate debate. The theme of his nationally ranked peace oratory, for instance, was the international community's bleak future as betokened by Mussolini's war of 1935 against defenseless Ethiopia and Hitler's destruction from the air of Coventry in 1940. Yet if he subscribed to the Republicans' slogan, "No Third Term," George did not have misgivings about Roosevelt's foreign policy. His research caused him to feel far more strongly about the affirmative side when debate resolutions endorsed the internationalist viewpoint and, as the national contention over the war reached high pitch, he came to see the America Firsters "as extremists, right wingers."[19]

One Sunday morning after church in the middle of his sophomore year, the family came home to listen to the New York Philharmonic on the radio. As George sat taking notes on the performance for a music course, a news flash about Pearl Harbor interrupted the broadcast. His father leaned over and turned up the volume. Literally overnight the devastation of the American base in Hawaii put an end to twenty-seven months of national debate. It also redirected national forensic competition. George and other debaters had their mettle tested on such topics as "The Spirit That Built America," "The Churchill-Roosevelt Meeting," "The U.S. Mobilizes for All Out War," and "What Does the Axis Really Want?" For a speech, "The Battle of the Far East," he won another blue ribbon, and the *Phreno Cosmian* invited him to write a regular column.[20]

Some of the installments of "As I See It" were the typical ruminations of a patriotic college student. In one, he declared, "We are fighting for freedom which has been bought with the blood of Americans for two centuries—from Valley Forge to Pearl Harbor." In another, he predicted that General Douglas MacArthur would be the next president of the United States. He described MacArthur as a "military genius" as well as "a shrewd politician" who "has proven himself to be a real red-blooded American leader."[21] Sometimes George ventured beyond simple flag waving. In his very first column, he reviewed the long domestic debate that had preceded the "day of infamy" in order to give the former opponents of intervention their due and thereby solemnize the prevailing of national resolution. America had been "torn by two factions—intervention and isolation," he observed, and Roosevelt had been "attacked daily from all parts of the United States." Then "in a single moment" the Japanese "removed . . . this dangerous spirit of disunity . . . which might have caused us to lose the war." Pearl Harbor constituted "the greatest moral victory which we Americans have yet won over an opposing country." The people were no longer divided; they were more unwavering than they otherwise might have been: "We stand united behind a capable, efficient government, 130 million strong."[22]

In the weeks following December 7, George's own experiences often determined what he wrote. For instance, it occurred to him that among those 130 million strong, "we can't all be soldiers, or sailors, or pilots." The realization dawned after he and nine of his classmates had decided, in January 1942, to enlist. None of them was sure which branch of the armed forces to join, but in two borrowed cars they drove to the recruitment centers in Omaha, Nebraska. Upon arrival they learned that the Army Air Corps was providing new recruits with hot lunches. Thus was indecision vanquished by roast beef dinners. All ten of the boys signed agreements to report for duty once the Air Corps had mustered sufficient numbers of flight instructors and training planes. They would be counted among the 64,530 South Dakotans who eventually went to war. In the meantime, they were to remain in school—for an entire year, as it turned out.[23] And so, George had begun to think about the variety of assignments Americans would need to take on in defending the nation: "Someone has to stay behind and make the equipment with which these men will fight . . . to render medical care . . . and even dig ditches and plow corn." As for his fellow college students, "we must not forget that we are fighting this war to preserve the life of democracy, the basis of which is educated leaders backed by intelligent voters. Let's resolve to get all the education we can before Uncle Sam calls us and then let us be willing to perform to the best of our ability the task to which we are called, whether it be piloting a dive bomber or teaching sixth graders how to be good Americans."[24]

Reports about Japanese advances in the Far East prompted his next piece. "We've got to beat these dictators at their own game or we're sunk," a friend had argued, assailing democracy as a form of government in times of national emergency. George had heard the argument before—that the ends justified the means. "More than once we have been caught flatfooted and unprepared by a ruthless dictator moving at a speed which cumbersome democracy can never hope to obtain," he admitted in his column. But history had "demonstrated that dictatorships fall almost as fast as they rise." The world's few democracies "have pushed steadily on, stubbornly resisting all attempts to check their growth," he continued, and their system "moves with a surety . . . [that] cannot easily be destroyed even in the face of overwhelming odds."[25]

The content of McGovern's commentaries were remarkably mature for a nineteen-year-old writing in 1941–42. Too much should not be read into them, but, along with other things, they reflected convictions that debate had instilled in him—particularly regarding education, the power of knowledge, and the notion that in a living democracy, means and ends were one and the same. In the first of the foregoing substantive commentaries his point was not that one side had been proven right and the other wrong. The point was that authentic debate was always legitimate and productive of good, and that the country would have been the weaker for its absence. It is also instructive that he did not question his opposition's loyalty. That tenet of civility informed the second example as well: Patriotism, he had reminded his draft-age readership, was not alone demonstrated by the willingness to take up arms. Each in his or her own way, including citizens who would never see combat (or those still in school), had an important contribution to make; as he was also wont to put it, "the mightiest warrior of democracy is the educated man or woman." Finally, in his essay about democrats and dictators, the thought about the indivisibility of means and ends was likewise grounded in the debater's elemental faith in American political institutions: In America, the full airing of the issues had to take place unimpeded no matter how grave the peril. Thus had McGovern already begun to compose a standard of principles that would guide him in time of both war and peace.[26]

———————

Even though military service impended from the middle of his sophomore year onward, George's days at Dakota Wesleyan were a kind of paradise. Despite his family's economic circumstances, advantages outweighed any obstacles he may have faced. Simply to be able to go to college placed him among the relatively privileged of his generation. (Just one out of ten of America's youth then was able to do so.) And Dakota Wesleyan's traditions created an ideal environment in which a young person of his inclinations could shine. Blessed with a keen mind and good looks, the class president/glamour boy was an academic and social success. In the classroom and on the debate circuit, that success tended to imbue him with a sense of purpose. Yet if Dakota Wesleyan was paradise, there was another reason why.

Neither George nor Eleanor Stegeberg had forgotten each other when their paths crossed again at the start of the winter term of their inaugural year of college and they found themselves together in an economics course. As the professor began to hand out a first-day current-events test of one hundred questions assembled by *Time* magazine, memories of their debate over American foreign policy came rushing back. The two warmed to the day's challenge and tied at ninety-eight, the highest score in the class. As they had done some months before, they also made strong mutual impressions. But just then he was entering the depths of his personal crisis.[27]

College was mainly a happy time for Eleanor and Ila, too. Yet student life was not quite as fulfilling as they might have hoped. Despite their aptitude, financial circumstances did not allow them to take part in debate. The activity required a considerable time commitment as well as money for travel, and they had to work as many hours as they could get just to stay in school. (George kept a part-time job, too, as a student recruiter for the college, but his scholarship covered tuition and he saved on room and board by living at home.) Still, the Stegebergs became a conspicuous presence on campus—as good students and very attractive twins. They were also cheerleaders, the one extracurricular indulgence they allowed themselves. Like other young men on campus, George admired them for their intelligence as well as for their prettiness. As he once put it, "they exuded a radiant beauty that seemed to come from within." But he was as bashful as a first grader as far as getting to know the famous twins was concerned. "They are so small I feel awkward around them," he confessed to a friend. "They may be only five feet tall," his friend scolded, "but they're all there and if you don't move, some other guy will."[28]

In April the freshman class held its annual skating party at the Mitchell Roller Rink. George glided past the twins a couple of times but still could not get up the nerve to invite either to skate with him. When "ladies choice" was announced, Ila (who, like Eleanor, had her pick of the crop) tagged George. A few weeks later, another boy asked Ila to the spring play at Mitchell High School. They decided to get Eleanor and George together and make it a double. A plan was set in motion. Ila called Eleanor at work. "There's someone coming into the Dean's Office and he's going to ask you for a date. Now, don't you dare turn him down," she said, declining to reveal his name. Eleanor was intrigued. As she hung up the phone, she noticed through the glass doors that George had entered the registrar's office, which adjoined hers. Could the mystery man, she wondered, be "the formidable debating rival, the handsome campus leader, the brain"? But he seemed to dawdle at the registrar's counter. No, she decided—it *couldn't* be George—and turned back to her work. Meanwhile, he had advanced finally to Eleanor's desk.[29]

A second date followed the first, then a third. The two were well matched, and a rapport began to blossom. Each was impressed with the other's intelligence, and their sense of personal values harmonized nicely. To education they both assigned the highest premium. They shared a deep appreciation for rural and small-town life, yet one mixed with a yearning to explore the world outside. Politics and international affairs were an endless source of conversation, and, if Eleanor was definitely a Democrat and George a Republican, their common concern for people in distress was instinctive. In becoming better acquainted, each learned that the other had known deprivation and loss, though (not withstanding his recent crisis) she had sustained harder blows.

Most of the diversions they enjoyed did not cost a lot—a nickel for a Coke at the "Rec" in College Inn, a dime or fifteen cents for movies at the Paramount or an outing at the roller rink or for a basketball game at the Corn Palace. For a dollar they could have a nice dinner for two at the Lawler Café. Sometimes they went dancing. That activity was prohibited on campus until 1950, but Dakota Wesleyan did permit the students a sort of side-by-side promenade around the gym floor as records played. More often, they went downtown with friends to "Dreamland" to hear local bands, or to the Corn Palace, where the country's famous Big Bands performed.[30]

Always would they remember the magical spring of 1941. "I had never known anything like it before," Eleanor recalled. "My only concern was that George might not care so much as I. Then on a beautiful clear afternoon he urged me to skip class with him and as we strolled slowly down the street south of campus, he reach down and touched my hand. I had my answer. A clasping of hands meant everything then." George also described that moment: "a simple touching of hands, then a slight squeeze of the fingers, and I was in love—hopelessly."[31]

The time had come to meet the parents. The day George brought Eleanor home, she fretted about whether to wear lipstick; she decided against it. Then, at the last minute, she changed her mind, feeling her prospective in-laws should see her as she really was. The trace of color did not seem to matter much; the McGoverns made her feel welcome instantly. Eleanor found Frances the warmer personality of the two; she could see that George was closer to and more like his mother than his father. But she liked Joseph's courtliness. For their part, they both knew they had just met the kind of young woman that every mother and father wanted their son to bring home for dinner. Before long she began attending Sunday services with the family.[32]

The couple would never have guessed that his first encounter with her father would have gone as smoothly as it did. On the appointed evening, they were all to meet at the Stegeberg farm and spend a few minutes chatting with Earl before George and Eleanor and Ila and her date would go to a dance. But that Saturday George was late—"unforgivably late," according to Eleanor—and they ended up leaving without him. It was ten o'clock when he arrived. The house was dark except for the movements of a lit cigarette on the front porch. As George approached, Earl stood up. He was impatient with the apology and suspicious his daughter's presumptive beau. Presently he invited the boy to sit. He began to speak of Marion and how she died. George could tell that this was a deeply lonely man. Then the subject turned to politics, religion, and Earl's views on chastity. They talked past midnight. When Eleanor came home, they were still at it. A chemistry had taken hold. People who knew Earl said later that his meeting George marked the beginning of his coming out of his shell. As for George, "From that day to this," he subsequently wrote a confidant, "I haven't had a closer friend than Mr. Stegeberg."[33]

———————————

By the end of their first year in college, the Stegeberg girls had come up against a dilemma: there was only enough money for one of them to return to school in the fall. Because she wanted to be near George, Eleanor decided to go to work full time as a legal secretary in Mitchell—with luck, she could reenroll next year—and she encouraged Ila to go ahead with her plans to begin nurse's training in Rochester, Minnesota. Yet the twins still faced a psychological hurdle. For the first time in their lives they were about to be separated. The cleaving proved tougher for Ila; she was 300 miles away from everyone, and she suffered a bad case of the blues. The following summer her mood brightened. Back in Mitchell, Ila would meet her future husband, Bob Pennington, a Dakota Wesleyan student about to enter the army, and George and Eleanor egged the romance on. Meanwhile, their own courtship was entering a more serious phase.[34] More than once that autumn they went by Dahles Jewelry Store on Main Street to browse the selection. For a hundred dollars, a fairly hefty price then, George purchased a little diamond engagement ring and presented it to Eleanor on her birthday in November.

"It took me my whole freshman year to realize that if I haven't gotten anything else out of Wesleyan those years were well spent because of the girl I got," he wrote to Bob Pennington. "I'm sure of one thing, and that is that when it comes to poise, sincerity and intelligence there aren't many girls who can stay in the race with the Stegeberg twins," he went on, partly playing matchmaker and commenting on his own good fortune. "I've observed those two girls under every circumstance imaginable, and I've yet to find a major flaw in either of them. As far as beauty and figures are concerned they've got the kind that isn't all put on—it's the real thing, Bob." ("Well, I guess I better shut up," went his next sentence.)[35]

This was the first of a series of letters that Eleanor and Ila's suitors would exchange throughout World War II. George and Bob quickly became mutual advisers—both on affairs of the heart and the war. The army already had sent Pennington to Ireland and back, and George wanted to know everything about his experiences. They also encouraged each other's ambitions to earn doctorates in history and go into college teaching. But the subject always came back, as George put it, to "the uncertainty this war has caused in a fellow's plans" and, as ever, to their girls. "Ye gods, Bob, you and Ila must have really gone all out for love in those few days you were here," George teased. "I'm honestly very glad that you kids have found each other and I'm hoping its something permanent." For his part, Bob had observed George and Eleanor enough to wonder when the wedding might take place. "If Eleanor had her way we'd be married by Christmas time," George replied, "but I'm afraid I love her too much to give her that kind of a deal." Wartime marriages seemed "pretty raw for the girl involved in an awful lot of cases," especially since so many fellows were going to be killed, and then what? "I for one hate to leave a swell girl with a Mrs. attached to her name. . . . A guy just feels like saying what in hell's the use of trying to make plans when they'll probably be smashed the next day anyway."[36]

At the same time, George was growing impatient to get into the war. Not until it was over, he and Eleanor had decided, could they be married. Also, he was beginning to hear stories "that make me hate those Japs like sin," he said. A classmate had just returned from the Pacific and told a campus gathering of his having shot down three enemy planes before being forced to bail out of his own craft. As he parachuted to the ground, Japanese fighters tried to machine-gun him. Miraculously, he escaped with only a leg wound. "I think when I get into this thing, I'll want to do all my gunning against the slant eyes," George told Bob, in a rare expression of racial enmity. In any case, he was "anxious to start doing something towards ending this mess."[37]

Then the waiting was over. On the night of February 12, 1943, George and Matt Smith and their fellow debaters were returning from their grand victory at the Red River Valley Tournament. Snow was coming down across the frozen prairie on the 300-mile route back from Fargo to Mitchell, and it was hard to keep the car on the road. Still, spirits were high, and they sang rowdy songs. When they finally pulled onto the campus, Dean Smith was waiting for them. Tearfully he handed George a large envelope, like the one that Walter Kreimann, the student body president, also had received that day. It contained greetings from the secretary of war. Both boys were to report for duty at Jefferson Barracks (near St. Louis) within seventy-two hours. Looking up from his orders, George's first thought was of Eleanor and his mother and how upset they were going to be. He worried more about his mother. How many times had he heard her exclaim after reading about the titanic struggles on the eastern front where Germans and Russians perished by the scores of thousands? "Oh, Dear," she would say. "There must be so many sad homes in Germany tonight," or "Isn't there some way that the heads of government can get together and stop this slaughter?"[38] Yet there was hardly time for George to do much more than pack a bag.

Because it was George and Walter Kreimann who were going off to war, theirs would be no ordinary farewell. Hundreds of Mitchellites—including a lot of the student body and the faculty of Dakota Wesleyan, and its marching band, too—turned out that evening to give them a send-off they would never forget. For a while, the occasion was almost joyous, what with all the cheers and music and tributes. But then the mood changed as the realization crept over the well-wishers that they might never see these fine young men again. Comparable scenes took place a thousand times a day throughout the country, intensely poignant leave-takings at the train station that overwhelmed the emotions. To George's sister, Mildred, suddenly "it was like the bottom had dropped out of everything. We thought the whole world was ending." Through most of it, George held Eleanor's hand tightly in his and tried to avert his mother's eyes; she "looked as though she were at my funeral," he would say decades later. Now that it was really happening, she "could not believe that they were going to take her son off to this miserable war." As for his father, Joseph remained stoic and, even at a moment like this, found it impossible to let his heart speak. (Only afterward, once George was flying missions over Germany, was he able to express himself to his "dear boy" in a letter: "You never caused us to lose any sleep. We always felt that we had one of the best boys in town and we feel that way yet, and I know the people of Mitchell feel that way.") Finally the conductor called out. George said his good-byes and kissed Eleanor one last time. As Mildred remembered it, "Everyone seemed to be crying except Dad and George. They just stood there talking gravely . . . until Dad finally shook his hand and it was time to go." George and Walter managed to get to a window and leaned out to wave as the wheels of the locomotive began to turn. The crowd, waving back, lingered on the platform until the line of coaches disappeared into the cold February night.

Dakota Wesleyan's brightest star had previously traveled by rail throughout the Middle West to debate issues about the war. But this departure from Mitchell was unlike the others. Although he still faced a grueling year of flight instruction before he would be shipped overseas, the train that George boarded this time carried him across the first great divide of his life.[39]

4 THE BEST B-24 PILOT IN THE WORLD

In April 1942, the US Army Air Forces took out a full-page advertisement in the *Phreno Cosmian*. The broadside featured a photograph of a B-17 (the "Flying Fortress") cruising above snow-covered mountains. "In the skies over America, the mightiest air fleet in the history of the world is mobilizing for victory!" the copy began. The service was in need of fliers and ground crews, and there was a place here "for every college man in America." The ad strove to make patriotic duty both attractive and practical. Ground crew could put their training to good use in a postwar profession—in armaments, communications, and engineering, for example. As for aviation, "the great career field of the future," cadets could count on more benefits and pay than any civilian job—$75 a month during training and up to $245 on active duty. Recruits in the enlisted reserves could remain in school until facilities could be built to accommodate them: "If you want to fight for America, this is where your blows will count."[1]

George McGovern had arrived at the same conclusion three months earlier, when he and his friends had signed up with the Army Air Corps in Omaha. He also had begun to chart the course for what lay ahead by enrolling in a civilian pilot training program, offered for credit at Mitchell Field in the spring of 1942. (He also thought it would impress Eleanor.) The course involved thirty-five hours in the air, and his group soon was introduced to a small, single-engine Aeronca equipped with tandem cockpits and two sets of controls in case the instructor had to take over. George showed evidence of having the keenest depth perception of anyone in the class, but when he went up for the first time, he discovered he possessed a liability for any prospective pilot—a palpable fear of flying. "I was scared to death," he told Eleanor, though the instructor said he had done just fine.[2]

In subsequent lessons, when the instructor demonstrated maneuvers such as stalls and spins, George was terrified. As Eleanor said, "He was afraid of taking off, landing, and every minute in between." His boyhood struggles with shyness, however, had taught him one of life's more important lessons. "I think if there's something you are particularly afraid to do," he observed many years later, "then it is all the more important that you go ahead and do it." It was a variation of one of his father's preachments to his children. "Make the best use of your time," the Reverend would say. "You can't make the best use of your time if you're going to live by fear." Born into an era when most Americans felt imprisoned by apprehension about the future, George tried to turn the good thought into a rule of life by the time he had entered college.[3]

The supreme test came the day he had to fly solo. Once at cruising altitude, he felt proud of himself, even at ease enough momentarily to regard Mitchell in wonderment. He had never thought about how his town might look from the air. Yet there it was, from two thousand feet: Main Street and the other boulevards that formed a grid disturbed only by the orbs atop the Corn Palace; to the south, the Dakota Wesleyan campus; to the east, the James River appearing as a great curving canal; and, finally, the issue of the farmer's labor, all laid out in orderly, quarter-mile squares of alternating shades of green and stretching endlessly in every direction. Then the amazement passed, dispelled by the reality of the hardest part of any flight—to land safely. When at last he heard the tires cuff the tarmac, he was overcome by a sense of relief. Much of the experience had been scary, but earning his license was "one of the happiest moments of his life," he said. For almost a year after that, thoughts of airplanes hardly entered his mind.[4]

"You smart college guys," Sergeant Trumbo called the would-be cadets charged to his care at Jefferson Barracks in the winter of 1943. From him they would learn how to march in close order, how to take proper care of a rifle and pistol, how to keep a neat barracks, and how to run through the surrounding hills in the snows of February. Although he drilled them from reveille to taps, Trumbo was never cruel or unreasonable. "We have a swell sergeant," George wrote to Bob Pennington the first week, "and [though] he is very lenient, our platoon works harder for him than any other." All of it was "probably pretty good training for a fellow," he added, "but it's just a little bit hard for me to get used to the strict discipline."[5]

Boot camp was mitigated not only by a decent drillmaster, but by familiar faces, too. Walter Kreimann and George bunked in the same hut, and the base was home to dozens of former debaters he had met at tournaments. "Our whole outfit seems to be made of good eggs," he wrote.[6] Even so, he was feeling homesick. "I've never been lonelier than I have been in downtown St. Louis," he confessed to Bob. There was, however, one big city experience that was the exception—a chance to hear Marian Anderson in concert. George remembered the 1939 controversy involving the great African American contralto and the Daughters of the American Revolution. In the spring before Hitler invaded Poland, the DAR barred her from performing at Constitution Hall. But at the St. Louis Opera House, Miss Anderson's voice ("such as one hears once in a hundred years," according to Toscanini) thrilled an audience of men in uniform. When she sang "America the Beautiful" at the end of the program, all the soldiers wept openly.[7]

After his thirty days of basic, the USAAF sent George to ground school at Southern Illinois Normal University, in Carbondale, for four months of specialized training. College instructors taught the hundreds of aspiring pilots courses in mathematics, meteorology, and navigation. The university's football coach put them through a physical regimen designed for athletes. Doctors and psychologists subjected the men to tests to determine everything else about them—from acuity of eyesight and finger dexterity to blood pressure and the capacity to hold up under stress. Examiners even asked questions to ascertain tendencies in the ranks toward bed-wetting. (The main cause of "wash-outs" was the eye exam, at a rate of 20 percent.)[8]

"I'm not nearly as crazy about flying as most of the fellows are, but I think I'd enjoy the air corps if they decided to put me in a bomber," George wrote to Bob Pennington after ten hours in the air at Carbondale. "There's something about these huge flying forts that fascinate me and I think it would be a real experience to fly one of them." At his next post, in San Antonio, he moved rapidly and entered upon nine months of preparation for air combat known as "the grind to the wings." But by then he was on the verge of a decision of greater moment.

On rare occasions, he and Eleanor had been able to talk long distance on the telephone, a luxury that only made them miss each other the more. Then, in June, his father fell ill, and he was granted a ten-day furlough. When the visit was over, the Reverend was feeling better; George and Eleanor, however, were not. George's departure was as difficult for them as the first one in February. "We may get married before fall," he told Bob. Prudence dictated that they should wait, he admitted. But there was one reason why they no longer could, "and that is we've simply got an old fashioned love affair on our hands, and it's pretty hard to stop love even for a war."[9]

The decision took the parents by surprise. Everyone had assumed that they would not be settling down together until the war was over. The McGoverns were accepting, if not especially happy about it, and George's father agreed to preside over the ceremony. Earl Stegeberg, however, was inconsolable. Whereas he admired George and approved of the engagement, he would not consent to his daughter's leaving home for a wartime marriage. "It's ridiculous! No! I'm not coming to the wedding!" he vowed. Never before in her life had Eleanor defied him. "The wedding plans unfolded cheerlessly," she wrote.

There was not a lot of money or time for a big to-do. George was in the middle of primary flight training in Muskogee logging some seventy hours in the air; he could only wrangle a three-day pass, two days of which would be consumed by travel to Mitchell and back. All the last-minute details were left to Eleanor. She made sixteen dollars a week as a secretary and could not afford a formal gown. Ila helped her shop for fabric, and a friend hurriedly made her a two-piece outfit. The wedding ring that matched the little diamond that George had purchased at Dahles cost too much as well. For a few dollars each, Eleanor bought two simple gold bands, one for herself and one for George. George's mother threw a bridal shower, and other relatives and neighbors organized a reception to be held in the basement of the Methodist Church in Woonsocket after the nuptials, set for October 31. By mid-morning on that Halloween Sunday the register of deeds had arrived with a license and the town's Book of Marriages. The mood was festive, except for Earl's absence. Then, only moments before the principals were about to take their places, in he walked—"my disappointed, uncommunicative, beloved dad," as Eleanor described him—to give his daughter in marriage to the sturdy young man in uniform. Everything was perfect. The Reverend McGovern smiled and began to read from the Bible.[10]

Marriage during the months of his aviation training was more like "a series of dates under enormous pressure," George once said. Indeed, the bride and groom had to spend their wedding night at his parents' home in Mitchell. Early the next morning they entrained for Muskogee. While waiting for a connection at the Kansas City terminal someone stole their luggage, leaving them without even a toothbrush. Every coach was packed, and they had to stand the entire way in a crowded aisle. As the train pulled out, they exchanged gazes, frazzled and worn out, and they both started to cry. After a long hug, they looked at each other again and started to laugh. The train did not reach Muskogee until midnight, and George had to get up at 5:00 a.m. to be at Hatbox Field in time for a crucial check flight.[11]

Army regulations made few allowances for newlyweds. Wives had to live off the base, so Eleanor rented a room in a private home in Muskogee, as she would in other towns. "I became a camp follower," she recalled. Only for a few hours on Saturday nights and on Sundays were cadets permitted to leave the base. Wives could visit on Wednesdays; they all rode in together on a bus and met their book-toting husbands in the lounge to help them cram for exams. Yet none of these impediments to normal married life seemed to matter. Just to live with George in new places was "a great adventure," Eleanor said. "I loved being a cadet wife." He was no less ebullient. "When we're together on weekends the time just seems to race away," he told Bob a month after the wedding. "Eleanor seems to be happier than she has been since I've known her, so . . . if being married under the handicap of a war is so wonderful, it must be nothing short of marvelous in peace time."[12]

But there were tragedies along the way. More than once, fate abruptly ended the idyll of young love for other couples they knew. After Muskogee, for instance, George was sent to Coffeyville, Kansas, for basic flight training. Early on there, during a routine takeoff in a single-engine BT-13, a trainee pulled up too quickly, sending his craft into a stall and an uncontrollable nosedive to the ground. The full gas tank exploded on impact. "The fire engines were out in nothing flat," George recalled, but the pilot was already dead and "his body was like a lobster." This kind of misfortune was far from uncommon, and there would be many more at Coffeyville. (Throughout the war, in simply teaching them how to fly, the air force lost 3,492 pilots—half again as many as the number of servicemen killed at Pearl Harbor.) "I don't think I'll ever get used to it," George said about the futility of death by training accident. The wives could not get used to it either. Living in constant fear for their spouses, they formed close bonds. An unwritten code governed their sisterhood—never to give in to foreboding or to talk about the war, on pain of being frozen out by the others. In this, Eleanor's cheerfulness and ability to cope amazed her husband. "As yet she's never even breathed a whimper or complaint of any kind," he wrote to Bob. "I guess she never will stop going up in my estimation." But practically every cadet wife, even Eleanor, lost control at some point.[13]

From Coffeyville they moved on to Pampa, a dusty town in the Texas Panhandle, where the Army Air Forces sent potential pilots for advanced training in twin-engine planes. George had already mastered such elementary aerobatics as loops, spins, rollovers, and the "Immelmann turn." Now, within two months, he had to pick up far more complicated skills that involved both good instincts and blind dependence on instrument flying: how to fly in formation, the main cause of midair collisions; how to keep the plane steady when the trainer shut down one of the engines; and how to navigate without benefit of a map, using only topography and landmarks such as water towers and train tracks. "Advanced is a little rougher than we had anticipated," he told Bob; it would be "really tough to wash out now after a year or more of working for wings." That was the greatest fear for all the cadets, and it happened to 40 percent of the 317,000 who took the wartime training—but not to George.[14]

For the pregraduation dance held in honor of the cadets and their wives and girlfriends, the auditorium on the Pampa base was turned into a ballroom. It was a relatively cool Texas evening in April 1944. Scores of couples were on the floor. The music was "soft, romantic," Eleanor recollected, mainly songs of Frank Sinatra and Tommy Dorsey. Later that night she and George gave each other presents. For him, Eleanor had an engraved identification bracelet—"an unimaginative gift," she felt, but "symbolic for me that I was Lieutenant McGovern's wife." For her, George had a little box that he had ordered from Mitchell. He gave it to her shyly, as if they were recommitting to their vows, it seemed to her. The box contained the wedding band from Dahles Jewelry Store that matched her engagement ring. "I wore both wedding rings the next day," she wrote in her memoir, "and I have ever since."

The graduation ceremony itself was held outdoors on the airfield, replete with speeches and the men marching past the reviewing stand, singing their anthem, "The Wild Blue Yonder." Then they received their commissions, their wings, and their assignments—in George's case, to train as a B-24 pilot, at Liberal, Kansas. No one looked prouder on this special day than Lieutenant McGovern and his wife; the photograph of her pinning his wings on him would have made an effective recruitment poster. "I knew then that I was going to be afraid and lonely," she nonetheless wrote.[15]

———————————

Among its crews and passengers, the B-24 could boast of some of the era's most celebrated public figures. The actor James Stewart commanded a squadron of them in England for the Eighth Air Force. Winston Churchill traveled in his, the *Commando*, to summits with Roosevelt and Stalin. The *Gulliver* transported Wendell Willkie on his famous global tour on which he based the decade's best-selling work of nonfiction, *One World* (1943). And Eleanor Roosevelt flew in one aptly named *Guess Where II*. Between 1942 and 1945, American factories turned out 19,256 B-24s, making it "the most numerous" and thus, arguably, the most important airplane ever built.[16]

The B-24 was a clear-cut case of function over form. The fuselage, sixty-seven feet long and eighteen feet in diameter, resembled a giant stout cigar. Visually, its most distinctive attributes were its dual rudder wings, attached vertically at either end of the tail section and the size of barn doors. Its most innovative feature was the main wing, the "Davis wing," named for its engineer, David R. Davis. Spanning 110 feet and mounted near the top of the fuselage, this airfoil was longer and much narrower than those of comparable bombers. While giving the ship a somewhat ungainly appearance, it afforded tremendous lift, an essential capability for what was then the heaviest plane in service. At the same time, the slender wing was more likely to crumple and break away if flak hit it or if an engine began to windmill. Then, too, its placement provided no shock absorption during crash landings, in contrast to the low-mounted wing of the B-17. Whereas Consolidated Aircraft officially dubbed it the "Liberator," flight crews called her the "Liquidator" or the "Flying Coffin." Charles Lindbergh pronounced an early prototype "the worst piece of metal aircraft construction" ever conceived.[17]

Nonetheless, the B-24 was a formidable battleship. Its four supercharged Pratt and Whitney engines generated the power of 4,800 horses upon takeoff and sustained a cruising speed of 278 mph at an altitude of 25,000 feet. Until 1945, no American bomber exceeded its round-trip mission range of 2,000 miles. Weighing some 70,000 pounds fully laden, the manifest included a crew of ten, up to 8,000 pounds of bombs, 16,000 pounds of high-octane gasoline (contained in the Davis wing's fuel cells), and 4,716 rounds of ammunition to supply ten .50 caliber Browning machine guns—two each, located in the nose and tail and in the dorsal and ventral turrets, and one each at either side of the waist. No other air ship did more to sap the strength of the Nazi juggernaut on the ground. Its greatest achievement was to carry the Allied war effort directly to the industrial centers of the European theater. By V-E Day, B-24s would fly 226,773 sorties and drop nearly a half million tons of bombs on enemy installations.[18]

From the moment he reported for transitional training, George McGovern was smitten by "these clumsy old Liberators." But they presented a host of bewildering challenges. To begin, B-24s were hard to fly. The steering was stiff—which made for a delayed response to the pilot's handling of the controls—and it demanded physical strength that taxed the muscles of all four limbs. The pilot had to turn the wheel, or "yoke," with the left hand and manage all the throttles with the right, while his feet and legs kept constant pressure on the floor pedals to steady or to turn the broad surfaces of the dual rudders against the force of 300-mph winds. Long runs, flown in tight formation with scores of other planes on either side and above and below, could be likened to driving an eighteen-wheel tractor trailer along a twisting mountain road without the aid of power steering. "I've seen pilots after a ten to twelve-hour mission who were so exhausted that they literally had to be physically lifted out of the cockpit," McGovern said.[19]

Getting in and settled was hardly any easier. The crew, carrying backpack parachutes and garbed in electrically heated flight suits to protect against the subzero temperatures, had to climb through the bomb bay doors, the only port of entry besides the well of the nose-wheel. In the pilot's domain, George had to master an array of gauges and devices. In addition to directional controls, each of the four Pratt and Whitneys had three pairs of levers. Before ignition, pilots also went through a checklist of thirty-four items; then, ten more switches in order to taxi, eighteen just before takeoff, and seven immediately after. Landing involved a total of twenty-nine procedures. None of this took into account the intangibles of taking off and touching down; nor the specifics of navigation, of arming 500-pound bombs and dropping them, or of defending against an onslaught of enemy fighters. The latter responsibilities belonged to the rest of the crew, but the pilot and copilot were required to learn the tasks of everyone else. Once he completed the instruction in air combat in late June, George traveled to Lincoln, Nebraska, to meet his crew, and then, together with them, to Mountain Home, Idaho, for gunnery practice and simulated bombing runs.[20]

By 1944, it was a convention of wartime Hollywood movies to portray a cast of GI characters as a cross section of American society—wholesome young men of widely diverse backgrounds, thrown together by chance, yet working together in a common enterprise so that good eventually would triumph over evil. Whether the setting was a Flying Fortress, a submarine, or Wake Island, audiences encountered in the typical screen story a farmer's son from Iowa, a ladies' man from a wealthy family, a soft-spoken bookworm with a religious bent, a Jewish kid from Brooklyn, one thirty-five-year-old dubbed "Pops," and somebody named "Tex." So it was in life on a Liberator.

For example, there was McGovern's copilot, Bill Rounds, a sexually precocious scion of a lumber magnate of Wichita, Kansas, who really wanted to be a fighter pilot. Then there was Sam Adams of Milwaukee, the navigator, whose charge was to let slip the bombs and whose aspiration it was to become a Presbyterian minister. Flight engineer Mike Valko was a former carnival roustabout from Bridgeport, Connecticut. The scar-faced Valko fulfilled several stereotypes. Thirty-three years old and five feet five, he was both the oldest and shortest man as well as the one with a drinking problem. Brattleboro, Vermont, supplied the gambler of the group, the twenty-year-old nose gunner Bob O'Connell, who always won at poker. For good measure, there were two boys from Texas—the witty, cowboy-booted radioman, Kenneth Higgins, nineteen, from Dallas, whom McGovern came to regard as the finest man on the crew; and waist gunner Bill Ashlock, eighteen, from Hereford, whose nickname was, indubitably, "Tex." Bill McAfee of Port Huron, Michigan, occupied the ball turret, which offered 360-degree views of the earth 20,000 feet below as well as the most exposed and cramped position on the plane. Finally, there was Isadore Seigel, the Jewish tailgunner from Omaha. Seigel was given to odd behavior, which included brandishing guns and hunting knives and running around in the barracks stripped head to toe, with nothing but a bayonet cinched around his body.[21]

They were a varied lot and something of a cultural cross section. They did share one demographic, however, common among fliers. Excepting Valko, they averaged barely twenty-one years of age, much younger than the GI average of twenty-six in World War II. (For the Vietnam War it would be nineteen.) McGovern himself turned twenty-two when the crew was formed, and he was initially self-conscious about his youth. At a point in life when a difference of two or three years seems significant, he decided to grow a moustache for a more sagacious appearance. He need not have worried; his demeanor and character were quickly evident to everyone, as his skill as a pilot soon would be. "From the day I first met him I liked him," Isadore Seigel said. "McGovern seemed mature, a person who commanded respect." Bill Rounds saw him as "a big brother type," and wrote his parents, "He's a very nice, refined, quiet man, and I know that we will make a fine team." George shaved his moustache and, a month into the training, reported to Bob Pennington, "I've really got a top notch crew. They were all pretty green at first as was their pilot, but we're getting hot I believe." He was pleased, too, that the boys also thought a lot of his missus. "We all just loved Eleanor," Bill Rounds said. Since George was the only married man on the ship, they all decided it should be named for her. Thus the *Dakota Queen* was christened.[22]

The nice gesture did not make her any less anxious for her husband's well-being at Mountain Home. Throughout the war, aircrews accounted for 43 percent of all the US Army's noncombat fatalities (nearly 36,000) at home and abroad; accidents involving B-24s alone claimed the lives of 850 fliers in 1943. Eleanor realized that luck was keeping George's crew from increasing those numbers—for instance, on one terrible afternoon when his squadron was practicing defensive maneuvers. As part of the exercise, a twin-engine B-25 was supposed to dive down on the formation of B-24s and then swoop under them, as an attacking fighter plane might do in combat. Instead, it flew into one Liberator head-on, the explosion engulfing two others. Gone in an instant were four ships and all the men inside them. ("I can still hear them yet," McGovern said fifty-six years later of the cries of anguish that night as the chaplain made his way through the barracks to inform the widows of the married men.) Not long after that, Eleanor experienced her moment of raw panic. She had been hospitalized with a mistaken diagnosis of diabetes, and George was away on a night flight. Around 10:00 p.m. the sound of a plane crash and then the sirens awakened her. For an hour she waited alone in the corridor, tortured by her imagination, until George at last appeared in the doorway to comfort her.[23]

There were blessings to count, too. Her doctor, it turned out, apparently did not know diabetes from morning sickness. Now George became the worrier—because of the nature of her mother's demise and the fact that he soon would be an ocean away. "I'm honestly just a little bit scared when I think about Eleanor going through the whole thing alone," he wrote. "If anything ever happened to her it would just be the end of me." At length, her gladness overcame his anxiety. "Even the fact that I in all probability may miss the big event doesn't worry me a whole lot anymore," he was presently telling Bob. "Eleanor is happier than I've ever seen her before."[24] The folks back home were happy, too, but for one exception. Eleanor's father openly disapproved. Who knew better the problems of single parenthood than the Widower Stegeberg? "He thought having a baby was foolish," she wrote, "for the exact reason that I was overjoyed—if George didn't come back from the war, at least I would have his son or daughter."[25] That sentiment ran deep in thousands of war brides about to be separated from their husbands, and it helped to set the "Baby Boom" in motion.

In the meantime, as their expertise and trust in one another grew week by week, the men of the *Dakota Queen* had become a team. In September, orders came through. Their destination would be a base near Cerignola, twenty miles inland from the southeastern coast of Italy, where they were to join the 741st Squadron of the 455th Bombardment Group of the Fifteenth Air Force. George was granted a short leave to take Eleanor home to her father in Woonsocket before proceeding to Norfolk, Virginia, for embarkation.

In all, the previous year had been the most eventful of his life. He had learned to fly one of the largest bombers ever built. He and Eleanor had been married and now were expecting. And, though the AAF obliged crews to carry out thirty-five daylight combat missions, he was already musing to Bob about the future—about finishing college, going on to graduate school at Northwestern, and about being with Eleanor forever. "I love her more every time another day goes by," he had said in the letter in which he had disclosed his anxiety about her pregnancy. "We've lived in a funny era and sort of a mixed up one, but I'm still glad I'm living in this age. If we can just get this war completely over with and make damn sure we've won it we may be able to spend the rest of our lives doing the things we've been dreaming about for so long."[26]

Each member of the crew had his own vivid memory of the twenty-six-day voyage to the Mediterranean. For Isadore Seigel, it was being seasick the whole time; for Ken Higgins, it was shaving in cold salt water; and for Bill Rounds, it was the abundance of red wine onboard. George's particular recollection of the journey was their convoy's entrance, on October 29, 1944, into the harbor at Naples. There on the pier, dozens of ragged children had gathered to beg for food—"spindly-legged kids with pale faces," as he described them. He was used to seeing a certain kind of poverty in South Dakota, but this, he said, "was my first exposure to people on the edge of starvation." That night he awakened to the rattling of garbage cans by women "looking for scraps of food that they could take home to their kids." (In retrospect, Bob Pennington believed these experiences had some impact on the sort of politician George eventually became, that they "made him a Democrat.")[27]

Two days later the men were loaded into boxcars for a jouncing hundred-mile train ride across the peninsula to the railhead near Cerignola, the site where, in 216 BC, Hannibal's legions had stored supplies prior to the battle of Cannae. More recently the town's occupiers had been Germans, until the British Eighth Army had liberated it during the first phase of the Allied invasion of September 1943–May 1945. Now the Americans had taken over, expanded the airfield, and established a colony alongside an olive grove just outside Cerignola. "We sleep in tents, with no lights or running water," Bill Rounds recorded in his diary. The officers—McGovern, Rounds, and Sam Adams—shared one such army tent; the six enlisted crewmen took another nearby. They spent their spare time improving their quarters. They hired Italian laborers to pour concrete floors and rigged each structure with an oil drum heater and other amenities. "Our tent is now in good shape—good stove, clothes rack and front door," Rounds noted, and George said it was "a cozy little place." As wartime journalist Ernie Pyle wrote in 1943, "The American soldier is a born housewife."[28]

In mid-November, in accordance with AAF regulations, McGovern flew his first five missions with a combat-seasoned crew, rather than with his own, and sat in the copilot's seat. Four of these were so-called milk runs—meaning no encounters with enemy fighters or antiaircraft resistance, or an aborted mission due to weather. His men were glad to ascertain that he held the controls for half the time on each flight. On the third anniversary of Pearl Harbor, they would undertake their first assignment over enemy territory together as a team—their target, the marshaling yards at Graz, Austria.[29]

Awakening at 4:00 a.m., McGovern, Rounds, and Adams ate a powdered egg breakfast and attended the briefings for pilots and navigators as the others went about their own preparations. Making ready would become routine, but on this red-letter morning nothing felt ordinary to them, especially to George, who had yet to prove himself worthy of combat command. They had already seen two Liberators blow up on the runway and incinerate everybody on board due to pilot error, one taking off, the other landing. Until McGovern turned in his postflight report, there would not be a moment's reprieve from responsibility and stress.[30]

Clad in boots, gloves, and flight suits, all of leather and lined in sheep's wool, the men climbed through the bays as their captain finished his visual check with the ground mechanics. Once inside the cockpit, he and Rounds went through three-dozen procedures to start the engines and taxi across the field. Two entire bomber groups—the 455th (theirs) and the 456th, each consisting of four, seven-plane squadrons—were rolling out together. Nose to tail, side by side in two separate lines, and raising a deafening, grinding roar, fifty-six Liberators moved toward the runway. They took off in pairs at thirty-second intervals. As the two bombers just ahead rumbled into the distance, McGovern set his brakes and pushed the engines' throttles forward to obtain maximum rpm. The ship lurched against its restraints. Upon signal, he set the wing flaps at twenty degrees then released the brakes. Rounds began to say a prayer. She moved slowly at first, so slowly they feared she would eat up all of the 4,800 feet of runway before reaching 160 mph, the speed required to become airborne. Suddenly, miraculously, they were up, though not by much. Rounds retracted the wheels and reset the flaps. For a mile or so they skimmed along just above the trees. "It seemed forever before I could climb," McGovern said. At last they gained altitude and circled the airfield. Ashlock, Higgins, McAfee, O'Connell, and Seigel each fired off a burst to test their machine guns. The *Dakota Queen* was away.[31]

It took an hour to get into formation over the Adriatic. The seven B-24s of each squadron flew in echelons, to create a "box." The lead plane was flanked, port and starboard and half a length back, by two others, the wingmen. Trailing by both forty feet behind and below came the second three-plane echelon, and behind it, the lone seventh bomber. After all four squadrons were configured (and stacked in a lead, a low, a middle, and high box) they would rendezvous with up to three additional groups and navigate a course to their Initial Point, then directly northward to the target. They flew close to one another, practically wingtip to wingtip—the tighter the formation, the more concentrated the bombing pattern and the harder for attacking enemy fighters to get between them, yet also rendering midair collisions more probable, owing to the B-24's sluggish response to the hydraulics. As they reached 20,000 feet, "the sky was full of planes," Ken Higgins exclaimed with undiminished awe a half century later, "just miles of airplanes." What with vapor trails streaming from the four engines of each of more than a hundred Liberators, he said, "it was quite a sight to see."[32]

At that altitude there was no oxygen to breathe and the temperature fell to about forty degrees below zero, inside the plane as well as outside. (Frostbite put more fliers out of action than wounds suffered in combat.) Every few minutes over the intercom, McGovern would make sure each man had his heated suit plugged in and oxygen mask screwed on properly, as he would do on all missions. McAfee especially appreciated the solicitude, as no one was more vulnerable to hazard than the ball turret, even on a milk run. And that, for all their nervous anticipation, was how their maiden flight ended. As the fleet passed over the Alps, the approach to Graz grew impossibly dense with clouds. The lead plane turned homeward and the rest of them followed. They dumped their lethal cargoes into the sea. Back at the airfield, McGovern managed a textbook-smooth, three-point landing.[33]

On the morning of December 4, while he was pheasant hunting with friends, the Reverend Joseph McGovern collapsed and died of a heart attack. He was seventy-six. Because of the usual wartime delays, word did not reach George for ten days. "He was an ideal dad and a genuine Christian," he wrote to Bob Pennington. "His example will never cease to influence my life," and he knew when he had left for Cerignola that his father "would breathe a prayer for me almost every hour that I was gone." Now he prayed for him. In such circumstances, pilots were entitled not to fly for a while. The *Dakota Queen*'s second mission, however, was scheduled for two days hence. George was not conflicted; just weeks before, his father had written to say how proud he was of him. "But, my dear boy," he counseled, "these are times when we need to be redeemed by God's saving grace and you must learn to draw upon the spiritual strength that is available to those who seek it." That thought confirmed George's decision not to stand down.[34]

The second mission—to the railroad yards at Linz, Austria, where Hitler had spent his adolescence and through which the Germans currently were moving troops both east and west—would introduce the crew to real combat. As before, the Liberators flew in a tight formation of layers of boxes. But German antiaircraft units employed their own version of "boxes"—intense barrages of shells timed to explode at the altitude of the attacking planes, saturating an air space sometimes as great as a half mile square, and one after another and another. From a distance, the detonating shells looked like "little black flowers that grow in the sky," airmen said. Yet each was an eruption, for thirty feet in every direction, of a hundred pieces of steel shrapnel known as flak. Flying into this sort of hell, B-24 crews struggled to stay in formation and hoped their number had not come up.[35]

The bombing of the rail yards went according to plan. Over the target for a minute or so, the lead plane's bombardier/navigator controlled the mission. Using his Norden bombsight, he alone determined the most opportune moment to release the bombs. His counterparts in all the other planes would let go their loads when they saw his falling. Whereas the close-in formation helped to assure coverage, it presented the antiaircraft guns with their best mark, too. At first, the flak "just added to the tension, rather than generating fear," McGovern said. "I really didn't become afraid of it until we took our first hit." The assault started with what sounded like pings on the fuselage, then the raps of a hammer. But as they passed beyond the target, the storm of bursts all around them stopped as suddenly as it had begun. No planes were lost. Three hours later the *Dakota Queen* landed uneventfully.[36]

Flak would continue to be the awful specter—for example, the following day, over the oil refineries of Brüx, Germany. "It was a raging inferno of black smoke and red fire, maybe 2,000 feet thick and 2,000 feet wide," McGovern recalled. "I frankly didn't see how an airplane could fly through that." Neither did the squadron leader. Rather than sacrifice seventy or so crewmen, he deliberately peeled off and led them away—a judgment about which everybody felt relieved, if somewhat ambivalent. On December 26, there was the enemy barrage at Oświçim (Auschwitz), Poland, that came close to decapitating McGovern and to shattering Mike Valko's nerves. Their prey was an oil field and "the flak was so thick you could walk on it," as the saying went. The *Dakota Queen* had just emerged from the bomb run when a chunk of metal crashed through the windshield of the cockpit, hit the bulkhead just above McGovern, and fell at Valko's feet. It was hot and jagged and about the size of an orange. "Lieutenant," Valko cried, "if that had been a few inches lower, it would have taken your head off!"

If the lieutenant was shaken, he showed no sign of it. "All I could do was just sit there and do my job," he said in relating the story. Indeed, by all accounts of their exploits, McGovern's demeanor became the crew's reassuring tonic, though Valko began to rely on alcohol between missions. The effect of their pilot's steadiness owed at least partly to "that midwestern twang" on the intercom, waist gunner Tex Ashlock thought. "It came through without any sign of stress or swearing or anything." The crew's sense of well-being also derived from a burgeoning faith in McGovern's proficiency. They felt safe with him. That trust was evident after the second and third missions; their fourth would set them to bragging about him.[37]

Between 8:15 and 8:45 that morning, December 17, two bomber groups left Cerignola as part of a force of 142 Liberators bound for the refineries of Odertal, Germany. Just as the *Dakota Queen* was lifting off, the crew felt a hard bump. Ken Higgins looked out his waist window in time to see a blown right tire on the retracting landing gear. McGovern immediately called the tower. It was up to the ship's commander, the control officer said, whether to let the crew bail out and then try to land, or to fly now and worry later. None of them was inclined to tempt fate by parachute, and landing fully loaded with 5,000 pounds of bombs and 2,000 gallons of enriched gasoline, with or without a flat tire, was tantamount to suicide. McGovern decided to proceed with the mission. According to briefings, 133 heavy guns and thirty-five enemy fighters guarded the target area; for the while, then, the blowout was a moot point.

By the time the armada reached the objective, five aircraft of the 455 had turned back because of fuel leaks or other problems. But the *Dakota Queen*, cruising at 21,000 feet as the left wingship of the second attack unit, was able to contribute its 5,000 pounds to the seventy-five tons of explosives the group dropped. (Flak was inaccurate, though true enough to bring down one plane and wound several others.) Four hours later, when the shores of Italy came into view, the crew could take some consolation in being shed of the bombs and most of the hundred-octane. Valko nonetheless had worked himself up into trembling hysteria. Yet with only a single serviceable main wheel, there was not a man onboard who could not help wondering whether the captain was skillful enough to save them from a fiery grave.

Approaching the landing field, the crew assumed their crash positions. The other planes had already set down, and McGovern could see scores of fliers and mechanics on the ground watching him descend.

He came in almost level. As the good tire under the left wing met the landing mat, simultaneously he cut back the power on that side and pushed the throttles forward on the right side. For a few seconds the tireless wheel rim hung inches above the runway and then it touched down. The plane fishtailed, but McGovern had slowed it enough to gain control and straighten out. They came to a halt on the side of the strip. That evening, amid all the jubilation, there was talk of a Distinguished Flying Cross.[38]

The next mission was more or less routine. Their sixth, three days later, would be the crew's most harrowing journey so far; after it, McGovern would loom forever heroic in their eyes. The intended destination of the 455th and 456th was Brüx; however, strong headwinds bucked the formation, throwing it off schedule and diverting it to an alternate site—the enormous Skoda munitions works at Pilsen, Czechoslovakia, which were commensurately defended. About an hour from the target the *Dakota Queen*'s number two engine (inboard left) lost oil pressure and quit. McGovern dropped out of his box to "feather" the prop, a push-button function that turned the edges of the four blades into wind, thus preventing inordinate drag. In this situation, many pilots would have felt free to abort. "So we're minus an engine," he said to Rounds, and they increased the power on the other engines to catch up with the formation. But on the final approach to Skoda, number three (inboard right) blew a cylinder, and the propeller windmilled out of control, slowing the plane perceptibly. McGovern instructed Adams to release the bombs. Just then, as Rounds recounted in his diary, the engine "began throwing oil and smoking badly." A moment later it burst into flames. Repeatedly, McGovern pushed the feather button, but to no response. They all knew from training manuals that the flames would burn through to the fuel cells within five minutes; barring that, the burden of the runaway prop might tear off the wing. "It looked real bad," Ken Higgins said. McGovern feathered again—this time, successfully, and the force of the wind doused the fire. Even so, they were far from home and losing altitude at the rate of a hundred feet a minute in a crippled Liberator. To lighten the load, he ordered the crew to throw overboard all nonessential items—ammunition belts, machine guns, everything.

Navigator Sam Adams all the while was studying the maps. Forty miles off the Dalmatian coast, he said, there was a small island where the British had built an emergency landing strip for fighter planes, albeit half the length that a B-24 required. It was called Vis, some fifty-eight square miles of alpine terrain, captured from the Italians in 1943 by Yugoslav partisans led by Marshal Tito. McGovern had Adams chart a course. By the time the isle appeared on the horizon an hour later, the *Queen* was barely 600 feet above the Adriatic. The runway was not a reassuring sight in any event, surrounded as it was by mountains, its perimeter strewn with the wreckage of other bombers that had crashed, either short of the gravel strip or into the promontory rising at the far end. "If you were down to two engines and had to pull up, I don't think we could have gone round again," McGovern said. "You had only one shot at the thing." At the very tip of the runway he managed to set down. With the exertion of weightlifters doing squats, pilot and copilot rode the floor pedals the whole length of their progress, the brake pads screeching and smoking all the way. Then the right tire collapsed, wrenching the plane to the side and nearly off the runway. "You almost felt we were going to ground loop," Tex Ashlock recollected, "but we bogged down in wet clay and stopped." Clambering out of the belly of the spent ship, the crew hugged one another and kissed the ground.

What happened next, though, crimped their exhilaration. No sooner had they piled into the back of a waiting truck than they heard the sputtering of another Liberator in distress. Immediately they could see that it was coming in too high and too fast. Pitching up and toward the side of the narrow valley, the plane plowed into one of the mountains that skirted the runway and exploded in a huge ball of fire. The following day McGovern and his men were transported back to Cerignola in a C-47. Among the 455th Bomber Group, alone, the mission to Skoda had claimed sixty of their brothers, killed or missing in action. Never, for the rest of their lives, would any of the men of the *Dakota Queen* have the slightest doubt that their captain was the reason why that number had not swollen to seventy.[39]

It was the nature of the air war that combatants would experience hour upon hour of almost unbearable tension of the foregoing sort for four and five days in a row; then there could be as much as a week's lull because of inclement weather. From December 15 to 26, McGovern's crew had flown seven missions, which included the ordeal of the blown-out tire, the potentially fatal detour to Vis, and the one during which McGovern almost literally lost his head to a piece of flak. After that, the *Dakota Queen* was grounded until the last day of January 1945, Europe's worst month of winter weather in a generation. For several weeks the men did not have much to do. Some played poker or ping-pong while others drank wine or courted Italian women. McGovern wrote letters to Eleanor, did a lot of reading, and cultivated friendships, particularly with Bill Rounds and Sam Adams.[40]

McGovern had long ago come to overlook his copilot's crazy antics and amorous adventures on the ground, neither of which had abated in Italy. Bill Rounds was a superb flier. ("He is especially good in flying formation," George wrote to Bill's parents, which "is the surest way in the world to live in combat.") And he did rather enjoy the Kansan's frequently crude tales of sexual athleticism. Yet it was Sam Adams with whom George formed the deepest bond. The two were of similar habit and temperament. They both read more than any of the others and often had reflective conversation about the war and politics and life in general. Sam disapproved of the way George indulged Rounds's bull sessions, but he knew he was a serious person with a good mind— someone who instinctively understood why he wanted to become a minister, just as George knew that Sam appreciated his own aspirations to become a college professor.

Then, too, McGovern respected and depended on his navigator's composure and skill as much as he did his copilot's. When the *Dakota Queen* was down to two engines over the Adriatic and all but grazing the whitecaps, one might have made the case that Sam could share the credit in retrieving an otherwise hopeless situation. Adams fully reciprocated. He dreaded going aloft with anybody other than George, but he and the others would have to do so five times in order to fulfill their thirty-five-mission obligation. (Crews were always behind their pilots by five and flew substitute service on other ships as opportunities arose.) It was during one of these catch-up journeys that Sam lost his life. On March 12, over Vienna, his plane was struck by antiaircraft fire; only two of its members survived. For weeks, George recalled, "we lived with Sam's empty bunk, his treasured photographs and his neatly hung clothing, waiting for further word that never came." Then one day someone at headquarters came to collect his things. George held on to the pen and pencil set and sent it to Sam's mother. His three-page letter to her took him several drafts.[41]

"I worried and worked and worked and worried," Eleanor once said about the months of separation from her husband. But of her fear she uttered not a word to anyone. She did not need to. By 1944–45, some fourteen million Americans were in the armed services, and the Allied war effort on the European continent was at its absolute height. As Eleanor observed, "by that time, foreboding permeated the house, the town, the country." A sudden knock at the door and "I would feel a stab of fear," she said. Every night she wrote to George and then read from the Bible—including the passage that began with, "To every thing there is a season" and ending with "A time of war, and a time of peace." Every morning she waited anxiously for the postman. Taking up to two weeks to arrive, George's letters, like hers to him, contained expressions of love and anecdotes of how a given day had gone, but, whereas he always noted his current tally, he spared her stories of combat. "I'd go through the letters hurriedly, looking for the number, to see how many missions he had flown," she said. "And then I went back and read the letter."[42]

She stayed busy. In addition to her job at the law office in Mitchell, she managed her father's household and, after George's father died, she divided her time between Earl and her mother-in-law, for Frances seemed "more grief-stricken and helpless than many widows." But by midwinter it was the pregnant Eleanor for whom both families felt the greater concern. Because she was so diminutive and the baby weighed seven pounds, her labor lasted thirty-six hours. Everyone was at the hospital for the event—her father, Ila, Phyllis, George's mother, and Mildred, who was now a nurse in obstetrics. As Eleanor described it, "they brought me a delicate, beautiful baby girl, every bit as lovely as my mother, for whom she would be named." Ann Marian McGovern, she cabled George, was born on March 10, 1945.[43]

The news of Ann's birth reached Cerignola on March 14. George was jubilant, and the crew drank to him and the baby in the old stone stable that was the officers' club.[44] But a heavy heart also plagued George that afternoon. Only two days before, Sam Adams had been reported missing in action, and he had just returned from a mission that would haunt him for decades. It had started as a milk run. Over the marshaling yards at Wiener-Neustadt, Austria, they had dropped their payload, except for one 500-pounder, which had gotten stuck in the racks. George left the formation to bring the plane down several thousand feet to give the men time to dislodge the hazard over open country on the way home. They were still struggling as the *Dakota Queen* neared the Italian border. Finally one of them jerked something loose; then, the moment the cylinder was rolling out, a farmhouse suddenly came into view through the bomb bay doors. "I'm watching the thing, and it looked like it went down the chimney," Ken Higgins explained. McGovern saw the explosion and glanced at his watch; it was noon, the time most farm families come in to have their main meal of the day. "I got a sickening feeling," he remembered. "It just withered the house, the barn, the chicken house, the water tank. *Everything* was just leveled."[45]

The crew returned to base to learn that George had become a father. During the impromptu celebration, he wondered to himself what Ann Marion looked like. But the thought kept creeping back into his mind that he probably had wiped out an innocent family, perhaps one like the Stegebergs of Woonsocket, and maybe the Austrian farmer's wife also had recently had a baby. "Just a peaceful farmyard. Had nothing to do with the war. Just a family eating a noon meal," he muttered.[46] After twenty missions he had encountered the war's harshest reality.

World War II killed more civilians than soldiers. Some portion of this carnage was accidental. On July 24–25, 1944, for example, at Normandy, B-17s and B-24s mistakenly bombed American infantry, killing 136 and wounding another 631. On D-Day itself, incontinent bombing and shelling slaughtered some 12,000 French and Belgians.[47] But the numbers of civilian casualties due to blunders were minor in contrast to those that were not. In an air assault over Tokyo (five days before McGovern's unfortunate incident) American incendiaries ignited tornadoes of fire that asphyxiated, boiled in the city's canals, or incinerated about 100,000 noncombatants. A month earlier, the same methods of the AAF and RAF burned to death some 40,000 citizens of Dresden. Between 300,000 and 600,000 German civilians perished as a result of all types of Allied bombing, as did perhaps half a million Japanese city dwellers in Allied raids in the war's final year (not counting Tokyo or Hiroshima and Nagasaki).[48]

The policy of inflicting such grief remains a flashpoint of debate among historians. It was a function of mathematical calculation proceeding from the confidence that policy makers placed in US industrial and technological capabilities, combined with righteous indignation. It evolved incrementally. The terror bombing of population centers, alongside so-called precision bombing of militarily significant targets, at first was rationalized because of the evil that Hitler represented and the assumption that it would end the war more quickly. As of 1944, however, findings of the US Strategic Bombing Survey (USSBS) revealed that even precision bombing in the European theater of operations had yet to show a serious diminution in the enemy's ability and will to carry on the war. For the Germans performed amazing feats in repairing damaged factories, ports, and marshaling yards, while their arms production actually increased through 1944. The official Army Air Forces history judged the air offensive of 1942–43 to be "flat, repetitive, and without climax." Consequently, the USSBS urged the air force to bring to bear a more efficient and humane method of destruction against the Third Reich as well as against Japan when that aerial war swung into high gear in 1945. Yet once it became apparent that the campaign was beginning to undermine Germany's economic strength in areas such as oil production, those successes fed a certain mindset— that massive terror bombing could not help but force Axis capitulation sooner rather than later.[49]

The men and boys who carried out the policy had no particular reason for questioning the AAF slogans, "Precision Bombing Will Win the War" and "Victory through Air Power," except for the extraordinary dangers they had to cope with. In addition to their 35,946 noncombat fatalities, airmen accounted for 52,172 of the official total of 291,557 battle deaths for the United States. Moreover, the odds of being captured were far higher in the air force as well, and its officers died in combat at double the rate of any other branch of the army. No form of combat service, then, held greater risks than warfare in the skies.[50]

Yet battle-induced emotional disturbances among crews were relatively rare, and just 2 percent were diagnosed with "nervous breakdowns." (On the *Dakota Queen*, only Mike Valko required psychiatric treatment.) Psychological problems that did occur almost never attached to the mass killings they participated in, but rather to the stress—the feeling of helplessness during antiaircraft barrages or the loss of a friend. Then there was the plane itself, a potential coffin irrespective of enemy fire. All of these perils loomed more terrifyingly in Europe, where aircrew casualties were twenty-six times greater than in the Pacific war.[51]

On any given mission, the immediate motivation was simply to survive. In general, fliers carried out their orders without ideological passion or moral apprehension, nor with much hatred toward the Germans. The absence of remorse regarding enemy noncombatants owed chiefly to the fact that, except for firestorms like Dresden or Tokyo, bomber crews did not see the effects of the skills they employed; nor, at a remove of four miles above, could they always be sure they had hit their targets until reconnaissance photographs were processed.[52] McGovern himself had dropped scores of tons of bombs and admitted of little sense of guilt about collateral civilian casualties. But an atypical sense of purpose evidently sustained him. "I so detested the whole Nazi system that I never really thought about it," he once said. "I was never aware it was killing large numbers of people. I always thought in terms of hitting strategic targets."[53] Not until his twenty-first mission did something else take hold. In the span of two days random circumstance had visited upon him the birth of his and Eleanor's first child, the loss of his best friend in the service, and the sobering reality of having served as the instrument of death of "just a family eating a noon meal." For the preacher's son from America's heartland the coincidence was appalling. Still, with fourteen missions still to go, he did not allow himself to become obsessed by it. All the same, he said many years later, "It really did make me feel different for the rest of the war."[54]

In a letter to Pennington some months before he became a warrior for democracy, George mused about the years ahead: "after this thing is all over," he and Bob and their wives could be together "and really enjoy whatever it is we're supposed to be fighting for."[55] Those lines captured the grousing of the typical letter from a GI. But the offhanded remark—"whatever it is we're supposed to be fighting for"—could not have been more profound, even if answers to it seldom were. For example, the famous war correspondent and novelist John Hersey once asked marines on Guadalcanal what they were fighting for. After a pause, one of them whispered, "Jesus, what I wouldn't give for a piece of blueberry pie," while another gave the more common reply, "to get the goddamn thing over and get home." When the *Saturday Evening Post* asked the same question, responses varied from a "nice little roadster" to "America and Christianity." In 1944 the assistant secretary of war for the AAF detected "very little idealism" among returnees and "not much willingness to discuss what we are fighting for." Ernie Pyle sought opinions about the proposal for the United Nations. "The run-of-the-mass soldiers didn't think twice about this bill," he reported. "It sounded too much like another Atlantic Charter."[56]

It is no reflection upon their sacrifices to point out that the vast majority of GIs were, as Bill Mauldin ascertained, so "tired of having their noses rubbed in this stinking war that their only ambition will be to forget about it." But there was an alternative perspective among men like McGovern. He was one of those apparent few to be "carried away," as he put it, "by the vision of Roosevelt and Churchill and the Four Freedoms and the United Nations." From the beginning, the struggle against fascism seemed to him unambiguous, and he believed "western civilization was at stake."[57] He also cared about the politics and diplomacy of the conflict. As early as January 1943, he was already "a little worried about the peace fight after the war," and disappointed with the recent Roosevelt-Churchill conference at Casablanca because the other principals were not represented there. "I'm afraid that Russia, China, and India . . . aren't going to cooperate with us as well as some people think," he wrote to Bob, asking him, "what do you think is going to come of this war? Are we really going to be any better off than before or will it be the same old thing for our kids 25 yrs. from now?" McGovern's main concern was the future of the Grand Alliance. "When a person stops to think that our objectives in this war are so vastly conflicting with those of the Russians," he wrote in March 1943, "it seems inevitable that we are going to clash sooner or later." He was mindful of Roosevelt and Churchill's great dilemma in dealing with Stalin, a subject he and Matt Smith had once debated—that the Soviet Union's contribution to Allied victory over fascism was at least as vital as that of the United States and Great Britain. Yet his apprehensions did not dampen his gratitude: "The Russians are really coming back into their own, aren't they," he exclaimed to Bob on the day before the Big Three met at Yalta in February 1945. "From where I sit the map looks plenty good. Those boys are kindly removing some of our roughest targets for us."[58]

That winter he nonetheless experienced a rough patch, intellectually, though it was short-lived. "I can't seem to keep my mind centered on a really good book long enough to digest it," he told Bob; he was even finding his "intense interest in history beginning to cool off." Then, after Sam's death, Ann's birth, and the Austrian farmhouse incident, he started reading again. His most significant diversion was Charles and Mary Beard's *The Rise of American Civilization*, a work read by tens of millions of students in the first half of the twentieth century.

Charles Beard was one of the most influential American historians who ever lived. He was also controversial. In *An Economic Interpretation of the Constitution* (1913), for instance, he had attempted to demonstrate that men of wealth seeking chiefly to secure their power over civil society crafted the Constitution. By the late 1930s he had become FDR's harshest critic among academics as well as a leading anti-interventionist (some would say isolationist).[59] Early editions of *The Rise of American Civilization*, however, were published before the war and did not address contemporary foreign policy. But the economic interpretation was woven into its arresting tapestry, the most brilliant redaction being devoted to the Civil War. That catastrophe the Beards likened to the French Revolution, explicating a veritable "social cataclysm in which capitalists, laborers, and farmers in the North and West drove from power in the national government the planting aristocracy of the South." Hence the Civil War was actually "the Second American Revolution." In its time, that particular analysis "had the force of revelation," Richard Hofstadter averred, and the work set an untold number of historians on their path. It also struck a chord among a more general audience reeling from the Depression and in search of an understanding of American institutions.[60]

McGovern fit both categories of readership. At 1,700 pages, the two-volume text was formidable, but, often into the late hours by candlelight in his tent, he read it from cover to cover, underlining heavily. He was especially enthralled by the Beards' broad-gauged thesis that American civilization (as of 1936) was the product of discord and conflict rather than of some divine purpose implanted in the minds of a favored people. But the story's outcome had yet to be arranged. And so McGovern bracketed the Beards' paraphrase of Emerson, who once had advised Americans, "in search of the full life, to stand fast where they are and work out their destiny in the place allotted to them by history for the fulfillment of their capacities."[61]

In subsequent years, McGovern's military experience would earn him membership in an exclusive pantheon. Among presidential candidates in the twentieth century, none save Eisenhower could boast of a more impressive combat record. And yet World War II is important in understanding McGovern's public career not alone because he had shown such a "high degree of courage and piloting skill . . . intrepid spirit . . . and rare devotion to duty" as affirmed by the citation to the Distinguished Flying Cross he would be awarded in the spring of 1945. For those exploits took place in the context of an ongoing endeavor marked by the sort of historical ruminating he had begun at Mitchell High and Dakota Wesleyan. Moreover, the war was not merely a patriotic adventure to him—in part because it had blown away certain illusions while reinforcing certain convictions he held. "If I thought about the war," he once said, "almost invariably I would think about that farm." In its climactic chapter, an array of experiential and intellectual influences crowded in on him, each playing its part in keeping him true to the path he had staked out long before. In May, he would decline a lucrative offer to go to work for Bill Rounds's father. A PhD in history was what he *really* wanted. "I've discovered that old driving interest to learn rather than make money is still dominant," he reported to Bob. "I'm afraid I'm 'doomed' to the life of a student and teacher."[62]

In the meantime he still had a job to finish. In these months the *Dakota Queen* flew missions against more marshaling yards and refineries as well as the bridges at the famed Brenner Pass on the edge of the Alps. On the first of April, on a mission to Germany, McGovern's crew for the first time saw indications that the end was coming—the movement of Russian ground troops advancing against Nazi front lines. While the Russians and Americans pushed into the Fatherland from east and west, the *Queen* also participated in tactical support for the Fifth Army in northern Italy. On the fifteenth, they struck German gun emplacements and troop concentrations near Bologna, in a twenty-four-hour operation involving more than 2,000 aircraft. The next three days presented similar assignments to Verona and to the Po River valley. On their thirty-third mission, on April 23, the 455th destroyed road bridges at Padua. Forty-two B-24s went out and forty-two returned unscathed.[63]

For all crews the prospect of mission thirty-five was the occasion for high hopes and worry, although by this point—the week before Hitler committed suicide—they counted on an easy time. But the *Dakota Queen*'s thirty-fifth was a return to Linz, the Führer's "hometown," still one of Austria's most heavily fortified rail hubs. Although the crew did not expect a milk run, they could hardly have guessed they were embarking upon their most desperate journey of all.

Because supplies and tens of thousands of German soldiers continued to move through Linz, the Fifteenth Air Force decided to send up every bomber available on that crisp twenty-fifth of April—altogether, 557 B-17s and B-24s, escorted by two hundred fighter planes. As the attacks commenced, a crystalline sky offered visibility for thirty miles, perfect weather not only for the bombers but also for the sixty-eight antiaircraft guns deployed in each of the city's quadrants. Within a two-hour period, a thousand tons of bombs fell on station buildings, railroad tracks and rolling stock, and industrial workshops. Severe explosions and fires erupted everywhere. Havoc, however, was not limited to ground zero.[64]

The 455th was among the four bomber groups that constituted the first wave. Of those sixteen seven-plane squadrons, McGovern's would receive the highest ratings for accuracy and results, "very good," according to the official report. But inside the *Dakota Queen* nobody felt even *pretty* good. They had barely come out of their run when flak began hitting the plane like machine gun spray. The first big burst cut through the ship's nose and destroyed the hydraulic lines. Then two other hits put the number three engine out of commission. Moments later more flak broke through the fuselage, a piece of it sawing up the length of Tex Ashlock's leg. For several terrible minutes, bedlam reigned. Everyone in the nose was slipping and falling in the hydraulic fluid streaming everywhere. Carroll Cooper, Sam Adams's replacement as navigator, was completely soaked and trying to trap some in flak helmets. In sheer terror Mike Valko was shouting out the locations of what looked to be scores of hits they had taken. And through the din, Ashlock's wails—"I'm hit! I'm hit!"—resounded over the intercom.[65]

Then the captain came on the system, telling them all to pipe down—"as cool, calm a deal as you would ever want to hear," as Ashlock recalled, although he was the only one who did not respond to it. (He "was making quite a racket on the intercom," Ken Higgins said, "so we finally just unplugged him.") McGovern ordered the men to report in to him, station by station, as he feathered number three and Higgins tore off Ashlock's pants leg, applied sulfa, and gave him a shot of morphine. No one else was injured, and they had passed beyond the danger zone. But their heat suits had gone cold and the oxygen supply was failing; accordingly, McGovern brought the *Queen* down about fifteen thousand feet. By then, the rest of the formation had long since disappeared. Now the only noise inside the ship came from the engines and the frigid air rushing through the big hole in the nosecap. They were already reported missing in action.[66]

The real crisis settled on the mangled hydraulics. The wing flaps were working only intermittently. The landing gear would have to be cranked down by hand. And even if they made it back to Cerignola, they had no brakes. When they were finally close enough to establish radio contact, McGovern reviewed the options with the control tower—to bail out, to ditch in the Adriatic, or to try to crash land at the base. He decided to brave the latter peril. He also had ideas about slowing the plane once it touched the ground: Higgins and McAfee were to secure two parachutes at each waist window and pull the cords upon his command; everybody else was to move to the rear in hopes that their weight would bring the tail down and cause it to drag. Meanwhile the men took turns at the crank until the main wheels locked in place.

At last they sighted the field. In the circumstances, it was not going to be one of McGovern's better landings. He came in too high and cut the power too soon and, at 150 mph, slammed onto the runway. Instantly he ordered the chutes released. They caught the wind, but the tail stayed up. Onward they careened, out of control and off the tarmac, roller-coastering down into a ditch, the tail pitching up forty-five degrees, then up the other side, the tail smacking back down with tremendous force. There she came to stop. Medics arrived and carried Ashlock away in an ambulance. The others walked back to their encampment, but not before surveying their all-but-shattered Liberator, perched upon her final resting place, riddled with sixty-seven holes and destined for the scrap heap. The next morning the Army Air Forces in the European Theater were ordered to stand down. The *Dakota Queen* had flown her final mission on the very last day of the air war against the Third Reich, which had now ended.[67]

Virtually overnight everyone's thoughts turned homeward. Yet McGovern's B-24 service was not quite over. The AAF found itself with huge surpluses of all sorts of rations—cornmeal, peanut butter, powdered eggs, Spam. For six weeks bombers ferried these cargoes to various locations for distribution to Italy's destitute population and to thousands of German POWs. McGovern liked this work.[68] To deliver food to the hungry seemed a fitting bookend to his arrival at Naples and the sight of starving children so many months ago.

New orders came through in June. He had always wanted the chance to fly a B-24 across the ocean. Now he was getting it. The crew could return stateside together. Tex Ashlock was still in the hospital and was upset that he could not go with them. The moment he saw McGovern enter the ward to say goodbye he started to cry. "I wouldn't leave you here if there was any doubt at all about your coming home," he assured the nineteen-year-old, praising his bravery and reliability. "You'll be back there soon." The crew left Cerignola on June 18. The route included refueling stops at Marrakesh, the Azores, and Newfoundland and ending at Boston.[69]

The memory of that Atlantic crossing would stay with McGovern forever. That night there were no antiaircraft batteries and close-in formations, nor flak, nor wind milling props to worry about. As everyone else on the plane slept, there was only the steady drone of the engines, a full moon overhead, and banks of clouds below. For a while he thought about his four-month-old daughter. Then he turned up the cockpit light so he could see the worn billfold photograph of Eleanor he had set on the instrument panel on every mission he had flown. He wondered what it would be like to hold her in his arms again. He also pondered what he had done.

"The members of my crew were boys when they entered combat," he would write many years later. "They emerged as serious men." That description certainly included himself, for gone was the physical aspect of the college debater self-conscious about his boyish looks and innocent of death and destruction. He had flown thirty-five potentially fatal missions and brought his crew back alive every time. For having overcome incredible odds, his superiors had judged him worthy of the Distinguished Flying Cross, burnished with three oak leaf clusters. Carroll Cooper called him "the best B-24 pilot in the world." But McGovern always blanched at that sort of thing. He would have understood what Admiral Nimitz meant when he wrote in his memoirs of his men at Iwo Jima, "Uncommon valor was a common virtue." He was content just to feel "a kind of glow that I had come through this," and to say, "I had survived."[70]

There was one other component to his reverie. Within a single generation America had fought two great wars, and he would be fated to devote virtually the rest of his life to trying to comprehend and interpret their meaning, and to delineating what his country afterward might do with its unexampled opportunity. Just then, though, as the moon's rays reflected up from the clouds far beneath the plane, he felt a kind of satisfaction. Most of it had to do with Roosevelt and the Four Freedoms and the United Nations, as well as with the Allied victory and his own exploits. Together, they imbued him with fresh confidence in the future and nurtured "that old Wilsonian view that this time it was over." For the present, it appeared that America was "going to continue the wartime cooperation with the British and Soviets and . . . we would weigh in on the side of collective security and cooperation." His first step would be to resume his history studies, the better to understand this good fortune that Americans had come into—"to work out their destiny in the place allotted to them by history for the fulfillment of their capacities," whatever that might be. For many reasons, it was "a great, quieting, wonderful experience" that would endure in McGovern's memory of coming home: "I thought all was right with the world. The United States had done the right thing. I was going back to participate in the launching of a new day in world affairs."[71]

5 I WOULD HAVE TO CALL HIM A PROGRESSIVE AGRARIAN

When his B-24 set down at Gander, Newfoundland, ten months had passed since George had heard the sound of Eleanor's voice, and he could not resist an extravagant impulse to call her. He would catch the first available troop train out of Boston to Minneapolis, where he would be discharged from the service, he told her. He could hardly wait to see her on the station platform in Mitchell in just another three days. But Eleanor had thoughts of her own about that moment. She did not intend to share it with anyone else—not with friends or family, not even with the baby. "I want it just to be the two of us when you first come in," she said. So they met for a two-day rendezvous at the Hotel Nicollet in Minneapolis before proceeding to Mitchell.[1]

George's mother and his brother and sisters were waiting for them as the train pulled into the old depot on June 23, 1945. The homecoming was joyous. His father had died the previous December, but Ann was there in his stead. The ride through town with his tiny daughter on his lap, then arriving at his home at the corner of Fifth and Sanborn, made George muse about the continuity of life. He was also taken aback by how unfazed everyone in Mitchell appeared to be as they went about their routines, almost as if the war had never happened. Like so many other returnees, he looked forward to picking up where he and his wife had left off. In many respects they would, but not entirely.[2]

"When George came home," Eleanor said, looking back, "we were almost strangers." More than anything, she lamented that the separation had occurred at such a crucial point in their marriage. Nothing could ever compensate for that time lost; their relationship had been "irrevocably altered by unshared experiences." This was rendered in one particularly jarring way early on. In his waking hours, George seemed completely normal, as he was, albeit a bit more serious and worldly than before. But he suffered from terrible dreams. Fifty years later Eleanor remembered being shaken from sleep in the middle of the night by George, thrashing about in a sweat and screaming, as if to his crew, "Get out! Get out! The plane is on fire!" Then they would talk, sometimes until dawn. The nightmares persisted for months.

The nature of their separation had another impact that also accounted for "the ambivalence of our postwar reunion," as she frankly characterized it. In their wartime letters they had enthused about having a real honeymoon and about living "as newly married lovers, free at last from the fear of death." For both of them it was hard to concede that they "would never have that period of abandon." They were a family of three now. "I suspect that even though he worshipped little Ann, he must have felt temporarily cheated out of being a couple," Eleanor wrote. "I knew we had both changed, that things were different."[3]

What she could not know, of course, was just how eventful their lives together were going to be, nor the accelerated pace. In less than a decade, he would finish his bachelor's degree, undertake to become a Methodist minister, start graduate school, teach at his alma mater, and complete his PhD dissertation. Then, having undergone a political metamorphosis, he would give up academics for politics and run for Congress. During the same span, Eleanor would bear four more children while being her husband's helpmate in all of his endeavors. From the standpoint of American family history, this beginning was a microcosm of a certain social stratum in the postwar years. In their case, the transition in their personal lives was affected more so than most by the larger events of a crowded decade that would turn out to be one of the most profound transitional periods in the history of the United States.

By 1945, most Americans had come to the conclusion that all veterans were worthy of government assistance—and quite a bit more. Even before Pearl Harbor, they had been making all kinds of provisions for their heirs, based on the proposition that it was both the decent and sensible thing to do. The young people who served in World War II may, or may not, have been "the greatest generation any society has produced," as the journalist Tom Brokaw declared in 1998 in his popular anthology of wartime reminiscences.[4] Without question, they were one of the most historically distinctive of generations; in childhood and adolescence, they had had to endure the worst depression ever to befall the United States and then, in early adulthood, to shoulder their country's burden in fighting the worst war in history. But they carried another distinction: They were the children of parents who accorded them more opportunities to make a good life than any generation had ever done for another. Most of those opportunities derived from three words—the New Deal.

For example, because of the New Deal's banking legislation, Americans would be free of the elemental fear of having their savings accounts wiped out overnight. Neither would they have to worry much about their parents falling onto hard times as retirement age approached, because of Social Security. Then, too, the Wagner Act and the Fair Labor Standards Act secured for blue-collar workers the right to organize unions and bargain collectively and a minimum wage. The New Deal also took steps on behalf of those, like the Stegebergs of Woonsocket, who fed the factory workers. In 1933 only 20 percent of the nation's farms had electricity. Within a decade the Rural Electrification Administration had more than quadrupled that proportion, while the two Agricultural Adjustment Acts (of 1933 and 1938) had established crop insurance, loans, and price supports—the goals of farmers since the Populist movement. In addition to transforming country life, the federal government befriended suburbanites trying to hold onto middle-class status in legislation that guaranteed home mortgages, which, in turn, benefited banks and the construction industry.

No less significant were the New Deal's massive public works projects, which had created jobs for nearly one-third of the nation's fourteen million unemployed. By 1940–41, these workers had constructed literally tens of thousands of bridges and public buildings (including thousands of schools, hospitals, and courthouses, plus six hundred airports) and 500,000 miles of roadways, not to mention a network of TVA dams and improved harbors. From manufacturing and the money exchange to real estate, textiles, and transportation, these programs exerted an enormously salutary effect upon virtually every area of the economy. Liberal reform not only had saved American capitalism, it also had made the economic system more dynamic and more humane (even though the plight of the very poorest citizens had not been substantially altered). In tandem with the repercussions of the vast wartime expansion, the New Deal had bequeathed to its children the essential civil works infrastructure, so to speak, upon which they would build the previously elusive American Dream.

There was more to come. Parents welcomed home serving sons and daughters with open wallets as well as open arms. In the summer of 1944, President Roosevelt signed the "bill of rights for G.I. Joe and G.I. Jane." The Servicemen's Readjustment Act provided money for college and vocational school tuition for up to four years, and low interest loans for homes, farms, and small business start-ups. By 1952, the federal government would spend $13.5 billion for veteran's education (roughly the amount expended on the Marshall Plan) and would guarantee $16 billion worth of loans for the other good purposes—in all, the greatest such investment by any government in history. The generation led by Franklin Roosevelt had no peer in America's past in showing such imaginative gratitude to its children and in furnishing a rising generation with so many means to the pursuit of happiness.[5] So it was that George McGovern was able to lay plans for getting his life and career under way.

During that discomfiting summer of 1945, he was understandably restless, not only with the prospect of school and the responsibilities of a family man, but with a heightened sensitivity to events, too—especially in light of the way the war in Asia had ended. Like the rest of the country, he was astonished and relieved by the suddenness of it. In "a harnessing of the basic power of the universe," as the White House called it, a single bomb in a single B-29 had delivered upon Hiroshima and then Nagasaki the equivalent of 12,000 and 22,000 tons of explosives. Together, the two cities sustained approximately 200,000 civilian deaths, a third of them within seconds, the rest within days or weeks. In terms of McGovern's knowledge of conventional war, to match the Nagasaki device would have required an inconceivable mission of 4,000 Liberators, a striking illustration of how much warfare had changed since Pearl Harbor. Just then he felt that President Truman had made the right decision.[6]

About the necessity of the second bomb, though, he would soon have second thoughts. His doubts were perhaps inevitable for a veteran who remained troubled by the thought that he had destroyed a single family of innocents and who continued in his nightmares to fear for the lives of his crewmen. Reams of articles appeared in August and September 1945 that explored the far-reaching implications of the blasts as "bright as a thousand suns." The *Christian Century*, among the few harsh assessments, referred to "the impetuous adoption of this incredibly inhuman instrument." Dwight MacDonald, in the journal *Politics*, did not see it as impetuous; rather, it revealed "how inhuman our normal life has become." The vast majority of publications did not criticize the deed itself. Hanson Baldwin of the *New York Times* captured a pervasive strain in wondering whether atomic energy would usher in "a new world [of] . . . common brotherhood, or . . . of troglodytes." Robert Hutchins of the University of Chicago likened the bomb to a kind of "damnation" to "frighten us into . . . [taking the] steps necessary to the creation of a world society, not a thousand or five hundred years hence, but now."[7]

Essays like these convinced McGovern that "this was a weapon too terrifying" ever to use again, and he beheld the United Nations Organization (of which the United States became a member on the day before Nagasaki) as the best hope for containing the "nuclear monster." That particular faith—that Woodrow Wilson's ostensible vindication in the creation of the United Nations meant something substantive—was fairly common among college-bound veterans, and it was one of the forces motivating him as he resumed work on his bachelor's degree. "There was a great spirit of hope and a great wave of practical idealism running through the campuses," he recalled. And he aimed "to be a part of that postwar effort to build a structure of peace on the smoldering ruins of war." The question was, "how best to contribute to the peace of the world."[8]

About five hundred students at Dakota Wesleyan had answered the call to duty as of 1945. The drain of its male population had pulled enrollments down by more than half, to 130. When McGovern returned that fall, the GI Bill was causing a different problem. The number of students suddenly quadrupled; over half of them were veterans, and the campus was skirted with makeshift housing for them and their wives. Because the university granted him credits for flight school, McGovern would finish his degree in one year. He earned solid As in philosophy, sociology, international economics, French, and Latin American and world history. But by far his favorite course was "The Making of the Modern Mind," taught by Donald McAnnich, a newly minted PhD from Boston University, who exuded intellectual freshness in this, his first year as a teacher. McGovern was "looking for nothing less than an answer to the ultimate questions of man, society, and the universe," and McAnnich swept him away.[9]

McGovern was searching mainly for ideas that could "serve the needs of my time" when McAnnich trained his attention on writings of the Social Gospel, a movement that had arisen in response to the abuses of concentrated wealth and industrial capitalism of turn-of-the century America. The founders of this new school of religious thought believed that the Protestant Church had a vital social mission to fulfill. Social Gospelers demanded that the church face up to the appalling conditions of American urban life in which it had so long acquiesced. If, for example, factory workers and coal miners were compelled to toil in circumstances that threatened life and limb from moment to moment, and capital and the political system refused to do anything about it, then the time had come for Christians to apply the message of Jesus to the workplace. The Social Gospel would become the primary religious agency of the burgeoning Progressive movement.[10]

The leading light of this activist outlook was Walter Rauschenbusch, a professor of church history at Rochester Theological Seminary who had ministered for eleven years to a church next to Hell's Kitchen in New York. At McAnnich's urging, McGovern read the theologian's seminal work, *Christianity and the Social Crisis*, published in 1907. He was immediately struck by the epigraph on the dedication page: "Thy Kingdom Come, Thy Will Be Done on Earth." McGovern had never thought about the Lord's Prayer in quite that way. He turned the pages "hungrily."

As he outlined how the crushing conditions of modern industrial America had come to be, Rauschenbusch argued that "the church must either condemn the world and seek to change it, or tolerate the world and conform to it." Just as new thinking in politics and journalism was beginning to raise public awareness, so must the church embrace new methods "to rally the moral forces of the community against everything that threatens the better life among men." The problem was industrial capitalism, a "mammonistic organization with which Christianity can never be content." Not every Social Gospeler was as politically "radical" as Rauschenbusch, however. But his book enjoyed an international readership and multiple printings; it became the catalyst for a movement within the church in support of labor unions and federal social welfare legislation. The Social Gospel represented a kind of left-wing Protestantism, though it was never very far from the ministries of liberal reformers like Jane Addams, or Theodore Roosevelt and Woodrow Wilson.[11]

Rauschenbusch and other adherents such as Harry Emerson Fosdick directed their entreaties at "young and serious minds" of the 1910s already "absorbed in the solution of social problems." They also exhorted others not so absorbed to harness, in Fosdick's phrase, their "religious motive power and zeal . . . to the problems of human welfare." These were not the kind of sermons McGovern had heard as a boy. Although it renewed his appreciation for his biblical training, his reading gave him a critical perspective on his fundamentalist father's emphasis on doctrine. Suddenly, his religious faith and keenness for politics had been brought into harmony. "For the first time," he said, "Christianity appeared to me as a very practical code for dealing with social, political, and international problems." Of all the books McGovern would ever read, none surpassed the impact of *Christianity and the Social Crisis*.[12]

His epiphany inspired him to enter South Dakota's annual collegiate peace oratory contest. As he had done in 1942, he would capture first-place honors. His speech, "From Cave to Cave," began with an account of a largely forgotten atrocity committed in December 1945 by American troops stationed in north China as part of the Truman administration's effort to forestall conflict between the forces of Chiang Kai-shek and Mao Zedong. A Chinese (possibly a communist) killed or perhaps murdered an American soldier, and the commander retaliated by shelling the village that harbored the suspect, killing scores of innocent men, women, and children. McGovern asked why the American military should have insisted on such disproportionate punishment. He next described an instance of what in the twenty-first century is called outsourcing. In India, a steel mill owned jointly by British and American capitalists was reaping a 300 percent profit on its investment. Yet the Indian laborers worked under conditions that would have made Henry Clay Frick wince; they were paid slightly over a penny an hour, or about one-fiftieth the prevailing minimum wage in the United States. Perhaps this was what Gandhi had in mind, McGovern remarked, when he told Americans, "Bring your Christ, but leave your Christianity at home." Lastly, there was the news item about a group of scientists who called on America's industrial leaders to relocate their factories to huge underground chambers, in anticipation of another war. The headline was "The History of Mankind in Four Words—From Cave to Cave."

The foregoing sins had been committed, McGovern said, for the sake of military pride, profits, and expediency. They betokened "a set of values that advances the material to the exclusion of the spiritual." He doubted whether a solution lay in any discrete program, citing the debate over how to control the bomb, which seemed to be "only a screen for the feverish battle . . . in the quest for atomic supremacy." He offered two suggestions instead: ungrudging adherence to the international agreements to which the United States was already a signatory and to "the applied idealism of Christianity." To those "practical men" who might scoff, a *genuine* effort might demonstrate "that applied idealism is the only true practicality." Otherwise, the devaluation of human life and international cooperation, the "harvest of . . . practical men," was sure to go on.[13]

McGovern's speech was steeped in Rauschenbusch. It was also informed by his own wartime experiences—his exposure to malnourished Italian children; his missions to airlift food once hostilities had ceased; and a growing visceral reaction to the mass killings in which he was implicated, sown by the Austrian farmhouse incident and now magnified by the atomic apocalypse. If his sense of the imminence of "a new day in world affairs" was undiminished, he was obviously having inklings that the war might not be the last one, and that the United Nations might not get the hearing it deserved.

Sometime that winter he had heard about a graduate fellowship at Garrett Theological Seminary. It involved a student pastorate. Garrett, located in Evanston, Illinois, was an institution with its share of Social Gospelers on the faculty; it occurred to him that his father's vocation might be the right path after all. He discussed the plan with Eleanor. She did not like the idea. She did not say, "No, you can't do it," but just now she preferred not to be away from home. Their second child was due in March and she felt unprepared for the responsibilities of a minister's wife. Mother McGovern, who had played that role for twenty-five years, was even more skeptical. What her son proposed would have pleased the departed Joseph, but she questioned the plan because it seemed to her entirely intellectual rather than "a calling." Nonetheless, come summer he set out by himself to begin his Garrett apprenticeship at the Methodist Church at Diamond Lake, thirty miles from Evanston. Eleanor, Ann, and little Susan were to join him in July.[14]

Writing sermons was hard work. Predictably, McGovern drew his themes from Rauschenbusch as well as biblical verses, such as "Whosoever will save his life will lose it; and whosoever will lose his life for my sake will find it." He preached the Social Gospel—about reaching "beyond immediate self-serving enrichment to consideration for the well-being of others," and about "a willingness to subordinate national rivalry and commercial greed to the larger needs of the human family." His flock was conservative, small, and well heeled. Yet it indulged the earnest twenty-four-year-old veteran, even if he stressed the social mission at the expense of doctrine. The congregation knew about his B-24 missions and the Distinguished Flying Cross, which no doubt shielded him from criticism when, for instance, one Sunday he declared, "Nuclear energy [has] rendered traditional nationalism obsolete." Attendance tripled within the month.[15]

By then Eleanor and the girls had arrived, followed a few weeks later by Ila and Bob Pennington and their baby daughter, Sharon. To save money, the Stegeberg twins and their husbands decided to live together in one big house. Since Bob was about to start the PhD program in history at Northwestern across the way from Garrett, he and George could carpool the twenty-five miles to Evanston. Eleanor and Ila were delighted to be under the same roof again and to be able to raise their girls together. For his part, George loved his courses at Garrett while meeting the challenge of weekly sermons. Yet several things about being a minister bothered him. "Every time the Methodist Church hierarchy comes through to check on me," he complained to Bob, "they want to know only two things: 'Has your congregation increased and have your collections increased?'" That emphasis caused him to wonder whether his sermons were making any impression. He felt even less at ease with his ministerial functions; in particular, he was embarrassed and ill equipped when parishioners brought their marital problems to him. He also disliked being regarded by the men as some sort of priest. Gradually he began to envy his friend engaged in the study of history, his own first love since high school.[16]

Bob Pennington had never considered not sticking to his original plan. A sense of purpose ran deeply in him. As a boy, despite the Depression, he had lived in affluence. His mother was a schoolteacher in Redfield, South Dakota; his father ran the town's electric company and earned $3,600 a year, an upper-middle-class income in the 1930s. Although Bob's parents were Republicans, the school of life changed his politics. His father died just before the war and his mother remarried—to a farmer, a Democrat. Bob was curious why his stepdad was not a Republican. "I'm an uneducated man and I've got problems being a farmer," he explained. "The only ones who have come through for us are the Democrats." Bob had to admit the observation had some validity. But the turning point occurred in 1940, after he had read about John Collier and the so-called Indian New Deal and spent that summer as a missionary on several of South Dakota's reservations. On one reservation, during a single week, sixteen small children died. "No doctor, no nurse. Nobody knew why they died. Some bug went through them, and that was it," he recalled. "When you're exposed to that sort of thing . . . you want to look for a solution." It was the spark of a lasting concern for Indians, and he would dedicate much of his career to the Bureau of Indian Affairs. But first he needed to gain historical perspective; so he would go to Northwestern to study with the rising scholar of the American frontier, Ray Allen Billington.[17]

One afternoon in the spring of 1947, Bob invited George to come along to his mentor's course in American social and intellectual history. The lecture was about the "Know Nothings," the nativist political party of the 1850s, about which Billington had written a book. Billington was one of the university's heavily subscribed professors. His lectures—for their blend of wit and rigorous analysis—were legendary. McGovern thought him brilliant and exciting. "By the end of that lecture I knew I had to get out of that seminary and move across the campus," he said. Eleanor had no qualms when, come fall, he plunged into the life of a born-again history student.[18]

With but a dozen faculty and twice that many graduate students, Northwestern's PhD program in history was exceptionally strong for its size. Several of McGovern's classmates would go on to great success in their fields. Alfred F. Young, for example, would become one of the nation's leading specialists on the American Revolution and social and labor history. Lawrence W. "Bill" Towner, another Early Americanist, would achieve eminence as the director of Chicago's Newberry Library. And William H. Harbaugh would have a celebrated career at the University of Virginia and write one of the finest one-volume biographies of Theodore Roosevelt ever published. Practically all of this band were mature combat veterans whose politics had been affected —in some cases "radicalized," according to Al Young—by their war experiences. Towner, for one, had seen hazardous action flying supplies to Chiang Kai-shek's army over the Hump from India and across the Himalayas; having witnessed the regime's corruption, he was troubled by the State Department's support of the dictator now.

Most of the graduate students shared one other attribute that stemmed from their personal experiences and impelled them toward a view of American politics and foreign policy at once critical and hopeful. McGovern was representative. "He was like so many of us who went into history," Harbaugh observed. "He became a historian because he wanted to change society." The atmosphere in the department encouraged that outlook. "There was a pervasive, progressive liberalism," said Young, which embraced the idea that "the study of history was a way of fulfilling a social and political purpose." The majority of the cohort aspired to become an "activist historian."[19]

The department also had some remarkable professors. There were, for instance, Billington, a Harvard PhD and his generation's successor to Frederick Jackson Turner; the erudite, punctilious Richard Leopold, one of the deans of American diplomatic history in the postwar period; and Lefton Stavrianos, a Greek immigrant who specialized in Eastern European and Russian history and who was author of a world history textbook that would stay in print into the twenty-first century. Above all, there was McGovern's dissertation supervisor, Arthur S. Link, barely thirty years old yet already on his way to becoming Woodrow Wilson's greatest biographer and one of the most distinguished figures in the annals of the history profession. During his career of ten years at Northwestern and thirty-four at Princeton, he would write a five-volume biography of Wilson (two of them winning the Bancroft Prize) as well as several monographs, scores of scholarly articles, and widely adopted textbooks. His most monumental achievement would be to edit, between 1966 and 1996, *The Papers of Woodrow Wilson*, in sixty-nine volumes. Link's devotion to the Progressive Era, Wilson, and American internationalism would influence McGovern in both conclusive and subtle ways. But other professors would make their mark on the future US senator and Democratic presidential candidate, too.[20]

As anyone who has braved the experience knows, graduate school imposes a kind of vow of poverty. That was certainly the case for the McGoverns and the Penningtons. Each couple (and their children) lived on a monthly allowance of $120, courtesy of the GI Bill. This time they shared expenses on the third floor of a ramshackle building of Victorian vintage at 710 Clark Street, in Evanston. Their lodgings consisted of a kitchen, bath, and living room and a single bedroom for each family at either end of the common space. A closet served as Ann and Susan's bedroom, where they slept in converted dresser drawers. The couples made the place livable. They bought secondhand furniture, Eleanor and Ila made slipcovers and curtains, and George and Bob gave the rooms a fresh coat of paint. The dwelling's only insurmountable peculiarity were the roaches—"so big you didn't know whether to kill them or throw a saddle on them," Bob said, and against which residents periodically conducted futile warfare.[21]

For all the graduate students these were the times of the home economics of canned soup and peanut butter, and macaroni casseroles. One did not hesitate to share with friends whatever leftovers happened to be the evening's fare, and Al Young was grateful whenever Eleanor stopped by his room to ask the bachelor to supper. Most of the professors also understood the importance of hospitality, too. Arthur and Margaret Link never had Thanksgiving dinner without graduate students gathered around the table, while other faculty invited them over for a filling buffet from time to time. Ray and Mabel Billington were noted for turning their home into a *salon*, where the first round of drinks was invariably double scotches, to loosen people up. Conversation was therefore lively, with the host brandishing a cigarette holder and punctuating political discussions with roisterous limericks. Eleanor would remember the young scholars and their wives and mentors as "comfortably clannish."[22]

That disposition extended to the seminar room. Under Billington, McGovern began his first serious study of American intellectual history, in a course that spurred his interest in politics. Its foundation was the work of America's three most eminent historians between the Populist movement and the Cold War—Frederick Jackson Turner, Charles Beard, and Vernon L. Parrington. Middle Westerners all, these scholars had made enduring contributions through historical interpretation that also illuminated the issues of their own time, an era of growing discontent with the constriction of opportunity and the physical dangers of industrial America.

Among this "holy trinity," Turner would attain immortality for a single essay, "The Significance of the Frontier on American History" (1893). What had made the United States unique, he submitted, was the existence of a western frontier throughout its history, a frontier that had offered opportunity in the form of free land, out of which had sprung America's leveling democracy. Turner also reported that, by 1890, the frontier had disappeared, "and with its going has closed the first period of American history." Critical engagement with Turner's "frontier thesis" has persisted into the twenty-first century. In its day, it was universally accepted and, for some, with alarm: If the source of national identity and opportunity had receded, and if the wave of the future now was industrial capitalism, unfettered and unconcerned for the welfare of the common people, then what was to become of democracy (or opportunity) in America? To progressive reformers the implication was clear. The federal government would have to assert itself like never before and find a way to compel Big Business to behave in a socially responsible way.[23]

Beard and Parrington advanced another of the ideas inherent in the foregoing perception—that conflict was one of the wellsprings of meaningful change in the progress of the United States. In 1913, as the sun rose over the Progressive ferment, Beard made the famous case, in *An Economic Interpretation of the Constitution*, that even the nation's organic document was the product of a kind of class conflict. McGovern had not read this work until Billington's seminar. He was impressed with Beard anew. Then came Parrington, the author of *Main Currents in American Thought* (1927), a three-volume study that analyzed the political skein running through American literature and, according to Alfred Kazin, "the most ambitious single effort of the Progressive mind to understand itself." (*Main Currents*, Al Young wrote, "bowled me over with its hidden riches of the dissenting tradition.") Parrington, in part because of his prairie upbringing, also had contemplated the importance of the West, but he was more radical than Turner. The farmer's revolt had given him his "first real insight into economics and political science," and he shared Beard's view of the natural clash between large-scale capitalism and democracy. Parrington put it this way: "On one side has been the party of the current aristocracy—of church, of gentry, of merchant, of slave holder, or manufacturer—and on the other the party of the commonalty—of farmer, villager, small tradesman, mechanic, proletariat." He was, as Bill Harbaugh said, "an impassioned Jeffersonian agrarian."[24]

When Arthur Link later assigned him readings on politics, McGovern learned that both Theodore Roosevelt and Woodrow Wilson, historians in their own right, admired Turner, while Turner declared TR "the most important single force in the regeneration of this nation in his day," and Wilson a statesman who would "rank with the great ones of the earth." For his part, Beard hoped to embolden presidents through his writings to do combat with the new corporate class in the interests of democracy.[25] Roosevelt, to check the power of the corporations and ameliorate some of the farmers' grievances and horrors of the factory system, accomplished breakthroughs in regulating the railroads and sided with coal miners in the biggest labor strike of his presidency. In other firsts, Wilson introduced a degree of public control over the nation's financial system and commerce in the Federal Reserve and Federal Trade Commission Acts and established the eight-hour day for railroad workers and restrictions on child labor.

Such governmental activism might not have seemed necessary in the preceding century, when classical, or laissez faire, liberalism had nurtured individual enterprise and gradually expanded the privileges of democracy. But now, the Jeffersonian notion of "that which governs best governs least" was simply inadequate. For most progressive reformers, whether they engaged in scholarship or politics, the goals of liberalism had stayed the same—"to promote the general Welfare, and secure the Blessings of Liberty." The means of achieving them, of necessity, had changed dramatically.[26]

The Progressive movement became the point of departure in McGovern's understanding of modern American liberalism. At Dakota Wesleyan, he had surveyed the Age of Reform through the eyes of Social Gospel activists. Everything he studied at Northwestern at Billington's and Link's behest seemed to fall into a pattern. And it was instructive to know that the two most significant presidents between Lincoln and Franklin Roosevelt were former scholars themselves, and that Turner, Beard, and Parrington, who practiced the historian's craft, had left an imprint on the affairs of their own time as well.

It is little wonder, then, that McGovern would warm to Arthur Link's suggestion for a dissertation topic, the Colorado Coal Strike of 1913–14. The subject would give him the opportunity to put the Progressive interpretation of American history to the test. This was the story of the bloodiest labor upheaval of the twentieth century—some eight months of violent struggle that manifested all the elements of class warfare, culminating in the "Ludlow Massacre" perpetrated by John D. Rockefeller Jr.'s private army. McGovern did not know much about it. But his mentor's authoritative manner and enthusiasm won him over. Although this would be the first doctoral dissertation that Link would supervise, his judgment about it could not have been better. As McGovern later said, "That subject was tailor-made for me."[27]

The dissertation is that crucial endeavor that measures the PhD candidate's capacity to become a professional historian. The process begins once the student has completed several semesters of course work, has passed a grueling oral examination in chosen fields of study, and has already done smaller research projects. A good history dissertation sheds light on a topic previously unexplored or puts a fresh interpretation on familiar subject matter. Its foundation is original research in manuscript collections and printed documentary sources as well as immersion in the existing scholarly literature surrounding the topic, and it usually requires two to three years' solitary effort.

In facing such a task as a married man with children, George was fortunate to have a wife like Eleanor. While tending to Ann and Susan and the household, she did all of his typing for him and even helped with his research. Moreover, before he completed the work, Eleanor would give birth to their third daughter, Terry, in 1949, and to their son, Steven, in 1952 (just hours after she finished typing the final draft). He benefited from Arthur Link's advising perhaps only slightly less: "You would have thought he had been doing it all his life, because he did it with such absolute certainty about how to proceed," McGovern explained. "He would say things like 'There's a whole cache of documents at Johns Hopkins or Princeton or at the New York Public Library.' And I went there and there they were. And he said, 'You should go to Colorado, probably spend the summer there. Take your family, rent an apartment, and stay [in the archives] all day. Come home at night and read until you fall asleep.'" Link would never let him slow down. "He set a production schedule. He would say that he wanted the first chapter on such-and-such a date, and there was no compromise."[28]

And so, off McGovern went on his quest—to the great public libraries of Boston and New York to find printed references to the coalfield war; then to Princeton to visit the Industrial Relations Section of Firestone Library; and, after that, to Johns Hopkins to study its extensive collection of labor periodicals. At the National Archives, for the role federal troops played in the strike, he examined War Department reports. At the Library of Congress he sought access to the Woodrow Wilson papers, which were still controlled by the president's widow. He also worked in the library's collections of key members of Wilson's cabinet and turn-of-the-century newspapers. Once good news from the former First Lady arrived, he was thrilled to discover a trove of materials on the conflict kept by the president himself. Before departing Washington, he interviewed Edward Keating, the former Colorado congressman who had fought to establish the federal investigation of the strike and had coauthored the historic child labor bill that Wilson signed in 1916. These forays into the raw materials of history left McGovern ecstatic. "Thanks," he wrote to Link, "for selling me on this exciting dissertation topic that promises to give me so much satisfaction along with the headaches. . . . No one has ever had a more challenging topic . . . I find myself fearing that I cannot do it justice."[29]

The next leg of his journey was Colorado, where thousands of pages of documents awaited him. He leased a house in Denver and made it a family affair. Throughout the summer, excursions occupied Eleanor and the kids while the scholar logged twelve-hour days in the archives. When "Grandpa Earl" visited, George enlisted Eleanor's aid in plowing through manuscript records in Boulder. "Everything is ideal for us," he enthused to Ray Allen Billington. "We have plenty of housing space, the recreational set-up is out of this world, and the research conditions couldn't be better."[30]

Within days of his arrival, it began to settle in on him just how controversial his subject remained among Coloradans, some thirty-five years on. "No one out here takes a middle position on the subject and the 'scholars' don't even want to talk to me about it," he reported to Link. "Believe me, this topic is still red hot."[31] He referred to it as "Colorado's Thirty Years War." That would have made an apt title, given the roots of the tragedy. The miners' attempt "to secure their industrial, legal, and political freedom," as McGovern put it, went back to the nature of the state's mining society since the 1880s. Stretching out over 25,000 square miles, the coalfields were yielding over ten million tons annually, 2 percent of the nation's supply, by the 1910s. The leading producer was the Colorado Fuel and Iron Company (CFI), accounting for a third of the state's output, most of it coming from Huerfano and Las Animas Counties, south of Colorado Springs. John D. Rockefeller was CFI's biggest stockholder; a majority of its trustees lived in New York and John D. Jr., was its director. According to McGovern, "it would be difficult to find a more clear-cut example of absentee capitalism and indifference toward the welfare of employees."[32]

Immigrants made up two-thirds of those employees, native born the remainder. They eked out a bleak existence. In the camps and towns that CFI maintained, family accommodations were typically small, boxcar-like houses of wooden frame or cement block, rented for eight dollars a month. Some camps were barely fit to live in. Coal and coke dust covered everything and tainted the water supplies. Open cesspools made typhoid a recurring problem. Just before the strike, a federal commission said of one settlement near Ludlow, "We do not believe more repulsive looking human rat holes can be found in America."[33]

The miners and their families otherwise enjoyed little freedom in their day-to-day lives. For example, "the company store" was not the only place to buy supplies, but it might as well have been, as a miner's wife who dared to look for fairer prices elsewhere courted the family's eviction. CFI protected its interests by other methods, too. In the little schools and churches, the corporation effectively controlled the hiring of teachers and preachers, and no Walter Rauschenbusches were suffered. Likewise, in the saloons, a miner never knew whether the fellow next to him was a spy nursing his brew in order to overhear casual talk of unions. Armed guards and barbed wire blocked many of the camp towns as a further way of thwarting union organizers.[34]

None of this assessed the human costs the coal barons levied. Whereas the technology of extraction had been modernized, in matters of life and death the miner's lot had not markedly improved since McGovern's grandfather had swung a pickax. In 1900 there was no more dangerous work in the industrialized world than mining in America. Based on the number of men killed relative to the tonnage mined, Colorado mining safety was the poorest of all the states, double the national average in 1909; by the year of the great strike, the accidental death rate had grown to three-and-a-half times the national. (Since 1892, the toll was four times and eight times that of Illinois and Montana, both of which were unionized.) Nor did Colorado have workmen's compensation laws. To avert court trials, the coal companies voluntarily offered indemnities, but these were not generous. In 1913, to cover all of the serious injuries in the state, including 110 fatalities, they paid out a total of $33,500. Families had little recourse but to accept. Sheriff-appointed juries regularly asserted negligence on the part of the dead and injured. This situation was all the more insidious because owners had no incentive to make the mines safer. The truth was that half of the accidents could have been avoided if the state had enforced its own codes or if a thriving union had insisted on enforcement.[35]

Colorado Fuel and Iron's indifference to other grievances only heightened the frustration and outrage. In 1913, the miner's workday was ten hours and often extended to twelve. That day might render a gross pay of $3.50, based on the tonnage he shoveled; however, after CFI deducted its fees for this and that, the average net came to $1.67. Because the work also was seasonal (two hundred days in a fair year) the miner's annual earnings conferred subsistence and no more. Irregular procedures made "short weighing" epidemic—by as much as four hundred pounds for a day's load, which translated into a full day's unpaid work per week (a full month in the work year).[36] Political corruption was the suture that held the system together. CFI wielded influence over judges and legislators sufficient to violate with impunity the statutes that mandated the eight-hour day and the miners' right to choose their own weight-check men and to form a union.[37]

In 1903, the United Mine Workers had led a strike for a wage increase and enforcement of Colorado's eight-hour-day law. Unionized workers of the northern fields secured their rights. But in Huerfano and Las Animas Counties, CFI prevailed through the combined powers of the courts, Pinkerton agents, and strikebreakers. By 1913, the southern fields stood out as the only unorganized mining region west of the Mississippi. That was the precipitating issue. Repeatedly, CFI officials refused even to meet with their employees' representatives. In essence, the corporations drove them to militancy.[38]

On September 23, 1913, 80 percent of the workforce of the southern fields responded to the UMW's call. Loading their families and belongings into carts, some nine thousand miners abandoned the pits and the company towns and set up tent colonies near the canyons. CFI lost no time bringing in thousands of strikebreakers and 871 armed guards equipped with machine guns and a makeshift tank called "The Death Special." Tensions exploded into violence in the form of several skirmishes, a pitched battle lasting forty hours, and indiscriminate machine-gun rakings of the tent communities. By the end of October, at least eighteen people, mostly miners and a twelve-year-old boy, had been killed. The governor then sent in the militia, a thousand strong, to restore order. But between the embittered miners and CFI's private army, mutual depredations and vendetta killings continued. Soon the militia was collaborating with the operators. The great coalfield war, as it was now known, was headline news across the nation.[39]

Ever since the rise of corporations in the late nineteenth century, the federal government habitually had come to the rescue of Big Business in clashes with labor. Rutherford B. Hayes had cut the pattern when he used the army to crush the national railway strike of 1877. Grover Cleveland dispatched troops to Chicago and made a bloody melee of the American Railway Union's reasonably orderly protest against the Pullman Company in 1894. Not until Theodore Roosevelt did the workingman and woman find a friend in the White House. In the Anthracite Coal Strike of 1902 Roosevelt judged the mine owners contemptible in their refusal to meet their workers halfway. Using his "bully pulpit," he ultimately forced capital to submit to the give and take of arbitration. "The citizens of the United States," TR declared, "must effectively control the mighty commercial forces which they themselves have called into being."[40]

The bloodless coal strike in Pennsylvania was a church social compared to the situation Woodrow Wilson faced in Colorado. When, in November 1913, he proposed arbitration, CFI reacted as if Wilson himself had organized the strike. Board chairman Lamont M. Bowers claimed the administration was conspiring with the United Mine Workers, in part because the secretary of labor was the former official of that union. The strike was the work of socialist agitators, Bowers told the White House, and recognizing the UMW would mean "inevitable revolution in this country," he told Rockefeller. Wilson appealed again after his own representative, Ethelbert Stewart, reported that Bowers was disingenuous to say that state law covered the workers' grievances. In fact, CFI stubbornly ignored those laws and had thus provoked the crisis. This was "a strike of the twentieth century against a tenth century attitude," Stewart said. Once more Bowers rebuffed Wilson, vowing that CFI would never treat with "ignorant, blood-thirsty anarchists." There things rested as the president authorized a federal investigation and a harsh winter fell over Colorado.[41] In mid-April 1914, UMW officials beseeched the junior Rockefeller for a personal meeting in order to find an honorable settlement. But Rockefeller, as obsessed as Bowers was about union recognition and wanting the camps dismantled, chose not to reply. Thus he set in motion events that would plunge southern Colorado into virtual civil war.[42]

On Sunday, April 19, 1914, the militia of Company B looked on while the Greek and Italian families of the 150-tent community at Ludlow celebrated the Easter holiday with a game of baseball. To the inhabitants the presence of those particular troops seemed to be a deliberate provocation. Company B's commander was known for his pathological hatred of the strikers, as was its second-in-command for his service in the Indian campaign that culminated in the Wounded Knee massacre in 1890. As the game proceeded, the strikers and their wives traded taunts with the soldiers, though the day ended without incident. Early the next morning the guardsmen returned, demanding to search the tents for an antiunion miner allegedly being held against his will. (He in fact no longer lived there.) Pulses already were pounding when a detachment of mounted troops, machine gun in tow, suddenly appeared on the crest above the camp. Scores of agitated strikers ran to fetch their

Winchesters and streamed out to defensive positions along the arroyo and the sand cuts.[43]

No one was ever able to answer the question of who fired the first shot at Ludlow, but bullets had begun to fly before panicked mothers could roust their children from sleep and get them out of harm's way. The initial deadly exchange lasted ten minutes. Then bombs started exploding in the rear of the colony. The militia was able to force a large group of armed resisters to retreat to the surrounding hills, and by noon the battle had devolved into guerrilla-like skirmishes at various locations. In the meantime, some of the women and children remained trapped inside their tents, taking refuge in sizeable interior pits dug for just such a contingency—the only protection against the machine guns that the troopers let loose upon them throughout the day. At sunset, reinforcements arrived and the militia elected to destroy the village. Brandishing torches, they set fire to it, tent by tent. Down in one pit, their escape barred before they realized what was happening, two young women and eleven children (ranging in age from three months to nine years) clung to one another as burning debris fell in on them and flames consumed the oxygen.[44]

By daybreak, the settlement that once had sheltered a thousand people had been reduced to smoking ruins. The discovery of the thirteen corpses in what soon would be called "the Black Hole of Ludlow" set off a cry that reverberated throughout the land. Sickened and outraged, the miners would not be stayed in their pursuit of justice. In units as large as three hundred, they furiously attacked strikebreakers and militia across two counties. At six CFI installations, they burned buildings and dynamited mineshafts, entombing some thirty-five of their adversaries at Empire. At Walsenburg the miners were repulsed by cannon fire. At Forbes, they succeeded in wrecking the entire place and killing nine of its defenders. Nearly a hundred combatants on both sides had so far paid such a price. As McGovern wrote, "Anarchy and unrestrained class warfare had this time reached a new peak in the long and bitter history of industrial warfare in Colorado."[45]

The Colorado state government had lost all control over the situation. It was now "indisputable," Wilson's secretary of war told him, that the militia's intentions had been to "provoke rather than allay disorder." When Rockefeller a third time slammed the door on union recognition, the president accepted the necessity of federal intervention. The miners welcomed his decision. Advance units of, ultimately, 1,600 federal troops arrived on April 30, there to stay until January 1915; their first act was to demand withdrawal of the militia and a surrender of arms from all others, including Rockefeller's army. Peace at last had come to Colorado. Given previous presidential interventions, McGovern was on firm ground in crediting this one as "the most successful police action by soldiers in American history."[46]

In the aftermath, John D. Rockefeller Jr., was shamed in the national press. McGovern described him as an industrialist "ill-equipped by temperament and training to grasp the social implications of the industrial age." For his part, Wilson reprimanded Colorado's governor and appointed an arbitration commission. Yet even after Wilson had persuaded the United Mine Workers to drop its demand for recognition in exchange for other concessions, Rockefeller still refused to cooperate. By December 1914, the UMW was forced to end the strike because its financial resources had run out.[47]

McGovern allowed that Rockefeller and Colorado Fuel and Iron had nonetheless learned something. Their eventual concession to "the social implications of the industrial age" was a precursor to "company unions" of the 1920s. Approved overwhelmingly by the miners, their plan established workers councils and insured long-overdue enforcement of safety regulations, the election of check-weight men, and improvements in company towns. Although Rockefeller no longer closed CFI to union organizers, he never yielded on recognition. Not until the Wagner Act in 1935 would the miners secure their full rights to collective bargaining. "Under the shaking impact of this long and bitter struggle," McGovern concluded, public consciousness had been raised by the miners' revolt; corporate heads to some extent had come to see that the old days were gone. "Although the strikers lost their campaign for union recognition, in a larger sense they achieved a truly significant victory."[48]

McGovern's 470-page dissertation was (for many years) the definitive work on the single most deadly labor conflict in the history of the United States, and a pioneering contribution to the field of labor history, which then was in its adolescence.[49] It also constituted the author's investigation into the merits of the emphasis of Turner, Beard, and Parrington (and Rauschenbusch) regarding social conflict in the making of American progress. Through his scholarship, McGovern had become a firsthand witness to the exercise of power without accountability, and he soon surmised that people who held such an advantage rarely surrendered it voluntarily. The strike itself would never have taken place, he observed, if the nation's system of large-scale industrial capitalism had shown a decent respect for its workers to begin with. Perhaps the violence, especially the miners' resort to arms, was necessary in the end, for that was what compelled the federal government to impose its authority. McGovern thus could see that political radicalism, a vital element of the American democratic and revolutionary traditions, still had its place. The miners' clash with the corporations lent validity to the broader interpretation of the Progressive school of historiography. But there were yet other important lessons—about political reaction and modern-day liberalism—embedded in the seams of Colorado's coal.

"The age of machinery, of the factory," Frederick Jackson Turner once wrote, "was also the age of socialistic inquiry." Few politicians were more sensitive to that fact than TR and Wilson. In his life of Roosevelt, Bill Harbaugh would make a great deal of his frustration over the "gross blindness of the operators" during the anthracite strike in 1902. "Do you realize that they are putting a heavy burden on us who stand against socialism; against anarchic disorder?" TR complained to a friend. The "violence and unreason" of corporate malefactors, as much as anything else, was why the progressives' redefinition of liberalism was called into being in the early twentieth century. Roosevelt's purpose in expanding the powers of the federal government was not to destroy Big Business, but to curb its excesses—"to destroy privilege, and give to . . . every individual the highest possible value both to himself and to the commonwealth."[50] Thus also Wilson intervened in Colorado and two years later signed the bills establishing the eight-hour day for railroad workers and restrictions on child labor. And so, these two archetypal progressives sought not revolution, but orderly change and some semblance of decency. As events played out, they achieved enough of both to undermine the radical appeal.

Yet Roosevelt and Wilson did not exert themselves to ameliorate some of the worst aspects of industrial capitalism merely in order to preserve it. "There can be no equality of opportunity," Wilson averred in his first inaugural address, "if men and women and children be not shielded in their lives . . . from the consequences of great industrial and social processes which they cannot alter, control, or singly cope with."[51] Even so, one could wonder whether TR and Wilson would have thus recast liberal politics in the absence of concerted pressure from quarters to their left. However McGovern might have answered such a question, he apprehended the persistence of reaction on the right and the radical challenge on the left of liberalism. For him, the progressives' approach seemed the irreducible minimum for any efficient and humane form of government that called itself a democracy.

In the very process of becoming a historian and rendering the Ludlow Massacre, McGovern's view of politics and social conflict had begun to crystallize. In retrospect, practically all of his academic strivings constitute a sort of compass; if not quite revealing the final destination, the arrow pointed in an unmistakable direction. "George was always concerned with public policy . . . and he was a reformer," Bill Harbaugh said of their days at Northwestern and of the impact that Parrington, in particular, had on his friend. "In terms of domestic policies, I would have to call him a progressive agrarian." Yet, he added, "McGovern went far beyond that, in the sense that his liberalism was a very inclusive liberalism. He was much concerned with the lot of the laboring man as well."

One final chord registered in a highly personal way as he contemplated his research. His paternal grandfather, Thomas, had inhaled coal dust and suffered various injuries in the mines for most of his working life. And his father, Joseph, had spent a blighted childhood and adolescence as a breaker boy until professional baseball emancipated him in his late teens. Neither could the young scholar help but weave into the pattern his own Depression-era experiences—vivid memories of South Dakota's farmers and small merchants struggling against forces beyond their control, and then of the salutary impact that the New Deal had had on his community and state.[52] All of these factors seemed to be of a piece; they galvanized his sense of kinship with the Progressive historians, which, in part, grew from the regional identity he shared with them and made their scholarship all the more persuasive. Al Young, the city boy from the New York Jewish left, made the connection this way: George's liberalism was, yes, unquestionably an intellectual evolution, but it also "came out of that kind of lived experience," he said. "I had to read *The Grapes of Wrath* to get that."[53]

Thus had McGovern embarked upon a wide-ranging examination of Progressive America through the eyes of scholars and the everyday working people and political and social activists who had lived it. He did so also through communion with his peers and mentors who aspired to interpret the American past for the post–New Deal generation. The enterprise was terribly exciting and relevant to a history graduate student in the late 1940s and early 1950s, and it engendered in him a preference for critical analysis of the country he had risked his life to defend. If one sought a better world, then one had to cultivate a *serious* sense of history—not merely "a ravenous appetite for Americana," as Richard Hofstadter once put it, in decrying popular tastes. The same principle would obtain in the realm of international relations, with which McGovern soon would be linking the fate of contemporary domestic reform. Indeed, the direction of postwar American foreign policy, as it happened, would stir him to activism even before he had begun to plumb the significance of the Great Coalfield War.

1. The McGovern family, c. 1931, Mildred, Olive, George, and Larry, and their parents, Joseph and Frances.

2. The Stegeberg twins, Ila and Eleanor, 1939.

Glamour Girl

Miss Harriet Long, a sophomore from Armour, was given the
title "most glamorous" girl on
the campus by a majority vote of
the entire Wesleyan student body.

Glamour Boy

George McGovern, a sophomore
from Mitchell, was elected by a
majority vote of the entire student
body of Dakota Wesleyan as the
"Glamour Boy" of the campus.

3. Dakota Wesleyan University's "Glamour Boy" of 1942, in the *Tumbleweed* yearbook.

4. On the campus of Dakota Wesleyan University, Old College Hall as it looked when George and Eleanor were students. Chartered in 1883 and affiliated with the United Methodist Church, the institution was established in an era when religious denominations built colleges to accompany settlers into the West. By the 1930s DWU had cemented its position as a powerhouse in national collegiate debate and oratorical competition.

5. The *Phreno Cosmian* headlines George's triumph in the Red River Valley Forensics Tournament, February 9, 1943. When he returned to campus his formal induction papers into the US Army were waiting for him.

6. Conceived by real estate developers to promote an annual agricultural exposition, "The World's Only Corn Palace" occupies a block on Main Street in Mitchell. Since 1892, the entire structure's exterior has been covered with large mosaics contrived of corncobs and tufts of wheat, requiring up to 3,000 bushels of corn and tons of other grains. Over the years it has functioned as hippodrome and civic hall, hosting the likes of John Philip Sousa, Harry James, Duke Ellington, Roy Rogers and Dale Evans, and Peter, Paul, and Mary. The list of politicians who appeared at the Corn Palace includes William Jennings Bryan, William Howard Taft, Franklin Roosevelt, Wendell Willkie, Adlai Stevenson, John F. Kennedy, Richard Nixon, and George McGovern himself. (Carnegie Resource Center, Mitchell, SD)

7. Home on furlough from flight training in Texas, June 1943. Shortly after this visit George and Eleanor decided they would get married before he shipped overseas. Their wedding would take place in his father's church on October 31, 1943. As George explained to a friend, "We've simply got an old fashioned love affair on our hands, and it's pretty hard to stop love even for war." (Left to right, Eleanor, George, sisters Mildred and Olive, and Frances and Joseph.)

8. Eleanor pins his wings on newly commissioned Lieutenant McGovern's lapel, April 1944, Pampa, Texas.

9. Officially dubbed the "Liberator," flight crews sometimes called the B-24 the "Liquidator" or the "Flying Coffin." Here, much like several of McGovern's missions in the *Dakota Queen*, B-24s have just loosed their bombs on an enemy oil refinery and flown through an intense barrage of flak as fire rages below, May 1944. American factories turned out 19,256 B-24s, "the most numerous" airplane ever built. By V-E Day, they would fly 226,773 sorties and drop nearly a half million tons of bombs on enemy installations in the European theater. (Library of Congress)

10. McGovern with his copilot Bill Rounds (left) and his navigator Sam Adams (right), in Cerignola, Italy, November 1944. Sam was the only member of his crew who was killed (when he flew with another crew on a catch-up flight).

11. The billfold photo of Eleanor that George set on the cockpit dashboard on every mission he flew in the *Dakota Queen*, including the flight back home to the US, in June 1945, from Cerignola, Italy, to Boston.

12. In transition as a student pastor, 1946–47. After completing his bachelor's degree at Dakota Wesleyan, McGovern enrolled in Garrett Theological Seminary in Evanston, Illinois, but soon realized he was ill suited for the ministry. He then entered the graduate history program at Northwestern University. (George and Eleanor with Susan and Ann.)

13. While completing his PhD dissertation, McGovern taught history and international relations at his alma mater for about three years and became Mitchell's most controversial citizen. He also chalked up the best record of any debate coach in the region, and the students dedicated the college yearbook to him in 1952. (Members of the national honorary forensics society, Pi Kappa Delta. Back row: Mait McNamara, Chuck Horner, McGovern, and Elmer Schwieder. Front row: Donna McLain, Margie Uhrich, Dorothy Hubbard, Gerry Morris, and Tom Bintliff.)

14. The Executive Secretary of the South Dakota Democratic Party with Adlai Stevenson (the Democrats' presidential nominee in 1952 and 1956) and state chairman Ward Clark in the autumn of 1954, in Sioux Falls.

15. In his first campaign for Congress, McGovern received former president Harry Truman's blessing when he visited South Dakota in April 1956.

16. The McGovern children campaigning for their Dad in 1956 (Steve in the car, and Susan, Terry, and Ann in the trailer).

17. McGovern (pictured with Eugene "Gene" Hoyt) never stopped talking to farmers throughout his career. On long stretches between towns, if he saw one plowing, he would pull over, climb a fence, cross a field, and start a conversation. As he became a leading agricultural expert on Capitol Hill and the champion of Food for Peace, farmers became the key to his political success in South Dakota and voted for him in sizable majorities.

18. With Sam Rayburn of Texas, the legendary Speaker of the House and a most important patron, 1957.

19. Congressman McGovern with Miss Blanche Johnston and Miss Valentine Preston, his civics and music teachers at Mitchell High School (and their friend Miss Thelma Tusia of Yankton, SD), July 1957.

6 AMERICA WAS BORN IN REVOLUTION AGAINST THE ESTABLISHED ORDER

Like most history PhD students before and since, it was second nature for George McGovern to follow the events of his own time as intently as he studied the past. His friend Bill Towner suggested why this was so for their cohort: "I remember coming back for my first year of graduate school in 1946 and thinking, well, we've really done it. We've licked Hitler, set the world in order, and now we can all live in peace. Then—wham—I turn on the radio and Walter Winchell is predicting we'll be at war with Russia in four years. They taught us during the war that Russia was our friend." Skeptical of the sudden turnabout, he wondered, "My God, what can we do now?"[1]

Battle-tempered, idealistic veterans like Towner and McGovern were troubled far more by other voices. Already, in March 1946, Winston Churchill had visited Fulton, Missouri, and shocked Americans by telling them that "an iron curtain" had descended across Europe, separating East from West. Then, in September, just as Towner arrived at Northwestern and McGovern started classes at Garrett Theological, President Truman abruptly fired Secretary of Commerce Henry Wallace, the last remaining Roosevelt appointee in the cabinet and Truman's predecessor as vice president. The blow-up was ignited by a speech that Wallace had made about the administration's emerging hard line toward the Soviet Union. To a full house at Madison Square Garden, Wallace had called for greater support for the United Nations, a halt to atomic weapons development, and a rejection of economic nationalism and imperialism on the part of all the great powers. The United States, he also said, had nothing to gain "by a 'Get tough with Russia' policy," and the Soviets should stop preaching that their "form of communism must, by force if necessary, ultimately triumph over democratic capitalism."[2]

The message pleased no one. The *New York Times* and the communist *Daily Worker* alike criticized it, and the State Department demanded its author's head. Truman, despite having personally cleared the speech, complied.[3] Then about a year later, as McGovern finished his first semester of graduate school, Wallace launched a third-party campaign for the presidency. The newly formed Progressive Citizens of America, an organization made up of left-liberal and labor groups critical of Truman's foreign policy, endorsed his candidacy. Wallace and company called themselves the Progressive Party, the name Theodore Roosevelt and Robert La Follette adopted for their third-party challenges in 1912 and 1924.[4]

Twenty-three out of twenty-six graduate history students at Northwestern, including McGovern, decided to support Wallace. They did so, as Al Young explained, mainly for two reasons: "Truman stood for an aggressive anti-Soviet policy, which seemed very dangerous, threatening war" and he had set in motion an ill-conceived federal loyalty program, the first ever in peacetime. McGovern also had admired Wallace since boyhood for his achievements in agricultural science.[5]

From 1933 to 1940, Henry Agard Wallace had been the right man in the right place at the right time. Scientist, businessman, and philosopher, in 1933 he bounded almost literally out of the cornfields of Iowa to become the greatest secretary of agriculture in American history. Since his teens his main interest in life was seed corn and how to improve its yields. In 1926, after years of crossbreeding various strains, he achieved a breakthrough—the first and ultimately the most commercially successful hybrid seed corn ever developed. Although the Depression forestalled adoption of his high-yield methodology, the war occasioned a sudden great leap. By 1942 his hybrid seed was generating 80 percent of the nation's corn, and yields would increase by the tens of bushels per acre with each decade—from thirty-one at the time of Pearl Harbor to 109 bushels per acre by the 1980s. By then, America's corn output required but one-third the acreage of fifty years before, and the innovation saved an incalculable number of lives around the world. This was the beginning of the "green revolution" and no individual was more responsible for it than Henry Wallace. His Pioneer Hi-Bred Corn Company would make him a multimillionaire by the late 1940s, and his children billionaires by the 1990s.[6]

No member of the cabinet would exert more influence on the New Deal than the secretary of agriculture. Across the nation, in communities like Mitchell, South Dakota, his name was a household word. From the mid-1920s to the end of Herbert Hoover's presidency farm income had dwindled by more than two-thirds. The chief causes were staggering surpluses and the absence of any national planning. Secretary Wallace met the crisis with the "domestic allotment" solution, embodied in the Agricultural Adjustment Act of May 1933. In thousands of local committees, some 3.5 million farmers agreed to drastic restrictions on production in exchange for federal subsidies to help them get by until market forces brought supply and demand in line with each other. This approach was not an unmitigated success, but it halted the free-fall in prices. By 1935, farm income had doubled. (Farm income rose from $73 million to $119 million between 1933 and 1936 in South Dakota.) Wallace also secured legislation to bolster prices, provide loans, and promote crop rotation and other forms of wise land use. His great dream was to achieve "balanced abundance," which he called an "Ever-Normal Granary." Its purpose was to stabilize prices and guarantee a steady food supply by building government-owned grain warehouses to buy up and store surpluses in bountiful years and release them in spare years. His plan came to fruition in a second Agricultural Adjustment Act, in 1938.[7]

Endlessly quirky, rumpled in appearance, and socially awkward, Wallace was never accepted by big city Democratic bosses and other party regulars as one of their own. But as Truman once said, he was "the best damn Secretary of Agriculture we ever had." Once considered radical, his ideas would be embraced as orthodoxy and hold sway for half a century. During World War II, the Ever-Normal Granary's contribution to national security ranked second only to the vast war industries, and his programs provided the tools of prosperity for American farmers in the postwar era.[8] His huge grain bins would become one of the great resources in waging the Cold War; in that enterprise McGovern would play a principal role.

As vice president from 1941 to 1945, Wallace was the party's champion of the labor movement, civil rights, and small business interests.

His status cost him dearly among corporate leaders and southern Democrats. His outspoken appreciation for the sacrifices of our Russian allies, along with his "visionary" outlook on international relations, added to his liabilities. Whereas he was the unexcelled voice of trade expansion and tariff reduction, his liberal internationalism took on a humanitarian and ideological temper. "I say that the century on which we are entering . . . must be the century of the common man," he declared in 1942, in his most famous utterance. "No nation will have the God-given right to exploit other nations. Older nations will have the privilege to help younger nations get started on the path to industrialization, but there must be neither military nor economic imperialism."[9]

Translated into twenty languages, "The Century of the Common Man" in pamphlet form reached tens of millions of people around the globe. In many quarters it was interpreted as a rebuttal to the self-congratulatory concept articulated by Henry Luce, the founder of *Time* and *Life*, in 1941. "The world of the 20th Century," Luce had written in *Life*, "must be to a significant degree an American Century." Like Wallace, he believed that postwar trade held "possibilities of such enormous human progress as to stagger the imagination." But his was a conservative form of internationalism intended to serve primarily nationalist ends. As "the most powerful and vital nation in the world," he maintained, Americans were *entitled* "to exert upon the world the full impact of our influence, for such purposes as we see fit and by such means as we see fit." Thus Luce sketched a plan for remaking the world in America's image.[10] In contrast, Wallace's vision was for a more authentic Wilsonian community of nations in which the United States would show leadership by exercising restraint. Even before World War II had ended, the two Henries had set the parameters of the domestic debate over the Cold War.

By 1944, the vice president had become a problem. He "wants to give a quart of milk to every Hottentot," went the standard complaint at home, and his remarks about self-determination for colonial peoples reportedly drove Winston Churchill to the heights of apoplexy. The State Department much preferred Luce's "American Century" to the notion of a postwar "century of the common man." Meanwhile, many Democrats worried that their commander in chief was a dying man, and Wallace now had enough detractors to depose him—unless Roosevelt insisted otherwise. But FDR did not insist. Meeting with party bosses, he settled on Truman as his running mate—a team player from a border state and sufficiently prounion to satisfy organized labor. As for his indispensable lieutenant of eleven years, according to one biography, "Roosevelt betrayed him utterly," then dawdled in granting his request to be appointed secretary of commerce. Nonetheless, Wallace performed splendid service for the ticket in the fall campaign, drawing larger audiences than his replacement, and even held the Bible for Truman as he swore the vice-presidential oath.[11]

On April 12, 1945, the day Roosevelt died, a rising young Minnesota Democrat wrote to Wallace, "I simply cannot conceal my emotions. . . . How I wish you were at the helm." Hubert Humphrey, who would become McGovern's first important political mentor, went on to tell Wallace that the country needed him "more than ever" and that admirers expected him to become the party's nominee in 1948.[12] Humphrey could not see it just then, but the fact that Truman was president, and Wallace was not, symbolized the beginning of the Democratic Party's transition from New Deal liberalism to Cold War liberalism. The struggle to reconcile the two would become the defining dilemma for the politicians of Humphrey and McGovern's generation.

"We do not agree on the nature of the Soviet Union entirely," McGovern once acknowledged in a letter to Arthur Link. But the Cold War was not just a matter of the Russians' "stubbornness and opportunism," he said. It was "the logical result of U.S. blundering and allegiance to reactionary regimes" as well. He worried that hot war would come "unless we can quickly replace the 'Get Tough Policy' with the thought and action that characterized Roosevelt's relations with the Russians." His was not the majority opinion, but neither was he alone when he wrote, "I cannot help feeling that . . . our course has been basically faulty since 1945."[13]

Mystery will always shroud what the Great Man might have done had he survived a fourth term. But between 1945 and 1947, foreign policy under Truman did appear to have turned away from FDR's attitude of cooperation toward the Soviets. Despite conflicting interests, Roosevelt had seen no alternative but to try to sustain the Grand Alliance. In February 1945, at Yalta, he had won Churchill's and Stalin's consent to a United Nations organization and secured Stalin's agreement to enter the war against Japan within ninety days of victory in Europe. Upon Roosevelt's insistence, Stalin also had acceded to vague promises to hold democratic elections in Eastern Europe, though Churchill refused to permit them in Britain's colonial holdings. Owing to military circumstance, both FDR and Churchill were resigned to a "spheres-of-influence" arrangement. Indeed, in October 1944, the prime minister had traveled to Moscow alone to strike with Stalin a bargain conceived in realpolitik—a swap, of sorts, that virtually assured Soviet domination in Eastern Europe in exchange for British control in Greece and the eastern Mediterranean. Republicans after the war decried a "Yalta sell-out" allegedly perpetrated by Roosevelt. Yet if any act of diplomacy ratified Stalin's position in Eastern Europe and prefigured Yalta, it was Churchill's nine-day mission to Moscow.[14]

In holding the Grand Alliance together, Roosevelt had proved himself the incomparable "juggler," as the historian Warren Kimball has characterized him—a statesman of flexibility and subtlety. Yet Roosevelt had his shortcomings as a diplomatist. Rarely did he take the State Department into his confidence, and in those ranks there had been deep divisions all along. He hardly helped the situation in failing to acknowledge the cosmetic nature of many of the Yalta provisions or to make plain to the American people why nothing could be done right now about the fate of Eastern Europe. Nor did he confide in his vice president. When FDR died, hard-liners rushed in to fill the vacuum, eager to guide the impulsive, untested Truman.

Among chief executives who entered office upon the death of a predecessor, only Andrew Johnson in 1865 faced problems of gravity comparable to those that confronted the man from Missouri eighty years later. In seeing the war through to its climax, Truman performed creditably in the eyes of most Americans. But he also badly mismanaged the reconversion to a peacetime economy. Runaway inflation, housing shortages, and labor unrest (involving millions of workers) unnerved the public. In November 1946 the Republicans captured both houses of Congress for the first time since Hoover. Democrats now talked openly about dumping Truman in 1948. In a sense, the Cold War would save him from becoming another Andrew Johnson.

Within days of Roosevelt's passing, the Soviets had begun to perceive a change in the Americans. For example, when they first met in late April 1945, Truman bawled out foreign minister V. M. Molotov over Eastern Europe even though the president admitted being "hazy about the Yalta matters." In May he halted Lend-Lease shipments to Russia and instead offered an unacceptably small reconstruction loan. These decisions only complicated the haggling over German reparations to which the Soviets thought they were entitled. The Americans' resolve to keep nuclear weapons a monopoly was final proof to the Russians that the Grand Alliance had been but a temporary marriage of convenience. Near the end of 1945, Harry Hopkins, FDR's adviser, despaired to Eleanor Roosevelt, "I think we are doing everything we can to break with Russia which seems so unnecessary to me."[15]

American foreign policy thereafter would take on aspects of Henry Luce's "American Century." Indeed, in the wake of World War II, the grandiose formula seemed practicable. From the Ruhr to Stalingrad, most of the continent's cities and towns, its river and rail transportation systems, its networks of communications, its agriculture and industrial plants—all had suffered destruction on a scale to defy human comprehension. As for the human toll, along with Russia's twenty million, 4.5 million Germans and nearly six million Poles were dead. In East Asia, in addition to vast expanses of physical devastation, two million Japanese and almost as many Chinese had been killed. Among the western allies, the losses were far lower, but significant—for France, 600,000 war-related deaths; for the United Kingdom, 324,000; and for the Netherlands, 200,000. The French, British, and Dutch would endure another humbling consequence of the war (one that eventually confounded the Americans, too.) Social revolutions were erupting in the distant provinces that made up their empires, the sources from which they continued to derive much of their own wealth.[16]

In contrast, the United States appeared to have reaped nothing but good fortune. While exercising hegemony over the Western Hemisphere, it occupied Japan, dominated the Philippines, and acquired more naval and military bases across the Pacific than all the other belligerents combined. Its boundless economic resources made it arbiter of Western Europe's future as well, while it controlled the oil in the Middle East in partnership with the British. By 1947–48, Americans at home were producing 40 percent of the world's good and services, half of the world's industrial output, half of its electricity, radios, and telephones, and 92 percent of its bathtubs. And they possessed the world's greatest navy and air force and held the patent on the atomic bomb.[17] For the first time in its history, the United States had a serious stake of some sort in every part of the globe. Its statesmen would develop a commensurate foreign policy, one driven by national security, ideology, economic self-interest, and domestic politics alike. US foreign policy makers often exhibited a double standard and not a little hubris in their conduct, and neglected to show much appreciation for the wartime sacrifices of their most important former ally.

The Soviets' behavior did not help matters, even though their grip on Eastern Europe was less than ironclad before 1947–48. Until then, elections in Czechoslovakia and Hungary had produced coalition governments, and communist Yugoslavia would maintain its independence throughout the Cold War. But the Soviets had bent Poland and Romania to their will almost from the start. In February 1946, Stalin unveiled a program of reconstruction for Russia and its satellites and superfluously predicted the imminent collapse of capitalism. Among other responses, the address prompted the American chargé d'affaires in Moscow, George Kennan, to send to Washington what would become known as the "Long Telegram." In it, the doctrine of "containment" was first expounded authoritatively.

Kennan's knowledge of Russian culture and Soviet politics was unsurpassed by any other American. To begin, he did not believe that Stalin would venture beyond the Yalta demarcation. After all, Russia lay in ruins, a quarter of its population was homeless, and half of its army was still horse-drawn. Nonetheless, because of "the Kremlin's neurotic view of world affairs," Kennan advised that the United States prepare a "vigilant application of counterforce at a series of constantly shifting geographical and political points." He had in mind primarily economic and psychological means; the problem, though critical, could be solved "without recourse to any general military conflict." Thus he counseled dispassion and patience in his strategy of containment. Eventually, the Soviet system would implode of the weight of its own "internal contradictions," he said. The "Long Telegram" quickly found its way to the Oval Office and earned its author a key position in the State Department. Coincidentally, in 1946–47, the British government determined that it could no longer persevere in Greece, where it had been propping up a right-wing monarchy beset by local communists since the end of the war. Here was the Truman administration's opportunity to make known the bold new doctrine Kennan outlined; it would guide American foreign policy for the next forty years.[18]

The immediate situation was a little complicated, however. Much of the Greek populace esteemed their native communists for having resisted Hitler's occupation force, whereas the royal government had worked hand in glove with the Germans. Then, too, Stalin had kept his Moscow bargain with Churchill and avoided involvement in the ongoing Greek civil war. Finally, there was American domestic politics. Truman's approval ratings had plunged from 87 percent to 32. Any initiative in the Mediterranean would require the wholehearted support of a war-weary electorate and of Republicans who now controlled Congress and expected to recapture the White House in 1948. In the circumstances, Truman's advisers (including Republicans in the Senate) urged him to "scare hell out of the American people." Accordingly, in his address to Congress, on March 12, 1947, he dispensed a form of "shock therapy." The president pictured a divided world—"free peoples" on one side versus "terror and oppression" on the other. The American people had to "choose between two alternative ways of life," he said in requesting $400 million in aid for embattled Greece (and Turkey). Nine days later, to press his case for the "Truman Doctrine" and refute charges that he was "soft" on the communist threat at home, he appointed his federal loyalty review board. He also secured legislation to establish the CIA and the National Security Council. Congress soon approved the aid package.[19]

The economic and military assistance to Greece and Turkey did what it was intended to do. But Truman's call to arms disturbed many Americans, and not only George McGovern, Bill Towner, and Al Young. "How does support given to the undemocratic governments of Greece and Turkey aid the cause of freedom?" asked Henry Wallace. Even Secretary of State George Marshall and the Russian expert Charles Bohlen thought the speech had "too much flamboyant anti-communism" in it, and Kennan worried about an indiscriminate crusade.[20] The next stage in the evolution of containment was more to Marshall's and Kennan's liking; they were its principal architects, and this time the tone was humanitarian.

As of 1947, Great Britain, France, Italy, and West Germany were still mired in economic torpor. If they did not recover soon, political parties on the left would come to power in those countries, or so the administration believed, and Soviet intentions would cease to matter. Moreover, economists had forecast another depression for the United States unless it expanded its export trade; a robust Western Europe could generate 10 percent of America's gross national product. These were the main considerations that shaped the European Recovery Plan, introduced by the secretary of state in his Harvard commencement address in June 1947. The four-year, $13 billion program would meet expectations. The Marshall Plan helped to revitalize Western Europe's economy and shore up the political structure in the process. It also stimulated the purchase of American manufactured products and food, thereby exorcising the phantom of depression. Yet the recovery program was elsewhere perceived as the capitalists' iron curtain dividing East from West and as a factor behind the Soviets' repression in Czechoslovakia in 1948.[21]

And so it would go. The United States and the Soviet Union would behold each other's actions and motives darkly, their search for economic and military security refracting as aggression and imperialist expansion from opposing vantage points. Soon the two great powers would begin a potentially suicidal nuclear arms race and the second Red Scare would plunge the United States into a series of domestic witch hunts that would warp American politics and foreign policy for years to come.

———————————

As the foregoing events were taking place, George McGovern began to believe "there would be no possibility of survival" if the United States and the Soviets failed to work out some kind of decent relationship.[22] And he made the prospect of humankind being forced back into caves the theme of his prize-winning peace oratory in 1946. For these and other reasons, at Northwestern he enrolled in Richard Leopold's seminar in American diplomatic history. But it was his course work on Eastern Europe and Russia with Lefton Stavrianos in 1947–48 that left the indelible imprint on his thinking about American foreign policy.

Of all his professors, McGovern formed his closest friendship with "Lefty" (aptly named in the double sense). The two of them often went on long walks across campus to talk politics. Lefty was struck by his student's maturity as well as by his "visceral reaction to his wartime experiences, which he voiced frequently" and which the professor would come to regard as a "key to understanding" him.[23] For his part, McGovern was impressed by the Greek American's mastery of the big picture and how he underscored connections between past and present in his observations about the Cold War. Stavrianos made sure his students grasped the magnitude of the Soviet contribution to victory over the Third Reich. One day he brought a map of the United States to class and, as McGovern recalled, he said, if the Germans had "bombarded every city and destroyed the principal buildings and bridges and water systems, burned the crops, destroyed the forests, tore up the infrastructure from New York to St. Louis to Chicago, everything between the Mississippi and the East Coast . . . [and] killed sixteen million Americans in that area, instead of the 300,000 we lost in the war," then one "would have some idea of what happened in the Soviet Union."[24]

Such information seldom appeared in US history textbooks. Moreover, not until the invasion of Normandy, less than a year before V-E

Day, had the United States at last opened the Second Front. Even then, whereas Hitler had deployed ninety divisions to repel the onslaught of Americans and Britons, some two hundred German divisions battled the Red Army in the East.[25] For every American who had lost his life in the war, at least fifty Russians had lost theirs. (Then, too, during the First World War, the Germans had plowed through Eastern Europe to attack the Motherland, and millions of Russians had perished.) To Stavrianos, these basic facts—perhaps a crude way of measuring who did the most to defeat Germany—were essential to understanding the Soviet point of view in the Cold War. He absolved neither the United States nor the Soviet Union for the current metastasis, and Stalin was a "son-of-a-bitch." But the two world wars naturally had intensified the Kremlin's fear and mistrust of the West. By 1947–48, all the Russians could see was that the Americans were about to revive German economic (and perhaps military) power. "He just took it apart, day after day," McGovern said. "I could never again get enthusiastic about the Cold War after that course."[26]

McGovern's readings honed his skepticism. Already journalists and scholars had begun to assess the opening phases of the Cold War. Among such works, McGovern discovered Theodore White's *Thunder Out of China* (1946), E. H. Carr's *The Soviet Impact on the Modern World* (1947), John K. Fairbank's *The United States and China* (1948), Owen Lattimore's *The Situation in Asia* (1949), and Howard K. Smith's *The State of Europe* (1949). All were first-rate rough drafts of history; subsequent scholars would challenge very little of what these authors wrote in this period.

Smith's *The State of Europe*, for example, provides a tour d'horizon drawn from his on-the-scene reportage throughout the 1940s. The Soviets had smothered liberal democracy in the rare cases in which a semblance of it could be found in Eastern Europe, the future ABC News anchor observed. Yet before the war, fascistic governments had ruled most of the satellite countries, and the "economic integration" the Soviets imposed on them had brought the people there the highest standard of living they had ever known, and no less freedom than before. The West's protest over the absence of democracy "was admirable," he added, but it would have been more persuasive "if some of the same concern were felt for victims in Spain and Greece."[27]

Indeed, in Greece, the rulers the president characterized as democratic were, in fact, former Nazi collaborationists who did nothing to improve their country's social and economic conditions while they arrested or executed thousands of Greek communists who had risked their lives to fight the Germans. "There are few modern parallels for government this bad," Smith wrote. The Truman Doctrine was legitimate, but behind containment lurked the intention to cure America's economic slump by expanding foreign trade and "stirring up warlike anti-Communist emotions in the west European vacuum." Truman had deliberately overstated his case to incite Congress, and anticommunism had become "a bogey to intimidate critics at home and an excuse for keeping arms production high enough to avoid economic crisis."[28]

As for the Marshall Plan, Smith could envision no substitute, and he criticized the Soviets for breaking off discussions about taking part in it. Their reaction was unfortunate because it militated against moderation in the debate in the United States. Alongside Truman's alarms, it fed "a genuine fear of Russian imperialism" and provided "the neo-imperialists" a rationalization to extend "American control over other nations." The European Recovery Program also served colonialism: Great Britain still ruled much of the Middle East while France and the Netherlands strove to reattach themselves to Indochina and Indonesia. And, what *was* one to make of an American foreign policy that elsewhere discouraged "direly needed social changes" and propped up fascistic classes that had driven Germany and Italy into aggressive war? Some form of containment was necessary, but the West was allowing the Russians to pose as the agents of social change. In a time of revolution, Smith concluded, America should "*be* the revolutionary power."[29]

To McGovern, books like *The State of Europe* confirmed his own concerns about American foreign policy as well as what he had gleaned from Professor Stavrianos. Thus he was, he said, "receptive to an alternative to the Truman-Dewey bipartisan policy of 1948." Henry Wallace was a fairly logical option. "We were turning to him," Bill Towner said, "because we wanted to build a better world, and he seemed the man to do it." To Al Young, the Iowa maverick emerged out of that "tradition of native American radical protest," as Parrington had limned it in *Main Currents in American Thought*. Their South Dakota friend regarded Wallace as a progressive agrarian and a "practical internationalist" who grasped the need to repair fences with the Soviets while espousing "a progressive American capitalism."[30]

In the early months of 1948 the three of them had begun agitating against the first antisubversive legislation of the Cold War. This measure, an example of how Truman's loyalty program played into the hands of the GOP, called for federal registration of members of the American Communist Party and its "front" organizations, along with public disclosure of the names of their financial contributors. (Aborted in the Senate, the bill was named for South Dakota's own Karl Mundt and Richard Nixon of California.) On any given day, McGovern, Towner, and Young could also be found in the teaching assistants' lounge typing and cranking out leaflets for Wallace on the mimeograph. They also canvassed for Curtis McDougall, a Northwestern journalism professor running for the Senate on the Progressive ticket.[31]

If his critique of American foreign policy was the main reason why they gave Henry Wallace their support, McGovern, Towner, and Young also felt comfortable with the new party's domestic program. Wallace and the Progressives of 1948 advocated equal rights for women, free trade, national health insurance, increases in Social Security payments, collective bargaining for federal employees, capital gains taxes, and expanded farm programs. Refusing to speak at segregated gatherings in the South, he called as well for the elimination of Jim Crow laws, desegregation of the public schools, and open housing legislation. Some scholars have suggested that his stand on civil rights forced Truman to embrace the cause to the extent that he did. (The president still used the word "nigger" in private conversation and once said that Eleanor Roosevelt "spent her public life stirring up trouble between whites and blacks.") Wallace's claim as the heir to the New Deal contributed to Truman's decision to recast himself as a more thoroughgoing liberal.[32] The third party's potential thereon motivated McGovern, Towner, and Young, despite the impossibility of victory. For McGovern, Charles Beard's observation, that "the philosophy of any subject (that is, the truth of it) is not at its center but on the periphery," took on new meaning. Billington's lectures on "third parties as catalysts of change in American history" reinforced that outlook. For Al Young, with his roots in New York City politics, getting elected the first time around did not matter. "I came out of a tradition where you ran candidates to put forward your cause."[33]

Even so, campaigning for Wallace was not easy; it required not only making the case for détente with the Soviets, but also defending him against charges of naïveté or, worse, of running while under the influence of communists. For, in their fear that he would siphon off enough votes to throw the election to Dewey, the Truman campaign engaged in red-baiting. Clark Clifford, the president's top political adviser, outlined the strategy in a memo in November 1947. "Every effort must be made . . . to identify and isolate [Wallace] in the public mind with the Communists," Clifford wrote. "The administration must persuade prominent liberals and progressives . . . [to] point out that the core of the Wallace backing is made up of Communists and fellow travelers." Thus, to New Yorkers, Truman would declare, "I do not want and I will not accept the support of Henry Wallace and his Communists." The latter five words became a mantra for mainstream Democrats. The president, in a speech on foreign policy, stooped to advise Wallace "to go to the country he loves so well and help them against his own country if that's the way he feels." Wallace replied over the radio: "Mr. Truman appealed to prejudice because he could not answer with reason."[34]

And yet this Gideon did make things difficult for his small army trying to save Israel from the Midianites. To be sure, with the insight of the prophets, he denounced the armaments race as "senseless" in the conviction that "Atomic power means 'one world or no world.'" And even as he criticized American foreign policy (the Soviets' less often), he knew enough to wish that American communists would desert him and nominate their own presidential candidate, and he publicly said so twice. Nonetheless, he refused to repudiate "any support which comes to me on the basis of interest in peace." Steadfastly he held to his principle: "Defense of the civil rights of Communists is the first line of defense of the liberties of a democratic people." Thus spoke the only bona fide capitalist and multimillionaire among the candidates for president in 1948.[35]

As the summer conventions neared, both the exaggerations and the facts about the people around Wallace gradually took their toll. The apartment at 710 Clark Street, where the McGoverns and the Penningtons resided in Evanston, was a microcosm of the Democratic house divided. Bob was a Truman man, and the arguments that he and George had across the kitchen table strained their brotherly friendship. "It got pretty hot and heavy," Bob recalled. "He couldn't understand why I was still for Truman, and I and couldn't understand why he was wasting his vote on Wallace." Eleanor and Ila would mix it up, too, with Ila defending her choice, Norman Thomas, the anticommunist Socialist. Of the four, Bob felt the most aggrieved, not because of his temporary rift with George, but because others around the History Department cut him from their circle.[36]

From a pragmatic perspective, mainstream Democrats like Pennington stood on a firm foundation. Yet as late as the eve of their convention, great numbers of Democrats still harbored doubts about Truman's abilities and his convictions as a reformer. Most of them abided, though, because they agreed with the main lines of his containment policy. Whereas very few questioned the Soviets' essential contribution to vanquishing fascism, they now were convinced that Stalinist totalitarianism was as sinister as Hitler's had been. At home, the liberal historian Arthur M. Schlesinger Jr. had written in *Life* in 1946 that the Communist Party of the United States appeared to be infiltrating parts of the federal government, several labor unions, and a few liberal political organizations. None of this constituted a dire threat to the Republic itself. But, he said, "Communism presents the most serious danger" because it was "dividing and neutralizing the left." As for those noncommunist "knaves and fools" who accorded communists legitimacy for any reason, Schlesinger advocated banishment from the ranks of American liberalism.[37]

Thus the issue of whether they could work to useful purpose with the Wallace movement was to be fought out bitterly among liberal activists and leaders of the farm and labor movements. Just weeks after Wallace announced his candidacy, a constellation of New Dealers and other prominent anticommunist liberals gathered in Washington to establish the Americans for Democratic Action (ADA). Feeling alienated from the Truman administration for their own reasons, this "government-in-exile" accentuated its support for the United Nations, civil rights, and the New Deal. Then, to distinguish themselves from Wallace and the Progressive Citizens of America, ADA liberals drew the line: "We reject any association with Communists or sympathizers with communism in the United States as completely as we reject any association with Fascists or their sympathizers." The Progressive Citizens of America glared at the authors of the new liberalism. In excommunicating others for their tolerance, the ADA was allowing the reactionary right, not communists, to divide the liberal movement. "Those who make anti-Communism the sole basis for organization," the PCA cautioned, "will find themselves so busy witch-hunting that they will have little energy left to work on the important issues."[38]

It all became too much for McGovern. "I'm tired of listening to the thoughtless jeers and charges of 'crackpot' and 'Communist' being thrown his way," he unburdened himself in April 1948 in the *Mitchell Daily Republic*. "I take my hat off to this much smeared man who has the fortitude to take his stand against the powerful forces of fear, militarism, nationalism, and greed." McGovern's intention was to counter the imputation that, because the American Communist Party supported him, Wallace was "therefore a Communist." This was rather "like assuming that because criminals are in favor of prison reform, all prison reformers are criminals." It amounted to a "mass movement to discredit Russia and the Wallace campaign" and anyone else who rejected the idea that "Russian communism and American democracy cannot live at peace in the same world."

He also invoked FDR's phrase about "fear itself." Having spilled so much blood to defeat the Nazis, Soviet Russia was "scared to death of atomic armed America," he said. "She quakes as she listens to the U.S. military and civilian leaders declare: 'Let's hit the Russians now before she gets the bomb,'" all of which at least partly explained Soviet "stubbornness, suspicion, loud talk, and superficial aggressiveness." But the tragedy was that "Americans, at the pinnacle of power and opportunity," had worked themselves into "a state of near hysteria because of the ideological competition." Now, under "the blinding light of the current Red Scare, we are going all out for nationalism, militarism, suspicion, and power politics." Battleships and bombs were not the way to contain communism, nor was the "futile policy" of military aid to Greece "to prop up a decadent, reactionary monarchy." The problem was that the administration had not tried "to honestly understand the Russian position" and had not "been true to the ideals of the Atlantic charter, the U.N., or any of those tenets so vital to the American way of life."

Finally, he asked, "Have we forgotten that the best way to challenge one dynamic idea is to meet it with a better one—one that we believe in enough to apply to all areas of life?" The solution lay in "American democracy" itself. For, "if it is really practiced at home and abroad, [we] need have no fear in the ideological struggle with communism." In thus defending Wallace, no one could accuse McGovern of not being daring. Once he attained elective office himself, the piece would wind up in the confidential FBI file that J. Edgar Hoover personally kept on him.[39]

George and Eleanor certainly expected to see democracy practiced over the long weekend of July 23, 1948, at Philadelphia's Convention Hall, the same site where both Dewey and Truman had been nominated earlier that summer. Whereas it had its share of notables,[40] the gathering was far more a "people's convention" than those held by the Republicans and Democrats. To begin, the new party's 3,240 delegates exceeded by five hundred the combined number attending the other two conclaves. A large percentage of them were a lot younger; according to one source, the typical Wallace delegate was twenty years younger (and thirty pounds lighter) than Truman's and Dewey's. (Eleanor and George were both twenty-six at the time, but ages ranged from sixteen to eighty-eight.) Almost a third of the conventioneers were women; war veterans made up at least a quarter. A reporter estimated that about half of the delegates belonged to trade unions and that a third was Jewish. African Americans represented upwards of 20 percent, which included the keynoter and another featured speaker who described herself as a "Negro woman come to Philadelphia to help write a platform for me and my children." Farmers also were conspicuous. To Fred Stover, president of the Iowa Farmers' Union, went the honor of formally nominating Wallace. And three-fourths of the delegates had never before attended a national political convention. Not until 1972 would either of the major parties hold one distinguished by such grassroots diversity in race, class, gender, and age as the Progressive Party convention of 1948.[41]

It was different for several other reasons. Hardly half an hour went by that the music of a thousand voices did not fill the hall. The delegates showed an unusual propensity for singing—ballads, folk songs, hymns, as well as old campaign songs with updated lyrics. They were led alternately by Pete Seeger and Michael Loring, an organist and hallelujah chorus, and by their guitar-strumming vice-presidential candidate, Senator Glen Taylor of Idaho, whose theme song was "Oh, Give Me a Home by the Capitol Dome." With Seeger's banjo accompanying them, the delegates sang "Friendly Henry Wallace" and the inevitable "Iowa Corn Song." Paul Robeson performed "Old Man River." At times, the entertainment carried McGovern back to his days at Holiness Camp above the James River, and he and Eleanor joined in with great feeling for the big chorus's rendition of "Battle Hymn of the Republic."[42]

The most spectacular event was the staging of Wallace's acceptance speech, delivered outdoors and attended by more people than any other before or since, until Barack Obama's in Chicago in 2008. Some 32,000 people poured into Shibe Park, home of the Philadelphia Athletics, leaving not a seat unoccupied. The party charged admission (one dollar on average), still another departure from custom, which raised enough money to defray the entire cost of the convention. Wallace entered the stadium in an open convertible as the beams of giant searchlights played over him and his cheering admirers as his vehicle rounded the bases. At the podium it took several minutes to quiet the crowd before the nominee could utter his first sentence: "The future belongs to those who go down the line unswervingly for all the liberal principles of political democracy regardless of race, color, or origin."[43]

The business that garnered the heaviest commentary took place the next day, when the delegates reassembled at Convention Hall to vote on the party platform. With little ado, they adopted a foreign policy plank, hammered out by the platform committee and commended by Wallace. It stated, in part, "Responsibility for ending the tragic prospect of war is a joint responsibility of the Soviet Union and the United States." Then a farmer from Vermont offered an amendment, read over the loudspeaker: "Although we are critical of the present foreign policy of the United States, it is not our intention to give a blanket endorsement to the foreign policy of any nation." This, the so-called Vermont Resolution, was meant to refute accusations that the Progressive Party was pro-Soviet; it caused a stir on the convention floor, though not a major one. Some delegates regarded the sentence as an accommodation with red-baiting and therefore unacceptable. But apparently most of the delegates simply deemed it superfluous in light of the "joint responsibility" statement they had just approved; they rejected it overwhelmingly on a voice vote. The vast majority of reporters, however, would interpret this outcome as further evidence of communist influence.[44] The more prominent among the three hundred journalists attending the proceedings included Marquis Childs, H. L. Mencken, Dorothy Parker, and Norman Thomas, none of whom was a friendly witness. Joseph and Stewart Alsop's syndicated column was typical of the coverage: The convention was "a dreary and sometimes nauseating spectacle, carefully and quite obviously stage-managed by the American communist party in the interests of the foreign policy of the Soviet Union."[45]

Exactly what or who was behind the controversial turndown remains a matter of dispute. According to one careful scholarly study of the convention, "the Progressive party organizers had barely noticed the Vermont Resolution and made no concerted effort to defeat it." Nonetheless, several of Wallace's advisers, notably Rexford Tugwell, anticipated trouble. So did Eleanor and George, who had called out "aye" when the vote on the amendment was taken. "I didn't think it was Red-baiting," he said long afterward. "No one should assume that when Americans criticize American foreign policy that this carries with it the assumption that Soviet foreign policy is beyond criticism." Ultimately, the McGoverns left Philadelphia disturbed by, in George's words, "a certain rigidity and fanaticism on the part of a few of the strategists." Whatever the case, the party's closing session was a public relations disaster.[46]

Wallace already was mired in the "communist issue" when the convention convened. His standing in the Gallup polls since January had dropped from 7 percent to 5; it would continue to fall. Throughout the autumn, however, he kept up a full schedule. In New York and California, he drew bigger crowds than Truman or Dewey. But elsewhere, as often as not, audiences were hostile. Almost daily he had to cope with shouts of "Did Stalin tell you to say that?" or "Go back to Russia!" as he tried to speak. Violence threatened in the South; in several cities audiences pelted him with eggs, and hotels refused his entourage accommodations. ("Am I in America?" he wondered to himself.) In Illinois one of his aides was hit by a stone. A car chase ensued in West Virginia. Ugliness of this sort swayed the coverage of his campaign; otherwise, the press and the voters gradually stopped paying attention to him.[47]

Meanwhile, the Democrats, too, had held a convention with shades of disaster about it. Before yielding up the nomination to Truman, ADA liberals led by Mayor Hubert Humphrey of Minneapolis had pushed through the first serious civil rights plank in the party's history, whereupon a majority of southern delegates marched out of the hall. On the final night, other distractions kept the president from making his acceptance speech until 2:00 a.m. Then the rebels reconvened in Birmingham, Alabama, to become the "Dixiecrats," a rump party "dedicated to complete separation of the races." As their standard-bearer, they chose Governor Strom Thurmond of South Carolina. With his party splintered three ways, it appeared to practically everyone that Truman had managed the dissolution of the Roosevelt coalition.[48]

Of course, practically everyone turned out to be wrong. For, as Tom Dewey, icy and overconfident, trudged along in his peculiarly inert campaign, Truman was just getting charged up. Moreover, in tandem with Clark Clifford's artful blueprint for victory, circumstances in both foreign and domestic affairs were starting to favor the incumbent. For instance, there was the "war scare" of 1948, which had begun in February with the Soviet crackdown on the coalition government in Czechoslovakia. At home, the Czech coup summoned from liberal Democrats ever-stronger support for the Marshall Plan and tended to undermine Wallace's views on the Cold War in general. Then, on June 24, just as the Republicans were nominating Dewey, the Soviets cut off all rail, river, and road access to Berlin in reaction to the American and British attempt to form a separate West German government. The president's swift response—the famous airlift to keep the city's western sector supplied—conveyed the impression of a resolute leader and won the backing of most Republicans and Democrats.[49]

Of greater consequence to the election's outcome were recent legislative missteps of the Republican Congress. These included a lighter tax schedule for corporations and higher income groups and the proposed elimination of the school lunch program. The Taft-Hartley Act imposed restrictions on union activities as well as a noncommunist loyalty oath on labor leaders, and a farm bill cut back on subsidies and federal crop storage ("a pitchfork in the farmer's back," Truman called it). Thus the GOP gave the scrappy Missourian his opportunity. In his "whistle-stop" campaign across the nation, he effectively portrayed his conservative opponents as the "Do Nothing Congress," a reactionary party unconcerned about the problems of average workers and their families. Thus he demonstrated to liberals his own progressive instincts while obviating the allure of Henry Wallace. The Dixiecrats provided a comparable assist. Partly to compensate for southern defections, Truman finally embraced civil rights more than tentatively and appealed directly to northern black voters, again impressing liberals and stealing Wallace's thunder, and ultimately carrying Ohio and Illinois for his exertions.[50]

Even the Republicans' "sure-fire issue" seemed not to work in their favor. The summer of 1948 opened a new chapter in the hunt for "communists in government." In sensational testimony before the House Un-American Activities Committee, the ex-communists Elizabeth Bentley and Whittaker Chambers leveled accusations against several prominent former New Dealers. Among many other names, Bentley claimed that Laughlin Currie, the architect of the International Monetary Fund and the World Bank, had in previous years passed along information to Soviet agents. Chambers made similar charges against Alger Hiss, the president of the Carnegie Endowment for International Peace, who had served in the State Department. Republicans thus expected to make election-year capital out the allegations. Yet because of Truman and Wallace's differences over foreign policy, the potential scandal simply was not sticking to the Democrats (for the time being). As the journalist Robert Donovan once observed, "Wallace had become so entangled with Communists that, with generous help from the Democrats, the Communist issue was turned against him instead of Truman, as Dewey, too late, was ruefully to acknowledge."[51]

On Election Day, out of the nearly forty-nine million popular votes, Henry Wallace won 1,157,172 (or 2.38 percent nationally) and no electoral votes. New York and California accounted for two-thirds of his total. Truman won 24,105,812 popular votes and 303 electoral votes, and Dewey won 21,970,065 and 189. Strom Thurmond, with 1,169,021 popular votes, took third place and carried four states in the Deep South. By the next day it was clear not only that Truman had scored an upset victory, but that the Democratic Party had recaptured both houses of Congress as well.[52] Throughout the country, feelings ran high as partisans on all sides tried to figure out what had happened and how. The Northwestern campus was no exception.

Bob Pennington remembered seeing his friend Martin Ridge (future editor of the *Journal of American History*) that morning in the crowd of students that packed the hallway outside the History Department. "Marty, we won!" Bob exulted, forgetting for a moment the scores of Wallace supporters who glowered at them. Consistent Truman supporters like Pennington and Martin Ridge, however, did not explain the president's triumph or Wallace's poor showing. According to Gallup polls, "as many as one-third" of the people who had declared for Wallace some months before had switched to Truman in the final days of the campaign. The administration's entreaties to liberals and the "insulation of Henry Wallace" had done much to seal his fate. The pattern held steady even among historians at Northwestern. "I was going to support him, but didn't," Bill Harbaugh, for example, said about his own last-minute decision. And so it went with others. "I thought most of [them] were going to be for Wallace," Al Young later said, "but then, when they went into the voting booth, they voted for Truman." None other than Ray Allen Billington told his students, "I just couldn't see myself electing Dewey."[53]

In these instances, however, a Supreme Court decision two weeks before undoubtedly tipped the balance for Truman. It also affected the unexpected course that George McGovern ultimately chose. Illinois was one of three states that denied Wallace a place on the ballot; all the way to the high bench his party contested the obscure law that the state's Republicans had invoked. Not until October 21 did the court rule, six to three, against the plaintiff. By then, it was too late for George to change his registration back to South Dakota after he had transferred it to Illinois in order to be a convention delegate. Unlike many of his associates, he could not bring himself to accept the only expedient alternative. Despite his work on the campaign, he ended up not voting at all.[54]

McGovern's decision was at once odd and principled; his chastening at Philadelphia had something to do with it. Yet his postconvention disillusionment did not run so deep that it prevented him from making a speech about the Progressive Party to the Kiwanis Club of Mitchell in late September, long after it became obvious that Wallace would be drubbed asunder. McGovern wrote about the experience in a letter to the editor of the *Daily Republic*. He had expected a hostile reception, but his audience listened and asked questions "on the highest possible level," he reported. "There was no 'red-baiting' or bitterness of any kind." It was "a genuine lesson in democracy," an illustration of "the free exchange of ideas." As for others who resorted "to egg-throwing, smear charges, witch-hunting, or intimidation of their employees," he supposed that they "are still a minority," though a great danger, for they would have a prescribed national political orthodoxy. He ended on a defiant note: "America was born in revolution against the established order. It grew strong on dissent and freely offered criticism. It became great through a willingness to experiment with the new and untried."[55]

––––––––––

It is interesting to note how McGovern had once regarded Roosevelt's bid for a fourth term. "I'm going to be more than a little disgusted if Dewey doesn't win," he had written to Bob Pennington on November 4, 1944. "I really think we need a man like Dewey in there now."[56] Only recently arrived at the Army Air Forces base at Cerignola, he could not have predicted the jostling that his patriotic outlook on American politics and foreign policy would sustain by the next electoral cycle. But such were the wages of the critical thinking he had begun once he returned to Dakota Wesleyan and carried on in graduate school at Northwestern. After 1948, he stayed unimpressed with Harry Truman, not only throughout his unhappy second term but decades later when the president was elevated to the status of folk hero. McGovern would always hold him responsible for setting the United States on an irreversible path—for having "too quickly abandoned the possibility of cooperation with the Soviet Union," for his "enormous overreaction to the crisis in Greece and Turkey," and for "taking the lead in the arms race and in the development of nuclear bombs." It was not that he could not see some justification for "standing firm." But he saw also that the Soviets were "reacting out of paranoia and fear and defensive purposes, even as we were," as each side terrified the other "beyond the realities of the threat that either one posed." Then, too, there was the "sardonic twist on things"—that Truman Democrats shortly would have to defend themselves against the same kind of loyalty questions that they had inflicted on Wallace and his followers.[57]

In contrast, McGovern would never stop believing that Wallace had been "essentially right" on many things. He continued to find him appealing because of the candidate's and his own faith in the power of positive thinking—that "America's great power was in its agriculture and its industry and its technology and its capacity to feed people and nurture them and educate them and minister to their physical needs," as he once put it. He would never ridicule Wallace as others did, even as he gave critics among Democrats some benefit of the doubt that they were sincere in the argument "that they prevented something even worse in terms of Soviet behavior."[58] He remained unconvinced "that the Soviets were poised and eager to launch World War III," and regretful that Truman and ADA liberals had "lent a certain legitimacy" to the tactics that McCarthyites and other opportunistic right-wing Republicans later used against them.[59]

Within two years of its founding the Progressive Party would disband. In the meantime, McGovern accepted a teaching position at his alma mater and completed his dissertation research. As much as those undertakings and his family meant to him, the affairs of state and of the world had become his daily bread. By the end of 1950, events had taken place that would shape the whole of his political career: Mao Zedong had prevailed in the Chinese civil war and sent Chiang Kai-shek fleeing to Formosa; the Truman administration redefined containment to cover, not just Europe, but the entire world, and thus began to finance the French in their futile quest to reclaim Indochina; the Korean War broke out; and Joseph McCarthy began his four-year reign of terror. As far as McGovern was concerned, a sort of political Frankenstein monster was at large. In its rampages against mainstream Democrats he took no satisfaction, but their refusal to acknowledge their part in building the laboratory in which the brute had been stitched together would continue to pain him. In the years ahead he would make his peace with them, and he would count several prominent ADAers among his most intimate friends. Even so, as late as the era of Bill Clinton, he would remark, "I don't know why they aren't more repentant."[60] For now, though, he was content to continue to study American history and soon to teach it. Intellectually and temperamentally, George McGovern had entered upon a life-long lover's quarrel with his country.

7 THE CONFUSED AND FEAR-RIDDEN TEMPER OF THE TIMES

"I cannot remember being bored—exhausted, yes, but never wondering what to do with my time," Eleanor McGovern once said. "I had my own private goals: to be the world's best mother; to be supportive of George if he needed me; mainly, to be a significant person, somehow, no matter what I was doing."[1] It was during the Wallace campaign that she had arrived at that state of mind, and she marveled at how much her life with George had changed, at how far they already had come and how stimulating their surroundings were. They had grown up in a stricken land during the most trying of times, yet the two of them had actually made it to college, and George had come home uninjured from the bloodiest of all wars. Eleanor reveled in being the mother of two healthy girls and took pride in her husband, the Northwestern University PhD candidate whom their friend Bill Harbaugh characterized as "the leader of the graduate students" and whom Margaret Link, the wife of one of George's mentors, described as "quite a dashing figure."[2] Every day through their door came energetic young people engaged in the world in transition around them. Eleanor herself had just been a delegate to a national political convention, and no ordinary one. She continued to read voraciously and to express her opinions. It required constant flexibility, but she liked her life.

Then, shortly before the November election, she discovered she was pregnant for the third time. But one morning as she watched Ann and Susan playing, she was suddenly miserable. The feeling had come out of nowhere; it returned the next day and the day after that. Eventually she would surmise that her melancholia was set off by an otherwise inconsequential evening out with a few of the graduate students and their wives. The conversation was about politics; then one of the women mentioned plans to take her children to visit their grandparents, and some of the men made fun of her for "going home to Mother." Eleanor was not amused. It was then she realized that she was overcome by an "inexplicable longing" for her own mother: "I wanted to go back to the farm, to find her there, to show off my girls, to share their first steps, to boast about their teeth." Although she looked forward to the birth of her third baby in June, "the child in me literally ached to be held," she wrote.[3]

Eleanor's depression took George unawares. As a husband and father, he was no less or more sensitive to the emotional needs of his family than most ambitious young men of the postwar era were—which is to say he was frequently inattentive to his wife and children. His lot as a graduate student placed a great burden on Eleanor. Often he was so absorbed in his studies that he was oblivious to Ann and Susan crawling under his study table. Other preoccupations exacerbated the tendency, for George aimed to play "a part in that postwar effort to build a structure of peace on the smoldering ruins of war."[4]

Eleanor's condition shook him up, though, and he set aside his work and became a better helpmate. He gave her the time she needed—to go on walks and to search out books in the library that might guide her. In the months before and after the baby arrived, she read about psychology and child development. Her studies convinced her that she was suffering from a delayed reaction to her mother's death. That tragedy "was the dominant force in my life," she came to believe. A repressed memory also reentered her consciousness. As a twelve-year-old she had overheard her father tell Grandmother Young about a dream he had had about his wife. It involved the beautiful Marion, attired in heavenly robes and sitting alone in a room, whereupon a young girl appeared and stood by her side. The girl was Eleanor. Grandmother Young's remark, "I hope that does not mean that Eleanor is going to die too," traumatized her for months. Because her mother had died some time after the birth of her third daughter, Phyllis, it seemed probable to Eleanor that her own third pregnancy had induced the depression. Now and then she would fret that her sadness had perhaps adversely affected the baby "during that early symbiotic period in our relationship." Over the years the feeling would come over her unexpectedly and leave the same way.

Eventually she concluded she had inherited a form of clinical depression. (Her mother's younger sister suffered terribly from it and their brother had committed suicide.)[5]

On the day Teresa Jane was born an early June hot spell hammered South Dakota. The maternity ward was stifling, and George used a magazine to fan Eleanor. The birthing turned out to be her easiest so far. Fortuitously, the McGoverns were back in Mitchell. Dakota Wesleyan had hired George to teach summer classes, which meant friends and family would be pitching in with the three kids. Their financial situation would improve markedly the following year. Once George had passed his PhD qualifying exams and completed his dissertation research, his alma mater offered him a full-time appointment as associate professor at the fairly decent salary of $4,500.[6]

For all kinds of reasons the 1950–51 school year, his first, would be the toughest. Dakota Wesleyan was "an excellent training field for green instructors," he would tell Arthur Link, but he was frustrated by how hard it was to find an hour in which to work on the dissertation. As is often the case at small colleges, DWU expected of faculty considerable interaction with students, and George found it rewarding to serve as the debate and forensics coach. Then, too, his school was in a protracted struggle between conservatives on the board of trustees and a progressive-minded university president, Samuel Hilburn, who had instituted a controversial interdisciplinary curriculum.[7]

A veteran of World War I, Hilburn had attended Southern Methodist University, in Dallas, and earned his PhD at the University of Chicago. Before the war, he had been a missionary in Japan and then an instructor in naval intelligence. At DWU his new curriculum—he called it "integrated education"—emphasized an individualized program of study and courses in human relations. It received high marks nationally but brewed contention among alumni and trustees. The president's disparaging view of sports at the university did not help. Even worse, he evinced a detached perspective on American foreign policy. He believed, for instance, that the road to Pearl Harbor had been paved by both the United States and Japan. His opinions fed grumbling in town that the college was an incubator for "un-American" thinking.[8]

But Hilburn was reckonable; he had defenders influential and numerous enough to keep him in place for five years. McGovern considered him "an excellent educator" who had "done more to improve the instructional aspects of the college than any" of his predecessors.

In George's opinion, Hilburn did what any good university president ought to do—he encouraged critical thinking in young people. Yet at a time when American higher education was becoming one of the domestic battlegrounds of the Cold War, the virtues that McGovern saw in Hilburn rankled others. In May 1951 the trustees pressured him into resigning on the grounds of declining enrollments and rising deficits. According to McGovern, however, Hilburn "was removed by bigoted, South Dakota Republicans who could not tolerate the liberal atmosphere of the college under [his] administration." McGovern assumed partial responsibility for the bad ending. "I was one of three professors known as 'too liberal' who had 'weakened' the president's cause," he told Link, concerning a last-ditch effort to save Hilburn.[9]

Being "too liberal" was already starting to have consequences on American campuses. In August 1950, thirty-one professors in California had lost their jobs for refusing to take a loyalty oath that the legislature insisted on. In the name of patriotism, lawmakers in Illinois attempted to do much the same thing; they established committees to ferret out "subversive" books in the public libraries and attempted to get faculty at the University of Chicago dismissed for membership in alleged communist-front organizations. A left-wing editorial in the student newspaper at the University of Oklahoma in 1949 prompted the legislature to impose a loyalty oath on state employees. Harvard provided the FBI with information on selected left-leaning faculty, while the freedom to express radical views in speech or writing was curtailed at universities in Kansas, Maryland, Massachusetts, Michigan, New Jersey, Wisconsin, and Washington. All of these incidents occurred before the term "McCarthyism" had been coined.[10]

The South Dakota legislature did not get around to imposing a loyalty oath on state employees until 1955. But after Hilburn's separation, the local American Legion had no trouble getting Dakota Wesleyan's administration to allow it to monitor certain professors from time to time. For example, when Bob Pennington taught a course on Russian history, Legionnaires showed up in his classroom one morning, unannounced—"two or three of them with their little caps on," as he told the story, "and they would sit there taking notes on my lecture." On another occasion the dean phoned him to say the Legion was coming in again and would he mind bringing over his collateral reading.[11] Pennington's politics were never a serious issue, however, at least not the way his brother-in-law's were. McGovern was suspect for his willingness to speak his mind on Cold War issues as well as for his involvement in the Wallace campaign. Yet he went about his work as a professor un-molested (for the most part) because he wore a suit of armor unique to Mitchell. The townspeople knew him as "that fine young man," the Reverend McGovern's boy. Dakota Wesleyan remembered him as one of its greatest debaters and honored his PhD studies at Northwestern. And everybody else knew about his combat decorations, a record no Legionnaire (or trustee) dared to slight. As for the students, George was immediately popular.

His courses nonetheless brewed trouble. One, "Human Relations," was designed around Hilburn's curriculum; in another, on American intellectual history, he assigned Vernon Parrington's radically inclined *Main Currents in American Thought*. His most heavily subscribed class, "International Relations," addressed current events—from the trial of Alger Hiss to whether Red China should be admitted into the United Nations.[12] Thus McGovern was destined to become Mitchell's most controversial citizen.

———————

The second Red Scare was entering its fourth year when, on February 10, 1950, Joseph R. McCarthy stood before an audience of Republican women in Wheeling, West Virginia, and claimed to hold in his hand a list of 205 known communists working in the State Department. What the junior senator from Wisconsin in fact held was a letter, printed in the *Congressional Record* in July 1946, in which the secretary of state dis-cussed the transfer of 3,000 federal employees into the department; for various reasons 205 of them would not be offered permanent employ-ment. There were no communists, "still working and shaping" Amer-ican foreign policy, as McCarthy averred, nor would he ever find any to expose. Yet over the next several years, he exercised power in wild disproportion to the evidence (which he could never produce) in sup-port of his charges. To much of the press and the public, however, that did not seem to matter. As one historian has written, Joe McCarthy had "found his oil gusher in communism."[13]

Until then, the most prominent American politician to use red-baiting for political advantage was President Truman, and it consti-tuted one of the keys to his victory in 1948. But in having destroyed Henry Wallace, the Democrats also had disabled their lightning rod. For the Republicans, stung through by Dewey's defeat, "communists-in-government" made for a big red umbrella that covered everything conservatives hated about Truman's multiplying shortcomings, not to mention FDR and the New Deal. The flashpoints included suspected wartime intrigue at Yalta and the Alger Hiss case and other alleged cases of communist espionage in the United States.[14] Then in August 1949 the Soviets exploded their first nuclear device, and the following year the Justice Department arrested Ethel and Julius Rosenberg for having furnished the KGB with atomic secrets stolen from the facilities at Los Alamos. But if there was a single event that had launched Joseph McCarthy on his course, it was the defeat of Generalissimo Chiang Kai-shek's Nationalist forces by Mao Zedong and his Red Revolution. After China "fell" to communism at the end of 1949, the politics and foreign policy of the Cold War would never be the same. China would also become McGovern's first passionate concern in international relations, and the position he staked out on it would become the chief weapon that Republicans wielded against him early in his political career.

On one level, it was odd that China's fate should have raised such a commotion. Until the prelude to World War II, "China remained an abstract concept in the minds of most Americans," as the historian Michael Schaller has observed.[15] Then, between 1937 and 1939, public sympathy for the Chinese increased significantly in the wake of Japan's unprovoked invasion. By December 1941, China, in the person of Chiang Kai-shek, had become "America's favorite ally."[16] This sentiment owed to the diligent work of several American organizations that would become the nucleus of the so-called China Lobby after 1945, informally led by Henry Luce, who himself had been born to missionary parents in China. The China Lobby's ostensible purpose was to help the country "emerge from the present conflict as a progressive democratic nation," said Luce, who on six occasions featured Chiang Kai-shek on the cover of *Time*. United China Relief reckoned that "the Chinese people [were] holding the western ramparts for us," and in the years ahead they would "turn to us for all the products that American industry . . . can produce"—to the tune of "four, five, ten billion dollars a year," added Luce in one of his "American Century" essays. During the war, *Life*, *Time*, and *Fortune* saturated the public with the same messages, as did Hollywood, the Office of War Information, and the Protestant Church. One scholar has dubbed this public-relations campaign "The Great China Hoax."[17]

China was then a war-torn country of one-half billion people, 90 percent of whom lived in poverty. Of its twenty-eight provinces, Chiang Kai-shek wielded authority in only two. After Pearl Harbor, one of the

United States' greatest difficulties was to get him to fight the Japanese. Chiang Kai-shek was dedicated to perpetuating his power base, the Kuomintang Party (KMT), and to eradicating his internal adversaries, the communists. Nonetheless, he demanded vast amounts of financial and military aid from the United States while rejecting advice on how to use it. Moreover, the Generalissimo practiced a brand of politics that conjoined feudalism and fascist theory.[18]

The Roosevelt administration was loath to acknowledge this shambling predicament, in spite of warnings from American advisers attached to the regime. In Nanking, the noted Asia scholar Owen Lattimore ascertained that Chiang regarded as a mortal threat any proposal for cleaning up the corruption within his government of warlords. Then there was his reluctance to engage the enemy. The legendary General Joseph Stilwell, serving as Chiang's chief of staff at FDR's behest, perceived two basic problems. One was an "inefficient system of political juggling," wrote Stilwell, the other was Chiang, "a grasping, bigoted, ungrateful little rattlesnake."[19]

But what made it a worse dilemma was the fact that many Americans in China had come to respect the Chinese communists, whose disciplined fighters in 1944 had prevented the invading enemy from overwhelming southeast China while the Nationalist forces ran for cover. In addition to killing Japanese troops, the communists also showed a penchant for another undertaking of no interest to the Kuomintang—land reform and tax reform for the peasantry. In a sense, these were the main reasons why Chiang ultimately failed and Mao Zedong succeeded. When the civil war recommenced, most American policy makers concluded that the country's future lay in a coalition of the two parties. (Apparently, Mao and Zhou En-lai envisaged a friendly relationship with the United States—partly so as to avoid overdependence on Stalin.)[20]

In December 1945, Truman dispatched George Marshall to Peking to conciliate the bitter foes. But Chiang's insistence that the communists fold themselves into his army spoiled whatever prospects for coalition government that survived the war. General Marshall was reasonably evenhanded, yet indisposed to taking sides against the KMT in disputes with the Chinese Communist Party (CCP). Likewise, though the president had pronounced Chiang's people "all thieves, every last one," the United States was still sending them aid. By the time Marshall came home in January 1947 to become secretary of state, the CCP was losing faith in the professed good intentions of the Americans. Republicans, meanwhile, were skewering the administration for even thinking about cooperating with Asian communists.[21]

The American people were not prepared for the military disasters the Nationalists suffered against communist arms; nor was it any easier to absorb the news that Chiang all along had been an inept general and a plundering dictator. In August 1949 Truman attempted to explain that the civil war had metamorphosed beyond the capacity of the United States to influence it. His admission only furnished the China Lobby more ammunition with which to assail the Democrats for "softness towards communism." In October, a new secretary of state, Dean Acheson, announced that the administration would withhold recognition of the "People's Republic of China." Two months later, Chiang and the Nationalists fled to Formosa. The United States since 1945 had squandered on this regime over $2 billion in what amounted to, as Owen Lattimore put it, "an extensive field test to demonstrate that America cannot control China."[22]

The fallout was comprehensive. Events in China lent credence to McCarthy's accusations of conspiracy in high places and became the catalyst for his second major speech and then an attack on Lattimore, whom he slandered as "definitely an espionage agent." Thereafter, the Republicans would draw more Democratic blood with China than with any other issue.[23] The reversal of fortunes sent the Truman administration reeling back to the drawing board. Within a few months, the National Security Council drafted a document known as NSC-68, a blueprint for containment on a global scale. Heretofore containment had focused practically exclusively on Europe; under NSC-68, the United States would resist communist expansion (or revolutionary upheaval) regardless of its scope, on any piece of earth near or far, by any means necessary. Gone forever was the comparative restraint of George Kennan's formula, which had stressed the need, even for a superpower, to acknowledge its own limitations and to have a sense of priorities.

NSC-68 was a secret document shaped as much by domestic political exigency as by national security. But its application would impel the development of the hydrogen bomb, the trebling of the defense budget within two years, and therefore a considerable increase in taxes. Intervention into the Korean War in June 1950 became the strategy's first test case. ("Korea came along and saved us," Dean Acheson later said, even though it ruined his boss's second term.) Of all the things one could read between the lines of NSC-68, in retrospect nothing would appear more legible than the origins of the American war in Vietnam.[24]

It was in his father's church that George McGovern initially encountered "strife-ridden China"—much like millions of other American Protestants had done in the late 1930s. But the propaganda leaflets had all the more impact on the Reverend McGovern's son when he learned that Chiang Kai-shek and his American-educated wife were converts not just to Christianity, but also to Methodism. Literature and motion pictures also shaped George's early impressions. Ever the devoted reader and filmgoer, he admired both the novel and the Hollywood version of the Nobel laureate Pearl S. Buck's *The Good Earth*, the epic story of a peasant family's triumph over daunting adversities early in the new century. Stirring war movies were George's regular fare, too; those set in the Far East might open upon a heroic portrait of Chiang or a montage of children being cared for by United China Relief, or depict a merciless Japanese air attack on Chinese civilians. As a *Phreno Cosmian* columnist and a debater, he followed the news from the Asian front; in 1941 he won one of his blue ribbons for a speech titled "The Battle of the Far East."[25]

His fascination with China intensified in the context of the Cold War. In his prize-winning peace oratory in 1946, he condemned atrocities committed by American troops stationed in north China early in the Truman administration. His Northwestern colleague Bill Towner, who had transported supplies to the Nationalists, bemoaned, "Chiang Kai-shek [is] rotten, corrupt, dictatorial, and the State Department [is] backing him."[26] By 1950 a new school of thought suggested that the Cold War had begun in Asia. Its more important works included Theodore White and Annalee Jacoby's *Thunder Out of China* (1946), John K. Fairbank's *The United States and China* (1948), and Lattimore's *The Situation in Asia* (1949). McGovern read all of them eagerly.

Theodore White would go on to win the Pulitzer Prize for *The Making of the President 1960* and write three more books in that series, ending with the 1972 campaign. For many readers, including McGovern, *Thunder Out of China* would stand as White's finest work. Its style was brisk and pungent as it explained the source of all the thunder three years before the storm subsided.[27] Characterizing it as "the greatest revolution in the history of mankind," White and Jacoby offered a perspective on

Chinese politics unfamiliar to most Americans. They reported grimly that Chiang Kai-shek "could not understand the revolution whose creature he was except as something fearful that had to be crushed." Moreover, his party's "leadership was corrupt, its secret police merciless." As for postwar reforms, as long as American representatives "were satisfied with a sack of wind, the [Kuomintang] government stood ready to meet its obligations."[28] The communists, in contrast, "lived not on taxes, but on the sweat of their own brow." They not only knew the peasants and understood their grievances but also practiced a form of alliance politics with them and the factory workers and petite bourgeoisie. In a peculiar way, according to the authors, the Chinese Communist Party (CCP) had "been more democratic than the Kuomintang." And it was not the KMT, but the CCP troops that "had fought, bled, and died for five years . . . [and] won the right in battle to occupy the strongholds of the defeated enemy."[29] Much to the communists' bewilderment, however, when the conflict with Japan ended, American troops had begun helping the Nationalists secure strategic positions. Suddenly, "Our flag flew in the cockpit of a civil war." Americans risked being seen as "the patrons of the decadent and corrupt, [while] the Russians become the patrons of the vigorous and dynamic," White and Jacoby argued finally. "We cannot defend a system of oppression, feudalism, and corruption anywhere in the world and tell people we are doing so in defense of their democratic rights. . . . We ourselves must become the sponsors of revolution."[30]

No study of contemporary history did more to stimulate McGovern's critical thinking about foreign policy than *Thunder Out of China*. But another, by John K. Fairbank, equaled it. A Rhodes scholar, a Harvard academic since the 1930s, and a native of South Dakota, Fairbank would gain eminence by the 1960s as the founder of Chinese studies in the United States. His seminal work, *The United States and China*, was based on seventeen years' research in libraries and in the field in both China and the West. On the subject of Chiang Kai-shek, the volume scarcely differed from *Thunder Out of China*. Fairbank regretted the Kuomintang's "record of incredible corruption and brutal terrorism" because it had destroyed the Chinese liberal movement, the political center around which the United States might have established a constructive policy.[31] But the book, which McGovern marked heavily, was even more powerful than *Thunder* for its detail on how a communist movement had put down roots in East Asia and for its authority as pioneering scholarship appearing in the last full year of the civil war.

In light of all the foreign intrusions and internal upheaval it had endured since the 1890s, "China was bound to experience shattering revolutionary movements," Fairbank cautioned, "with or without the aid of Marxism and the Comintern." Henry Luce's "American Century" notwithstanding, "we cannot remake Chinese society in our own image," he further explained. "We court disaster if we let our patriotic measures against Russian expansion, or purely doctrinaire anticommunism, dictate our China policy."[32]

Thus Americans needed to acknowledge their mistake of seeking a "divided objective"—of pressing the Kuomintang to introduce democratic reforms while sending material support that strengthened the dictatorship. American policy makers also had to realize that mankind was "going through a process of social and political revolution . . . our salvation lies in understanding this process . . . and adapting our policy to it, not in fearful efforts to stamp it out." The United States could not ally itself with despots and still "claim to be a force for democracy." In large areas of China, "we are known chiefly . . . as the source of the Nationalist planes and guns which strafe peasant villages." Reliance on military means to influence events was self-defeating, he continued. The "outcome of a social revolution among 450 million people does not depend upon us."[33]

Fairbank pointed out in his concluding chapter that if Americans truly embraced the principle of self-determination, then they must face "the rueful possibility that the Chinese people may actually decide to go Communist." But it would be a terrible mistake to dismiss the revolution as evil. Wisdom required the United States to stand for individual freedoms, "as opposed to police-state totalitarianism," and to offer as much assistance for agrarian reform as possible and not otherwise interfere. Americans must grasp something else, too: "In Asia, food comes before civil liberties and political self-expression. . . . [T]he ideal of economic freedom in China is much closer to 'freedom from want' than it is to 'freedom of enterprise.'" Food and other kinds of economic aid were "a form of intervention quite as potent as marines or gunboats." And so, "in the world-wide struggle for individual political liberty," the United States should be willing to help "other peoples in poorer circumstances to develop whatever degree of collectivist or socialized economy they need to meet their problems"—that is, to help by letting the people do things their own way. Finally, the historian advised, "Support of the political status quo will not save our position." At stake was nothing less than "the creation of a new social structure and new sources of political authority." The decisions would ultimately be made among the Chinese people themselves.[34]

After the publication of his book, Fairbank continued to advocate rapprochement with the People's Republic of China. He also defended Owen Lattimore and other experts against Senator McCarthy's charges that they somehow had assisted in the communist victory. In 1951, the State Department denied Fairbank permission to travel to Japan. Yet his deeds and the chastisement he suffered enhanced his stature in the eyes of fellow scholars. For one of them in particular, his words would take on living meaning. To shun the knee-jerk use of force and instead seek nonmilitary solutions to the problems of new nations in the grip of revolution would become an article of faith for George McGovern. Almost instinctively he understood why, in such countries, "food comes before civil liberties and political self-expression" and "freedom from want was part and parcel of freedom from tyranny." Within a few years he would have the opportunity to demonstrate how America's greatest asset in the cause of peace was its abundance of food, not nuclear force loads.

Fairbank's and White's influence was on display in McGovern's letters to Ray Allen Billington and Arthur Link just as the Sino-American standoff collided with the Korean War and McCarthyism. In July 1950, three weeks after Truman committed US forces to defend South Korea against North Korea's invasion,[35] McGovern wrote the following to Billington: "It seems to me that the events there are following the pattern of China where we saw a decadent regime get the axe under communist leadership but with the mass support from the peasants. Isn't that the case in Korea, with the Americans once again trying to support a regime that has already been repudiated by the majority of South Koreans that we are trying to save?" The Russians were "cagey enough to play along with the twin forces of nationalism and socialism," while the United States strained to uphold the status quo, which all of his readings had warned against.[36]

"Frankly, I'm scared," he told Link a month later. "We have thrown in our lot with decadent systems in Greece, China, Indonesia, [and] South Korea . . . whereas Russia has been quick to encourage uprisings against those very regimes that we have been trying so hard to peg down." Once again he regretted that Americans did not seem to know what to do about "the two forces of nationalism and socialism that are now convulsing the 'backward' areas of the world." Just where it would end in Korea, he could not say. But even before General

MacArthur had landed at Inchon and turned back the North's surge into the South, McGovern feared that "we shall find ourselves in an eastern war against 120 crack Chinese and Russian divisions," unless Truman changed course. "Would not a third world war make inevitable a world of communism on one hand and fascism on the other?" he asked Link. What was all the fuss supposed to be about "when we have such allies as Franco, Chiang, Rhee and the most reactionary elements of the Republican party?"[37]

McGovern made clear connections between domestic politics and foreign policy. He could see that China, Korea, and McCarthyism had stymied the Fair Deal, Truman's program to go beyond the New Deal (expanded Social Security, a modest public housing program, and increases in farm subsidies and the minimum wage). What chilled him most was the McCarran Act, the spawn of not only Republican witch-hunting but also the president's loyalty program, as he wrote to Link. On one hand, the Internal Security Act was the Mundt-Nixon bill repackaged; on the other hand, Democrats had amended this version to provide detention camps into which "subversives" could be herded if the president declared an "internal security emergency." McGovern considered this law "possibly a greater loss to freedom than any previous measure in our history as a nation—more so than the acts of 1798." Although Truman opposed the McCarran Act, his veto was easily overridden. McGovern held him as well as the Congress responsible for creating "the present atmosphere" that had egged it on. He worried that the events of 1950 might "mean the death blow to whatever liberalism remains in the United States."[38]

McGovern's apprehensions about Korea exploding into a bigger conflict were borne out during his first semester of teaching. By the end of September 1950 MacArthur had shoved the invaders out of the South. The White House then permitted US troops to move well above the 38th parallel. Simply to restore that line and contain North Korea had been the original goal; now it was to pursue enemy forces as far north as the Yalu River on the border of the People's Republic of China and unite all of Korea under the right-wing dictator, Syngman Rhee. Neither the president nor his field marshal could have exercised worse judgment in dismissing the warnings of Mao Zedong to respect China's frontiers. On November 26, 200,000 Red Chinese troops swept down across the Yalu; within days they drove the Americans out of North Korea and far below the 38th parallel. Over a piece of geography of dubious strategic value, MacArthur had perpetrated one of the greatest military disasters in American history.[39]

When Truman fired the general for insubordination in April 1951, McGovern called it "the most brilliant and courageous single act" of his presidency. Perhaps "the next logical step will be a negotiated settlement," he exclaimed to Link.[40] But Korea devolved into a grinding stalemate for still another two years, ensuring the longevity of McCarthyism as well as the election of a Republican president and Congress in 1952. The undeclared war would also increase the powers of the executive branch, while the riptide of domestic politics, in tandem with NSC-68, would mandate a defense budget of $50 billion. (The previous one was $14 billion.) A portion of this sum would provide financial aid for the stubborn exertions of the French to keep intact their colonial empire in Indochina. It was yet another situation that fitted perfectly the analyses of Fairbank, Lattimore, and White concerning what, and what not, to do in Asia.

———————

The foregoing events and historical studies had a decisive impact on McGovern's day-to-day responsibilities as a professor and on the direction of his life. His International Relations class was proving to be "a rewarding experience," he told Link innocently. But it made for additional material for the inquisitive J. Edgar Hoover to scrutinize, too, as McGovern would learn years later.[41] Not only Legionnaires (with and without their little caps on), but also his students and colleagues contributed to his secret FBI file, albeit not detrimentally in most cases.

One Dakota Wesleyan professor told an FBI investigator that a talk McGovern had given on campus towed "the pro-communist line." The assertion centered on his defense of Henry Wallace and his harsh criticisms of Karl Mundt, McCarthyism, and the House Un-American Activities Committee, whose members he supposedly said were "un-American." An unidentified observer (a member of the Legion post) sat in on three class meetings and reported that the holder of the Distinguished Flying Cross advocated Red China's admission to the United Nations and assigned Lattimore's current book, *Ordeal by Slander*. "McGovern could easily be duped by communists," he surmised. An undergraduate who took two of his courses concurred and resented having to read Lattimore and probably sincerely felt his instructor preached "communistic ideas." The student listed the following as examples: that the "the United States had no business fighting in South Korea," that "Roosevelt's major mistake during World War II was to help Nationalist China," that Alger Hiss was "a victim of a lie," and that no citizen should be required to say whether or not he is a communist.

McGovern would not have denied making such remarks, but whether they constituted "communistic ideas" was another matter. The FBI in any case had a hard time finding corroboration. Another member of the class revealed that the witness and the accused were "bitter enemies" and at least one of the faculty considered the student "unstable." McGovern's problem, according to his colleague, was that he "was always willing to listen to both sides of a political issue," which could "cause a dull student . . . to doubt [his] loyalty." Likewise, one other pupil commented that McGovern "strongly supported the United Nations" as well as various federal welfare programs, but admitted he was "completely impartial in class discussion."[42]

Evenhanded or no, he simply could not keep quiet on the subjects of China, Korea, and the United Nations. In June 1951 he gave a speech at the annual banquet of the regional Methodist Conference on Social Action. The result was a red fire that would take years to go out. "Christianity and the Challenge of Communism" was his topic and its argument was based on Fairbank. The "social revolutions going on in the world today are not a Moscow plot, but are the result of misrule [and] economic distress," McGovern said. The solution to such problems lay not in "guns, tanks, and planes," but more likely in historical understanding and in tractors; our Far Eastern policy was "shortsighted." It had "involved us in a debacle in Korea which has brought the death of many Americans and has seen us kill thousands of ragged Chinese peasants who had no more idea of what they were fighting for than we do." He laid out a four-point program that could alleviate the crisis: a cease-fire in Korea, an international conference on Asia, US recognition of China's new government, and economic and technical assistance for the country.[43]

The speech gratified the two hundred Methodist ministers, he reported to Arthur Link, but an account in the *Mitchell Daily Republic* provoked a letter to the editor that denounced the speaker for "following the Communist party line, point for point" and portrayed him as "muddle-headed."[44] Communism, McGovern responded, "feeds on poverty, misrule and ignorance," and he had tried to plumb its root

causes in part by applying "practical Christian principles to the threat."
As for his "extreme" positions, he reaffirmed his case that nonrecognition only served to drive China "into the arms of Moscow." An aid program and diplomatic relations, he reminded his assailant, had helped to keep Tito and the communists of Yugoslavia out of the Soviet orbit. Could not the same patience and peaceful means work with China? Was it not possible "that Stalin may be interested in keeping China out of the U.N. and isolated from diplomatic contact with the U.S.?" (Although the fact was not established until the 1990s, Stalin indeed dreaded a Sino-American rapprochement and perceived Mao as a "Titoist" rival.)[45]

McGovern, partly in anger, dismissed the attack as a "hysterical outburst . . . typical of the confused and fear-ridden temper of the times." But the letter was his first published declaration on United States foreign policy toward Asia—an unimaginative policy embedded in a narrow anticommunism, he asserted, which had resulted in an unnecessary war. Along with his service to Henry Wallace, South Dakota Republicans would never let the statement rest once he entered politics. "Christianity and the Challenge of Communism" made quite a capstone for his first year of teaching.

McGovern had proved not to be the typical prairie college professor, especially so in such "confused and fear-ridden" times. His views might have triggered some measure of social ostracism or a reprimand from the university. To the community's credit neither ever happened.[46] What prevented it is not clear, particularly when the state's most famous politician was one of the nation's leading anticommunists, Karl Mundt. (Dakota Wesleyan actually raised McGovern's salary by 10 percent the next year.) But it had something to do with McGovern's qualities as a teacher, which people would begin to remark upon more and more. In both casual and formal speech, he had a knack for making his views on any issue sound quite reasonable. The same position in print or spoken by someone else, however, might have struck some folks as radical in the context of Cold War politics.

Then, too, there was his persona, for which most of his students seemed almost to love him. Although he exhibited intensity when issues that really mattered to him came up, he was never a bore. By most accounts, he was easygoing and often funny; some students even called him by his first name. Indubitably, he personified the archetypal, inspired young professor, eager to instill in his students an appreciation for the discovery of unexpected facts and ideas and a sense of engagement with the world through critical thinking about the nation's history and current policies. For that, South Dakota did not seem quite so isolated to many of his students. In his own way, he motivated them in part by tapping into their innate idealism. According to one, he had a gift, "a way of making you feel like you could continue to do your best." That was apparently the attribute that meant the most to students—plus the fact that he showed interest in them as individuals.[47]

No one at Dakota Wesleyan was surprised when he turned out to be the best debate coach the school had hired in a long time. According to *The Tumbleweed* of 1951, he had begun with "a comparatively green squad." Yet the twenty or so debaters racked up "a remarkable record of accomplishment" under his tutelage. By spring, the women were doing particularly well. Although they lost to SMU and the University of Colorado, they beat Utah State and Denver Women's College, with Roberta McRae taking first place in oral interpretation and Donna McLain receiving a "superior" rating in extemp. In 1951–52, at the Rocky Mountain meet, Dakota Wesleyan won four out of five major debates, a "first" in extemp, and several "superiors." The next year, against a range of schools, the women's team won four of six debates, and sophomore Martha Jurgeson placed first in a major regional competition and followed it up with top honors against all women competitors from South Dakota in the·National Intercollegiate at Northwestern.[48]

George's most celebrated protégé was Barbara Rollins, the daughter of the university's business manager, Gordon Rollins. Barbara excelled in high school debate but really came into her own in college. In her opinion, George had no equal when it came to advice on how to make a sound argument in a ten-minute oration, or how to identify its weakness. His criticism was helpful also, she said, because of his relaxed personal manner. Debate clarified Barbara's outlook on American politics and foreign policy; in a Sioux Falls tournament she drew the affirmative on whether the United States should extend diplomatic recognition to Communist China. That subject, the Army-McCarthy hearings of the spring of 1954, and a debate in the state legislature, inspired an award-winning speech on fear, anxiety, and loyalty oaths. "Have we sought so diligently to become good anti-Communists," she asked, "that we have lost sight of the more difficult task of living as good Americans?" George guided her toward the topic and to the prestigious national women's peace oratory competition in Redlands, California, where she won the grand prize for her oration, "Loyalty and the Cold War." (He was responsible for her becoming a Democrat, Barbara also said, and for the founding of the Young Democrats Club at Dakota Wesleyan by mid-decade.)[49]

McGovern was on the faculty only two years when the students dedicated the 1952 *Tumbleweed* to him. That accolade was usually reserved for someone with much longer service, but the editors thought he was the exception. "George has found a place in the hearts of students both in and out of the classroom," read the citation, which highlighted his coaching of the debate squads and his advising of the student-run radio station KDWU. It also stressed how he commanded the students' respect "in the deepest sense of the word," "his excellence as a teacher, and understanding of all sides of student life." In February 1953, his peers among the Rocky Mountain Intercollegiate Forensics Association paid him tribute with a special coach's award "for having the best record of any team entered in the Rocky Mountain event over a three-year period."[50]

McGovern's controversialism and success as a teacher functioned as augury and spur. He continued to find teaching history and coaching debate "utterly rewarding" and derived "a lot of satisfaction" from his dissertation. Politics, however, held an irresistible attraction. One passion fed another. "My quickened interest in contemporary politics has sharpened my historical appetite and, of course, the reverse is true," he wrote to Link in early 1952, wondering, "How do some of our colleagues find it possible to remain so detached from current politics?"[51]

The words were no coincidence. A pattern of life was setting up. His career henceforward would turn on the years of presidential elections, and each one of them would be more important to him than the last. In 1948 there had been the Wallace campaign. Now, in 1952, he was making his peace with the party of Adlai Stevenson. For the first time he had begun to refer to himself as a Democrat and to ponder alternative paths to academia. "I can see a great challenge here in this state," he mentioned to Link in passing, after the chair of the Democratic organization approached him about becoming a full-time organizer. His Progressive Party association and forays into the local Cold War combat zone situated him a little to the left of respectability in the eyes of a lot of good people. The things he wrote and said about Red China and the Korean War even caused a few to identify him with "the pinks" and "the unwitting fellow-travelers." For far lesser offenses, one could be excommunicated from the ranks of the liberalism known as "the Vital Center," a matter of consequence that he had to confront whether he launched into politics or stayed put at the university.[52] In the four years since 1948, McGovern had read enough history to appreciate the role third parties had played in American history. The Progressive Party had fulfilled its purpose. There was no future in trying to revive the party of Henry Wallace, least of all in South Dakota. In the 1952 presidential primaries, South Dakotans cast 128,000 ballots for Republicans compared with 34,000 in the Democratic contest. If he was serious about a political career, the Stevenson boom might be the key to his transition.[53]

In the meanwhile, Eleanor was pregnant for the fourth time and George had a doctoral dissertation to finish. With his full course load and sponsorship of the debate squad (and helping out with the children at least a little), his dissertation had "really been a big load to carry these past two years," as he tried to explain to his adviser. The date for the formal defense, alas, had to be pushed back to December 1952. Even so, it might not have happened then, but for Eleanor who typed and retyped the entire manuscript and many sections several times to accommodate revisions. She was correcting the final pages when her labor pains began.[54]

Link and Billington were already putting McGovern up for top jobs in the year before his dissertation defense. For a tenure-track position at the University of North Carolina, Link certified him "the brightest student of American history . . . [and] the most effective teacher we have turned out since the war's end." Billington recommended him in still more glowing terms to the University of Iowa and ranked him among the top five graduate students he had ever known, among "the relatively few that can be designated as 'brilliant.' "[55] In the fierce competition for jobs at major universities, such testimonials were requisite. The Iowa History Department received eighty applications. Ultimately they were winnowed down to two—George and a newly minted Harvard PhD.

Yet he was ever more preoccupied with politics. The coming presidential race, with both parties showing fresh horses for the first time since 1928, fed his thinking about the possibilities in South Dakota, and he broached the subject when Professor and Mrs. Billington paid the McGoverns a visit during the summer. Eleanor frowned on that conversation as premature and afterward persuaded George to explain that he had gotten a little carried away. "Perhaps she is right (as she usually is) since nothing more than speculation may ever come of it," George wrote to Billington. "It may well be that I am experiencing a temporary burst of enthusiasm because of the Stevenson uplift to the Democratic Party." That much was true, if not the whole truth.[56]

As for Stevenson, he had made his first impression on the national political scene when he won the Illinois gubernatorial race in 1948, out-polling Truman and helping him to carry the state. By 1952, he was Eleanor Roosevelt's as well as the president's preferred candidate for the nomination. Whereas the governor was cozy with Mrs. Roosevelt, he kept his distance from the man he hoped to succeed. Most observers would have described Stevenson as a moderate northern liberal and a sincere Cold Warrior of the ADA sort: He was a solid supporter of the New Deal and the Fair Deal; he defended the Korean War and the loyalty program; and he often invoked "Godless communism" in his speeches. Substantively, very little set him apart from either Truman or Eisenhower.

Still there were some differences. He was, for instance, an ardent champion of the United Nations, a claim his opponent could not make unequivocally. Then there was Joseph McCarthy. Throughout the campaign, Eisenhower spoke not a word of reproof, publicly, despite that senator's scurrilous denunciation of General Marshall as a traitor for his role in the "sellout in Asia." But Stevenson traveled to McCarthy's home state and called on Wisconsinites to turn him out of office. About Eisenhower's silence in defending his old commanding officer, Stevenson remarked, "I'm wondering about his backbone." (Others also wondered.) For having a backbone himself, though, he suffered doubly—for the sins of the Truman administration and as a kind of Henry Wallace stand-in. Once he was nominated, charges of the Democrats being "soft on communism," the fall of China, and mounting discontent with the Korean War fell on his shoulders. Richard Nixon incessantly linked "Adlai the Appeaser" to "Acheson's cowardly college of Communist Containment" and squeezed all the mileage he could from Stevenson's testimony on behalf of Alger Hiss. Joe McCarthy relished referring to "Alger—I mean Adlai" in feigned slips of the tongue.[57]

The reason why he won McGovern's admiration and that of other liberals, however, was found in Stevenson's venerable status as "egg-head," a part he looked and played with uncommon charm. In his textbook, Arthur Link declared him "the most eloquent political leader since Franklin Roosevelt." Indeed, Stevenson was arguably the greatest rhetorician among all presidential candidates of the twentieth century, save Wilson. "There was a combination of high intelligence, character and common sense . . . which profoundly attracted me," McGovern wrote in his memoir. "I could not resist Stevenson's eloquence."[58] He had finally come home to the Democratic Party.

It was the acceptance speech in July that captivated him. The nominee did not get to speak to his national audience until almost midnight. George was painting the living room. He laid his paintbrush aside and listened spellbound when Stevenson said he wanted to talk sense to the American people. The message was that there were no easy solutions to the problems they faced, at home or abroad. His concern was "not just winning the election, but how it is won, how well we can take advantage of this quadrennial opportunity to debate issues sensibly and soberly," he explained. "I hope and pray that we Democrats, win or lose, can campaign not as a campaign to exterminate the opposing party as our opponents seem to prefer, but as a great opportunity to educate and elevate a people whose destiny is leadership, not alone of a rich and prosperous, contented country as in the past, but of a world in ferment. . . . Better we lose the election than mislead the people; and better we lose than misgovern the people."[59]

"That was it," McGovern confessed. "I was dedicated to the Stevenson campaign from that moment on." And *so* dedicated was he that, two days later, as Eleanor lay waiting to be taken into the delivery room and they talked about names for the baby, the thought occurred to him, "Well, if it should be a boy, why don't we name him Steven after Stevenson?" On July 27, 1952, Steven McGovern was born in the same hospital where all of his sisters had been. The family's storied regard for its hero did not end there. Some weeks after, George and Eleanor overheard four-year-old Terry announce to her playmates: "My three favorite people are God, Jesus, and Adlai Stevenson."[60]

———————————

To land the job at Iowa would be terrific good fortune, George knew, but if he did not, he resolved to see it as a sign from on high. He was aching for his counselors to say it was okay with them if he decided against the main-traveled roads of academia. It was what he had hoped to hear when the Billingtons visited in August. And he had put out a feeler in a letter to Link in July: "By the way, it would be awfully easy for a Democratic college professor to move into the political arena here in South Dakota. I think that I should talk to you about that possibility, or should I??"[61] But both mentors were reticent. They were important figures in the profession and they had lavished a great deal of time and energy to help George succeed in a field in which the majority of would-be practitioners never secure suitable jobs. Was he just going to throw it away—all that hard work to earn a PhD as well the endorsements they had bestowed regarding his potential to become an outstanding teacher and scholar?

Indeed, therein lay the paradox afflicting him. His historical training and teaching experience together had rendered him defenseless against the allures of politics. But it was dawning on him that his background as a scholar would never go for naught. It would be the element that made him stand out, that gave him the tools, the better to represent the interests of everyday people. His study of history, then, conferred a bolder sense of what he might be capable of achieving. In a letter to Iowa, Billington had explained that George once had chosen to be a scholar and teacher "based on the belief that he could do more good for mankind in that capacity." To McGovern, politics had become the next step; but for now he would wait on Iowa.

8 WHAT A LOSS TO HISTORY!

In April 1948, in a *New York Times Magazine* article, "Not Left, Not Right, but a Vital Center," Arthur M. Schlesinger Jr., coined a new political term. It was intended as a response to Henry Wallace. Barely thirty years old, Schlesinger was already famous for his innovative *The Age of Jackson* (1946), a Pulitzer Prize–winning study that cast the seventh president as the champion of the common man and "Jacksonian Democracy" as the enabler of the American dream of the 1830s—that is, as early national antecedents of Roosevelt and the New Deal. For Schlesinger, the Vital Center was a synonym for liberalism in the context of both domestic and world politics. It was America's answer, its antidote, to the two twentieth-century forms of totalitarianism—fascism and communism. Midway on the spectrum between those extremes, liberalism had been "fundamentally reshaped" by the experiment called the New Deal and by its encounters, first, with Hitler and, now, with Stalin. That meant two things for postwar American democracy: at home, a mixed economy based on capitalism, but augmented by partial governmental planning, as the best blueprint for prosperity and a minimum standard of living for those less fortunate than the affluent majority; in foreign policy, anticommunism, pure and simple—or, the welfare state and the containment doctrine.

The author elaborated on this formula the following year in a book, *The Vital Center: The Politics of Freedom.* Guided by the ideas of Americans for Democratic Action, the tract leveled criticisms at Wallace's followers, whom Schlesinger had dubbed "knaves and fools" in 1947–

48 and now called "dough-faced progressives." The title of the chapter on their campaign was "The Communist Challenge to America."
Schlesinger was unclear about how far to the left of ADA one could
stray before he might issue the "dough face" warrant, and he declined
to acknowledge any salutary impact that Wallace might have had on
the Democrats and Truman's comparatively progressive shift.

The Vital Center also skimped on liberalism's failings. About its historic myopia concerning Jim Crow, or the Cold War's mushrooming
costs, the creeping militarization of American society, and the capacity of nuclear weapons to destroy civilization, he said nothing. Yet he
strained to rationalize Truman's loyalty board. Thus, though McCarthy
was not yet the national figure Schlesinger would detest instinctively,
the book allowed elements of McCarthyism room to breathe.[1] Its main
shortcoming lay in its not drawing a sharp distinction between communism and socialism. This not to say that Schlesinger's manifesto
fanned the embers of McCarthyism, but neither did it help to douse
them. Republicans persisted in equating the New Deal with socialism,
ignoring the fact that anticommunism was a vital component of any
useful definition of Cold War liberalism.[2]

In the years ahead, McGovern and Schlesinger would become intimate friends. But if the Vital Center was the compass, on certain issues
McGovern had gone about as far as he could go without falling off the
map. His views stemmed from the two most significant experiences
of his adult life thus far. The first was World War II and his sense of
what America's motives and objectives were supposed to have been.
Second were his studies at Northwestern, which, he said, "introduced
me to some of the rawest aspects of American politics and society."[3]
McGovern favored liberal capitalism, and his faith in constitutional
democracy was profound, but he also believed that the United States
erred in attempts to impose its own values and institutions upon other
countries, especially emerging nations in revolt against colonial oppressors. Moreover, he was completing a dissertation about Colorado
mining families of the 1910s and the lengths to which corporations
went to destroy unions. The topic itself put him somewhat out of step
with the mainstream. "History from the bottom up" was not quite the
preferred form in the 1950s. Most historians tended, like Arthur Link, to
emphasize elites, not working people, as the makers of history. Owing
to communism's challenge, historians were starting to tout the virtues
of capitalism in a more prideful way than they had done during the
Depression and the war. They stressed the notion of *consensus* as the

outstanding characteristic of America's national development rather than *conflict* as the principal engine of its progress. The consensus school would supplant the progressive school by the time John F. Kennedy established Camelot on the Potomac.

McGovern employed progressive history as he tried to show South Dakotans why they should appreciate Adlai Stevenson (the very personification of the Vital Center). Partly owing to Governor Sigurd Anderson's portrayal of the 1952 contest as a struggle "between New Dealism and Americanism," McGovern aimed to advance Stevenson's cause by placing the Democratic Party's achievements in historical perspective. From August to October, the *Mitchell Daily Republic* published seven essays he wrote about the conflicts that divided Republicans and Democrats since early nationhood. His series constituted a declaration of principles upon the eve of his entrance into politics.[4]

The first piece dealt with recent events. Taking issue with predictions that the era of Democratic ascendancy was ending, he argued that the trend born in 1932 "was a permanent change in the course of American history." It had laid bare "the inability of individual, uncoordinated efforts to meet the problems of a complex and frequently dislocated economy." Americans had called upon the state "to direct the benefits of the economy to a larger number of people." Thus the Democrats shored up the banking system and created Social Security, the TVA, and programs for labor and agriculture. While many Republicans still opposed them, the majority of Americans embraced these initiatives. Far from dying of old age, the trend of 1932 was gaining new foundations. Adlai Stevenson would capture the imagination of voters "who yearn for greater equality, international cooperation and the right to enjoy the fruits of their labor with a reasonable degree of security," McGovern asserted.[5]

In a subsequent essay he explained that the American political tradition was marked by contradiction and conflict. The Founders had provided "government in the interest of the common people, freedom of expression, and social equality." Yet, "rule by the few . . . the suppression of dissent, and social inequality" often prevailed. These contradictions set in motion the first party system during the Washington administration. The Federalist Party, led by him and Hamilton, in many ways was the forerunner of the Republican Party; it preferred strong central government "dedicated to the control of the 'mob' and the advancement of the interests of the rich and well-born." Its Jeffersonian opponents, forebears of the Democratic Party, "believed that the backbone of America was the small independent farmer," a contrast McGovern stressed for his readership. He also singled out the Alien and Sedition Acts of 1798 (which John Adams aimed at the Jeffersonians because of their sympathy for the French Revolution) as "the first major example in our national history of the latter day manifestations of McCarthyism." To understand the present day was to understand "the *ongoing* struggle between the Hamiltonians and Jeffersonians."[6]

Schlesinger's influence was apparent in the fourth essay. It resumed with Jackson, Jefferson's heir, who made the Democrats a permanent party by championing the farmer, the day worker, and the small businessman. "Jackson symbolized the rise of the common man as a major force in politics," wrote McGovern. By the end of his two terms, the United States had attained universal white male suffrage, whereas in the Federalist era only one-fifth of the population could vote. After 1837, "no major political party has dared to ignore the farmer-labor vote." As for the deceased Federalists, their successors, the Whigs, sought to advance the interests of "the great manufacturers, merchants, and bankers" of the North, while trying to forge an alliance with the large planters of the South—a strategy that would founder on the rocks of slavery. Hatred of Jackson was the cement that held them together, much as FDR's legacy unified Republicans, McGovern suggested.[7]

The fifth essay, informed by Charles Beard, traced the rise of the Republican Party within the antislavery elements of northern Whigs in the 1850s. It was then that Democrats at last confronted formidable opposition. The brilliant, practical Lincoln was "not so interested in eradicating slavery as he was in checking its expansion into the vast undeveloped West." He appealed to "millions of working men and small farmers who viewed the continued expansion of slavery as a threat to their own social and economic status." The Republican coalition had a particular vision of the nation's future that necessitated the gradual termination of slavery—a modern, industrial political economy served by wage labor and fed by an agricultural complex grown on cheap land and free homesteads in the West, and the whole continent laced by a network of railroads created by private enterprise and government subsidies alike.[8]

Then came the tragic postscript to the war to overthrow feudalism in the South—Lincoln's assassination and then "instantaneous deterioration of the progressive leanings of the Republican coalition," McGovern lamented. A series of weak presidents presided over "the Great Barbeque" (so named by Vernon Parrington) as mining and railroad tycoons wooed Congress and whittled the country's politicians into the puppets of "raw, undisciplined capitalism." The result was "waste and ruthless exploitation of the oil reserves, mineral deposits, forests and land of the public domain," and attended by bipartisan corruption on a huge scale. "Little wonder that a new third party was called into being." The Populists of the 1890s made the Democrats pay attention to the farmer's plight and helped lay the foundation for the Progressive movement as the century turned.[9]

The sixth installment recalled that the Great Depression had begun on the farm early in the 1920s. This was the result of the collapse of the wartime market of 1914–18 and Republican policies that dismantled the progressive legislation of Wilson and Theodore Roosevelt. McGovern ripped the GOP for reversing the Democrats' low tariff policy and thus "transplant[ing] billions of dollars from the pockets of the farmers and other consumers to the coffers of the men of industry and finance." In scrapping Wilson's progressive tax structure, the Republicans showed a "skill in shifting the tax load onto the backs of the little people." In the era of Harding, Coolidge, and Hoover, "big business domination of Congress and the White House was taken for granted . . . [and] stock market manipulation . . . had the Easterners dizzy with artificial prosperity."[10]

McGovern also reminded his readers that the best of the Republicans representing agriculture bolted their party in 1932. Peter Norbeck, South Dakota's great Republican senator, endorsed the Democratic ticket in 1936 because his own party "had sold out the farmer," whereas "under Franklin Roosevelt, the farmers of the Midwest had achieved a fair deal, including price supports [and] conservation programs." It was a not-so-subtle history lesson: Both Eisenhower and Stevenson had endorsed the New Deal farm programs. But which party could McGovern's readers really depend on?[11]

In his final article, he pointed out that in 1952 two-thirds of the Republicans in Congress had "fought every welfare measure of the Roosevelt-Truman period," and the party's right wing, as ever, deplored the " 'Socialistic' New Deal." Yet the moderate wing, the one responsible for nominating Eisenhower in hopes of attracting independent liberals, "claims that it will preserve the social gains of the New Deal." So, who really spoke for the GOP? On the subject of foreign policy McGovern suggested that it presented another confusing Janus face. The Republicans wailed about Truman letting China fall to communism but did not acknowledge "the decaying Chiang regime" or that communism had come to China "largely as a result of poverty and misrule." He asked why they referred to "the needless Truman war." Had they not wanted "to save South Korea from communist aggression"? Had the Democrats not practiced bipartisanship in foreign policy? What frustrated him most, however, was Ike's bow to the party's right wing, which only weeks before had denounced him as "simply a reflection of the Roosevelt-Truman policies." Egregiously, Eisenhower had failed to repudiate Joseph McCarthy, whom McGovern called "a dangerous, pathological liar." Instead he allowed a "political hoodlum" to shape his campaign and impugn the patriotism of the party that had led the nation out of the catastrophes of depression and war. "Can this party of Lincoln," McGovern wondered in conclusion, "realize its plight before it is too late?"[12]

If any Democrat had any doubts about where he now stood, his essays had laid them to rest. "We need a strong two-party system in America," he affirmed. "Truman moved quickly to save South Korea from communist aggression," he boasted. He had even left out his own disapproval of the war. That omission and his carefully parsed defense of the administration were disingenuous. Yet he was also trying to say, if the Republicans did not want Truman "to act with vigor and power" regarding Korea, they should "cease talking about the alleged betrayal of China." Then, too, it took some guts to declare in print, in South Dakota in 1952, that Joe McCarthy was a "hoodlum" and a "pathological liar" nearly two years before Edward R. Murrow would do as much on his CBS television program.

McGovern had written his series partly to show South Dakotans how New Deal programs benefited the broad middle class (including farmers), and that these commonsense economic safeguards had created prosperity for great numbers of people. Because McCarthyite demagoguery had proved so insidious, he also had begun to fear for the future of competitive politics in his state. So he stressed domestic issues to counter the "smokescreen" charges about communism aimed at Democrats. The key was the New Deal farm policy. South Dakota farmers long ago had conceded the expediency of Henry Wallace's essential ideas—for example, the Ever Normal Granary, which could be had only through national agricultural planning. Thus they accepted the idea that government could help solve certain problems, and it was Wallace who had demonstrated the feds were up to the job. Here was ground on which a left-leaning liberal like McGovern and a centrist liberal like Hubert Humphrey could stand together—and so could conservative Republicans like Karl Mundt. In these circumstances, McGovern had made up his mind about the two-party system. In addressing voters, the crucial question was which party one could trust to preserve the New Deal's "fundamental measures such as social security and the farm price supports," which many Republicans still regarded as "un-American."[13]

McGovern was proud of his essays, and he believed he had done good work on Stevenson's behalf. All through the campaign he stayed high on the candidate. "We have just heard Adlai deliver a superb speech from Chicago by transcription," he wrote to Ray Allen Billington after his final essay came out. "That man inspires me more and more as the campaign rolls (or jolts) along." Eisenhower, in contrast, "proved to be a dismal flop."[14] A landslide of Rooseveltian proportions nonetheless was about to ensue, owing mainly to Ike's popularity, his prestige, and his memorable pledge, "I shall go to Korea" (alongside a vague desire for a change at the top). On November 5, he carried thirty-nine of the forty-eight states, polling 33,936,234 popular votes to Stevenson's 27,314,992. In the Electoral College the tally was 442 to 89. Quipped Stevenson, "I was happy to hear that I had even placed second."[15] (The Republicans also won control of the 83rd Congress—by 48 to 47 in the Senate and 221 to 211 in the House, with one independent elected to each chamber.)

Most of McGovern's readers apparently had not been convinced either, although in South Dakota it was a case of trying to push a boulder up the steep mountainside of history. Since statehood in 1889, it had sent only five Democrats to Washington and, except for Bryan in 1896, FDR was the only Democratic presidential candidate it had ever favored with a majority, though not in 1940 or 1944. And so South Dakotans gave Eisenhower 203,857 votes as against 90,426 for Stevenson, a record 69.3 percent of the total. Republicans were victorious in the congressional races, too; in the bicameral legislature they won 108 seats out of 110, for yet another record. To quote McGovern, the Democrats had been "all but wiped out." To paraphrase Governor Anderson, who had won reelection by 70 percent, Americanism had triumphed over New Dealism.[16]

If the Iowa job went to his competitor, he had written Link in January 1952, he would accept the decision "as a clue to my next move." Already the state's Democratic chair, Ward Clark, had pitched a full-time organizational job to him. To Link, McGovern described the young law-yer from Canistota as "an extremely intelligent, high-minded individ-ual," who sympathized with his academic ambitions. For Clark, George presented a combination of qualities almost too good to be true, and he was becoming well known for a college professor. If anyone could resuscitate South Dakota's Democratic Party, he thought, it was this ar-ticulate former bomber pilot with the beautiful wife and all those kids and a PhD in history. But Clark did not press the thirty-year-old for an immediate decision. He knew to bide his time. Months later, after the *Daily Republic* published McGovern's widely discussed articles, Clark invited him to give a speech on Stevenson's behalf over the state's big-gest radio station. As Election Day closed in, he arranged for George to deliver his first campaign address, in Platte, a town of about a thousand. That evening, at the local café, Clark made the hard sell. The GOP was going to sweep the state, he conceded, but therein was the opportunity: with "attractive candidates backed by a strong grassroots organization, the Democratic Party could make a comeback." Of course, "it would require the full-time effort of an imaginative, hard-working person."[17]

According to Bob Pennington, "George asked everybody he knew whether he should do it, and everybody told him 'no.'" Pennington was stupefied to learn that his brother-in-law would even think about giving up a tenure-track position. Organizing Democrats in South Da-kota? He might as well have said he was switching over to something dependable like acting. "George, you'd have to be crazy to take that job," Bradley Young, the manager of Penney's, snorted. Across the street, two politically minded lawyer friends dismissed it as hopeless, though they seemed intrigued.[18]

"Stevenson's defeat," Eleanor was of the opinion, "merely hastened George's move from the classroom." When Iowa did not offer him the position, he concluded that it was for the best; now he could try out that executive secretaryship come summer. So in June, he did. After a week he realized he could not run away from it any longer. "I'm sure that all of you will think that I am slightly nuts," he wrote Billington. "I have agreed to accept a two-year appointment as executive-secretary of the S.D. Democratic Party." Matthew Smith, Dakota Wesleyan's president, wept as he tried to get George to change his mind. Bill Harbaugh heard about the decision from their mutual mentor. Shaking his head as he finished the story, Link exclaimed, "What a loss to history!"[19]

Thus had McGovern taken the different road. Others had played a part, but Ward Clark had given him the push when he needed it most.

Indirectly, Billington and Link had a hand in it, too. "You have to assume part of the blame for my liberal zeal, you know," he told them. (If they felt a little let down, they recovered quickly; later they took enormous pride in the part they played in his career.) And so, in the little upstairs office he rented in the Western Building on Main Street, with no air conditioner or secretary, but fortified by Lincoln, Roosevelt, and Stevenson peering out of picture frames, McGovern began laying plans for rebuilding the Democratic Party of South Dakota.[20]

"There is certainly a big job to be done," he wrote to Link within the month. That was so mainly because Democrats in South Dakota stayed in the closet. To help find them and figure out what else had to be done, McGovern gathered some daring sorts to advise him—from Mitchell, Jack Weiland, and Ezra Brady of the *Daily Republic*; Goldie Wells of Aberdeen; and Cobb Chase of Watertown. Soon Dennis Jensen of Spencer, Jim Magness of Miller, and Katie Kuhns of Worthing joined them. Half of this doughty group hailed from urban centers (the state's third, fifth, and sixth largest cities), ranging in population from a high of 23,000 down to 12,000; the other half lived in towns of 300 to 600 inhabitants.[21] They represented varied demographic perspectives on life and work in South Dakota. "I learned early that a few committed allies of this kind are better than an army of drifters who go with the prevailing wind," McGovern later reflected.[22]

Their first course of action was to assess the party's situation through the eyes of the Democratic chairs in each of sixty-seven counties—with regard to local organizations, precinct committees, and fund-raising and recruiting candidates for office. McGovern drafted a letter that prompted exactly seven replies; this suggested he needed to tour the state to meet these happy few and to track down the unresponsive sixty. Anything he would ever achieve in politics flowed from that simple ascertainment; he would end up organizing the entire state, as Eleanor put it, "almost Democrat by Democrat."[23]

He logged a lot of time on the road that summer, visiting farms and offices and small businesses and talking to hundreds of everyday citizens. On the family's old Chrysler he racked up thousands of miles until it literally collapsed on US Highway 16 during the second summer. (He replaced it with a Ford.) Sometimes he traveled alone, but just as often with a companion such as Ward Clark, or Peder Ecker, who founded the state's Young Democrats, or George Cunningham, a University of South Dakota law student who eventually became his administrative assistant in Washington. In searching for fellow partisans, their first hurdle was to overcome their party affiliation. "If you were a Democrat," Peder Ecker submitted, "people just found it hard to take you seriously." Things were especially tough for small shopkeepers because being a Democrat was bad for business. George Cunningham liked to tell the story of William Bryan Jennings Doyle. One day he and McGovern arrived in the town of Dimock (population 198) and went straight to the general store. Bounding up to the counter, Cunningham blurted, "Are there any Democrats around here?" Proprietor Doyle, worried that patrons had heard the question, shushed him. He then motioned his visitors to follow him to the rear and out into the alley. "*I'm* a Democrat," he gasped. People "*suspected* that he was a Democrat," he confided; maybe "there are others around here." The two Georges would encounter innumerable variations of William Bryan Jennings Doyle on their statewide tours.[24]

It did not take them long to realize the importance of note taking in rebuilding a political party. "We always carried 3 × 5 cards. If you'd find anybody who admitted they were a Democrat, you'd get their name and address and phone number," Cunningham explained. They also made notes about the person's family, occupation, and so on. McGovern kept the index cards in a shoebox, subdividing it with sixty-seven orange tab markers, one per county, and green tabs for sizeable towns within them. "People were amazed when I saw them again," he remarked. "They were impressed that I cared enough to remember." He was disciplined and sincere in the effort. Besides a teacher's facility for name recall, he could also ask how many merit badges Joey still needed to become an Eagle Scout or whether Sophie had finally gotten over those measles. Eventually he would amass forty thousand cards.[25]

The shoebox of cards had immense practical value. McGovern studied them to see who might make a good precinct manager or county chair, and they comprised his direct-mail list for fund-raising, which was essential to having a functioning political party and to putting food on his family's table. He was responsible for procuring not only funds for office rent, supplies, and travel, but also his salary of $6,000. That meant raising $10,000 a year. With the aid of the note cards he invented the "Century Club," a simple plan to persuade one hundred Democrats to contribute $100 to the party annually. Soon the Century Club had 130 members. He also inaugurated moderately priced county dinners at five and ten dollars a plate, and state dinners at never more than $25.[26]

McGovern attended countless coffees and receptions, dialed hundreds of phone numbers, issued weekly press releases, and sent out thousands of mimeographed letters. Keeping up with the Republicans even required him to set up a booth at the state fair in Huron. In this, the opposition held the advantage, as they could show off candidates who were well-known incumbents. But what really griped the Democrats' new executive secretary was not the glad appearance of Senators Karl Mundt or Francis Case, but "Bingo," an elephant hauled in from the Omaha zoo. To best them, he borrowed a donkey from a nearby gas station and tied it to the main pole supporting the Democratic tent. To gales of laughter on the midway, it yanked down the little big top. After it bit a small child, McGovern was convinced that this donkey had stayed too long at the fair.[27]

The purpose behind all of this activity was to improve the party's position in the coming midterm elections. McGovern and Clark hoped to recruit dozens of candidates formidable enough to make their way either to Pierre or Washington. On one hand, 1954 had produced for South Dakota Democrats a bright opportunity, owing to the farmers' economic woes under Eisenhower, and, on the other, a substantial challenge rooted in the voters' conservative leanings since the mid-1930s. In that era, South Dakota was the odd state out. The Democrats had swept it clean in 1932 and held on in 1934. But in 1936, despite the magnitude of FDR's reelection victory, South Dakotans bucked the trend, giving the president 50,000 fewer votes against Alf Landon than they had given him against Hoover. They also returned the governorship to the GOP and chose newspaper editor Francis Case as their congressman and very nearly Karl Mundt. In the 1938 midterms, Republicans captured every statewide office and control of the legislature by 90 to 18, and Mundt won a seat in the House of Representatives in his second attempt.[28]

Two-party politics would not thrive easily in this soil. Part of the explanation had to do with the lack of key elements in South Dakota that made up the Roosevelt coalition elsewhere in the country. First, organized labor hardly existed in the state (and would remain relatively small in the postwar period). As for the Democrats' agricultural base, a split occurred between the conservative Farm Bureau and the more militant Farmers' Union that backed Henry Wallace's reforms. A related breach—the Jeffersonian tradition of small government versus big government ushered in by FDR—divided other blocs. Lastly, along with African Americans, the coalition's Eastern European components were in scarce supply. The plentiful northern Europeans and Scandinavians leaned toward the GOP. There were some other reasons why the Democrats had lost their grip on power.[29]

The Works Progress Administration had helped ten of thousands of South Dakotans survive the Depression. Yet once the worst phase of the crisis had passed, conservatives declined to give such programs the credit and began to argue that the improved conditions would have come anyhow and had "derived from the effort of businesses and ordinary citizens." President Roosevelt "was determined to interfere with normal recovery of the capitalistic system," grumbled the Republican *Argus Leader* of Sioux Falls, the largest circulating paper. "The New Deal way leads inevitably to social revolution and ultimate enthronement of either a fascist or a communist dictatorship," warned the South Dakota Republicans' platform of 1938, and some of their candidates complained of a "lack of Americanism in the Democratic platform."[30]

Then there was Karl Mundt, who had introduced his own distinctive brand of red-baiting to neutralize the competition in 1936. Mundt appropriated and denigrated the Democrats' achievements, then accused his opponent, congressman Fred Hildebrandt, of being tinged with communism.[31] He lost the election, but in 1938 began to call himself "a liberal Republican," and he said he wanted "government to go forward the American way." In careful language, he explained himself. For farmers he advocated "cost of production, with profit," for old folks he desired "liberal and adequate pensions," and he professed to be "sympathetic with the purpose and program of organized labor." Yet as he had done Hildebrandt, Mundt crucified as an extremist his rival, Emil Loriks, a farmer and high school science teacher. Because Loriks had been a consultant to the Department of Agriculture, the *Argus Leader* slammed him for "endors[ing] policies that are communistic in nature" and for "stirring class hatred." Said Mundt privately, "The mere fact that he is recognized as a friend of Henry Wallace . . . will serve as a whole array of red flags." He also asked the new House Un-American Activities Committee to investigate whether Democratic candidates in the state had fallen prey to communist influence. As one South Dakota historian has written, the 1938 campaign provided "a case study of McCarthyism before McCarthy."[32]

By 1954, as McGovern was learning, the state's politics had hardly changed since the late New Deal, though certain elements of the broader environment had. Whereas Mundt's pursuit of Alger Hiss had catapulted him, like Richard Nixon, to national fame, McCarthyism seemed on the wane. Ironically, nothing had done more to sap its strength than the Republican restoration. Until then, McCarthy had been a considerable asset for the party. But with his latest wild charges about the US Army "coddling communists," and his steady exposure on television as an ill-mannered lout, he was fast becoming an embarrassment. A growing number of moderate Republicans, including the president, wished to be rid him. Mundt, too, was unhappy in the spring of 1954 to find himself cochairing the Army-McCarthy hearings, the historic thirty-six-day televised event that delivered the mortal blow to his confrere. The hearings gave McGovern the chance to nail Mundt for his own "fanatical charges of treason" and "irresponsible investigations." From other quarters the senator won poor ratings for losing control of the hearings. His advisers worried that voters might connect him with McCarthy's dishonor. Then, upon Francis Case fell unwelcome membership on a committee to decide whether the Senate ought to censure McCarthy. When Case resigned from it in November, his attempt to portray his resignation as an act of conviction backfired. Republicans accused him of bad faith, and McGovern publicly chided him for "desertion." For the while, association with McCarthy, if not anticommunism, had become a millstone even in South Dakota.[33]

Incumbency held one other major disadvantage in 1954 that the executive secretary intended to exploit. It settled on agriculture and was rendered the worse for Eisenhower's showy pledge, in 1952, to uphold 90 percent parity payments. This, the Holy Grail for many American farmers, was hardly true Republican policy. Dewey's defeat had compelled its adoption, as too much loose talk about "flexible" price supports in 1948 had caused midwestern farmers to stampede over to Truman. To make his "Golden Promise," candidate Ike had traveled to Brookings, South Dakota—a stroke of good luck for McGovern's Democrats, as events unfolded.[34]

Farmers started feeling the crunch in 1953. Their enormous productivity (stimulated by fertilizers, hybrid grain seed, and machinery) together with slackened demand upon the ending of the Korean War eroded commodity prices. Eisenhower did not create the circumstances but he badly aggravated them by naming Ezra Taft Benson as secretary of agriculture. A devout Mormon and self-styled "rugged individualist" from Utah, Benson was a friend of agribusiness and a foe of New Deal farm policies. His opposition to high price supports in the Agricultural Act of 1949 provoked cries of betrayal that the president had reneged on his "Golden Promise." Moreover, while income in every other area of the economy increased substantially, farm income would fall 23 percent by 1960. With one or two exceptions, farm organization leaders would never stop demanding Benson's head.[35]

No one was more eager to plow a row straight and deep with this issue than McGovern, and he proceeded to demonstrate why Bill Harbaugh would dub him "a progressive agrarian." In May 1954, as keynote speaker at the North Dakota Democratic State Convention, he said a lot of growers were thinking about joining the "Never Again Club." According to a recent poll, 52 percent of the nation's farmers wished they had voted for Stevenson. With Benson as the scythe, the GOP had undercut the farmer's income while federal grain bins bulged with surplus carryovers. Then, too, South Dakota was losing hundreds of farms each year. Numbering 83,000 early on in the Depression, they were down to 62,500. McGovern always reminded his audience of the new slogan sweeping the farm belt: "Vote Democratic, the farm you save may be your own."[36]

Throughout the campaign, he also enlisted the help of both rising and established stars in the Democratic firmament—including Hubert Humphrey, former vice president Alben Barkley, and Adlai Stevenson. McGovern wanted Stevenson to be sure to direct "some of his skillful wit" against Mundt during his speech. "We would love that," he said. Naturally he asked all of the visiting dignitaries to hit the farm issue hard. A preelection poll indicated that Republican candidates were leading overwhelmingly in towns and cities. *But the farm vote was going Democratic.* In the gubernatorial race, farmers preferred Ed Martin to the incumbent Joe Foss by 56 to 44 percent, and challenger Ken Holum enjoyed an edge of 54 percent over Senator Mundt in the rural areas. Here, parity was the central concern. To deflect attention from Benson's policies, Mundt imported major firepower, notably Vice President Nixon and Barry Goldwater. In September, he wrote to President Eisenhower, "Communism is still our next best issue to peace." Reverting to form in the final week of the campaign, he claimed the state was awash in propaganda from New York City communists trying to dethrone him.[37]

Although they captured not a single federal office, Election Day 1954 gave South Dakota Democrats grounds for optimism. In every contest they had significantly reduced Republican margins of victory of 1952— by 25 percent in Mundt's case, 50 percent in E. Y. Berry's, and by 65 percent in the case of three-term incumbent Harold Lovre. In the legislature, instead of two Democrats contending with 108 Republicans, the new count would be 24 to 86. Behind these numbers lay other gains.

Democrats actually felt energized, and they were getting favorable editorial comment all over the state. As McGovern boasted to Adlai's assistant, the party was "in the best condition that we have known in a great many years."[38] Nationally, the Democrats regained their majorities—just barely in the Senate but by 232 to 203 in the House.

He was excited to send the election news to his mentors. "I must admit that I have enjoyed my political apprenticeship thoroughly," he told Billington. "It has given me an opportunity to know and try to understand people of every possible type." That included the chance to host an ex-vice president; to develop friendships with rising Senate liberals like Humphrey and Wayne Morse; and to have an all-night bull session with his hero, Stevenson, and later to drive him across the state. He relished telling Arthur Link about the banquet for Sam Rayburn in DC, where two former First Ladies received big ovations: "Eleanor Roosevelt and Mrs. Wilson did much to create a rich emotional atmosphere for the evening." It was fitting that on Woodrow Wilson's birthday he announced to Link: "The present plan is that I should run for Congress."[39]

––––––––––––

In 1954, in pursuit of his fourth term in the House, Harold Lovre had been South Dakota's biggest vote getter. Married, fifty years old, and the father of four daughters, he had grown up near the village of Toronto, five miles west of the Minnesota state line, in an era when horses still outnumbered automobiles. Bright and hardworking, Harold left behind his prairie boyhood to study at St. Olaf College, in Northfield, then transferred to the University of South Dakota, in Vermillion, where he earned his LLB. For several years he practiced law at Watertown, and he served two terms in the state legislature before his first election to Congress, in 1948. He also owned a fair-sized spread and occasionally called himself "a farmer operator," though he did not toil there. Like South Dakota's three other national representatives, he paid attention to every piece of farm legislation and advocated the 90 percent support program for wheat and corn while praising Secretary Benson's far less generous Soil Bank proposal.

Lovre otherwise could be described as moderate-to-conservative. Whereas his voting record on the Rural Electrification Administration was spotty, he had introduced a bill to extend the School Milk Program and another to provide federal insurance for loans to improve ranch and farm homes; Congress had enacted both. He voted sparingly for Missouri River development projects and against federal aid to education. In international relations, he never questioned the defense budget, but he opposed foreign aid, with the exception of surplus agricultural commodities to assist friendly countries. Isolationism he no longer countenanced, yet he believed "there are limits as to how far we can spread our wealth and manpower." To Lovre, Eisenhower had struck the proper balance, which accorded with the GOP's slogan—"Peace, Prosperity, Progress." As the *Sioux Falls Argus Leader* described him, Harold was "calm and studied," the sort of capable, self-effacing representative South Dakota seemed to want.[40]

Perhaps he sensed he was vulnerable, or perhaps he was sincere, when he met his rival in early 1956 and said, "You're a nice young man, George. I'd hate to see you get beat your first time out." McGovern was courteous, but the encounter only stoked his determination. They both knew Lovre enjoyed many advantages—incumbency under a popular president in prosperous times, senior rank on the House Agriculture Committee, unlimited campaign funds, and the state's Republican tradition. Even so, his recent victory margin had shrunk 65 percent over the previous one and Ezra Taft Benson still ravaged the countryside. It was conceivable that a sharp, young whippersnapper could fell him. "If the Democrats nominate George McGovern," said the *Brookings Register*, "they will be putting their best foot forward." By the time he declared, George in effect had been laying the foundation for his campaign for something over two years. Once the battle was joined, the Republican *Argus Leader* would not only describe him as "personable, likeable, and energetic," but also as a "political professional." From his grasp of the issues to the physical demands of campaigning across the 38,000 square miles that the East River district added up to, the challenger could not have been better prepared.[41]

As executive secretary, he had learned three crucial things about the workings of South Dakota politics. First, organization and persistence were essential for good results. Second, regardless of one's most passionate concerns, if one failed to attend to farm issues, all other bets were off. Third, because there were not enough Democrats to make a majority, one had to find a way to appeal to independent-minded Republicans. And so, besides exhorting Democrats to stand up, in 1955 McGovern had begun "reaching out beyond the party," as he called it. This required courting the Lions and the Rotarians and church groups and chambers of commerce. It also meant sidestepping overt partisanship. Thus, to citizens who maintained, "I'm a registered Republican, but I vote for the man," he would make this case: There is no escaping the impact of politics on one's life; everyday people hold the power to determine the quality of government; and this state is on the verge of "one-party government," the root of most of its problems, he said. *Then* he would light into Ezra Taft Benson, not just to woo farmers but also to show other voters how their own welfare and that of the farmers depended on one another.[42]

"So, really, I was building two organizations," he acknowledged, "the party's and my own." Some Democrats gave him some heat for being self-serving. "George rebuilt the party alright," one official complained, "but it wasn't the Democratic party, it was the McGovern party." Yet as the faithful Cunningham countered, South Dakotans had not sent a Democrat to Washington in eighteen years and everyone knew George was going to be a candidate for something. The question was when and for what. "We all urged him to do so," Cunningham said. According to the *Watertown Public Opinion*, "The Democratic Party couldn't have picked an abler contender for the job."[43]

His first practical step was to sift through all the note cards he had amassed and identify coordinators in every East River town. He hoped these individuals would be glad to distribute campaign literature, talk up his candidacy, write letters to the editor, solicit donations, and even form a local "McGovern for Congress Club." His campaign staff numbered a trio. His friend Bob Verschoor, who owned the Mitchell Chevy dealership, became financial director. (The campaign would cost about $14,000, which Verschoor raised mainly through contributions ranging from $1 to $10.) Cunningham served as aide-de-camp and driver. Patricia Buchanan, a housewife and part-time journalist, was the secretary and lone paid staffer.[44]

The candidate got from place to place usually in Cunningham's little red-and-white Rambler station wagon with "McGovern for Congress" painted on the side. A typical day might begin at dawn at a factory where he could shake hands with workers as they arrived. Breakfast at the local diner presented another opportunity. Before taking a booth, McGovern would say hello to the manager and the waitresses and kitchen help, and then to customers. After his cereal, he would introduce himself to more patrons, then drive to the next community and walk from store to store and chat with employees and managers. Before lunch he might address an assembly at a high school. By noon, if he was not speaking to the Kiwanis club, he could hit another restaurant and repeat the breakfast routine. Then it was on to the next town. At day's end he might seek out a church supper or even a tavern—any place where voters gathered.[45]

George had real conversations with people. He was at his best with small groups of five or so and he actually asked folks what they were thinking and discussed their concerns with them. He was also good at "one-on-ones," and he did a lot of them on the long stretches between towns. If he saw a farmer plowing, for example, he would pull over, climb a fence and cross a field if necessary, and explain to him why he had decided to challenge Harold Lovre. Sometimes he might drive up to a farmhouse and ask for a drink of water and start a conversation. That impressed people who lived miles from their nearest neighbor. And there was a multiplier effect. When the family went to town for Saturday shopping, they would tell their friends about this well-spoken young fellow running for Congress who stopped by, and that he got them to wondering just how much more of Ezra Taft Benson they could take.[46]

McGovern circulated his message in other ways, too. On one hundred roadside billboards he had his name and face displayed around the state. In three fifteen-minute televised speeches in late summer, he informed voters about his views on agriculture; argued on behalf of a new, competitive two-party politics for South Dakota; and pledged himself "to the struggle for a peaceful world." These ads aired long before Lovre's did, and they were followed by six weekly broadcasts of five minutes each. Days before the election, an attractive brochure, featuring photos and favorable editorial comments, were mailed to every household in the state.[47]

Oftentimes McGovern would conjoin certain issues in a fresh way. At Lake Preston, in September, he articulated one of his signature lines on foreign policy—the pursuit of peace and agriculture. In depicting the farmers lot and roughing up Secretary Benson, he said, "I regard the productive power of America's farms as a blessing instead of a curse." Rather than curtail production and pay farmers to destroy crops, would it not be better "to use our food abundance to fight human hunger?" But this "moral obligation" should not be limited to needy American families. Citing the proportion of the federal budget devoted to containing communism, he reasoned that the United States "could very wisely use a small fraction of that amount to fight the hunger which breeds communism." He also voiced this theme in his summer telecasts: "We know there are mountains to be moved—mountains of fear, oppression, ignorance, poverty and disease. These are the real enemies of mankind. These are the obstacles on the road to peace that cannot be removed by military power alone."[48]

On August 10, the American Institute of Public Opinion published a national survey of 2,900 Democratic county chairs. Its purpose was to see what they considered the party's "strongest argument" against Republicans. According to George Gallup's report, 49 percent of these grassroots leaders put the "plight of the farmer" at the top of the list. "Business favoritism" came in second, at 25 percent. Four days later McGovern testified before the platform committee of the party's national convention in Chicago. "It is ridiculous that the farmer and small businessmen should be in trouble at the same time that big business is making the largest profits in history," he said, pressing his case for 100 percent parity. In his state, farm income in 1955 was $65 million less than it was in 1954, and it had dropped another $22 million by June 1956. "The only way we can keep young farm families on the land and maintain prosperity on Main Street," he went on, "is by reversing the downward spiral of farm prices." Then he called for "a reasonable price floor" for storable grains, hogs, and cattle; credit expansion for small businesses and farmers; and a food stamp program to put surpluses to work for families in need.[49]

The platform committee adopted the food stamp proposal but opted for 90 percent parity for commodities like corn, wheat, cotton, rice, and tobacco. (Republicans promoted "flexible" supports ranging as low as 75 percent.) McGovern left for home before the convention nominated Adlai Stevenson and his running mate, Senator Estes Kefauver of Tennessee. "If I'm going to give Mr. Lovre a vacation in November," he said, "I've got to beat him in South Dakota, not Chicago." The *Argus Leader* pronounced Lovre versus McGovern "the hottest congressional race in South Dakota in the last twenty years."[50]

In contrast, the second Eisenhower-Stevenson match would prove tepid. For a while the president's health was a worry because he had suffered a heart attack in 1955 and a serious intestinal disorder in 1956. Stevenson spoke of a "part time presidency" and attempted to raise the specter of "the Republican heir apparent, Mr. Nixon." But Eisenhower had fully recovered by September and even topped the list of "America's Ten Best-Dressed Men" (trailed by actor William Holden and J. Edgar Hoover). The issue receded. Anticommunism seemed less the obsession this time than it had in 1952, though Harry Truman threatened to revive it. For the former president to say that Stevenson was not a "fighting" candidate and "can't win" was one thing. It was quite another for him to insist in an interview that Alger Hiss was neither a communist nor a spy. A storm brewed. Nixon and Mundt demanded to know Stevenson's position on the "shocking" statement. The nominee ended the commotion by disassociating himself from it; he maintained that Truman was "a help, not a hindrance" to his candidacy.[51]

Two broad issues in particular gave the campaign its form, and nobody hammered them harder than Nixon or Mundt. "Historians will point to Eisenhower's record as a peacemaker and peace preserver," Mundt predicted, touting the swift end that the soldier-statesman had brought to the Korean War in 1953 and his steady hand on the ship of state ever since. Over and over the vice president boasted about an irrefutable fact: "The great majority of the American people have enjoyed the best four years of their lives."[52] Stevenson had trouble coping with this peace-and-prosperity theme, yet voters in several farm states, including South Dakota, remained unconvinced by the second part of it.

On the eve of the Republican convention, the *Sioux Falls Argus Leader* reported on the front page of its Sunday edition that personal income in South Dakota had fallen by 6 percent in 1955 and by comparable rates in Iowa, Kansas, and Nebraska. The Commerce Department reported the slump "traceable to a reduced volume of farm income." All through the campaign, newspapers featured accounts of bumper harvests and busted prices. Thus Stevenson received a respectful hearing in the upper Midwest when he emphasized that for every four dollars the farmer received in 1952, he was getting less than three dollars in 1956.[53] Still, the numbers of farmers willing to punish President Eisenhower himself were not decisive.

There was a different story to tell in many congressional races. At the South Dakota State Fair, for example, countless fair-goers dropped lots of coins into the large tin can Democrats had set up for the "Retirement Fund for Ezra Benson." McGovern repeatedly challenged Lovre to debate the declining purchasing power of the farmers under Benson and Eisenhower. Lovre dismissed the idea, kept quiet about the secretary, and tried to muddle through by backing the party's Soil Bank proposal, though he said it needed revisions.[54] On that point, McGovern focused on the fact that it was "a soil conservation and crop control program" originally proposed by Democrats and opposed by Republicans. In it the farmer, in exchange for a modest subsidy, could take some acreage out of production to reduce surpluses, but it was not "a miracle drug." The Soil Bank would "not protect farm income in normal years unless it [was] joined to a good price support program." McGovern accused Lovre of "overselling" in an "eleventh hour effort to buy their votes." A similar argument flared between Ike and Adlai.[55]

As his prospects and September slipped away, Harold Lovre made his situation worse by refusing to debate his young opponent. One in a flurry of letters to the editor lamented his rejection of the Lincoln-Douglas tradition while another advised, "If Mr. Lovre is that timid, he has no place in the Republican party." Yet another copartisan declared that he would "not vote for a coward." According to the *Daily Republic*, Lovre had in fact appeared with McGovern at the Aurora County farmers' annual picnic, but only after the sponsors had agreed to let him speak last and not to allow rebuttals or questions from the audience. The piece also charged that he had dodged a joint interview with McGovern on *Siouxland Speaks*, a television show on which Governor Foss and Senator Case had faced their Democratic adversaries. The *Daily Republic* titled its Lovre editorial "Running Scared."[56]

On Sunday, September 30, the *Argus Leader* published the results of a statewide poll conducted by three newspapers. South Dakota's major Republican candidates were all ahead, with one stunning exception. "McGovern Shades Lovre, 51 to 49," the front-page headline read. Although the incumbent had a clear advantage in the towns and cities, a whopping 65 percent of the farm vote favored the newcomer, enough to nudge him into the lead. An editorial suggested that the state's other Republicans, like Eisenhower, enjoyed an overall edge, but somewhat less so than in 1952. The poll was heartening for McGovern, yet he had not a moment to savor it. As the *Argus Leader* was quick to say, Lovre's current disadvantage could easily be reversed by the tendency of loyal Republicans to vote a straight ticket.[57]

More importantly, the campaign just then was taking a very ugly turn. A group of Republicans had decided the time had come to unsheathe the ultimate weapon. They would remind voters that their man's antagonist not long ago had advocated diplomatic recognition of the People's Republic of China and its admission into the United Nations. Only days before the report came out that Lovre trailed McGovern, a group called the "South Dakota Volunteer Bipartisan Committee in Opposition to the Admission of Red China to the United Nations" materialized and began sending telegrams to congressional candidates to ask how they stood on that issue. In several newspapers, this committee ran quarter- and half-page-size advertisements that displayed a clipping of the *Daily Republic*'s story (of June 8, 1951) about McGovern's speech calling for recognition for Red China. Framed in a jagged black border, it displayed ludicrous paraphrases and quotations taken out of context, obvious to anyone who read the clipping.[58]

McGovern countered with a ten-minute televised address. It was the night before the publication of the polling results, and he began by calling the committee with the long name a "phony front for a Congressman who is afraid to debate openly the real issues of the campaign." He explained the remarks in question—that he had made them five years before, in an address titled "Christianity and the Challenge of Communism," to a conference of Methodist ministers in Mitchell. "I pointed out that it was better for us to fight China across the conference table than across the battlefield," he said. But he was pledged to uphold the Democratic platform, which opposed membership for Red China in the United Nations, so the point was moot. "I fought Fascism with all my strength," he concluded, referring to his World War II service, "and I am just as determined to safeguard America against Communism."[59]

In a way, this was McGovern's version of Richard Nixon's Checkers speech of 1952, albeit shorter and less mawkish, but less effective than Nixon's in laying to rest the accusations against him. The controversy would hijack the campaign thereafter. In the first week of October, for instance, Karl Mundt's chief assistant pronounced McGovern "not qualified to sit in the House of Representatives" because of his "inability to spot the dangers of communism," adding that he "has never said that he has changed his mind" on China. Two days later, Lovre weighed in. Accusing McGovern of "fuzzy thinking" and of "a vicious attack" on the anti–Red China Committee (for labeling it a "phony front"), he said the *real* questions were "not only where he stands now on the Red China issue but also why he has been an advocate of such measures in the past." He acknowledged his adversary's "exceptionally fine war record" and concluded by protesting, "I do not question his loyalty or patriotism." McGovern spurned such assurances. "Lovre is trying to smear my Americanism," he insisted. Instead of "hiding behind a motley assortment of committees [and] . . . incendiary newspaper ads," he ought to "come out in the open and meet me face to face in public debate." Yet McGovern obviously felt threatened. "In light of present world conditions," he said in a limited retreat, "I would oppose Red China's entry in the U.N."

Meanwhile, the Reverend Frank Lochridge of the Methodist Church of Mitchell had had enough. As a Republican, he was offended by the attacks against the son of his old friend and fellow churchman, Joseph

McGovern. To the *Daily Republic*, Lochridge fired off a letter vouching for the candidate he had watched grow from boy to fine young man, and several newspapers around the state reprinted it. Within days remorse plagued John Ehrstrom, a Republican insurance executive of Watertown. "I did not realize the unethical manner in which this committee was to be used by . . . Lovre's supporters," he told a journalist upon pulling out of the group. George "is a thoroughly reliable, loyal American with a distinguished record of defending his country . . . [and] will, if elected to Congress, be dedicated to the advancement of his country's best interests." But the drama was far from over.[60]

In terms of the letters to the editor it generated, China overwhelmed even the farm issue. Whereas some people charged Lovre with "adopting the imported McCarthy method," a few defended both him and the zealous committee. "Certainly it is not a smear for South Dakotans to quote the very words McGovern used himself," aptly wrote one who also referred to Henry Wallace and 1948. Others, including the state's Republican chairman, wanted to know why (after five years) McGovern had suddenly turned against UN membership and economic aid for China. "1956 is an election year and he is a candidate," ventured Lovre. Yet, if expediency was the motive behind the timely adjustment (as it obviously was), then what of the apparent aspersions the Republicans claimed that they were *not* casting on the Democrat's patriotism? That mystery was solved when Lovre answered criticism of his stand on Rural Electrification programs. McGovern had several times disparaged his rival's "amazingly sorry record on REA issues," especially votes against federal funds for flood control and public power projects on the Missouri River upon which the farmers depended. To this, Lovre responded: "Let McGovern run on his record of support for the Red Chinese and Henry Wallace and I'll run on my REA record."[61]

That the GOP had stepped over the line in trying to paint George red, none felt more strongly than his wife or his aide-de-camp. To be in the limelight would have been difficult in the best of circumstances for Eleanor. "I had pretty thin skin at that time," she said. But in their very first campaign, to hear people call her husband a radical or even a communist, "That was awfully hard." There were limits to her forbearance: "Once I unexpectedly lashed out . . . against smear tactics at a sedate tea for women; another time I burst into tears on the street when a friend offered sympathetic words."[62] The attacks upset George Cunningham at least as much, although they did not cause him to stop reading the newspapers as they did Eleanor. Indeed, all the Republican flag-waving made him curious why Lovre never spoke of his service in World War II, and it prompted him to visit the county courthouse. According to his draft record, Lovre not only had *not* served; he had secured his exemption by crossing out "lawyer" and writing in "farmer" as his occupation. "Where did this guy get off saying stuff about McGovern's patriotism?" Cunningham wondered. A few days later, at the University of South Dakota, he stood up after Lovre finished speaking to an audience of five hundred and inquired about his wartime draft status. The candidate could only stammer and question the validity of the document bearing his signature that Cunningham had brought along. Mrs. Karl Mundt, known as "a tough lady," turned in her seat and eyed the accuser, muttering audibly, "Who is that little son-of-a-bitch?" For the while, the revelation did not generate any more of a blip than that. In time, though, it would make the rounds among veterans' groups.[63]

On Sunday, October 21, the *Argus Leader* published a new poll that placed Lovre in the lead, 49 to 45 percent. Harold's points had not gone up, but George had lost six, with the drop attributable to an increase in "undecideds" among farmers—to 8 percent, up from zero. An opinion piece ("The Republican Fence, Can McGovern Jump It?"), however, suggested that the Red China controversy would "not necessarily be the deciding issue." It was "a battle against South Dakota's voting tradition."[64] With two weeks left to reverse the tradition, he decided he must highlight his three most effective issues—how Democrats served the interests of farmers and small businesses better than the GOP did; education; and the urgency of the pursuit of world peace in a nuclear world.

In the first instance, Ezra Taft Benson seemed glad to lend a hand. He had written a book touting "flexible supports" and, near the end of the campaign, announced that he wanted to get "government out of the grain storage business." McGovern was thrilled. Benson's intention, he said, amounted to "another long stride forward in his plan to rid the country of three million family farmers"—yet more proof that he was "a complete captive of the giant grain firms and processors." Business failures had doubled in South Dakota and a thousand families a year had left their farmsteads since the Republicans had taken over the White House. "When family farmers are forced to leave the land, family businesses are eliminated too." McGovern said he would seek appointments to the House committees on small business and agriculture and reminded voters of his opponent's "warm praise" for the secretary of Soil Bank. "Are you a Benson man or a 90 per cent of parity man?" he now asked at every opportunity.[65]

Education worked almost as well for the college teacher, although the more acute issue was *federal aid* to education, about which Lovre had his doubts. Two factors would eventually overcome the constitutional and philosophical scruples conservatives often marshaled against the idea. The first was the baby boom. Since 1945 the multiplying numbers of children had put greater and greater strains on states and localities to find money to build new classrooms. The second factor was the Cold War. As it happened, the conservative publisher of the *Argus Leader*, John A. Kennedy, had recently toured the Soviet Union and had begun to make education his cause in much the way McGovern sometimes did. "Schools and colleges—not jet planes nor H-bombs—are the greatest Russian threat to America and the West," Kennedy warned in September on the front page. "The Soviet Union has 70 per cent more students in colleges and universities than we; tuition is free . . . [and it] has the stiffest primary-secondary system of six-day per-week, 10 months-per-year schooling in the world."[66]

Lovre would say differently, but he had taken the wrong side. During the previous congressional session he had helped to defeat a generous act to send federal funds to the states for school construction. For that, McGovern slapped him with an F. But the congressman argued that the bill would have given the ten wealthiest states one-third of the monies while the ten poorest states would have received barely one-fifth. "If Professor McGovern wants to tax South Dakotans to build schoolhouses in New York or California, he can," he said. "I will have no part of it." That explanation was "an insult to the intelligence of South Dakota citizens," McGovern rejoined. "Federal funds were to have been made on a matching formula based directly on the school population," and naturally their share would not be as large as New York's. Invoking the authority of Mr. Kennedy, he declared, "I want South Dakota to know that I will fight for an American educational system that will best anything the Soviets can offer."[67] Never did he stop challenging Lovre to debate the issue either. The banner of one of his final campaign ads read, "For Better Schools, Elect George McGovern." Its text construed federal aid as a kind of tax relief for property owners and underscored his experience as an educator. Another hard hitter protested, "it is inconceivable to me that Mr. Lovre would vote against a measure that would have given us some educational assistance." Again he cited Kennedy of the *Argus Leader* and asked, "How can we afford, even from the standpoint of national defense, to neglect the needs of a rapidly growing school population?"[68]

In light of other circumstances, the Cold War context was a shrewd way of framing an issue that McGovern deeply cared about for its own sake. He followed suit on world peace. The approach provided a means of airing his trust in the United Nations, of reminding voters of both his war record and his PhD in American history, and of countering the imputations regarding his statements on Red China. In the homestretch, newspaper readers could take note of a political ad topped by the quotation, "I did not fully realize the urgency of peace until I had witnessed the destruction of war." The copy told about his Distinguished Flying Cross for heroic action and his learning "first-hand how poverty leads to instability, tyranny and war." "Working through the United Nations, the United States must take the lead in a constructive attack on poverty, oppression, disease, and fear," the combat-pilot-turned-scholar declared. "America cannot follow a static or negative policy in a revolutionary age." The next week a bigger broadside began, "George McGovern Is Dedicated to the Task of Building a Peaceful World." The text told of his having seen "close friends blown out of the skies," and deciding that, if he survived, he would study "all phases of history and government" and "dedicate the rest of his life to the cause of peace."[69] South Dakotans had never had the issues put to them quite like that. Lovre's background did not afford him the same reach.

In the meantime, the imbroglio over Red China was coming to its climax. McGovern's detractors had redoubled their pursuit, adding his Progressive Party membership to the list of his sins. The author of a letter to the editor suggested that his "endorsement of Henry Wallace's socialistic program indicates . . . indifference to the disruption of our free enterprise system." Another pointed out that "McGovern's so-called Chinese-socialistic-communistic speeches" were not surprising, because college professors were prone to such utterances. On the other side, an advocate portrayed him as "one of the most sincere Christian men we have." Then a Republican banker wrote in, "I cannot in good conscience vote for Lovre." He held nothing against him for not having served in the war, he explained. "But I do condemn him for slurring one of my fellow veterans whose judgment and integrity I admire." George was not only an "educated gentleman, but he has a distinguished record of defending his country in wartime."[70]

It was along these lines that the whole thing broke in McGovern's favor. On the Thursday before election, fourteen prominent members of East River's American Legion and VFW posts published a rebuke of Lovre. "Instead of discussing problems now facing the people of South

Dakota, you have deliberately tried to cast doubt on the Americanism of our comrade in arms," their statement began. "You have resorted to unethical attacks on a highly respected citizen who risked his life defending his country while you were free to advance your political ambitions at home." Describing McGovern as a loyal person of sound judgment "who despises any moment that threatens the American way of life," they branded Lovre "a desperate politician who has outlived his usefulness as a representative in Congress."[71]

As if the weight of such words were not enough, on that day the *Argus Leader* printed a letter about a current book, *Eisenhower: The Inside Story*, by Robert Donovan, quoting lines of relevance to the Lovre-McGovern knock down. "The President was not convinced that the vital interests of the United States were best served by prolonged non-recognition of China," the journalist-historian had written, paraphrasing remarks Eisenhower had made privately. "He has serious doubts as to whether Russia and China were natural allies. . . . Therefore, he has asked, would it not be the best policy in the long run for the United States to try to pull China away from Russia rather than drive the Chinese deeper into an unnatural alliance unfriendly to the United States?" If he had read the book, McGovern might have stemmed the assault by quoting those lines and another in which Donovan revealed that Ike "felt it was unfortunate that a climate had developed in which . . . it was looked upon almost as un-American even to debate the merits of recognition." Alas, it was too late for that, at the end of a race now too close to call.[72]

For both Harold Lovre and George McGovern, November 6 was a nerve-wracking day. Precincts all around Sioux Falls were reporting record turnouts. "It beats anything we've ever had in this precinct," said one ward captain. "We're running way ahead of 1952," confirmed another just after lunch. Clerks at various polling places described their numbers as either "far ahead" of the usual vote, or as the "heaviest ever." At the courthouse precinct the noon total was "double that for the last general election." By any other yardstick as well, this election in South Dakota was destined to be historic; the Associated Press likened the results to "crazy-quilt pieces . . . stitched together."[73]

To begin, for the first time since 1936, the state had elected a Democrat to Congress. By a majority of 116,516 to 105,835, McGovern could celebrate "a convincing victory," conceded the *Argus Leader*. Moreover, in legislative competition, whereas four years earlier his party had captured a grand total of two seats, this time they took seventeen out of the thirty-five in the Senate (one seat shy of majority control) and twenty-six out of seventy-five in the House, along with several county court benches. "Democrats scared the stuffing out of Republicans," one reporter surmised, even in losing some major offices. Out of nearly 290,000 ballots cast in the election for the US Senate, for example, Ken Holum came within 4,000 of upsetting Francis Case. Then, too, although President Eisenhower carried it by 58 percent—or 171,569 votes to 122,288—his margin in the state had fallen eleven points below that of 1952, or 32,000 fewer votes, the same number by which Stevenson's had increased. As the AP observed, "some strange things happened in South Dakota."[74]

To the question of how McGovern managed to pull off his first election, his wife, his chief campaign aide, and his brother-in-law offered answers that centered on personal attributes. "I think it was because he really worked hard to meet people of both parties, and people liked him," Eleanor said. "The Republicans liked him. So many, of course, didn't agree with him, but they liked him." Cunningham believed that McGovern, who lost twenty pounds during the campaign, simply outworked Lovre: "He really wanted to be in Congress and he ran against almost impossible odds, and he never, never stopped focusing on what he was gonna do." Bob Pennington maintained that people actually "didn't vote for George on the issues. They voted because they had met him, shaken hands with him, and the second time he remembered their name." In his election night victory statement, McGovern cited the simple fact that "many Republicans supported my candidacy." He then reviewed his promises. "I have campaigned with all my strength for programs in the interest of the family farmer and the small businessman, for better schools and improved programs for the aged and the underprivileged," he said. "I have pledged myself to work, too, for a peaceful world." The *Argus Leader*'s editorial offered this: "It was obvious that there was sharp disaffection in the farm areas, a discontent that was reflected to a considerable extent in the voting two years ago."[75]

And so, if the overwhelming majority of South Dakotans still liked Ike, some several thousands of them from the president's own party nonetheless had joined Democrats to send him a message—in the form of a young representative they believed understood their problems better than the four-term incumbent. That message manifested a ratio of sometimes two to one in some areas of the state where agriculture was the most important source of income. For instance, in Brule County, McGovern beat Lovre by 2,031 to 1,095, a pattern that held more often than not in East River's rural counties. But what was more striking was the fact that he actually carried Minnehaha County, the state's most populous and urban, by 17,711 votes to Lovre's 16,933—an astonishing outcome alongside Eisenhower's majority of 22,285 to Stevenson's 13,093. Only partly, then, were the results a case of farmers sacrificing Harold Lovre on the altar of falling commodity prices. For in and around Sioux Falls, he fared no better for being the lone major candidate in the state to refuse to debate his opponent. Nor did his vote against federal monies for school construction seem evenhanded in light of persistent increases in local property taxes or his vote for the $10,000 pay hike that members of the House had recently given themselves.[76]

Beyond those concerns and the farmers' woes, there remained McGovern's position on Red China. The evidence indicates that the issue ultimately backfired on Lovre because his campaign raised it so crudely—to the extent that, in the eyes of many Republicans, it came across as an attack on a brave man's patriotism. (The Reverend Frank Lochridge's letter in the *Daily Republic*, Eleanor believed, "was what probably turned things around.") Furthermore, Lovre's absence from military service in World War II embarrassed Republicans and prompted veterans in their ranks to come to McGovern's defense publicly; the evidence suggests that ample numbers of them voted for the former bomber pilot out of indignation toward Lovre.[77]

———————————

"I am an object of curiosity," he wrote to Arthur Link at Thanksgiving, and he was. George was not just the first Democrat the state sent to Washington in twenty years, but the youngest the First Congressional District had ever elected. He was credited with ending the long political "drought" in South Dakota in other ways, too. A study by the Democratic National Committee determined that, proportionately, he had run further ahead of Stevenson than any other Democratic candidate for Congress in the country.[78]

The actual experience underscored for him the importance of the irreducible ingredients of success in South Dakota politics—to wit, unflagging diligence and sincerity in pressing his party's positions on farm issues. These constituted the key to winning over "independent-minded" Republicans and therefore to winning elections, though they were not merely a means to an end. "I think it was my study of American history and the conviction that the Democratic Party was more on the side of the average American," he said to a reporter who asked why he had become a Democrat. Thus the cause of the farmer was his foremost article of faith (which meant he was keeping part of Henry Wallace's legacy alive as well). Being on the side of average Americans also would afford engagement with other issues that stirred him and the chance to try to explain to his constituents why, for instance, there might be room for doubt about America's course so far regarding China. The opposition would always have its own corresponding passions, and they had taken him by surprise and nearly undone him. But having triumphed, McGovern seemed to generate only greater self-confidence that told him that most people were fair-minded and willing to give him a chance.[79] Even so, politics had turned out to be harder than he or Eleanor had expected, and they had no real inkling of the full price of such a career upon which they were about to embark. "But on the crisp Monday before election George and I were suddenly convinced that we were going to win," she recalled with some ambivalence. "That is about all I remember until we started packing the kids and our shabby old furniture into a Ford station wagon and headed for the nation's capital."[80]

An entire decade had passed since he had made his decision "to be a part of that postwar effort to build a structure of peace." During that time, he had undertaken a PhD in history as "a way of fulfilling a social and political purpose," and by 1948 he had become an "activist historian" involved in the Progressive Party campaign. Thereafter, his ambition progressed naturally—from the classroom to politics and leadership in the Democratic Party of South Dakota and then on to a smart campaign. Professor Link no longer regarded his former graduate student's decision to leave academia as a "loss to history." Like the congressman-elect, he had always understood that one did not have to write history in order to make his mark upon it. McGovern's years of preparation were over, and now the real thing was coming.

9 WASHINGTON, DC

On December 22, 1956, at the end of a 1,300-mile drive, the McGoverns reached the outskirts of the first metropolis in which they would live. The feeling of a new beginning started taking hold as traffic hemmed them in and they could see the Capitol dome and the Washington Monument glowing through the damp night. Just then, to Ann, Susan, and Terry, it did not matter that moving had canceled out Christmas in Mitchell or that they would have to stay in an apartment a few days before they could move into their new home. The house was in Chevy Chase, next door to Hubert Humphrey, who had told George and Eleanor about it—two stories, four bedrooms, gabled attic, two baths, and a sizable lot. Now, in their excitement, they all wanted to see it. George found the way to Coquelin Terrace, the street where they would live for the next twelve years, and stopped the car. The house was dark; their eyes were drawn to the Humphreys' and the bright Christmas tree in the window. Then George pulled away.

The holiday week was full of sightseeing. The federal city that the McGoverns explored never looked more impressive. Much of its modern-day aspect had been achieved during Franklin Roosevelt's reign, when the government had embarked upon the greatest expansion of its physical plant in its history. In the midst of depression, the New Deal had ushered in a construction boom. In addition to five thousand new apartment and office buildings and homes, this explosion included the Supreme Court building, the annex to the Library of Congress, and the Longworth House Office Building (where George was assigned his suite of offices), as well as the National Archives on the mall and Federal Triangle along Pennsylvania Avenue. The improvements completed during the war included the National Gallery of Art, the Pentagon, and the Jefferson Memorial, a project FDR had set in motion and monitored closely.

Washington would afford the McGoverns other cultural amenities that simply did not exist in Mitchell. Constitution Hall, for instance, not only was home to the National Symphony Orchestra but also featured ballet and opera and renowned soloists such as Édith Piaf. The National Theater offered first-rate dramatic productions; in December 1956, Julie Harris was playing in Jean Anouilh's *The Lark*, to be followed by Melvyn Douglas in *Inherit the Wind*. Come spring, the National would stage the world premiere of *West Side Story*. Downtown offered grand cinemas such as the RKO Keith's and the Loews Capitol and Palace, newly retrofitted with widescreen technology to lure midcentury audiences away from their television sets. When the McGoverns arrived, Cecil B. DeMille's *The Ten Commandments* was several weeks into its four-month reserve-seat engagement, and *Friendly Persuasion*, starring Gary Cooper, was finishing a run of two months. Christmas openings included *The Teahouse of the August Moon* with Marlon Brando and *Anastasia* with Ingrid Bergman. As for open-air activities, the family would be living near one end of Rock Creek Park; the kids especially would all grow fond of outings there because of "Candy Cane City," a popular playground.[1]

The more important coincidence of adjacency for the McGoverns, though, was the celebrity next door. It was not entirely because he was a United States senator that a lot of Americans knew of Hubert Horatio Humphrey in the 1950s. Many of them also remembered him as the brash young mayor of Minneapolis whose speech on behalf of a civil rights plank had electrified the convention that nominated Harry Truman in 1948. "The time has come for the Democratic Party to get out of the shadow of states' rights and walk forthrightly into the bright sunshine of human rights," Humphrey had declared, and it would remain his finest moment.[2]

Ten years George's senior and the son of a pharmacist, Hubert was reared in Doland, a town of six hundred in the flat center of eastern South Dakota. Like McGovern, he had been the ideal son and student as well as a debater in high school and college, winning prizes for his oratory and essays on politics. After earning a bachelor's degree at the University of Minnesota, he went to graduate school at Louisiana State

University and wrote his thesis on the New Deal. He taught political science at Macalester College, in St. Paul, and helped to forge Minnesota's Democratic-Farmer-Labor Party (DFL) in 1944. The following year, and again in 1947, he won the mayoralty race, and then his seat in the US Senate in 1948. At that point, his and McGovern's parallel paths diverged; Humphrey had become a founding member of Americans for Democratic Action as well as the instigator of a struggle to purge the DFL of leftists and alleged communists. He was quick to condemn Henry Wallace yet slow to endorse Truman. In 1950 he became a leading advocate of the McCarran Act and, on the eve of his reelection campaign, a sponsor of the Communist Control Act of 1954. In January 1949, *Time* magazine put him on its cover, calling him "a hard-working, fast-talking fireball from the Midwest" and "the most articulate spokesman for the Fair Deal among the newcomers." When McGovern entered the House, Humphrey already had completed two years of his second term in the Senate and sat on its committees on agriculture and foreign relations and helped majority leader Lyndon Johnson as his link to the liberal wing of the party. No politician of the Middle Border region was more powerful.[3]

Because he was South Dakota–born and frequently came to speak there, the state's Democrats claimed Humphrey as their own senator, and not the least did George. From 1953 onward, whenever he needed him for a fund-raiser or to stump for his campaign for Congress, Hubert was there. "For me," he told George, "your victory helped overshadow the national landslide for Ike." The bond grew still stronger once their wives became close friends and their children started running in and out of one another's house every day. Dougie Humphrey and Terry, who in 1957 turned nine and eight, developed a close pal-ship. So did the senator and Terry; she called him "Humfey" and truly loved him, and he dubbed her "the Queen of Coquelin Terrace." Hubert's banter and famed effulgence appealed to most of the neighborhood youngsters. Now and then he would gather all of them up ("like the Pied Piper," said Eleanor) and buy them ice cream. On birthdays he always gave each child a dollar. Arthur Link liked to tell graduate students about a visit to the McGoverns when he watched Hubert drive up to his house, calling out the window by name to the children playing on the sidewalk. George had a fond story, too—of hearing "shouts of exultation" one morning and looking outside to find his next-door neighbor alone in his backyard exclaiming, "What a wonderful day! What a wonderful day!" No one appraised his exuberance more fittingly than

Mary, the youngest of the McGovern family. "When I was a little girl," she said, "I thought that Hubert Humphrey was Bob Hope."[4] Of course, he was her dad's mentor, too.

Boxes of unopened mail spilling onto the floor awaited McGovern as he unlocked the doors to Suite 120 of the Longworth House Office Building on a cold morning in January 1957. It was to be a day of learning. Scarcely five minutes went by that one of the phones did not ring. At noon, a delegation of South Dakotans, in town for a Chamber of Commerce convention, arrived to say hello. George invited them to lunch but he was unfamiliar with the underground passageways connecting the office buildings with the Capitol, and they got lost three times before the dining room appeared. That afternoon, a staff member who had gained her understanding of politics in the county courthouse of Chamberlain, South Dakota, answered the telephone: "George? No, we ain't seen him," she told the caller just as he returned from lunch. "It's some Douglas feller calling you," she explained to George, and it happened to be Justice William O. Douglas of the Supreme Court wanting to welcome him to Washington.[5]

McGovern's heart probably could not have taken another day of blameless incidents like these, but they made him realize he had at his side not a single savvy person with a Capitol Hill education. All three of the staffers he had brought along were as green as he was, and only one of them (Robert Nelson, formerly of the South Dakota Farmers Union) proved to be a shrewd choice and eventually a well-regarded Washington hand. What he really needed was a superb executive secretary.

At the end of the week, he interviewed Patricia Donovan, a native Washingtonian employed by Harold Donohue, Democrat of Massachusetts. Pat had ten siblings and a widowed mother, and she had gone to work right after high school. Sacred Heart Academy, from which she had graduated in 1954, had imparted rapid typing speed, a grammarian's knowledge of English, and the self-confidence, as McGovern put it, "to be bluntly critical of slipshod work on the part of anyone, including me." She regarded Donohue as "an absentee congressman, not really involved," whereas she later said of her interview with McGovern, "I could just tell he would be an activist congressman." After twenty minutes he offered her the position at a generous salary of $5,000.[6]

Pat Donovan's intuition was well tuned. But her boss had luck going for him, too. Although his request to join the Agriculture Committee was in vain for someone so junior, he nonetheless drew a decent assignment on Education and Labor.[7] By chance, both of those fields of duty would throw the House of Representatives into hard combat over issues of national significance in which the rookie would make his presence known. Then, too, McGovern was fortunate that Sam Rayburn was Speaker of the House. Like his fellow Texan who ruled the Senate, "Mr. Sam" exercised great power, but he was not the domineering, vindictive master of his domain that Lyndon Johnson was. Rayburn believed devoutly in the seniority system and in fairness otherwise. As for younger members, he wished not to control, but to give them a fair chance to show what they could do. He once told Adam Clayton Powell, in 1945, that freshmen "are supposed not to be heard and not even seen too much." But by the mid-1950s, according to LBJ, Rayburn had become more indulgent of younger members. The seventy-five-year-old appreciated McGovern's eagerness to learn and his good manners and, in part because his own district was rural, he was receptive to any earnest freshmen who represented farmers and ranchers. As it happened, the first domestic issue McGovern got swept up into had to do with price supports as a means of bringing about a decent income for farmers relative to the rest of the country's prosperity, or "a farm dollar that is in harmony with the city dollar," as the *Argus Leader* once explained parity.[8]

There were few policy questions more combustible than this one, and none of greater interest to McGovern's constituency. It was complicated by the paradox that American agriculture was too productive for its own health. To note but basic staples, between the late 1940s and the late 1950s, average output per acre had increased by an average of 41 percent for potatoes, corn, and wheat, and 70 percent for cotton. Such yields on fewer acres nullified whatever benefits might have accrued from Ezra Taft Benson's Soil Bank, a plan that offered a subsidy to farmers who agreed to limit the acreage given over to a particular crop. Thus farmers continued to suffer as prices collapsed under the weight of mounting surpluses, which Benson's "flexible" price supports practically abetted.[9]

But yet another market-related development further undercut a fair return. In the otherwise prosperous ten years preceding 1957, the farmer's share of the retail price his produce fetched on the grocery shelf had fallen by more than 25 percent, even as he faced rising costs of living and of production. (The overall parity ratio had fallen from 115 to 79 during that decade as well.) Ironically, farmers received less for the food they grew while consumers were paying more for it. This was a predicament that McGovern decided to address near the end of January on the House floor, in two resolutions—to hold an investigation of the causes behind the insidious "price/cost spread" and to raise supports to 90 percent of parity.[10] A month later, in his formal maiden speech as a congressman, he distilled Ezra Taft Benson's offenses.

His point of departure was Benson's claim that the drop in net farm income since 1947 was due to the high wages that American workers were wringing from employers. To the contrary, McGovern said, "The American farmer, like the merchant, has no better friend than the adequately paid worker." Benson was attempting "to drive divisive wedges" between three interdependent groups. The real culprit behind the decline, the congressman argued, might be "the fact that corporation profits have soared to record peaks." To pit struggling farmers against prosperous industrial workers was "an irresponsible effort to cover up" the administration's failure. What was needed was a "price support structure that will enable the farmer to meet the higher cost of living that comes with a constantly rising American standard of living." Thus had he introduced his bill "to prevent farm prices from falling below the 90 percent of parity level . . . in relation to the cost of what the farmer buys from the rest of us."[11]

"American agriculture today is grievously ill," traceable to the "cost-price squeeze" and "the discredited theory of flexible price supports," McGovern advised. Using the Ag Department's own statistics, he compared the purchasing power of family farms in the period between 1947 and 1949 with that of 1955. He found that farms that fattened hogs and beef, for instance, had realized an average annual return of $4,299 in purchasing power in 1947–49, but that that had shrunken to $379 in 1955. Likewise, cash-grain farms had averaged $3,068 in 1947–49 but only $983 by 1955; wheat-roughage-livestock growers had achieved the purchasing power of $2,070, which then slipped to $940. The USDA tabulations showed sheep ranchers at $1,772 for 1947–49, and then at *minus* $112 after three years of the Benson policy. Was it any wonder, he asked, that South Dakota was losing a thousand family farms and that, nationally, 100,000 farmers were going out of business each year?[12]

McGovern then held up a copy of President Eisenhower's economic report dated January 1957. Corporate profits now ranged 20 percent higher than in 1947–49, interest income and dividends were up 93 percent and 69 percent, and weekly earnings for labor in manufacturing had climbed by 51 percent and for all workers across the board by 36 percent since 1947–49. But what of those who herded or plowed for a living, those hard-working folks who comprised 13 percent of the population, yet received only 6 percent of the income bounty? This was the crisis in American agriculture, and it warranted consideration on the basis "of solid economic measures and true human and spiritual values instead of a cold materialistic concept," he said. "Farmers do not ask for any special favors. They only seek the same right their city cousins long ago attained through legislation—a decent return on their land and their labor."[13] With that, he yielded.

Institutional custom obliged several member to bid him welcome on the occasion of his inaugural speech. Congresswoman Coya Knutson of Minnesota said she wished "to commend the people of South Dakota for their wonderful intelligence and good sense in sending to us such a champion as you." Carl Albert, majority whip from Oklahoma, and LeRoy Anderson, a Montana freshman, complimented his presentation, too. "The gentleman from South Dakota has made an outstanding statement," Lee Metcalf, another Montanan interjected. "Already he has shown a broad knowledge of the farm problem and a deep sympathy for our family farmers." Anson Yeager of the *Argus Leader* remarked in his column that the "Ph.D and political salesman" not only was "new and different," but also "looks like a hard man to beat." Even better reviews would be his the next month, when the debate resumed—"the first shot fired in the 1958 congressional elections campaign," a leading Washington journalist would write.[14]

This was a serious political conflict about corn, the commodity that Benson's Soil Bank plan favored over all others by requiring smaller cuts in production by farmers in the Republican Midwest where it was grown in abundance. Thus "King Corn" threatened to fracture the mutual aid alliance between the two main components of the farm bloc—Republicans of the corn and wheat states and Democrats of the cotton and tobacco—though Republican wheat growers (McGovern's constituency) felt as deeply wounded by the Benson policy as Democrats did.[15] The problem started upon the introduction of controversial legislation hammered out in the Agriculture Committee. The authors of the majority measure, under the direction of Chairman Harold Cooley of North Carolina, acknowledged its imperfections along with the fact that the committee had recommended it on a partisan vote of fourteen to twelve. Some thirty representatives, for about as many hours, did battle on the floor, but no one shed more light on the contents of Chairman Cooley's bill than Coya Knutson.

The Democratic proposal neither favored nor disadvantaged one grain over another, the committee's only woman explained, be it barley or wheat or commercial versus noncommercial corn. ("Commercial" corn was grown for sale and in far greater volume; "noncommercial" was the corn farmers grew for feeding their livestock.) The program aimed, first, to realize an uncompensated, voluntary 20 percent cut in all feed grain acreage in order to take a bite out of runaway surpluses. Subscribing growers also would agree to reduce their feed grain acreage by an additional 15 percent, but here the Soil Bank would compensate them at the particular feed grain's rate per acre. To receive this replacement income, farmers would be required to set aside *productive* feed grain acreage, not scrub land or fields used for other purposes. In this way, Knutson continued, the Cooley bill, in effect, would raise grain prices to "approximately 84 to 87 percent of equivalent parity prices" and reduce significantly the surpluses (some of which the government could sell overseas to offset part of the Soil Bank payments).[16]

The Republican substitute zeroed in on corn. Bearing the stamp of August Andresen of Minnesota, it sought to cut down to fifty-one million acres the Democrats' allotment of fifty-eight million acres for commercial corn production while continuing with Benson's lower price supports. But no production limits would be imposed on any other feed grains, including noncommercial corn; nor would price supports be improved for them. (Parity for corn then stood at 66 percent.) The Andresen bill also contained a sweetener. It would allow growers to receive Soil Bank payments for setting aside land that they perhaps did not intend for grain anyway, or on which they might have sown commercial corn. This would mean a potential windfall mainly for large producers of that crop. And so the Democrats contended that the Benson system, as modified by the Andresen bill, would put a greater strain on government finances and stimulate still larger surpluses, while family farms would continue to lag further behind. For their part, many Republicans reviled the majority measure as a "budget-buster" and a "monstrosity" and accused Democrats of ingratitude for their help with drought relief in the South.[17]

As the partisans charged each other with pushing wrongheaded legislation, time was running out for midwestern farmers. Decisions would have to be made about spring planting, and price-supported corn for the coming season had been limited to thirty-seven million acres—one-third fewer acres for commercial corn than the previous year—with supports at only 75 percent of parity. The worry was, if

Congress did not act quickly to improve the terms, growers would opt out of the regime, and the upshot would be yet more gigantic surpluses, with all sorts of dire ripple effects. "The house of agriculture is divided," Chairman Cooley intoned. Recriminations such as "I do not believe everything the gentleman says, by a jugful," and "You have horsed around with this bill until it is now the middle of March" began to fly.[18]

Toward the end of the day, after all of the convolution over commercial corn versus noncommercial, the chair recognized McGovern. He had an amendment at the clerk's desk. It was as easy to understand as it was radical. If adopted, it would overthrow Benson's flexible support system (as well as both parties' corn laws) and make available payments at 90 percent of parity for grains and livestock *of every kind*. McGovern called it the "family farm parity amendment." The chamber settled down to listen.[19]

He was offering it for two reasons—because he believed that farmers were "entitled to at least 90 percent of a fair return" and that "Federal farm programs should be geared primarily to the family-sized farm." Benson's attempt to reduce surpluses by cutting parity was a colossal failure, he said; if nothing else, that "should now be clear to all." Since the Eisenhower administration had come in, surpluses had tripled and farm income had dropped 25 percent, and yet the consumer's grocery bill was "higher than ever before." McGovern stressed that his proposal was "not offered in the interest of any one farm group" but would apply "to the whole range of farm production." The terms, however, were set purposely to the well-being of the family farm. Therefore, eligibility would be "limited to commodities not to exceed in value at the parity price of 14,000 bushels of corn or 10,000 bushels of wheat"—or, converted into gross sales, a maximum of $25,000. As for Soil Bank payments, no individual producer could receive more than $5,000 a year. This would prevent the program from becoming the trough of corporate agriculture. And that was it—this "family farm parity amendment."[20]

Before the vote, a few members had advised its author not to expect more than fifty or sixty ayes in the midst of the bitter debate. Yet to the astonishment of all, the tally topped out at 168 to 172, or four votes shy of adoption—a "sensationally close margin," McGovern wrote Ward Clark. He later attributed the near success to the $5,000 cutoff provision for Soil Bank payments. Whatever the explanation, journalists across the country discussed the amendment as the one bright spot within the grim stalemate that Congress and the Agriculture Committee had reaped in failing to pass any legislation at all. In the *Washington Post*, Carroll Kilpatrick made McGovern's initiative the pivot of his column about the acrimony. A national agricultural newsletter informed its readers: "The vote for the McGovern bill represents the strongest support ever manifested in the House for protecting farm prices and incomes. It was a remarkable tribute to a freshman congressman." The *Minneapolis Tribune* deemed it amazing, especially for a newcomer "who was not even a member of the Agriculture Committee." And then a gift of gold: "His effort for 90 per cent of parity came very near passing because he made such a splendid argument in its favor," declared Speaker Rayburn. "He has impressed us all with his character and ability since the beginning of this congress." The *Daily Republic* reported that McGovern after three months was "rapidly making a national reputation for himself." In another story, he admitted, "I've never done anything I've enjoyed as much as this job and I've never worked harder."[21]

He knew, of course, that his efforts on behalf of farm issues would determine his fate in politics. But it was not simply the righteous attack on Ezra Taft Benson or the populism of the Family Farm Parity Amendment that roused the voters of East River. In January, he had introduced legislation to investigate the spread between farm prices and consumer prices. In February he protested to the comptroller general about shortfalls in Soil Bank payments to South Dakota farmers. The next month, he intervened on behalf of durum wheat farmers for a longer Soil Bank sign-up period. Then, in June, he called upon the secretary of agriculture to exercise his powers to bolster egg producers, since farmers now received just 21 cents for the dozen that sold for 70 cents in the cities. (In October, Benson was met by a hail of surplus eggs as he rose to speak to a crowd at the annual corn-picking contest in Sioux Falls. By local standards, this form of protest was extreme, yet not utterly inexcusable. Five average farmers had thrown the eggs. "We have seen friends and neighbors go down the drain," said one to a group of Republicans. "You have backed away from almost everything benefitting the little guy.")[22]

During the second session of the 85th Congress, in the struggle against Benson's effort to lower supports still further, McGovern might as well have been a member of the Ag Committee for the central role he played. In February, he introduced his "Family Farm Income Improvement Act of 1958," his response to the 25 percent drop in farm family net income and the mounting surpluses. This proposal addressed the plight of family farms (not corporate agriculture) seeking to improve their income "at a net effective level at not less than 80 percent of full parity income." The concept of "parity of income," McGovern explained, "would enable farm people to attain a standard of living enjoyed by people in other walks of life." Alongside referenda for marketing agreements, the program would allow commodity prices to rise and fall, but the farmer would be protected against "income deficiencies" by payments of up to $3,500 a year, depending on the size of the enterprise and the drop in prices. H.R. 10966 prompted a lively colloquy. On both sides of the aisle McGovern garnered praise from former cattle ranchers and farmers as well as the urban dwellers among his colleagues.[23]

By spring, however, a temporary holding action was needed to prevent further cuts in price supports and acreage allotments until Congress could craft a complete package. In the debate, again, McGovern explained the imperative of maintaining the current year's levels as a bare minimum. The Montanan LeRoy Anderson went out of his way to associate himself with McGovern's "thoughtful and very constructive remarks," and Edmond Edmondson, a third-term Democrat from Muskogee, lauded him for "the fight he has made" as well as for a "splendid" analysis, which was "on all fours with the conditions in Oklahoma."[24] But on March 31 a presidential veto rendered it for naught. This opened the way, in August, for the Agricultural Act of 1958, the final major farm legislation of the Eisenhower years. McGovern called it "the poorest farm legislation . . . in a quarter of a century." Humphrey described one version as "unbelievably bad." The impossibility of overriding a second veto caused Democrats to accept some reduction in supports to a floor of 65 percent of parity on basic commodities.

And yet East River folks seemed not inclined to hold this Bensonite victory against McGovern. He had made an indelible impression as an astute and knowledgeable young representative who had tried, as hard as anyone could, to improve the lot of families on the land, and who had observed as he set his own legislation before the Congress, "Deep in the heart of every farmer is the desire to be a good farmer."[25]

————————————

There were reasons why he could not have acted or spoken with any less resolve. No sooner was McGovern sworn in than he confronted a controversial resolution related to presidential war-making powers; its contents would soon be dubbed the Eisenhower Doctrine. This was the administration's response to the turmoil in the Middle East, sparked by the Suez Crisis and the fading influence of British and French imperialism; its purpose was to deter Soviet intervention in the region as well as local communist or nationalist uprisings. Before a joint session of Congress, on January 5, 1957, the president requested $200 million for economic and military aid to help friendly governments in the Middle East resist "overt armed aggression from any nation controlled by international communism." All they had to do was ask and the aid or the marines or both would arrive. Thus did the United States intend to preserve its inestimable strategic interests in that part of the world. This kind of foreign aid initiative was part of Eisenhower's "New Look" in foreign policy, which stressed economy in the implementation of NSC-68. To contain communism yet avoid bloody bogs like Korea, the New Look put nuclear weapons in the forefront while cutting the size of the armed forces. The strategy also called for new alliances modeled on NATO as well as expanded covert actions in which the CIA would undermine unfriendly governments and replace them with friendly ones in the Middle East, Latin America, and Asia. Such interventions often succeeded in the moment but carried untoward consequences. (For instance, to control Iran's oil and thwart an alleged communist takeover, the CIA destroyed a parliamentary government led by Prime Minister Mohammed Mosaddeq and installed the dictator, Shah Reza Pahlavi, in 1953. Iranians would never forgive the United States.)

In light of the recent campaign uproar over McGovern's tolerance of Red China, his vote on the Eisenhower Doctrine resolution was potentially consequential. Although Congress would pass it overwhelmingly, the bill had detractors. Humphrey, for instance, called it "a predated declaration of war," yet he ended up supporting it and urged his neighbor to do the same. On January 30, the roll was called in the House; 355 members voted for it and 61 against. McGovern was among the latter. "I hate to see you make a judgment like this so early," Hubert said. But, always a loyal Democrat, he would never be "a safe party man."[26]

McGovern explained himself on the floor the following day. Whereas he did not doubt the reality of "an incendiary political problem stemming from the Arab-Israeli dispute," he regarded advance authorization to commit troops as a usurpation of the constitutional prerogatives of the Congress; and he questioned whether "the Russians would be so stupid as to launch a military attack in the Middle East" anyway. His main concern was that the president's proposal represented "a dangerous illusion of policy where there is no policy." On the one hand, it would bestow precious economic resources on feudal despots;

on the other, it would leave untouched the social and political problems that *really* threatened the peace and stability in the region, for it provided "no practical plan to use American aid . . . to eradicate the swamplands of poverty and disease that open the way for Communist inroads." How, then, he wondered, could the United States hope to secure its own long-term interests, let alone improve the lives of the impoverished people of these lands? To illustrate his point, he referred to the impending visit to Washington of the sovereign of Saudi Arabia. A heavy drinker and sworn enemy of Israel, King Saud spent $54 million annually to maintain his palaces and innumerable Cadillacs and concubines, while the country's per capita income was $42. Because he had built only ten elementary schools and two high schools, the Saudi rate of illiteracy stood at 99.5 percent. If this were not bad enough, slavery was a governmental enterprise, with 45,000 people auctioned on the block each year, according to the United Nations. "Do we build strength against communism by contributing American tax dollars to prop up rulers who embody everything that is alien to our tradition of liberty and equality?" McGovern asked. It would be a far better thing for the United States, the Arab states, and the United Nations together to draw up plans for "a series of constructive, well-defined [civil works] projects," he concluded. This was the way to "build for true strength against Communist subversion, by a full-scale attack on those ancient evils—poverty, ignorance, and disease."[27]

In defying the obvious political hazards, McGovern's very first foreign policy interposition as a congressman was quite bold. Sometimes he would not be able to "get along by going along," as Rayburn once advised him. That he spoke and voted his conscience turned out to be fortuitous, however. Public response to the Eisenhower doctrine was cool. Congressional mail in February ran eight to one against it. "Instead of bribing dictators not to give our oil interests too much trouble," grumbled the *Daily Republic*, the administration could do worse than to cooperate with the United Nations, "and we congratulate McGovern for refusing to be a party to such temporization." His case against subsidies to potentates even prompted the *Argus Leader* to commend his "questioning attitude" toward "wasteful expenditures."[28]

McGovern's stand stirred the American Christian Palestine Committee, a well-respected nonpartisan, nonsectarian organization, to offer him a fellowship to travel the Middle East. "We simply want you to use your skills as a humanitarian and as a keen student of modern social, economic, and political problems," its executive director explained, "[to study] the region both in terms of its conflicts and of its prospects for development and human progress." (It was the latest reason why South Dakotans "may take pride in the excellent reputation McGovern is making," said the *Daily Republic*.) For two weeks during the Easter recess, George and Eleanor visited Israel, Egypt, Jordan, Iraq, and Lebanon. Their journey would become the subject of a Drew Pearson column and a segment on the *Today Show*.[29]

After visiting Israel and Lebanon, the McGoverns' arrival in Jordan coincided with an attempt by pro-Nasser partisans to overthrow King Hussein. The upheaval resulted in the first invocation of the Eisenhower Doctrine. On April 25, the president ordered the Sixth Fleet to the eastern Mediterranean and sent $10 million to bolster the young monarch's government. Meanwhile, McGovern met with foreign minister Mahmoud Fawzi in Cairo. He expressed hope that "the Egyptian government would see fit to recognize the existence of the state of Israel and her right to use the Suez Canal and the Gulf of Aqaba." Fawzi replied that his "government hadn't criticized [the US] for not recognizing China, and by the same token Egypt would recognize Israel when she wants to, not before." McGovern gathered the impression that US prestige among Arab nations was deteriorating. This owed partly to its support for Israel; but more than one of his hosts complained, "American policy seemed to be based largely on our desire to arm other nations so that they can defend our military positions abroad." Assistance of that kind (which Hussein received) seemed a "wasted effort" to McGovern, especially when he had encountered undernourished people (in all, thousands) everywhere he went.[30]

It was just two weeks and five countries, but the trip definitely helped the congressman clarify his outlook on American relations with the former colonial areas of the world, the scene of the Cold War's severest tensions in the 1950s. His observations of the Middle East confirmed what his historical studies of Asia had taught him about foreign policy conducted in the name of rigid anticommunism—about the failure to try to understand the "forces of nationalism and socialism that are now convulsing the 'backward' areas of the world," as he had once written to Arthur Link.[31] Like Truman, Eisenhower seemed to emphasize military solutions practically to the exclusion of all others. And in the context of battles over defense appropriations, McGovern began to say so publicly and to outline alternatives as well.

"Any major cut in the presidential budget will have to come in the military field," he informed the Mitchell Chamber of Commerce on May

31, 1957. Given the ten-to-one ratio of dollars spent on military versus economic assistance in countries whose people did not have enough to eat, "more of the foreign aid program should be of bread rather than guns," he reasoned. In June he blasted Eisenhower's new $72 billion budget for exceeding the total of all federal expenditures from 1933 to 1941, with over half of it going to military purposes. Billions could be saved, he held forth on Sioux Falls television, if only the armed services applied basic rules of efficiency and competitive bidding in procurement. In July he referred to these matters in an Op-Ed piece in the *Daily Republic* that focused on the big increases in agricultural production in tandem with the 20 percent cut in price supports. "I have made up my mind," he wrote. Declining farm income was "the greatest threat, not only to farm families, but to the merchants who depend upon them." But he wanted South Dakotans to see how all the threads in the skein intertwined: "I have never accepted the view that farm surpluses constitute a curse. What is needed in a world where two out of three people are hungry and where there are many hungry people even in the United States is a more intelligent food use program. *Food is our greatest weapon for peace.*"[32]

Accordingly, McGovern cast a surprise protest vote when the final foreign aid bill came up in August because the $3 billion package was so heavily weighted on the military side of the scales. "I see very little to be gained in handing a gun to a man crying for bread," he remarked.[33] In September, he announced at the state capitol that his other major priority therefore would be to secure "a fuller and more constructive use of American farm commodities." Alluding to his Middle East tour and his critique of the Eisenhower Doctrine, he said, "The Russians can match us gun for gun in any such arms shipments, but they can't compete with us in food production." That was the way to stop the spread of communism—with "our greatest national asset in the Cold War." It required imagination, he said, referring to the Agricultural Trade Development and Assistance Act, an administration program established in 1954 to reduce the gluts of commodities by distributing them abroad. He was calling for a creative expansion of the scope of the legislation. "The time has come when we should re-evaluate this foreign aid program of ours," he exhorted blue collar workers in Mitchell. To counter "the real threat of communism," the United States must "increase materials which will increase the dignity of man" and make possible "a better standard of life." A few days later, to a thousand farmers at the rural electric cooperative in De Smet, he stressed "the need for small communities to work together to raise food to fight the cold war." The everyday people he had seen in the Middle East "wanted food, not arms and ammunition," he said.[34]

It is unlikely that the citizens of any other congressional district in the United States heard from their representative the kind of message that McGovern's heard from him. In the foregoing series of speeches, the professor not only attempted to demonstrate connections between domestic and foreign policy; in effect, he was appealing to his constituents to expand their capacity for critical thought while they served their own interests through commonsense humanitarianism. The conundrum of agriculture, he enjoined, gave South Dakota a serious stake in the conduct of the Cold War, and that involved the rejection of the military option at the first sign of trouble in favor of a blend of practicality and idealism. "We have allowed ourselves to become identified with those who seek to freeze the status quo," he would lament in a floor speech on the Middle East in early 1958. "Most of the people of the world are not looking primarily for military hardware. They are hungry, sick, or illiterate. They yearn for better standards of life." The test for foreign assistance should be "how effectively it enables the people of the underdeveloped areas to build up the kind of society where those better standards of life are possible."[35] Thus had he embarked upon a path from which he would rarely stray.

The first-term congressman's presence mattered in another significant area of policy making and it, too, captured well the essence of his mission in politics. In his campaign, he had berated Harold Lovre for helping to defeat federal aid for classroom construction. His first chance to make good on his slogan, "For Better Schools, Elect George McGovern," came just after the hoopla over his family farm parity bill. Assigned to the Committee on Education and Labor, he was involved in a floor debate over the new rural library services program that Congress had authorized in 1956. In certain parts of the United States the program's good effects were wonderfully disproportionate to the small obligation of federal money, and the education subcommittee wanted to increase the funding from $2 million to $5 million. The "bookmobile"—a genus of van equipped with stocked bookcases inside—was its most salutary innovation. Motoring along its circuit through the countryside, a bookmobile could transport as many as two thousand volumes to an isolated community; both schoolchildren and grown-ups could browse the bookshelves and check out two or three selections for a month, and perhaps request a particular title for next time. The enhanced legislation could help extend the opportunity to "about 27 million people living in rural areas who have no libraries . . . and another 53 million that have inadequate services," according to Peter Fogarty, Republican of Rhode Island. Al Ullman of Oregon knew what it meant "to the people of the little towns . . . and the farms of this country," describing his district. "This is essentially a program for underprivileged children . . . who have been deprived of the sustenance of the mind—books." Democrat Gracie Pfost of Idaho disclosed, "More than half of the population of my state has no library service at all," noting that matching funds had induced some states to upgrade library budgets by as much as 150 percent.[36]

If the argument for putting more bookmobiles on the road verged on the poignant, those against it invoked principles about overspending. John Byrnes of Wisconsin chided Democrats for criticizing the president's huge budget and then recommending increases like this one; for economy's sake he urged a $2 million cut. Others questioned not the worthiness of rural education but whose responsibility it was. John Taber, a New York Republican, fretted that approval would "encourage idealists to try to create another agency and set up another Federal department."[37]

McGovern regarded this sort of reasoning as "fatuous" and "shortsighted." In the full flush of the Cold War, half of the population of the United States did not have a library within practical reach. Just $5 million dollars (out of a $72 *billion* budget) would correct that inadequacy. There was "no true economy" in slashing these funds, he told colleagues. The American people expected them to invest their tax dollars "in enterprises that will bring the greatest possible benefit to the greatest possible number." Quoting Jefferson on essential ingredients for democracy, he asked, "How can we better promote 'the diffusion of knowledge' than through the rural, traveling library service?" His constituents wanted "to bring the blessings of good books to farm boys and girls" the same as "they expect the Congress to stabilize farm prices at a fair level."[38] Yet this stinginess was but a preview of the debate that the revived schoolhouse bill would ignite in July.

It was called the School Construction Assistance Act of 1957, a $1.5 billion request over five years. In light of the emergency it was intended to cope with, compared to the $3 billion the government spent each year on highway construction, supporters thought it a modest commitment. In 1950, elementary and high school enrollments stood at 30.3 million students; by 1955, the total had climbed to 37.4 million. It would jump to 46.3 million by 1960. Already the secretary of health, education, and welfare had affirmed the need for 159,000 new classrooms; in 1957–58 the forty-eight states planned to build 69,000. That number was both unprecedented and insufficient. Over a million additional students would enter the system each fall in the coming decade, while at least 10,000 classrooms annually would give way to obsolescence. According to the US Office of Education, to arrest the shortage would take sixteen years. In Gallup surveys, 76 percent of the American people agreed that federal aid was the answer.[39]

Nonetheless, large numbers of politicians from both parties either did not believe the polls or cared not what they said. For instance, Martin Dies, the cantankerous Texan and founding chair of the House Un-American Activities Committee, denounced the bill as extravagant in "a period of reckless spending." Paul Schenck, a former Dayton schoolteacher, not only doubted Ohio had a shortage but figured, on the basis of cost and tax redistributions, his state would lose $10 million. The program was needs based, and wealthier states would be helping poorer states. New York would lose $38 million, for example, although Governor Averell Harriman said it was an investment in the nation's future. But Schenck's concern lay elsewhere. "History has shown that dictatorships have . . . developed by controls exercised over the minds of growing children through the schools," he said. "I do not want Uncle Sam sitting on our local school boards." Clare Hoffman, Republican of Michigan, sounded a recurring tocsin: Communists "realize they can further their cause . . . if they control the teaching of our youth," and persuade citizens "to place the Federal Government in [charge] of our educational program."[40]

Of all the speakers Chairman Graham Barden recognized, only the education subcommittee's formally trained historian was granted "such time as he may desire." To begin, McGovern invoked his status as an educator and father of five; he also emphasized that 60 percent of South Dakota's school districts fitted the "distressed" category with regard to buildings, teacher salaries, and tax levies. He pointed to Alexander Hamilton's report that ranked "the general interests of learning" as first among the government's concerns "as regards the application of money." He quoted Washington's first message to Congress that nothing was "more deserving your patronage than the promotion of science and literature," and then Jefferson's Notes on Virginia: "An amendment of our Constitution must here come in aid of the public education." The Northwest Ordinance of 1787 also had obliged townships to reserve their 16th section for that purpose. He spoke as well about Andrew Jackson distributing $28 million to the states for educational purposes in 1836 and Lincoln's epochal land-grant college act of 1862. "Federal assistance to public education [was] not new," and it had been continued in the New Deal, wartime training programs, and the GI Bill. And there was "no evidence . . . that time-honored local control of American education had been jeopardized."

He also turned the Cold War argument on its head. He quoted John A. Kennedy, publisher of the *Argus Leader*, who had testified before the subcommittee that the Soviet Union had graduated "two-and-half times as many engineers and scientists as we did in 1956." Then McGovern asked, "Do we build real national defense when we concentrate on bigger and better guns and bombs while permitting the Russians to overtake us in the education of our youth?" Conservative antagonists were untroubled by his conviction, "the diffusion of knowledge is a fundamental responsibility of a democracy." For the rest of the day they drummed three arguments: "this bill is not necessary," it "is intended to give the Federal Government control over the public-school system," and, "if passed, [it] will greatly endanger the future freedom of our people."[41]

Throughout the struggle, the issue of civil rights cut into the bill at its own peculiar angle, as it had done before, in 1956. In that version, Adam Clayton Powell, the Harlem Democrat, had secured an amendment that would require schools to comply with the Supreme Court's recent desegregation ruling in *Brown v. Board of Education* in order to receive federal funds. A coalition of conservative Republicans and southern Democrats, some of whom had voted for the amendment, then defeated the legislation altogether. Liberals and moderates now feared a repetition, even though Powell this time did not insist on his amendment. New York Republican Stuyvesant Wainwright revived it, however—only out of antipathy to the bill, which he would vote against once more.[42]

All the while everyone was waiting for Eisenhower. Opponents recited his statements about the evils of federal control over local affairs and proponents quoted him on the critical shortage of classrooms. "It is a lot easier to 'like Ike' than to learn what it is that Ike likes," McGovern cracked, alluding to parity and the school bill that actually conformed to the administration's wishes. Now, because of Wainwright's maneuver, it needed the president's unqualified support. Yet he balked at muscling copartisans and even canceled a scheduled press conference in order to duck questions about it. On July 25, with 411 members voting, the school construction act collapsed in the House, shy of five votes. When Eisenhower claimed he had done everything possible to help, Cleveland Bailey of West Virginia called him "a lousy liar," and Augustine Kelley, a Pennsylvania Democrat, said, "If he had come out with a strong statement we could have won." Vice President Nixon, too, criticized his boss. This setback and the bookmobile allocation left McGovern incredulous. But the story was about to take a dramatic turn.[43]

On October 4, 1957, the Soviet Union sent the first man-made satellite into space. Barely the diameter of a basketball and weighing 184 pounds, the shiny silver sphere both alarmed and astounded the American people. Commencing its earth orbit just two months after the Russians had launched the world's first intercontinental ballistic missile, "Sputnik" gave birth to fears of a "missile gap." The president rightly denied such a gap existed, but quite in vain. The Democrats readily exploited the military and political implications of the Soviets' achievement. Auspiciously, however, Sputnik jolted the cause of federal aid to education back to life.[44]

McGovern seized the moment. "Not since Pearl Harbor have we been faced with so dramatic a challenge as the Soviet satellite," he told the Chamber of Commerce of Brookings, South Dakota, in November, though not to play the warmonger. "There can be no permanent security for America on a scale of values that spends vastly more on luxuries than we do on the schools and colleges of our country." Because of Russia's strides in science and education, he said to a convention of four thousand teachers in Mitchell, "The long-range struggle between East and West will be won or lost in the classroom." His remarks were part of a barrage of criticism pointing to a "failure of leadership in the White House," although his priority was a bit different from that of most Democrats. Senator Humphrey voiced the more typical call for a missile program "equal to the demands of national security and survival and commensurate with the scope of the Soviet menace." Lyndon Johnson's judgment was similar: "We know that we are faced with some grave problems because of the Russians' Sputniks and their missile advances. Congress is coming back here in a 'can do' mood."[45]

Eisenhower responded with recommendations for a boost in the defense budget and the creation of the National Aeronautics and Space

Administration, but no massive build-up of ICBMs. His ongoing program nonetheless would triple the number of nuclear weapons in the arsenal to 18,000 within three years. He also acknowledged grave shortcomings in federal education policy and the need to train more scientists. At year's end the White House approved a four-year, billion-dollar spending program that involved federal scholarships and matching grants to the states. McGovern liked certain parts of the package. But the single-track emphasis on science and math "violates the concept of educating the whole person," he said to the Washington press corps. "What good is technology if you don't have human understanding?"[46]

On that basis—the "importance of education to human welfare"—he made it his task to plead the case that some of the federal benefits should be extended to college students regardless of their major. On March 6, 1958, he introduced legislation to that end in the form of scholarships, loans, and fellowships as well as grants to local school districts to meet urgent needs, "be it teacher salaries, school construction, or equipment." In a follow-up newsletter to constituents, whereas he agreed that America needed better science education, he urged support for the study of history and foreign languages and other areas of endeavor: "It is fine to talk about accelerating science," but "we must accelerate our understanding of those social, political, and moral forces that will determine whether science is a blessing or the means of our destruction." His argument so impressed Senator J. William Fulbright that he entered the newsletter into the *Congressional Record*, and the South Dakota Education Association published it in its quarterly journal in April.

McGovern's views eventually prevailed within the five-member Subcommittee on Education, though not without a sharp debate between the freshman and Carl Elliott of Alabama. Serving his fifth term, Elliott argued that the urgency of the Soviet challenge demanded that the scholarship provision bestow special consideration to superior students in science and math. McGovern rebutted on two counts. First, he contended that Congress did not have jurisdiction to impose preferences, and that they would violate the tradition of local control of education. Second, he asserted that Americans needed "well educated men and women in all fields of knowledge . . . if we are to survive and flourish," then asked, "who are we to say that a physicist contributes more to the security of the nation than, for example, an elementary teacher, a clergyman, an agriculturalist, a diplomat, or a journalist?" By the time the so-called National Defense Education Act (NDEA) came to the House floor in August, his expertise was widely acknowledged, and Elliott capitulated in favor of an amendment to offer scholarships "on the basis of financial need only."[47]

The subcommittee conducted months of research and heard more than two hundred witnesses. Some of the things members learned about the state of American education in the middle of the American Century were alarming. The nation had a deficiency of properly trained teachers at every level. One-third of elementary school teachers did not hold a bachelor's degree; less than half of the nation's college teachers held doctorates. As for math and the sciences, only one out of three high school students studied chemistry and one in four, physics. Forty-three percent of America's high schools offered no courses in physics, and 20 percent offered neither physics nor chemistry. In contrast, every Russian high school student was required to take four years of both math and science. Then, too, in the "nation of nations" that presumed to lead the Free World, only 15 percent of either high school or college students studied a foreign language; half of its 26,000 high schools offered no foreign language classes of any kind. A larger percentage in high school studied foreign language in 1890 than in 1955.[48]

It was rather fitting, then, that McGovern should begin his remarks on the floor of the House, on August 8, by quoting H. G. Wells: "Human history becomes more and more a race between education and catastrophe." As one of the committee's designated pitchers, he explained how the bill would remedy the foregoing inadequacies. Over the next four years it would provide grants totaling $260 million to the states to make improvements in science, mathematics, and foreign language instruction in the public schools. In the name of national defense, a generous program of loans would be offered at favorable terms to provide $1,000 a year for college students no matter what their fields of concentration, for graduate students in order to meet the next decade's demand for as many as 20,000 qualified college teachers; plus 10,000 scholarships for college students concentrating in math and the sciences.[49]

McGovern highlighted the NDEA's preamble, which both validated shared responsibility for improving the quality and "prohibited Federal control of education." As ever, though, plenty of members challenged that assertion and derided the "Sputnik scare." Charles Brownson, an Indiana Republican, deplored "federal aid to education dressed up in a bright new uniform," seeing the bill as a slippery slope and its champions as disingenuous in the matter of the scholarships. As many as two million students might apply, he said, and then the authors of Title II would come back "asking for another 10,000 scholarships, and another 10,000, and another."[50]

West Virginia's Robert Byrd was among the authors. "We are in a one-game world series, and we cannot afford to lose any more innings," he declared, attributing objections to anti-intellectualism. "America needs more eggheads and fewer fatheads." But Title II drew other criticisms. Iowa Republican Fred Schwengel considered it unfair to reserve scholarships only for science majors. "The most important phase of education is the humanities, and the great leaders in education will tell you that," he argued, not unlike McGovern. Walter Judd of Minnesota deemed scholarships simply not a proper undertaking for the federal government; he thought the funds should be folded into the loan program with no restrictions on what to study. At length, supporters in both parties accepted the latter change, and opposition melted away.[51] Even so, Republicans divided up after reviewing the conference report of the House and Senate two weeks later. "If this bill passes," the conservative Edwin Thomson of Wyoming warned, "it will be indeed a dark day for America," whereas Henry Dixon, a moderate from Utah, believed it would mean "the beginning of a new educational awakening in America."[52]

As McGovern pointed out in his closing remarks, the revised legislation would devote $435 million (out of the total of $887 million) to student loans over the next four years. That would make it possible for countless young people to go to college who otherwise could not afford it, a category that included half of the students who ranked academically among the top 10 percent in the nation. The conference committee also lowered the interest rate on loans to 3 percent, and half of the entire loan would be forgiven for persons who taught school for five years. As for graduate work, the federal government would pay up to $6,600 of the cost over three years—a sum of $82 million in fellowships to alleviate the shortage of teachers at the university level. The committee also added $60 million for vocational schools, provided the states matched those funds, and $300 million to aid in the teaching of math, science, and foreign languages.

"A literal explosion of school-age population is upon us," McGovern went on, referring to the current college enrollments of three million that could triple by 1970; "anti-intellectualism is a luxury America cannot afford in the nuclear age." What, after all, could be said of this legislation? First, "it represents at least one significant answer to the educational challenge of communism." Second, "it preserves local control while extending a helping hand from our National Government." And third, "It seeks to encourage and underwrite scholarly attainment." The National Defense Education Act, he said, thus "seeks to build a better America." A few minutes later the clerk called the roll; 212 members voted yea, 85 voted nay, and 131 (including 57 pairs) did not vote. The House of Representatives had passed the most important legislation of its kind theretofore in American history.[53]

In these exciting last days of the second session of the 85th Congress, McGovern would hardly rest. Concurrent with the climactic debates over the agriculture and education, he played the principal role in several other significant legislative exploits. These included his successful sponsorship of three bills, each of which concerned issues of human welfare and reaffirmed his objective "to build a better America." One aimed to do right by the Crow Creek Sioux Indians of South Dakota, who had been displaced by the construction of the Fort Randall Dam, a 160-foot-high earthen structure across the Missouri River that had created a reservoir 140 miles long. The legislation authorized payment to the tribe of $1.6 million to cover the losses—of land, homes, timber, and wildlife—they suffered due to inundation and to relocation. The bill passed the House on July 24 and the Senate soon thereafter. In mid-August, Congress enacted McGovern legislation authorizing the secretary of health, education, and welfare to furnish printed captions for motion pictures to be loaned to schools for the deaf and other institutions that catered to their needs, much like the talking book program for the blind. "This program will cost very little," he said, "but it will enable the deaf to enjoy some of the benefits available to the rest of us."[54]

Finally, in late August, came the first federal boost to the new field of special education—to afford mentally retarded children the kind of education that a decent life required, by granting assistance to state agencies and universities to improve the numbers of properly trained teachers. But his initiative would never bear its sponsor's name. The minority leadership denied him that credit as retribution for the stand he had taken in a showdown over labor reform the week before. Les Arends, Republican whip from Illinois, thwarted his motion for unanimous consent until John Fogarty, a Rhode Island Democrat and defender of library development, agreed to sponsor an identical bill. "It is regrettable that someone would play politics with handicapped children," McGovern complained after the "splendid" legislation passed. But such were the wages of politics.[55]

The American labor movement underwent tremendous change and disruption in the time of McGovern's ascent. The most salutary change was the merger, in December 1955, of the American Federation of Labor and the Congress of Industrial Organizations. With that, some 90 percent of the country's eighteen million organized workers belonged to a giant federation of unions—in pursuit of safety in the workplace, regular wage increases, and family health insurance and old-age pensions. Yet on the dark side, a wave of corruption had engulfed a small segment of organized labor—the worst perpetrator being its single largest union, the Teamsters, led by the notorious Dave Beck and Jimmy Hoffa. A Senate investigating committee held a series of sensational hearings in 1957–58, which the nation followed closely. The result was the Kennedy-Ives Act, an effort to correct the abuses through greater democratic accountability. Favored by the AFL-CIO and public opinion, the bill passed the Senate, 88 to 1, in June 1958. But not until August did Speaker Rayburn place the bill on the House calendar, too late into the session for the Committee on Education and Labor to hold hearings on it. Republicans accused Democrats of purposeful delay. Only by suspending the rules, a procedure that barred amendments and required a two-thirds majority, could the House pass the bill before Congress adjourned.[56]

McGovern had an interest in the legislation, and he volunteered to lead the case for suspension, along with his friends Frank Thompson of New Jersey and Stewart Udall of Arizona. His influence with Rayburn was decisive in getting it to the floor. By then, however, the measure had become highly politicized; midterm congressional campaigns were virtually under way. McGovern's opponents in South Dakota already were saying he was a stooge of the AFL-CIO. "I thought that this bill would dramatize my true position which was one of independence of either management or labor," he subsequently told a Senate staffer. But passage of Kennedy-Ives would rob the GOP of one of its few serviceable issues. Although virtually all Republicans in the Senate (including Karl Mundt and Francis Case) had supported the bill, in the House they now began to unite with southern Democrats, the US Chamber of Commerce, and the National Association of Manufacturers to block it because the measure lacked overt union-busting features while it imposed certain constraints on employers. The arch anticommunist Clare Hoffman pronounced it "worse than no bill at all" and "merely a cover-up for politicians of both parties." Likewise, Jimmy Hoffa opposed the reform—but because it threatened the power of labor bosses, its main purpose.[57]

The majority of Democrats considered the bill workable, if imperfect. It would keep corrupt union officials from "prey[ing] with impunity on the American workingman and the American public," McGovern argued. He professed to be "at a loss to understand the tremendous objections that are being raised now by . . . people that endorsed this measure" in the Senate. The "extremists on both sides" were the trouble. The choice before the House was whether to "act boldly in an area desperately in need of legislative attention . . . [or] slump into the depths of inaction." The *Daily Republic* defended the bill as "the best possible . . . that could be gotten at this time" and suggested there were "those who would like to place the labor movement in a vise . . . and those who for political or other selfish reasons would like to see no labor legislation at all." After rounds of debate in mid-August, the question of suspending the rules was answered with 190 yeas and 198 nays (77 percent of the Republicans among the latter). "McGovern fought the good fight," said the *Daily Republic*, "and he is deserving of acclaim of all of those citizens who wanted to see a reasonable and realistic labor reform bill." That was maybe true. But McGovern was privately "very grateful" at least to have gotten a roll call vote in advance of the fall election "even though the measure did go down to defeat."[58]

"In the seed-time of our Republic, young men carved out stunning careers in public affairs," *Esquire* magazine observed in September 1958 in an article profiling fifteen rising Democrats and Republicans in their twenties and thirties. Among these "Bright Young Men in Politics" was a first term congressman, "both 'an egghead' and a war hero, who had won the Distinguished Flying Cross." Once he came home from Europe, continued *Esquire*, he had earned a PhD in history, taught college, and then, in a Republican state, had rebuilt "a moribund Democratic party virtually from scratch." On Capitol Hill he was well known "for his clear discussions of farm and foreign policy, and his interest in education is unflagging." It was all proof positive that "even in historically solid Republican or Democratic bailiwicks, voters today are more willing to cross party lines, if an attractive candidate (like McGovern) comes along."[59]

His inclusion on such a list was a proper valedictory for an exceptional Washington debut. Although the breakthrough education bill was the product of the cooperation of many lawmakers, no one was more responsible for its final progressive form than McGovern. His work on agriculture also set him apart from most of his forty-three fellow freshmen; many senior Democrats considered him the head of his class. And that did not begin to account for his three sponsorships brought to fruition or for his forthright criticism of Eisenhower foreign policy. So far, South Dakotans seemed willing to consider that on its own merits—in part because of his good work on farm issues. In all, he had made an excellent record on which to run for reelection, and then some. It was not without reason that Republicans worried about finding someone who could beat the upstart come November.

10 THE APOSTLE OF AGRICULTURE, EDUCATION, AND PEACE

The first choice for Congress of practically every East River Republican was a reluctant warrior who had taken not quite a year to make up his mind. Yet once he did, party members across the state breathed a collective sigh, not the least Senator Mundt. The candidate was Joe Foss, the current governor and one of the most celebrated heroes of World War II. Since the age of twelve, Foss had been inspired by Charles Lindbergh's solo flight across the Atlantic in 1927. The Sioux Falls farm boy wanted to become a flier; he succeeded on a historic scale. As a marine fighter pilot in the South Pacific, he shot down twenty-six enemy planes, a record. For that and other displays of "indomitable fighting spirit," he was awarded the Bronze Star, the Silver Star, and the Purple Heart. In May 1943 President Roosevelt presented the Congressional Medal of Honor to him at the White House. *Life* magazine put Foss on its cover and the Office of War Information sent him on a triumphal war-bond tour. Factory workers, movie stars, and politicians alike treated him as their own. In the estimation of journalist Lowell Thomas, Joe was "the American ace of aces," "the perfect fighting man,"—"Tall, handsome, modest . . . the embodiment of the frontiersman of old."[1]

In the world of politics, he had shown enough natural skill to win election twice to the state legislature and to the governorship in 1954 and in 1956. Although reasonably popular, the cigar-chomping Foss did not always wear well. To many South Dakotans, he seemed a bit too colorful, even cocky, and some questioned his qualifications for office or felt he traded on his war record. In 1956 his margin of victory had declined, and his second term coincided with a marked increase in property taxes as well as in marital problems in his personal life. His wife, June, whose hero was Albert Schweitzer, did not like politics; she was displeased when Joe set family considerations aside to run for Congress. Then, too, like all farm-state Republicans, he would have to cope with the backlash against Ezra Taft Benson's grim reaper policies—the tougher still because Democrats were calling an ongoing economic downturn "the Eisenhower recession." Nonetheless, Foss was optimistic. The state's entire Republican establishment, not to mention the White House, would be behind him. And George McGovern was a fluke.[2]

Since the summer of 1957, long before they knew Foss would parachute in, a small corps within the South Dakota GOP had begun sniping at the incumbent. State chairman Glen Rhodes wondered in print "who furnished the money for Mr. McGovern's Camel Caravan in the Middle East last spring," and charged him with "serious absenteeism." The editor of the *Rapid City Journal*, too, insinuated a sojourn "at the expense of the taxpayers." But the Republican *Sioux Falls Argus Leader* joined the *Mitchell Daily Republic* and House Majority Leader John McCormack to refute the attacks as "ill-conceived and reprehensible." Said McCormack, "I have never known a more conscientious member than Mr. McGovern," and the *Daily Republic* reminded readers that the American Christian Palestine Committee had awarded him the travel fellowship. The *Argus Leader* hinted that an unnamed party boss had prodded Rhodes to go after McGovern and "shoot blindly in his general direction." The fusillade subsided due to the shield of editors who wished the young man well, one noting, "the people of this state are dedicated to fair play and decency in politics."[3]

The charges resumed more insidiously the next summer. The campaign of 1958 had yet to commence when Glenn Martz, an associate of Karl Mundt and editor of "The Low Down," a Washington-based farmer's newsletter, reported that McGovern was a sponsor of "a communist-front known as the American Peace Crusade." McGovern then filed a $250,000 libel suit against Martz. "I am getting sick and tired of being forced to prove that I am a loyal American every time an election comes around," he said. This variant of McCarthyism was based on an incident dating back to 1951 in which his name had appeared on the Peace Crusade's petitions without his permission, and he had protested to the group in writing. In July, on behalf of the House Un-American Activities Committee, Morgan Moulder, a Missouri Democrat, detailed on the House floor the fraudulent nature of Martz's accusation, describing McGovern as a "patriotic" and "outstanding member of Congress." The chair of the Democratic National Committee called upon Foss to repudiate the smear. McGovern fingered Senator Mundt in September for having instigated Martz and for having talked Foss into running for Congress. "What really worries them is that thousands of members of their own party voted for me in 1956," he asserted.[4]

"Karl Mundt has been firing the shots so far, and Foss has not yet opened his attack," George wrote to Arthur Link on September 10. "I hope we can begin a campaign on the issues soon." A day later, Joe Foss and Glen Rhodes together unveiled the campaign issue that the Republicans had divined their most potent—the depredations of organized labor. "South Dakota should know that George McGovern received at least $4,000 from out of state labor unions in 1956 and that he voted as the labor bosses wanted in Congress," said Rhodes. To an audience in Miller, Governor Foss declared that his opponent had supported Walter Reuther, president of the United Auto Workers and the vice president of the AFL-CIO, more often than he had President Eisenhower. The next day, in Sioux Falls, the rivals sat on the same stage. Foss acknowledged receiving $300 in out-of-state contributions before alluding to labor's gifts to his adversary in 1956. "How much was it, George?" he asked. "$4400," McGovern replied flatly.[5]

Few Democrats doubted that this strategy was the brainchild of Karl Mundt, who never stopped railing against the labor movement. To cite but one of countless examples, on a CBS news program in August, he blamed the shortcomings of the Kennedy-Ives bill on Walter Reuther and accused "his political henchmen" of invading rural states to stump for Democrats. As the ranking minority member on the Senate "rackets committee," Mundt was obsessed with Reuther and habitually referred to him as a socialist. But the formidable Reuther was a member in good standing of the anticommunist left, and he had helped to purge the CIO of communists in 1949. Admired for his honesty and resourcefulness, he usually supported Democrats. When called before Mundt's committee in April 1958, he easily bested the senator. Even the *Argus Leader*'s editor found "no trace of graft" about him and observed, "if the U.S.

economy has nothing more to fear than men such as Reuther, I'm not too much worried about it."[6] In contrast to his antipathy to the UAW president, Mundt treated Republican Jimmy Hoffa amiably when the committee examined him. During one of their exchanges the senator practically led the Teamsters president by the hand in drawing invidious comparisons between his own political philosophy and that of Reuther's.[7]

Indubitably, George McGovern was guilty of sympathy for organized labor as well as of accepting its support. Just three months into his tenure, he gave a commemorative floor speech for the forty-third anniversary of the Ludlow massacre, depicting the impact of unchecked power on the lives of thousands of immigrant miners in the Colorado coalfields. His intention was to honor the sacrifices of families "who fought for the dignity and freedom of labor that we enjoy today" and to remind Americans that not all labor leaders were Jimmy Hoffa and his lieutenant, Dave Beck. He based his remarks on his dissertation, which had touted "the vital relationship between a strong, healthy labor movement and effective political democracy." He also supposed his reelection potentially depended on organized labor in South Dakota. Even though its numbers were not overly impressive—about 12,000 out of a voting population of 300,000—they were enough to tip the balance. Throughout his term, McGovern spoke at various union gatherings—the International Union of Electrical Workers, the Textile Workers of America, and the Farmers and Workers Conference, and so on—and in the summer of 1958 he took up the cause of Kennedy-Ives, "a good bill" that he later admitted was "important to my own campaign in the fall."[8]

Whether any of this justified what the *Daily Republic* dubbed "gutter-type politics" was another matter. In order to discredit McGovern, for example, Foss attempted to capitalize on public outrage against labor racketeers by "stooping to guilt-by-association tactics." Moreover, the *Daily Republic* highlighted a Senate study of the 1956 elections that revealed that the nation's largest oil companies had contributed $344,000 to Republican candidates but only $14,650 to Democrats. If Republicans were unconcerned about that, then surely there was no peril in a labor political action committee giving a small amount to "this patriotic and religious young man." As for Reuther's "must" agenda, several commentators pointed out that it included legislation for a family farm parity program, an inquiry into the causes behind the "price/cost" gouge, and an expansion of social security for the disabled. McGovern in any case resented the implication that anyone "who accepts campaign support from working men and women is a tool of corrupt labor bosses." More than once he asserted that the Kennedy-Ives Act "would have put the Becks and the Hoffas out of business," whereas Foss had praised representatives who had voted to kill it. "Dave Beck and Jimmy Hoffa gave their donations to Republicans," McGovern added, "not to me, or to my party." (His aide Bob Nelson liked to quote Mundt's description of Kennedy-Ives as "legislation of which we can all be reasonably proud." But, "when he saw McGovern working for its passage in the House, he said it was a terrible bill.") In October, the governor alleged that labor leaders were sending paid organizers into South Dakota to canvass for Democrats. That was "utter nonsense," McGovern told the Mitchell Chamber of Commerce. "Mr. Foss and his sponsor, Karl Mundt, seem to think the best way to win this election is to . . . arouse hatred and fear between the farmer, the workingman, and the businessman."[9]

If Joe Foss's main strategy was to run against Walter Reuther, it was not nearly as effective as McGovern running against the secretary of agriculture. "My opponent has spent most of his time . . . talking about the dangers of labor leaders, but he has had nothing to say about the number one danger to farmers . . . Ezra Taft Benson," he repeated in town after town. "Agriculture is the number one issue in the 1958 congressional campaign." Then he would review the record since 1953: Prices for crops were down 16 percent, farm purchasing power was down 29 percent, agricultural surpluses had tripled, and 600,000 families had been forced off the land. "A vote for my opponent is a vote for Benson" was his pet refrain.[10]

On October 7, George and Joe shared the stage before an audience of thousands at the state corn-picking contest (the event where Benson was egged the year before). The secretary's policies had "cost the American farmer the equivalent of 1 1/2 years in income," the congressman figured. As a remedy to constant reductions in price supports, he laid out his own plan to bring family farm income in line with other groups in the economy, expand resources for rural loans and crop insurance, and accelerate irrigation and conservation projects. He also wanted to use more of the surpluses to feed hungry people at home and abroad. For his part, Foss told his rival to stop calling him a Bensonite; he was neither for nor against the man. "I regret my opponent has taken up the Benson line in almost every detail," McGovern replied, and the *Daily Republic* marveled, "Joe Foss after six years of Benson can't make up his mind which side he is on."[11]

Education was McGovern's best issue after agriculture. "I am opposed to federal aid to education," Foss had told a Republican gathering on August 22, declining to explain why, except, "For every dollar we get from the federal government, we also get $10 worth of instructions on how to use it." McGovern struck back in debate. The governor not only had "permitted our school districts to roll up a debt of $25 million, while South Dakota sinks to the bottom in terms of state assistance," but also had let "our aged and handicapped citizens languish under one of the poorest state programs in the nation." During another debate, at Brookings, McGovern explained the importance of the provision for low-interest loans in the National Defense Education Act in helping worthy youth go to college. Foss reaffirmed his state rights dogma. "They dictate where to build and how to build your schools and you take it or leave it," he said, not coming off very well for it. A week later, McGovern accused him of apathy. "Never before in the history of our country has education been so clearly on trial as it is today," he said and pointed out that South Dakota ranked forty-sixth out of the forty-eight states in school assistance, regardless of the hike in state taxes that the Republican legislature had ratified.[12]

By mid-October, it was apparent to most voters that the candidates were not evenly matched. Too often Foss was ill prepared or nervous while the articulate McGovern seemed to know everything there was to know about agriculture, education, and even labor. This made for an odd problem. "I was worried when George and Joe were going to have a big debate at Brookings," Eleanor recalled. "Joe just wasn't well-informed on the issues and George had to be so careful not to show him up too much." Indeed, the debate became known as the "slaughter at Brookings." George's manner was courteous, but there was no hiding the truth that the two men were in different leagues. Then, on October 15, the *Sioux Falls Argus Leader* published data from an extensive survey. In the First Congressional District a substantial majority favored McGovern over Foss—55.8 to 42 percent, with farmers preferring Mitchell's favorite son by 71 to 29 percent, and town dwellers choosing likewise, 51 to 46. City folks bucked the broader trend, giving Foss 58 percent to McGovern's 37. But a polling question about party affiliation produced the most unsettling news for Foss. Although 61 percent of the state's population belonged to the GOP, 34.8 percent of the Republicans of East River said they intended to vote for McGovern. (About 26 percent of them also backed the Democratic gubernatorial candidate, Ralph Herseth.)[13]

With only three weeks to go, Foss continued to complain that he was running against "eastern labor bosses." But letters to the editor started to criticize him; one considered it "strange that 'labor' is one of the main issues . . . [in] the most agricultural state in the union." Then, too, his neutrality on the Benson program impressed no one.[14] Foss campaign strategists thus decided to resurrect the patriot's issue—on two counts. First, they distorted McGovern's vote against a version of an internal security bill that would have denied government employees the right to confront an accuser and to examine the charges against them. McGovern forthrightly clarified his intention "to protect the legal rights of American citizens," but the soft-on-communism implication was nonetheless disturbing. Second, the Republicans enlisted the aid of Glenn Martz, whom McGovern was suing and now identified as Karl Mundt's former publicity agent. "This man is flooding the rural areas of the State with letters charging me with un-American activities," he told the citizens of Clear Lake. A few days later, Republican campaign workers were seen distributing "a little scandal sheet" in Sioux Falls that alleged that McGovern had sponsored communist organizations.[15]

"I feel a Congressman should be firm and not weak when it comes to dealing with Communists at home or abroad," Foss insisted. For some, that was not a worthy explanation. On October 26, Drew Pearson's "Washington Merry-Go-Round" came to McGovern's defense. The syndicated columnist did not mention Foss by name. Instead, he laid responsibility at the door of "the chief surviving McCarthyite in the Senate" for arranging the massive mailings of Martz's "Lowdown." By other means, too, Karl Mundt had cast suspicion on the loyalty of the Democrat most likely to challenge him in 1960, Pearson concluded; politicians were watching "to see whether McCarthyism still pays." That weekend, in a major address in Sioux Falls, Richard Nixon cautioned a big coliseum crowd about the possibility of "radicals" among Democrats taking over the House. Foss deserved to win, the vice president averred, because he stood for "peace with honor and without surrender." President Eisenhower put it less crudely in a public endorsement four days later: "I know you will bring hard realism to our overriding task—the building of a just, enduring peace." Mundt continued to tell audiences they could sleep soundly where "internal security is concerned" by voting for Foss.[16]

McGovern had endorsements, too. Sam Rayburn predicted "he will rise to a high place in the Councils of the House," and majority leader John McCormack christened him "A People's Congressman." Hubert

Humphrey came home to tell his neighbors that no one in Congress had "worked more diligently for a good agricultural program for family farmers" than George, and that a Foss victory "would be interpreted as a vote for Benson's policies." Jim Wright, Fort Worth's rising star, and the charismatic Frank Church of Idaho stumped for McGovern in October. No other representative, Congressman Wright declared, had "earned more universal respect in so short a time." Senator Church, after denouncing the GOP's "irresponsible brand of opposition," lauded McGovern's as "the most successful record of all 43 new members of the House."[17] Finally, the *Daily Republic* weighed in with "McGovern Has Earned a Second Term." Building a statesman's reputation in less than two years, the editorial said, he had expanded educational opportunity, defended the family farm against Benson, forced the House to vote on labor legislation, and otherwise campaigned on "vital issues"—the need to preserve small businesses and close up tax loopholes for big corporations; to respond to the concerns of the elderly; to support the United Nations; and to feed "the world's hungry as a defense measure and a means of using our huge farm surpluses." In contrast, Foss had based his campaign on the "big lie." It had backfired on Lovre in 1956; it "should backfire this year."[18]

In the home stretch McGovern ran several newspaper ads, including one bannered, "McGovern Works for Peace and a Strong National Defense." It underscored his Distinguished Flying Cross and his plan "to use our food abundance as an instrument of foreign policy to eliminate hunger and poverty abroad which breed communism and war." He followed up with an ad quoting the *Esquire* profile and, in two others, spelled out his stands on national security and labor. "We must not permit our fear of Communism to lead us into adopting the very methods of those whom we scorn," went one. The other observed: "The overwhelming majority of the leaders and members of labor are upright citizens. I welcome their support. Workers, businessmen, and farmers are dependent upon each other."[19]

On the Sunday before election, the *Argus Leader* published its final polling survey. McGovern's percentage was unchanged at 55.5. Foss had picked up two points, bringing him to 44 percent but still trailing by eleven. Curiously, among farmers he had improved his position by nine points, raising him to 38, to McGovern's 62 percent. But Foss's standing in the cities suffered an eight-point drop while McGovern's had shot up twelve points, to 49.4, nearly tying the governor's 50.6 percent. Some 31 percent of Republican voters still preferred McGovern.

If this was not enough to confound Foss, fortune took one last crack—during a live, election-eve television broadcast that turned into a 1950s sitcom. Surrounded by his wife and children and the family dog, he was delivering his spiel from a teleprompter when his seven-year-old son suddenly joined in, reading the lines just a few words behind his father. The governor stopped. He decided to introduce the dog and, as he patted it on the head, it snapped at him. Foss turned to his wife and said, "Well, honey, what do you think?" "Think about what, Joe?" she replied vacantly. "The election, honey," he pleaded, "The election."[20]

A few days later, McGovern reported to Arthur Link: "The campaign was a bitterly fought, rough and tumble affair. Mundt, Foss and company spent an enormous sum of money for a rural state election. Nixon went all out for Foss in his S.D. visit. But in spite of what seemed like a great conspiracy of the press, money, and TV, the people gave me a 14,000 vote majority, which compares favorably to the 10,000 margin of 1956."[21]

November 4 proved to be a great day for Democrats everywhere. The turnout in South Dakota broke the record high for midterm elections. McGovern triumphed over Foss, 107,202 votes to 93,388, and Ralph Herseth beat his opponent by 132,761 to 125,520 to become the state's first Democratic governor since 1937. Likewise, the party took several other executive offices and gained control of the state senate, 20 seats to 15. The Republicans held on to the lower house, 43 to 32, as Democrats increased their numbers by five. Nobody any longer doubted McGovern's assertion, "Most people recognize there are now two strong, evenly balanced political organizations in South Dakota." Indeed, newspaper editors across the state voted the Democratic victory as the top news story of the year. Many observers would have agreed with George's friend, Gilbert Fite, the noted agricultural historian at the University of Oklahoma, who wrote: "The state owes you a great debt of gratitude for having rebuilt the Democratic Party." Competitive politics had come at last to South Dakota.[22]

Among reasons why, Governor-elect Herseth suggested that a "determined Democratic party reinforced by liberal independent Republicans ready for a change made this possible." McGovern agreed, citing their opponents' "lack of concern toward educational problems." A teachers' organization had endorsed him because of "his understanding of the challenge to the educational system," while Foss wanted to shut down the state teachers college at Springfield. The GOP also had failed in its exertions to coil the issues of labor and "right to work" laws around the Democrats' necks. The *Daily Republic* stressed the GOP's "desperation tactics." McGovern was an "intelligent, hard-working and religious young war hero," and the opposition pictured him "as a dupe of the Reds, a stooge of labor bosses and so on ad nauseam." South Dakotans "proved anew that they can think for themselves." As for "the mastermind" behind the GOP campaign, Mundt was the "big loser."[23]

On the morning after, McGovern thanked the people for their "heartening vote of confidence." This referendum had demonstrated that a significant bloc of Republican farmers believed he was on their side and that he had done as much as any mortal could have to help them against the onslaught of Benson's flexible price supports. No less important, Democrats and Republicans alike knew that McGovern had played a central role in bringing about federal legislation that would make it possible for their sons and daughters to go to college. They knew, too, that Foss had discouraged such initiatives. As for big labor and the communist menace, in the end these issues did not amount to much more than what McGovern said they were—distractions from the things that really mattered to most people in South Dakota. The Republicans had hardly nicked him.[24]

The trend in national politics abetted McGovern's victory. Indeed, the sweep exceeded the Democrats' fondest hopes. Whereas the previous composition was 49 to 47 in the Senate and 234 to 201 in the House, the party of Roosevelt had swelled its majorities to 64 to 34 and 283 to 153. And Democrats now held 34 out of 48 governorships. The party of Eisenhower thus had suffered a stunning rebuke. One of the leading factors behind it was farm policy. In one agricultural state after another—in California, Minnesota, Nevada, Ohio, Utah, and Wyoming— voters ousted incumbent Republican senators. Moreover, Democrats won nine Republican-held governorships—including those in California, Nebraska, New Mexico, Ohio, Wisconsin, Wyoming, and South Dakota—while keeping Michigan and Minnesota. In six midwestern states the Democrats seized a total of twenty seats in the House of Representatives that Republicans had held for years. Other issues were at work, too. Sputnik had diluted confidence in the administration, revealing apparent deficiencies in national defense and American education and symbolizing the president's "complacency." The recession and rising unemployment revealed shortcomings in the GOP's economic policies, while antagonism to organized labor provided a lesson in how not to woo the union vote. Finally, the elections buoyed the Democrats' prospects for capturing the White House in 1960 as well as McGovern's for replacing Mundt. "It looks as though King Karl is already campaigning," wrote Gilbert Fite. "He is obviously scared stiff and will undoubtedly spend a lot of time in South Dakota the next two years."[25]

Dwight Eisenhower later claimed 1958 was the "worst year" of his political life. His own analysis of the greatest midterm landslide since the New Deal told him the electorate preferred "spenders," his euphemism for proponents of bigger government. Even so, he did not interpret the returns as a personal repudiation. For six years he had practiced government by coalition and veto, and he expected to do so again. Among the new total of 347 Democrats, he could depend on a hundred conservative southerners in the House and as many as thirty in the Senate to join their Republican counterparts to check the progressives of both parties on certain issues. In the 86th Congress, as before, his copartisans fell mainly into two categories. The GOP's liberals mostly came from the Northeast, its conservatives from the Middle West and (ever more) the Far West. These contending wings each set their sights on gaining control of the party by 1960, not knowing they had entered upon a struggle that would go on for the next twenty years.[26]

The Democrats now divided into three categories. First were representatives and senators from the sixteen border and southern states, many of whom reviled the big government legacy of the New Deal and bristled at the mention of civil rights. They accounted for over half of the party's electoral strength. Next in number came moderate Democrats of the large urban centers of the North representing ethnic and working-class groups that still venerated Roosevelt. Lastly and smallest was a rising generation of somewhat more liberal reformers from the West as well as the North whose ranks had been augmented by the election. Seeking new approaches to the Cold War and civil rights and other social issues, they formed a "Democratic Study Group" that aimed to redefine liberalism beyond the bread-and-butter issues of the New Deal era and to counter the influence of more senior and of southern Democrats. McGovern inclined naturally toward these progressives (who numbered about a hundred) and joined their strategy sessions. In any event, Sam Rayburn, like Lyndon Johnson in the Senate, would continue to guide Democrats straight down the middle; their watchwords remained compromise and moderation and, regarding the White House, cooperation, even though Eisenhower would tend toward more conservative positions in his final quarter.[27]

McGovern would go along with his elders even as he questioned some things. Although he respected the president, he was far more critical of the "New Look" in American foreign policy than the Democratic leadership was. In dealing with the communist world, the strategy of amassing thousands of nuclear weapons to the point of (in George Kennan's words) "grotesque redundancy" and relying on the threat of "massive retaliation" struck the congressman as just shy of insanity. In contrast, Johnson and Kennedy (Humphrey less so) berated Ike for not spending enough on missiles. The emphasis on military assistance to despotic governments in the Third World was equally objectionable to someone who considered hunger and disease as "the very roots of strife" and the United Nations as "the greatest instrument for peace in the world today." Yet McGovern knew that the administration's foreign policy had not diverged fundamentally from Truman's. Nor had its domestic policy. Ike called himself a "dynamic conservative," which was another way of saying he embraced Schlesinger's notion of the "Vital Center."[28] He had appointed the first secretary of health, education, and welfare, increased the minimum wage by one-third, expanded Social Security coverage for millions of senior citizens, and had signed the National Defense Education Act. In the form of the interstate highway system, he had launched the single greatest public works project in American history. Thus the first Republican president since Hoover had acted to consolidate the New Deal as much as any Democratic president might have done, and perhaps quite a bit more.

Where the president fell short was on the farm. Evidently Eisenhower just did not get it, and Ezra Taft Benson did not care. But agriculture was a force as powerful as any other in American politics; as the midterm harvest demonstrated, progressive Democrats were the better workers of those fields. McGovern put both heart and substance into his proposals, such as the family farm legislation, to enhance his state's livelihood. He was becoming especially adroit at integrating agriculture into his own nascent program and plying its intrinsic connection to both the New Deal and his concerns about American foreign policy. And progressive agrarianism was proving good for the party. At least a few conservative Republicans, including Karl Mundt, who very much liked Ike, were starting to wonder how he could still like Secretary Benson.

––––––––––––––

On December 10, 1958, 175 members of the Kiwanis, Lions, and Rotary groups of Mitchell assembled at the Masonic Temple to give their congressman a send-off. He had just returned from a NATO conference in Paris for which Rayburn had handpicked him. Upon explaining to these leading citizens how NATO acted as a deterrent to war, he issued a call for a "complete re-examination of American foreign policy." His summons had little to do with military alliances. Rather, he advocated an exchange program between America and the communist bloc—of goods and ideas, technical knowledge, and people—to improve mutual understanding and "increase our chances of maintaining the peace." The plan embraced two premises—that the "obstacles on the road to peace . . . cannot be removed by military power alone" and that "constructive use of our surplus food and fiber . . . will win more friends than giving away guns to the poor people of the world." A day later, he addressed a gathering of 150 Davison County farmers who tied their criticism of Secretary Benson to criticism of foreign policy. "We need more surplus agricultural commodities overseas and less military aid," they said. This was music to McGovern's ears. It was also "Food for Peace." And the progressive agrarian was going to conjoin it to his responsibility to agriculture upon his return to Washington for his second term.[29]

On January 15, he won appointment to the Agriculture Committee despite a record sixty applications for the nine vacancies that the political earthquake in the farm belt had created. The plum was yet another sign that South Dakota's junior congressman enjoyed the patronage of the Speaker of the House. Moreover, on the session's first day McGovern introduced legislation to stabilize family farm income. His bill would curtail certain abuses of the Soil Bank, which he deplored as a terrible substitute for a parity program. Many others held it responsible for the cracks in the farm bloc's bipartisanship. Benson's conservation reserve was "a dagger aimed at the heart of every farm family and the communities that depend on the farmer," he said, and a bonanza for "the absentee speculator" who could pick up whole farms "for investment purposes and put them in the Soil Bank."[30]

Increasingly, though, McGovern jousted with the reality of modern times—the plain fact that fewer farmers were producing greater volumes of agriculture than ever before and on fewer acres. In 1945 farmers could coax thirty-five to forty bushels of corn out of an acre; by 1960 that fair yield had doubled. As for wheat, World War II's final year marked an output of 1.1 billion bushels on sixty-five million acres; yet that volume increased to 1.3 billion as Eisenhower was leaving office and on fifteen million fewer acres. Agricultural production also now required only about half the labor as in 1945, or about ten million work-hours as opposed to nineteen million. These figures contained other portents: a decline in the number of farms from six million down to 3.9 million, with an increase in their average size to 300 acres, up from 175; and a halving of the number of people who farmed or did agricultural work—from thirty million in wartime to 15.8 million by 1960. At that point, 13 percent of the nation's farmers owned one-third of all the farmland and produced nearly 52 percent of all of America's market agriculture.[31]

The foregoing data suited Ezra Taft Benson just fine; his regime of flexible supports helped to bring them about. Payments should be "insurance against disaster," not an income supplement, he believed, and only market forces, not a high parity policy, would curb overproduction. The lower the supports, the smaller the surpluses, he argued. Ostensibly seeking efficiency, his Soil Bank favored the larger operations. On the one hand, a wheat farmer could receive $19.80 for retiring an acre of land for the year; a southern cotton grower could do the same, and receive $40 for the acre. But problems abounded. As McGovern pointed out, only about 125,000 of the nation's farm families participated in the program. The majority of farm families did not have enough land to set any aside and still make a go of it. According to Ag Committee member Tom Abernathy, the average cotton farmer in Mississippi was able to retire thirteen acres. On the other hand, an investor or a large operator could put an entire five-hundred-acre farm into the Soil Bank reserve for several years in a row and make a bundle. Again, that was okay with Secretary Benson, though politically it did not help when he coldly declared that smaller farmers should get out of the business if they could not make do on lower supports. Fairness was not his responsibility. Yet the evidence was slight that his policies had improved anything; they had failed utterly to dent the excessive supply and they continued to upset as many Republicans as Democrats.[32]

Scarcely a week went by that McGovern did not call attention to these manifold misfortunes. "In the 1952–57 period, farmers absorbed an aggregate loss of nearly $18 billion in income," he lamented to constituents in his first "Washington Report" of the session. "Four million farm folks have left the land, and 600,000 farms have disappeared." In the meantime, farmers had attempted to offset the dwindling price supports with greater production, federal stocks of commodities thus had quadrupled, and per capita farm income had fallen to half that of nonfarm per capita income. Then, in February 1959, Benson announced a cut in payments to 60 percent of parity on major feed grains. (In South Dakota this would mean a loss of $16 million to farmers.) The secretary was "seeking to demolish the entire farm program," McGovern charged, and colleagues introduced legislation to reverse the cuts while he offered an amendment to an appropriations bill to reduce salaries in Benson's office by 60 percent.[33]

In the spring McGovern sponsored new legislation to address "the pileup of wheat surpluses." Within the fifty-five-million-acre national allotment, wheat farmers could choose via referendum to reduce acreage by 25 percent in exchange for 90 percent parity on the remainder. After two years, his plan would bring wheat production down by 480 million bushels and, notwithstanding the high supports, cost half a billion dollars less than the Soil Bank's provisions for the grain. It was "a good solid wheat bill," he remonstrated when the White House vetoed it.[34] He exerted himself again in the passing of a measure to divest the secretary of his powers over the loan-making authority of the Rural Electrification Administration, which Ike vetoed too. "Mr. Benson speaks to the President and our efforts are killed off," McGovern cried in a sharp speech after the House fell four votes shy of an override. "We might just as well recognize that this administration is not going to approve strong legislation designed to help the farmer."[35]

What bothered him most was Benson's apparent lack of appreciation for the tradition of the family farm, for the unique combination of individualism and cooperative values that characterized it. As historian Gilbert Fite once wrote, the family farm was "to many Americans a symbol of democratic government, social stability, and agricultural abundance . . . and any threat to it seemed to many people an attack on the nation itself." To be sure, McGovern understood that one could not build a future on Jefferson's sentiment that "those who labour in the earth are the chosen people of God." Agriculture was in the throes of tremendous change. But Benson's policies were doing nothing to ease the transition.[36] To innumerable congressmen, senators, and governors the preservation of the family farm was about a living, interdependent community, something of vital importance to regional economies. In March 1960 the governors of ten midwestern states (many of them newly elected Democrats) gathered in St. Paul as a bloc to endorse the new family farm income legislation sponsored by McGovern and nineteen other members of the House. Governor Orville Freeman told the *New York Times* that the annual income of 63 percent of Minnesota's farms had fallen below $2,000. Wisconsin's governor Gaylord Nelson explained that the average dairy farmer in his state had to get by on one-third the income of that of the country's average family. And Governor Ralph Brooks of Nebraska said bluntly, "The farmers are going bankrupt." Seven other governors shared the apprehension "that small towns relying on farm customers were dying." Meanwhile, the *Daily Republic* observed, "until a new Secretary of Agriculture provides the leadership," nothing was going to get better.[37]

Of course, the congressman who venerated the works of Franklin Roosevelt and Henry Wallace and who often rode up to Capitol Hill with Hubert Humphrey grasped the implications of the impact of industrial capitalism, science, and technology on agriculture. He also studied it through the lens of American foreign policy and beheld a wider range of possibilities. Already he had been pressing for an expansion of the pilot food stamp program and stronger dietary standards for the school lunch program. Improved nutrition for millions of needy Americans meant an increase in consumption, and that would help erode the mountains of stored food. Also, just three weeks into the session, he introduced his "Food for Peace Resolution," in effect a critical review of the Agricultural Trade Development and Assistance Act of 1954, known as Public Law 480. The Eisenhower administration had conceived of this legislation as a way to dispose of the agricultural surpluses the nation had been amassing since World War II. Because the accent was "surplus disposal," recipient countries had come to regard it with suspicion. As conditions for obtaining the food, Greece, for example, was pressured into accepting tobacco while cotton was forced on India. Critics had branded PL 480 a Republican "dumping" program. Democrats, notably McGovern and Humphrey, decried the administration's narrow construction and the absence of any overtly humanitarian component.[38]

In his resolution, McGovern struck a tone of idealism and pragmatism. Citing the near cessation of the barter program in 1957 and a sharp drop in exports shipped under the law in 1958, he pointed out that American storage bins soon would be bulging with a record carryover of 1.3 billion bushels of wheat (double the annual domestic requirement) as well as comparable stocks of corn, rice, and dairy products. "Here are the instruments with which we can build a sound foreign economic policy to promote peace, stability and free institutions," he exclaimed. Instead of spending $1 billion for storage each year, would it not be wiser to use those resources to feed the world's hungry and help to build more just societies? Eisenhower's "cautious, reluctant approach" was pitiful. PL 480 required "leadership which will stimulate a spirit of adventure and a sense of dedication in all persons connected with the program."[39]

By April 1959 he and Humphrey had crafted new legislation to transform PL 480 from a temporary expedient into a creative, permanent enterprise, replete with a special administrator and officially the new name, "Food for Peace." Stressing humanitarian goals, the Food for Peace Act of 1959 called for long-term credit to finance sales under Title I, significant outright grants of food to underwrite construction projects in the Third World, and for the return of the accumulations of foreign currency to recipient countries in order to encourage social development, including education. Like McGovern, Senator Humphrey accused Benson and Eisenhower of a "negative" attitude. The term "surplus disposal" was an "insult [to] the people of the world who live in . . . hopelessness and despair." Should not this program, he asked, be used "positively and constructively for the relief of human hunger, for promoting economic and social development, and for serving the foreign policy of the United States by helping to build essential world conditions of peace?" The paragon of Vital Centerism also invoked Cold War precepts alongside America's duty to help others less fortunate. "Russia cannot supply food," Humphrey remarked, "the United States can." McGovern, in a report to constituents devoted to Food for Peace, asked, "Does anyone wonder what the crafty Khrushchev could do if he had American surplus food to use in his international operations?" He also underscored the imprudence of sending military hardware "to undemocratic governments that rule over people suffering from hunger, poverty, and disease." America's "most powerful material asset" was the bounty that sprang from its farms. That productivity, "if properly used, can be a more decisive factor in the struggle between freedom and communism than . . . any number of jets and sputniks," he told the folks back home. "We could literally convert surplus farm commodities into education and health."[40]

Near the end of the session, the president signed an amended PL 480 and a new food stamp bill that satisfied both cosponsors (for the while) and prompted the *Daily Republic* to note that the White House at last had "seen fit to endorse a program which our own . . . George McGovern has been promoting since he first announced for Congress." He would still continue to prod Eisenhower and Benson to jettison their "myopic view of this extremely important program" in favor of "vigor, boldness, and imagination."[41]

The country would soon be hearing a great deal about "vigor, boldness, and imagination" as the presidential movement of John F. Kennedy got underway in 1959–60. And he hoped to have the support of the young South Dakotan who, like his brother Robert, had made *Esquire*'s honor roll of young statesmen, and who was also a party leader in an area of the country where the candidate from Massachusetts did not have a following. After the 1958 midterms, Kennedy's assistant, Ted Sorensen, sent a letter brimming with record-shattering facts about the senator's reelection victory—this, to demonstrate his broad appeal and willingness to engage controversial issues. McGovern was impressed but, among the competitors, he preferred Humphrey, even though his foreign policy views were indistinguishable from JFK's. In the New Year he told Hubert he considered his election "the most important project open to young liberal Democrats today." (Eleanor Roosevelt said that, of the contenders in 1960, only Humphrey seemed to possess "the spark of greatness.") In May 1959 McGovern formed a group of House Democrats to promote Humphrey's candidacy and became his most "avid and powerful supporter" in South Dakota, which disappointed Sorensen. "I thought that Hubert was more committed on civil rights, domestic programs for farmers [and] small merchants, and had a better sense of the problems of ordinary Americans," McGovern later reflected. "Kennedy always struck me in that period as a more cool and detached person on most civil rights and economic and social issues." Also, owing to his Catholicism, he would be a hard sell among the Lutherans and Methodists of the Plains states; McGovern initially even felt his nomination "would be disastrous." Nor was Kennedy exactly an expert on the "farm problem," a question that largely bored him. "I don't want to hear about agriculture from anyone but Ken Galbraith," he once quipped, "and I don't want to hear about it from him." Many Democrats believed he had lost his bid for the 1956 vice-presidential nomination because farm groups doubted whether he understood their problems.[42]

Since then, however, Kennedy had begun to display contempt for Ezra Taft Benson and due sympathy for high price supports. He now paid close attention to the Humphrey-McGovern endeavors to remake Food for Peace. Their approach appealed to him; it linked an ostensibly unexciting domestic issue to foreign policy in a dynamic way. In June 1959 he decided to join McGovern in sponsoring a bill to help millions of malnourished Americans. Their legislation would also reduce the costs of the farm program by moving the task of distributing surplus food out of the Department of Agriculture and over to the Department of Health, Education, and Welfare (HEW). Benson was "basically opposed to the idea of donating food," Kennedy and McGovern argued. HEW was better suited "to carry on a humanitarian food distribution program." Their proposal would demonstrate that food abundance was "a great national asset," not a "calamity."[43]

The two had first met in the previous Congress in conferences on the Kennedy-Ives Act—"the beginning of a growing respect on my part for his ability," McGovern recorded. They each had been engrossed in it for political reasons and were once again when they worked on a similar package known initially as Kennedy-Ervin in 1959.[44] This bill would require unions to publish their financial records and expenditures and insure the fair election of officers and convention delegates by secret ballot; it would also prevent racketeering in part by prohibiting convicted criminals from holding office and restrict certain kinds of picketing. A bit tougher than its predecessor, the new measure would "make it unprofitable for hoodlums to infiltrate the union movement," said Kennedy. The Senate passed a penultimate rendering by 90 to 1; then the House Labor Committee amended it slightly and replaced Ervin's name with Chairman Elliot's. McGovern became the first sponsor of both versions in the House; he called the latter "a reasonable bill designed to end the corruption, racketeering, and undemocratic practices in a small . . . portion of an otherwise honest labor-management field."[45]

Yet to President Eisenhower and many Republicans and southern Democrats in the House, the Kennedy-Elliot bill was not nearly strong enough. Late in the summer a bitter struggle ensued upon a substitute bill offered by Phillip Landrum, Democrat of Georgia, and Robert

Griffin, a Michigan Republican. Backed by the president's conservative coalition as well as the Chamber of Commerce and the National Association of Manufacturers, Landrum-Griffin insisted on three unprecedented restrictions on organized labor that went far beyond the anticorruption provisions. The first two would amend sections of the Taft-Hartley Act by outlawing virtually all picketing (even for such basics as higher wages and safer work conditions) except in the case of a formal strike, and the secondary boycott, wherein a union might attempt to pressure its employer to boycott another employer's goods. The third provision would place smaller unions under the jurisdiction of state labor boards whenever the National Labor Relations Board declined to hear a dispute. Among Democrats, only southerners took exception to those who denounced the legislation as "an administrative monstrosity." Nonetheless the coalition held firm. On August 13, with 434 members in their seats, the substitute prevailed, 229 to 201.[46]

McGovern immediately found himself entangled in a dilemma. Because of the coming electoral contest, he was just as anxious about composing the issue as he had been in 1958. It was "essential" and "imperative," he had averred over and over, "that this Congress pass a strong and effective labor reform bill." But now the only alternative was the more restrictive measure he had just voted against or no labor reform at all. He called Dave Beck and Jimmy Hoffa "hoodlums" and their tactics "disgusting." He recounted for the House his promise to devise legislation to root out corruption but not to crush the labor movement. Then he announced, "I am voting for this substitute measure on final passage." A majority in both parties in both chambers chose the same course, including Senators Humphrey, Johnson, and Kennedy, and for the same reasons. The House vote was 303 to 125.[47]

Naïvely he hoped his explanation might lay the matter to rest. The legislation had yet to arrive at the White House when Karl Mundt's patron, the editor Fred Christopherson, declared in the *Sioux Falls Argus Leader*: "The issue at stake is how McGovern voted on the Landrum-Griffin bill." His second vote, the one in favor of it, Christopherson submitted, was merely "a technicality," a "ratifying vote." His first vote the day before—*against* substituting it for the Elliot bill—was "the crucial test, the vote that really counted." The editor wanted his readers to notice two things: "if McGovern had had his way, the strong bill endorsed by President Eisenhower would not have passed," and Jim Carey, AFL-CIO vice president, had sent McGovern a note of thanks for his exertions. The *Aberdeen American News* offered an interpretation: "McGovern on Side of Labor Bosses."[48]

He had done his "best to steer a reasonable course," he rejoined to reporters. He had shown "not the slightest hint of inconsistency or hypocrisy" in voting against, and then for, Landrum-Griffin: "When the bill I thought was the fairest one was defeated . . . I had no honorable course left except to support the only possibility remaining." But an editorial crony of "a certain talkative South Dakota Senator" had "deliberately twisted" his position. If Mundt and Christopherson had worked harder "to straighten Secretary Benson out" instead of "beating the working man over the head . . . we would all be a lot better off." The *Argus Leader* denied twisting anything; it had printed "the official voting record" and simply applied a *New York Times* analysis to McGovern, whom the Machinists' Union weekly listed as having "voted right." State Republican chairman Glen Rhodes added that the "double shuffle vote" revealed his true loyalties—"for labor bosses first and South Dakota second." In a speech in Rapid City, McGovern rebutted the charge that he had been "two-faced" and again rationalized his votes as an attempt to clean out vice without destroying unions. "Mr. Christopherson has gone to great lengths to show that many laboring men support me in this position," he said. "If that is a crime, I am proud to plead guilty."[49] Yet even some of McGovern's friends wondered whether he had been misguided, if not disingenuous. The flare-up over Landrum-Griffin (in a state with a minor stake in it) was a harbinger of the campaign barely a year away.

In the meantime, the congressman did focus on other things. For example, there was the matter of congressional dereliction regarding the National Defense Education Act. In March it dawned on lawmakers that they had appropriated only $40 million of the $183 million authorized for fiscal 1959. This translated into a meager $19 million to fortify the instruction of the nation's students in science, math, and foreign languages instead of the allotted $70 million. The student loan program was supposed to disburse $47 million in this first year, yet the previous Congress had provided only $6 million despite Eisenhower's request for at least another $24 million. "It is inconceivable to me that this Congress would establish a worthwhile and necessary program and then leave it high and dry," said the Republican John Lindsay of New York upon introducing a measure to restore the funds. James Roosevelt found it "incomprehensible" that "there is a possibility that we shall start to undo what we recognized was so important to do in 1958," while John Brademas, Democrat of Indiana, denounced its Republican governor who had blocked NDEA funds from getting into their state.[50]

When his turn came, McGovern spoke proudly of having been a part of the group that carved out the legislation. "It is my conviction that the minds of our young people constitute our most precious national resource," he said, offering examples of how three colleges in South Dakota could not get any help under one of the titles because of the absence of funds. More worryingly, out of one thousand NDEA graduate fellowships authorized to address the shortage of university teachers, money for only 160 had been granted. Clearly there was "urgent need for these funds to carry out even a minimum part of the program," he said in conclusion. "High quality education is not only good for the soul and mind of man; it has become an essential ingredient in our national defense."[51]

In April he spoke to the needs of the rural library service. That legislation put over two hundred bookmobiles on the road, serving over one million citizens. It was nothing less than "vital to the national welfare," he said, explaining how two South Dakota counties were able to procure bookmobiles for the first time, and three others had purchased 14,000 volumes and circulated some 42,447 books in the previous year—all owing to the program. He also spoke plaintively about another fund request "small in size" but which could go far to overcome a shortage of trained nurses in the United States and enliven "the time-tested field of vocational education." He expressed gratitude to the Appropriations Committee for recommending a $1 million expenditure for his initiative to expand the pool of qualified teachers for the nation's mentally handicapped children, of whom only 15 percent had trained specialists to educate them.[52]

McGovern continued to involve himself in important foreign policy issues, too, besides PL 480. The first was the controversy over the $3.9 billion foreign aid appropriation for fiscal 1960, needed, the president said, to thwart "a fanatic conspiracy of international communism." A sizable proportion of this amount went to economic and technical support, including the Development Loan Fund created by the 85th Congress. Sixty-two percent, however, was earmarked for direct military assistance to thirty-seven countries, with fourteen receiving most of it.[53] Many liberal Democrats, such as McGovern and Senator J. William Fulbright, objected to weighting the scales so heavily on the side of weapons for dictators. But some Republicans made a bigger fuss by disparaging the broader enterprise, often in isolationist terms. Harold Gross of Iowa called it "the annual multibillion dollar, giveaway carnival." For him, the "real deterrent to communist aggression" was "the ability of U.S. military forces to destroy the nerve centers of communism." Taiwan, Korea, Greece, and Turkey served as buffers against communism, but they required a fraction of Ike's request. Gross's "great rule of conduct" permitted commerce with most countries, but "as little political connection as possible." He had no patience for "building a bunch of outhouses on the fringe of the jungle near Manila."[54]

It is likely that McGovern saw no harm in the latter prospect. But he had an amendment of his own—to cut the administration's $1.6 billion military provision down to $1.24 billion after the Committee on Military Affairs had already reduced it to $1.44 billion. "I think the American mutual security program, along with the United Nations, constitutes the chief cornerstone of world peace," he said. At the same time, he believed that, in the Middle East, Southeast Asia, and Latin America, "we have overemphasized the military aspects of the foreign aid program." Iraq, for instance, suffered "from misery, poverty and instability . . . [and] from a lack of heath [and educational] facilities." Yet the United States had sent the Iraqis mainly military hardware, and a group of officers recently seized it and then replaced the government with a communist regime. Then there was the oversized arms package to Pakistan that provoked India into diverting $100 million from its five-year plan to purchase weapons from Britain and France. "It seems to me," McGovern argued, "that we ought to be giving a little less attention to building up military machines and more attention to the human problems."[55]

Clement Zablocki, a Democrat on the Foreign Affairs Committee, decided to press him. Where would he trim the program and in which countries? The bulk of the military assistance went to Greece, Turkey, South Korea, Taiwan, and South Vietnam—"five allies who are on the border of the Sino-Soviet bloc." Was McGovern advocating cutbacks to any of them? If so, he wanted to assure him "the committee cut was as deep as it could possibly be." McGovern replied that he was as concerned as Zablocki about "turning back communism wherever it threatens us" but reiterated his point about disease, illiteracy, and poverty, adding that, "you cannot build a very effective bulwark against communism by trying to impose a military monument on a shaky foundation like that."[56]

The McGovern amendment failed, 87 to 107. A week later he declared to an American Legion convention at the Corn Palace that, "in some parts of the world our foreign aid military shipments are doing more harm than good." Citing Iraq and India's reaction to Pakistan, he said, "This kind of so-called foreign policy is a threat to the peace of the world." More generally he observed, "A man who is hungry and sick and poorly governed doesn't make a very good soldier against communism." In the undeveloped world "we could do more to stop the communist menace . . . [with] surplus farm commodities than with costly military hardware." In Congress he offered no further opposition to the committee bill and voted for the final compromise authorization of $3.55 billion, which the House approved 257 to 153 and the president signed.[57] With great conviction, however, he had sustained a good fight on behalf of critical thinking about American foreign policy. Despite his impending contest with the Senate's most ardent anticommunist, he would do so again that summer. The occasion was the transfer of atomic weapons from the United States to seven NATO members, including Jupiter missiles to Turkey.[58]

It was not surprising that none of his party's presidential aspirants joined McGovern in resolving to void this transfer. From the moment the White House had unveiled its defense budget in 1959, Majority Leader Johnson had complained "that we are not going farther and faster with the missile program." John F. Kennedy was about to make an alleged "missile gap" a major feature of his campaign, accusing Eisenhower of letting the country fall behind the Russians in the arms race. He would not point out, as McGovern did, that in January 1953 the United States had brandished about 1,500 nuclear weapons (mainly in the lower registers of kilotons in magnitude) but that, six years later, the administration had seen to the manufacture of an additional 4,500 nuclear weapons as part of the New Look, or about two per day since Ike had taken office. In their tests in 1958, the two superpowers had exploded into the atmosphere some eighty-one devices, most of them in the one-megaton range (fifty times greater than the Hiroshima bomb). That same year the Joint Chiefs of Staff developed a top-secret war plan involving thousands of targets inside the Soviet Union as well as thousands of nuclear weapons averaging 3.5 megatons. The emplacements in the NATO countries were part of this strategy.[59]

The fact that mainstream Democrats failed even to ask questions about the reliance on the threat of "massive retaliation" troubled McGovern. Rarely did he speak stridently, but he led with his chin in introducing his resolution on July 2. "I feel very strongly that it will be a tragic mistake to further extend nuclear weapons around the world," he said, noting the impediments to finding common ground with the Soviets on arms limitation. But that goal surely would recede if this transfer went forward: "It is difficult to imagine that we are improving either our national security or the chances for world peace by placing in the hands of additional countries the destructive power of a nuclear weapons system." The risks far outweighed any advantages, and Congress had the power to delay the deployment; if it did so, maybe it could take more time to investigate "the deadly danger to civilization posed by nuclear weapons," he advised. "We need to be reexamining constantly the validity of our present policy of military deterrence." It was not just a short, unpretentious speech on a subject of incalculable significance. For McGovern, this was the beginning of a life-long commitment to try to persuade the American people and their government to consider the ramifications of a nuclear holocaust. Only three colleagues enlisted in his cause that day, and the building program continued at a staggering pace. By January 1961 Eisenhower would be able to hand over to his successor an arsenal of 18,000 nuclear weapons.[60]

The adjournment of Congress in September 1959 marked the opening of the 1960 electoral season. Already Hubert Humphrey had formally announced his candidacy for the presidency, and John Kennedy was shifting into high gear in most of the primary states. The autumn recess was demanding for House and Senate candidates, too. McGovern came home to mounting speculation not about whether, but when, he might declare his challenge. A preference poll conducted by the *Argus Leader* gave him 41.6 percent to Mundt's 43 percent. Across both West and East River he traveled to report on his work. In a single October week he spoke at the State Corn-Picking Contest in Redfield, Watertown's Cosmopolitan Club, and Yankton College on Pioneer Day, not to mention a ceremony in Huron to anoint the World's Largest Pheasant. Wherever he spoke his message was crafted around Nikita Khrushchev's recent visit to the United States, the first ever by a Soviet premier.[61]

For two unforgettable weeks in September 1959 Khrushchev and his American hosts had alternately delighted and perplexed each other. The tour began at the United Nations, where the rotund, unpredictable leader unveiled a plan for "general and complete disarmament" and gained some notoriety for pounding the podium with his shoe. But his stay ended on a hopeful note that spawned the phrase "the spirit of

Camp David." For there, at the Maryland retreat named for the president's grandson, Khrushchev and Eisenhower came to a tentative understanding on the future of Berlin and agreed to hold a summit on disarmament in May 1960. McGovern surely welcomed the breakthrough, yet for him the fact that Khrushchev had insisted on tarrying two full days on a farm in Iowa was equally instructive. Some four years earlier Iowans had initiated an exchange of agricultural delegations with the Soviets. Among the Americans traveling to Moscow was one Roswell "Bob" Garst of Coon Rapids, an expert of the Henry Wallace ilk who evangelized on behalf of the use of nitrogen in the growing of corn. Khrushchev admired Garst and afterward wrote him more letters than he did Eisenhower; upon coming to America, it was the Iowan's famed "mile of maize" that he wanted to see firsthand and about which he would always exhort his own farmers when they fell short of production goals.[62]

Khrushchev's sojourn gave McGovern's precampaign speeches their form and content. In Rapid City, he posited that "the cold war struggle . . . is rapidly shifting" and cited evidence that the Kremlin desired to avoid nuclear war. But Khrushchev "repeatedly declared war on us," albeit "with the new weapons of economics, science, political manipulation and foreign trade." While many Americans remained skeptical of federal aid to education and farm supports, the Russians were busy "upgrading schools, strengthening their laboratories . . . and increasing both their industrial and agricultural production." Whereas we were sending weapons to Asia and the Middle East, "they are training thousands of technicians who can speak the local language to work in the uncommitted areas" of the world. "I have no fear of our ability to win the contest with Communism," McGovern said. But to do so, "we must take Khrushchev's visit, not as an excuse to relax, but as a challenge to strengthen our economic, educational and moral muscles." That was why he told the Huron PTA that "Russia intends to compete with the United States in the field of science and economics," while Huron's own schools could not hope to vie effectively without federal aid. "Khrushchev knows that education is a powerful factor in the modern world," he assured students at Centerville High the next week, and "education will play an important role in deciding the contest between Communism and Democracy."[63]

In these talks McGovern never missed a chance to remind folks that Secretary Benson's policies, "if continued, will destroy our agricultural economy and the towns dependent upon it," as he did at another gathering of Centervilleans. "We strengthened Public Law 480 to use the farm surplus in foreign countries," he reported. "A food stamp plan was authorized in six major cities on an experimental basis." He then drew their attention to Coon Rapids. "If Khrushchev had our farm surplus he would use it to strengthen his international position. Why scold the farmer for production? He should be given a reasonable return and we should use the surplus for those not as fortunate as we. Let's put food to work to win friends, not as a club to drive down prices." Once more he appealed to his constituents' self-interest and sense of world citizenship in telling an overflow crowd in Edgemont about Food for Peace and that "the world's biggest problem" was that nine out of ten of the planet's inhabitants suffered from malnutrition or starvation. In Aberdeen, he told the local United Nations Association that "in the nuclear age . . . there is no longer any alternative to peace except annihilation" and that, alongside "strengthening the U.N. at every point," this country could make its "greatest contribution to world peace by fully utilizing our agricultural abundance."[64] And so it went. Throughout his statewide swing he posed his distinctive progressive agrarian synthesis of concerns and his activities on behalf of South Dakotans in the context of the Cold War—in other words, the interrelatedness of education, agriculture, and foreign policy, and the *right* way to reckon with, and prevail over, the Soviets.

County Democratic chairs, impressed by "his record as a courageous spokesman for agriculture, business and working professional people," began to issue statements to urge him on. "His keen knowledge of public affairs, his humanitarianism and broad insight into problems of all walks of life clearly demonstrate that he should seek the office of U.S. Senator . . . where he could put his skills to work for even greater service to this State and our Nation," went a typical endorsement.[65] On January 6, 1960, the heralded event took place at a dinner in his honor at Mitchell. Some six hundred people packed the hall and another two hundred were turned away for lack of standing room. "I do not underestimate my opponent, for he is a clever campaigner who has been running for Congress since I was a boy," the thirty-seven-year-old said of the fifty-nine-year-old. Some had wished he would "play it safe" and run for a third term in the House, he admitted. "But I am firmly convinced that a majority of South Dakotans recognize that the time has come to make a change," and he sought "a greater field of service." He then declared, "I intend to seek election with all my strength and if elected I will do my very best to promote South Dakota's future and the peace and well-being of our nation."[66]

The announcement dominated the state's front pages and editorials for days. They all agreed it was going to be an arduous and exciting race, especially in concert with a campaign for president that already seemed to signal a changing of the guard. (In addition to determining South Dakota's future, this clash was just as likely to have a direct impact on the race for the White House as the other way around.) Mundt versus McGovern, the *Mobridge Tribune* observed, "sets the stage for the hottest political battle South Dakota has ever seen." The contest would be "a battle of giants . . . of a young congressman against an older generation," Anson Yeager wrote in the *Argus Leader*. "It will be fought up and down South Dakota from now until November. Main Street, the farm communities, and the cities will constitute the arena." Some observers pictured an arena beyond the Plains. "From time to time, a battle for a Senate seat occurs which for symbolic reasons takes on national importance," submitted columnist William V. Shannon of the *New York Post*. "In 1960, it appears that the most important Senatorial race will be fought in South Dakota."[67]

11 THE QUEST FOR THE SENATE

From the moment the McGoverns moved to Coquelin Terrace, Eleanor valued her next-door neighbor. Muriel Buck Humphrey was not just her "good, good friend." She became her mentor in Washington, guiding her through the shoals of being a political wife and sponsoring her membership in the Women's National Democratic Club. The two had much in common—a South Dakota heritage, a well-developed sense of civic engagement and considerable savvy, not to mention the role of adviser to their respective husbands. A generation later either might have run for office herself. Of course, neither did. "We felt very subordinate, and I think with good reason," Eleanor once told an interviewer, quoting Muriel's remark about the men they married: "Both of them needed wives like us." The two women were willing to give their husbands "the freedom to do what they wanted to do and take over responsibilities of the family," Eleanor said, describing the circumstances of most political couples of the 1950s. "There really are sacrifices that a family has to make . . . because no politician can be in any political office without being totally immersed in it. You can't go halfway. Certainly George and Hubert didn't."[1]

Nothing about this kind of life was easy. Eleanor characterized their initial decade in politics as "the circus years" and their lives from 1956 onward as "simultaneous juggling acts in three separate rings." The first ring was their responsibility to the people of South Dakota; the second, the power politics and social obligations of Washington; their life as a family formed the third. They had hardly unpacked when the official activities started with Eisenhower's inaugural ball. George put on a rented white tie and tails and Eleanor wore "a long iridescent taffeta dress" she had bought on sale for $3.97 in Mitchell. They were terribly excited about the pageantry and riding to the gala with the Humphreys in a limousine. The realization that "governors are accorded royal treatment while freshman Congressmen rate very, very low on the totem pole" did not faze them, Eleanor noted. She quickly learned the separate protocol that wives had to master—such as how to address an ambassador as opposed to a senator, the proper seating of guests (a senator's wife outranks a congresswoman), and the sorts of invitations one should accept and those one might decline. There were thrilling encounters with celebrated figures. Eleanor met Eleanor Roosevelt and Indira Gandhi, the Kennedy brothers, and Adlai Stevenson. For her introduction to Queen Elizabeth, she practiced curtseying and sewed herself a blue velveteen dress and matching hat. And she was able to travel with George on two missions overseas, her first ever, to the Middle East and to Europe. Occasionally she accompanied him back to the First District for his speaking engagements.[2]

Eleanor also had *five* children to rear. A large portion of her life was dedicated to housework, grocery shopping and preparing meals for seven (and always with concern about nutrition), making clothes for the children, settling sibling squabbles, and trying to be sensitive to their needs in the transition. In 1956–57, Ann and Susan were in the sixth and fifth grades, respectively; leaving their school and the small-town life they had always known were difficult adjustments. For Ann, the fact that "Grampa Earl," her great friend and Eleanor's father, had suddenly died in October was a painful complication. She called the move to the nation's capital "a great rupture." For Terry, a second grader, it was less traumatic, while Steven was just four and Mary Kay was an infant. When school let out the family would return to South Dakota. As she would do most summers, Eleanor loaded up the children (and their pets) into the station wagon and made the 1,300-mile haul, doing all the driving herself. George stayed behind until the House adjourned in August, so she had no help with the driving. As Ann recalled, "She really worked sort of around the clock." In all of this, Eleanor refused to let her mind shut down. Her interest in politics never flagged and she kept up with the important issues before Congress.[3] Meanwhile, George had a special houseguest that first summer. Arthur Link came to do manuscript research at the Library of Congress and gladly accepted his former student's invitation to "batch it together." The two of them and Hubert, a summer bachelor himself, spent many an evening drinking beer on the porch and talking politics. Link had "the best time imaginable" and later learned from George that Senator Kennedy's literary tastes included his Wilson biography. Link thought it "significant that Kennedy is reading the first [*The Road to the White House*] instead of the second volume."[4]

As a representative and legislator, George was a recurrent absentee father. The children gradually came to understand why and tended not to nurse resentments. "To my young mind, he was the wisest, best man in the world," Steve said years later of his attitude toward his father at that stage. "I felt secure and happy." Even so, at the age of six he asked, "Mommy, when are we going to move back into the house in Mitchell where Daddy used to play with me?" To Ann and Susan, their father's absence was nothing new; his work as a professor and debate coach had sometimes intruded on evenings or Saturdays at home. But things were definitely different now. "The main change was we didn't see as much of him," Susan remarked. Once, when she and Ann complained about it, their mother spoke frankly: she believed strongly that the "work that he was doing was very, very important" and that everyone would have to make some sacrifice. Disappointments inevitably were mixed in with their appreciation for their father. "I was somewhat in awe of him," Ann said. "I liked to hear him talk about the issues." And Susan acknowledged, "Up until I was in my twenties I thought my father had all the answers and his opinions were the last word on an issue." During his House terms, Eleanor did not draw him into family problems as much as she wanted to. "He was more patient and effective with the children than I was," she felt, whereas the kids were frequently "mother-deaf" to her. Still George confessed after they left home, "I wish that on more nights and weekends I had left my briefcase at the office and given time to fun and conversation with my children."[5]

But if there was an aspect of his career throughout "the circus years" that bothered the entire family the most, it was the endless campaigning and having to endure mean-spirited public criticism of their favorite patriarch. In 1960 Ann would turn fifteen years old; Susan, fourteen; Terry, eleven; Steven, eight; and Mary Kay, five. And so, as soon as the prospect of challenging Karl Mundt arose, Eleanor did not simply encourage George's ambitions, she urged him on. "Anything," she wrote, "was better than campaigning for reelection every two years, living with one foot in South Dakota and the other in Washington with a pre-occupied husband and five growing children who had no idea where they belonged."[6]

"I think that I had had my eye on an eventual race with Karl Mundt from the day I entered politics," George once said. The *Lake Preston Times* remarked that his announcement "formalized a campaign that has been going on by both men for some time." The first lap had been run in 1958. According to the *Grant County Review*, McGovern had "won it [by] defeating Joe Foss despite . . . the help of Sen. Mundt."[7] The candidates were both "articulate, personable and intelligent professionals," the *Aberdeen American News* observed, while another opinion page noted that for the first time Mundt faced a formidable adversary who would make South Dakotans "take a more critical attitude toward him." The *Argus Leader* lamented McGovern's endeavor to oust an incumbent who, for ten years in the House and twelve in the Senate, "has constantly worked with vigor, effect, and purpose" for South Dakota. The *Brookings Register* agreed: "Seniority means very much in the Senate and it would appear to be folly to lose Senator Mundt's position." Variations of that doubt burdened some Democrats. McGovern was their biggest vote getter, a shoo-in for reelection to the House, but his withdrawal from that race could enable the GOP to recapture his district while victory over Mundt was by no means assured.[8]

The concern was substantive. To begin, Mundt brought a determination and passion to his work that matched McGovern's, augmented by twenty-two years of experience in the political frays of South Dakota and Capitol Hill. Before that, again like McGovern, he had been a highly successful educator in the social sciences and speech. As a student at Carleton College, in Northfield, Minnesota, he had met his wife-to-be, Mary Moses. They became an inseparable couple. Karl and Mary taught at the same high school, in Bryant, South Dakota; since they did not have children, they were able to pursue graduate studies together at Columbia University for four consecutive summers and earn master's degrees; they moved on to positions at Dakota State University, in Madison. By the 1930s his renown as an inspirational speaker and debate coach had spread across the Plains, capped by his cofounding the National Forensics League. His background had primed him well for his ultimate vocation.

In 1938 he had won election to Congress by savaging his opponent, Emil Loriks, for his support of the New Deal and "leftist" leanings. With the partial exception of the farm programs, there was little about the New Deal that Mundt did not denigrate. Like most Republicans in the prewar period, he was also wary of Rooseveltian diplomacy. He supported America First in 1940, voted against Lend-Lease in 1941, and stayed harnessed to isolationism until the morning of Pearl Harbor. Always mistrustful of big government, by 1945 he had readjusted his foreign policy views to accommodate a form of conservative internationalism, its rationale being anticommunism. Mundt joined the House Un-American Activities Committee (HUAC) in 1943 and became adept at investigation, a skill he honed on the Senate rackets committee in the 1950s against organized labor. He saw connections between these assignments. Along with the Army-McCarthy hearings, his admirers believed that his single-mindedness in the Hiss case in 1948 had helped to make HUAC an indispensable weapon to thwart communist attempts to subvert America. In the eyes of many people his investigations of the labor movement worked as an antidote to the more subtle domestic threat of the New Deal's "creeping socialism." (The Senator once pulled these themes together in a memorable estimation of "New Dealers, Fair Dealers, Misdealers and Hiss dealers who have shuttled back and forth between Freedom and Red Fascism like a pendulum on a cuckoo clock.") He was responsible not only for one of the earliest antisubversive bills of the Cold War—the failed Mundt-Nixon Act of 1948—but also for what one scholar has cited as the "last vestige of McCarthyism in federal legislation." Mundt insisted on putting into the National Defense Education Act a provision that required students to sign a noncommunist affidavit and swear an oath before they could receive their school loan. (Even Eisenhower found this distasteful and joined McGovern in recommending its repeal.) Then, too, no one could claim greater responsibility than Mundt for the passage of the McCarran Internal Security Act of 1950, a direct descendant of the 1948 bill, which McGovern once described as "possibly a greater loss to freedom than any previous measure in our history." By 1960 the terms "Mundtism" and "McCarthyism" had become synonyms among midwestern Democrats. McGovern held Mundt responsible for Joe Foss's attacks on his patriotism. Liberals elsewhere associated him with Nixon and regarded the two as the kindred heralds of the *ism*.[9]

They did not call him King Karl for nothing. He was the most famous politician South Dakota had ever produced, a close friend of

J. Edgar Hoover and of the vice president, whom everyone expected would be elected president. Mundt was "a giant in Republican politics," the journalist David Kranz observed. "You turned on the Six O'clock News, and he was there. You listened, you read the paper, and he was there . . . he knew how to play the political game too." George Cunningham and Pat Donovan had their own takes. Cunningham mocked his contrived radio performances. Mundt wrote out both the questions and the answers in advance but wanted his weekly program to sound unrehearsed. On the air, the interviewer would inquire on cue about some issue. Whereupon the senator, as if taken unawares, would exclaim, "Well, Bob, you threw me a hot potato that time!" Pat Donovan characterized her boss's nemesis as affable as well as "a marvelous debater, " but her summation was brutal: "He drove an old broken down, second-hand car in South Dakota, and he had a Lincoln or a Cadillac in Washington. That's Karl Mundt."[10]

Mundt himself provided another insight into his political discernment. After it was over, he told George Cunningham that to prepare for the coming marathon, he had started going to the Senate gymnasium for the first time. The press had always drawn attention to his rotundity. Even William Shannon of the *New York Post*, in describing a "contest of opposing philosophies," had made note of it. "McGovern is a slim, handsome six-footer," he wrote. Mundt was "the roly-poly playmate of Joe McCarthy." That he set about to lose forty pounds was a sign of his respect for the junior congressman.[11]

In mid-January, a week after McGovern announced, the *Argus Leader*'s first preelection poll revealed that South Dakotans favored David over Goliath, 47.8 percent to 44.2. In East River, where over 60 percent of the population lived, the challenger's numbers improved to 49.8 percent to the incumbent's 40.8; whereas west of the Missouri the flow reversed to 50.6 percent for Mundt against 45.9 for McGovern. Mundt scored highest in cities and towns, 56 points to McGovern's 38, statewide. McGovern's best numbers came from the farmers, a whopping 59 to not quite 31, with 10 percent undecided. Thus his declaration of purpose in the *Daily Republic*: "The preservation of the family farm is an economic and moral necessity." He chose to run for the Senate "to further the cause of the farmer." Mundt devoted his "time to sensational televised hearings on problems not related to agriculture," said McGovern, and after his election in 1954 "he became strangely silent about the Benson program."[12]

Karl Mundt, however, was not a pro-Benson Republican, and his differences with most Democrats over agriculture were not fundamental. He and Senator Case had cosponsored the original PL 480 legislation out of which Food for Peace evolved, and he worked cordially with Hubert Humphrey on the Senate Ag Committee. He publicly disagreed with Benson on a regular basis. (When he heard Benson was planning a fall trip to Europe, Mundt said that it would be "a nice place for him to spend the campaign.") Yet no Democrat had ever used the farm issue to greater advantage against Republicans than McGovern did. Mundt could not let him repeat what he had done to the hapless Harold Lovre and Joe Foss. The old pro enlisted surrogates to hit his rival where he was vulnerable.[13]

On January 12, Fred Christopherson of the *Argus Leader*, Mundt's journalistic ally who had hounded McGovern about his votes on the Landrum-Griffin bill, published the editorial, "Hoffa Will Be Happy If Mundt Loses." The union boss's "cup of joy would be overflowing" because Mundt supposedly had exposed his criminality and thwarted the kind of labor legislation he desired (single-handedly, one would have thought). The *Argus Leader* followed up with more sensationalism: "The record shows that the official publication of the Teamsters Union . . . has listed Mundt as a candidate to be defeated and McGovern as one to be supported." For weeks newspapers across the state reprinted or embellished both the assertion and the falsehood. The *De Smet News* suggested that McGovern was the cat's paw of unions while the *Lemmon Leader* construed him as Hoffa's "fair-haired boy."[14] On January 28, the *Argus Leader* published a letter from McGovern about Christopherson's claim: "I challenge you to support your charge that Hoffa and the Teamsters have endorsed my election." He reiterated his opinion of Hoffa and Dave Beck and reminded readers that these "unscrupulous racketeers" were Republicans who "have contributed liberally to Republican campaign coffers." Christopherson retracted his statement that the Teamsters cited McGovern as their candidate. "There is no such listing," he admitted, but insisted, "Hoffa would be happy should Senator Mundt be defeated."[15]

Only a few publications defended McGovern, by clarifying events in recent labor history and the difference between Hoffa and Beck of the Teamsters and Walter Reuther of the AFL. Mundt was at it again, "trying to pin a phony labor rap on George," grumbled W. R. Ronald, editor in chief of the *Daily Republic*, while the *Salem Special* pointed out, "Hoffa's

Teamsters withdrew from the AFL-CIO under pressure of the internal crack-down on racketeering." Both newspapers reprised Hoffa's $5,000 contribution to the Republicans and their misrepresentations of the initial Kennedy-Elliott bill, which was "designed to end the corruption and undemocratic practices," as McGovern had said in introducing it. Hoffa hated that legislation for its stress on union corruption, Ronald explained, and "Mundt made Hoffa happy by failing to lend support to the Kennedy measure." According to the *Salem Special*, Hoffa had "commented favorably" on Landrum-Griffin (the bill Mundt favored). Although it restricted some activities of organized labor, it "was not nearly as tough on racketeering—the greatest evil of unions headed by such men as Hoffa," said Ronald. "King Karl's forces undoubtedly are hard-pressed for issues."[16]

Then, on March 15, the *New York Herald Tribune* printed an actual purge list of nine senators and seventy-eight congressmen—an addendum to a front-page story about a Teamsters rally at Madison Square Garden where Hoffa had given a ranting speech. Hoffa's list included Kennedy as well as Mundt, but a total of fifty-nine out of eighty-seven were Republicans. Even so, the *Herald Tribune* referred to JFK as the "No. 1 target for political oblivion," and Hoffa's speech heaped scorn on him and Robert F. Kennedy. Mundt was merely included, yet it provided him ample license to vow, "I shall not be intimidated by Hoffa's threats or dissuaded by his boasts." He announced his candidacy for reelection the next day, accompanied by a round of editorials. "It is unthinkable that the people of South Dakota will follow Hoffa in his determination to retire Senator Mundt," said the *Brookings Register*. The *Selby Record* fretted he not only would have to "battle McGovern but will have to fight labor money which will be poured into the state." In papers across the state, letters to the editor using identical phrases came to Mundt's defense in response to the purge list. McGovern could not help a little sarcasm: "Mundt's brave pledge . . . has firmly established the fact that Hoffa will not be the next senator from South Dakota."[17]

He had lots of reasons to be edgy. Soon South Dakotans once again found literature in their mailboxes accusing him of affiliating with communist front organizations, the same propaganda that Glenn Martz—Mundt's former publicity agent whom McGovern was suing for libel—had circulated in 1958. A letter by a former student of McGovern's surfaced as well. "A man who will betray his trust in the classroom just might betray his country," Lionel Stacey, the student, had written during the contest with Lovre in 1956. "Why did you make communist propaganda compulsory reading?" These materials were sent from Sioux Falls, in envelopes from Florida hotels, with no return address. Among the recipients was one Arvid Carlson, a county chair of McGovern's campaign, who wrote to three newspapers protesting "a filthy smear campaign." Carlson called on Mundt to repudiate the mailings. Mundt obliged; he declared them "repugnant" and vowed that neither he nor the Republican central committee condoned such tactics. McGovern and Carlson said they were glad he had denounced anonymous mailings but implied he had shed crocodile tears. Probably they had a point. "Mundt made heavy use of the letter," his biographer has written; his "rumor squad did its job." Then Lionel Stacey returned in a 750-word follow-up in the *Watertown Public Opinion*. Confirming McGovern's sympathy for Alger Hiss and Owen Lattimore and his subservience to organized labor, Stacey's intent was to praise Mundt— "who was neither soft on communism or bossed by Walter Reuther." The Hansen County Republican Committee spun the letter into a paid newspaper advertisement.[18]

There was still more conjoining of the communist threat, unions, and the New Deal. In April, Arthur Motley, publisher of *Parade* magazine and president-elect of the US Chamber of Commerce, delivered an address in Rapid City deriding McGovern as "a hired hand of the AFL-CIO." Another out-of-state hatchet man arrived from Virginia in May to give a series of talks to Rotarians around the state; in most of them he extolled Mundt's "courageous stands" and blasted McGovern for his farm subsidies and "socialized medicine" and for voting nine times "in favor of Walter Reuther."[19] Then, an unfortunate postscript to Nikita Khrushchev's visit to America also made a contribution to Mundt's campaign.

On May Day 1960, a Soviet missile had brought down an American U-2 spy plane over the Urals, 1,300 miles inside Russian territory. The event occurred just two weeks before Eisenhower and Khrushchev were to hold their summit in Paris. The United States initially claimed a weather plane had gone astray, but Khrushchev embarrassed Eisenhower on May 5 by revealing that the pilot and parts of the U-2 had been retrieved. The president acknowledged he had authorized high-altitude surveillance flights over Russia since 1956, "a distasteful but vital necessity," he said. Khrushchev did not take this at all well, interpreting the flights as technical acts of war. On the summit's opening day, May 16, he let loose a denunciation of the man he believed had betrayed him and demanded apologies and a halt to future flights. Ike sat and listened, feeling wronged as well. Soon he would terminate the U-2 missions but he rebuffed any act of contrition. The two *had* intended at Élysée Palace to strive toward a nuclear test ban and reductions in strategic arms. Now they grieved for "the spirit of Camp David."[20]

On the evening that the president flew to Paris, McGovern drove to Aberdeen. "The administration's handling of the spy plane incident is one of the most serious diplomatic blunders in our national history," he told the UN Association of South Dakota. The White House at first had refused to own up to its violation of international law; then, caught in a lie, it asserted the right to conduct the flights from allied bases. It was a "highly dangerous announcement," he continued, that gave cause for "prayerful thinking of our leadership role in world affairs."[21]

History would confirm everything McGovern had said, but his timing was flawed. Coming before the Paris talks had yet to collapse, he opened himself up to censure. His remarks "sounded like what the Russians would be expected to say," observed the *Aberdeen American News*. "Khrushchev's indictment of President Eisenhower . . . was hardly more severe than McGovern's." The *Selby Record* likened it to "slapping Eisenhower in the face." Quoting Lyndon Johnson—that "Khrushchev could not use this incident to divide the American people"—the *Record* said it wished "McGovern would have said something like that."[22]

Mundt knew just how to play it. At a rally of Young Republicans in Sioux Falls, he comported himself like a senior adviser to the Oval Office. "America is showing Khrushchev and the world that our hearts are with Mr. Eisenhower," he said. The Democratic leadership had exhibited "statesmanship of the highest order" and proved it "draws the line when danger threatens the country," though there were one or two exceptions, he added, "who demonstrated they belong in the minor leagues." If, in the realm of foreign policy, McGovern had gained credibility among his constituents because of his critical perspective, in this instance he had overreached. The first phase of the campaign was not going quite the way he had hoped.[23]

"The trouble with us Democrats this year," McGovern said to the "Dollar-a-Month Club" of Aberdeen in May, "is that we have so much Presidential talent that we don't know which one to choose." He was commenting on the quandary in which South Dakota delegates to the national convention found themselves. Hubert Humphrey, their "native son," had just quit the race after losing the West Virginia primary to Kennedy. McGovern saw no need for haste in deciding whom to support; he had already concluded that Adlai Stevenson's moment had come and gone and that Johnson, though he considered him "the most masterful Senate leader in our national history," could not beat Nixon. So he arranged to have a cup of tea with Kennedy and offer his endorsement. McGovern realized that his was not exactly the nod from Mayor Daley, but the senator was glad to have it. Afterward they drove together to a House reception. "It was my first really casual visit with him," McGovern later said. "I just saw him as a more serious forceful, committed individual than I had before." He had become a Kennedy man.[24]

That did not mean he had disowned the others. "I am proud of my political party when it can produce not only a Kennedy and a Humphrey but also a Symington, a Stevenson, and a Johnson," he declared publicly. The tribute was sincere—the five contenders constituted an exceptionally strong field of presidential aspirants—and McGovern was held in comparable esteem. Eleanor Roosevelt, in a rare endorsement, had recently cast him as a young man of "character, independence, and intellectual fibre," suggesting that his ascendance was "a political opportunity second only to the presidential election." In June a luncheon on his behalf in Washington drew the Big Three. Humphrey spoke warmly of his next-door neighbor's family and said George's opponent personified the "forces that have needed a good whipping for a long time." The majority leader hailed "a fighting Liberal on the side of the people." And Kennedy said, "I can think of no two more valuable results of the 1960 senatorial campaign than the retirement of Karl Mundt and the election of George McGovern."[25]

The presumptive Democratic nominee arrived in Aberdeen the following week to court uncommitted delegates. Preceded by advertisements inviting people to come hear "Two Bright Young Men, Honored in Peace . . . Decorated in War," the Kennedy charm worked its magic. The *American News*, which supported Nixon and Mundt, described him as "remarkable," his primary campaign as "brilliantly successful," and his family as "amazing." More crucially, though, the senator laid out an "agricultural bill of rights." It was the Gospel according to George and Hubert. JFK was "a 100 percent convert to the farmer's longtime struggle to achieve parity," McGovern assured the crowd at the auditorium. The first right—"the right to a fair share of the national income"— echoed a McGovern refrain, as did those about the preservation of the family farm, democratic referenda in adjusting output, and the expansion of rural credits and telephone service. The candidate also portrayed Nixon as a committed Bensonite. And not only McGovern, but Kennedy, too, now claimed that agriculture was "the No. 1 problem the next president will have to solve." Whether or not he really believed that, the issue held precedence in South Dakota politics, and the national Democrats were about to organize "Farmers for Kennedy and Johnson." Alert to the fact that the presidency could be within the gift of the people of the Great Plains, JFK would return at harvest time.[26]

As for McGovern, once more he was touting his Family Farm Income Act, revised to reckon with falling income and the 1.3 billion bushels of surplus wheat the government owned. His bill entailed a 25 percent reduction of wheat acreage with price supports at 85 percent of parity. Another section would expand the school lunch program and surplus food distribution to poor families. Average-size farmsteads stood to prosper by these provisions, which would go into effect if two-thirds of producers in a nationwide referendum agreed to them. Benson's alternative was an unrestricted wheat program with supports up to 75 percent, and a doubling of the Soil Bank to sixty million acres. It favored larger operators, and had the approval of Nixon and the conservative American Farm Bureau. McGovern condemned it as tantamount to "destroying most of the communities of rural America."[27]

Senator Mundt now took pains to remind people, "I do not agree with Ezra Taft Benson and I said so first in 1953 [when] I first asked for his resignation." That did not dissuade his challenger from trumpeting the tenacity of flexible supports or Mundt's advice that farmers give unlimited production a try—"the same Benson philosophy that has driven farm income down by 24 percent since 1952," McGovern said. In July, statewide polls conducted by the *Argus Leader*, the *Huron Daily Plainsman*, and the *Watertown Public Opinion* brought him good news. Despite the red-baiting, McGovern had a nine-point lead, 54 percent to 45, and a twenty-point advantage among farmers. The bipartisan "Farmers for McGovern" was soon founded to promote "the best friend of agriculture South Dakota ever sent to Congress." He publicized as well his perfect voting record for Rural Electrification Administration (REA) programs, lifelines that Mundt supported erratically. This issue tilted against Mundt further when the state's Young Republicans attacked the REA as "socialistic." The REA cooperatives had 70,000 members in South Dakota, the Democrats retorted, and there was "nothing socialistic" about them. McGovern considered them "one of our finest examples of free enterprise." Meanwhile, the Mundt campaign had set in motion a stratagem designed to throw McGovern off his game.[28]

On August 17, Jimmy Hoffa made a startling statement in response to a query from the *Omaha World Herald*. "Information correct," he replied. "I am supporting the election of Congressman McGovern because he was one of 201 courageous members voting with labor for the desired substitution of [the] Landrum-Griffith Act."[29] Few Democrats doubted that Hoffa had been put up to it—to discredit McGovern. "It's politically inspired," governor Ralph Herseth was the first to say. "George has repeatedly denounced Hoffa and has supported legislation to straightjacket such leaders." Pointing to Hoffa's recent endorsement of Nixon, McGovern declared to a gathering at the Shadehill basin in West River: "I have never sought the endorsement of Hoffa. I do not want it and I refuse to acknowledge it." The story went national when Drew Pearson picked it up in his column. The McClellan Committee had given the Teamster chief a working over, Pearson explained, and "the only friend Hoffa had was Sen. Karl Mundt . . . [who] interceded to ask friendly questions." By coming out for McGovern, "Hoffa has reciprocated . . . which is anything but a blessing in anti-labor South Dakota."[30]

The Hoffa "endorsement" was not the only poison loosed in August. In the run-up to the planned debates the Mundt campaign also had circulated an article from the ultra right-wing magazine, *Human Events*. The piece described McGovern's agenda—increases in foreign aid and in federal aid to education, housing, the minimum wage, and Social Security—as "left-wing extremism." Undeniably, he was the tool of "militant left-wing groups," such as the AFL-CIO and ADA. And beware the term, "Family Farm," "a slogan in radical circles" for discredited farm programs "just as the slogan 'peace' covers strange diplomatic policies." No less subversive were McGovern's evident belief in the "'one world' philosophy" and "all-out drive for world government" and his opposition to Mundt's loyalty oath for students with federal loans. A vote for McGovern, warned *Human Events*, was a vote for "a yielding attitude toward the Communist challenge to everything for which we stand." When congressman E. Y. Berry of West River called him "a socialist" at the Young Republicans convention, McGovern supposed things were "getting pretty raw, even for an election year." Berry also said that labor had pumped $250,000 into his campaign, a distortion multiplied by thirty-five. This, then, formed the prelude to what was being hyped as "a modern-day version of the Lincoln-Douglas debates."[31]

The first of the "Big M" meets, before two hundred members of the Methodist Brotherhood of Sioux Falls on September 15, was cordial and spirited. The Kennedy campaign informed the first question from the audience: "What are we going to do about regaining America's prestige?" Mundt stepped forward. "You're looking at a man who says it's not slipping," he said, contending that a "team of experience and of record" had prevented war with the Russians for more than seven years. McGovern, too, believed "America is strongest today," yet wondered what lay ahead. He accused Eisenhower not of a missile gap, but of "complacency in leadership." He worried that US policy in the Third World lacked imagination and had "failed to meet the rising needs in Africa, Iran, and other areas." What had become of the Good Neighbor Policy in Venezuela, he asked, when in 1958 Vice President Nixon had been spat upon and his car stoned? "Republicans," Mundt rejoined, "have always managed to keep us at peace and every time it was the other fellow that failed to keep us out of war." The implication was that Democrats were the "party of war" in 1917 and 1941; it irritated McGovern enough for him to point out that Mundt had voted against Lend-Lease and measures to expand the army and navy prior to Pearl Harbor.[32]

Inevitably agriculture dominated the debate. Mundt observed that neither party had found a satisfactory solution; the answer was "largely one of curtailing or expanding production." He envisioned a future in which the surpluses could be converted to industrial purposes such as fuel from grain alcohol. His "basic difference" with McGovern was supply versus demand, and he believed the farmer's best hope was "expanding and stimulating markets." McGovern insisted on the practical need for restricted output coupled with 90 percent parity for which there was "no substitute." Industrial use of agriculture was forward looking, but it tended to put "us in a bad light with the hungry people of the world." The great opportunities for American farmers lay instead in the expansion of Food for Peace.[33]

At the next debate, members of an association of television and newspaper journalists asked McGovern about the funds he had accepted from organized labor and the aspersions on his patriotism. He had received $4,500 in both 1956 and 1958 and probably would receive that amount in the current campaign, he answered. "My basic support in 1960 will be from the rank and file of South Dakotans." ("Historians for McGovern," organized by Ray Allen Billington, would contribute some $2,000.) As for the "hate literature" and the Stacey letter, he said,

"It's all false." Mundt then volunteered that he had been "shown the letter two years ago and said 'no' to its circulation."[34] For his role in inflating the issue, though, Karl might have suffered some pangs of remorse at their next appearance, at Sioux Falls on September 20.

The discussion, presided over by Fred Christopherson and attended by Senator Case, centered on conservation. But the friendly mood suddenly changed when Walter Bones, a former state chair of the Young Republicans, arose to put a question. Why, asked Bones, did McGovern not salute during the presentation of the fifty-star American flag earlier in the evening? "I was one of the first persons to salute the flag," McGovern replied. Editor Christopherson, who sat beside the accused, intervened. "I stood up with him when the flag was being presented," he said. "He did precisely what I did." Then an attorney at the main table assured Mr. Bones of the salute and Christopherson broke in again, "I believe I am expressing the viewpoint of the group when I say I regret this question was asked." The *Daily Republic* reported the incident as "one of the more dramatic in what has been an increasingly tense campaign," and it discomfited everyone who witnessed it. The veteran of thirty-five air combat missions against the Axis kept his composure. The editor of the *Argus Leader* acquitted himself nicely. Mundt kept silent. That a "flag incident" had occurred at all was not simply a matter of one Young Republican's bad manners. No doubt everyone welcomed the respite that the presidential candidates were soon to provide.[35]

The year 1960 was not a normal political year anywhere in the United States and certainly not in South Dakota. Mundt versus McGovern was the object of national attention and Nixon and Kennedy each visited the state twice, despite its prize of only four electoral votes. On successive days they came to speak at the National Plowing Contest, a major annual event just outside Sioux Falls. Kennedy touched down on Thursday afternoon, September 22, "National Level Land Day." Although it had been drizzling most of the week, the crowd on the main plow field was huge—some 70,000 people. They listened respectfully as the candidate read from his prepared text on agriculture and struggled with wind and light rain for twenty minutes or so. His audience seemed indifferent, and McGovern worried that he was not at ease. He also noticed Mundt in the front row, smiling benevolently and enjoying the damp reception Jack was getting. On the return to the airport, the entourage of Democrats agreed it had not gone well. Boarding their plane for Mitchell, George suggested that Kennedy speak extemporaneously there and be sure to underscore his commitment to Food for Peace and generous parity payments.[36]

Not since Wendell Willkie in 1940 had a presidential nominee stumped in McGovern's hometown, and folks showed their appreciation. The rain had stopped, a motorcade conveyed all the dignitaries into town, and hundreds of people lined Main Street and cheered them on their way. Someone on the press bus caught sight of the Corn Palace and asked, "My God, what is that?" The venerable structure overflowed with what one reporter described as "a jammed and roaring crowd" of 6,000 as the Kennedy party walked onstage. "We Back Jack" and "Vote Democratic" signs abounded. The candidate told Jim Magness it was "the most heartwarming" welcome of his midwestern tour. His spirits were lifted and he took George's advice. Discarding his text, Kennedy promised to allow farmers to conserve upwards of a quarter of their land and to support a program of 100 percent parity for commodities grown for domestic consumption. Then, "with great feeling and compassion," as McGovern recalled, he said his administration would also devote a greater volume of their productivity than ever before to feeding the hungry here at home and in foreign lands. The exuberant throng punctuated his sentences with applause and cheers. "I don't regard the agricultural surplus as a problem," he continued, adopting McGovern's rhetoric and a lively cadence. "I regard it as an opportunity to use it imaginatively, not only for our own people, but for people all around the world." Theirs was "a new generation with new problems which must have new solutions." In the decade ahead, no group could do more to bring about lasting goodwill and peace, for America or for the world, than farmers—not "if we recognize that food is strength, and food is peace, and food is freedom, and food is a helping hand to people around the world whose good will and friendship we want."[37]

If Sioux Falls had bordered on disaster, the trip to Mitchell was triumphal and, for McGovern, the highlight of the campaign. His many friends in attendance would remember it forever, and Kennedy was grateful to George for having helped him find his voice. Yet Mitchell was an aberration. Kennedy was not the choice of the people. The polls suggested he was a big drag on the party ticket. And at no point did Nixon not own South Dakota. On September 14 their percentages in the state were 57 to 40—a low for Nixon and a high for Kennedy. Two weeks later, Nixon climbed to 60 and Kennedy had fallen to 36. For that same date, September 28, the Senate race registered at 51.6 to 48.4 in Mundt's favor, whereas McGovern had held the lead in every survey since January until Kennedy's nomination in July, holding then at 54 to 45 percent. Mundt at last had captured it starting in August, with 52 percent to McGovern's 47. It was still early in a competitive heat, public opinion was on a seesaw, and any number of factors could have explained the data. But the downward drift for Democrats in other races after the Los Angeles convention was conspicuous, most surprisingly for the popular Governor Herseth.[38]

Kennedy appreciated the hospitality and the smiles that McGovern, Herseth, and House candidate Ray Fitzgerald wore as they joined him onstage. He was aware of the trends as well as of the tone of Mundt's campaign. Of McGovern, he said to his brother after their departure, "Bobby, I think we just lost that man a seat in the Senate." This was, in part, a reference to his religion, one of the reasons why he ran behind Nixon in certain regions of the country. Having Kennedy in South Dakota was a plus for everyone, and he probably did himself some good. But "the overall result was not good," McGovern believed; a day later he wrote Professor Billington, "Anti-Catholicism is still running high and hurting all Democratic candidates in this state."[39]

In the Dakotas it reached back to the territorial days, when the pioneer generation of Protestant immigrants arrived from Europe and from east of the Mississippi. Protestant versus Catholic then translated into Republican versus Democrat. (According to one scholar, the antipathy between Irish Catholic Democrats among miners in the Black Hills and the Protestant Republican majority was a carryover of relationships in the Northeast in the pre–Civil War era.) In the 1920s both Dakotas had had an active Ku Klux Klan that harassed Catholics rather than African Americans. Fear of the papal threat to public education was pronounced well into the 1940s. A marriage between a Lutheran and a Catholic was a source of family shame well into the 1960s. Eleanor remembered how "terribly distressed" their grandmother was when Ila had dated a young Catholic man. Campaigning in small towns she frequently encountered prejudice. So many Protestant ministers said to her, "Why, it's unconstitutional for a Catholic to run for president," that she avoided homes next to churches. Eleanor always greatly admired Jack Kennedy, but she had to admit, "He didn't help us out in South Dakota."[40]

After the "Plowtown" extravaganzas, Mundt and McGovern began outwardly to show irritation with each another during their debates. Their sixth took place before a crowd of 1,400 on September 26, just two hours before the first historic televised Kennedy-Nixon debate. Republicans packed the Huron Arena. "They cheered everything Mundt said and booed and hissed everything I said," McGovern complained. The focus was the farm programs of the presidential candidates. Mundt touted Nixon's plan for expanding markets and his own for turning commodities into industrial products. He also noted that Kennedy had cast a few Benson votes in his past. McGovern hammered the perpetual decline in farm income since 1952, questioning "uncontrolled production when surpluses are depressing the markets" and arguing for high supports, limits on output, and using the surpluses to boost Food for Peace.[41]

Of the final debate, held on October 4 in Sioux Falls, the *Argus Leader* reported that the candidates "discussed Crow Indians, fought like Sioux, and faced an audience that seemed to be on the warpath." The *Daily Republic* noticed that all 1,500 partisans at Washington High School indulged in immoderate booing and catcalls. The chair of the Young Republicans set the tone. As he introduced Mundt, he held up a sheet of paper listing the enacted legislation McGovern had sponsored in four years. It included "a couple of Indian bills," he said dismissively. Then he unrolled across the footlights a list twenty feet long—the legislative record of Mundt's twenty-two years. When his turn came, McGovern said, "There's nothing ridiculous about legislation to help Indians." Then he plunged in. Mundt had accepted $2,500 from oil companies, he charged, for voting against sharing tidelands oil revenues with all the states (thus depriving South Dakota of $38 million), whereas Senator Case had voted the same way but refused the reward money. Mundt the patriot fired a broadside of his own. He wanted to know how his opponent would have voted on the Mundt-Nixon antisubversive bill of 1950.[42] "I would have voted against it at that time," McGovern replied, for its unwarranted restrictions on individual freedoms while merely driving communists underground.

Agriculture, however, ruled the agenda. If the Kennedy program were enacted, a "million people would lose their jobs," Mundt maintained. Nixon had the right answer—"expanding markets instead of shrinking supply." McGovern reiterated his case about family farms and observed that this day marked the eighth anniversary of Eisenhower's promise to uphold 90 percent parity, which ended in "the greatest betrayal in history." Mundt provided the most memorable moment. Religion had come up only in their first debate, when he noted simply that he and McGovern were both Methodists. Now he grazed it in talking about agriculture—by mocking Kennedy's accent and labeling him "this new Pilgrim from Massachusetts." Said Mundt: "He calls it a 'faam' program, and I'm old-fashioned enough to think a man should be able to pronounce a problem before he solves it." A young Democrat stood up and said he was glad his party "cares for people who speak a little differently." The next day's *Daily Republic* chided Mundt and others who ridiculed Kennedy's accent, as if it detracted from his qualifications. Nixon's running mate was a Bostonian, too, the editorial observed.[43]

It was hard to gauge the debates. But Mundt may have believed they had done him less good than McGovern. Five days after the final duel, he and Christopherson unleashed one of the mothers of all "October surprises," a matching bookend to Hoffa's "endorsement." This time it was one for Mundt and from none other than J. Edgar Hoover. Christopherson had solicited him to name "the most experienced members of Congress with knowledge of the Communistic threat." The FBI director maintained a feeble pretense of impartiality; he and Mundt were longtime mutual admirers. On October 4 he named, "in all fairness," four members of Congress, two from each party and "fearless men" all.[44] Of his South Dakota ally Hoover declared: "The communists, both here and abroad, have felt the heel of Senator Karl Mundt. . . . [A]s an active, courageous member of several committees seeking to expose and fight this menace, he has truly combined experience, knowledge and farsightedness."[45]

For the *Argus Leader*, this was worthy of page-one headlines in the Sunday edition. The missive itself deserved printing from the top of page five to the bottom, three columns wide and in a font twice the normal size. A main editorial interpreted it as "a source of gratification" for the state, coming from "a leader so well qualified as Director Hoover." The next day's letters to the editor carried the colors too. "Every loyal South Dakotan should be thrilled," for voters now "have a clear cut choice November 8," said one. A second wondered how McGovern could "have voted against the Mundt-Nixon bill" and yet "permit himself to be identified with the [AFL]." Another marveled "how our great senator has grown in influence."[46]

A week passed before Christopherson published the contrary view of Daryl Stahl, a minister dismayed by the editor's "attempt . . . to exploit the use of [his] newspaper's function of gathering news" as well as by "Hoover's entrance into . . . South Dakota politics." With the campaign in full swing, the *Argus Leader* had petitioned Hoover to commend Mundt and then ran the story on Sunday's front page as "half-news-half-editorial," the insinuation being "that McGovern is not fighting communism as vigorously as Mundt." There were many ways to fight communism, such as "using imagination and vigor in foreign aid programs, working on a farm program which will function," the Reverend Stahl added. "You have every right to support whomever you please, but I hate to see you do it at the expense of your integrity and the integrity of your readers."[47] Then came the coup de grâce. On October 20 the *Argus Leader* formally endorsed the incumbent's reelection for twenty column inches, highlighting his "inestimable assistance in fighting communism," which "had induced" Hoover's praise. In the home stretch it offered up a final editorial titled "Hoover for Mundt; Hoffa against Him."[48]

To McGovern's people, there was nothing King Karl's court would not stoop to, and it opened the gates for more bad behavior and bad judgment all around.[49] Just as the GOP was spreading the word of J. Edgar, Governor Herseth released an explosive report on local land sales and the new interstate highway. It revealed influence peddling on the part of many South Dakotans and appeared to implicate Mundt for profiting by inside information. For in 1949, a small investment group, of which he was a member, had purchased lots at bargain prices near the proposed route for Interstate 90 and later sold them to the federal government at a profit. The idea that Mundt was caught in a scandal was irresistible to McGovern. Assuming the charges were indisputable, he let his campaign run with it, but he did not have all the facts. It turned out Mundt was innocent of wrongdoing, if not wholly of avarice. He had not belonged to the investment group when the land was purchased and the highway legislation was then six years in the future. Now it was Mundt who was being sullied. The *Argus Leader* slaughtered McGovern for "a dirty smear" and called on him to apologize. Mundt made a display of patience with the younger man's brashness. It was a bitter pill for McGovern to read of sympathy for Mundt whose campaign was now handing out cards that read: "Protect America's Time-Honored Separation of Church and State. Vote 'No' on Kennedy, McGovern, and Fitzgerald."[50]

As of October 12, Mundt had improved his polling position to 53 percent over McGovern's 46. But public opinion was poised on a hair trigger. On October 26, McGovern regained a slim advantage, 50.1 to 49.9, keeping a fourteen-point edge among farmers while his "city" numbers had risen from 38 to 47 and Mundt's had dropped eleven points to 52 percent.[51] That Mundt had fallen behind was significant, given that virtually all of the state's editorial pages, save the *Daily Republic*, had endorsed him. Then in the final weeks he extricated himself from the highway report at McGovern's expense. The journalists' consensus was that the imbroglio helped Republicans by eclipsing the farm issue. On Sunday before election, the final poll put Mundt way ahead, at 57 to 40.7. Democrats cited another, however. McGovern and Mundt were set at 52 and 48, according the Lou Harris research firm of New York.[52]

Both candidates released a surge of ads in the final weeks. McGovern ran a "This I Believe" series. One of these focused on his "key role" in enacting the NDEA and his ratings as "one of the top congressional friends of education." An ad on "Leadership" stated that a strong national defense involved being first, not only in missiles, but also "in ideas and programs to win men's minds to freedom." To "secure the peace" in the "uncommitted areas of the world" required education, medical assistance, and technology. Election eve ads stressed agriculture. "The family farm is the cornerstone of our state and Nation," one headline stated. "For the good of all it must be preserved."[53] As for the Republican's ads, "Karl Mundt's Seniority Is a Great Asset for South Dakota," went one featuring him and Nixon. In another, about "Labor Bosses," Barry Goldwater testified on how he had fought racketeers. One final ad stated: "Today this country is blessed with the stillness of Peace, the quiet of long-silent battlefields." This could continue only with "South Dakota's distinguished statesman" at the helm—"the man best equipped through his record of . . . clear comprehension of the Communist menace."[54] Thus the curtain fell on the months of intense political drama. In all, the campaign had been one of the more emblematic contests of the Cold War era and the most bruising in South Dakota history.

———————

It was going to shatter all the records. The expected historic turnout would easily exceed the sixty-two million voters of 1952. In the excitement of 1960 it seemed as if the entire country got up early on that Tuesday morning. Vice President and Mrs. Nixon voted shortly after the polls opened in Whittier, California, and then took a drive along the Pacific coast, "to get away from it all for a little while," Nixon said. The Kennedys cast their ballots at the West End branch of the Boston Public Library, then flew to the family compound in Hyannis Port. The Mundts voted in their hometown of Madison, and the McGoverns, at the Corn Palace. George spent most of the day driving people to the polls.[55]

The first returns in the nation came at dawn from New Hampshire, a precinct tally of forty-nine votes for Nixon and eight for Kennedy. In South Dakota, Westover Township in West River was the first to check in, seven for Nixon and one for Kennedy. Across the continent most precincts were reporting their highest turnouts ever. "We haven't even had time for a coffee break," bemoaned one overworked election official in Sioux Falls. The earliest count had McGovern leading; by late afternoon Mundt was ahead, 105,000 to 101,000. Back and forth it went into the night. A Republican year otherwise was in the making in South Dakota, except for the dead heat of Herseth vs. Gubbrud. Kennedy trailed Nixon by tens of thousands.[56]

Sixty-three percent of the voting-age population of the United States cast ballots in the presidential election. Out of slightly over 68 million, Kennedy received a mere 112,827 more votes than Nixon. In South Dakota, where 78 percent of the qualified voters came out, the Republican candidate scored his fourth biggest landslide among the states he carried. Nixon took it by 58.2 percent as against Kennedy's 41.8 percent, or 178,000 votes to 128,000. Mundt did only one-third as well in securing his third term by 160,000 to 145,000 votes. McGovern had given him the closest shave of his life while attracting 17,000 more votes than Kennedy. This was major ticket splitting. Thereon Herseth had even more reason for regrets. The senatorial contest had been a real horse race, but Herseth had been favored to win by many lengths. Ultimately, he lost by 4,000, or 154,000 to 150,000. In the meantime, the Second District gave E. Y. Berry his sixth term in Congress, 42,000 to 28,000. Voters in the First District chose the Republican Ben Reifel over Ray Fitzgerald, 126,000 to 103,000, to replace McGovern. Elsewhere in the nation the Democrats lost twenty-one seats in the House of Representatives and two in the Senate, retaining their majorities in Congress by 263 to 174 and 64 to 36, no thanks to the president-elect. As for the bicameral legislature in Pierre, the Republicans increased their hold by 22, to a combined total of 80 seats out of 110.[57]

"The people have expressed their will and I accept it with no bitterness in my heart," said McGovern in conceding. He was grateful that South Dakotans had allowed him to represent them in Congress for four years, and he hoped "Americans everywhere will unite behind our courageous new President, John F. Kennedy." He finished on a graceful note: "God speed to Karl and Mary Mundt and to all others who have been called to service in the critical 1960s."[58]

Since the two previous elections had created a semblance two-party government in the state and this time the nation had gone Democratic, the big question remained: Why did South Dakota yield such a sweeping victory to the Republicans? To begin, Vice President Nixon was very popular in the farm belt; his coattails definitely helped his fellow Republicans on the ballot. The senator from Massachusetts was demonstrably less than helpful to his copartisans in the region. The closeness of South Dakota's gubernatorial and senatorial elections, coupled with the Kennedy's massive defeat, pointed toward a different outcome in those contests if the Democrats had nominated someone other than JFK for president. Harold Milner, a leading reporter in the state, put religion on the top of his list of explanations, "although most were reluctant to admit it," he said. The highway investigation was second. It had backfired on McGovern and Herseth and diverted attention from issues that would have served them. Milner also emphasized the Republicans' superior organization in getting their propaganda across. According to the *Argus Leader*, "the course of wisdom" and Mundt's character and seniority decided the Senate race. Some analysts cited McGovern's decision not to seek reelection to the House; almost certainly he would have won and then "would have wielded considerable influence with the new Kennedy administration," said the *Sturgis Press*. In any event, there was "little doubt that McGovern's alliance with [labor] . . . cost him the election." Another explanation settled upon the growth of federal programs and spending and "traditionally conservative" South Dakota voters.[59]

McGovern's main concern, in an interview with the *Daily Republic*, was that the people had not "intended to kill two-party government when they voted," and he predicted a restoration two years hence. But he was "convinced that emotional factors beyond our control and a loaded Republican press defeated the Democratic candidates." Kennedy's religion "caused thousands of South Dakotans to vote Republican," he asserted. (Kennedy attributed the *narrowness* of his overall victory to both the perception of "peace and prosperity" under Eisenhower and anti-Catholic sentiment.)[60] McGovern revealed his deeper feelings in letters to well wishers.

Most admirers had attributed the outcome to "the blizzard of straight Republican balloting" and to anti-Catholicism. McGovern would also cite the Hoffa "endorsement," J. Edgar Hoover's intervention, and the South Dakota press. But he agreed with friends that the religious issue was "fundamental." It was "the sleeper that had me worried all fall," he told Robert Nathan, the Washington economist. "Mundt exploited it skillfully in combination with his usual fear-mongering tactics, related to labor, big spending, and the Communists." To Jim Symington, the son of the Missouri senator, he wrote: "We worked so hard [but] we were overwhelmed with the concerted effort to stir up the religious issue." He found it impossible "to describe the intensity" to Arthur Link; it was as if "religious hysteria [had] struck the state." To Al Young he quipped, "I don't think Abraham Lincoln could have won this one." Occasionally he belied anger. "I came out of that campaign feeling as though I had literally been covered with mud," he confessed to Daryl Stahl, who had chastised the *Argus Leader*. "I am completely convinced that Karl Mundt is one of the most evil men in American politics."[61]

Then, suddenly all of that passed. Everyone conveyed the same message, from senators Ernest Gruening, Eugene McCarthy, and Ralph Yarborough to historians Billington, Link, and James MacGregor Burns, as well as friends like Adlai Stevenson and the owner of Mitchell's propane gas company. In so many words they all said, as Link did, "The country needs you and men like you now more than ever." He was "one of the most able and promising and best trained of the young Democratic leaders." His defeat was "only a momentary setback." Even the *Argus Leader* granted that McGovern's "potentiality for service is great," and "we will hear from him again in the future and it is well that we should."[62]

As it happened, arrangements to that end were already under way at Hyannis Port. The president-elect of the United States was meeting with advisers before departing for a few days' rest. He liked McGovern very much. He appreciated his credentials in agriculture and education and his fine personal qualities. The South Dakotan's steadfast loyalty to the national ticket and the battle scars he sustained in his own race only enhanced his worthiness in Kennedy's eyes. McGovern was one of four younger liberals whom "he wanted in particularly important positions," he told Arthur Schlesinger.

The following evening George and Eleanor were dining with friends in Mitchell when the phone rang, long distance from Palm Beach. It was quite a surprise, but there was no mistaking that fresh and confident voice: "George, this is Jack Kennedy. I'm awfully sorry about what happened up there in South Dakota on Tuesday. I think I cost you the election." McGovern momentarily stammered. All kinds of factors had been involved, he started to say. "No, George," Kennedy cut in. "I understand what happened. I hope you will come and see me before you make any plans."[63]

The conversation was short, but McGovern would never forget how it "really put me back on the mountain top." Eleanor and their dinner companions were all abuzz. The president-elect had not been explicit, he told them, but there were at least two distinct possibilities. And so the quest for the Senate had ended in a call to service that McGovern had never anticipated. His fortunes now pointed the way toward a New Frontier.

12 FOOD FOR PEACE

In the weeks after the election McGovern mused about the irony that he actually might become Ezra Taft Benson's successor. The *Kiplinger Agricultural Newsletter* had reported him on a short list for secretary, and word of Kennedy's phone call only spurred the speculation. The *Pierre Daily Journal* sniffed about whether two years on the House Ag Committee were sufficient qualifications, whereas the *Des Moines Register* considered McGovern's background strong and noted that colleagues on the Hill and most farmers groups liked him. The National Farmers Union president said he would be "most happy" to see him in the post. The *Daily Republic* also ran a piece on his heading Food for Peace instead and quoted him as "vitally interested in both" positions.[1]

Robert Kennedy was the first Kennedy to realize that McGovern was an "action intellectual" of the sort who populated his brother's inner circle. He respected George's background in agriculture as well as his enthusiasm and intelligence and wanted to bring him onboard. The two had first worked together on the Kennedy-Ives labor bill in 1958. Then came the presidential campaign. George had impressed Bobby because he stood by Jack despite his own uphill battle against Karl Mundt. In the final week, when he found himself in trouble, George asked the organization for help. On the Friday before election, as McGovern told the story, Bob did "a very remarkable thing." He was his brother's campaign manager and was "badly needed elsewhere." Yet he flew from Washington—and he was afraid of flying—to a state with four electoral votes that Nixon was sure to take, to speak for George at a rally in Watertown. He returned in a small plane in dangerous winds at midnight.[2] Bob had impressed George, too.

In advancing McGovern for secretary of agriculture, both Kennedys had to bear in mind suitors of clout, including Democratic governors of Iowa, Kansas, and Minnesota. Senior members of the House and Senate Ag Committees also weighed in. Chairman Cooley protested on the grounds of McGovern's inexperience; his objection proved decisive just when the president-elect was on the verge of naming McGovern. But Robert told him the real plum was Food for Peace, especially if he entertained ever running for office again. The problems at Agriculture were "virtually insoluble," he said; "it was a rather unpopular job." McGovern would learn his fate when he met with Jack in Georgetown on December 16.[3]

Although George and Eleanor would have celebrated a cabinet appointment, Bobby's opinion prompted a rethinking, and Al Young was urging, "Get something exciting that will take you all over the world before you settle down again." On second thought he did not want to crimp his options in the nearer term, and Food for Peace held tremendous appeal. In the same way he had helped JFK see agriculture in a new light, McGovern warmed to such issues when he could connect them to foreign policy and America's position in the world. By November 1960 Kennedy had gained an understanding of the program's potential. After his swing through South Dakota, he became excited about it and played on the theme in all the farm states. In October he appointed a committee to consider ways that the New Frontier might turn "Food for Peace" into "a long-term investment in progress" and also create "a world food agency." He would weave the idea into portions of his inaugural address that issued the call to national service: "To those peoples in the huts and villages of half the globe struggling to break the bonds of mass misery," he pledged his administration's "best efforts to help them help themselves"—for however long it might take and "because it is right." With this consolation prize McGovern would be thrilled.[4]

The president-elect announced his selections for the first "director" of Food for Peace and for secretary of agriculture (Governor Orville Freeman of Minnesota) at the same press conference, as if to imply that the former had virtual cabinet rank. At his brother's behest, he also gave McGovern the co-curricular title of "Special Assistant to the President" and placed the program in the Executive Office to insulate it against bureaucratic depredations. (PL 480 had been the shuttlecock of the Departments of Agriculture and State, with its "coordinator" operating in an administrative twilight zone.)[5]

Thus on his third day in office and in his second executive order, President Kennedy formally created the post and charged the director with the responsibility of making "the most vigorous and constructive use possible" of American agricultural abundance to narrow the gap between the haves and the have-nots. "Humanity and prudence, alike," he stated, "counsel a major effort on our part." Suffice it to say that an auspicious intersection in the history of Public Law 480 and the life of George McGovern had occurred.[6]

"Food aid," as political scientists call it, had not become commonplace in American foreign relations until the second half of the twentieth century. The earliest instance of it took place just before the War of 1812, when Congress appropriated $50,000 to purchase food for the victims of an earthquake in Venezuela. During the Russian famine of 1891, donations poured in from America to the people of St. Petersburg. In 1908 Theodore Roosevelt dispatched ships laden with food and supplies to ease suffering after a terrible earthquake in Sicily.[7] During World War I Herbert Hoover helped save millions of Belgians from starvation. By 1919, however, he was advising the peacemakers at Paris to withhold food shipments from a communist regime in Hungary, which contributed to its overthrow. (Hoover became the first diplomat to demonstrate how America's agricultural abundance might serve political ends.)[8]

It would take another world war and the Soviet-American confrontation before economic assistance would become a pillar of US foreign policy. In the Marshall Plan (1948–51), food aid had its most dramatic application in US history. By the time it had ended, a total of 29 percent of all Marshall Plan funds had been allocated to food for humans and feed for livestock.[9] Thus had the United States wielded food to contain Soviet communism, to restore confidence to the people of Western Europe, and, not incidentally, to shape their political economies in accord with American economic interests.

Even so, a coherent concept concerning food and foreign policy had yet to be invented. The first steps were taken in 1954, with the passage of the Agricultural Trade Development and Assistance Act, otherwise known as Public Law 480. The legislation had three titles. Title I provided for the sale of farm commodities to "friendly" governments, and the food could be purchased with their own currencies. Along with cutting down the surpluses, then, PL 480 became a source of foreign exchange. Title II concerned disaster relief; a recipient country could use food grants to alleviate hunger as it saw fit. Title III authorized distribution of surpluses by private voluntary agencies such as the Catholic Relief Services as well as the barter of food for strategic raw materials such as industrial diamonds and ferromanganese from Ghana and India.[10]

On its own terms, PL 480 was a modest success. But during Eisenhower's time, one-third of the economic assistance to developing countries had taken the form of loans, not grants, and the accumulation of foreign currencies had become an embarrassing problem. And the line between military and economic assistance was increasingly blurred. Although some PL 480 food resources were set aside for humanitarian purposes, the main purpose was to "get rid of surpluses," as chairman Charles Francis of General Foods insisted; even PL 480's coordinating body was named the Committee on Agricultural Surplus Disposal. Humphrey and McGovern, however, in their International Food for Peace Act of 1959, aimed to fight the Cold War more creatively with a new emphasis on humanitarian goals and outright grants of food. They also favored returning the foreign currencies to the host countries. A generous expansion of the program not only would relieve hunger but also could underwrite projects for economic and social development. Although Eisenhower adopted the new term "Food for Peace" in 1959–60, he paid little more than lip service to the goals of the authors of the revised legislation.[11]

"I have always believed that one person, despite weaknesses and mistakes, can make a difference," McGovern once wrote. Food for Peace would turn out to be one of those instances in a political career in which this was really so. Indeed, for someone of McGovern's background and inclinations, the assignment was well-nigh perfect. Feeding the world's hungry had been a concern of his since his encounters with Italians on the edge of starvation during World War II. In Congress he had probably talked about Food for Peace more than any other subject except agriculture itself. As director, he intended to bury forever the old "surplus disposal" concept, engineer a vast expansion of the program, and turn it into a bona fide progressive instrument of American foreign policy. When Kennedy asked what actions were needed in order to make "the maximum effort," McGovern sent a memorandum, on January 26, urging a series of missions to Latin America, Africa, and Asia.[12] He received a response four days later, though not in a letter.[13]

On the evening of January 30, 1961, the president delivered his first State of the Union message to Congress. In many respects it was a postscript to the inaugural address that everyone was still talking about, and much of it was cast in comparable rhetoric. Yet this speech would not dwell exclusively on matters of foreign policy. Kennedy began with the economy he had just inherited—an ongoing recession, high unemployment, a balance of payments deficit, and nine years of declining farm income. Twenty-five million US citizens lived in substandard housing. The public school system contended with two million more students than it had rooms for, and the college-age population was going to double in the coming decade. There were shortages of hospital beds and medical care for old people. At least one million American families did not have enough to eat. The denial of civil rights on account of race, he also observed, "disturbs the national conscience, and subjects us to the charge of world opinion that our democracy is not equal to the high promise of our heritage." He promised to send to Congress legislation to deal with most of these matters without delay.

By his lights, domestic problems paled against the dangers posed by the Soviet Union and Communist China. Invoking the premise of amassing a "force so powerful as to make any aggression clearly futile," he recommended an acceleration of the country's nuclear missile and Polaris submarine programs as well as an increase in rapid deployment capabilities to transport conventional forces to "any spot on the globe at any moment's notice." He noted as well the difficult challenges in the Third World—in Laos, the Congo, and Latin America, in particular—which necessitated an emphasis on education and social justice and a commitment to long-term economic development. He then announced the New Frontier's first overseas mission of any kind—a Food for Peace mission to Latin America, as McGovern had just proposed—"to explore ways in which our vast food abundance can be used to help end hunger and malnutrition in certain areas of suffering in our own hemisphere." For that purpose as well as to aid economic growth around the globe, his administration would expand Food for Peace "in every possible way." He had also asked the program's director, he said, to explore ways that the bounty of America's agriculture could "advance the interests of world peace" and the establishment of an international food bank. He concluded in the style of "an idealist without illusions," as his wife Jacqueline once described him: "Life in 1961 will not be easy. Wishing it, predicting it, even asking for it will not make it so. There will be further setbacks before the tide is turned. But turn it we must. The hopes of all mankind rest upon us."

McGovern could not have imagined a more exciting response to his first official recommendation. Kennedy had actually devoted a portion of his State of the Union message to introducing Food for Peace, not only to the people of the United States but also to the entire world. Arthur Schlesinger, now a special assistant to the president, no doubt captured McGovern's feelings when he recalled returning to the White House after the speech "exhilarated by the sense of taking part in a great new national adventure." In that spirit, their boss would ask them to undertake this mission to Latin America together.[14]

The president's men boarded a plane out of New York's Idlewild Airport bound for Buenos Aires on the night of February 12. They barely knew each other, but the 5,000-mile flight was the beginning of a lifelong friendship. McGovern was acquainted with Schlesinger's books on Andrew Jackson and Franklin Roosevelt and his treatise on Cold War liberalism, *The Vital Center*. For his part, Schlesinger knew of McGovern's work in Congress and the battle he had just waged against Mundt. Their common background as scholars, he wrote, "established an immediate bond." Fascinated by his companion's wartime experiences as a B-24 pilot, he was able to pull some of his more harrowing stories out of him "over many drinks."[15]

The mission to Latin America, specifically to Argentina and Brazil, had several purposes behind it. McGovern had laid his own plans with the objective of ascertaining effective ways of using food abundance to improve the lives of Latin Americans and thus US relations with their governments. A few days before his departure, Kennedy had called to say that Schlesinger would be coming along "to look into some things for me." Schlesinger's task, not entirely unlike McGovern's, was to persuade the leaders of the southern continent that the New Frontier was not the conservative, business-oriented Eisenhower administration but, rather, "a liberal-minded administration in the tradition of FDR that had a genuine interest in Latin America besides making as much money out of it as possible." The historian was also supposed to sound them out on their attitudes toward Fidel Castro.[16] For Kennedy, then, this mission was a starting point for a major initiative to halt the deterioration of inter-American relations of the Eisenhower years, culminating in the Cuban Revolution of 1958–59. In March 1961, he would proudly unveil the "Alliance for Progress"—a ten-year, $20 billion commitment to help Latin Americans develop their economies, reform their systems of landownership and taxation, and encourage political democracy—thereby preventing any further communist footholds in the hemisphere.[17]

That Fidel Castro had come to power was partly a story of neglect going back to the immediate postwar period and the suspension of Franklin Roosevelt's "Good Neighbor Policy." Like Hoover before him, FDR had refrained from military interventions of the sort perpetrated by Theodore Roosevelt, Taft, Wilson, and Coolidge. Even so, the Trade Agreement of 1934 conferred control over the region's one-crop economies. Then, too, noninterventionism abided dictators such as Anastasio Somoza of Nicaragua and Fulgencio Batista of Cuba, strongmen who served the interests of their countries' oligarchies and of the United States.[18]

During World War II, Latin America made a signal contribution to the Allied victory over fascism. In all, it supplied the United States with $2.4 billion worth of strategic raw materials. In exchange for their commodities, Latin Americans accepted credits with which they hoped to purchase capital goods once the war was over. After 1945, however, the United States lifted price controls, and Latin Americans quickly depleted their credit reserves on fewer and more costly manufactured products than they had anticipated. Because the war had destroyed the economies of its European trading partners, Latin America had to depend more than ever on the goodwill of its neighbor to the north.[19]

The Cold War did not rejuvenate goodwill. For Latin America there would be no Marshall Plan. The United States would promote only one-crop export economies and provide but sparse investment capital for diversification. Nor would Truman's or Eisenhower's administrations do much to encourage democracy. Secretary Dulles's directive was to "do nothing to offend the dictators" who ruled thirteen out of the twenty Latin American states, and he refused to allow human rights on the agenda of any inter-American conference. In 1954 the CIA went so far as to destroy a fledgling democracy. In Guatemala the popular government of Jacobo Árbenz Guzmán had tolerated labor unions, instituted a form of social security, and (worst of all) expropriated the uncultivated lands of the United Fruit Company and parceled them out to thousands of peasants. Claiming Guatemala had "succumbed to Communist infiltration," Eisenhower launched a covert operation

to overthrow the liberal reformer, much like the coup against Moham-
mad Mosaddegh in Iran the year before. A military dictator replaced
Árbenz only to plunge the country into a nightmare of repression and
violence.[20]

By the 1950s, nationalist uprisings throughout the Third World against
colonial oppressors had raised the stakes in the Cold War. Eisenhower
and Dulles equated such nationalism with communism. In the name
of national security, they armed national guards and upheld entrenched
elites while disregarding the poverty and illiteracy that the vast majority
of the people of Latin America endured. In 1958 Venezuelan students
stoned Vice President Nixon's motorcade on a visit to Caracas. That
event caused Eisenhower to reconsider demands of Latin America's
leaders and its middle class for help in realizing their aspirations for
modernization. His response, an Inter-American Development Bank,
was hardly a radical change in policy, and much too late, as Castro
demonstrated in overthrowing Batista.[21]

The new director of Food for Peace regarded Eisenhower's Latin
America policy as comparable to that in the Middle East. As ever, the
United States "offered no practical plan to use American aid . . . to
eradicate the poverty and disease that open the way for Communist
inroads," while it "overemphasized . . . the military aspects of the foreign aid program." To be sure, McGovern apprehended that Kennedy
was an ardent anticommunist and that part of Schlesinger's assignment
was to appraise opposition to Castro (and even encourage it) among
the elites. Yet to him, they both seemed sensitive to the shortcomings
of a blindly anticommunist foreign policy that ran contrary to the nation's best ideals and best interests. It was a complex challenge, but he
relished the chance to attack hunger and ameliorate the broader threat
of communism, whatever its nature, with surplus American farm commodities.[22]

In Argentina, McGovern and Schlesinger had an audience with Ar-
turo Frondizi, its democratically elected president. Frondizi was favorably disposed to the new administration, yet not indisposed to Cuba's.
He disparaged the idea that the United States should regard Castro as
the source of Latin America's problems and resisted a direct answer
when Schlesinger pressed him on supporting collective anti-Castro
measures. "What is required is an attack on the conditions which produced him," he said. McGovern might have offered the same analysis.[23]

Frondizi was not excited about Food for Peace. Argentina was a major
exporter of beef and grain, and he did not appreciate the Eisenhower

accent on "dumping." The pervasive complaint was that shipments of American grain, no matter the motivation, threatened unfair competition.[24] McGovern came to realize that PL 480 could no longer be driven solely by whatever commodities happened to be overspilling storage bins; he took pains to assure the Argentines that the United States would respect their export interests in any expansion of Food for Peace. Frondizi nonetheless doubted whether humanitarian food distribution was much of a solution to anything. Like other leaders of the more prosperous economies, he believed capital investment in heavy industry was the key to redressing their social problems. McGovern insisted food was "a complement rather than a substitute . . . in promoting economic growth" but realized that a major undertaking in Argentina was unwelcome. A year later Kennedy announced that Argentina, a "representative democracy," would receive $150 million in loans for economic development under the Alliance for Progress. By then, the wary Frondizi had moved a little closer to "the general U.S. position" on Cuba, yet the United States did not protest when his own military deposed him in mid-1962.[25]

Brazil was another matter altogether. Nothing in their experience prepared McGovern and Schlesinger for the misery they beheld in the favelas of Rio de Janeiro and the countryside. "Her face bore the unmistakable signs of under-nourishment and neglect as she sat on the mud floor of her hut," McGovern wrote of "a shapeless young woman" he encountered in a village in the northeast. "Lying with their heads on her lap were two frail children, their eyes open but without childish delight." Their seven-year-old brother only that day had expired from smallpox and malnutrition. (Life expectancy in the region was twenty-nine.) "I had never seen such an area of despair," Schlesinger recorded, "one bleak, stagnant village after another, dark mud huts, children with spindle legs and swollen bellies, practically no old people." The two were shaken by other pitiful scenes as well—particularly of listless children covered with sores or dying of hunger or measles before their eyes, and reaching up to be comforted.[26]

President Jânio Quadros "displayed a lively interest in Food for Peace." The Brazilians wanted to purchase one million tons of wheat, under the generous terms of PL 480's Title I, because of crop failure in Argentina, their normal supplier. But McGovern worried that this by itself would not have an immediate impact on hunger. One-third of the country's population—900,000 in Rio de Janeiro alone—lived on the verge of starvation. The Brazilians were similar to the Argentines, however, in their perception that the need for capital development and jobs was as exigent as "relieving today's hunger." McGovern did not disagree. As he put it, "to be really useful, any long-range program of feeding the hungry should be linked to incentives for self-help and with orderly progress in economic development." But he also believed that conditions in the city slums and the drought-ridden rural areas required emergency action now.[27]

Brazil's financial and political straits complicated the situation. Quadros had to struggle with the repercussions of the deficit spending of the previous president; the charismatic Juscelino Kubitschek had given the people an automobile industry and the dazzling futuristic capital city, Brasília. But the attendant runaway inflation would undo Quadros. Then there was the leftist Francisco Julião who appealed to the peasants of the northeast to rise and destroy the feudalistic system that kept them ill fed and in rags. The indictment of the "counterpart Castro" challenged the basic prescriptions of both the Alliance for Progress and Food for Peace. Finally, Quadros rubbed both the White House and his own military the wrong way. A week after McGovern and Schlesinger's visit, Adolf Berle arrived with an offer of $100 million in assistance. But the United States wanted Brazil's approval of its planned actions against Castro. Quadros refused, and no one accompanied Berle to the airport to see him off. Soon Quadros's "attentions to Che Guevara" and his pursuit of an "independent" foreign policy began to worry secretary of state Dean Rusk and CIA director Allen Dulles.[28]

Although McGovern was not unconcerned about the communist issue, he returned to Washington flushed with humanitarian purpose and noticeably impatient. "You just knew that, somehow or other, without violating the law, things would have to move," his assistant Nelson Post said. Within weeks, the million-ton wheat sale was under way, and the United States agreed to accept local currency and then channel it into Brazilian economic development. In March, at McGovern's request, President Kennedy sent Jonathan Garst (Bob's brother) to Brazil to begin a pilot project to convert surplus feed grain into badly needed protein. Some months later, the United States dispatched to northeast Brazil 6,000 tons of corn and 10,000 tons of beans and enough dried milk (300 hundred tons) to feed two million people for a year. In the meantime, deputy director Jim Symington led a month-long mission to Bolivia, Colombia, Ecuador, Paraguay, Peru, and Venezuela, and McGovern conducted a country-by-country survey for a report to the president.[29]

It did not take the director long to learn that every country in need was different from the next, and that Food for Peace could not work miracles in every case. To make it more effective he recommended a two-pronged recasting of the program. First of all, in keeping with Kennedy's preference for the "tough, pragmatic" approach to foreign aid, he told the president that they needed to allocate agricultural resources to stimulate foreign economic development and to help Third World countries improve their agricultural methods, leading toward self-sufficiency. Second, Food for Peace should dedicate itself as well "to the cause of feeding hungry people even if the economic benefit [to the United States] is an indirect one." Justifying humanitarian programs on moral grounds, he made the case that they would win "friends for the United States among population groups which could easily drift toward communism," while the "greater physical strength derived from better nutrition will ultimately be reflected in high productivity."[30]

Food was "a building block in the development of a foreign economy," McGovern wrote in his thirty-page report. It was the "long-term investment in progress" he and Humphrey had contemplated since the 1950s, and it neatly dovetailed with deputy national security adviser Walt Rostow's *Stages of Economic Growth* and the notion of the 1960s as the "development decade." And so McGovern would underscore the importance of a reliable, "continuing supply of food during the development period." This would necessitate long-term authorizations from Congress for Title I sales to supplement those emerging nations that had stronger economies. India, a country that remained "nonaligned" in the Cold War, offered the most vivid illustration. Its five-year plan depended on the annual shipment of four million tons of wheat from the United States. For the poorer countries of the Third World, however, Title II of PL 480 would have to play a principal role through a "Food for Wages" program. Because laborers in most developing countries spent half of their earnings on food, the idea was to provide cheap food and fiber to fuel labor-intensive economic development projects. In 1958–59 the Eisenhower administration had shipped 44,763 tons to that end in a temporary experiment in two countries.[31]

Kennedy encouraged McGovern's initiative, and within six months the United States had shipped out 264,173 tons for "Food for Wages," nearly six times the total that the Eisenhower administration had put into it. At the end of 1961 eleven countries were participating. Food for Wages provided partial wage payments to hundreds of thousands of workers in all sorts of projects—from land clearance, reforestation, irrigation, and reclamation to the construction of roads, bridges, and dams as well as provincial hospitals, schools, and agricultural cooperatives. By 1963 the program was operating in twenty-two Third World countries and generating scores of millions of "man-days" of work. The annual volume of commodities reached 968,000 tons and the number of workers upwards of 700,000. Of added significance, these workers received food not only for themselves but for their families as well. In some cases, a quarter of a partaking country's population thus benefited directly. No one before McGovern had given much thought to any of this, or on such a scale, but Food for Wages was improving the nutritional health of many millions of people while launching essential public works projects that otherwise might have been delayed indefinitely.[32]

Yet this was only the half of it. The children that McGovern had seen in Brazil exerted a powerful force on him. "I would certainly agree that our food exports should fit into economic development programs," he said to Kennedy. "But I would urge most strongly that we should . . . not ignore the vital need for purely humanitarian programs to feed the hungry." Mindful of the dangers of dependency and the skepticism of government officials and private commercial groups in the recipient countries, he argued, "We must not let our fear of such consequences paralyze us into non-action." Here, then, dearest to the director's heart was the overseas school lunch program. The project, begun in Egypt in 1954, was being phased out in many places. McGovern demanded an abrupt change. In twelve to eighteen months, he predicted, the new administration could double the volume of this Title II program. ("No other single effort returns such high dividends," he would say after overhauling it.) With Prime Minister Beltran of Peru he signed his initial school lunch agreement, known as "Operation *Niños,*" in May 1961.[33]

What was involved? A bakery, clean cans for the milk, clean water, basic kitchen facilities, kettles, and utensils, and a constant supply of the food. As for the "high dividends," these included dramatic improvements in the health of millions of children as well as in increases in school attendance as high as 40 and 50 percent and better academic performance, not to mention good will for the United States. It also made for smiles and a happy time of day in the lives of the children. Sometimes the nutrition might be a soup of beans and tomatoes or a bit of meat on a bed of bulgur or rice, or perhaps only milk in a tin cup and a roll. But the children could count on it—and this midday meal was a magnet to get them into school and learning. (Preschoolers and nursing mothers often came at lunchtime, too.) Ambassador John Kenneth Galbraith remarked about the program in Madras: "I hope that those who look at the power plants of the Five-Year Plans will also spare a glance at the children who are better fed and better read as a result of this progressive vision." In terms of sheer scope, it was extremely impressive. By mid-1962, some thirty-five million children worldwide were receiving daily Food for Peace lunches. By 1963–64, the children at the Food for Peace table numbered one million in Peru, two million in South Korea as well as in Mexico, three-and-a-half million in Egypt, four-and-a-half million in Brazil and the Philippines, nine million in India, and over ten million throughout Southeast Asia.[34] The Peace Corps not excepted, between Food for Wages and the school lunch programs, George McGovern had superintended the single greatest humanitarian achievement of the Kennedy-Johnson era.

It took just two overseas missions to spark in him the desire to find multilateral solutions to global hunger. Four months into his tenure he traveled to Rome for an intergovernmental meeting of the United Nations Food and Agriculture Organization (FAO). Since its inception in 1945, the FAO had frequently proposed remedies, including a world food bank, to supplement bilateral arrangements (like Food for Peace), but so far to no avail. In the fall of 1960, the General Assembly had passed a resolution instructing the FAO to explore the possibilities. Having listened to the discussions in Rome and studied the recommendations, though, it was clear to McGovern "that somebody was going to have to make a concrete proposal." Two fellow delegates from the Departments of Agriculture and State suggested a plan for getting it off the ground. From Rome McGovern contacted the White House late on a Saturday night to ask permission to pledge on behalf of the United States some $40 million in commodities (and $10 million in cash, pending congressional approval), in order to generate an initial $100 million international fund. His audacity and his connections yielded results that might have taken Congress two years to achieve. Kennedy gave the go-ahead within twenty-four hours. The startled delegates in Rome gasped audibly as McGovern read out the terms of his proposal and the amount of the American pledge. It was an auspicious beginning. By early 1962 a three-year pilot program was in place in which some forty countries contributed to a multilateral world food bank—intended to meet emergencies and augment development projects and child-feeding programs—and all of it endorsed by the president, personally and publicly. McGovern had planted the seed for what was to become, in 1963, the FAO's World Food Program.[35]

As a result of all of these exertions, Food for Peace suddenly seemed to be everywhere at once. Although foreign aid was always subject to heated congressional debate, the *Milwaukee Journal* honored McGovern's version as "the Kennedy Administration's most successful achievement to date." Bernard Brenner, the United Press International's expert on agriculture, touted its "tremendous impact around the world," while Senator Humphrey pronounced it "a twentieth century form of alchemy." Drew Pearson hailed the program as one of the "most spectacular achievements of the young Kennedy administration," adding: "Live-wire ex-Congressman George McGovern of South Dakota has put three times as much life into the Food for Peace Program in six months as in eight years under Eisenhower." In countless newspaper articles and magazine features, from the *Wall Street Journal* to *The Progressive* and in Sunday supplements, particularly in western states, Americans learned about "The Coming War on Hunger." When he was not overseeing allotments in Egypt or Hong Kong, McGovern himself put out reams of press releases, appeared on television shows such as *Issues and Answers*, and traveled the speaker's circuit. He sponsored a national contest in *Parade* magazine to design a Food for Peace logo and oversaw the production of a promotional documentary film. Moreover, he took the lead in creating the American Food for Peace Council, with the author James Michener as cochair and a distinguished membership of serious-minded celebrities that boasted Marian Anderson, Yul Brynner, and Danny Kaye, the beloved champion of UNESCO.[36]

It was ironic that foreign aid programs always encountered serious congressional opposition. Kennedy referred to the problem as "one of the most extreme" paradoxes that ever beset him in politics. Despite its potential as an enlightened way to combat communism, Congress cut requests by 20 and 30 percent. To the National Conference on International Economic and Social Development, he complained: "I cannot understand those who are the most vigorous in wishing to stem the tide of communism around the world and are at the same time bombarding the Congress and the Administration with attacks on this program."[37]

In certain respects, McGovern felt the same frustrations. In recounting the successes of Food for Peace to his audiences he would highlight its practical advantages for the United States. It was obviously a godsend to American agriculture in helping to absorb the surpluses. But the shipments abroad also saved the federal government hundreds of millions of dollars in storage costs. And, because PL 480 stipulated that half of all the exports be carried in American ships, the program was a boon to the merchant marine. McGovern usually would begin a talk with statistics on social disparities in the recipient countries. In Ghana, for instance, there were four doctors for every 100,000 people; in Vietnam, fourteen teachers for every 10,000 people; and so on. Then he would describe the school lunch program and the misery it had ameliorated with "corn meal from Iowa and Illinois" and "wheat flour from the Dakotas and Kansas." And he would explain how "milk powder from Wisconsin" and "rice from Arkansas" constituted "self-help capital" for social and economic development in the Food for Wages program. America's heartland, once the cradle of isolationism, was now a dynamic force in *foreign policy*. "The American farmer," he declared, "is the new internationalist."

Finally, because "communism feeds on hunger and poverty," America's food was the greatest weapon in its arsenal. McGovern would remind his audience that Khrushchev was more interested in agriculture than in any other subject. The Soviet premier knew and worried about one astonishing fact: Farmers represented just 8 percent of the population of the United States, and yet they were five times more productive than their counterparts in Russia who made up nearly half of that country's labor force. Small wonder that the man who bragged, "We will bury you," spent two days with Bob Garst to see Iowa's tall corn firsthand. Food for Peace was indeed "a constructive instrument of foreign policy that illustrated the success of free American agriculture as . . . against some of the failures in the communist world." It was all rather crisply summed up by Walt Rostow—"Marx was a city boy."[38]

Yet McGovern was ambivalent about employing anticommunist rhetoric in selling Food for Peace. "My own inner sense of the program was that it should not be used in any major way as a Cold War tool," he said privately. A reliable applause line, such as "American food has done more to prevent . . . communism than all the military hardware we have shipped around the world," was an argument "against shipping arms around the world."[39] Then, too, in 1961 and 1962, he tried to convince Kennedy to ship surplus wheat to the People's Republic of China to relieve famine. The president listened carefully but told him twice, "The second term would be the time—not now." McGovern also talked to Walt Rostow after discovering a legal provision that would permit the sending of food to "friendly people 'without regard to the friendliness of their government.'" Such pleas did not move the deputy national security adviser, who viewed the famine through the lens of what Henry Kissinger would later call "linkage." In a "Memo for the Thanksgiving Weekend" (1961) Rostow wrote to Kennedy: "I would take even money that the Chinese Communists are in such bad economic trouble that they would do a good deal we would like them to do for a dose of PL 480." Rostow proposed to address tensions in Southeast Asia by persuading Australia and Canada to delay their grain shipments to China; the idea was to inform Beijing that Food for Peace could supply 350,000 tons of grain, but only "after a successful Lao settlement and if Hanoi calls off the attack on South Viet-Nam."[40]

McGovern never deluded himself that Cold War politics could be kept out of the humanitarian enterprise. The overarching question about Southeast Asia for American foreign policy makers was whether it would go "the India way" or "the China way."[41] Under the Kennedy administration Food for Peace would become politicized in South Vietnam and undermine much of the goodwill with which McGovern had imbued it. As for India, it did not have to contend with internal upheaval and foreign intervention as Vietnam did, but its problems were gargantuan. India could not feed itself, four out of five of its people were illiterate, and the average daily income was nineteen cents. In February 1962, McGovern traveled to Bombay to celebrate the delivery of the fourteen-millionth ton of wheat, making India the largest of all PL 480 consumers. School lunches were then reaching nearly four million Indian children and, on this mission, the director inaugurated a CARE program to nourish an additional half a million in the Punjab (which would double within two years). "It's hard now to emphasize how important Food for Peace was," Ambassador Galbraith recalled of the time McGovern came to India. "If two tankers loaded with wheat didn't come into Bombay every week there would be starvation somewhere." Yet India's neutrality in the Soviet-American confrontation was a sore point for Washington, and it would get sorer later when Indira Gandhi outraged President Johnson by sending birthday greetings to Ho Chi Minh. But just now McGovern could delight in reporting to Kennedy that, out of all the foreign aid the United States sent to the country, 62 percent was food. (For several other Food for Peace recipients the proportion ranged from 50 to 79 percent.) The program would prove indispensible in helping India to achieve self-sufficiency.[42]

By the end of his directorship, Food for Peace had become the most extensive foreign aid program of its kind of the twentieth century. McGovern had fully tripled the volume of commodities exported under PL 480. Under Title I, he had doubled the sales of food for foreign currencies and returned up to three-quarters of the proceeds to the various countries in the form of grants or loans for development purposes. Through Food for Wages he had created an international Works Progress Administration. Adding in the school lunch program, he had coordinated the feeding of more hungry people than any other individual in American history. And the world's first food bank had been established. Moreover, the president himself now talked regularly about the program at press conferences and emphasized it in State of the Union addresses. "Food for Peace," he declared in his second, "has become a vital force in the world."[43]

Food for Peace would have a lasting impact on McGovern's thinking about the ways that powerful nations, for weal or for woe, might figure in the life of weaker nations; indeed, it was probably the most important formative experience in his evolution as an anti-imperialist and political progressive. Even so, notwithstanding his decidedly milder brand of it, anticommunism was one of the causes the program had served and, in a way, anticommunism would do it in, though that misfortune lay down the road a ways. Meanwhile, whereas he would sustain a keen proprietary interest in Food for Peace, McGovern had never stopped longing to be a senator.

———————

It had become more than a reverie as early as the summer of 1961. This was partly because he had had to spend that June and July in the Georgetown University Hospital recovering from a severe case of hepatitis. The White House dispensary had infected him with a reused needle when inoculating him for his Latin America trip. His bedside reading included Theodore White's bestseller, *The Making of the President 1960*, and it prompted him to contemplate taking on Francis Case in November 1962. The president discouraged him when he broached the subject in January 1962, but McGovern raised it again in the spring with the younger Kennedy. "Can you win?" Bobby asked bluntly, for hardly anyone considered Case even slightly vulnerable. The attorney general also quizzed him about his health and said, "What I think you really ought to do is rest for about six or eight months." Yet McGovern was nothing if not self-confident, and another chance would not come along until 1966. "I don't think you should run," JFK said once more in April, "but you make the decision and whatever it is, I'll be with you."[44]

On the list of compelling reasons why not to run, the incumbent senator ranked first. Born in 1896 in Clay County, Iowa, Francis Case was a Dakota Wesleyan alumnus who, like McGovern, had won the national peace oratory prize and had gone on to Northwestern for graduate school. After years as a newspaper editor and publisher in Custer and Rapid City, he had served in seven Congresses before winning a Senate seat in 1950. On the Hill he earned the title of "the legislator's legislator." Case had few peers when it came to securing passage of major bills for interstate highway construction and for waterpower and irrigation development on the Missouri River. Water, an editorialist wrote, was "his very gospel." His constituents recognized that his work had improved their lives; they also admired him as a foe of profiteering during World War II and as a stickler who spurned improper corporate campaign contributions. Yet if any politician could deny him a third term in 1962, it was South Dakota's most prominent Democrat, who happened also to be a special assistant to the president.

But other complications perplexed McGovern. The selection of his successor was not a casual matter. And with a wife and five children to support, he could not afford to resign from his $22,500-a-year job. Nor did he want to start drawing fire back home too soon. He decided to postpone his resignation until August 30.[45] That begged still another problem. Some South Dakota Democrats thought McGovern should stay where he was and give someone else a shot at the race; others were annoyed he had not made his intentions known. His allies Peder Ecker and Bill Dougherty set off a rocket in April when they persuaded former lieutenant governor John "Frank" Lindley to declare candidacy for nomination. McGovern flew to Sioux Falls that week. Dougherty and Ecker thus smoked his plans out of him, and it turned out that Frank Lindley had no taste for battle with George. What Lindley really wanted was to be governor; he would gladly step aside if the three promised to move mountains for him in 1964. They did so immediately.[46]

McGovern announced his candidacy after a conference with the president on April 18. The same day the opposing chairs of the state-party organizations tried out some themes for the campaign. Jim Magness boasted, "No state in the union will have a stronger candidate for the Senate." The GOP's Leo Temmey was not impressed. "McGovern is being forced into this race by the Kennedy clan," he said. "They want to take over the whole country." One or two Republican newspapers followed that lead but gave McGovern his due. The *Argus Leader* observed that only he could mount a real challenge to Senator Case, and the administration knew it. According to the Rapid City *Daily Journal*, he was in the race "because the White House said so." The *Watertown Public Opinion* noted that McGovern frequently had expressed admiration for Case. "Both are scholarly and well grounded in government" and "the campaign . . . will be conducted on a high level."[47]

In a bit of larking, McGovern ostensibly confounded that forecast when he and Case met for a debate in June at the Hutchison County fair. As George Cunningham recalled the incident, the candidates' platform was set up outside a burlesque theater where dancing girls performed nightly. George and Francis were two stern Methodists, he reminisced, "And George said to me, 'You watch Francis and see what I do to him.' So this crowd was out there and McGovern got up and said, 'I want to thank Senator Case for giving us the opportunity to speak here today on the stage in front of his headquarters.' Francis just turned white. The audience roared and clapped. It was 90 percent Republican but they thought that was a pretty good joke. Francis thought it was kind of funny too." Then they turned to more serious matters. Alas, fate would grant these adversaries this one joint appearance. On June 21, the sixty-six-year-old Case complained of chest pains, checked in to the Naval Medical Center in Bethesda, and died the next morning. Their grief had yet to subside when the Republicans fell into disquiet over who was to be both his successor and the party's nominee for the next Senate term. The complexion of the campaign had changed before it had begun.[48]

The 126-member Republican Central Committee would select the party's nominee to face McGovern. The field included two former governors, the current East River congressman, and lieutenant governor. The convention took place at Pierre in the stifling house chamber of the capitol, galleries packed and no air conditioning. After twenty ballots and "a lot of hard feelings," Joseph Bottum, the lieutenant governor, emerged. Governor Archie Gubbrud appointed him to serve out Case's unexpired term as well.[49] Most copartisans considered the fifty-nine-year-old Rapid City lawyer more conservative than Case. Editorials described "a political scrapper" and "a Republican handyman." He portrayed himself as a devoted family man, an accomplished pianist, patron of the Boy Scouts, and an avid baker of cookies. One GOP committeeman said he was "a tireless campaigner who will retire Kennedy's fair-haired boy for good." As for Democrats, George Cunningham characterized him as a "hard drinking . . . guy who had fought bitter Republican battles all the way up the line." John Engel, the new state chairman, predicted he would "wage a clever and no-holds-barred campaign." But to Bill Dougherty, Bottum was "the worst guy they could have picked. That was the damnedest campaign I had ever been in. I mean it was just fucking balls to the wall the whole way."[50]

The Republicans lent some credence to Dougherty's recollection as they drafted a platform and a strategy. They cast McGovern as "a tool" of a "power grabbing" administration, but Kennedy would edge him out as the bête noire. The platform denounced the administration for its "exertion of centralized dictatorial power over our people." West River congressman E. Y. Berry accused the president of "turning the United States into a welfare state," and Bottum asserted JFK would go to any lengths to see McGovern elected. Karl Mundt said the Democrats let Kennedy pick their candidate. The keynote speaker, too, played on fears that he supposed afflicted South Dakotans. "The Kennedy lust for power bared its stark brazenness in a night time coup held high in the skyscrapers of New York," he warned. Hubert Humphrey and Arthur Schlesinger had "assembled a select group" to plan how to "buy a senate seat in South Dakota cheaper than they could in populous New York." These "arrogant, left-wing Democrats" then collected untold sums of money from their "suave international set." (The event, a cocktail party hosted by Averell Harriman, in fact had raised $980.)[51]

McGovern had taken a different tone upon his nomination by acclamation at Pierre on July 2. Food for Peace was the emphasis—that is, how "wheat and milk and corn from South Dakota are clearing up the swamplands of hunger on which communism breed[s]," and that there was "no stronger asset in our competition with Mr. Khrushchev than the American Farmer." Kennedy had not "in the slightest" affected his decision to run, he said. "But would it not be helpful for South Dakota to have one Senator who has some influence with the President of the United States?" The "deadening one-party Republican monopoly" had held the state back for decades. Now it was helping to obstruct national legislation for agriculture, medical care for the aged, and expanded trade with Europe. The Republicans "talk about the Government as though it were an enemy of the people," he said. They seemed to "have lost faith in the capacity of the people to advance through positive government." The question was "whether South Dakota is going to stand still or move ahead." The very first statewide poll, completed on July 25, put him at 48 percent to Bottum's 52.[52]

———————

McGovern hoped to run more or less on the New Frontier agenda. Yet it was as much of a handicap in South Dakota as Catholicism had been two years before. JFK's legislative score card, one of the least impressive of any president's in the twentieth century, complicated the situation. This was not entirely of his making. He had been saddled with a depressed economy, and the coalition of southern Democrats and conservative Republicans continued to thrive. Then, too, hardly any Democrat was beholden to the president; like McGovern, a record number of them had run ahead of the national ticket in 1960. As for his power to persuade, to liberal Democrats JFK's sense of connection to Roosevelt's domestic legacy seemed tenuous and lacked passion. "What is at stake in our economic decisions today is not some grand warfare of rival ideologies," Kennedy believed, "but the practical management of a modern economy." Hence, in his first two years, victories were few and modest—an increase in the minimum wage from $1 to $1.25; a $400 million appropriation for redevelopment in distressed parts of the country; and the Trade Expansion Act of September 1962, which permitted reciprocal tariff reductions to stimulate trade with the European Common Market (in retrospect, momentous).[53]

At the same time, the conservative coalition had beaten back the legislation of greatest potential. This included an expansion of the National Defense Education Act—to allocate to the states some $2.3 billion for school construction and teacher salaries and an additional $3.3 billion for colleges and scholarships. Then, conservatives cut by two-thirds his $2.9 billion request for public works projects to relieve unemployment and scuttled the administration's proposal to create a department of urban affairs. As the midterm contests heated up in July 1962, the Senate roll was called on a coalition-backed motion to table Medicare. A vote of 52 to 48 rendered the bill dead on arrival. Three weeks earlier the House had stunned the president by rejecting his farm bill 215 to 205; it had aimed further to reduce surpluses through restrictions on output in exchange for reasonable price supports. A single Republican supported the measure while forty-eight Democrats jumped ship.[54]

Kennedy nonetheless had gotten behind Medicare, education, trade expansion, and youth employment programs. Facing a political cross-cut saw, McGovern affirmed at Aberdeen, "We're not going to soft pedal the issues of this campaign." He would also argue that the New Frontier had halted the downward trend in agriculture: Farm income was now $1 billion higher than in 1960 and, with help from Food for Peace, the surpluses had been reduced. Even so, by Labor Day, JFK the legislator had provided his party with little by way of substantive results to campaign on. In South Dakota, however, it did not matter that his liberalism lacked efficacy. The Republicans reproached him for Big Government excesses anyway. Right after voting to table Medicare, Joe Bottum claimed he had become one of five White House "targets" for punishment—"another example of how this ruthless administration operates." As in 1960, anti-Kennedy sentiment was the hurdle McGovern had to overcome.[55]

Naturally, then, Republicans criticized the president for coming to Pierre in mid-August with McGovern at his side to dedicate the gigantic Oahe Dam. Not all of Bottum's supporters protested, however. Robert Lusk, publisher of Huron's *Daily Plainsman*, considered the visit "a signal honor" and its purpose not partisan. Kennedy, Lusk pointed out, would be the first president to see the world's largest earth-rolled dam, 242 feet high at the crest and embankments stretching almost two miles. In addition to flood control, the structure would irrigate half a million acres in eastern South Dakota and supply three billion kilowatts of hydroelectricity to nine states.[56] Indeed, the focus of the event, prompted by a letter to the White House from fifth-grader Jamie Damon, whose father worked on the dam, was a perfect illustration of McGovern's vision of "the capacity of the people to advance through positive government."

Kennedy kept his remarks "nonpolitical." He invited Jamie's family to join him on the platform. He likened the dam's national security importance to that of "any military Alliance or missile complex." He stressed the need for cooperation between public and private institutions—as Oahe showed—if, his *text* stated, "we are to make certain . . . America will always have the soil and water to feed the world's hungry and homeless, as George McGovern has demonstrated so ably these last eighteen months." But he decided not to mention his protégé. This gesture failed to assuage the state's congressional Republicans, none of whom attended the ceremony or could appreciate Jamie's uncomplicated greeting to the president, "I'm glad I invited you." Joe Bottum was certain his purpose was "to further the political ambitions of one of the candidates he wants to vote implicitly for the New Frontier programs." To state chairman Temmey, JFK had attempted "to threaten South

Dakotans into delivering a Democrat to the United States Senate."[57] On every front they continued to attack the president; in newspaper ads, Bottum declared his behavior "not many steps removed from those a dictator might employ" and alerted voters, "Democrats try to hide their liberal, often socialistic views, their desire to control everything."[58]

Yet all along Joe refused to debate George. Two joint appearances without direct interaction were all he would concede. In the first, before Mitchell's Municipal League in September, he assailed Big Government and the Kennedy administration for spending beyond its means and for "taking nearly $200 million from our state." McGovern reminded the audience that those tax dollars had gone to agriculture, highways, and national defense. As for the $200 million, the feds returned $400 million to South Dakota in the form of Social Security, Missouri River development, and the Rural Electrification program.[59]

The rivals addressed agriculture at a large gathering at the State Corn Picking Contest two weeks later. Bottum advocated "sufficiently high" supports and opposed the limits on grain output that Secretary Freeman advocated. McGovern contended that the Kennedy-Freeman program had enriched South Dakota farmers by $35 million for two years running, but Bottum wanted to go back to Ezra Taft Benson's policies. He then turned to Temmey's latest outburst, that Freeman wanted to "communize" US farming. Temmey, said McGovern, had spoken in "bad faith" against Kennedy and Freeman who worked "night and day to improve the lot of the farmer." He also made Bottum look foolish for boasting that he had killed Medicare.[60]

Most people seemed to think McGovern had won, but that morning he could barely get out of bed. Just to raise an arm was a struggle. Eleanor and his doctor, concerned about his hepatitis, had tried to keep him from overdoing things. Now a serious relapse had gripped him. Yet he refused to cancel the debate, which was to be broadcast over the radio. He had Eleanor put a mattress in the rear of their station wagon so he could rest on the long drive to the fairgrounds. As Bottum spoke over the loudspeaker George listened on his back from the parking lot. Then he made his way to the platform. "Operating purely on nerve," he later said, "I gave what had to be one of the most effective public performances of my life." But he was seriously ill, and he worried about the news getting out. Later he checked in to a hospital in Sioux City, Iowa, as G. Stanley McGovern. A nurse recognized him and the local television station called. That ended his anonymity. He remained bedridden for most of October.[61]

He might have fallen behind and lost, but for three factors. The first was Eleanor, who filled in for him at engagements he was too sick to attend. Never before had she taken on such a role. For weeks she drove all over the state, sometimes with ten-year-old Steve as her navigator but often solo. "She did better before some audiences than George would have," one staffer said. (Humphrey stumped for him, too.) Second, at the behest of Jim Symington (his former assistant at Food for Peace), McGovern previously had commissioned Charles Guggenheim, a young filmmaker, to produce a twenty-five-minute documentary about him. It proved to be a wise investment.[62]

A Dakota Story opens on McGovern conversing with citizens on a street corner. Cued by thematic music, the scene fades to panoramas of the countryside on his drive home. "As a Democrat in our Republican state he can see an uphill climb, but he can also see a chance to work for the land he was born to," the narrator says, as Eleanor and the children greet him. The story harks back to olden times in a series of photographs of homesteaders and then to a rendering of Joseph McGovern's influence upon his son—"the faith and convictions of a Christian gentleman"—along with the impact of the Great Depression. Then two of George's teachers recall what a fine boy he was. A farmer speaks of him as "a man who'd help anybody anytime anyway he could." The account moves to Dakota Wesleyan, a wartime courtship, and on to a montage of aerial combat to reenact a crash landing of a B-24. Crewmate Bill McAfee attests to his commander's courage. The film then comes back home. Students are asking McGovern questions about the Cold War as seven-year-old Mary looks on. There must be an alternative between "the Wallace way of just hoping for peace" and "the extremists out on the right wing . . . [who] would lead us straight into a war to the death," he tells them. "There are certain constructive things that we . . . have to do if we want to see the world move in the direction of peace instead of war." The setting changes to his labors in Congress to show the state that the Democratic Party works for people and the nation. Views of giant grain elevators follow, pouring out America's great gift into Food for Peace to fortify the prospects of freedom for the children of the Third World. As music wells up, George salutes those who turned the frontier into thriving farms and cities: "The people of South Dakota have never been content to stand still. And I'm convinced that now they're not going to turn their backs on the future!"[63]

A Dakota Story was its creator's second such film—Guggenheim would win four Academy Awards in the years ahead—and a part of a pioneering body of work in the new field of political and historical documentary filmmaking. In 1962, radio, print media, and personal contact remained extremely important in South Dakota politics. (It was possible for a candidate to shake hands with every voter in the state.) But television had already emerged as the principal medium in national politics. Guggenheim's innovative propaganda was intended to educate and persuade via television. The campaign aired the film across the state repeatedly, and Eleanor showed it on her tours. "When the senator got sick," said Pat Donovan, "it was our life saver."[64] But the third factor also compensated for the candidate's disability—an international crisis of historic proportions and one deeply fraught with domestic political implications.

Revolutionary Cuba's prominence in American politics and foreign policy had never waned after January 1959. During the 1960 campaign Kennedy had exploited the issue unabashedly. "Today the Iron curtain is 90 miles off the coast of the United States," he said as often as Nixon might have done if Castro had come to power under a Democrat instead of Eisenhower. After the Bay of Pigs fiasco in April 1961, however, Cuba belonged to Kennedy.[65] Most accounts suggest it became his obsession. He accepted responsibility for permitting the hopeless raid—and privately regretted having been "so stupid"—but also refused to guarantee not to undertake another such assault. The administration had not relented in its resolve to destroy Castro's government. The president authorized acts of sabotage and secret economic warfare against Cuba and arranged for its ouster from the OAS. The CIA commenced an assortment of bizarre attempts to assassinate Castro. This determination played its part in motivating Castro to seek protection and in providing Khrushchev with a rationale for his supremely reckless decision, in July 1962, to mount medium-range ballistic missiles on the island ostensibly to shield it against the colossus to the north, though strategic factors were involved as well.[66]

Once the midterm campaigns were under way the Soviet build-up became the blockbuster issue. Republicans led by senators Homer Capehart of Indiana and Kenneth Keating of New York complained about the alleged presence of missiles and called for either a blockade or another invasion of Cuba. Karl Mundt sounded off as well. The president's initial response was to request a resolution approving a call-up of 150,000 reservists in an emergency, which the Senate passed. McGovern declared that Kennedy had "successfully isolated Castro's influence within the isle of Cuba" and made much of Joe Bottum's absence when the vote was taken. Meanwhile, in neighboring Iowa and Minnesota 80 percent of respondents said Cuba was a "serious threat" to the nation in late September polls conducted by the *Des Moines Register* and the *Minneapolis Tribune*. Another survey of six states revealed that four out of five Republicans favored a blockade as opposed to only one out of three Democrats.[67]

This divide obtained in South Dakota, too. "Cuba is the Democratic nightmare and the Republican dream-issue," the *Huron Daily Plainsman* posited a week before U-2 flights secured proof of the missile sites; citizens were angry because Kennedy had "allowed a Communist satellite to rise at our back door." House Republicans regarded the brewing crisis as their most promising means of gaining majority control. On October 9, Senator Bottum demanded "firm action against Cuba," perhaps a naval blockade, he said. From his sickbed McGovern called Bottum an "arm-chair general" and cautioned him not to "play politics . . . [with] our national security." Counseling "firmness instead of reckless talk," McGovern argued that there was no telling where a blockade (an act of war) would end, and that the congressional resolution, "which my opponent failed to support," would "bring instant retaliation" against any threat from Cuba.[68]

On October 16 Kennedy saw the photographic evidence and immediately convened the "ExCom," an advisory group he hoped could help him avert catastrophe. Secretary of defense Robert McNamara affirmed on the first of the "thirteen days" that the forty-odd missiles upset the strategic balance "not at all." The United States vastly outmatched the Soviets in every category, from nuclear force loads to numbers of ICBMs. What the administration faced was "a domestic political problem," he said. The president did not demur. But everyone agreed the missiles had to be gotten out before they became operational. The question was how. The range of choices was limited: negotiations that involved the removal of US Jupiter missiles in Turkey on the Soviet border; a surprise air strike, which could not ensure destruction of all the missiles; a military invasion sure to incur heavy casualties on all sides; and a naval blockade to halt further shipments to Cuba accompanied by a demand that the Soviets dismantle the sites.[69]

Kennedy chose the latter option and informed the Soviets and the American people at the same moment, in a solemn televised address on October 22. Two tense days later Soviet ships neared the line of "quarantine," then turned homeward. Yet the crisis had hardly subsided. On October 26 Khrushchev offered to withdraw his missiles in exchange for what Kennedy had previously refused—a guarantee not to invade Cuba again. Then, on the twenty-seventh, before the president could answer, the premier sent a second letter, demanding the United States dismantle its missiles in Turkey also. Some advisers now urged an air strike. But Kennedy judged Khrushchev's letters "reasonable." In fact, they formed the basis for a peaceful finale—although the ExCom stipulated that the Soviets must begin to take down their missiles forthwith and that the accord on the Jupiters must remain secret and might take a few months to complete. Scholars ever since have debated the implications of this settlement as well as the origins of the crisis and how well Kennedy managed it. As historian Walter LaFeber has written, however, "That the world survived the Cuban missile crisis was in part dumb luck." Indeed, not even the frazzled principals realized the full extent to which this was so.[70]

Although Americans gave the president credit for his courage and restraint, that did not mean politics had been adjourned. Senator Capehart said he knew "Khrushchev would put his tail between his legs" if only JFK would toughen up. Joe Bottum declared himself vindicated by the blockade, counsel his opponent had called "half-baked." McGovern rejoined that action taken any sooner would have been "premature and highly dangerous." Karl Mundt threw in, too. McGovern had "ridiculed [Bottum's] stand-up policy against Cuba," then "lamely switched positions." The senator also advised JFK to fire Rostow and Schlesinger, who had "induced him to delay his blockade . . . [and] to withdraw the air-cover from the Bay of Pigs liberation."[71]

These criticisms did not reflect the rank and file, for the missile crisis had transformed Kennedy's presidency. His quarantine speech in particular impressed his audiences, and South Dakotans were no exception. The *Argus Leader* ran a cross section of Sioux Falls opinion on the front page. "I thought his talk was excellent," an American Legion commander said. The head of the historical society felt "Kennedy acted in a most courageous manner." The United Nations Day chairman believed he was "wise" to wait "until all the facts were in, thereby assuring . . . our integrity in this crisis," though several people said the show of strength "probably should have come sooner." The *Daily Plainsman* headlined Samuel Lubell's national opinion report, "Blockade Will Aid Democrat Chances."[72]

Thus the crisis appeared to have turned the political liability of association with Kennedy into an asset. On November 2, in South Dakota's final poll, McGovern for the first time pulled ahead, 53 percent to 47, after trailing Bottum by an average of six points since July. An assistant to Francis Case believed Cuba was the "only single thing with sufficient force to make such a dramatic change." Just the week before, Ethel Kennedy, Bobby's wife, drew enthusiastic crowds in Aberdeen, Rapid City, and Sioux Falls, stumping for George. "Everybody in Washington wants him, the President needs him, and all the Kennedys love him," she said. Local press and television gave her visit maximum coverage. She "played the Kennedy thing in a humorous, light way that blunted a lot of the attacks about me being out there as a stooge," McGovern said. "I think it was a nice lift right at the end."[73]

Both sides kept up their attacks down to the wire. Leo Temmey asserted that Ethel's affection for her "great pal" made South Dakotans "more anxious than ever" to stay "out of the clutches of the Kennedy family." Bottum derided McGovern's "go soft on Cuba" policy and said the New Frontier intended to "bring us socialism a piece at a time." McGovern stuck to the administration's improved wheat and feed grain program and reductions in surpluses, and how Kennedy's trade bill, Food for Peace, and the Peace Corps together had "placed the Communists in a greatly weakened defensive position."[74]

On November 6, Kennedy managed an extraordinary feat in spite of his legislative woes and a problematical foreign policy performance until the run-up to Election Day. With the exceptions of 1902 and 1934, in the twentieth century the party in power always lost a sizable number of seats in off-year elections—an average of forty-four in the House and seven in the Senate. In 1962 the Democratic Party netted a loss of only four in the House and gained two in the Senate. Because so many domestic initiatives had failed by three or four votes, and early polls had warned that perhaps twenty-five Democrats were at risk, the president had decided he must wade into the campaign. Even with the distraction of Cuba, he logged more miles than Ike had in the midterms of 1954 and 1958 combined. The phenomenal outcome had much to do with the unexpected surge in Kennedy's popular standing. The composition of the 88th Congress would be 259 to 176 in the House and 66 to 34 in the Senate.[75]

South Dakota, in its second-highest midterm turnout ever, registered a Republican sweep of all statewide offices, including governor and the two House districts. But the contest in which more people voted than any other remained undecided. On Wednesday the unofficial tally for McGovern versus Bottum was 128,558 to 128,287. Although his phone rang constantly with calls of congratulation, McGovern declined to claim victory with a lead of 271 votes out of over a quarter million. Bottum filed for a recount at the end of the week.[76]

The process was tedious. President Kennedy sent the chief Democratic and Republican counsels of the Senate Rules Committee to oversee it. George Cunningham immersed himself in the state's case law on recounts as well as in the sixteen irregularities that might disqualify a ballot. He then developed a slide show to instruct election boards in counties where the McGovern campaign decided to lodge its own challenges. "Bottum's people were not as well prepared as our people," Cunningham said. On one day the auditor of Lawrence County reported a gain of twelve for McGovern while the official canvass in Pennington County determined no change at all in Bottum's vote of 8,396 and McGovern's of 7,458. On another day, McGovern's statewide numbers improved slightly, yet Codington County established gains of forty-seven for him and seventy-six for Bottum, while Mellette Township disqualified seventy-five and thirty-one of their ballots, respectively. A painstaking recount of the precincts of Minnehaha, the most populous county, gave McGovern another fifty-one the next week and Yankton County corrected clerical errors, netting him a 118-vote gain. Bottum's attorney acknowledged that the changes were "not encouraging."[77] Trailing by over five hundred votes, Bottum conceded on December 5.

One might have thought that McGovern should have walked away with this contest. But Bottum proved to be an awfully tough candidate; he had no qualms about running on "Americanism" or branding the director of Food for Peace as a socialist tool of a dynastic instrument of Big Government. To an extent, he made the election turn on whether South Dakotans liked and trusted the young Democrat enough to put him in the upper house where he might do the bidding of a president whom the state had rejected overwhelmingly in 1960. Bottum probably benefited from having been lieutenant governor as much as being the incumbent senator; he might have won had he not overplayed his hand in the Cuban situation. The *Argus Leader*, Senator Case's adviser, and local surveys suggested that the president's success in the missile crisis gave McGovern a boost. (So has a major historical analysis of the impact of the crisis on the midterm elections.) Moreover, he made Bottum pay a price for not showing up to vote on the "fight-if-we-must" emergency resolution. Nor did Bottum have anything to offset the modest improvements in farm income of the previous two years or McGovern's enhanced expertise in international agricultural economics. Then, too, as George once remarked, Ethel Kennedy's last-minute tour of three major cities may well have made the difference; he won by 597 votes out of 257,000; "that push right at the end on her part was decisive," he said. "Oh, yes," Eleanor remarked. "It really taught us that there really is value in one vote." They would have said as much about Guggenheim's film as well.[78]

Final certification of the results rested with the State Board of Canvassers, chaired by Governor Gubbrud, the man who had appointed Bottum in the first place. George Cunningham was prepared for anything as he stood before the board in Pierre. But he had barely begun his presentation when Gubbrud interrupted: "I have a dental appointment. I think I'll go." And so it ended. Cunningham drove back to Mitchell, certificate in hand. As he pulled up, all of the McGoverns poured out of the house whooping and wanting "to see the truth after going through all of that," as he recalled the moment. It was, said McGovern, "the best Christmas present anybody ever received."[79]

13 WE ARE DETERMINING THE PRIORITIES OF OUR NATIONAL LIFE

George McGovern believed he had the best job imaginable, save being president of the United States. At forty, he was among the youngest in the chamber, and he joked that only his seat mate in the back row, thirty-year-old Ted Kennedy, showed him "the respect reserved for an 'elderly gentleman.'" In contrast to 1957, however, McGovern already understood much of the workings of the Senate. He enjoyed a stellar reputation as a former representative, the champion of Food for Peace, and a favorite of the White House. (He even drew the suite in the Russell Office Building that President Kennedy had occupied.) Moreover, being a senator afforded him the sort of freedom he had always craved in politics but had never known. He and his family had endured four grueling elections in six years. Now he felt liberated to go about the work he was intended to do, beyond South Dakota. And luck favored him again; as with Rayburn in the House, he entered the Senate two years after Mike Mansfield had succeeded LBJ as majority leader. A learned, self-effacing Montanan, Mansfield disliked the way Johnson had operated, and he saw himself instead as one among equal colleagues; one of them once stated that his approach as leader was "to make it possible for every senator to do what he wants to do." For the likes of McGovern, that engendered a most conducive institutional environment. There was no friendlier soul on Capitol Hill more ready to accommodate others, yet he could also be a lone player, especially on the controversial issues. This did not mean he did not know a good horse trade when he saw one or no longer heeded the interests of his state. He used his pull with Humphrey and Mansfield to secure committee assignments on Agriculture and Interior, and he never feared to regale Secretary Freeman or the president himself about sliding beef prices.[1]

But these were not the realms in which he planned to carve his legacy. On January 31, 1963, McGovern had the honor of addressing the National Roosevelt Day Dinner at the Astor Hotel in New York City. Eleanor and Franklin Roosevelt's great strength, he said, lay in the fact that they did not seek selfish lives, but instead dedicated themselves to service to others. Their example could inspire new senators as they confronted the challenges of the 1960s. These included "the broad question of whether or not, in our affluence, we can be aroused to act in behalf of the voiceless Americans around us who still live in poverty and insecurity." Given that "we are involved in the lives of a hundred nations," the tasks of arms control, a nuclear test ban, and related issues beckoned also. With his own campaign and the missile crisis in mind, he warned, "beware the impatient men of the ultra right—those who . . . are ready either to retire from the world or annihilate it." Senators "desperately need a sense of history," so they might understand that "America's position abroad will be determined not only by what we do around the world but by the quality of our society, our institutions, and our service here at home."[2]

McGovern's perception about the indivisibility of politics and foreign policy was to become his central mode of political analysis; it delineated his ambitions for his country and his understanding of liberalism of the 1960s. In addition to helping to enlarge "the capacity of the people to advance through positive government," as he had put it in the campaign, he intended to play a role in international affairs so as to ameliorate the Cold War and further the cause of world peace. The Senate gave him the maximum opportunity to be heard and to have an impact. Although he esteemed his new colleagues, if truth be told he considered himself better equipped than most of them to bring to the forum distinctive insights, even wisdom—derived in part from his critical study of history.[3] McGovern's maiden floor speech on March 15 was an example.

"Our Castro Fixation versus the Alliance for Progress" was informed by his scholarly background, his earlier stands against military interventionism, and his education as Food for Peace director. He began by defending President Kennedy against right-wing attacks for his disinclination to undertake a post-missile-crisis invasion of Cuba. At the same time, though, he characterized the administration's trespasses against that island as a "tragic mistake," adding that the Bay of Pigs invasion "might have damaged our standing in the hemisphere more if it had succeeded." Neither Castro nor Khrushchev was at the root of Latin America's "explosive situation," he argued; they were "effects rather than causes." Too many in Congress seemed too willing to shed American blood in Cuba instead of giving attention to Latin America's "real problems." He submitted an inventory. The richest 2 percent of the region's people possessed over half its wealth while 80 percent lived in shacks or huts, with no prospect of ever owning the land to which they were bound. The rate of illiteracy exceeded one-third, and disease and malnourishment afflicted 50 percent of the people. There were also the burdens of swelling populations, one-crop economies, unjust tax structures, and military establishments designed to keep the system intact.

In time, history might honor Cuba's revolution, McGovern proffered, because it had confronted the ruling classes of Latin America as well as the United States "and forced every government of the hemisphere to take a new and more searching look at the crying needs of the great masses of human beings." The Alliance for Progress and the Peace Corps and Food for Peace were "our best answer to communism." But he doubted whether the ruling classes had been "aroused sufficiently . . . to make the Alliance succeed on a broad scale." As for his fellow citizens, they must not dissipate their energies "in a senseless fixation on Castro." They would do well to refrain from ill-advised military interventions in the name of anticommunism; their mission abroad ought to be "to point the way to a better life for the hemisphere and, indeed, for all mankind."[4]

His remarks would have been considered audacious for a seasoned member of the chamber, let alone for a beginner. Kennedy, for one, was not pleased; McGovern had neglected to send an advance copy to the White House. Notwithstanding his praise for the Alliance, he had implied that the administration, not just its right-wing critics, was hobbled by a "Castro fixation" that failed to plumb the causes of modern revolutions. When he inquired about JFK's reaction, Ted Sorensen told him, "I don't think he liked it very well. He thinks [Castro] is really bad news." It bothered Arthur Schlesinger too: "Basically this is a splendid piece," but he worried George appeared "indifferent to . . . Castro" and "overstated the national preoccupation with Castro." The *Wash-*

ington Post did not agree. "How right the senator is!" a main editorial exclaimed, praising him for setting forth revelatory facts about Latin America. "While Castro may not beat us, the Castro fixation could." Senator Wayne Morse, chair of the Subcommittee on Latin American Affairs, called it a "brilliant and eloquent statement." Mansfield said "it was a damned important speech that plowed new ground." The *New York Times Magazine* affirmed its significance by publishing an expanded version, "Is Castro an Obsession with Us?"[5]

Latin America formed the pivot of McGovern's gravest concerns. The region exemplified what, since his time in the House, he had regarded as the core problems with American foreign policy in the Third World. He worried that the administration's ongoing aid to noxious military regimes and its hostility to democratic leftists would unravel the Alliance for Progress. He admired the president's performance in the October crisis, but he apprehended how close humanity had lurched toward oblivion, to some extent the result of a potentially disastrous, systemic way of thinking. As he said in a follow-up speech in June, "Cuba is only one of a score of tension spots." It could happen elsewhere, or on that island again.[6]

Significantly, the initial stage of George McGovern's Senate apprenticeship occurred between the aftermath of the missile crisis and the escalation of the war in Vietnam. During that hopeful interlude, he perceived a historic opportunity for the United States to alter the trend born of the Cold War. His article in the *New York Times Magazine* brought him to the attention of leading academic critics of American foreign and defense policy such as Seymour Melman, a Columbia University professor of industrial engineering and a critic of excessive military spending; George McT. Kahin, a Southeast Asia expert at Cornell; and Sanford Gottlieb, the director of the National Committee for a Sane Nuclear Policy. They supplied McGovern with studies relevant to his concerns. The prevailing state of international relations, he believed, held promise for curbing the arms race and for dismantling (at least partially) America's colossal military-industrial complex by way of a gradual shift in the nation's economy toward more pacific industrial enterprises. If the United States intended "to fulfill its promise both at home and around the globe," as he had said in his Cuba speech, it must get on with the unfinished work of creating new jobs and educational opportunities for young people, and of addressing the high medical costs older people faced as well as the deeper causes behind poverty. It was "no longer possible to separate America's domestic health from our position in world affairs." He began to prepare extraordinary legislation to serve those ends.

McGovern assumed the White House would be sympathetic. In his State of the Union message in January, Kennedy once again had called for a controversial tax cut, new investment in the education of the nation's youth, and health insurance for its old people. "Now, when no military crisis strains our resources—now is the time to act," he had said. McGovern also liked the phrase, "We shall be judged more by what we do at home than what we preach abroad." But the president embraced incongruous goals. He spoke of humanitarian concerns—of the Alliance, Food for Peace, and the Peace Corps—yet framed them in Cold War rhetoric: "to arm and feed and clothe millions of people who live on the front lines of freedom." He advocated a nuclear test ban, but he also forecast for 1963 expenditures of $15 billion just for nuclear weapons (more than all the European allies' defense budgets combined). On June 10, he mixed his message again, in his first effort to confront the existential issues the missile crisis had raised.[7]

In this celebrated address at American University, Kennedy announced that he and his Soviet and British counterparts had agreed to begin talks about a comprehensive test ban treaty. To advance the cause he declared that the United States would halt all nuclear testing in the atmosphere. He then discoursed on détente and the pursuit of peace, "a topic on which ignorance too often abounds." Peace did not mean "a Pax Americana to be enforced on the world by American weapons of war." It was "a process—a way of solving problems," he said. He asked his fellow citizens to reexamine their attitudes toward their adversaries. Unlike any Cold War president before or since, he paid tribute to the Soviet people's suffering during World War II. "At least 20 million lost their lives," he instructed. "A third of the nation's territory, including nearly two-thirds of its industrial base, was turned into a wasteland." His point was that no people was utterly "lacking in virtue," regardless of their political system. "And if we cannot end now our differences," he concluded, "at least we can help make the world safe for diversity." To no one did Kennedy's remarks mean more than they did to McGovern, with one possible exception. Nikita Khrushchev judged it "the best speech by any American president since Roosevelt."[8]

On August 2, 1963, the senator took the floor to give a speech that would stand among the most significant of his career. It was about the arms race and the pending military budget of $53.6 billion for fiscal 1964, which accounted for over half of the entire federal budget and exceeded, he pointed out, the cost of all the programs of the New Deal from 1933 to 1940. He proposed to reverse course by cutting appropriations by 10 percent, or $5 billion. He made a powerful case for pruning. In virtually every category—from ICBMs to Polaris submarines and strategic bombers—the United States far outpaced Soviet capabilities. He noted that during World War II, his B-24 had carried the equivalent of five tons of TNT, a force rendered trifling "in the shadow of the 20,000-ton destroyer of Hiroshima." Then, only five years later, scientists invented the H-Bomb, its magnitude a thousand times greater. But today the US nuclear arsenal was more than "one and a half million times as powerful as the bomb that wiped out Hiroshima." Together, the two superpowers had amassed in their stockpiles the equivalent of some sixty billion tons of TNT, or a twenty-ton bomb for every human being on the face of the earth. Next he cited estimates of Secretary of Defense McNamara that an all-out nuclear exchange would yield ninety million fatalities in western Europe, 100 million in the United States, and 100 million in the Soviet Union. In light of such excessive "overkill capacity," a term that Professor Melman invoked, "what possible advantage" could accrue from spending "additional billions of dollars to build more missiles and bombs," McGovern asked. "How many times is it necessary to kill a man or a nation?" It went without saying that America required "a defense force that is second to none," but the time had come for a serious reconsideration of national security needs and their implications for American society. What, in this instance, could his proposed $5 billion savings mean? It could "build a $1 million school in every one of the nation's 3,000 counties, plus 500 hospitals costing $1 million apiece, plus college scholarships worth $5,000 each to 100,000 students—and still permit a tax reduction of a billion dollars."

The threat of annihilation was not McGovern's only concern. He felt discouraged, he said, that debate grew heated over whether the government should spend a mere $200 million for the nation's mental health facilities, or $100 million for a youth conservation training program. Yet staggering expenditures for armaments flew through the legislature with hardly a quibble. Not far from his mind in all of this was President Eisenhower's yet to be celebrated farewell address, which warned of the dangers that the military-industrial complex posed to democracy. Counseling a coordinated effort between industry and government, McGovern called upon Kennedy to establish an Economic Conversion Commission, to study, in consultation with the governors of the states, "any reasonable future opportunities for converting the instruments of war to the tools of peace." The president should also request major defense contractors to appoint their own committees to study ways to ease the coming transition to a peacetime economy. Systematic planning of this sort was essential to relieving the anxieties of all concerned who had grown dependent upon the "gigantic WPA" that the Pentagon had become. And it would "add new force to disarmament discussions by removing fear of the economic consequences" and "cause a boom, rather than a drag on our economy."

Alluding to Eisenhower's alarm over "the conjunction of an immense military establishment and a large arms industry," McGovern argued that the current level of military spending actually distorted the nation's economy—by weakening the competitive position of civilian industries and aggravating the balance of payments. For example, both Japan and western Europe were busy modernizing their civilian industrial plants at a much faster rate, yet the United States devoted three-fourths of all its scientific and engineering talent to weapons research and development. Although it once ranked first in machine tool production, the United States had slipped to fifth place by 1963. Meanwhile, thousands of public school teachers were failing to meet reasonable teaching standards. Apart from everything else, then, a gradual reordering of priorities seemed a matter of common sense. McGovern recognized that what he was proposing could not be accomplished overnight. A full tenth of the country's gross national product was devoted to military spending, and many corporations and members of Congress would oppose any substantial reductions. But perhaps his suggestions might "stimulate in some way the larger debate which needs to be waged."[9]

"New Perspectives on American Security" scored a great success. Several leading Democrats rose to associate themselves with McGovern. Frank Church, his kindred spirit from Idaho, declared the speech "the most important of the session" and urged absentee senators to read it. Jennings Randolph of West Virginia agreed that the nation's nuclear stockpile exceeded "any conceivable need" and that undue military spending wasted human resources. To make his case, Randolph cited the 1960 census, which had revealed that over 20 percent of American families lived in poverty on annual incomes of $1,000 or less. Wisconsin's Gaylord Nelson could not recall anyone who had ever focused the Senate's attention on this, "the all-consuming issue of our time." Senator Morse was gratified to find new colleagues who understood that Americans "shall have a stronger security program if we spend less."[10]

That evening on the ABC network news Edward P. Morgan devoted his commentary to the subject. A young senator with a fine war record was advocating some diversion of military appropriations "to peaceful purposes . . . to enrich the fabric of American society," he said. The Pentagon had conceded that the United States had "hundreds of times more nuclear weapons than [it] would ever use in an all-out war," continued Morgan, but there was "too much logic and good sense in the Senator's idea for it to have easy sledding." The *New York Times* also showed appreciation. On August 16, "the problem of economic adjustment to arms control" filled an entire page, based on interviews with McGovern, the country's twenty-five largest defense contractors, and the Defense Department. Over 2.5 million civilians worked in these industries and nearly one-third of all manufacturing jobs in the states of Washington, Kansas, and California were tied to defense, the *Times* reported. Yet major contractors indicated that, "although the transition would be difficult," they would shift into commercial manufacturing if the government said so. The Arms Control and Disarmament Agency agreed: "the [US] economy could be . . . adapted to any kind of arms control, including general and complete disarmament." The key was to start planning now, as McGovern proposed. As for nuclear "overkill," McNamara tried to refute it, but his prior testimony to Congress contradicted his denial that the arsenal had attained such grim levels of redundancy.[11]

Two days later the *Wall Street Journal* said McGovern's speech was "among the most widely read documents in official Washington." Noting that Senators Fulbright and Humphrey "were inclined to agree" on the matter of "overkill," the *Journal* thought few of their colleagues would vote against the recommendations of the Appropriations Committee. Still there was "restiveness" on Capitol Hill traceable to McGovern. Set in motion by a freshman's initiative, "for the first time Congress is seriously questioning in a coherent way the assumptions underlying defense spending," the *Journal* suggested. Leading publications ran similar stories throughout the summer in the context of the pending test ban treaty. As that vote neared, the *Washington Post* hoped McGovern's economic conversion would be "widely supported."[12]

The Limited Nuclear Test Ban—in prohibiting the testing of nuclear warheads in the atmosphere, the oceans, and outer space—checked the hazard of radiation poisoning in the Earth's air, food, and water. As Kennedy promised, the Cold War's first arms control agreement offered "a small but important foundation on which a world of law can be built," but it did not "slow down the nuclear arms race," as he also asserted. It simply forced the contest underground where the number of detonations actually would increase. Most Americans strongly favored the treaty in any case. On September 24, the Senate approved it 80 to 19, and more than a hundred nations eventually signed it; China and France conspicuously did not.[13]

McGovern presumed the pact would advance solutions to related problems. Opponents of the treaty, such Arizona's Barry Goldwater, however, fretted that the United States was relaxing its guard; and many Democrats, even as they voted aye, were nervous about conveying an impression of complacency. Senators had debated the treaty for sixty-seven hours over the course of twelve days before the vote. The same afternoon it took them just five hours to approve the defense budget (now upped to $54.8 billion) from which McGovern had wished to pare 10 percent. The South Dakotan was granted ample time to reiterate his arguments about overkill and the massive spending that had led "to the neglect of other vital sources of national strength." Only Jennings Randolph supported his amendment. On a roll call (demanded by Goldwater) the vote was 74 to 2. According to the *Washington Post*, a bloc within the Senate feared that, on any day other than this, as many as thirty of their colleagues might have voted for the cuts. But "powerful defense backers" contrived to move the two bills in tandem—to secure the defense budget and ward off accusations of "test-ban euphoria." Democrat Richard Russell of Georgia joined Goldwater to denounce McGovern's amendment as akin to "unilateral disarmament." Others, such as Paul Douglas of Illinois and Claiborne Pell of Rhode Island, disapproved of the amendment while welcoming McGovern's economic conversion bill. When he introduced it in October, he had thirty-one cosponsors; leading publications endorsed it as an idea whose time had come. The hard-liners' trepidations that a third of the Senate might have gone for his 10 percent cut were not misplaced, not when a third shared his thinking about economic conversion. The implications were profound. McGovern had been in the Senate a mere seven months. His principal initiatives since March, taken together, composed a critical treatise that called into question the basic assumptions that had guided American foreign policy since the 1940s. At a time when Vital Center liberalism was nearing high tide, it was a most unusual indictment.[14]

There was yet one more reason why the Senate's proceedings on September 24, 1963, were of some historical significance. As he criticized a strategy of containment that ignored other "important aspects of the international challenge," McGovern pointed to the "current dilemma in Vietnam" as "a clear demonstration [of] the limitations of military power." The $50 billion arms budget had proved useless in coping with "a ragged band of illiterate guerillas fighting with home-made weapons," he said. Even worse, the United States was financing a government in Saigon that tyrannized its own citizens. Alas, Kennedy's course was scarcely one of victory or even stalemate. It was, rather, "a policy of moral debacle and political defeat." American resources were being "used to suppress the very liberties we went in to defend." If senators neglected to reexamine the policy—the core of which could be traced to the military spending bill—they would "stand derelict before history." McGovern had offered comparable words before in letters to Arthur Link and in a few of his House speeches, but none that had rung so like this fire bell in the night. His was among the earliest trenchant commentaries on the nation's growing entanglement in Southeast Asia on the floor of either house of Congress:

> For the failure in Vietnam will not remain confined to Vietnam. The trap we have fallen into there will haunt us in every corner of this revolutionary world if we do not properly appraise its lessons. I submit that America will exert a far greater impact for peace and freedom in Asia and elsewhere if we rely less on armaments and more on the economic, political, and moral sources of our strength.

McGovern had been aware of the Indochina war since graduate school, when the works of Theodore White, John K. Fairbank, and Owen Lattimore had kindled his interest in China. "There would have been no American intervention in Vietnam if the views of Lattimore and other competent Asia scholars had been heeded," he would later write. Lattimore's *The Situation in Asia* introduced him to the subject in 1949, and he assigned it to students at Dakota Wesleyan.[15]

Five years earlier, when the French wanted to reclaim their prize colony after having surrendered it to Japan, Franklin Roosevelt had declared: "France has milked it for a hundred years. The people of Indochina are entitled to something better than that." FDR's impatience with colonialism would soon give way to Truman's anxieties about revolutionary upheaval in Southeast Asia and China at the end of the war. In Hanoi, on September 2, 1945, the charismatic leader Ho Chi Minh proclaimed his country's independence in phrases borrowed from Thomas Jefferson. Half a million fellow patriots and a handful of US Army officers cheered him as American planes flew overhead and a Vietnamese band played "The Star Spangled Banner."

Although Ho was as much a communist as an inveterate nationalist, FDR would not have taken exception to his priorities in dismantling the old structure. Ho's government abolished forced labor, established the eight-hour day and universal suffrage for women and men, and legalized unions. It also reduced rents and taxes—often employing brutal measures against landlords—and launched campaigns to wipe out illiteracy and ban alcohol and prostitution. To be sure, he and his comrades were hardly spotless democrats, but because he found much to admire in the Americans with whom he had joined forces against the Japanese, Ho sent Truman eleven letters about prospects for a trade relationship and a US naval base at Cam Ranh Bay.

The overtures went for naught. To begin, once the French Indochina War erupted in November 1946, Ho Chi Minh and his movement, the Vietminh, loomed as communists to Americans. In 1947 Truman implemented the containment doctrine, and he needed to have France firmly in the Atlantic alliance to assure western Europe's economic recovery under the Marshall Plan. Japan was a factor, too; the United States had to secure for its new strategic base in East Asia access to Indochina's markets and resources (which included most of the world's natural rubber and tin). Thus the Truman administration resolved indirectly to assist in returning Vietnam to imperialist rule. To this endeavor in "the most weakly held of all colonial possessions" (as Lattimore depicted it) France initially committed 100,000 troops. Yet by the end of 1949, the nationalist resistance controlled two-thirds of the country. In January 1950, both Beijing and Moscow recognized Ho. Then in March, as NSC-68 (the blueprint for global containment) was being drafted in the wake of the China disaster, Truman decided to extend direct aid to France. That June the Korean War broke out and McCarthyism festered at home. The Vietminh-led independence movement continued to prevail. According to Lattimore, American and British journalists on the scene believed "the French situation was hopeless."[16]

President Eisenhower's commitment eclipsed Truman's. In 1952 he won election by capitalizing on the political repercussions of the fall of China, McCarthyism, and the Democrats' inability to end the Korean War. He poured still more money into Indochina (80 percent of the cost of the conflict), while the crudely equipped nationalists humiliated a modern, mechanized western army. In the spring of 1954, the Vietminh prepared to strike a mortal blow at Dien Bien Phu, far to the north. Ike aspired to rescue the besieged French garrison there. But invocations of the domino theory and Munich did not convince congressional leaders or prime minister Winston Churchill of the wisdom of a joint military venture. He deferred to their skepticism and allowed the French to collapse.[17]

In the meantime, in Geneva a conference cochaired by the British and the Soviets had begun to hammer out a settlement to end the eight-year war. The United States and Red China attended along with delegates from France and both Ho's Democratic Republic of Vietnam (DRV) and southern Vietnam. The Geneva Accords called for the withdrawal of French forces from the country and DVR forces from the South and prohibited any further introduction of troops or war materiel into Indochina. For two years Vietnam also was to be divided at the 17th parallel and then reunited under one government via internationally supervised elections in 1956. No one doubted that Ho Chi Minh, whom the State Department described as the "ablest figure in Indochina," would triumph in this exercise in democracy. Mainly for that reason the United States refused to accede to the Geneva Accords.

A sturdy bipartisan Cold War consensus sanctioned Eisenhower's decision to spurn the accords. But after eviscerating the Democrats over China, the Republicans could hardly afford to have Americans wonder, "Who lost Vietnam?" As Geneva proceeded, the CIA carried out a coup in Guatemala against a democratically elected administration suspected of communist ties, much like the overthrow of Iran's antagonistic parliamentary government in 1953. The president associated nationalism in the Third World with communism; he replaced both regimes with pliable anticommunist dictators portrayed as friends of liberty. In Vietnam he hoped to find a similar solution and succeed where the French had failed. It is unlikely that he ever read a work like *The Situation in Asia*. "A sound policy . . . must operate within the laws of growth and change," Lattimore had written in pondering American policy. "It is almost always impossible to start over again in an attempt to do things the same way, only better."[18]

Eisenhower and Secretary Dulles hoped to turn South Vietnam into an independent noncommunist state. To superintend the task, they settled on Ngo Dinh Diem, a fervent nationalist and anticommunist, untainted by collaboration with the French. A devout Roman Catholic,

Diem had lived in seminaries in New Jersey in the early 1950s and cultivated the favor of prominent liberal anticommunists, including Senators Kennedy and Mansfield. In the fall of 1954, after pressuring the French puppet government in Saigon to appoint Diem as premier, the United States began to send financial aid to his regime and to train an army of 150,000.[19] By 1955 Diem and his brother Nhu had consolidated their authority over the armed forces and the bureaucracy and had won the support of the Catholics. In 1956 South Vietnam staged a rigged plebiscite (to get around the Geneva Accords) preceded by elections for a constituent assembly in which Diem became president. Eisenhower hailed him as a "miracle man." The following year the magazines *Foreign Affairs* and *Life* would both describe the country as a "police state."[20]

Although the government owed its existence wholly to the United States, Diem refused to practice anything other than ruthless "one-man government." Within a year, his secret police had thrown thousands of political opponents into "re-education camps." But the worst failing of America's mandarin was his apathy to the plight of three-fourths of his people, a mostly landless peasantry beholden to wealthy absentee landlords. Each year the Eisenhower administration pumped $250 million into Vietnam, 80 percent of which went to its Army of the Republic (ARVN). Almost none went to remedying an agricultural system that compelled desperately poor families annually to pay landowners as much as half the yield from a year's labor. During the war against the French, the communists in the South had redistributed the land or lowered rents to 10 or 15 percent. Now the landowners returned and raised rents to 40 and 50 percent. In time, the lack of any serious reform incited an insurgency. As the decade wore on, Vietminh cadres, aided by local villagers, clashed with government forces in countless incidents. In December 1960, encouraged by Hanoi, communists joined with noncommunists in South Vietnam to form an anti-Diem coalition, the National Liberation Front. The NLF's sense of purpose and its relentless guerrilla tactics undermined the efficacy and morale of the American-trained ARVN conscripts. The stability of Diem's regime began to erode. As the historian David Anderson has written, Eisenhower had only been "managing the Vietnam issue but not solving it substantively." For its part, Congress never questioned any aspect of his policy.[21]

George McGovern's service in the House of Representatives coincided with this experiment in "nation-building." His main foreign policy worries in those four years, however, related to the Eisenhower Doctrine and foreign aid to the Middle East. The United States was propping up reactionary governments "that ignore the basic needs of their own citizens" while "more than 80 percent of our entire foreign assistance program is devoted to military items," he lamented in January 1958, for example, in criticism that one could have applied to Vietnam. Typically he would ask, "could we not propose a world food bank . . . [and] use some of our agricultural abundance in relieving world hunger" and hold the line against communism that way?[22]

Vietnam and food aid had had a bearing on each other almost from the beginning. In 1959 and 1961, the CIA conducted studies on the nutritional needs of South Vietnamese soldiers and distributed enriched vitamin wafers until proper field rations could be put into use. The CIA reported also on food shortages in North Vietnam and "peasant disgruntlement over the regime's heavy-handed efforts at collectivization." McGovern's concerns, as director of Food for Peace, involved different things. In 1961 he built up a school lunch program and coordinated the emergency shipment of 4.5 million pounds of wheat flour and dried milk for thousands of flood victims in the Mekong delta. He also initiated "Pigs plus Corn plus Cement Equals Success in Vietnam." This was the brainchild of Earl Brockman, an Idaho farmer working for AID, who had been inspired by a radio talk McGovern had given on *Voice of America*. The idea was to provide thousands of peasant families with three pigs, eight sacks of cement (for a sty), and surplus corn with which to replicate American-style farm cooperatives. McGovern helped him set up a hundred cooperatives in thirty provinces. His alarm over the strife in September 1963, though, was coupled to his distress over what was happening to Food for Peace in Saigon.[23]

"It is no wonder that many of us hesitate to enlist our men and our treasure in a struggle which may go on indefinitely, and in which the justice of the cause is not completely and clearly on our side," John F. Kennedy said on April 6, 1954, in the most incisive speech he ever made about Vietnam. "No amount of American military assistance in Indochina can conquer an enemy which is everywhere and at the same time nowhere . . . [W]ithout a reliable and crusading native army with a dependable officer corps, a military victory, even with American support, in that area is difficult, if not impossible of achievement." The senator had toured Indochina three years before and had come home a staunch critic of the French. The siege at Dien Bien Phu, the occasion for his remarks, confirmed his judgment. But by 1956 he had become Diem's patron, plying rhetoric, now, about Saigon as "the cornerstone of the Free World in Southeast Asia." By 1963, as president, he was completing the foundation, begun by Eisenhower, for the greatest foreign policy disaster in American history.[24]

South Vietnam's importance grew under Kennedy because the battle against the insurgency was going so badly and nobody in Washington knew what to do about it. That predicament, a few historians have argued, owed mostly to the fact that neither Kennedy's nor Diem's people ever understood the central issue behind the revolt. Nothing had given the NLF a better recruitment tool than Diem's attempt to reinstate the landlords whom the Vietminh had dispossessed before 1954. In some provinces the regime and Diem's family had become the biggest landowners. By 1961 the Vietminh were able to gain the favor of a large majority of the villages and drive Diem's officials out, whereupon they redistributed the land or lowered rents once again. Kennedy' advisers could not grasp why peasants might side with communists, and their antidote only inflamed the situation. To deprive the NLF of shelter, peasants by the millions would be uprooted from the land they had lived upon for generations and relocated to "strategic hamlets" bound by moats and barbed wire. There would be no reform.[25]

Kennedy showed comparative caution when he initially considered how to turn the tide militarily. In the spring of 1961, the Vietcong (as Washington now called the revolutionaries) controlled nearly 60 percent of South Vietnam; this prompted him to authorize an increase in the size of ARVN by 50,000 and to expand the counterinsurgency operations, which had captivated his interest. In December, after General Maxwell Taylor and Walt Rostow returned from a fact-finding mission, the president agreed to augment the contingent of 900 Americans with 2,300 military and political personnel and to enrich the economic aid package to Diem's government. He rejected their recommendation to deploy 10,000 combat troops.

Yet as the struggle intensified in 1962, Kennedy reluctantly sent virtually that many "military advisers," as well as hundreds of aircraft, napalm bombs, and even the herbicide Agent Orange with which the air force began to spray the countryside. Contrary to the US mission's deceptive reports, progress was elusive. The Military Advisory and Assistance Group knew little of revolutionary war. According to Bernard Fall, the journalist-historian and McGovern's friend-to-be, it concentrated instead on training ARVN "for conventional war it could not conceivably have to fight"—that is, a Korea-like invasion from the north. And only rarely did the president hear about sullen ARVN troops refusing to engage the enemy or of their frequent cowardice under fire regardless of their enormous advantage over the guerrillas.[26]

Then, too, there was Diem's corruption and repression and his tendency to hold back his best troops. Hopes for his redemption faded after May 8, 1963, when he provoked a crisis in the city of Hue. Buddhists, who made up 80 percent of all Vietnamese, were forbidden to display religious flags during celebrations of Buddha's birthday. Into a crowd of thousands who violated the ban, Diem's troops fired weapons, killing nine. A wave of protests swept major cities, including, in June, the self-immolation of an elderly monk in downtown Saigon. As Kennedy beheld a front-page photo of that incident, his thoughts may well have run back to his speech of 1954. He and Diem had become each other's hostage.[27]

Meanwhile, in the countryside, the strategic hamlet program implemented by Nhu, Diem's brother, only caused the peasants to hate the government more. At the same time, these fortified settlements had proved utterly ineffective in isolating villagers from the Vietcong. Whereas over half of the population of fourteen million was living in them by June 1963, insurgents were collecting taxes in all but two of South Vietnam's forty-four provinces. If, as a leading authority has claimed, "it was the land issue that brought Diem to ruin," then perhaps it was Kennedy's failure, too, to appreciate the centrality of the land in an agrarian society that ultimately rendered his Vietnam strategy a disaster. No less an agricultural economist than John Kenneth Galbraith had admonished him in October 1961: "We are increasingly replacing the French as the colonial force and we will increasingly arouse the resentment associated therewith." The president could have done a lot worse than to heed the words of his ambassador to India or, for that matter, those of his former director of Food for Peace.[28]

McGovern would argue that the United States was not succeeding in Vietnam in part because policy makers had shown hardly any interest in the rural economy or in sustaining adequate agricultural and land reform. He had begun to think so in the summer of 1963, as it happened, after writing to a number of American embassies for status reports on PL 480. The reply he received in August from William Trueheart, chargé d'affaires ad interim in Saigon, was rather shocking. Trueheart assumed the senator would be gratified to learn that Food for Peace had "proven a valuable and flexible tool in the achievement of

U.S. policy goals in Viet Nam." For example, it had become "integral" to the feeding of militia trainees in the Strategic Hamlet program as well as to other counterinsurgency efforts. Title I programs were also useful, he went on, because the currency proceeds from the food sales were delivered over to Diem, which "enables the GVN to maintain a high level of military expenditures for the prosecution of the war." What the chargé did not mention, and McGovern did not know, was that the White House had been violating the spirit of the program this way since the Taylor-Rostow mission. On the highest authority, in November 1961, ambassador Frederick Nolting had secretly offered Diem the first installment (50,000 tons of rice) under PL 480, "the purchase price to be granted back to the GVN for their military budget."[29]

One week after Trueheart's letter arrived, Nhu launched plundering raids on the major pagodas of Hue and Saigon and imprisoned 1,400 Buddhists—yet more "acts of gratuitous savagery which reduced to shambles whatever rationale remained for American policies," wrote Bernard Fall. Now congressmen and senators demanded to know what was going on. In August and September, Mike Mansfield, Wayne Morse, and Frank Church were especially vocal. Major editorial pages wondered whether there were "limits to our toleration." Kennedy instructed his new ambassador, Henry Cabot Lodge, that Nhu had to go. In September, via televised interviews on CBS and NBC, the president sent Diem a message that he must correct course. "I don't think the war can be won unless the people support the effort," he said, "and, in my opinion, in the last two months, the government has gotten out of touch with the people." Still he declined to disassociate himself from either his client or the war. To both news anchors he reaffirmed his belief in the domino theory, that the war was "a very important struggle even though it is far away," and that to withdraw "would be a great mistake."[30]

On September 12, Senator Church, in cooperation with the White House, introduced a resolution to cut off assistance if Diem's government did not abandon "policies of repression against its own people." McGovern was one of thirty cosponsors; out of concern about his mentor's willingness to have waded at least knee deep into the Big Muddy, he decided to review the record of the intervention near the end of his speech on the arms race on September 24. McGovern spoke again on the twenty-sixth. The United States had 14,000 troops in Vietnam; so far it had spent the lives of a hundred of them, plus $3 billion in foreign aid. Yet the regime "is so tyrannical, self-centered and narrow that it

is not capable of maintaining popular support," he said. "Our identification with such a regime weakens, rather than strengthens, us in
the global competition with communism." Indeed, America's "position
in Vietnam has deteriorated so drastically that it is in our national interest to withdraw from that country our forces and our aid." Church
and Mansfield had threatened to pull the plug on Diem, but not on the
commitment. None save Wayne Morse had gone as far as the South
Dakotan had.[31]

If Kennedy had really been in search of the sort of disengagement
McGovern had in mind, the Buddhist crisis, together with all the other
offenses, may have offered sufficient political cover for it. But by then
Diem's days were numbered. US pressure on the dictator had made
him more obdurate than ever; a faction among his generals interpreted
it, correctly, as encouragement for a coup d'état. Ambassador Lodge,
since his arrival in August, had wanted them to strike against Diem
on the assumption they could then win the war. The White House remained deeply divided throughout October. Kennedy was ambivalent
to the last. Once the coup commenced on November 1, he did nothing
to alter the course of events. The next morning Diem and Nhu surrendered to the military junta, whereupon they were tied, thrown into
the back of a truck, and shot to death. General Taylor recalled he had
never seen the president more upset than when he learned of the brutal
nature of this change of government. "Awful, just awful," McGovern
remembered Kennedy saying to him three times at a reception at the
White House. For his part, the senator did not feel "any great sorrow
over the assassination of Diem," but neither did he celebrate. Six military governments would rise and fall in Saigon within a year, and he
came to regard the overthrow as "a tragedy." He also suspected it had
been more an improvisation than a well-deliberated administration
plan. Certainly, "there was no evidence of an American pullout," as he
had recently advocated. Its full purpose, then, was hard to fathom in
early November 1963—especially since the president himself did not
have much time left.[32]

Around lunchtime on that infamous Friday, McGovern's seatmate
Ted Kennedy was presiding over the Senate. Mike Mansfield entered,
motioned to George to take Teddy's place, and told the younger Kennedy that his brother had been shot. The majority leader made a brief
statement to the Senate and moved adjournment. McGovern's staff was
crowded around the TV set when he returned to his office; within moments a reporter announced the president was dead. Their working

relationship had been the closest McGovern would ever have with a chief executive—the only one who would ever be truly attentive to his career—and he had looked forward to years of association with him. "I thought that Kennedy represented the future," he later reflected, "he was so young and optimistic and such a graceful and gallant figure." He could not believe someone had snuffed out "this attractive, exciting, appealing figure who had really aroused the admiration and affection of the world. It was just an enormous shock."

Until he was laid to rest at Arlington National Cemetery four days later, the American people hardly did anything but mourn the president and follow the stages of the funeral on television. George and Eleanor attended the formal service in the Capitol Rotunda where the flag-draped casket was placed. At 2:00 a.m. that Sunday night, Eleanor and the children drove back up to the Hill where thousands stood in line to pay their last respects. The next day the family joined a throng of one million on the curbsides and watched as world leaders walked down Constitution Avenue toward the Lincoln Memorial followed by the horse-drawn cortege. Eleanor's grief was such that she "could not reach the hurt," she said. Ann was devastated. JFK had first captivated her in 1956 when he had sought the nomination for vice president, "an eleven-year-old's idea of the perfect candidate," she reminisced. In 1960, at the age of fifteen, she confessed, "I just fell in love with him," and enough so that her father's loss to Karl Mundt "was softened quite a bit by the fact that Kennedy won." Sometime later, like countless other Americans, she came to mark the assassination as "a turning point in my life," as "the end of innocence . . . in part because of what happened afterward." Her father had similar feelings: "I saw some limitations in Kennedy. I didn't agree with all his policies," but "to have him cut down like that . . . seemed to me just an enormous waste of a very precious political commodity that might have led the country into new and better directions."[33]

Exactly where those directions might have led—particularly in the case of South Vietnam—still lingers as a contentious issue. Although a small number of historians have attempted to argue that he planned to withdraw after the 1964 election, most scholars of the Vietnam War are critical of Kennedy for expanding US involvement—for having, in historian George Herring's words, "bequeathed to his successor a problem eminently more dangerous than the one he had inherited." His friend from South Dakota hoped that he would see the light once he won a second term. Yet he also realized that his "Castro fixation" analysis applied to Southeast Asia as well as to Latin America; that JFK's conflicted policy was a continuation of Eisenhower, built upon the domino theory; and that neither of the two presidents had ever tried to plumb the fundamental causes of Vietnam's revolution. In retrospect, McGovern tended to be lenient, though never uncritical. "I always felt that at some point Jack Kennedy would disengage from Vietnam," he mused decades later; then the historian added, "But I had no evidence of that." After all, he knew JFK's record quite well. It included the final remarks silenced by gunfire. "We in this country in this generation are . . . the watchmen on the walls of world freedom," the president had planned to say in Dallas. "Our assistance to . . . nations can be painful, risky and costly, as is true in Southeast Asia today. But we dare not weary of the task."[34]

The American people were living through perhaps the most traumatic week in their history when Lyndon Johnson addressed a Joint Session of Congress on Thanksgiving Eve, 1963. "All I have I would have given gladly not to be standing here today," he began. Never had he spoken with greater sincerity, nor was anyone more conscious of the fact than he that Kennedy had been killed in his home state of Texas. In the circumstances, the new president saw his task as twofold: to reassure his fellow citizens that their government would endure as the world's strongest and continue to keep its commitments at home and abroad, and to instill in them a sense of resolve to move forward with his predecessor's agenda. In this regard he dwelled on domestic issues, although the public did not yet identify them with their slain leader. "John Kennedy had died. But his 'cause' was not really clear," LBJ remarked after leaving office. "That was my job. I had to take the dead man's program and turn it into a martyr's cause." Indubitably, that is what he did; in doing so, he would make of himself half a great president.[35]

Like many politicians who came of age in the West and South before World War II, Johnson was reared in a lower-middle-class family that never quite attained middle-class status. This largely owed to the region's economic downturn in the 1920s. His father, Sam Johnson, an unsuccessful farmer near Stonewall, in the Texas Hill Country, served for twelve years in the state legislature. Sam devoted himself to the interests of working people. When the cotton market collapsed, however, he had to take up road construction to support his wife Rebeka and their five children. Of his two parents, Rebeka was the more demanding of Lyndon, who adored his mother. But he struggled to please her, as she withheld her approval as often as she bestowed praise, helping to create the insecure, intensely driven politician that her son grew to be.[36] More so through his father, Lyndon came by his humane, liberal political values. But it was through student government at Southwest Texas State Teachers' College that he actually first excelled in politicking—as a superb debater and a storied wheeler-dealer among the campus elite. He showed a bent for teaching, too. For a year before graduating, he worked as principal and taught fifth and sixth graders at an impoverished "Mexican school" in Cotulla; his students regarded him as heaven-sent. Afterward he taught public speaking at a high school in Houston and coached the debate team to a district championship. Thus had the seed of his conviction, that "education is the only valid passport from poverty," been planted.[37]

In 1931 Johnson wrangled a job as legislative aide to Richard Kleberg, the wealthy scion of the King Ranch and a congressman who stayed away from the office more than not. And so LBJ began his life-long immersion in politics. At the behest of Sam Rayburn, President Roosevelt appointed him the Texas director of the new National Youth Administration in 1935. Johnson ran a model operation. In six months he had put some 20,000 young people to work improving the state's infrastructure. Two years later, as a self-proclaimed New Dealer, he won election to the House of Representatives. Bringing public power and rural electrification to Texas ranked among his proudest deeds. Duly impressed, FDR remarked, "That's the kind of man I could have been if I hadn't had a Harvard education." Conversely, as Bill Moyers once observed, Roosevelt's impact on LBJ was "like the mark a prehistoric river leaves in a cavern."[38]

Although he was consistently more liberal on civil rights than most of his southern colleagues, Johnson took increasingly conservative positions after his election to the Senate in 1948—in keeping with his ambitions for party leadership, the interests of Texas oil barons, and political imperatives of the Cold War. His ascent was quick. He became majority whip as a freshman in 1951, then majority leader (the youngest in US history) in 1955. For the rest of the decade Johnson and the beloved Mr. Sam kept the action on Capitol Hill in the center of the Vital Center. By the time JFK tapped him, no one in the history of the Congress had a better understanding of the workings of its machinery—or of how to keep it lubricated through a mélange of favors, threats, flattery, and badgering, filtered through what one biographer called his "turbulent and infantile nature," and all of it leading to the desired outcome, "consensus." As the nation slowly emerged from Camelot's dark night, he would demonstrate that it was he who was the rightful heir to the New Deal tradition. The first step would be to memorialize the thirty-fifth president. "That way," as he put it, "Kennedy would live on forever and so would I."[39]

"George, I'll come to South Dakota and campaign for you or against you, whichever you think will get you the most votes," he had said in May 1960. McGovern respected Johnson and enjoyed his exuberance and self-deprecating humor. He was grateful that he showed up at his fund-raiser in DC and, in the presence of Kennedy and Humphrey, christened him "a fighting Liberal" and one of "the ablest men in Washington." A few days later LBJ came to speak at the groundbreaking for the Big Bend Dam, part of the Missouri Valley Authority established by an act Roosevelt had signed in 1944. To the crowd McGovern declared the majority leader "the most masterful" the Senate had ever had, lauding him as the "vigorous champion" of resource development, and for "the strongest legislation to assist our schools [the NDEA] ever to clear the Senate." He even predicted that, "if events should bring Senator Johnson into the White House, he [will] go down in history as one of our greatest presidents." The Texan was enormously pleased with that estimation and the fact that McGovern inserted it in the *Congressional Record*. He regretted the congressman's defeat in November. It was "a really serious" loss to the Senate, he wrote. "I particularly hated to lose South Dakota, because I know how much it meant to you."[40] On this basis, and a shared faith that a principal object of government was to enhance the means by which average Americans might pursue happiness, they sustained a cordial friendship.

There was nothing about President Johnson's first speech to Congress that McGovern did not like. To begin, he distilled foreign affairs into three paragraphs and without much Cold War boilerplate. The nation would stay the course "from South Vietnam to West Berlin." Yet in the nuclear age, the emphasis must be on "the obligation to match national strength with national restraint" as well as "unswerving support to the United Nations." His primary purpose was "the forward thrust of America" that Kennedy had begun. Education for all of the nation's children, medical care for its elderly, "an all-out attack" on mental illness, and a tax cut to provide "more incentive for our economy," he vowed, would be written into law. The "most immediate task," however, would be "the earliest possible passage of the civil rights bill for which he fought so long." Since JFK had braved to endorse it only 164 days before Dallas and failed even to mention it in his last State of the Union, the latter claim was a bit dubious. But Johnson's affirmation, that "no memorial oration or eulogy could more eloquently honor President Kennedy's memory," struck a chord throughout the land.[41]

To McGovern, it appeared that his and Johnson's priorities were in harmony. Whereas the senator advocated "military strength second to none," he also believed that the material and spiritual inadequacies in the lives of millions of Americans, of which the president spoke, owed much to the diversion of resources to the Cold War. A few days later, LBJ invited McGovern to fly with him on Air Force One to New York for the funeral of former governor Herbert Lehman. "The military has about four times as much of everything they need," Johnson said en route. "Whether you're talking about missiles or submarines or bombers or aircraft carriers, they quadruple everything." He wanted it known that he was "on to" the Pentagon. Coincidentally, the *Washington Post* had just run another favorable editorial on economic conversion legislation; McGovern hoped LBJ would lend his support, too.[42]

The president went further than that. On December 21 he established a high-level commission to study the impact of possible reductions in defense spending and procurement on communities that relied heavily on defense industries for their prosperity, and to ensure that such changes occurred smoothly and with a minimum of hardship.[43] "With an arsenal filled with tens of thousands of warheads, the time is approaching when weapons production must be curtailed," the *New York Times* observed in a series of articles; military spending made up 12 percent of the nation's GNP, and the committee's creation signaled "the first significant reversal in the upward trend in weapons production . . . since World War II." McGovern was thrilled to quote it. "Today, we need schools, housing, health facilities, modern urban transportation, electronic traffic control systems, water resources development, pollution control, modernization of industries," he held forth. These requisite enterprises were "enough to absorb all of our excess defense production capacities in civilian work." He also paid tribute to the "man of action." There had been "no lag, no pause, no suspension of initiative." The president had "not only kept the work of . . . Kennedy moving forward but has already initiated programs of his own."[44]

Johnson was just then about to deliver what many of his colleagues would consider "the most effective State of the Union message" they had ever heard. Invoking JFK's memory once again, on January 8, 1964, he demanded action on the massive tax cut and on civil rights to "abolish not some, but all discrimination." Moreover, this would be the Congress that "declared all-out war on human poverty." It would build "more homes, more schools, more libraries, and more hospitals than any single session" in its history. Simultaneously, the administration would cut the current deficit in half, reduce federal employment, and pare down the budget by 4 percent over the previous one. He also set out guideposts to "a world without war, a world made safe for diversity," including McGovern's goals to reduce armaments and, as LBJ said, to "make increased use of our food as an instrument of peace." In closing, he asked the Congress to join in helping to fulfill President Kennedy's promise—to build "a world of peace and justice, and freedom and abundance, for our time and for all time to come." This, then, was the dawning of "the Great Society," an idea Johnson would expound on in May in a commencement address at the University of Michigan, a manifesto on liberal reform akin to Kennedy's on détente and Soviet-American relations at American University.[45]

Two days before his State of the Union, a Harris poll found that 64 percent of the American people wanted the "J.F.K. program" enacted. Shrewdly, Johnson began with taxes—a $10 billion reduction over two years to stimulate economic growth and create jobs. On Capitol Hill conservatives objected on the grounds that the deficits incurred would unbalance the budget; liberals worried that the bill favored corporations and upper income groups. (About 45 percent of the cuts would go to the richest 12 percent of the population.) Opposition on both sides abated, however, when Johnson brought the federal budget in at $97.9 billion, trimmed down from Kennedy's proposed $102 billion. McGovern was impressed that half of the savings ($1.9 billion) came out of defense, the space program, and nuclear weapons. LBJ's remark, "I'm not going to produce atomic bombs as a WPA project," prompted from the author of the National Economic Conversion Act yet another round of speeches on arms reduction and poverty.[46]

The president had the controversial tax cut on his desk by February. Wall Street had not needed convincing. Corporate leaders understood the New Economics based on the work of John Maynard Keynes, which every president since Roosevelt had employed to some extent. Although the federal government would sustain a deficit, it would only be temporary; the freeing up of financial resources would stimulate new investment in the private sector, fuel demand through additional consumer spending, and thereby put more people to work. The combined multiplier effects would bring even greater revenue back to the federal government that would drive further stimulus in the form of new public spending. And that was what happened. By the end of 1964 the GNP would grow by 6 percent and unemployment would fall to 5 percent, with more feats to come.[47]

Johnson's plan was to put this burgeoning prosperity in the service of the War on Poverty. One-fifth of America's families had incomes "too small to even meet their basic needs," he had pointed out in his State of the Union. Before the tax bill had passed he was exhorting business leaders and conservatives in Congress that "poverty was not only wrong, it was something we could not afford." To give their "fellow citizens a fair chance to develop their own capacities," he said again and again, meant providing them with the proper tools—better education, health, housing, and jobs. In its early phase, however, Johnson limited his poverty program to the Economic Opportunity Act of 1964 (EOA). Preelection politics kept start-up funds just under $1 billion spread over three years. Yet the legislation constituted a breakthrough. Along with the Office of Economic Opportunity, it launched Job Corps, a vocational training program for inner city youths; VISTA, a domestic Peace Corps aiming at helping poor neighborhoods; and adult literacy and community action programs. Senator Pell remarked on the bill's modest scope but also said Rhode Island would receive enough funds to help a thousand work-study students go to college and put 48,000 citizens with less than a sixth grade education into adult education. McGovern, one of its coauthors, saw ways the act might have been expanded—for example, to address the plight of Indians, whose median family income was $1,500 while the poverty cut-off was $3,000. But he realized, when Senator Thurmond labeled it "a Trojan horse filled with socialism," a bigger program was unattainable just now. (McGovern was able to get some money tagged for tribal councils on the basis of "community action" guidelines.)[48]

The EOA and the tax cut supplied two of the initial pillars of the new edifice of liberal reform in the 1960s. It entailed purposes that Franklin Roosevelt had never contemplated. To be sure, the Great Society shunned designs to redistribute wealth; its success would depend instead on the Keynesian notion that a rising tide floats all boats and on what Kennedy had once called "the practical management of a modern economy." But it was more than that. In a time of exceptional prosperity, Johnson was enlisting willing capitalists and consumers alike in the cause of social uplift and a better life for the forgotten poor. The next year would bring the pillars of Medicare for older citizens regardless of station and opportunities for higher education for the children of factory workers and secretaries. All of it would enlarge the economy. Still further beyond the New Deal would Great Society liberalism go in seeking to ameliorate the worst aspects of racism in America. This task, said Johnson, could not wait.

The Civil Rights Act of 1964 and the Voting Rights Act of 1965 comprised the most significant domestic legislation enacted during McGovern's first Senate term, and he engaged them with ardor and intelligence. As he admitted much later, he had been slow to develop "deep feelings" to match his support intellectually. When the first civil rights bills since Reconstruction came before the House in 1957 and 1960, he did not participate in the debate but simply voted in favor. (Both pertained to voting rights and were very weak.) Steven McGovern once suggested that his father did not think he could be "a voice for Civil Rights" in part because he had grown up on the Plains where hardly any African Americans lived. He did not interact with black people regularly until the family moved to Washington.[49]

With a midcentury population of 800,000, the District experienced all the problems besetting major urban centers. Despite its architectural splendor, the most striking social aspect of the seat of government of the world's greatest democracy was its racial segregation. Nineteen fifty-four was the year of the Supreme Court's ruling in *Brown v. Board of Education* and the unveiling of the Iwo Jima Memorial adjacent to Arlington Cemetery, each among the nation's great monuments to the struggle for freedom. Yet, upon the McGoverns' arrival two years later, most of Washington's public facilities remained segregated, from playgrounds and parks (including Candy Cane City) to restaurants, swimming pools, and theaters.[50] This feature of life was common in the capital and elsewhere, if not in South Dakota. Even so, McGovern could not help but be aware of it. Now a senator, he was determined to speak; his first formal declaration followed Kennedy's long-delayed endorsement of a potent civil rights law by just four days.

Two events in the centenary of the Emancipation Proclamation had forced the president to act. On May 3, 1963, Bull Connor, commissioner of police of Birmingham, Alabama, turned his attack dogs and high-pressure water hoses on hundreds of black children and teenagers marching peacefully in the downtown district. Captured by television cameras, the brutal spectacle was viewed by millions of people around the world. Then, on June 11, governor George Wallace, backed by state troopers, created another ugly display by personally blocking the entry of two African American students trying to enroll for classes at the University of Alabama. Kennedy decided he must go on television that evening. In a powerful speech delivered with conviction, he outlined to the nation the sweeping civil rights bill that eventually would become law.[51]

McGovern's address, to the New York State Young Democrats Convention, was also prompted by the incidents in Alabama. In it he linked the struggle for equality to the American Revolution and to his plans for the economic rejuvenation of the United States and reversing the arms race. "We should not forget that once the colonists launched the war for independence from England, they unleashed forces that led to a social revolution in American life," the former professor said. "I think if we can understand the spirit of 1776, we can better appreciate the rising expectations that are convulsing the American Negro community." The expectation of civil justice was "greatly complicated by [the demand] for better jobs and better schools and better housing at a time when all of these are in short supply for both whites and Negroes." Meeting these needs was "so fundamental to the strength of our nation that we ought to shift some of our massive military budget to constructive purposes here at home." For McGovern, then, priorities in waging the Cold War had become an obstacle to simple justice.[52]

Upon Johnson's ascension, the legislation to end segregation in public facilities and discrimination in the workplace gathered momentum. The House passed it handily, 290 votes to 110, in February 1964. The Senate needed eleven weeks. During the debates McGovern listened to his white supremacists colleagues John J. Sparkman of Alabama and Herman Talmadge of Georgia argue that enactment would lead to a national police state. The letters he received from opponents across the country disturbed him just as much. The "so-called civil rights bill," one New Yorker claimed, was an "attempt to socialize America." An Alabaman suspected treason and wanted the "communist affiliations of integrationists" investigated. Only a few letters were overtly racist. "The Negro is still largely shiftless and unreliable," wrote a Californian, for example. Rather, the unifying theme was Sparkman and Talmadge's argument about "this extension of federal power." As letters from North Carolina and Florida insisted, "Communism has infiltrated our government," and the bill's proponents were "selling out the freedom of the people." McGovern's mail from home, however, was running two-and-a-half to one in favor by late May. He attributed the tilt to South Dakota's own law prohibiting racial discrimination in access to public accommodations; it had *not* brought disaster to his state, he said on the floor as he refuted the opposition's "picture of monstrous Federal power."[53]

McGovern reflected further on the subject on June 4, shortly before a historic vote of cloture ended a southern filibuster. His topics ranged from Medger Evers and the song "Jesus Loves the Little Children," to James Baldwin's "Notes on a Native Son" and the Cold War. He placed the cause in the context of Western imperialism and his concerns regarding the nation's role in the world politics. "Four out of five human beings of the globe are non-whites," he reminded his fellows. "Since World War II, they have been largely caught up in an irrepressible demand for national independence. They have sounded the death knell to colonialism and they are demanding the right to be treated as equals . . . and they will mock the pretensions of those who preach democracy but practice discrimination. We cannot possibly maintain our leadership in the world and close our eyes to our racial sins. . . . It is no longer possible to separate our domestic condition from our international posture." Communism possessed no weapon "so damaging as the stark truth about race relations in the United States."[54]

In January 1963, when he asked the question at the Roosevelt Day dinner —of "whether or not, in our affluence, we can be aroused to act in behalf of the voiceless Americans around us who still live in poverty and insecurity"—McGovern could not have guessed that fate would choose Lyndon Johnson to answer it, nor with such a resounding yes. But by the late summer of 1964 he was situating Johnson "in the tradition of Jefferson, Jackson, Roosevelt, and Kennedy" and saluting the 88th Congress as "one of the most productive in American history"—for the nuclear test ban, the tax cut, the civil rights act, and the antipoverty program. Moreover, the president seemed to grasp that "America's position abroad will be determined not only by what we do around the world but by the quality of our society, our institutions, and our service here at home," as McGovern had maintained in his keynote. The country "is on the eve of a major shift . . . away from military spending towards investment in people," he now told audiences in Michigan, Wisconsin, and North Carolina. "America's ability to live and compete in a world without war is clear. What remains is our willingness to make maximum use of our capacity." Indeed, after Kennedy had increased defense expenditures by 10 percent for fiscal 1964, to $54.8 billion, LBJ had brought them down for fiscal 1965, to $50.6 billion. Through commonsense economies, he actually had put into effect McGovern's "radical" proposal for a 10 percent cut. Not only that, he had begun to reallocate those resources to the War on Poverty, and he had even appointed a blue-ribbon committee on national economic conversion![55]

To challenge Johnson that fall, the Republicans—under the sway of conservatives long fed up with Eisenhower and Nixon's clinging to the Vital Center—were poised to nominate a candidate of severely different mettle. Barry Goldwater had voted against the test ban, the tax cut, the civil rights law, and the Economic Opportunity Act. He had suggested that Social Security was communistic. He advocated giving NATO commanders authority to use nuclear weapons in the event of a crisis with the Soviets. And he held extreme views about what ought to be done in Southeast Asia. Of course, no one could deny that Saigon had descended into anarchy since the death of Diem. But McGovern had no reason not to assume that Johnson would simply "hold the line in Vietnam until the 1964 election and would then move to extricate our military forces." He was convinced a sweeping Democratic victory was essential to that extrication and to the opening of a new era in the nation's history. Indeed, Johnson appeared to be the first president since the New Deal whose mind, as columnist Walter Lippmann would put it, was "not fixed upon the danger abroad, but on the problems and prospects at home." For McGovern, all of it was a "giant step in the right direction" toward the future he envisioned. [56]

20. A growing family, c. 1957. (Left to right, Terry, Susan, Ann, Eleanor, Mary Kay, George, and Steve.)

21. At Brookings in 1958, McGovern debates Governor Joe Foss, who tried to deprive him of a second term in the House. Foss had won the Congressional Medal of Honor in World War II and later became president of the National Rifle Association.

22. Congressman McGovern visits Senator John F. Kennedy in the Old Senate Office Building; the two worked together on labor legislation in 1958 and 1959. In 1963 McGovern would inherit the same suite and hang this photo over the green marble fireplace in the background.

23. Eleanor and George (center) and Ila and Bob Pennington to their left at a gala presidential campaign kickoff dinner for Kennedy in Washington, DC, in January 1960.

24. Four Democrats at the Corn Palace, September 1960: Kennedy, McGovern, Ray Fitzgerald (the House candidate hoping to succeed McGovern), and Governor Ralph Herseth, seeking a second term. JFK wowed the crowd in Mitchell, but not the state.

25. During his campaign for the Senate, Eleanor Roosevelt (in a rare endorsement) described McGovern as a young man of "character, independence, and intellectual fiber," suggesting that his ascendance was "a political opportunity second only to the presidential election."

26. McGovern at the Food for Peace table with Egyptian children in February 1962, during a five-week international tour.

27. At the Vatican on the final leg of the tour, an audience with Pope John XXIII, who blessed Pat Donovan's rosary and said to McGovern, "Ah, when you meet your maker and He asks, 'Have you fed the hungry, given drink to the thirsty, and cared for the lonely, you can answer, 'Yes.'"

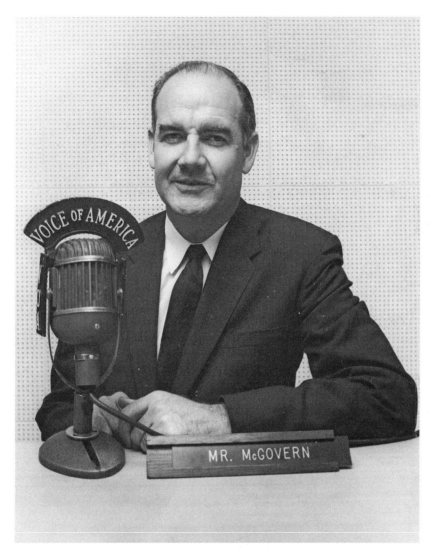

28. The Director of Food for Peace also spoke as a "Voice of America." One of his speeches would inspire an innovative development program in South Vietnam.

29. Despite waging the bitterest senatorial battle in South Dakota history in 1960, McGovern and the inimitable Senator Karl Mundt put it behind them. In January 1963, after McGovern defeated Joe Bottum in November 1962, Mundt graciously escorted his former rival into the chamber on opening day; according to McGovern, neither ever again uttered a word of criticism about the other.

30. Senator McGovern, 1963.

31. The McGoverns throw the Humphreys a block party at Coquelin Terrace to celebrate their next-door neighbor's nomination for the vice presidency in the summer of 1964. (From left to right, Muriel, Hubert, George, and Eleanor.)

32. Senator McGovern and President Johnson in a cordial mood.

33. George and Hubert in the Vice President's office before the Vietnam War put a frost on their long-standing close friendship.

34. On his first trip to Vietnam, in November 1965, McGovern was impressed by all the young GIs he met—"these splendid American servicemen," he remarked of his encounters in one battle area.

35. On the same Vietnam tour he also visited with children at the Food for Peace mission that he had worked to set up four years earlier during his directorship of the program.

36. Senate Democrats gather to congratulate their colleague upon the publication of his book, *Agricultural Thought in the 20th Century*, in 1967. (Left to right: Lee Metcalf of Montana, Frank Church of Idaho, Joseph Montoya of New Mexico, Fred Harris of Oklahoma, McGovern, Mike Monroney of Oklahoma, Birch Bayh of Indiana, and Quentin Burdick of North Dakota.)

37. Bobby Kennedy, accompanied by McGovern, arriving in May 1968 on a second trip to campaign in South Dakota's primary. His cocker spaniel precedes them.

38. A hearing at the Pine Ridge reservation, during RFK's first campaign swing in April 1968, to publicize poor conditions of life for the Oglala Sioux (followed by a visit to the monument to the Wounded Knee massacre of 1890).

39. This family portrait, taken in 1967, appeared in publicity materials for McGovern's bid for the Democratic presidential nomination in 1968. (Left to right: Susan, Ann, Steve, Mary Kay, George, Eleanor, and Terry; and Melody the collie, center.)

40. At McGovern headquarters at Chicago's Blackstone Hotel, Eleanor and son Steve watch some of the televised proceedings of the Democratic National Convention with dismay before the family set off to the International Amphitheater to attend Connecticut Senator Abraham Ribicoff's formal speech nominating George for president.

41. On the afternoon of August 26, as convention delegates debated a plank calling for a complete halt to bombing in North Vietnam and serious negotiations to end the war, thousands of antiwar protesters gathered in Grant Park, the prelude to the infamous street violence that evening. (Photograph © Jo Freeman; used with permission.)

42. Chicago police and demonstrators battle outside the Hilton and Blackstone Hotels along Michigan Avenue as the nominating speeches get under way at the convention. Some eighty-nine million Americans watched the shocking scenes on television. (Photograph © Getty Images; used with permission.)

43. Even in 1968, still one of the most effective ways of campaigning in South Dakota.

14 THE RIGHT SONG FOR THE WRONG SEASON

When Robert McNamara went on a fact-finding mission to Saigon in December 1963, the Vietcong controlled more territory than ever before, and his military hosts were unable to locate a single strategic hamlet that would be safe for him to visit. "The situation is very disturbing," he told the president upon his return, and CIA director John McCone lamented there was "no organized government in South Vietnam." Indeed, it was clear that the overthrow of the Ngo brothers had solved nothing; the Kennedy team had neglected even to think about a replacement for them. LBJ had roundly opposed the coup; now he confronted a situation that could "lead to neutralization at best or more likely to a Communist controlled state," according to McNamara. In the new year the administration would have no choice but to recognize the government of Nguyen Khanh, a young general who had ousted the military junta in Saigon. But conditions continued to deteriorate as the National Liberation Front expanded its assaults throughout the South. Khanh's regime would all but collapse by the end of 1964.[1]

LBJ had no appetite for the plate in front of him. Yet he could not ignore it in an election year. Memories of the McCarthy era haunted him. As a freshman senator he had watched China fall to communism, crush the Fair Deal, and ruin Truman's elective term. As vice president he had gone to Saigon in 1961 and anointed Diem the "Winston Churchill of Southeast Asia." He knew little about the regime but agreed with

Kennedy's remark in September 1963 that, "if South-Vietnam went, it . . . would give the impression that the wave of the future in Southeast Asia was China and the Communists." JFK's chief advisers—Rusk, McNamara, McGeorge Bundy, Walt Rostow, Maxwell Taylor—were now Johnson's, and they all subscribed to the domino theory. When, in early 1964, Senator Mansfield submitted a memo that asked whether the United States had a compelling stake in Vietnam and counseled "neutralization," McNamara said his plan invited a communist takeover. NSC adviser Bundy reminded LBJ how the Republicans had destroyed Truman by convincing the public he had not tried hard enough to save China.[2]

Thus in March 1964, McNamara characterized the conflict as "a test case of U.S. capacity to help a nation meet a Communist 'war of liberation.'" Johnson explained to colleagues what had to be done: "more of the same, except we're going to firm it up and strengthen it." Most Democrats understood. Senator Fulbright adopted LBJ's stance even as he delivered an important critique of American foreign policy, "Old Myths and New Realities." In it Fulbright raised doubts about the "master myth of the Cold War"—that the communist bloc was monolithic and dedicated to the destruction of the West—while affirming the United States would "continue to . . . fulfill its commitments with respect to Vietnam." Neither negotiation nor withdrawal was an option. George McGovern's position hardly differed at this juncture. He had proposed withdrawal in September 1963, but since JFK's death, he had decided that pressing Vietnam served no purpose. With the election on the horizon, he later said, LBJ "was not likely to make any fundamental changes, although I continued to have deep apprehension about it."[3]

Johnson was able to devote most of his energy to his legislative agenda throughout 1964, the best year of his presidency. Still he never stopped fretting that any change in the war's status might derail his antipoverty program or the civil rights bill. Whereas Democrats like McGovern were staying off the issue, Republicans were not. After a trip to Saigon in April, Richard Nixon declared the administration's policy too "soft" and implied that the war must be taken to the North. *Washington Post* columnist Joseph Alsop, whose influence rivaled Walter Lippmann's, considered military victory as essential. Others accused the commander-in-chief of having vague war aims. In May, on *Issues and Answers*, Barry Goldwater advocated "low-yield atomic weapons," instead of Agent Orange, as a way to defoliate Vietnam more efficiently, even if it risked war with Red China. (A moderate rival for the nomination wondered if he intended "to defoliate the Republican Party" as well.) "Don't try to sweep this under the rug," Goldwater declared in his speech to the national convention in July, "We are at war in Vietnam."[4] Then, just before the Democratic convention, the war's status quo did change.

The bleak outlook for Khanh's regime and the criticisms of Republicans prompted Johnson to ask Bundy to draft a congressional resolution to authorize the "selective use of force" against North Vietnam. To demonstrate resolve, he boosted the number of US personnel in-country from 16,000 to 22,000. And South Vietnamese and Americans began to cooperate in a battery of covert operations and sabotage against the foe in the Gulf of Tonkin.[5] On the night of July 30/31, South Vietnamese patrol boats attacked installations on two islands ten miles off the coast of North Vietnam. In response on August 2, as the destroyer USS *Maddox* plowed the waters near the islands, North Vietnamese PT boats suddenly appeared and began firing torpedoes. A small sea battle raged for twenty minutes. The *Maddox* emerged unscathed and damaged the attacking vessels as they fled.[6] On the next day Johnson sent a second destroyer, the *C. Turner Joy*, to join the *Maddox*. There ensued upon that order an ill-starred incident.

On the evening of August 4, the two ships notified Washington (where it was morning) that they had just begun to take evasive action against incoming torpedoes and to fire on three enemy PT boats in the gulf. Some hours later the captain of the *Maddox* reviewed the exploit and cast doubt on his earlier dispatch, in part because the crews had had to cope with heavy seas on a moonless night. "Freak weather effects on radar and overeager sonar men may have accounted for many reports," read his unwelcome correction. "No actual visual sighting by *Maddox*" or the *C. Turner Joy*. Yet despite contradictory messages, Johnson and McNamara believed the time was right to place Bundy's draft resolution before Congress. By afternoon the president had decided to strike back with aerial raids on several oil refineries and naval bases in North Vietnam. The retaliation commenced as he spoke to the nation about the incident on television. Earlier that evening he had called congressional leaders to the White House to ask for the resolution; naturally, he withheld information that the second attack may not have occurred. Only Senator Mansfield was skeptical. LBJ silenced him with a fabrication: "Some of our boys are floating around in the water." As for the American people, they were unaware their president could mislead so fluently when he told them, "Aggression by terror against the peaceful villagers of South Vietnam has now been joined by open aggression on the high seas against the United States of America." The Gulf of Tonkin resolution itself asserted that communist patrol boats had "deliberately and repeatedly attacked" American vessels; it would authorize the president "to take all necessary measures to repel any armed attack against the forces of the United States and to prevent further aggression." The Armed Services and Foreign Relations Committees jointly approved it thirty-one votes to the lone dissent of Wayne Morse.[7]

For his insights into American foreign policy there was no one McGovern more highly esteemed than J. William Fulbright of Arkansas, chair of the Foreign Relations Committee since 1959 and author of the resolutions calling for the creation of the United Nations in 1943 and the Fulbright Exchange Program for scholars in 1946. McGovern wondered how anyone so brilliant could oppose *Brown v. Board of Education* and the Civil Rights Act of 1964, but he never hesitated to express admiration for Fulbright's learned addresses on international relations. The two critics agreed on all the crucial issues—on the bloated nuclear arsenal, on the kind of foreign aid the United States should (or should not) be sending overseas, and on the causes of social revolution in Latin America. (Of "Our Castro Fixation," Fulbright had written, "I think you are entirely correct, and congratulate you.") The pair also had voted against the Eisenhower Doctrine of 1957. All of which made Fulbright's management of the Tonkin Gulf resolution (at Johnson's behest) both perplexing and formidable for some members of the Senate on August 6.[8]

Once the committee chair had finished his presentation, describing the president's actions as "wise and necessary" and the attacks as "unprovoked," McGovern began the questioning. He was "baffled," he said, as to why "North Vietnam should seek a deliberate naval conflict," and he cited speculation in the news about US Navy involvement in the South Vietnamese attack on the offshore islands on July 31. Fulbright assured that the latter foray and the destroyers' presence in the gulf were "entirely unconnected." McGovern then referred to General Khanh's petitions about taking the war to the North. Was there "any danger in this resolution that we may be surrendering to [his] position," he asked. Fulbright reiterated his faith in LBJ's televised statement, "We want no wider war." Gaylord Nelson, however, wondered what would prevent Johnson from landing "as many divisions as deemed necessary," or from launching "a direct military assault on North Vietnam" in other circumstances. "I would deplore it," Fulbright said. John Sherman Cooper of Kentucky asked, "If the President decided that it was necessary to use such force as could lead into war, we will give him that authority by this resolution?" "That is the way I would interpret it," Fulbright answered freely, to which Cooper replied, "I understand, and believe that the President will use this vast power with judgment."

Most senators evinced no trepidations at all. "Our national honor is at stake," Richard Russell, LBJ's friend and mentor, exclaimed. "We cannot and we will not shrink from defending it." Strom Thurmond seized on the words, "to prevent further aggression." He favored "a 'win policy' in the war which the Communist aggressors have initiated." Humphrey, soon to be LBJ's running mate, said, "I do not believe we show any love of peace by letting the Communists take the world over piece by piece." Ernest Gruening, Senator Morse's Alaska confederate, denounced the resolution as "a predated declaration of war." Vietnam was "not worth the life of a single American boy." Morse would remonstrate for an hour before the vote the next day.[9]

McGovern suspected these two naysayers might be right. But, away from the chamber, Fulbright persuaded his copartisans that the resolution did not mean anything; its purpose was to take Vietnam out of politics and foil Goldwater. Privately, to McGovern and other Democrats, he said: "You pass this thing and it gives Lyndon a tool in the campaign. I wouldn't support it if I thought it would lead to any escalation of the war." Nelson persisted with an amendment "to avoid a direct military involvement in the southeast Asian conflict," but Fulbright talked him out of it on the grounds it would delay action needlessly. His dual appeal—privately to party unity, publicly to national unity—prevailed. McGovern, like other skeptics, wanted to believe that Johnson "was more interested in domestic policy, that he did not quite know how to liquidate the Kennedy policy in Vietnam before the election," that the resolution was no more than a shot across North Vietnam's bow. And so, for the sake of a Great Society, he voted in favor, though with great misgivings. Of the ninety senators present only Morse and Gruening dared stand against it at the end of ten hours of debate. The House, having devoted forty minutes of discussion to the historic resolution, approved it unanimously, with 416 voting. Thus was Vietnam purged from the campaign and Goldwater thwarted.[10]

But second thoughts plagued McGovern. "This resolution is designed to make perfectly clear that the President has the support of the

Congress and the American people in meeting the recent aggression," he explained himself the next day. "I do not wish my vote . . . to be interpreted as an endorsement of our long-standing and growing military involvement in Vietnam." The better course would be a conference of the nations involved. "In my judgment an indefinite continuance of the military conflict in South Vietnam is a hopeless course that will lead . . . to defeat or entanglement in the kind of major war which we are ill prepared to fight in Asia. Let us seek a political settlement as soon as possible for a problem that is basically political." With that, he let the matter rest; the time had come to campaign for his party.[11]

For George and Eleanor the presidential campaign commenced with a block party they threw for the Humphreys two days after the Democratic convention in Atlantic City. Every one of the sixty-five children of Coquelin Terrace showed up to celebrate the vice-presidential candidate who knew all their names and exact ages. It was a joyous evening for Hubert and Muriel. The McGoverns would travel with them to several homecomings in South Dakota. It was the first election year since 1956 that George himself was not running, and he stumped for the national ticket with gusto.[12]

"The two great parties of this nation have sharply divergent views," he told South Dakotans shortly after announcing that their state was about to receive $1,287,000 in federal student loans, owing to recent improvements in the NDEA. "Goldwater has called for the end of farm programs, for ending REA, and for ending price supports," he reminded. In neighboring states, McGovern stressed Johnson's "wonderful leadership" and "the path of progress and peace" he had taken. All through October he pointed to the president's and Humphrey's staunch support of rural electrification and of the wheat certificate program, not to mention the expansion of Food for Peace, which put American farm surpluses in the service of school lunch and public works programs in twenty-five countries. He often spun his grander theme about the arms race and economic conversion and how a good foreign policy begins at home with a good domestic policy. In rapping Goldwater he harked back to the Arizonan's antagonism toward the test ban treaty and blasted him for sanctioning "colossal military waste," particularly when "our present preponderance of military power indicates that some of the funds for weapons can be safely diverted to such urgent national needs as job training, education, and conservation." McGovern also branded the challenger as an "extremist" and "unstable." In contrast, the incumbent was "a reasonable, responsible, restrained leader, suited both by intellect and temperament" for the job. He cited a Harris poll that found that 42 percent of the public viewed Johnson as "middle of the road" while 45 percent considered Goldwater a "radical." (Since Tonkin Gulf, LBJ's approval rating had shot up 30 points, to 72 percent, and forty-five of the nation's leading businessmen and industrialists had endorsed his election.)[13]

The results of the presidential campaign were everything McGovern had hoped for in rationalizing his vote for the Tonkin Gulf resolution. With forty-three million votes to Goldwater's twenty-seven million, the American people gave Johnson the greatest popular majority in US history, or 61.1 percent to 38.5. In the Electoral College he scored the biggest landslide since FDR in 1936, carrying forty-four states for 486 votes to fifty-two. (This included South Dakota's electoral votes, too. By 49 to 44 percent, LBJ and Humphrey became only the third Democratic ticket ever to take the state.) And Democrats amassed their biggest congressional majorities since that year as well, gaining thirty-eight seats in the House and two in the Senate. The party would control the 89th Congress, 295 to 140 and 68 to 32. Within a decade the significance of these data would become a subject of debate. Five of the six Goldwater states were in the Deep South—in retrospect, the first tangible indication of a coming ideological and sectional shift between the GOP and the Democratic Party. At the time, though, the meaning of Johnson's victory and Goldwater's defeat seemed clear to one and all, and no pundit put it more confidently than Arthur Link did. In the next edition of his textbook, *American Epoch*, the historian proffered "the real significance" of the election—"that the American people had overwhelmingly affirmed their allegiance to the progressive tradition."[14]

McGovern would not have disagreed; he had petitioned along those lines up and down the Plains. Yet he would conclude that LBJ's landslide owed much more to foreign policy. His fellow South Dakotans supplied the evidence. McGovern believed they "would have preferred [Goldwater's] more conservative approach" to domestic policy. But they "supported Johnson because they thought he would not escalate that war," he would say in an interview at the LBJ Library in April 1969. "They rejected Goldwater because they were afraid he was going to send their sons off to a major war in Asia." Indeed, the president had done everything possible to show the American people he was not the bellicose (but forthright) Goldwater. "We are trying as best we can not to enlarge that war, not to get the United States tied down in a land war in Asia, and not for American boys starting to do the fighting that Asian boys ought to be doing to protect themselves," the peace candidate claimed in Louisville. "Some others are eager to enlarge the conflict," he said in a speech in New York. "They ask us to take reckless action . . . [that] would offer no solution at all to the real problem of Vietnam." With a week to go, he told South Carolinians the big question in the election "is how to avoid war, not to provoke war."[15]

On Election Day itself Johnson's principal advisers began to lay plans, in William Bundy's words, "in terms of a maximum use of the Gulf of Tonkin rationale." This was to involve a series of bombing raids over North Vietnam to punish Vietcong offensives in the South and to buy time for its government to shape up. Once Saigon became more stable, a second phase of heavier aerial attacks on the North would start. When Rusk, McNamara, and Taylor presented the plan to LBJ on December 1, however, they agreed it might be necessary to begin "graduated military pressure" regardless of the progress Khanh's regime was able to make. These were momentous decisions, for they would render the introduction of US combat troops all but inevitable. Most historians of the war now agree it was at this point that the president "opted fundamentally to alter American involvement in Vietnam," rather than in July 1965, when he raised the number of ground troops to 125,000. Moreover, the decision to expand the war regardless of the viability of the Saigon government meant that LBJ had effectively ruled out negotiations with the National Liberation Front and Hanoi. Of all his men, only George Ball, his undersecretary of state, was willing to tell him the plan was wrongheaded—that bombing the North would have no impact on the struggle in the South; that nationalism, not communism, was the decisive force throughout Vietnam; that Saigon was not Berlin; and that the administration ought to extricate itself from a hopeless situation. The working group treated Ball's memorandum "like a poisonous snake."[16]

In the months ahead, Johnson would offer many reasons for his war policy. Most of them pertained to the lessons of Munich, stopping aggression, and to the Cold War. He cited the domino theory and how he could not allow all of Vietnam to fall to communism (like China under Truman) and undermine the credibility of the United States in the eyes of the world. In a postelection column, Joseph Alsop warned that appeasement in Vietnam would risk "all that we fought for in the Second World War and in Korea." In private, the president's favored explanation had to do with domestic politics and the War on Poverty. "Those damned conservatives are going . . . to use this war as a way of opposing my Great Society legislation," he said to visitors in December 1964. "They'll be against my programs because of the war. . . . They'll say . . . they're not against the poor, but we have this job to do, beating Communists. We beat the Communists first, then we can look around and maybe give something to the poor." Progress in the war on poverty, then, depended on progress in Vietnam. His most elemental fear, however, was not losing the Great Society; rather, it was "the thought of being responsible for America's losing a war to Communists," he confessed to Doris Kearns Goodwin years later. "Nothing could possibly be worse than that."[17]

Yet he was sincere in his pursuit of the Great Society. That, too, required the conspiracy—involving not many people—to mask their intentions to expand the war. As George Herring has written, the president covered "his tracks so skillfully that he deceived his contemporaries and misled a generation of historians." It would prove to be a cover-up of far greater consequence to the lives of more people than any in which Richard Nixon would engage in either Vietnam or the Watergate affair. At the moment, though, caution was the watchword. Any action prior to Inauguration Day was out of the question.[18]

Even so, talk of escalation began to spread over Capitol Hill in December. Senator Fulbright told an audience at Southern Methodist University that expansion of the Asian conflict would be "senseless." In a Wilsonian vein, he explained that "a peace without victory" was the best Americans could hope for in the struggle against communism in the nuclear age. More bad news came at month's end. Near the village of Binh Gia two hundred ARVN troops and five Americans advisers were killed in a clash with large numbers of guerrillas. On the heels of this Vietcong victory, a new military junta came to power in Saigon in early January 1965, the sixth coup since Diem's demise. News magazines ran major stories under such titles as "Vietnam: Where Will It All End?" and "Can U.S. Win in Vietnam?" Senators Cooper, Russell, Gore, Church, Mansfield, and McGovern called for a major debate.[19]

McGovern had been reading and thinking about the subject for weeks as these events transpired. He had also consulted with his friend Bernard Fall, a foreign correspondent and professor of international relations at Howard University who had written *Street without Joy* (1961) and *The Two Vietnams* (1964), important books that combined history and journalism. McGovern regarded Fall's work as his "most valuable" source of information on the war. In the 1950s, Fall had believed the United States could stop communism in South Vietnam; by the end of the Kennedy period he had begun to doubt it. He had hoped Americans would find *Street without Joy* instructive for its focus on the French debacle. In *The Two Vietnams*, he traced the origins of the current crisis to the discontent with Diem and argued that "concentrating on the external military symptoms" would not compose the "politico-socio-economic components" of the war. (For this the FBI placed him under surveillance.) In late 1964, he concluded that "set-piece" battles against guerrillas in a revolutionary war were no remedy "when one has to commit 5000 men for three days, with all the paraphernalia of a D-Day landing, to come up with a dead count of nine out of perhaps 500 enemy troops under attack." Such hard-hitting observations reflected McGovern's thinking on the Cold War since graduate school and the failure of the United States, as Fall put it, "to face up to the fact of revolution itself."[20]

Then, in early January 1965, McGovern engaged Hubert Humphrey in the Senate cloakroom. "I think this is a disaster," he insisted to his friend, "We just have to wind this thing up." The vice president elect was not unsympathetic but he was impatient. "We can't just pull out. We have to respond and take whatever measures are necessary," he retorted. "We're committed. We've got to see it through." Their conversation made McGovern uneasy; Hubert would not have spoken so unyieldingly, he thought to himself, if Johnson was actually preparing to de-escalate. It was the final prompt for his first detailed policy statement on Southeast Asia on the Senate floor, just five days before the inauguration.[21]

"We are not winning in South Vietnam," McGovern began in his appraisal of America's expenditures in blood and treasure from the First Indochina War to Binh Gia. "We are backing a government that is incapable of winning a military struggle or of governing its people. We are fighting a determined army of guerrillas that seems to enjoy the cooperation of the countryside and that grows stronger in the face of foreign intervention . . . [and] we are further away from victory . . . today than we were a decade ago." In such circumstances, he declared, "expanding the American military involvement is an act of folly." South Vietnam was "not basically a military problem, but a political one." The United States could "accomplish much through foreign aid and military support, but we cannot create strong, effective, and popular national leadership where [one] . . . does not exist." He opposed air strikes on the North because they could not weaken enemies a thousand miles away in the South "who depend for 80 percent of their weapons on captured U.S. equipment and for food on a sympathetic local peasantry."

Nor would bombing advance the goal of "bringing Ho Chi Minh to the conference table."

McGovern instead wanted to reconvene a kind of Geneva Convention, an idea that Charles De Gaulle, Walter Lippmann, and Mike Mansfield had pressed in the past months (though it had not been raised in the Senate since before the Tonkin Gulf incident). He laid out a five-point agenda. The conference would take steps, first, to bring about a "closer association or confederation" between the two Vietnams, ensuring "autonomy for the South as well as the North," and, second, to help foster that association with "renewed trade and rail links." (Fall had stressed the North's need for the South's food and rubber and the South's need for the North's manufactured goods and minerals.) The third point was cooperative development of the Mekong River to control flooding and to produce hydroelectric power for the benefit of all Vietnamese. "Neutralization" of North and South Vietnam—"guarantees that foreign troops and military advisers would gradually be eliminated as the situation permits"—was the fourth and most important point. The final term was the introduction of peacekeeping forces "to guarantee national borders, to offer protection against external aggression."

Although he opposed an increase in the number of troops, McGovern was not advising withdrawal. He recommended a military policy based on General James Gavin's enclave theory, "holding the cities while taking whatever attrition is possible of the guerrillas in the countryside," until a settlement could be effected. He also speculated that Ho Chi Minh might find his plan acceptable, as a way of avoiding both a destructive Korean-like conflict and an undesirable overdependence on Red China. The "key element" for the administration, said the senator, was whether neutralization would "pave the way for Communist takeover." The answer would rest on the rulers of South Vietnam. As ever, he held firm to his view that "the United States cannot offer American leadership or American soldiers as a substitute for popular and effective government from Saigon."[22]

Given the choices the White House had secretly made by January 1965, a formal appeal to pursue the middle ground and abstain from escalation was not likely to bear fruit. Even so, McGovern's five points made headlines. The *Washington Post* stated that his proposals based on neutralization had "broadened Senate debate." *The Nation* declared them "statesmanlike." We "must recognize our mistakes . . . and retrieve what we can by negotiation," its editorial continued. "Senator McGovern has shown the way." Indeed, the speech was well informed and well reasoned—prophetic in virtually all aspects. It marked his first concrete step on a journey fated to last many years as well as the beginning of a new strategy devised by him and Frank Church, who also spoke that day, to pressure LBJ to explore all avenues to peace. While being careful not to strike at him personally, they hoped to make it impossible for him to ignore a small but resolute minority of fellow Democrats. Public opinion encouraged them; a recent Gallup poll showed that 81 percent of the American people favored a compromise settlement. (Should that prove impossible, however, popular judgment supported sending more troops.)[23]

In the meantime, the administration intended to unsheathe a wider war. The opportunity came in the early hours of February 7, when the Vietcong (using captured US equipment, it turned out) launched a surprise mortar attack on the base at Pleiku in the central highlands. The enemy inflicted the highest number of American casualties so far— eight killed and 126 wounded, plus ten aircraft destroyed. A day later Johnson ordered retaliation against targets in North Vietnam as well as the evacuation of 1,800 American dependents in South Vietnam. Then, on February 13, he approved, but did not announce publicly, the second phase of the larger plan—the aerial attacks on the North named "Operation Rolling Thunder." (For three years they would go on, exceeding the tonnage of bombs dropped on Europe during World War II). Four days later McGovern, Frank Church, and Gaylord Nelson set off the Senate's first sustained debate on the "undeclared and unexplained war," as James Reston now portrayed it in the *New York Times*.[24]

Church spoke first. His broader thesis was that American foreign policy had "become over-involved in both Africa and Asia" and too concerned "with other people's ideologies." He wondered, in seeking to immunize nations against communism, whether direct US intervention was always productive in former colonial regions "where the specter of western imperialism is dreaded more than communism." As for Saigon, there were "limits to what we can do . . . if the people themselves will not support the Government." He approved the measured Pleiku reprisal but believed Johnson should "make clear that a peaceful settlement is our objective in Southeast Asia." Church rejected withdrawal but touted neutralization, lest the next step "be to send American land forces into battle, thus converting the struggle into an American war."[25]

McGovern, too, maintained that the president "has consistently acted with restraint." Yet he underscored the opinion that America's "deepening military involvement" and "embrace of South Vietnam's rulers" were at least partly responsible for the NLF's gains. The hard fact was that the problem resisted a military solution: "We could pulverize the great cities of China and North Vietnam and still not end the guerrilla war, or encourage the establishment of effective local government." His mail from home was running fifteen to one in favor of a negotiated settlement; the out-of-state ratio was twenty to one. Why *not* give a cease-fire and peace discussions a chance? Even if the effort failed and the fighting resumed, "we would have lost nothing of substance militarily, and our political position might be stronger."[26]

Because they were not the detested mavericks Gruening and Morse, McGovern and Church threw the White House into confusion. The two could only be described as respectful. That evening, however, the Republican leader Everett Dirksen phoned the president, thinking he "needed a little defense on the floor." "Good!" LBJ replied. "Really the worst problem that we have are the speeches . . . about negotiations." Then came the dominoes. "If they take South Vietnam, they take Thailand, they take Indonesia, they take Burma, they come right on back to the Philippines," he said. "The Communists take our speeches and they quote what Mansfield . . . or what McGovern says, and they think that's the government of the United States."[27]

The next morning Johnson asked McGeorge Bundy to meet with McGovern ("who's supposed to be an administration man," he complained) and Church, as well as Nelson, Eugene McCarthy, and Stephen Young to set them straight about the necessity of a united front. Bundy arranged it immediately. The NSC adviser had not reviewed the *Congressional Record* until then and, according to McGovern, "he was stunned by the apparent logic of these two speeches" and the fact that no one had called for withdrawal or criticized his boss. Still Bundy noted that Hanoi was circulating the commentaries to suggest "a breach in the unity of the country." The five Democrats held their ground.[28]

Meanwhile, Dirksen, with Johnson's complicity, was speaking in the Senate about "the strange experience" of having listened to Church and McGovern's "chorus of despair" on behalf of "the Red bear trap of negotiations." Theirs was "a proposal to run up the white flag before the world and start running away from communism." It would end only in retreat to "the inner line from Alaska and Hawaii," he said. Thankfully, the pair had not been with "the continentals at Valley Forge" or "our Marines at the Chosin reservoir." Democrat George Smathers of Florida seconded Dirksen. The Vietcong's provocations proved Hanoi had no interest in peace, he said, and "negotiating at this time would amount to a complete surrender of South Vietnam." Senator Mansfield then rose to defend the dissenters for having reflected "great credit upon the Senate." The New York Republican Jacob Javits also appreciated their skepticism because "it has not gotten over to the American people what the policy of this Government is with respect of Vietnam." Were the South Vietnamese determined to fight for their country? he asked. Did they want the Americans there? Are we willing to negotiate? McGovern and Church returned to the floor later that afternoon. Dirksen's "white flag" jab struck them as unhelpful. McGovern resented the innuendo that "it is somehow un-American" to take soundings for a conference to end the war, noting that in 1952 Dirksen had applauded Eisenhower's pledge to go to Korea for the same purpose. "It doesn't require any particular bravery to stand on the floor of the Senate and urge our boys in Vietnam to fight harder," he added. "It is just possible that it required more courage . . . to lead off this debate than . . . to try to squelch it." As for the United States retreating back to Hawaii, that was "nonsense." With its naval and air forces situated along the Asian coast, it remained the great power of the Pacific at the ready and "capable of utterly devastating China."[29]

Five days later supporters of the war on both sides of the aisle staged their own colloquy in the Senate. No one urged Johnson to shun negotiations with more fervor than Thomas Dodd, Democrat from Connecticut, who led off with a 20,000-word address, "The New Isolationism." Dodd was concerned about this brand of thinking, the context for which was "a growing national weariness with cold war burdens." Alluding to Church and McGovern, he cited its corollaries: The United States was "overextended in its attempt to resist Communism," and it must "reverse national priorities in favor of domestic improvements" and pursue neutralization in Vietnam. These propositions could be called "by no other name than appeasement," he declared. "The demand that we negotiate now over Vietnam is akin to asking Churchill to negotiate with the Germans at the time of Dunkirk." Dodd argued that Diem had not been a bad ruler, nor had he persecuted the Buddhists, and Vietnam was not a civil war. Americans would not repeat the mistakes of the French, he said. "We are not a colonial power." Nonetheless they must be prepared "to pay whatever cost . . . and to take whatever risk may be necessary to prevent the Communists from subjugating the Vietnamese people," he concluded. "The ultimate outcome of the cold war" depended on it.[30]

Many of Dodd's colleagues praised his line of reasoning. But the charge of neoisolationism against the likes of McGovern and Church was absurd and disingenuous. In their patronage of the United Nations, intercultural exchange, of the Peace Corps and Food for Peace, and the principle of international cooperation, they had few peers. But that was the problem; it would not be the last time the war's champions attempted to stigmatize its critics.

In any event, February 1965 marked the long overdue coming-out of congressional debate over Vietnam. It was a portent of the perils of respectfully challenging the White House about American foreign policy. To imply that the United States was wrong, or perhaps even on the wrong side, in its conduct overseas was hazardous. Dirksen's tone smacked of McCarthy's attacks on Democrats for "twenty years of treason," and Dodd's Munich invocation recalled the aspersions Democrats cast on Henry Wallace in 1948. In his *Washington Post* column, William S. White decried the "unconscious appeasers" and their "bookish isolationism" and "submission to 'negotiation.'" None of these hawkish exhortations would be lost on the president.[31]

On the last day of February, the *New York Times* conducted its first-ever debate on Vietnam—between two former history professors, Senators McGovern and Gale McGee of Wyoming—and filled an entire page of the Sunday edition with it. McGee, a Democratic hawk with a PhD, argued that Vietnam posed "a major threat to the security of the free world because its loss would open the door to an extension of Communist China's power throughout Southeast Asia." Citing the lessons of Cuba and Munich, he dismissed negotiations as a sign of weakness and set out a plan for escalation remarkably similar to the one about to come to pass. McGovern refuted his opponent's historical analogies and characterized the struggle as a civil war. He asserted that a political settlement would serve everyone's interests, for it simply was "not within the power of the United States, or any other combinations of nations, to guarantee a permanently stable political situation in Southeast Asia" by force of arms.[32]

An even bigger spotlight was cast on McGovern and McGee a week later, when CBS News invited them to join a panel to debate the issue on a prime-time special titled, "Vietnam: The Hawks and the Doves," hosted by Charles Collingwood. The hawks were McGee and Hanson Baldwin, the *Times* military editor. The doves were McGovern and, curiously, Roger Hilsman, a former Kennedy adviser on Asian policy and an advocate of Diem's ouster. McGee once more called for "planned escalation" before any negotiations could take place. Baldwin believed the war would "have to be won by ground forces" and contemplated not only an increase in US troops in Vietnam but also a naval blockade and a massive air and sea bombardment of North Vietnam. If the Chinese intervened, he explained, one could rest assured "the upper limit" of the US response would not exceed a million men. As for Hilsman, it was hard to tell where he stood. "I don't think any number of American troops can win in South Vietnam permanently," he admitted at one point, but then at another, "I agree with Mr. Baldwin that we've got to bite this bullet. We've got to make up our minds whether or not we intend to save Southeast Asia." Like Baldwin and McGee, his greatest concern was "the long shadow of Communist China." Thus McGovern was outnumbered three-to-one in this particular aviary. Yet his command of the history of the struggle, combined with his case for negotiations leading to neutralization, made for an impressive performance. His sharpest exchanges came with Baldwin. About the aerial campaign that the latter entertained, McGovern said in part:

> Even if we could obliterate North Vietnam, with the kind of massive bombing attacks that you suggest, the war would still continue in the South, the guerrillas would continue to fight, the political situation would continue to deteriorate, and we would have much the same situation in the future that we have today.

About the kind of ground escalation Baldwin had in mind, McGovern reckoned:

> I think there will be a staggering loss of life out of all proportion to the stakes involved and I see no guarantee that once we go through that kind of murderous and destructive . . . military effort that the situation out there will be any better. In fact, I think that there will be such enormous political instability, such enormous political chaos that indeed we invite a much worse situation than the one that exists.

It would be "better for politicians to take some political risks than for us to risk a course that might cost the lives of hundreds of thousands of our citizens," he continued. To reach a satisfactory settlement might not be possible just now, "but we must try." And the United States would be most ably represented at the bargaining table, for President Johnson was "one of the most masterful negotiators of all time."[33]

McGovern's tribute was not without purpose; he recognized the need to preserve the lines of communication with LBJ, especially given his ongoing legislative accomplishments. Indeed, that same week a domestic crisis erupted that reminded all of his liberal critics of their dilemma. On March 7, 1965, some six hundred civil rights workers endeavored to cross the Edmund Pettus Bridge near Selma, Alabama, on a fifty-mile march to Montgomery to protest restrictions on voting rights. (Only 19 percent of voting-age blacks were registered in Alabama; 6 percent in Mississippi). Their progress was halted, however, by a force of local police who charged into them on horseback, brandishing cattle prods, rubber hoses, and tear gas. The incident gave Johnson his opportunity. On March 15, before a televised joint session of Congress, he called for a new law to protect the right of all Americans to vote regardless of color. Should they fail to insist on this legislation, "we will have failed as a people and a nation," he said. "Because it is not just Negroes, but really it is all of us, who must overcome the crippling legacy of bigotry and injustice." Then, with palpable emotion, he added: "And we . . . shall . . . overcome!" The entire chamber stood and cheered. Martin Luther King, watching on television in Selma, wept. McGovern praised the president's "magnificent" address and his "superb" delivery of it.[34]

And yet what were liberals like McGovern supposed to think when, on the day after the civil rights movement arrived at the Pettus Bridge, the US commitment in Vietnam crossed a major threshold also as two battalions of marines, 3,500 strong, waded ashore at Da Nang with tanks and artillery in tow? Or for that matter when, during the week of Johnson's plea for voting rights, General William Westmoreland called for an additional 40,000 soldiers in order to stave off defeat in South Vietnam where, despite Rolling Thunder, both ARVN desertions and VC attacks were on the upswing? Sensing the imminence of escalation, McGovern called Bill Moyers on March 26 to ask, "Is it possible that I could come down and talk with the President about the war?" Johnson agreed to see him that night.[35]

McGovern arrived at the White House at 7:00 p.m., memorandum in hand. The president had "inherited a quagmire in Vietnam," the document emphasized. If he could "compensate for the mistakes" of his predecessors, future historians would consider it an achievement "greater than the Cuban missile showdown." From there McGovern stressed the need for a political solution and explained how it was that Vietnamese peasants could not distinguish American objectives from French. Johnson listened for a few minutes. His guest recounted the logic of negotiations and proposed a Mekong River development modeled on the TVA and a sweeping policy statement on the order of the Atlantic Charter or Wilson's Fourteen Points. Then LBJ interrupted with a monologue about communism and the Chinese moving inexorably from Asia to Latin America and Africa. "George, you know what they want?" he asked. "They want to take over the world. Vietnam is the very first point. We're not going to let them do it." McGovern refuted this article of faith. Ho Chi Minh was nobody's stooge, and the Chinese and Vietnamese had hated each other for centuries, he said. Ho the nationalist might well serve as a barrier against Chinese expansion. "Goddamn it, George, don't give me another history lesson," Johnson once more cut in. "I've got a drawer full of history lessons over there from Mansfield, another professor. I don't have time to be sitting around this desk reading history books!"[36]

When his half hour ended, McGovern did not feel reassured about anything, and certainly not by Johnson's boasts about his control over the bombing campaign or about his powers of seduction in "going up little Ho Chi Minh's skirt an inch at a time." Driving home, he later wrote, "I literally trembled for the future of the nation." The following week at Bucknell University he told students: "It seems clear that we are now on a spiral of blows and counterblows which could lead to a major war under the worst possible conditions for the United States." The speech, the senator offered in a note to LBJ, was "not easy to give."[37]

Coincidentally, two nights before McGovern's ordeal in the Oval Office, faculty at the University of Michigan had responded to Rolling Thunder by holding the first "teach-in." In defiance of governor George Romney, some 3,000 students gathered in Angell Hall to hear professors talk about this war and ways to stop it. The idea caught on. Within a week students and faculty staged teach-ins at thirty-five other campuses and a hundred more by year's end.[38]

The Michigan event was one of the earliest manifestations of a burgeoning citizens' antiwar movement. This crusade was a coalition of activists that included organizations such as the Women's International League for Peace and Freedom, the Fellowship of Reconciliation, and SANE, with which McGovern had ties. Overall, of course, college-age youth predominated. The guiding light of the more radical activists was Students for a Democratic Society (SDS), created by affluent northern white college students who wanted to help their black counterparts in the struggle for freedom in the apartheid South. In 1962, SDS leaders drafted a historic manifesto. The "Port Huron Statement" called for a New Left in American politics and university life dedicated to "participatory democracy," more rapid advances against poverty and racism, and (echoing McGovern's theme) a shift in government spending away from the military and toward education and social welfare. It was logical, then, that these and kindred groups should not only join in the debate but also spearhead direct action protests as the war began to escalate in 1965.[39]

On March 1, the journalist Joseph Kraft had written a column about certain Senate liberals and conservatives and the Vietnam debate. Kraft, a Cold War liberal, accorded McGovern and Church's brief some cogency, but he called it "a case, as W. H. Auden once put it, of 'the right song for the wrong season.'"[40] LBJ probably agreed, but he could not exorcise the senators' melody. By mid-March the state of the war had demoralized him. The criticisms of his fellow Democrats scoured. The faculty-led dissent had gotten under his skin. According to Bill Moyers, he was "morose, self-pitying, angry." Lady Bird worried about "this heavy load of tension and fog of depression" that weighed on him. Then, just days after the teach-in and McGovern's visit, he decided to accept an invitation to speak at the Johns Hopkins University to clarify his Vietnam policy for the nation and answer his critics on the matter of negotiations.[41]

On the afternoon of April 7, before he was to deliver this important address, Johnson invited McGovern and Church to the West Wing for a private reading. For an hour and a half he kept them there, in part to get them to defer speeches they had slated for the next day. His text ostensibly offered to negotiate an end to the war, stating, "we remain ready . . . for unconditional discussions." As an inducement to Hanoi, he outlined a plan involving the idea McGovern had raised in the Oval Office and the Senate for cooperative economic projects throughout Southeast Asia—in this instance, a $1 billion proposal to harness the power of the "vast Mekong River . . . on a scale to dwarf even our own TVA." In language McGovern might have written, LBJ also pledged to expand Food for Peace resources for "the needy in Asia."

Yet these sections of the speech were preceded by a defiant case on behalf of war. "We are there because we have promises to keep," the lines read, referring to commitments going back to Eisenhower. "Our objective is the independence of South Viet-Nam, and its freedom from attack," he said. The American people would defend South Vietnam against the Vietcong's stepped-up attacks because their "own security is at stake." The United States had no choice but to strike North Vietnam from the air to instill confidence in the Saigon government and to convince Hanoi of America's determination: "We will not be defeated. We will not grow tired. We will not withdraw, either openly or under the cloak of a meaningless agreement. . . . And we must be prepared for a long and continued conflict."[42]

McGovern and Church liked some of what they heard. Johnson not only appeared to have yielded on negotiations, but, in the plans for a Mekong TVA and expanding Food for Peace assistance, he also had articulated the kind of liberal vision that all three of them shared—faith in "the capacity of the people to advance through positive government," in McGovern's phrase. But he and Church were dubious about what "unconditional discussions" meant. McGovern later remarked that it was as if Johnson was saying, "I'm giving you what you've been asking for, an offer to negotiate. Now I hope you bastards will shut up." But he praised the president in a floor speech the next day.[43]

Johnson had conceded a central point to two responsible critics who worried him. Yet the Johns Hopkins speech was in retrospect a substitute for a war address to Congress that he would never deliver. At that, it was sparse on details about the oncoming surge in troop numbers, which would transform the conflict into "an American war very ineffectively assisted by the South Vietnamese," as Walter Lippmann observed in his next *Newsweek* column. Still the speech garnered mostly positive reviews. Editorials in the *New York Times* and *Washington Post* praised Johnson for his overture to negotiate. For a time it quelled a chorus of staunch advocates of a negotiated settlement among the Western allies, too, especially Great Britain and France. Ten days later, however, to the surprise of everyone in the nation's capital, SDS organized the largest antiwar demonstration theretofore in American history. After picketing the White House, some 22,000 protesters gathered at the Washington Monument where Joan Baez and Judy Collins sang for them and Ernest Gruening gave the featured address. Gruening's was a step McGovern had yet to take, though he felt a natural connection to the young activists. In July he would state publicly, "The important thing is that they are speaking out of their consciences, from their minds, and from their hearts on issues which affect their lives perhaps more than any of the rest of us." At the same time he tried to convince himself that Johnson was, in fact, ready "to explore the possibility of a peaceful settlement without precondition."[44]

For his reasoned dissent and getting the president to consider his alternative, the senator won plaudits nationally and back home as well. In March the *Daily Republic* had applauded his "courageous stand" and characterized "gradual disengagement" as the "only sane solution." In April, his leading detractor, Fred Christopherson of the *Argus Leader*, seemed to concur. Shortly after LBJ's speech, McGovern drew an overflow crowd at the Sioux Falls Chamber of Congress. Judging from the reception, "there were many in the audience who shared his opinion [that] negotiation was both desirable and feasible," Christopherson wrote, affirming that the United States was "in a position to negotiate from strength." The White House would not acknowledge it, he also said (paraphrasing McGovern again) but, "We have the power in the Pacific and Asiatic waters to smash Red China to bits." So why not try in Vietnam what Eisenhower had achieved in Korea? McGovern occupied the middle ground between the extremes of "an all-out smash or withdrawal," he added, and "it is well that our minds be kept open." The *Watertown Public Opinion* agreed: The junior senator had "increased his stature" for his willingness "to have so adamantly opposed a major policy and commitment of his own party and administration."[45]

In the wake of the Johns Hopkins gambit, McGovern did relent in his criticism, but not for long. In late April rumors were rife that Johnson had granted Westmoreland's request for the 40,000 troops. Then the Vietcong shot down the helicopter of Joe Thorne of Brookings. "He was a hero to thousands of South Dakota schoolboys," said McGovern in a floor speech, on April 28, about one of the state's greatest collegiate football players; the twenty-four-year-old was married and the father of a three-year-old son. "It's too late to save Joe," his parents had written to McGovern, but implored him to "do everything you can to get those other boys out of there before it's too late." The senator read from the letter and another that the lieutenant had sent his family before he was killed: "Today the Vietnamese are having another coup (a shakeup in the government). The Army and Air Force (Vietnamese) are fighting among themselves. To be honest, the cause is lost. We can't possibly win (at least as long as the Vietnamese do things the way they do)." McGovern cited the number of troops about to be deployed and asked, "Does this mean that we are prepared to sacrifice a hundred thousand Joe Thornes in the highly questionable venture in the southeast Asia jungle?"[46]

Into the summer of 1965 McGovern, Church, and a small band of like-minded colleagues persisted in their endeavor to draw the White House away from the gathering disaster. Fulbright at last had awakened and called for a bombing halt. Joe Clark of Pennsylvania and New York's senior and freshman senators, Javits and Robert Kennedy, stressed the imperative of Johnson's conferring with them. But in early May the president decided to coerce Congress into sustaining his course by requesting a $700 million supplemental military appropriation, presenting it as an issue of whether or not patriots would support "our boys in Vietnam." The ploy worked. The House voted 408 to 7. In the Senate only Morse, Gruening, and Gaylord Nelson registered nays. (Both McGovern and Fulbright were absent that day.) Near the end of May another coup in Saigon brought to power two young, French-trained military officers, Nguyen Cao Ky and Nguyen Van Thieu. Ky was well known for his boisterous behavior and showy attire, which included pearl-handled pistols, and for his admiration of Adolf Hitler. Thieu was capable but corrupt. William Bundy would refer to the pair as "absolutely the bottom of the barrel." Yet they were to become the Ngo brothers' permanent replacements. Then Westmoreland set off what McNamara called a "bombshell," with a plea on June 7 for an additional 93,000 troops. "Desertion rates are inordinately high," the general reported about ARVN forces, "and their steadfastness under fire is coming into doubt." LBJ now deployed his advisers to make known on the Hill their construction of the Gulf of Tonkin Resolution as legal permission to do whatever they wanted—"a blank check," McGovern said in chagrin.[47]

The White House also had begun to lean on friends of its critics as a way to rein them in—in McGovern's case, Arthur Schlesinger and the vice president. "A friend of mine in South Dakota expressed concern lest you find yourself being portrayed as opposing the President's policy," Hubert wrote to George. For his part, in May 1965 Schlesinger had agreed to replace McGeorge Bundy in a televised Vietnam "teach-in" transmitted directly to a hundred campuses; though he had advocated neither escalation nor withdrawal, by the summer he began to turn against the war. George was one of the first to press him on it "in a rather urgent way." As Schlesinger recalled, he "had an impact on me."

One extended discussion took place during a weekend seminar at Ken Galbraith's farm near New Fane, Vermont, in July 1965 (a critical time in the evolution of the war). Among the participants was the journalist Gloria Steinem, soon to become a leading women's rights activist. McGovern impressed Steinem because, she wrote, he was the only person there "who is as content to listen as he is to expound his own theories." At one point, she suggested that a serious draft resistance movement was underway. The others dismissed the possibility. McGovern did not. "Yes, it's going to happen," he said. "I sense it around the country." The next day he passed around a copy of a Vietnam speech he intended to give in the Senate. Steinem was "surprised by the flat-out anger" of it; she wondered "how this unpretentious honest man became a politician." As for Schlesinger, he sometimes thought that George was "overexcited" on the subject, but before long realized he was "very prescient."[48]

Critics saw no good reason *not* to carry on the debate. "We are not yet in a full-scale war," Church exclaimed in the Senate. "There are still ways to be explored to find an honorable settlement." The commitment of so many American soldiers, McGovern argued, "does not give us any excuse to remain silent."[49] On June 17 he had spoken on the futility of bombing either the South or the North. The number of sorties increased from 3,600 in April to 4,800 in June, but whereas the B-52 strikes had not made a dent on the Vietcong, they were turning the peasants against the United States. "These guerrillas have lived for 20 years largely off the countryside," he said. "They are a part of the people and the terrain in which they fight . . . and in many cases are farmers by day and fighters by night. To bomb them is to bomb the women and children, the villagers and peasants with whom they are intermingled. To destroy their crops is to destroy the countryside on which the general population depends." Such action would only "strengthen the guerrilla's cause." An expansion of this warfare "would simply destroy the moral and political influence of the United States in Asia." Johnson claimed he welcomed "unconditional discussions." Now he refused to negotiate with the Vietcong. Hanoi found this unacceptable. To exclude the NLF, McGovern held, was to obviate the offer to parley—like King George III negotiating "with our French ally but not with George Washington."[50]

The speech troubled Johnson. He phoned McNamara and quoted McGovern's lines about the bombing and the guerrillas and the peasants as well as the need to talk to the Vietcong. McNamara was dismissive; the decision had already been made; the announcement was only a matter of time. Yet according to the secretary they "remained in constant turmoil over Vietnam" well into July. In the early hours of July 22, Lady Bird was awakened by her husband's voice; he was talking to himself: "I don't want to get in a war and I don't see any way out of it. I've got to call up 600,000 boys, make them leave their homes." Then, over three days the Vietcong blew up seven bridges, blockaded four highways into Saigon, and made an attempt on the US ambassador's life. "Physically and psychologically," *Newsweek* reported, "South Vietnam showed unmistakable signs of crumbling in the clutches of the Communist guerrillas."[51]

The fateful communication came at a televised midday press conference on July 28. It was all very low key. He had asked General Westmoreland what more he needed "to meet this mounting aggression," the president said. "He has told me. And we will meet his needs." Thus "almost immediately," he was raising the commitment from 75,000 men to 125,000. He did not say so, but he would send another 50,000 by December. Nor did he explain why he was not seeking a declaration of war, mobilizing the reserves, or asking for war credits. He hesitated to do these things, though, because he feared to provoke the Chinese as Truman had done in Korea, and he aimed also to forestall a formal debate in Congress while appealing to the public without unduly alarming it. Nonetheless he mustered all the tocsins—the credibility and indispensability of United States, the domino theory, Munich, the pledges of three predecessors since FDR. "We cannot be defeated by force of arms," he averred. "We will stand in Vietnam."[52]

One can only wonder how things might have worked out if his announcement had conveyed the message of one of the several speeches in the Senate the day before. In "How to Save Lives and Political Face in Vietnam" (the draft he had shared with the Galbraith group) McGovern spoke of "a major land war in Asia . . . involving thousands of American casualties, the expenditure of billions of dollars, vast bloodshed and destruction for the Vietnamese people, and an uncertain outcome . . . to say nothing of the impact on our own hopes for a better society." Once again he refrained from calling for withdrawal and instead outlined a formula for showing determination in the conflict while pursuing negotiations. He valued the lives of Vietnamese and Americans alike. First, Rolling Thunder must be suspended because it was "ineffective in a guerrilla war and more often than not kills the wrong people." Second, he advised a resolute military posture restricted to the cities and coastal enclaves (that is, the Gavin plan), which would keep casualties low on both sides. This strategy would avoid "self-defeating jungle warfare, which we are ill-equipped to fight" and at the same time "demonstrate that we are not going to be pushed out." McGovern could support such a holding action for as long as it might take, until "an acceptable settlement of the struggle" was reached. He was not insensitive to Johnson's burdens. "He has always been a man of peace," he said, and, as ever, his legislative record was "virtually unprecedented in American history . . . the pride of our country and the envy of the world."[53] Even in the face of the escalation it was not easy to go against the authentic heir to Franklin Roosevelt's legacy.

Indeed, as the president moved by stages toward his decision, a month did not go by that he did not bring to fruition legislation that would improve the lives of millions of disadvantaged Americans (including the lower tiers of the middle class). In these strivings, he could count on McGovern's undivided fealty—particularly in education, the field in which both of them had toiled before entering politics. In April, with his first grade teacher beside him at Junction, Texas, LBJ signed the Elementary and Secondary Education Act (ESEA). Its chief mission was the "compensatory education" of the children of poor families. Mississippi's public school system spent $241 a year per pupil, for example, while New York's spent $705; the federal government contributed only 3.5 percent of the total cost of all primary and secondary education. The ESEA was the first federal law to allocate major resources ($1.3 billion for 1965–66) to impoverished public school districts. In May came Project Head Start, a federal-state partnership to benefit preschoolers from families earning less than $2,000 a year. By June McGovern was heaping praise on South Dakota's twenty-five Head Start centers. The summer program in Rapid City, he reported, had enrolled 120 children, including seventy Indians. Its first step was to provide immunizations and dental and eye exams for the children; then came orientation to classroom learning and social interaction. With transportation and lunch, the eight-week program to prepare these five-year-olds for the first grade cost the federal government $135 per pupil. The local director called it "the most exciting thing in which we ever have been involved."[54]

In the fall Congress passed the Higher Education Act, a major revamping of the National Defense Education Act that McGovern had helped to formulate in 1958. The new legislation provided scholarships averaging $500 and guaranteed low-interest loans for tens of thousands of needy students (at both two- and four-year institutions) who otherwise could not have afforded tuition. Thenceforth it would no longer be uncommon for the daughters and sons of blue-collar workers or farm families to go to college. The act also pumped money into university libraries, expanded the work-study program, offered fellowships to encourage graduates to become teachers, and created a National Teacher Corps to send young instructors into poverty-stricken districts.[55]

McGovern also proudly cosponsored Johnson's Medicare and Medicaid legislation. Like the education bills, they were as much a part of the War on Poverty as of the Great Society. For example, whereas the cost of hospital care per day was $9 in 1946, it had increased to $40 by 1965—while half of the country's over-sixty-five-year-olds lived on $1,000 a year and the median for senior couples was about $2,800. Since the defeat of Kennedy's version of the bill in 1962, two out of three Americans had come to regard the health and welfare of older citizens as a collective responsibility. Medicare was "a reasonable and practical solution," McGovern said to his constituents, a pay-as-you-go insurance policy for basic health and hospital care, which increased Social Security assessments then to 5.2 percent of one's earnings. It was the most popular and significant social legislation since the New Deal—a blessing to the middle class as well as a health-care safety net for those a lot less well off. On July 30, two days after he had unveiled his war plans, Johnson flew to the Truman Library in Independence, Missouri, to sign the bill as the aging former president, who had first proposed it, looked on.[56]

On August 10, McGovern spoke in the Senate about a Harris poll that found a majority of Americans in a "progressive" mood. Eighty-four percent "often, or sometimes" worried about hunger in the United States, 77 percent felt concern for those without proper medical care, and 69 percent and 64 percent believed that old people and Negroes had been neglected or ill treated. "Prosperity had not made the majority complacent," Harris concluded. McGovern paid Johnson unstinting tribute a few weeks later for creating the consensus that had made the array of progressive programs possible, suggesting that he had even surpassed FDR.[57]

Yet if he believed LBJ had in two short years "earned himself a high place in American history," he also feared the goal of a Great Society could come undone just as quickly. And if he "never doubted the President's commitment to peace," he still did not think the White House was searching for it hard enough. "Our high officials ought to quit preaching that the fate of the human race and the cause of all mankind center in Saigon," he had said on July 27; they should devote more of their energy and talent to "more important issues such as the strengthening of the Atlantic Community, the Alliance for Progress, Soviet-American relations, the control of nuclear weapons, and other steps toward peace that promise a better life for the people of the earth."[58]

The war also claimed victims of the kind McGovern had not anticipated. His plan for conversion to a peacetime economy was one example. In 1964 LBJ had buoyed his hopes by establishing a committee on it and by squeezing the Pentagon for about $2 billion for the War on Poverty. But by March 1965 his legislation had slipped beyond resuscitation. "I don't think defense spending is going to drop drastically next year or the year after," he admitted at a United Auto Workers conference.[59]

Then there was Food for Peace, which, since 1963, had had a direct impact on his concerns about Vietnam. In June 1965 he called for a major expansion of its projects around the globe in the belief that the United States "ought to declare an all-out war on hunger." Johnson had hailed the program in 1964 as "a monument to high moral purpose . . . [and] the cause of freedom and human dignity by every peaceful means." Yet whereas the Kennedy administration had initiated the ravaging of Food for Peace in Saigon, it was about to mutate into "Food for War" under LBJ. The devolution began in earnest in October 1965 when he turned it over to the State Department. (There was "no reason to maintain within the White House a bureaucratic structure created primarily to elect George McGovern to the Senate," he reportedly said.) "The free ride is coming to an end," Dean Rusk soon told the Food for Peace Council. "We have to think about hard-headed facts." Vietnam was putting "a large strain on the Federal Budget," and there was going to be "a sharp reduction in Food For Peace." In fact there was no reduction; commencing with the American invasion, it was actually stepped up in Vietnam. From May 1965 to March 1966 the State Department negotiated a record eight PL 480 agreements with Saigon, the $230 million in proceeds to go to war purposes. What occurred, then, was a massive diversion of resources—nearly half of the total program—to subsidize the Thieu-Ky regime so more money would be left over for fighting the Vietcong. If Johnson and Rusk could have gotten away with it, McGovern mourned years later, "I think they would have been willing to put the whole thing in Vietnam." What Arthur Schlesinger had once extolled as "one of the visible embodiments of the idealism of the New Frontier" was becoming one of the invisible casualties of the war.[60]

If McGovern had any doubts that he might be mistaken in his manifold apprehensions, then his first trip to Vietnam, for five days in late November 1965, obliterated them. In Saigon he attended well-orchestrated intelligence briefings. He met with Ambassador Lodge and spent a memorably weird evening at the villa of the storied Colonel Edward Lansdale, Ngo Dinh Diem's erstwhile mentor upon whom Graham Greene had partly based *The Quiet American* (1955) and cosseted now by several young Vietnamese women. The senator was far more impressed by all the young GIs—"these splendid American servicemen," he remarked of his encounters in one battle area. His reputation as war critic preceded him to the extent that Westmoreland accorded him a private two-hour parley. As McGovern recalled, the general's office was "totally bare except for a huge family Bible." He "conducted himself with dignity and restraint" and was "utterly devoted to his mission." He "invited questions and tried to explain as best he could what we were doing and why we were doing it. I couldn't fault him in any way."[61]

Yet most of what he experienced sickened him. At the Tan Son Nhut Air Force Base he happened upon a convoy of flatbed trucks loaded with row after row of coffins addressed to destinations back home. (In 1965, American casualties would total 1,369 killed and 3,308 wounded.) The former bomber pilot was not unaccustomed to scenes of war, but his visits to American military hospitals shook him to the core; so many fine young men lying there putting on a brave face for him—eighteen-year-olds without arms or legs or genitals; a handsome marine lieutenant, a Purple Heart pinned to his gown, who had had both feet blown off. The hospital for wounded civilians in Da Nang horrified him; it was overcrowded with hundreds of villagers (often two on a cot and children among them) suffering from shrapnel wounds or burns from napalm. As for the enemy, McGovern was struck by their elusiveness. The Vietcong "are everywhere and nowhere," he would tell a South Dakota audience. "They are farmers during the day and fighters at night." Flying over the countryside, he beheld the endless jungle and thought to himself, "How are we going to fight in this?"[62]

Both *Newsweek* and the *New York Times* covered his journey, which included a stopover in Rome for the World Food Conference. The *Argus Leader* reported his account at a sold-out appreciation dinner at the Corn Palace. "I do not want future historians to report that brave American soldiers died needlessly because of the weakness of our diplomats or the indifference of our politicians," he said. "I continue to fear that we are staking the lives of our men on a shaky political foundation in Viet Nam." Again he called upon the administration to face up to the political and social factors and find some way "of getting the struggle off the battlefield and into the conference room." His report on the World Food Conference put it in perspective. "The war against hunger is really the most important war," the one "America is best equipped to fight," he said. "If we fight that war as we should, it will not only bring unprecedented prosperity to our farmers, but it will help remove the swamplands of hunger on which Communism breeds."[63]

It had been a signal year in both the history of American politics and foreign policy and in the life of George McGovern. By December 1965 he had ascended to a position of central importance among critics within the liberal establishment, which itself had conceived the Vietnam War. "To me, his arguments are unanswerable," Joseph Clark said of his colleague's analysis on July 27; he hoped the president would "give prayerful thought to the viewpoint" before taking further action. Frank Church quoted a *Watertown Public Opinion* editorial that saluted McGovern for "a brand of nerve one doesn't see very often in politics." From the start, George had never hesitated to speak his conscience, Church said, and his position "has often been a lonely one."[64] Of course McGovern had never been alone in this. Besides Morse and Gruening and Church himself, a dozen of his colleagues had questioned escalation publicly and a like number did so privately. But few of them matched the clarity of his insights or his grasp of the historical circumstances that surrounded the looming detonation.

Of all the counterfactual scenarios for avoiding a full-scale land war in Asia, perhaps the most tempting is what might have happened if Johnson had taken neutralization and negotiations seriously in 1965. In 1961–62 Kennedy had pursued neutralization in Laos with some success and Eisenhower's concurrence. In 1963 de Gaulle had aspired to apply it to Vietnam through an international conference, which the British (and Walter Lippmann) fervently endorsed. But LBJ always disdained the idea as a white flag. (McNamara thirty years later admitted "how limited and shallow our analysis and discussion of the alternative to our existing policy in Vietnam—i.e., neutralization or withdrawal—had been.") Then in January 1965, McGovern offered his five-point variant to advance negotiations. With this "statesmanlike" proposal, *The*

Nation magazine declared, "McGovern has shown the way." Debate was soon under way on Capitol Hill. In April, Fred Christopherson of the *Argus Leader* vouched for McGovern and the benefits of the doubt. "Negotiation may or may not be the answer," he wrote, "but surely we should explore its possibilities in detail." If, at this juncture, South Dakota's leading Republican editor could see the merits a settlement of the sort Eisenhower had secured in Korea (where "the fighting was stopped and our prestige was unharmed"), why could not Johnson and his advisers?[65]

McGovern believed that they could have and should have. In April 1969, when the war's full measure had become palpable, he was asked during an oral history interview at the Johnson Library whether LBJ "could have reversed the situation" as he had found it. "Absolutely," the senator replied. "And the greatest single political tragedy of my lifetime was the failure of President Johnson to use that enormous mandate he got in November 1964 to end the war." The electorate "had just repudiated the hawkish, militaristic recommendations of Goldwater." South Dakota, he added, did the same, going Democratic for the first time since 1936. "The president had a clear mandate in 1964 to end that war and the American people would have gone with him. He told us . . . he wasn't going to send American troops over there to resolve an Asian struggle that they ought to resolve themselves. If he had held to that decision I think that we not only could have ended the war but that Mr. Johnson might very well have gone down in history as the most effective president we've had since Franklin Roosevelt."[66]

Scholarly analyses of the decision-making process and public opinion since the turn of the twenty-first century (most compellingly, Fredrick Logevall's *Choosing War*) have tended to confirm McGovern's judgment that there was indeed a politically feasible alternative to war—if Johnson's inner fears and concerns about his own credibility had not consumed him. Public opinion was malleable before escalation had produced the customary rallying to the flag. Americans were "apathetic and permissive" about Vietnam, George Herring has written, and they "would likely have gone along with a skillfully executed disengagement." A Roper poll in June revealed that, whereas 47 percent supported sending more troops, 53 percent did not; 23 percent were unsure, 19 percent favored the status quo, and 11 percent wanted to pull out. And 73 percent gave the Saigon government a vote of no confidence—hardly a battle cry of freedom. To McNamara on June 21, LBJ acknowledged "the division that we have here and particularly the potential divisions." Nothing "gives me much hope of doing anything except just praying . . . and hope they'll quit," he said regarding the enemy. "And I don't believe they're ever goin' to quit."[67]

Pessimism of this sort was common in establishment circles, although it was expressed mainly in private correspondence or in one-on-one conversations. LBJ's dear friend Richard Russell had never betrayed a doubt on the Senate floor, but ten weeks before the Tonkin Gulf incident he had told him: "It's the damn worst mess I ever saw. . . . It's just one of those places where you can't win. . . . We're just in quicksands up to our very necks. And I just don't know what the hell . . . to do about it." Many senior and mid-level officials at State and NSC foresaw only a grim outcome in escalation. Britain and France simply did not believe the American interpretation of the struggle or that Vietnam had any bearing on the credibility or security of the United States. Even the devout anticommunist Humphrey had cautioned his boss in an unsolicited memorandum in February. People did not want to go to war for a country that "is totally unable to put its house in order," he wrote. Like McGovern, he wanted gradually to reduce troop levels. They were "in a stronger position to do so now," the vice president pointed out; 1965 was "the year of minimum political risk for the Johnson administration." Goldwater had lost by a landslide and "we stressed not enlarging the war." With his "political ingenuity," LBJ could achieve "the best possible outcome . . . a Vietnamese settlement" and stop worrying about "the Republican right." When Humphrey repeated his case at an NSC meeting, LBJ barred him from its sessions for an entire year and from meetings on legislation indefinitely. In July the intermittently brave George Ball decided to abjure his Cassandra role rather than court exile. In March 1966 he would tell McGovern and three other senators there was "no option to do anything other than . . . to see the war through and at the price of substantial increased effort."[68]

Along with his embrace of the precepts of the Cold War, the president's massive insecurities and his urge to dominate everyone around him made for a deadly combination. In his fear that he might not measure up—that he might be held responsible for losing, in Joseph Alsop's words, "all that we fought for in the Second World War and in Korea"—he chose war in Vietnam. He did so, "by stealth," insisting there had been no change in policy and concealing the costs as long as possible, ostensibly to prevent his domestic programs from being starved. Johnson assumed that in order to conduct his War on Poverty he must fight communism in Vietnam; McGovern believed that in order to achieve a Great Society the United States must curtail military interventionism in the name of anticommunism.

If a body of argument and evidence, of which McGovern was a principal author, had been heeded, it could have saved the lives of tens of thousands of Americans soldiers as well as those of at least a million Southeast Asians. In being right about these things the forty-three-year-old prairie statesman would never take any pleasure. He would have been pleased just to coax the Senate into holding a "painstaking debate about the essentials of our present policy," as he had tried to do many times, in order to ascertain what the intervention foretold. His comrades in dissent "spoke out as a matter of conscience and conviction," McGovern later observed, but "it would be inaccurate to say that there was a carefully organized wing of dissenters" in 1965.[69] As much as Johnson fretted about them, they could never match the resources of the executive branch. In the meantime, the American people had no reason to suspect that their government could be so wrong, or that it might lie to them about something so important as war.

15 THE CUP OF PERIL IS FULL

"The house was never quite large enough for our family," McGovern once wrote about Coquelin Terrace. Add-ons and renovations seemed constant in the early years. The first one involved turning the attic into a dormered bedroom for Ann and Susan, which their friends envied for its seclusion; next, the carport was converted into a study for George; then the screened back porch became an all-purpose room with large windows looking out upon Eleanor's ever-expanding flower garden. For Terry, Steve, and Mary, Coquelin Terrace became the home of their childhood. As the "adored baby," Mary was the member of the family who received more attention than anyone else. Steve, his mother once wrote, was always the shy and "independent only brother, who rolled down hills instead of walking, climbed over fences instead of open-ing gates." His favorite boyhood pastime was reenacting the Civil War in his bedroom with his armies of toy soldiers. Terry was "our ray of sunshine," Eleanor said. The middle child and the most outgoing of the five, she was also the tidiest, and for that, her parents indulged her with a special set of bedroom furniture that she treasured all of her life. George called her "the Bear" and for morning wake-ups would gently tap her on the nose. "There was a special relationship between Terry and me," he wrote. "We thrived on a shared sense of humor."[1] Terry and Steve were reasonably happy kids but were fated to be troubled teenagers.

More than once McGovern would write of "the conflict between politics and normal family life," of his regret over how his "political career and personal ego demands deprived . . . [his] children of time, attention, direction—and fun with their father." He noted that many fathers of his generation "spent no more time guiding their children . . . or just enjoying them than I did." But his five did express their appreciation for his good humor when he was home and took pride in his work. He and Eleanor had their failings, he would declare, but they "provided models . . . of social conscience, decency, and tolerance in human relations, a love for books and music and cultural affairs, and a constant concern for their well-being." Even so, coping with the children's adolescences was "beginning to rock my complacency," Eleanor said. "I felt it was beyond me, and of course it was beyond both of us, as it turned out."[2]

That was not a commentary on Ann or Susan, whose 1960s experience was markedly different from Terry and Steve's. Most of Ann and Sue's adolescent problems that created turmoil at home were not really determined by the temper of a decade. There was friction, for instance, when their parents made them come home from dates earlier than any of their friends had to, and one time George even ordered a boyfriend of Susan's to leave the house when he stayed too late. Then, too, they had both gone off to college and no longer lived at home by 1965, when "the sixties," per se, seemed to begin. They were mature for their ages as well—Susan was married in 1967 and Ann in 1968—and neither was particularly susceptible to the more harmful cultural excesses characteristic of the times.[3]

But Terry and Steve succumbed, and fairly early. By the age of fourteen or fifteen, just as Johnson was expanding the war and their father was emerging as an outspoken war critic, they had begun drinking and were about to experiment with drugs.[4] Alcohol, however, would ultimately be their undoing in life; it contributed to a sudden, severe emotional trauma in Terry's youth, too.

She was thirteen and in the company of a few neighborhood teens, including her boyfriend, Bill, the first time she ever drank a beer. This was not abnormal adolescent behavior, but in a year or so she had graduated to five beers a week, plus the occasional vodka pilfered from the family liquor cabinet. The unstable Bill compounded Terry's problem. No matter how many times she resisted, he frequently pressured her to go to bed with him. One night in the spring of 1965, angry over another refusal, he went home, put a rifle to his abdomen, and shot himself. The suicide attempt was not fatal, but Terry blamed herself. After his recovery, Bill renewed his advances at the earliest opportunity; for the first time, barely sixteen years old, Terry gave in. Soon she realized she was pregnant.

Once the shock of it settled in on them, George and Eleanor's greatest concern was, as he put it, "the impact on Terry's emotional life of trying to deliver a child under the circumstances of the pregnancy." Their family doctor concurred, and he contacted a trusted colleague in Florida who agreed to perform an abortion, an illegal procedure then, unless the mother's life was clearly endangered. Susan would travel to Florida with Terry. The McGoverns chose not to confront Bill or his parents or to make them privy to their decisions. The whole incident left Terry devastated. Many years later, to her father, she confessed doubt about terminating the pregnancy. And though he never once berated her or raised his voice, she also told him, "I thought my special relationship with you was over." (George's thoughts must have run back to his own troubles in January 1941. Yet the context for that painful story and the ages and statuses of the protagonists were too dissimilar to offer much direction for Terry's predicament; moreover, he had yet to tell even Eleanor about it and would not do so for another ten years.)

That summer he and Eleanor decided that Terry should leave Coquelin Terrace in the fall and take her junior year at a well-regarded Quaker school for girls in Providence, Rhode Island. She weathered the loneliness and came home in June. Some normality returned to her life, but she still drank on the sly, and before long she was smoking pot and taking amphetamines. For her senior year she enrolled in a Quaker school in the District.[5]

Politically, the McGovern family never endured a "generation gap." Susan's concern about Vietnam, for instance, went back to 1964, and she deeply respected her father's stand on it. By 1966–67 she was moving to his left on a number of other issues and was immersed in antiwar activity at the University of Wisconsin, but these were never cause for discord. "No, none of that kind of disagreement," said Steve. In his case, as with Terry, what brought on the conflicts were his drinking and pot smoking and related activities starting in his early teens. "I remember there was a time of sheer panic for me," Eleanor recalled. She and George sent both of them to psychiatrists for a while, which apparently helped a little. "But the psychiatrists didn't know any more than we did. It was such a new thing that it seemed it just exploded on the scene." In retrospect, Steve felt nothing but compassion for what his parents, especially his mother, had to contend with. "There weren't any road maps for either side," he remarked without rancor. "I think my dad coped . . . pretty much by staying out of it." And, through all the difficulties that ensnared them, he and Terry remained in sympathy with their father's career and especially "his desperation, almost" as Steve called it, "about getting the United States out of Vietnam."[6]

It was indeed becoming a matter of desperation for him. McGovern listened to Lyndon Johnson's third State of the Union address, in January 1966, in a very different frame of mind than he had the second. Its content and the president's tone had changed, too. The year before, his emphasis had been prosperity, opportunity, and enriching life for all Americans. Vietnam had been accorded only a few perfunctory sentences. Now, the war consumed over half of the speech. "This nation is mighty enough, its society is healthy enough, its people are strong enough, to pursue our goals in the rest of the world while still building a Great Society here at home," LBJ asserted at the outset. A flourishing economy was his evidence: The number of Americans working had increased by two and a half million and the gross domestic product had risen by $47 billion over the previous year. Income for the average worker was up 33 percent and for farms by 40 percent since 1961, and corporate earnings had soared 60 percent and the balance of payments deficit had been cut in half. The federal budget of $112.8 billion, moreover, would incur only a small deficit of $1.8 billion. Thus (despite his economists' warnings) the president declared, "I believe that we can continue the Great Society while we fight in Vietnam."

Yet he admitted, "Tonight the cup of peril is full in Vietnam." The United States had 190,000 soldiers there and expenditures would consume 10 percent of the $58.3 billion defense budget for the fiscal year. Alluding to a pause in the northern bombing campaign that he had ordered on December 24, he could not predict what it might yield, but he said he would meet anywhere to discuss any peace proposal advanced by any group. "I wish tonight that I could give you a blueprint for the course of this conflict," he concluded heavily. "The days may become months, and the months . . . years, but we will stay as long as aggression commands us to battle."[7]

The reference to the "Christmas Bombing Pause" was misleading; he called it his "peace initiative." It would last thirty-seven days. One aim, owing to a personal plea from McGovern, was to impress domestic opinion and the allies that the United States was determined to start negotiations. But because in the South there was no let-up in the aerial or ground war, Ho Chi Minh would deem it not a serious overture. In reality, its purpose was to justify an impending intensification of Rolling Thunder—"to prove to the Vietcong and the North Vietnamese that they could not win in the South," McNamara later revealed.[8]

McGovern was about to launch an escalation of his own. To be sure, he would still pay LBJ due obeisance. But more openly than before he would express his alarm—in the Senate and increasingly through national publications and network television (where he was starting to develop important friendships). On January 5, 1966, just before the State of the Union, both the *New York Times* and the *Today* show invited him to assess the war for them. "I think the best we can hope for is a negotiated settlement," he said to Sander Vanocur of NBC. "I don't see how either . . . side can score a decisive military victory." In lauding the "superb" servicemen he had met in Vietnam, he spelled out the "overwhelming odds" they faced—the difficult climate and terrain and the fact that "if we were to destroy the Viet Cong, we'd have to destroy a large part of the civilian population." Although thankful for the Christmas pause in the North, to the *Times* he suggested that nothing would come of it unless the Saigon government accepted the National Liberation Front at the negotiations. Thus he was "not convinced . . . that the United States was doing enough to obtain peace."[9]

Neither interview endeared him to the White House, but McGovern's first floor speech of the new session, on January 20, riled Johnson so much he ordered McNamara and Rusk to prepare a rebuttal.[10] It was part of a debate over whether the bombing pause should be extended or terminated. (Sixteen senators and seventy-six representatives would request LBJ formally to extend it.) McGovern believed his colleagues faced a decision of great consequence—to permit or prevent "a major war on the Asian mainland." For five years they had indulged military solutions, which proved futile. "Now let us be equally patient in the effort to find a peaceful solution," he said. There was "nothing to gain and much to lose by resuming the bombing of North Vietnam." It had never stemmed the flow of enemy soldiers into the South and it was not cost effective. In a recent attempt "to knock out a little bridge of secondary importance," he had learned, "we lost three highly trained pilots and three expensive bombers." Nor did any advantage accrue from air raids on the North that "infuriate and unite a people behind their government" or from those on the South that killed two or three civilians for every guerrilla killed. (The *Times* had just reported the governments of Britain, France, and Japan were "pleading for several more weeks or even months of restraint.") McGovern also invoked the authority of Generals Bradley, MacArthur, and Ridgway in warnings against committing US troops to an Asian land war. Realism required the administration to recognize that the rebels, who controlled half the population and two-thirds of the countryside, must play a role "in both the negotiations and a postwar provisional government." This, then, was McGovern's "plea for patience and courage." (Only the day before assistant secretary John McNaughton had warned McNamara: "The PAVN/VC are effectively matching our deployments. . . . We are in an escalating stalemate . . . we will probably be faced . . . with a continued stalemate at a higher level of forces and casualties.")[11]

To make sure they did not miss it, he sent the speech to the editors of *Newsweek* and *Time* and to columnists such as Walter Lippmann and I. F. Stone. "Your leadership on the Vietnam issue—in and out of Congress—is a national asset," replied Norman Cousins of *The Saturday Review*. "You have managed to sort out the essential issues and speak to the question of national morality and purpose." At the *Times* James Reston also complimented him, and then asked, "But do you think anybody is listening to your comments and my columns on Vietnam these days?"[12] It was an apt question. Bombs began to fall again on North Vietnam on January 31. On that day two senior Republicans, George Aiken of Vermont and John Sherman Cooper of Kentucky, joined with the Democrats Mansfield, Morse, and Albert Gore Sr., of Tennessee to protest the resumption on the Senate floor. Aiken envisioned a disastrous war, perhaps one culminating in a conflagration with China; he wondered whether "we have been mousetrapped into letting Russia and China choose the arena for a major showdown." Gore was worried about China too: "The communists have us committed on a battlefield where we suffer the greatest possible disadvantages." Cooper stated his concerns and pulled back: "But the president has made his decision."[13]

Some of the strongest backing for Johnson's action came from southern Democrats. "When we are in a war we should fight to win," Russell Long of Louisiana said in disputing Aiken's commentary. As for China, if the United States did not stand fast, what would become of India, Pakistan, and Indonesia? Sam Ervin of North Carolina maintained US servicemen were in South Vietnam because of the aggression of North Vietnam. Skeptical of the critics, Ervin asked, "is it not possibly true that the admirals and generals can make a more accurate determination of what is advisable, not only to win the war . . . but to protect the lives of American boys?" And on CBS News the previous day John Stennis of Mississippi had come to "the painful conclusion that we must see it through." The communists had made the war "a test of our national purpose and our will to win," he said. "We are there and we are committed."[14]

The foregoing views probably represented the position of the majority of legislators. Yet McGovern spoke a week later of apprehension among both constituents and colleagues finding themselves waist deep in the Big Muddy. Opinion polls did not always "get at the heart of people's thinking on issues as complex as this one," he said. In South Dakota "large numbers of people" had told him "of their concern over what they believe to be a mistaken U.S. course." After private conversations with fellow senators, it was his "studied judgment that at least 75 percent of them feel we should never have become involved militarily in Vietnam." LBJ's advisers, he warned, "will gravely misinterpret public opinion if they assume they have an overwhelming mandate for a growing war." Dean Rusk claimed the North Vietnamese had exploited the bombing halt to stream more regiments southward, but McGovern cited evidence that they had managed to pour soldiers in and repair bridges even when Rolling Thunder was at full throttle. (The CIA in fact had told Johnson all along that aerial attacks had little impact on the North's capacity for infiltration.) McGovern's main concerns were twofold. Renewed bombing would harden Hanoi and destroy all hope of finding a way to negotiate, and it might cause the conflict to spin out of control and risk "a major war with the limitless forces of China." Little wonder the president soared to heights of apoplexy at the mere mention of McGovern's name. "The boss gets wild about him sometimes," Harry McPherson told Joe Califano in February.[15]

Perhaps the resumption's most important result was to provoke Senator Fulbright, who considered the resumption unconscionable. The chair of the Foreign Relations Committee had always kept his counsel private. Now, tutored by Bernard Fall and still regretting his lapse in the Tonkin resolution, he resolved to hold hearings on the war—his purpose, to educate, forewarn, and enlist the public in heading off a huge escalation. For several days in February 1966 distinguished practitioners and scholars of American foreign policy testified, and were cross-examined, before the committee and the nation via live broadcasts on network television. James Gavin explained his enclave strategy, which McGovern advocated and LBJ dismissed as "hunkering down like a mule in a hail storm." George Kennan, author of the containment doctrine, elucidated why Vietnam was not an area of vital interest to the United States and expressed "great misgivings about any deliberate expansion of hostilities." He proposed that the United States limit its commitment, adopt a secure defensive posture akin to Gavin's idea, and show "a little patience" until some diplomatic solution opened up for extrication. Only Rusk's and Taylor's defense of their strategy produced any fireworks—particularly the latter's remark that dissenters had "badly misguided" the public.

The first of their kind ever televised, the hearings created a moderate sensation. Johnson considered them an assault on him personally and soon placed Fulbright under FBI surveillance. In January a Lou Harris poll had accorded the president's Vietnam policy a 63 percent approval rating; by late February, though, that support had fallen to 49 percent, and 34 percent wanted him to "do more to bring about negotiations."[16]

The hearings had affirmed McGovern's every utterance on the war. Yet regardless of their apparent impact on public opinion, on March 1 he and his fellows faced a critical vote on a supplemental defense appropriation to fund the war into 1967. To oppose such a measure (an extra $4.8 billion, for starters) at this point in the evolution of events was politically impossible. "So long as our men fight there," as Gaylord Nelson put it, "they must have the best equipment and support we are able to give them." McGovern said the same thing, and would about every bill for military appropriations for Vietnam thereafter. But he also warned about the possible price in lives lost "in trying to settle a Vietnamese civil conflict with American troops." The United States had deployed 250,000 men, however; they had to be protected, "no matter how mistaken the policy may be that sent them to that battlefield." He voted to provide the GIs with the means of defending themselves; it was "not an endorsement" of the policy. "I only wish more Senators had been involved in the debate . . . a year ago," he remarked, still hoping they would "do everything in [their] power to avoid an all-out war in Asia." The bill passed unanimously except for the two Tonkin Gulf rebels. Rejecting the reasoning of hawks and doves alike, Gruening spoke for himself and Morse: "I cannot in good conscience lend my vote to this needless and unjustifiable slaughter."[17]

Since the night Lyndon Johnson had ranted to him about China's designs for taking over the world, McGovern had been mulling the idea of a major speech about Sino-American relations. Bundy had said to him that the fear of Chinese expansion and a communist takeover in Saigon were inseparable elements behind the American presence in Vietnam. China had figured in virtually every Vietnam discussion McGovern had ever taken part in, and since Northwestern he had been pondering "the greatest revolution in the history of mankind." The works of Fairbank, Lattimore, and White had shaped his outlook on the Cold War. No factor had been more important than Red China in making him a controversial figure at Dakota Wesleyan. His advocacy of its entry into the United Nations was part of his FBI record; it had almost ended his political career when Harold Lovre tried to exploit it in 1956, and it may have given Karl Mundt victory in 1960.

Out of political expediency McGovern had backpedaled in these incidences. But over the years his opinion on UN membership had grown sturdier. Some colleagues (notably Church and Fulbright) agreed with his position. Many more did not. In the spring of 1965 "The Committee of One Million," a group opposed to People's Republic of China (PRC) membership in the UN, boasted three hundred congressional endorsers, including several liberal Democrats. "I rather pray that Red China would give us provocation to attack her military and atomic installations," Barry Goldwater said in print. Yet a House subcommittee in April had approved of cultural exchange with the People's Republic "at an appropriate time," and the president of the US Chamber of Commerce declared, "It makes no sense for the United States not to be in touch with a country of 700 million people."[18]

McGovern had always viewed Vietnam as a consequence of a failed China policy. Now he worried that the escalation had set the United States on a collision course with the PRC. As the Fulbright hearings proceeded, editor Norman Podhoretz of *Commentary* invited McGovern to join him and Richard Goodwin (former special assistant to both JFK and LBJ) for a public forum in New York titled "Containing China." By then he was at work on his Senate speech, and scholars to whom he had sent drafts were replying with kudos. George Kennan called it "one of the really great contributions to the discussion . . . of our foreign policy in this present period." Even more gratifying was John K. Fairbank's opinion. "I feel sure that China specialists . . . including myself, would subscribe to practically everything you say," he wrote. "Few could say it as well." Thus fortified, on May 3 McGovern took the floor to explain why the time had come for a "fundamental reappraisal" of US policy toward Asia.[19]

Since the collapse of European imperialism after 1945, he began, "the most powerful forces moving in Asia have not been communism, but nationalism and the 'revolution of rising expectations.'" Ho Chi Minh's eight-year war of independence against a crumbling colonial power was a vivid example. Had the United States not interfered, McGovern held, "Vietnam would have united under Ho" and "might have served as a more effective buffer to Chinese penetration of Southeast Asia than the . . . warring two Vietnams we helped initiate." Americans often had "become identified with corrupt, stupid, and ineffective dictators who made communist revolutionists look appealing by comparison." The "blinding light" of anticommunism had "even more clearly" shaped policy toward China since 1945. He recounted Americans' apprehensions when Chiang Kai-shek's regime had fled to Formosa, and how McCarthyism, recriminations over "who lost China," and Truman's refusal to recognize Mao's government "combined with a bristling military containment." The Red Scare made matters worse for the purging of specialists on East Asia in the State Department. The result was a "paralysis of policy" while the "the peace of mankind demand[ed] that we open the curtain of ignorance."[20]

The senator observed that China lacked a navy and an air force and confronted the problems of too many people and too little food. It feared both the United States and the Soviet Union. Whereas China had felt great antipathy for the Soviets (her unreliable ally) for the past five years, the United States exercised the Seventh Fleet off her shores. Americans also had aircraft capable of dropping nuclear bombs at the ready in Japan, Thailand, South Vietnam, the Philippines, Okinawa, and on Formosa, where they backed Chiang's army of 600,000. But McGovern believed the United States was wise enough to reach "reconciliation with the people and government of this vast country." To begin, the president should appoint a special commission to study the troubled relationship. The State Department needed at last to secure the services of experts on Chinese affairs, like George Kennan and Charles Bohlen in the field of Soviet studies, and it should invite China to the coming disarmaments talks at Geneva. As for the United Nations, perhaps Americans did not have to advocate China's admission, but neither should they any longer oppose it.[21]

Yet that hurdle necessitated a solution to the "Formosa problem." Since 1949 the United States had acceded to Chiang's insistence that his was the legitimate government of China and that he would one day reclaim the mainland. Whereas the United States could never abandon

Formosa to Peking, McGovern argued that Chiang's delusions were not a credible basis for American policy. The absence of self-determination for the Formosans themselves (who regarded Mao with fear and Chiang with resentment) complicated matters further. McGovern proposed a role for the United Nations in resolving the dilemma: The United States "would be happy to see a 'One China–One Formosa' solution with maximum self-determination for the people of Formosa."[22]

A series of first steps—to encourage tourism and an exchange of artists, business people, doctors, and scholars—would kindle results, he said. Agricultural conferences would be another. Universities in the American heartland, such as South Dakota State and Iowa State, would gladly host the Chinese. No less important, as all of its allies had done, the United States needed to "open the door for trade" with the PRC. Japan, not the Soviet Union, he noted, was now China's leading trading partner. He stressed as well how Peking's demand for huge volumes of wheat stimulated the agricultural economies of Canada, France, and Australia. McGovern wanted Americans to think about their own farmers struggling under acreage restrictions and surpluses; they could anticipate $250 million in grain sales to China annually if Congress removed the political barriers.[23]

These steps to encourage communication and friendly relations carried no risk to American security. "We have neither the mission nor the capacity to play God in Asia by a unilateral U.S. police action," he declared. "Vietnam should have taught us the futility of this role." His suggestions simply made it clear "that while we would resist any military aggression by the Chinese, we want to see them prosper in a climate of peace." Yet China's leaders were "not in a happy mood." Memories of the West's depredations and Japan's invasion were still fresh. The Chinese felt estranged from the Soviets while encirclement by American nuclear power and the war in Vietnam only engendered more bitterness. It was urgent that the United States begin to "take reasonable steps to quiet their fears" rather than "answering hysteria with hysteria." Perhaps it all came down to an appreciation of the "spirit of liberty," he said, quoting Judge Learned Hand—"the spirit which is not too sure that it is right . . . which seeks to understand the minds of other men and women . . . which weighs their interests alongside its own without bias."[24]

The speech was an unalloyed success. Echoing Kennan and Fairbank, Fulbright, who had recently held hearings on China, congratulated McGovern for this, his "latest of several speeches" on foreign policy, and doing the American people a "great service." The two then commenced a lively dialogue. Ted Kennedy had spoken on China more briefly that afternoon and evinced admiration for his seatmate's superior work. Fred Dutton, adviser to all three Kennedy brothers, would call it "the most thoughtful and comprehensive statement" he had seen on the subject. Sargent Shriver, director of the War on Poverty, said it was "a masterpiece . . . of statesmanship." And Ray Allen Billington hailed his former student for "the courage and knowledge to state the case for a policy revision so convincingly." Newspaper coverage was excellent and extensive across the country. At a time when not many people were speaking out on it, McGovern had composed a creative alternative to the country's outdated China policy—six years before Richard Nixon's opening to Beijing.[25]

Johnson, predictably, fretted about the impact of McGovern's proposition and ordered his vice president to refute it. Red China, Humphrey dutifully averred, could not gain UN admission because it "stands as yet designated an aggressor in the resolution of the United Nations Assembly on the Korean war"—hardly a primer to help Americans understand the problems plaguing US-China relations. Thoughtful public discourse on the subject had been years overdue. McGovern and Fulbright and a few others helped to break the long silence. Curiously, LBJ had left the initiative to them, even though the issue was on his mind.[26] He vowed not to become the president who saw Southeast Asia go the way China went. But because of their presence in North Vietnam, he lived with the Sword of Damocles of war with the Chinese (and Soviets) hanging over him. China fortified the North to create a buffer against the encroaching Americans as well as to excel the Soviets as a friend.[27] The Chinese warned Washington of stark consequences in June 1965 if their support of North Vietnam should "bring on American aggression against China." Communism, though, was never the suture that held together North Vietnam's "alliance" with the two great communist powers. The relationships were not unlike Saigon's and Washington's—the product of circumstance rather than affinity. The North Vietnamese remained dedicated to independence against any foreign interloper, and Ho Chi Minh never ceased to propagate the history of China's past invasions.[28]

In the weeks and months after his China speech, McGovern was afforded opportunities to follow up. The National Press Club and several universities invited him to speak, and the *American Legion Magazine* and the *New York Review of Books* asked him to write on the subject.

In September, Metromedia of New York broadcast "The Eagle and the Dragon," a live ninety-minute debate between McGovern and Gale McGee and several pundits and Asia scholars.[29] In June, news of expanded B-52 raids on oil depots on the outskirts of Hanoi and Haiphong had sparked a major colloquy among McGovern, Church, Joe Clark, and Vance Hartke. These senators (and some editorial pages) saw the attacks as a dangerous new phase of the escalation. The move "toward a bigger, bloodier, perhaps longer war" would do nothing to build a stable government in Saigon, said McGovern, omitting his customary nod toward LBJ's "restraint." This intensification risked making "a political and military wasteland" of Vietnamese society and driving the North into the arms of China. The senators were also concerned about the commitment to holding credible elections in the South at the earliest possible time. McGovern urged the White House to demonstrate its support by curtailing ground operations and the bombing until the election could take place. To assure the integrity of the process he wanted a special UN mission to oversee it.[30]

Elections back home also loomed, and most Democrats saw trouble ahead. Even though the economy was humming for most Americans, the inadequately funded War on Poverty had not delivered sufficient prosperity where it was needed most, and that put some tarnish on the gleam of Johnson's achievements in civil rights. The consequences were laid bare in the heat of consecutive summers. In August 1965, a week after the president signed the Voting Rights Act, a race riot had erupted in the Watts district of Los Angeles. Watts was a stable community of black families, but a routine arrest of a black drunk driver by a white policeman set off six days of violence, resulting in the deaths of thirty-four people and the arrest of 4,000 more, and the burning of 250 buildings. When Martin Luther King surveyed the battleground, black youth jeered him as an Uncle Tom who did not understand the plight of African Americans living outside the South. A dispute between police and black teens over an open fire hydrant in a Chicago ghetto in July 1966, let loose another veritable guerrilla war just as revealing as Watts, though less injurious to life and property. Comparable incidents occurred in Cleveland, Dayton, and San Francisco that summer. Constitutional rights were being restored to blacks in the South, yet in the North and West, crime, high unemployment, and the lack of decent housing and schools continued to afflict urban black neighborhoods. "They've lost faith in the democratic process," despaired Dr. King, whose movement was plainly fragmenting. "They've lost faith in nonviolence." The patience of others was wearing thin, too. LBJ was both furious and un-comprehending. To many blue-collar and middle-class whites the riots seemed senseless, and they began to question the value of the War on Poverty.[31]

Neither did the war in Vietnam appear to be any closer to victory. Public opinion was mercurial. In December 1965 a solid 64 percent ap-proved of LBJ's general conduct as president and 75 percent approved of his handling of the war. But by June 1966, those scores had fallen to 46 and 40 percent, while 42 percent actively disapproved of his han-dling of the war and 36 percent considered it a mistake to have gotten involved militarily. In September, another poll disclosed that Demo-crats, by 40 to 38 percent, preferred Robert Kennedy to Johnson as the 1968 standard-bearer. The party's midterm prospects were not helped when the first week of October turned out to be one of the bloodiest so far for US casualties in Vietnam, with 142 killed and 825 wounded.[32]

The Democrats suffered a record setback in the 1966 elections. On November 8, their rivals netted gains of forty-seven in the House and three in the Senate, as well as 540 state legislative seats and eight governorships—the GOP's best showing since 1938 and fairly stunning in light of the Goldwater debacle. (In South Dakota the Republicans swept the state from top to bottom.)[33] The president's party would still control the 90th Congress (64 to 36 in the Senate and 248 to 187 in the House), but the conservative coalition had been replenished, and he would face greater pressure from war hawks than ever before. This prelude to 1968 heartened Republicans, and none more so than Richard Nixon. The former vice president had stumped tirelessly for the party's candidates. Repeatedly he accused Johnson of not pursuing military victory aggressively enough in Vietnam and portrayed his gestures to-ward negotiations (tepid as they were) as offers "to surrender a decisive military advantage." He also declared him "the first president in Amer-ican history who has failed to unite his party in time of war." Nixon, his comeback clearly revving up, earned more credit for the GOP's score card than anyone else—except perhaps for LBJ. At their annual gather-ing in December, Democratic governors laid the blame at their leader's feet. Elsewhere, the midterms set in motion talk of whether he could be deposed. Chet Huntley, coanchor of NBC News, declared, "Johnson will probably be defeated in 1968." In the opinion of Frank Mankiewicz, Rob-ert Kennedy's press secretary, it was now "a brand new ball game."[34]

McGovern was inclined to agree. In July, during another seminar weekend in Vermont, he had raised with Ken Galbraith and Arthur

Schlesinger the prospect of New York's junior senator challenging Johnson. He had even broached it with Kennedy himself, in the summer of 1965 during a visit to Hickory Hill, RFK's estate near Washington. Just then, the notion was quite premature. Neither Ted nor Bobby had yet made a significant speech on the war, let alone enlisted in the opposition. Bobby was still "in transition," as McGovern put it; he continued to mourn his brother and felt a measure of responsibility for their part in getting the country involved in Vietnam. Also, within the administration, McNamara and Maxwell Taylor were his "most trusted and cherished friends." But the biggest complication was the storied enmity between himself and LBJ.[35]

Bobby had been the first to draw blood, in his bitter objection to his brother's choice of running mates in 1960. To him Johnson had been an object of ridicule, a crude and vulgar Texan—and then, after Dallas, an inconceivable usurper to be shunned. To Johnson, the younger Kennedy was JFK's disrespectful messenger boy, the spoiled upstart. Whereas LBJ honored the slain president's public memory, he remained wary of RFK's capacity to overshadow him or to mount a popular coup d'état. If he ever faltered in Vietnam, he once remarked, Bobby would be "telling everyone I had betrayed John Kennedy's commitment to South Vietnam . . . [and] let a democracy fall into the hands of the communists. That I was a coward, an unmanly man." This, then, was his "Bobby problem." Bobby, however, did not nurse a "Lyndon problem." For his own and the party's sake, he tried not to inflame the situation by openly criticizing the president or the war. The press kept constant watch on the feud.[36]

McGovern appreciated the unique position Bob occupied and his need to avoid confrontation. Even so, Kennedy "welcomed the dissent" and told George that he was "especially high" on him and Frank Church as the Senate's "more thoughtful critics." He invited them to his Hickory Hill seminars, along with his hawkish friends such as Averell Harriman, and often provoked debates among his guests as a way of honing his education on Vietnam. George became one of a few senators around whom Bobby really felt comfortable, and they would develop one of the closest friendships that either had on the Hill. "There is nobody that I feel more genuinely about, whether we are in politics or not—about the importance of his contribution and . . . his understanding and feeling—than George McGovern," Kennedy once said. And Pat Donovan observed: "Their instincts, their guts were so much alike. It was two kindred souls, I think."[37]

Although a rupture had not occurred between McGovern and LBJ, the midterms suggested one was not far off. So far Johnson had refrained from retribution. But before the campaign got under way he sent Dean Rusk on a mission to South Dakota to dedicate a new dam on the Missouri River and to praise Karl Mundt. One of the war's strongest supporters in the GOP, Mundt was up for reelection. Putting his arm around him, the secretary of state dubbed the former McCarthyite "a great American absolutely essential to the well being of the United States." The endorsement, given the campaign's outcome, confirmed McGovern's thinking on two points—"that it was going to be difficult to turn the President around on Vietnam and that Bob Kennedy was the only person who had the national stature, the name, the money and the organizational power to do it."[38]

In the new year, as the bombing runs on the North increased, Kennedy finally decided the time had come to make his first major speech on the war. On the evening before, he had Frank Mankiewicz take the text to McGovern's home for his review. Its principal authors were Schlesinger and Richard Goodwin. McGovern judged it "fine," though privately he thought it was too cautious on the idea of coalition government in Saigon. But that did not matter. He was relieved the heir to Camelot at last was about to carve a role for himself regarding his own great obsession.[39]

Kennedy took the floor on March 2, 1967, the day after the Senate appropriated yet another $4.5 billion to finance the war. Most senators were in their seats and the gallery was full. LBJ, he began, had "for years . . . dedicated his energies" to achieving "an honorable peace," and *three* presidents shared the burden of the war. If "fault is to be found," he added, "there is enough to go around for all—including myself." But the war had become an "unending crescendo of violence, hatred, and savage fury" fraught with possibly mortal peril for all concerned. Thus Bobby was calling on the White House to suspend Rolling Thunder and express its readiness to embark upon negotiations "within the week." The sole condition he would impose on this cease-fire was that neither side "increase the size of the war in South Vietnam—by infiltration or reinforcement." Nothing prevented the United States from breaking off the negotiation, and no advantage would be lost by the bombing halt. He worried that the ongoing bombardment "may have already stiffened our adversaries' position and dimmed the prospect for peace."[40]

There was little in the speech that McGovern or Church or other critics had not aired before. But this was the Kennedy treatise on the war and thus front-page news. LBJ did his damnedest to discredit his proposals and to defend the bombing in a disingenuous four-page letter to Senator Henry Jackson, the Democratic hawk from Washington State, who released it during the colloquy following RFK's speech. By this juncture it seemed to McGovern that Johnson was "out of touch with practically all the leading critics in the Senate." His fellow dissenters acted responsibly, he felt, but he also knew that the president was "pained and angered by the refusal of the doves to give him any credit for the restraint that he was exercising."[41] Hawks in both parties rapped him, too—for micromanaging the war and allegedly making the military "fight with one hand tied behind its back." But they did not apprehend the potential disaster of losing control of the bombing, as LBJ, to his credit, did. It was the principal factor behind the kind of "limited" war he fought—by his lights the center between two extremes.

Its magnitude was nonetheless staggering. In December 1966, US troops in Vietnam numbered 385,300. Of these, 5,008 were killed in action that year and 16,526 were wounded. By the end of 1967, troop levels would climb to 485,600 and an additional 9,377 GIs would be killed and 32,370 wounded.[42] These losses were the result of Westmoreland's strategy of attrition. Often preceded by saturation bombing, the general's "search and destroy" missions might involve as few as thirty troops in an attack on a single village, or as many as 30,000, as in the assault on the NLF bastion known as the "Iron Triangle" north of Saigon in early 1967, where the area afterward "looked like giant steel claws had raked the jungle," according to Bernard Fall. Success was based on "body counts." Because of the difficulty of knowing whether the dead were guerrillas or innocent villagers, the GIs' common verdict was, "If it's dead and Vietnamese, it's VC." Yet which army was wearing down its enemy remained debatable. Even as the United States upped the ante by 100,000 troops in both 1966 and 1967, twice that number of North Vietnamese came of draft age annually—a perfect formula for stalemate.[43]

No country in the history of warfare had been subjected to more intensive air assaults than Vietnam. Sorties against North Vietnam had come to 25,000 in 1965 and quadrupled in 1967. B-52s carried a payload of nearly thirty tons (six times that of McGovern's B-24). From March 1965 through December 1967 they rained down upon the country a total of one-and-a-half million tons of bombs—a half million in the North and a million in the South—which exceeded the combined tonnage dropped by all belligerents in World War II. Most of North Vietnam's infrastructure by then lay in ruins. Napalm and Agent Orange had destroyed half of South Vietnam's forests—1,570,114 acres in 1967 alone.

In addition to the hundreds of thousands killed, one in four southern peasants was homeless. In Saigon, Nguyen Cao Ky and Nguyen Van Thieu, the quasi-dictators who once had fought alongside the French, controlled the government through corruption and repression. To accomplish these feats, the United States was spending $2 billion a month, a sum exceeding the War on Poverty's budget for 1966, roughly equal to what the Soviets and Chinese together expended in North Vietnam from 1965 to 1968. And still, the enemy's capacity and will to carry on the struggle seemed undiminished.[44]

It was this insensate destruction of innocent lives and Vietnam's countryside—as well as the waste of resources that might have been put to better use at home—that by 1967 had wrought the greatest antiwar movement in American history. The movement attracted a variety of groups. But as their collective impact grew in strength, they were not always of the same mind. In October 1965, for example, 36,000 young men were conscripted into military service. This, the largest one-month call-up since Korea, stoked a series of draft card burnings, a form of protest that SDS encouraged but that McGovern and his colleagues could not condone. In November his friend Sanford Gottlieb of SANE led a demonstration of 30,000 people in Washington. It included Dr. Benjamin Spock, the socialist Norman Thomas, and Carl Oglesby of SDS, and advocated the program of the Senate doves—a cease-fire, a bombing halt, and a negotiated settlement.[45]

In 1966, the year of greatest support for the war, antiwar activity was smaller in scale. Prominent clerical leaders such as William Sloan Coffin and Rabbi Abraham Heschel formed interfaith organizations while college students continued to leaflet and take to the campus soapbox. But antiwar protesters began to encounter resistance. Campus police at Texas A&M arrested students for passing out flyers; conservative youths at Ohio State burned Senator Gruening in effigy; and Barry Goldwater denounced the Fulbright hearings for lending "aid and comfort" to the enemy. In 1967, as US troop levels increased by 10,000 a month, the scope of antiwar demonstrations grew. On April 15, the "Spring Mobilization," a coalition of civil rights and peace activists, led 75,000 protesters through the streets of San Francisco and 200,000 in New York City, with perhaps twice that number gathering afterward in Central Park. Soon the National Committee set about making plans for rallies of a more militant nature for the autumn.[46]

McGovern deemed the opposition within the academic community "one of the most revealing factors about our Vietnam experience." In

June 1966, he had printed in the *Congressional Record* a list of 6,000 university professors from around the country who had signed a statement published in the *New York Times* calling for negotiations. Some of them were acquaintances of his, and by then his daughter Susan and future son-in-law, James Rowen, participated in the movement at the University of Wisconsin. In August the AFL-CIO's executive council declared, "disruption by even a well-meaning minority can only pollute and poison the bloodstream of our democracy," and McGovern countered, "For the sake of our sons and the future vitality and health of America, I hope that free and honest discussion of policy in Southeast Asia has not ended." Johnson's "strenuous moves to kill" Kennedy's speech in March 1967, disturbed him just as much. Defending the dissenters, McGovern wrote in the *New Republic*, "Seldom in our history have so many enlightened and morally sensitive political, religious, and educational leaders joined in opposing a wartime policy of our government." These now included Martin Luther King, who had exhorted from the speaker's platform that he shared with McGovern in Los Angeles on February 26, 1967: "Those of us who love peace must organize as effectively as the war hawks.[47]

In the spring of 1967, McGovern, Fulbright, and several other senators began to suspect the administration of preparing a major military surge in Vietnam, attended by a political one at home to undercut dissent. Arthur Schlesinger and Ken Galbraith had the same feeling. In early April McGovern began to work on a new speech when reports surfaced that the Russians and Chinese, at Hanoi's bidding, had agreed to put aside their differences and work closely to provision North Vietnam. The expansion of the war was becoming even more dangerous, for it was pulling the two great communist powers together. Then LBJ decided to call Westmoreland home, "to keep the American people informed, particularly in view of manifold misinformation disseminated by antiwar activists," the general recorded in his memoir. Never before had a field commander been summoned from a combat theater for such a purpose. His first assignment was to address 1,500 journalists at New York's Waldorf-Astoria on April 24. That morning Air Force F-105s attacked rail yards two miles from Hanoi and two Russian MIG airfields. In his formal remarks Westmoreland applauded the attacks and said that the enemy had "lost the chance of military victory he had two years ago."

And yet the enemy "clings to the belief that he will defeat us," he continued. This was because, "both here and abroad, he has gained support which gives him the hope that he can win politically that which he cannot accomplish militarily." It was costing lives on both sides. Then, as if to hurl a second brick into a beehive, he remarked that the GIs in Vietnam were "dismayed, and so am I, by recent unpatriotic acts here at home." The next morning McGovern responded with one of the era's greatest speeches about the war.[48]

The hawks were frustrated, McGovern observed in his preface on the floor of the Senate. They were "trying to blame the failure of their policy on their critics." He did not hold Westmoreland responsible for his comments in New York, though; fine soldier that he was, he was carrying out the orders of his commander-in-chief. But to imply that the dissent in America was behind the refusal of the North Vietnamese and the NLF to quit the war amounted to an admission by the White House of "the weakness of its own case." The critics had simply "exposed the contradictions, the falsehoods, and the resulting credibility gap which surrounds administration policy." Worse still, the new forays into the North courted intervention by the Chinese. "Thus," he explained, "I do not intend to remain silent in the face of what I regard as a policy of madness."[49]

The Vietnam conflict represented "the most tragic diplomatic and moral failure in our national experience," McGovern said, for it was "degenerating into a defeat for America whether we 'win' or 'lose.'" He quoted Douglas MacArthur's line, "Anyone who commits American forces to a land war in Asia ought to have his head examined," and warned that, if the fighting continued on its present course, "our dreams of a Great Society and a peaceful world will turn to ashes." He noted as well that only "by a crude misreading of history and a distortion of our most treasured ideals" was anyone able to rationalize the policy. "After all the dead are counted—American and Vietnamese— and the countryside is laid waste, what will we have accomplished?" he asked. "We fight in Vietnam . . . because of a highly questionable notion that this is the only honorable course. . . . We fight, also, perhaps, to save the professional reputation of policy planners who have recommended a series of steps . . . seemingly prudent and restrained, yet each one inexorably setting in motion the next step to a larger war."[50]

He then spoke of "a climate of intimidation designed to silence . . . meaningful discussion" and of the war hawks' incessant invocations of Hitler and Munich and the domino theory. "This, I think, is a piece of historical nonsense," he said. "There is no analogy between Munich and Vietnam, and countries are not dominoes." (He noted the irony that Adolf Hitler was vice president Ky's "only political hero.") Ho Chi Minh, though a Marxist, was first a nationalist, and the war was "a civil conflict among various groups of Vietnamese," not one of northern aggression against neighbors to the south, as the administration claimed. In any case, the challenge of communism could not be met "by forcing an American solution on a people still in search of their own national identity." Deploring the war's magnitude—"a scale heretofore used only against Nazi Germany and Tojo's Japan"—he reminded his listeners of Barry Goldwater's pitch for "victory in Vietnam through bombing . . . and a major escalation of American forces." Voters resoundingly rejected that proposition on the strength of Johnson's promise, "We seek no wider war." The "mandate for peace of 1964" nonetheless had been "translated into the Goldwater prescription on the installment plan."[51]

The United States had "no obligation to play policeman for the world and especially in Asia, which is so sensitive to heavy-handed interference by even well-meaning white men." Above all, Americans must learn that "conflicts of this kind have historical dimensions that are essentially political, economic, psychological; they do not respond readily to military force from the outside." And "corrupt regimes do not deserve to be saved by the blood of American boys." Finally, he reckoned, "Congress must never again surrender its power under our constitutional system by permitting an ill-advised, undeclared war," thus rendering its function "very largely one of acquiescence." To be sure, dissent in Congress recently had been sharp; alas, it had come "late in the day."[52]

"The Lessons of Vietnam" captured the depth and range of his thoughts perhaps better than any other of McGovern's speeches so far. (Decades later it reads like the summary pages of the best scholarly monographs on the subject.) Major newspapers accorded it front-page headlines and frequently quoted the phrase, "a policy of madness." The *New York Times* devoted a full page to the text and featured it in the Sunday "Week in Review." It was "a remarkable performance" by "a notably fine Senator" and "an act of political, moral, and intellectual courage," said *The Nation*. *The Progressive*, which published it in April and sold copies in bulk for years, called it "the finest single analysis of the past, present, and future U.S. in Vietnam." Back home, the *Mitchell Daily Republic* commented, "McGovern has shown courage . . . [and]

turned his back on political expediency in favor of conscientious opposition." Congratulating him on the completeness of his indictment despite "an unparalleled effort to silence dissent," the *St. Louis Post-Dispatch* declared, "It is essential to the very integrity of American democracy that brave men like Senator McGovern decline to be intimidated."[53]

Colleagues offered their support, too. In a colloquy Bobby Kennedy considered it "one of the most courageous speeches delivered in the Senate" since his election in 1964. His friend had "touched the conscience of this body and reminded the people of the United States that war is not always the answer." Fulbright as well called it "one of the best and most thoughtful speeches" on Vietnam he had ever heard. "I know that I am one of those to whom he referred, and properly," the Arkansan acknowledged, "having been too slow to recognize the war and to do anything about it to warn the country." By the end of the week several moderate Republicans—George Aiken, Thruston B. Morton of Kentucky, Charles Percy of Illinois, and Mark Hatfield of Oregon—had seconded his criticisms of the escalation and LBJ's flag-waving ploy. In their columns, Drew Pearson openly admired McGovern for his daring and Marquis Childs and Tom Wicker praised him as a "courageous dissenter."[54]

Three days later, on April 28, Westmoreland capped his visit with an address to a Joint Session of Congress. Whereas he avoided the subject of dissent, he still managed, as the *New York Times* remarked, to "put on display the political power of patriotism," and the Congress gave him four standing ovations. (A few members only applauded politely.) On the day before, he had been summoned to the Oval Office to clarify his secret request of March 17—for 200,000 troops on top of the 470,000 already in Vietnam. He estimated that without such strength, it could take five years to win the war, but with the optimum 670,000, it could be done in three years. Incredulous, Johnson asked, "When we add divisions, can't the enemy add divisions? If so, where does it all end?" In July he indulged the general with 55,000 more troops.[55]

On May 2 the *Washington Evening Star* reported that McGovern had received a thousand letters a day since his speech, at a ratio of sixty to one in support. When the *Aberdeen American News* asked how the speech might affect his relationship with the White House, he offered dryly, "I think it's been banged up a bit." He also said he could potentially support a Republican for president if he advanced an alternative "likely . . . to lead us to an honorable settlement of the war." He attacked the administration's farm policy that week, too. For months he had been calling its approach to Food for Peace "timid and uncertain." Wheat growers barely realized 74 percent of parity for their harvests and rural state Democrats charged LBJ with making farmers the "scapegoats of every attempt to control inflation," and war-induced inflation at that.[56]

Events of summer and fall would rule out any chance for reconciliation between Johnson and McGovern. To begin, the president's failure to address the problems that underlay the previous summer's racial disturbances was about to be exposed, no matter his historic nomination of Thurgood Marshall as a justice of the Supreme Court in June. A month later a series of small incidents between whites and blacks in Newark exploded into five terrible days that left twenty-six dead and entire neighborhoods destroyed. The next week, Detroit became the scene of the worst race riot of the era: forty-three people killed, 2,250 injured, and thousands of homes and businesses burned. Order was restored by 4,700 federalized national guardsmen equipped with Hueys (the helicopters used in Vietnam).[57]

As before, middle- and working-class whites of the North were not sympathetic. In some polls, crime and "law and order" was displacing Vietnam as the country's greatest problem. Unable to fathom the grievances of the urban ghetto that had spawned this nightmare, few of them had ever contemplated the poverty, unemployment, the lack of decent housing, and the separate and unequal schools that northern racism still countenanced. The president was caught in a political cross fire. Conservatives of both parties blamed the riots on him and liberal coddling along with the communist conspiracy that many of them said suffused the civil rights movement. Among liberals the Marshall nomination had little staying power, and McGovern was ready with an itemized list to show how funds spent on Vietnam could be channeled into a dozen worthy domestic programs, including enhancements of 40 percent in the budgets for education, housing, and community development. "He's through with domestic problems, with the cities," Bobby Kennedy said of LBJ to Frank Mankiewicz in the wake of the riots. "He's not going to do one thing. And he's the only one who can."[58]

That summer the nation also faced the prospect of a budgetary deficit of $29 billion for fiscal 1968 as well as the onset of inflation. The solution Johnson reluctantly embraced was a 10 percent surcharge on personal and corporate income taxes. His new budget totaled $137 billion. It allotted $12 billion for the war (half of what really would be needed) and an increase of only $1.9 billion for the Great Society. The conservative coalition wanted to control both the deficit and inflation by slashing expenditures for social programs by five to ten billion dollars. A growing number of liberals located the source of the economic woes in Southeast Asia, which LBJ was only making worse by pouring in an additional 55,000 GIs. Together, the sequence of summer crises had pushed his approval ratings down to 39 percent, an all-time low.[59]

McGovern's August newsletter was the bleakest ever. "The truth is we cannot win this struggle by the course we are following," he declared, decrying the deployment of still more troops. At a monthly average of 1,200, "our men are dying by the thousands . . . [while] South Vietnamese soldiers are deserting by the thousands." ARVN had "all but quit the fight." Turning to the bombing in light of deficits and rising taxes, he asked, "Does it make sense to use a $2 million plane . . . carrying a $10,000 bomb load to knock out a grass hut or a rope bridge that will be repaired by nightfall?" He also remarked on Saigon's forthcoming election in which most opponents of the Thieu-Ky ticket for president and vice president had been disqualified on the grounds that they were either communist sympathizers or neutralists. (In September the two generals would win with barely 35 percent of the vote. Their closest rival, subsequently arrested, placed at 17 percent.) "One wonders if this kind of 'freedom' is worth the death of 15,000 young Americans," he said. But whatever its outcome, he wanted the election to be "the best possible arrangement for ending this war or turning its conduct over to the Vietnamese." He assured constituents he would continue to support the appropriations their soldiers needed, but added, *"The best way to back our men in Vietnam is to change the policy that sent them there."*[60]

On September 22, LBJ invited the senator to a stag dinner at the White House along with eleven others, including several of his tormentors on the Hill. Sometime between the presentation of the prime rib and the peach melba, the subject inescapably turned to Vietnam. "He seemed to be almost begging for political advice," McGovern wrote in a memorandum, "yet, when we would try to interject, he would immediately break in. I think one time—I didn't time him—but he went on for 45 minutes without interruption." When he asked whether the formal election of the Thieu-Ky government meant that the United States might entrust it with greater responsibility for fighting the war instead of sending yet more American draftees, Johnson lectured for twenty minutes without really answering. "The President is a tortured, confused man—literally tortured by the mess he has gotten into in Vietnam," McGovern recorded. "He is restless, almost like a caged lion, as if some great force has overtaken him." By the end of the evening he feared his host was going to pieces, as "he reacts violently to suggestions that our involvement is immoral, or that he is following the Goldwater line." LBJ soon resolved to banish McGovern from all White House functions.[61]

By then the president was apprised of a "Dump Johnson" movement, and he suspected the South Dakotan had a hand in it. A disgruntled Sioux Falls Democrat had been feeding such accusations to Joe Califano, and the *Argus Leader* had run an editorial about McGovern's criticisms, Bobby Kennedy's ambitions, and the implications of the pair's friendship. Yet LBJ knew that McGovern had discouraged attacks on him by Americans for Democratic Action that summer. And though McGovern and RFK continued to have reveries about a Kennedy challenge, neither knew how to go about it short of tearing the party to shreds.[62]

George was easing off RFK also because he knew what it was like to be pressed. Delegations of academics and church groups had come to talk to him about running for president. In July, James Wechsler of the *New York Post* and Joseph Rauh of ADA had cajoled him—that he might take 25 percent of the vote in the New Hampshire primary, perhaps enough "to frighten Johnson into changing his policy," they said. Bobby, he answered, would make the strongest race. Next came the scholar-activists Marcus Raskin and Richard J. Barnet, cofounders of the Institute for Policy Studies in Washington; in late August came Allard Lowenstein, an ADA officer and the zealous organizer of "Dump Johnson." Lowenstein's first choice was Kennedy, who had resisted the young man and convinced him that George was the most attractive alternative.[63]

"I rather enjoyed having someone tell me they thought I ought to run for president," McGovern admitted years later. It had crossed his mind as early as 1961. Along with working for JFK, his political experience and historical studies had made him feel the way was open to anybody. He believed Kennedy had prevailed "against all odds," not so much owing to his charm and privileged upbringing as to his "having the imagination and courage" to attempt it. "I began to see that there wasn't any miracle about this." McGovern himself had come from "out of nowhere to be elected to Congress," and that gave him confidence to see that "the White House was really winning five or six states in the primaries." As his friend Arthur Schlesinger once remarked, "George, in his quiet way, is an ambitious man."[64]

If McGovern had beaten Karl Mundt in 1960 and then won reelection in 1966, it is a safe bet that he would not have hesitated. But in this moment, caution tempered ambition. In 1962 he had won his Senate race by a mere 597 votes; in 1968 he would face a bloc of largely Republican voters as the Democrat who was one of the war's most unrelenting critics. Regardless of how unpopular LBJ was in South Dakota, no one on the senator's staff thought a challenge was a good idea, and none of his solicitors thought he could deprive LBJ of renomination. It was unreasonable, then, to demand so much of someone facing reelection, he told Lowenstein, who argued fervently that his candidacy had the potential to turn Johnson around on Vietnam. But his suitor did not want him to lose his Senate seat either, so Lowenstein flew to Sioux Falls to do "a little looking around and see what the people think about this possibility." Bill Dougherty and Peter Ecker—leading South Dakota Democrats, Kennedy men, and McGovern disciples—heard him out. "Jeez. Run for president? Are you kidding?" Dougherty said. "Hell, we've got to get him elected to the Senate again." Then Ecker reprised the labors of raising the state's party from the dead in the 1950s. Lowenstein gained the impression that here the war was not the stark tragedy that divided other parts of the nation, and that George could do himself harm in undertaking two campaigns. Yet he persisted. Finally, in October, McGovern ascertained that, among the acceptable prospects, only Lee Metcalf and Eugene McCarthy did not face reelection in 1968. They might have been "peripheral doves" (a year or so late in coming to the cause and sometimes short on ardor), but one of them would say "yes" to Lowenstein.[65]

As that search was ending, the antiwar movement approached a not unrelated culmination of its own. October 1967 would become the movement's most important month so far—even if the nature of some of the protests worried activists in ADA and SANE. On Monday, the sixteenth, in Philadelphia, Cincinnati, and Boston, hundreds of young men destroyed their draft cards. "Stop the Draft Week" began that day in Oakland, California, where a hundred students held a nonviolent sit-down demonstration at an induction center; it climaxed on Friday in a fierce clash between 10,000 protesters and 2,000 of the city's police. At that same time in the Middle West, a sit-in against the presence of Dow Chemical Company (a major provider of napalm) at the University of Wisconsin turned into hand-to-hand combat between students and Madison police. Susan McGovern and her husband Jim Rowen took part in the protest. The police "just beat the hell out of everybody" inside the building and turned dogs and tear gas on the large crowd of supporters outside. "We went to the demonstration as good liberals and left as radicals," said Susan, describing a provisional transformation that many young people underwent after encounters with force exercised unreasonably by those in authority.[66]

On Saturday, October 21, the peace march to end all others took place in Washington, DC. Neither SDS nor SANE agreed to endorse this event—the "March on the Pentagon"—organized primarily by the radical Jerry Rubin. The day began on the National Mall with the amassing of about 50,000 protesters, songs by Peter, Paul, and Mary, and speeches into the afternoon. Then, upwards of 30,000—looking "like the legions of Sgt. Pepper's Band," wrote Norman Mailer—moved across Memorial Bridge and onto the grounds of the Pentagon. Awaiting them, a phalanx of disciplined troops standing shoulder to shoulder had encircled the huge building. McNamara kept vigil on the roof. Some accounts say the protesters' behavior undermined their effectiveness. Many in the front ranks taunted the soldiers, and Abbie Hoffman attempted to "levitate" the Pentagon. Had they been more "Gandhi-like," McNamara later reflected, "they could have achieved their goal of shutting us down." The siege receded by nightfall; there were some arrests and violence. NBC's David Brinkley called it a "coarse, vulgar episode." Johnson could not shake his conviction that "communist elements" had instigated the throng despite the fact the FBI and CIA could produce no evidence to sustain it.[67]

Despite its frivolous aspects, the March on the Pentagon had an impact on politics. The spectacle was nothing if not a boost for the Dump Johnson movement. In a matter of weeks the exhausted secretary of defense—at odds with his boss and nearly estranged from his seventeen-year-old son—decided to resign his post. By late October, Gallup polls found that only 28 percent of the public approved of LBJ's handling of the war and 46 percent considered it a blunder to have sent troops to Vietnam in the first place. In November the *Saturday Evening Post*, the purveyor of Norman Rockwell's America, pronounced the war "a national mistake."[68]

For Eugene McCarthy the events of autumn became food for thought when Allard Lowenstein, at McGovern's behest, had begun to woo him. On October 17, McCarthy hailed McGovern in the Senate to thank him and say he had decided to run against LBJ in four primaries. Arthur Schlesinger saw the development as good news when George phoned to tell him. "It might, indeed, open the way for a serious draft-RFK movement," he entered in his diary. But Kennedy called George that night "in great mental anguish." McCarthy would get a lot of support, he said. "I can tell you right now, he'll run very strong in New Hampshire." McGovern guessed that, "Bob had intended all along to run if . . . [the] disaffection in the country continued to mount," but it had not occurred to him "that somebody else might jump in." How to keep his options open and, if need be, to induce McCarthy to abandon his quest would preoccupy RFK for the next three months.[69]

Throughout this period, though, most politicians did not take McCarthy's candidacy seriously. The Minnesotan had served for ten years in the House and eight in the Senate. But, whereas he was "a most intelligent and attractive man," as Schlesinger granted, he was also "a disappointing senator, especially in his laziness." Gloria Steinem, once she started to work on his campaign, found him "autocratic, standoffish, sarcastic, and belittling of people." Another activist considered him a "deeply cynical man." Some colleagues privately questioned his motives. It was known that McCarthy was still bitter toward Johnson for not selecting him for vice president instead of Humphrey, and that he considered the Kennedys deficient as Catholics and resented their success in politics. More substantively, his voting record was mixed from a liberal standpoint and he was a loyal friend of Big Oil. Not until February 1967 did he make an unvarnished public statement against the war, nor did he question the basic tenets of the Cold War or feel comfortable with most elements of the antiwar movement. Had he been LBJ's running mate in 1964, his biographer has written, "it is unlikely he would have become an outspoken opponent of the war."[70]

Even so, as early as 1966, McCarthy had begun to raise questions about the usurpation of power by the executive branch. And, "particularly for students and young people," the *New York Times* editorialized, he "provided constructive political leadership in a hard, confused time." As McGovern said in the Senate, McCarthy showed "courage and dignity which justifies the respect of us all." Still, as a campaigner, his flat speaking style and personality were problematical. Steinem wrote that he had "a gift for diffusing enthusiasm," and British author Henry Fairlie compared him to Calvin Coolidge. A friend told Joe Rauh that his performance was "so weak he makes even Johnson look good." Polls sustained that verdict. One national survey in December gave LBJ a five-to-one advantage over McCarthy. Yet to convince him that he needed to campaign in New Hampshire was nearly impossible. When he at last acceded in January, his lectures caused more supporters to fall away. In February he would plummet to 11 percent in a Roper poll of the state's Democrats.[71]

Meanwhile, the counselors of Robert Kennedy were wrestling with his dilemma. His brother and Ted Sorensen all along had agreed that 1972 would be Bobby's year; they resisted any venture that might jeopardize it. In November Fred Dutton contended that it would be "political suicide" to run in 1968. Schlesinger perceived a limited potential for McCarthy by December, believing that party leaders soon would seek out RFK to rescue the Democrats from being pulled down by LBJ. McGovern had the same hunch, but neither had hard evidence as to who might support his candidacy. "You really have no business urging him to run," Ted Sorensen scolded him, and twice Ted Kennedy told George he did not want his brother to do it: "Now, be careful what you tell him because he's thinking seriously about going in." Just before the holidays, Bobby asked George to sound out Frank Church, Gaylord Nelson, and a few others. "No one was ready to stick his neck out," he reported, to Bobby's dismay. "The ordeal continues," Schlesinger would write in January. "I have never seen RFK so torn about anything."[72]

Long before McCarthy appeared to career toward disaster, McGovern fully expected LBJ to be renominated. It was no more than "a continuation of the debate," he wrote an acquaintance when McCarthy declared, and he doubted whether "either party will nominate a candidate more devoted to peace than Johnson." Some weeks after the stag dinner, his sense of resignation prompted him to send the president one last proposal in October. It recommended an indefinite bombing halt in North Vietnam on the grounds that all significant military targets had been destroyed and the costs of the attacks—including "the disunity of our own country"—exceeded the benefits. He also urged the enlistment of the Soviets to secure a pullback of North Vietnamese forces; the replacement of the bloody "search and destroy" with "clear and hold" operations in the South; the start of American troop withdrawals and Saigon's assumption of "a greater responsibility for its own defense." These latter sections anticipated "Vietnamization."[73]

It was ironic that, in his final policy report to Johnson in November, Secretary McNamara advocated a course of action that reflected every point on McGovern's list (especially that ARVN take on a greater combat burden) and embraced the essence of his inclusive analysis as well. (A Carnegie study a month later advised that the "clear and hold" strategy could both reduce US casualties and stabilize the struggle in the South "without surrender and without risking a wider war.") Yet LBJ was still asking, "How are we going to win?" The argument that the fighting had reached a stalemate rankled him, not to mention the antiwar protests and the growing number of mainstream editors advocating an "honorable alternative to an endless war," as McGovern reminded him.[74] "The major threat we have is from the doves," Johnson concluded in September. And so, despite the controversial public relations blitz in April, he decided on still another such offensive, obliging his field commander once more to take center stage.

Westmoreland's predictions would turn out to be notorious. "We are making steady progress without any question," he assured members of Congress at the White House on November 16. At the National Press Club on the twenty-first he emphasized, "It is significant that the enemy has not won a major battle in more than a year. . . . His guerrilla force is declining at a steady rate." And then: "We have reached an important point where the end begins to come into view." (The American embassy in Saigon would send out invitations to its New Year's Eve party that read, "Come see the light at the end of the tunnel.")[75]

On the previous evening he and his wife had dined with the president and Lady Bird at the White House. The men talked alone afterward. LBJ disclosed that soon McNamara would resign and Clark Clifford would replace him. Near midnight he broached another sensitive subject. He told Westmoreland he was tired, and he alluded to Woodrow Wilson's stroke and invalidism. His health was "not good." His wife and daughters doubted he could survive another term. These "were not the words of a man feeling his way," the general wrote years later. "He had obviously made up his mind."[76]

McGovern would have felt sadness for the revelation, but just then he knew only that Johnson was back to his old tricks, trying to silence dissent. And now his own future was starting to overtake his thoughts and actions. After his Vietnam speech, the *New York Times* and *The Nation* had featured him in significant pieces. On its front page, the *Times* posited that the politics of war threatened the incumbency of six Senate Democrats in 1968, including Church, Clark, Fulbright, Gruening, and Morse. McGovern was among "the most outspoken" of critics while "representing a constituency that is mainly hawkish," and he was "no longer invited to the White House." William S. White and Marquis Childs wrote similar columns. *The Nation*'s editorial, however, had a different take altogether. McGovern had advanced his state's "best interests in ways that can only enhance the pride of his constituents," and they appreciated his excellent service. The editorial gave South Dakotans an important benefit of the doubt: "Whether spontaneously or grudgingly, people admire acts of political courage." LBJ was known for "deviousness," McGovern for "forthrightness." Hawks acknowledged as much. "By challenging a major Administration policy, the Senator may have helped rather than hurt his chances."[77]

And yet, who could say? In April the state's Federation of Young Republicans attacked him "for statements that encourage the enemy to continue the war." In July, after the *Washington Post* reported that Schlesinger and Galbraith had raised $13,000 for McGovern at a cocktail party in New York, South Dakota Republicans nailed him for accepting great sums of "outside money" from "the more radical fringes of Eastern liberalism." In June a Sioux Falls friend had written to say he had seen in the *Chicago Tribune* a photo of George at Northwestern University and an announcement on the cover of the *Village Voice* "that you are speaking to the Hippies in the Village." It was, the friend teased, "a tribute to your versatility and wide ranging acceptance." McGovern had in fact addressed the Foreign Policy Council of New York Democrats, not "hippies." But he replied in good humor, "I will be far more relaxed if you are able to observe any broadening of my appeal in South Dakota!" He was making trips to the state almost every weekend, he explained. "I don't know how long the energy is going to hold out." The pace would become so hectic that, in November, he sent Eleanor a playful note regarding his scarcity at Coquelin Terrace: "I am only sorry that the schedule pressures under which I was operating prevented us from having a longer chat. I will look forward to seeing you again the next time I am in your area. With warm personal regards."[78]

At the end of May, a major South Dakota poll published the results of its public opinion survey taken in the weeks after his hard-hitting "The Lessons of Vietnam." His constituents defended his right to voice his dissent by 73 to 21 percent, even as 50 percent disliked his stand and 47 percent approved. Among farmers, 66 percent supported his Vietnam policy. Then, just before Christmas, a South Dakota poll seemed to bear out *The Nation*'s interpretation in full. McGovern's likely opponents were Nils Boe and Archie Gubbrud, the current governor and his predecessor. And he trounced them both—Boe by 60 percent to 36 and Gubbrud, 66 to 29. The senator ran strong in East and West River and among farmers and ranchers as well as in the towns and cities.

The Associated Press, moreover, named him the state's top individual newsmaker of 1967. Republicans started to worry that McGovern might be unstoppable! Nonetheless, his office manager and secretary, George Cunningham and Pat Donovan, were of a different mind. For a Democrat in South Dakota, the only way that numbers like these could go was down. Not that he needed to be told.[79]

16 BUT THERE ARE STILL PEOPLE WITH HOPE

In the history of the United States, 1968 was a year of multiplying disasters. It was the year that ended in the election of Richard Nixon as president, an event that was preceded in August by the Democratic National Convention, remembered mostly for clashes between the Chicago police and antiwar protestors. In June, Robert Kennedy had been assassinated in Los Angeles, as had Martin Luther King in Memphis two months earlier. Four days before that, Lyndon Johnson tacitly acknowledged the failure of his presidency by announcing his withdrawal from politics. It was not altogether unfitting, then, that such a year should have started with the Tet Offensive in Vietnam.

Devised by Ho Chi Minh's government, the purpose behind this daring onslaught was to take advantage of the stalemate that LBJ refused to recognize and to force him to de-escalate the war and negotiate a settlement. The National Liberation Front, backed by DRV forces, launched the surprise attacks at dawn on the lunar holiday, Tet, on January 31. They did so not in the countryside but, for the first time, in the major urban areas; in many instances, the NLF had infiltrated in advance. On that morning detachments of Vietcong spread throughout Saigon and fired mortars into President Thieu's palace and the Tan Son Nhut airport. Even more shocking, nineteen guerrillas stormed the American embassy and kept it in jeopardy for six hours until they were killed. Units of VC captured the ancient citadel at Hue as well. By nightfall, a total of 84,000 warriors had assaulted thirty-six of South Vietnam's forty-four provincial capitals, including its five largest cities.[1]

American and ARVN troops responded effectively, although in Saigon it required 11,000 to oust 1,000 invaders. In retaking Hue, US-ARVN forces suffered 500 killed while inflicting 5,000 deaths on the enemy. The capital of Ben Tre was destroyed by American artillery and bombers "in order to save it" from the communists. In the course of two months, Tet would cost the lives of nearly 4,000 American and 5,000 South Vietnamese soldiers, and upwards of 58,000 Vietcong and North Vietnamese. About 12,000 civilians were killed and one million made refugees.[2]

From a strictly military perspective, General Westmoreland rightly claimed a major victory. "The enemy's well-laid plans went afoul . . . and he suffered heavy casualties," he told incredulous journalists in Saigon in the immediate aftermath. In a press conference on February 2, LBJ likewise characterized the offensive as "a complete failure." This time, however, many on Capitol Hill were not having it. "If this is a failure," Republican Senator Aiken retorted, "I hope the Viet Cong never have a major success." Hawks among Democrats, too, were hard to convince. Senator Robert Byrd accused the president of having been ill prepared and of underestimating the Vietcong. Richard Russell called for "a complete reappraisal of Vietnam."[3]

Tet changed everything. Public support for the war initially surged then plunged. Television news heretofore had hardly ever been critical of Vietnam. But Americans now saw on their TVs combat in downtown Saigon; the police chief's street execution of a handcuffed guerrilla by pistol shot to the head; and a US Army major try to explain why Ben Tre (a city of 35,000) had to be leveled in order to save it—a scene, McGovern remarked, that captured "the irony of this whole war." Then, on February 27, Walter Cronkite of CBS, the nation's most admired news anchor, dealt the resounding blow. "To say that we are mired in stalemate seems the only realistic, yet unsatisfactory, conclusion," he submitted after three years of having gone along with it; "the only rational way out then will be to negotiate, not as victors, but as an honorable people who lived up to their pledge to defend democracy, and did the best they could." Only the next week's news, that Westmoreland had requested an additional 206,000 troops, did more to cause Americans to wonder where they had gone wrong.[4]

By early March the implications of Tet had settled in. A national poll showed that for the first time, by 49 to 41 percent, more Americans than not believed Vietnam was a "mistake." Barely 26 percent approved of the president's handling of the war. Adding to the doubts, Fulbright called for hearings on the hazards of another buildup of US troops and aired evidence that the White House had fabricated some of the facts about the Gulf of Tonkin incident. McGovern and Robert Kennedy sounded their own alarm about a superfluous escalation and condemned the war in moral terms.[5]

The chief political beneficiary of Tet was Eugene McCarthy. On February 10, the national board of ADA endorsed his candidacy. New Hampshire voters began to pay the maverick some heed, and money started flowing into his campaign. Suddenly, with this more conservative bloc of Democrats, McCarthy's calm style turned into an asset. About LBJ's promises of light at the end of the tunnel in Vietnam, he said, "Only a few months ago we were told 65 percent of the population was secure. Now we know that even the American embassy is not secure." The criticism was undeniably factual; the tone was reasonable and thoughtful. Yet as Gloria Steinem would write, "It was the kids, of course, who transformed McCarthy into a symbol of hope." For in the wake of Tet, thousands of college students, chiefly from eastern schools, poured into New Hampshire. Centrist liberal in their politics, they got shaved, brushed, and "Clean for Gene," and canvassed the state door to door, interacting on an individual basis with three-quarters of the entire electorate. In the course of doing so, they lifted McCarthy's campaign to a new plane. On March 12, the challenger won a stunning 42 percent of the vote to the incumbent's 49 percent. Yet the polls revealed that a majority of those who voted for McCarthy saw themselves as hawkish; the results, then, appeared to be more a repudiation of Johnson than of the war.[6]

As for Robert Kennedy, Tet had thrown him back into his agony as college youth began to rally to McCarthy as the only practical alternative candidate. "God, I'm going to lose them," he said of the students. By late February he was asking again whether he should get in. Advisers and family remained divided. McGovern feared that, if Bobby announced before the New Hampshire primary, it would spark a write-in campaign and split the dissenting vote with McCarthy. "Let him have his big day and hold off a while," he told him. After McCarthy's "victory," Ethel and Jackie encouraged him to run. But Ted Kennedy and Sorensen still thought it was a bad idea. Schlesinger recommended that he endorse McCarthy as a gesture of good will so that "when McCarthy reached his limit, he would be obliged to come out for RFK."[7]

Two days after New Hampshire, Kennedy called McGovern. George was finishing lunch in his office with his former House colleagues, Frank Thompson, Senator Metcalf, and secretary of the interior Stewart Udall. Bobby joined them. "I have never seen anybody who looked so desperately weary," Pat Donovan thought as she brought him coffee. McGovern remembered their two-hour session as "tortured." RFK paced the floor as he reviewed not only Vietnam but also Johnson's ambivalence toward the findings of his own Commission on Civil Disorders. "Gene McCarthy is not competent to be President of the United States," he said, and he would not still be struggling over whether to declare if George "had made the race in New Hampshire." Bobby wanted to tell the press that the four of them had urged him to run; he left "a little disappointed with us," according to McGovern who counseled a week's delay. The rest of the group advised him to back McCarthy. When he jumped in two days later, he beseeched the voters of Wisconsin to support McCarthy in their primary on April 2. This gesture did not stem the resentment of McCarthy or his followers.[8]

In the meantime, LBJ's political fortunes and energy were ebbing. Tet shook the country's confidence in his leadership; McCarthy exposed his vulnerability; and his nemesis Bobby, not Gene, threatened his renomination. And now his Council of Economic Advisers was warning about a "possible spiraling world depression" if he did not address the gathering gold crisis. Things were catching up with him. The president had deceived on many levels about the war, including its costs; all along he had refused to raise taxes in order not to heighten outcries against it or the one on poverty. By 1968 budgetary sleight of hand no longer served. War expenditures had spawned inflation, a balance of payments deficit, and the drain on gold reserves. In the last quarter of 1967 the United States realized a $7 billion trade deficit and, from February to March 1968, European creditors withdrew $1 billion in gold bullion owing to the weakened dollar. On New Hampshire primary day McGovern pointed out that the United States held barely half the gold reserves it had held in 1945. The war's price tag had mushroomed to $30 billion a year; the defense budget crowded $80 billion. "If we want to stop the drain on gold," he said, "let us stop trying to settle other people's civil wars." Arguing that America's security commitments to forty-one countries exceeded its capabilities and interests, he added, "Now we are told General Westmoreland wants another 200,000 American boys sent to Vietnam."[9]

Clark Clifford would not have faulted anything McGovern had said. Since becoming secretary of defense in February, he had undertaken a review of all the calamities the conflict was visiting on the United States. Clifford was deeply troubled by the "hopeless bog" that the war had become, by the absence of a plan for winning it, and by dwindling support among business elites. Further expansion would put an unconscionable strain on the economy and invite unprecedented domestic unrest. The time had arrived, he concluded, to begin a de-escalation leading to negotiations. In all of this, he was able to carry a majority of the Wise Men, the former presidential advisers and architects of containment led by Dean Acheson, whom LBJ periodically consulted. The country, Acheson gloomily informed him on March 26, could "no longer do the job we set out to do in the time we have left and we must begin to take steps to disengage."[10] Johnson accepted the verdict. He had already decided to bring Westmoreland home for good.

Thus in a televised speech on Sunday, March 31, he spoke to the nation "of peace in Vietnam and Southeast Asia." He was willing to "de-escalate the conflict" by halting the bombing of North Vietnam except for the area just north of the DMZ, and he named Averell Harriman his envoy to any peace forum this initiative might set in motion. He then addressed troop levels and the economy. ARVN had recently expanded its strength to 800,000, he said, so the United States needed to mobilize no more than 13,500 of its own troops, not 206,000. And if Congress passed his tax bill, the huge deficits in the budget could be brought into balance. Then he observed, "There is division in the American house." He did not wish to add to it in this year of partisan politics. "Accordingly," he told his astonished audience, "I shall not seek, and I will not accept, the nomination of my party for another term as your President."

Editorialists applauded him for his peace overture and self-sacrifice, but some noted his untenable electoral position. In two days he would lose the Wisconsin primary to McCarthy, and Democrats preferred Kennedy over LBJ by 54 to 41 percent in recent polls. His main critics were generous. "Lyndon Johnson's finest hour," McGovern called it. He had "put the well-being and the unity of his country above other considerations." Fulbright saluted "an act of a very great patriot." Privately Schlesinger admitted to a "non-exuberant, incredulous feeling that RFK would be our next President."[11]

The American people hardly had time to think things through when, on April 4, a white assassin shot and killed Martin Luther King as he stood on his motel balcony in Memphis, where he was to march with sanitation workers on strike. Almost immediately riots broke out in Washington, Chicago, and a hundred other cities. Four days of upheaval would leave forty-six people dead and thousands injured. Moments after King died, Kennedy arrived in Indianapolis on the campaign trail. Despite the pleading of police and his wife, he refused to cancel his appearance in the city's black ghetto; it was he who told the crowd the grim news. He spoke to them about the values that King had dedicated his life to. Some black people will be "filled with bitterness . . . and a desire for revenge," he said. "Or we can make an effort, as [Martin] did, to understand . . . with compassion and love." Kennedy knew the grief in their hearts. "I had a member of my family killed," he continued, "but he was killed by a white man." Finally, he asked them to pray for King's family and for the nation and quoted Aeschylus: "In our sleep, pain which cannot forget falls drop by drop upon the heart until, in our own despair . . . comes wisdom." There would be no riots in Indianapolis. For several days Kennedy and McCarthy suspended their campaigns while Johnson brilliantly spurred the House into joining the Senate to pass the Civil Rights Act of 1968, the beginning of fair housing practices in America.[12]

The two foregoing events would alter the course of American politics as much as Tet had. LBJ's pending retirement and peace proposal temporarily downgraded Vietnam as a campaign issue and opened the way for another seeker of the Democratic presidential nomination, Hubert Humphrey. King's murder and its violent aftershocks raised the broader issue of the health of American society, of its very soul. Much of it was about race relations. For blacks, limited opportunities and the quality of life for the have-nots in the Land of the Free continued to be their main concerns. For blacks and whites alike, but especially whites, law and order and personal safety were the top priorities. These issues had been roiling since the summer of 1967. LBJ received his loudest applause during his State of the Union address in January when he urged Congress to pass the Safe Streets Act and said, "Americans have had enough of rising crime and lawlessness."[13]

These were inevitable issues for the Kennedy-McCarthy contest. Both candidates echoed McGovern's long-standing views on the indivisibility of domestic and foreign policy—that Americans could fix most of their problems at home if they would put some constraints on misguided interventions overseas. Thereon, McCarthy stressed the federal government's role in vocational training, job creation, and housing, which languished because of Vietnam. Kennedy, however, preferred to see private enterprise and local groups play a larger part in regenerating ghetto communities and to keep government as an employer of last resort. Yet their goals and solutions were similar.[14]

They held comparable views on Vietnam as well. Like McGovern, they now advocated a complete bombing halt and the inclusion of the NLF in the peace process. In this, McCarthy had a certain advantage. Unlike Kennedy, he had adopted McGovern's historical perspective, arguing that uncritical acceptance of the containment doctrine was at the root of the disaster. McCarthy made a point of holding not just LBJ, but also Eisenhower and JFK—and therefore Bobby—responsible for the war. He also advocated US recognition of China and its admission into the United Nations. Not until the spring of 1968, however, had he taken these positions and only by a couple of months had he preceded RFK in uttering his first sustained critique of the war, in 1967. Schlesinger worried that McCarthy had, "by a single act of prior entry, captured Bobby's constituency and, with it, a lot of the dynamism of the campaign."[15]

Even so, Kennedy's chances of winning the next several primaries were brighter than his rival's. McCarthy enjoyed an edge among educated, middle-class whites but faltered among blacks, Hispanics, and working-class whites—who perceived him as distant and professorial. To them, the depth of Kennedy's feeling for disadvantaged people was palpable. With an inimitable charisma, RFK was able to captivate black youth in the ghettos on one side of town and the old-time pols in the blue-collar ethnic neighborhoods on the other side. He fared well with farmers also—in Indiana, Nebraska, and South Dakota—joking about being from "the great farm state of New York." Oregon was McCarthy country, its population centers resembling white, middle-class suburbs.[16]

In the South Dakota primary, McGovern resolved to be neutral. As he had said before LBJ withdrew, the Kennedy-McCarthy contest was a "healthy, useful exercise." And in his own campaign, he could not afford to alienate McCarthy Democrats. The editor of the *Daily Plainsman* wondered, though, how long he could keep this pledge, in light of "his association with the Kennedy family." But what made neutrality difficult was McCarthy. McGovern had recommended him to Allard Lowenstein and the week before New Hampshire had entered the *Times* editorial endorsement of his candidacy in the *Congressional Record*. Yet McCarthy pouted. He "had not been asked" to come to South Dakota.

McGovern assured him he would be glad to introduce him whenever he visited. Then, in May, as he boarded a flight home for a day's tour with him, George learned that Gene had canceled the trip without letting him know. Still he hosted him when he came to the state a week later.[17]

Humphrey was a different case. He was eager to have George introduce him at major gatherings at Sioux Falls and Huron. There was an element of poignancy about the situation. "He has the potential to become one of the great presidents," McGovern said of his former next-door neighbor and, regarding Vietnam, none of the contenders was "so close to the problem." Indeed, that regrettable fact had strained their friendship. Except for the war, McGovern considered him "an authentic liberal Democrat" and "on the right side of every issue." The bond between their families was "one of our most cherished blessings," he had written to Hubert and Muriel in 1966. As Eleanor explained, "the four of us had closed all discussion about Vietnam." But George and Hubert still had a terrible quarrel about it in the spring, during a weekend the two couples spent at a resort in West Virginia. According to Eleanor, a "frost" settled upon the relationship. But the vice president's conversion to chief crier for the crusade in Asia ran true to form. As early as his sponsorship of the Communist Control Act of 1954, his Cold War liberalism had allowed assorted bids to outflank the Republican right. Even so, Schlesinger lamented in 1966, "It was a new and different Hubert—hard-faced, except for some unctuous smiles, and uncharacteristically coarse in his language."[18]

Kennedy came for his first swing through the state in mid-April, after his brash young admirer, Bill Dougherty, had filed a slate in the South Dakota primary against the candidate's wishes. Bob assumed he would not do well because it was Humphrey's home state. As for McGovern's neutrality, there was no doubting who had won his heart and mind. In Sioux Falls, he compared his "gallant friend" to Lincoln and Wilson and predicted that, if elected, he would "become one of the three or four greatest Presidents in our national history." Commenting on how JFK had become "a greater man with each passing month," George iterated his conviction that RFK, even more so than his brother, would "bring to the Presidency a deeper measure of experience and a more profound capacity to lead our troubled land into the light of a new day." Said Bobby in reply: "I would like to win this election in South Dakota, but what is more important is to have George McGovern in the Senate."[19]

Besides speeches in Sioux Falls and Rapid City, Kennedy, as chair of an Indian affairs subcommittee, spent the afternoon on the Pine Ridge reservation of the Oglala Sioux. With McGovern assisting, he held a hearing to shed light on the realities of Native American life—a 60 percent school dropout rate, a 65 percent rate of poverty, uniformly substandard housing, and no Job Corps. Afterward they drove out to Wounded Knee, the site of the infamous massacre of 146 Indians by units of the Seventh Cavalry in 1890. Kennedy said he favored making it a national monument. For both him and McGovern, Indians illustrated the problems of poverty and race in America and the connection to Vietnam. If they could expend $30 billion on the war, RFK remonstrated, "It seems we could spend some money to help the Indians in this country."[20]

When he returned in May, he was mobbed in Huron like a teen idol. At Brookings and Aberdeen, and sounding very much like George, he promised to reverse the decline in farm income and the rise in farm-loan interest rates that in 1967 had set in. "The farmer should be rewarded for what he has done for this country," he said, highlighting agriculture's boon to the underfed in America and overseas. In pursuing these themes for the crowds at Mitchell as well as why the war had to be ended, he praised George for his "courageous criticism of the conduct of the Vietnam War when it was not popular to do so," singling out "The Lessons of Vietnam." He observed that his own speeches drew attention because of his last name. Yet "of all the speeches . . . on that subject, the one that . . . had the greatest influence across the country was Senator McGovern's speech." Food for Peace, he continued, had been merely a surplus distribution venture until George "changed the whole program . . . really almost single-handedly" and made it "mean something around the rest of the world."[21]

His listeners realized he was not just being courteous. Many of them had heard about his remark to Richard Reeves in the *New York Times*— that "he would not have become a candidate if George McGovern of South Dakota had been the dove who first challenged Johnson." Now he told the audience at the Corn Palace that, of all his fellow senators, George was the one "who has the most feeling and does things in the most genuine way," that he "is so highly admired by his colleagues not just for his ability but because of the kind of man he is." In paying such tribute, Kennedy drove the issues home, suggesting that he and George were of one mind, and that the state could play an important role in the life of the nation by supporting them both. For their part, South

Dakotans appreciated RFK's attentions. He wooed them in a dozen cities. They knew that the California primary (on June 4, the same day as theirs) was the big payoff—the second largest of all—and yet he was staying with them another precious day and night. George was grateful, too. Of their farewell at the airport in Mitchell he later said: "I remember that morning just being seized with a feeling of sadness. For some reason, he looked so small. Bob, at various times, appeared different sizes to me. It depended, I guess, on the angle of vision. But, as he walked away, he looked like such a frail and small person." They would never see each other again.[22]

McGovern's reelection prospects meanwhile looked better and better. In late February, in the first statewide poll after Tet, South Dakota gave him more than a 40-point edge over both of his potential rivals. Farmers and ranchers preferred him over governor Nils Boe by 79 to 15 percent, prompting Boe's withdrawal and clearing the way for the nomination of former governor Archie Gubbrud, who was not eager to take on McGovern. The poll also indicated that South Dakotans held the war critic in much greater esteem than they did the war president. Like *The Nation* months before, the *Daily Plainsman* suggested that his attacks on Johnson's policies had "enhanced his popularity in the state."[23] A South Dakota poll published on May 1 trimmed his overall margin, but to a still commanding lead of 59 to 35 percent; in any event, Gubbrud could not have been pleased to see that, along with 90 percent of Democrats, 40 percent of the state's Republicans supported McGovern.[24]

Kennedy's and McGovern's campaigns buoyed each other. Before RFK's first visit, South Dakotans showed a natural preference for Humphrey by 48 to 33 percent. But after Bobby's mid-April tour he climbed to 45 percent and the vice president fell to 31 in the state canvass. McCarthy drew 16 percent and "undecided," 8 percent. Kennedy won the Indiana primary on May 7, taking 42 percent of the vote to McCarthy's 27 percent, the rest going to the Humphrey-LBJ slate. A week later he swamped McCarthy in Nebraska, 51 to 31 percent. On May 28, however, Oregonians revived the McCarthy campaign. By 45 to 39 percent, he meted out the first defeat any Kennedy had ever suffered. On June 1, they faced each other in a nationally televised debate in California.[25]

In South Dakota, the last poll before the June 4 primaries kept Kennedy in the lead with 38 percent and Humphrey-Johnson and McCarthy unchanged at 31 and 16 percent; "undecideds" had jumped to 15. In all areas—rural, urban, small town, and among the state's 45,000 Indians— the New York senator's strength was comparable to McGovern's. In the closing days, the three candidates cranked up their operations and spent heavily. Humphrey had most of the editorial pages behind him, including the *Daily Republic*. But RFK's forces were the most vigorous. In the final weekend Ethel Kennedy and pop singer Andy Williams staged events in Sioux Falls and Rapid City, and brother Ted traversed the state for two days, shaking thousands of hands. Everything about the three-way race pointed to a record-breaking turnout.[26]

Indeed, some 64,676 Democrats—over half of those registered in South Dakota—cast votes to establish a new presidential primary record for their party. Surpassing all expectations, Kennedy carried sixty out of sixty-seven counties, capturing a full 50 percent of the vote, with 30 percent going to Humphrey and 20 percent to McCarthy.[27] He ran well with every group on both sides of the Missouri River, with unusually big margins in Indian precincts. The *Daily Republic* called it a "crushing" victory and likened RFK to "a prize fighter delivering a one-punch knock-out."[28]

That evening McGovern was home in Washington collecting reports from all over the state. Although swept up in the tumult of his other impending victory, Bobby was thrilled with the data when George phoned his suite at the Ambassador Hotel in Los Angeles. He was especially pleased with the Pine Ridge reservation—59 votes for himself, 6 for Humphrey, and 9 for McCarthy. Bill Dougherty also checked in and remarked that Bob "seemed happier about South Dakota than about California." Before going downstairs to the hotel ballroom to make his victory statement, Kennedy told reporters that South Dakota's results "confirm absolutely that the people of the nation want a change from the policies of the Humphrey-Johnson administration." In his comments to the throng, he conjoined the two victories. With his notes from McGovern in hand, he reflected on the balloting in California, "the most urban state," and in South Dakota, "the most rural." They were a microcosm of the nation, and his campaign had been "able to win them both," he said. "I think we can end the division in the United States."[29] Then, as he left the ballroom, a deranged Palestinian shot him in the head; he died twenty-six hours later.

During the bleak days that followed, grief mingled with a sense of nightmarish déjà vu. "It is beyond belief," Schlesinger wrote in his journal, "but it has happened—it has happened again." The expressions of sorrow across the nation were extraordinary—in particular, the public response to Ted Kennedy's eulogy at St. Patrick's Cathedral and the thousands of mourners of all walks who turned out along the route of the train bearing the coffin from New York to Washington for its interment near President Kennedy's grave. Among those who knew both slain brothers, many felt the same emotion: They were more stunned by RFK's assassination than JFK's. McGovern was definitely one of these. Eleanor had never seen him cry before, and "he shed a lot of tears over Bobby's death," she recorded. When he spoke of him afterward, he often evinced pride in their friendship. "He made the most extravagant statements about me which were very touching to me because he had a reputation of being a very tough, hard-boiled cookie," he reminisced, "but he was always quite, I thought, sentimental around me." He also thought that Kennedy would have become one of the nation's three or four greatest presidents. Now millions of Americans wondered what was next for their country.[30]

McGovern did too, but his grief and worry were complicated. He was among the close friends whom Ethel had asked to stand a half-hour's watch over her husband's coffin at St. Patrick's on the night before the service. (Such intimates ranged from Bill Dougherty to Averell Harriman.) The next afternoon, as he stared out the window of the funeral train, he could not help wondering whether his comrade might still be alive if he had agreed to be the candidate to challenge LBJ. Just the day before, the *Argus Leader* had quoted Bob's remark in the *New York Times* that he would have stayed out if George had gotten in. Had he really meant it? Then someone tapping him on the shoulder interrupted George's numbing reverie.[31]

It was Bill Dougherty, chair of the South Dakota delegation to the Democratic National Convention as of Tuesday's primary. He had been talking to Jesse Unruh, the speaker of the California Assembly and chair of his delegation. Both men had loved Bobby. But the issue now was what was to become of his delegates and who would lead them. Neither man relished having them go to either Humphrey or McCarthy. "Do you think George would be interested?" Unruh wondered. They decided to ask him. "A replacement for Bobby" would have to be found soon, Dougherty said to McGovern. Unruh stressed the bad blood between Kennedy's and McCarthy's people, and Humphrey remained, in effect, the war candidate. Someone had to hold RFK's delegates together, Dougherty added. "I think it's up to you." McGovern was annoyed. It was not the time, certainly not the place, to talk politics of this sort, he said. And if anybody was the heir to Bobby's mantle, Ted Kennedy was, not himself. Nor did he consider it unreasonable if some of their delegates went over to McCarthy. As the funeral train neared its destination several other Kennedy men onboard came to him with the same proposition.[32]

"By God, he will lose the Senate!" George Cunningham shouted over the phone to Dougherty, hoping he would back off in case McGovern reopened the conversation. "We did not need that diversion," Pat Donovan said flatly in retrospect, though she would waver once Gloria Steinem got involved. And John Holum, despite being one of the bolder, younger members of the staff, shared their alarm. That South Dakota had "a Democrat in the Senate was a tremendous achievement," he said, "and something you didn't want to jeopardize."[33]

More powerful voices counseled otherwise. As Schlesinger observed, "A lot of Kennedy people . . . for various reasons, did not want to go to McCarthy and they thought George was the natural heir." For instance, Frank Mankiewicz, RFK's press secretary, called McGovern shortly after the funeral to urge him to declare. "It seemed to me there was an enormous number of delegates who were looking for a place to go and a candidate like McGovern," he explained, and if Humphrey failed on the first ballot, almost anything could happen. "It was a long shot, but I thought it was a legitimate candidacy." Some of his legislative aides lobbied George, too. They reasoned that he could keep Bobby's bloc of delegates intact, draw other delegates to his side, and make sure the platform included a Vietnam plank that embodied the position of Kennedy, McGovern, *and* McCarthy. Then, on June 26, in the first South Dakota poll since the assassination, McGovern's standing in the Senate race shot up to 67 percent to Gubbrud's 29; he carried farmers 71 to 27. The poll only made his staff more nervous; the numbers were liable to persuade him that he could afford to give a presidential campaign a try when it was sure to dent his lead.[34]

Other developments also kept him on the path. To begin, despite the bombing curtailment above the 17th parallel and the start of the Paris peace talks in May, the war's intensity had not abated one iota. In a Senate colloquy on June 25, William Proxmire of Wisconsin and McGovern pointed out that, between Tet and the California primary, the United States had dropped 441,368 tons of bombs on South Vietnam (the volume that fell on the North through 1967). From March to May, the largest search-and-destroy missions of the war took place around Saigon, engaging 100,000 American and ARVN troops. These facts, said

McGovern, reflected the view that "more military escalation is justified in order to redeem the original mistake." Hanoi would retaliate by stepping up infiltration in the South, and the NLF launched a series of heavy mortar attacks on Hue and Saigon well into summer. At the same time, the number of antiwar demonstrations rose to record levels—two hundred on a hundred different campuses from January to June—confirming a growing radicalization among some activists fed up with the establishment.[35]

In early July, in a conversation with McGovern in the Senate, McCarthy said he believed Humphrey had the nomination sewn up, thus he would only be going through the motions of a campaign now, "to keep up the spirits of my supporters." McGovern was incredulous. Not to continue the quest for delegates into the convention seemed to him terribly premature, given all that both Bobby and Gene and their adherents had been through. It made him doubt whether McCarthy really wanted to be president or if he understood the imperative "to maximize the impact of the antiwar effort at the convention," regardless of Humphrey.[36]

During the same week, Gloria Steinem had an epiphany on a radio talk show in New York. Suddenly, while discussing the ups and downs of the campaign, she said, "Probably, George McGovern is the real Eugene McCarthy." Steinem's disillusionment with McCarthy had caused her to switch to Kennedy once he entered the race. Then, his assassination became the "great cataclysm for us all." Humphrey was unacceptable and had to be stopped on the first ballot. In desperation she decided to give McCarthy another chance; it proved to be a mistake. By this pass, many progressive activists had begun to look seriously at McGovern. Steinem's remark on the radio generated dozens of phone calls and telegrams. Soon she met with the Kennedy Action Corps, a group in New York of a hundred or so who asked her to seek out her friend, George.[37]

Steinem had admired him since the Ken Galbraith seminars in Vermont three years before. She realized now that George had been "the one who had the visceral, principled anti-war position, and he really was a populist and a democrat in behavior." Over dinner in Washington he listened intently as she argued that "he was the only person" who could stand effectively for the antiwar cause at the convention. In New York, two thousand former Kennedy volunteers awaited the go-ahead to open a "Draft McGovern" storefront. There were groups in California, too. Although he remained undecided, he did let slip to Steinem his concern about McCarthy's defeatist revelation. He also expounded on his reelection predicament, his ongoing regret for having declined to run in New Hampshire, and his feelings of guilt over Bobby's death. "Not a day goes by that these thoughts don't rattle around in my head," he said.[38]

Meanwhile, in South Dakota, the Kennedy-McGovern forces prepared to take control of the state Democratic Party. Because he "best exemplifies the ideals and goals of Robert Kennedy," the delegation to the national convention was about to endorse McGovern unanimously as its "favorite son." And Bill Dougherty was organizing a Kennedy memorial dinner to be held in Huron on July 13, the eve of the state convention (even though George and Eleanor would be at a conference of the National Council of Churches in Sweden). Ted Sorensen agreed to be the main speaker, and the guest list included Jess Unruh, Richard Goodwin, and the Kennedy campaign coordinators for Nebraska, Massachusetts, Wisconsin, Iowa, and Maine.[39]

The event made national news. At a predinner press conference, Sorensen and Unruh interpreted the burst of interest in McGovern as an effort "to prevent a lock-up at the national Democratic convention." Unruh said, "the people of California are looking for an alternate candidate and McGovern might be the one." Sorensen said his candidacy "found us a good spot to land." In his address, he spoke respectfully of Humphrey and McCarthy. They were both "of the Midwest progressive mold" and "devoted to the public good," he observed, "but neither one has yet measured up to the standards of Robert Kennedy." In his opinion, "we have no single, strong, clear voice to show us the way." Thus he was not endorsing either candidate; however, he said that South Dakotans "ought to be proud they can place in nomination a man with the qualifications of George McGovern." Ten days later, at Sorensen's request, McGovern agreed to allow his name to serve "as a rallying point" for uncommitted Kennedy delegates at the convention in Chicago. What that meant for a favorite son candidate was not clear. But he took pains to tell South Dakotans that he was running only for reelection to the Senate in 1968.[40]

Things might have rested there if Jesse Unruh had not invited him to Los Angeles to give the keynote at a gathering of hundreds of Kennedy delegates and volunteers on July 27. His ambition and ego aside, what mattered to McGovern was the destruction of Vietnam and the concomitant political and social upheaval in the United States. With conventions almost at hand, Unruh provided him a major stage on which to insist, as he paid tribute to Bobby, that the war simply had to be stopped. McGovern told his youthful audience, "it is for us to carry on . . . the causes in which he led us such a short moment ago." Bombs still fell on villages, and the fighting continued on the ground, "while people starve in Vietnam and in our own rich country," and the White House persisted "in a needless disaster," he reminded them. "I am convinced that any President with the will to do it could end the war in Vietnam on terms acceptable to the American people in 60 days." But to correct a mistake, it was first necessary to admit it. "We cannot do this by accepting a platform which sacrifices the future peace to the vindication of past error." The California delegation had "a special role to play in shaping the platform." It was "imperative that we nominate a standard bearer who can run with a clear mind and conscience," he said. "That is why I have declined to endorse the candidacy of an old and dear friend—the vice president."

McGovern spoke about his and RFK's concerns at home, too—for neglected farmers and urban ghettos, the plight of the Indians, the poor in the rural West, and the starving children of Mississippi. Kennedy had "fired the conscience of America" with the proposition that everyone had to play a "part in solving the great problems." It was that "profound, personal, moral commitment that we are here to reaffirm, a commitment to personal effort, to passion and action in the service of the nation we love and of our fellow man." Perhaps, then, he said in a final peroration, "from the meaning of his life and of his too great sacrifice we can take a new measure of conviction, a new courage, a new resolve that he shall not have died in vain." Instantly his listeners were on their feet, not just cheering, but chanting, "We want McGovern! We want McGovern!"[41] He had not expected such an ovation.

Nor, on this particular day, could he savor it as he might have done. For the night before, after he landed in Los Angeles, a frantic Eleanor had called from Chevy Chase to tell him that Terry and another Dakota Wesleyan student had just been arrested for possession of narcotics at a Rapid City motel. (A third student turned herself in the next day.) Terry and her companions were part of a cohort of volunteers canvassing the Black Hills region on behalf of her dad's reelection. Earlier the motel manager had detected the scent of marijuana and noticed related paraphernalia in the room. She decided to tip off the police and local Republican leaders.[42] McGovern delivered his midday address and then left promptly for Rapid City. Eleanor and the rest of the family soon followed.

The story of the arrest was reported across the country starting on July 28. Terry's real anguish settled on the fear that she may have ruined her father's chances for reelection. Yet George and Eleanor were far more worried about their daughter's emotional state and South Dakota's severe new narcotics law. A first conviction for possession mandated a prison term of not less than two years and up to five. Terry "has first claim on my time . . . [and] political considerations will not be allowed to enter into the case," McGovern said to reporters at her arraignment on Monday, July 29. "These are difficult times for young people and parents, and in some ways political life is especially hard on family life. But Terry's mother and I believe she is not only a precious member of our family, but that she has the capacity to emerge from this painful experience a stronger and better member of society."[43]

Within forty-eight hours, the students' attorneys discovered an irregularity in the arrests. The search warrant had been signed at 7:20 p.m. on that Friday by a magistrate filling in for the municipal judge who was away on vacation, but this temporary appointment had expired at 5:00 p.m. Thus the attorneys moved that the evidence was inadmissible, and the presiding judge eventually dismissed the charges. Although the case would not be fully settled for months, the crisis passed within a week.[44] Happily, the South Dakota press declined to dwell on a young girl's troubles, and the McGoverns received nothing but expressions of sympathy from around the state. Such responses probably owed to the senator's forthright admission of Terry's wrongdoing without condemning her and to the reality that lots of families identified with the situation. (Newspapers estimated one in four of the state's high school youth smoked marijuana occasionally.)[45] The incident would prove to have no untoward political repercussions, and George decided to take the family on a retreat to Sylvan Lake in the Black Hills.

The getaway and quieting of Terry's ordeal allowed him to reexamine his future. He was now very much in the news. On July 31, a story by Carl Leubsdorf was picked up around the country about his California speech, his concern for the party platform, and his potential attractiveness to uncommitted delegates. On August 1, Flora Lewis devoted her *Newsday* column to why Democrats dissatisfied with McCarthy and Humphrey were "now focused on one figure . . . [even at] this 'impossibly' late date." Reviewing the party's want of unity "in a year of broken precedents," she observed, "'unity' must have a name. It could be McGovern." On the same day "New York Citizens for McGovern" declared publicly that his candidacy would proffer "a truly open convention" and give "disenfranchised delegates a unified voice in assuring a strong anti-war and anti-poverty plank in the Democratic platform." A few nights later, as Republicans gathered at Miami Beach to nominate Nixon, McGovern dined in a Black Hills restaurant of his friend, Karl Burgess, and asked him whether he thought he should run. Burgess, a Republican, wrote a check for $5,000 to "McGovern for President" and handed it to him. That clinched it.[46]

The following Saturday morning, August 10, with his family and staff at his side, a self-assured McGovern stood before the press in the Senate Caucus Room. Making no claim to the Kennedy mantle, he stated his belief "in the twin goals for which Robert Kennedy gave his life—an end to the war in Vietnam and a passionate commitment to heal the divisions in our own society." It was "those inseparable aspirations" that he intended to serve. "I have spoken out on the hard issues," he said in outlining his career since 1956. "If I have any special asset for national leadership, it is, I believe, a sense of history—an understanding of the forces that have brought this country to a position of power and influence and an appreciation of what is important in our own time." He continued: "For five years I have warned against our deepening involvement in Vietnam—the most disastrous political and military blunder in our national experience. That war must be ended now—not next year or the year following—but now." It had cost the lives 25,000 GIs and $100 billion; it was the Democrats' "responsibility to take to the American people a platform and leadership determined to reverse this grievous error."

McGovern also advocated replacing the draft with a voluntary program and scaling down the military-industrial complex so that "excess resources may be diverted to long-neglected areas of our national life—the reconstruction of our cities and the strengthening of rural America." "Finally," he said, "we need to harness the full spiritual and political resources of the nation to put an end to the shameful remnants of racism and poverty that still afflict our land. Just as brotherhood is the condition of survival in a nuclear world, so it is the condition of peace in America. . . . It is for these purposes that I declare myself a candidate for the presidential nomination."[47]

In the Sunday papers all over the country McGovern was front-page news. Under the headline, "A Dove Who Flew Bombers," the *New York Times* profiled "a shy and modest professor [who] . . . long ago demonstrated his willingness to accept tough challenges." The *Washington Evening Star* touted his "gentle, understated, professorial approach to the great political issues." And Marquis Childs, in the *Washington Post*, pronounced him "one of the most honorable and high-minded men in the Senate," whose opposition to the war was "early and unwavering." According to Pierre Salinger, no other candidate possessed "the idealism, the understanding, and the compassion of the late Senator Kennedy" as McGovern did. "A war hero, a scholar, a brave and eloquent senator," Arthur Schlesinger appraised him, "he has the breadth of experience, clarity of purpose, and the passion of commitment to make a great president."[48]

The press seemed implicitly to echo Schlesinger for the contrast McGovern presented to the other candidates. As *U.S. News* noted, he was "an unusual politician." Virtually all the coverage emphasized his reputation for integrity and likeability and the fact that he had been years ahead of practically everyone on Vietnam, and that South Dakota conservatives did not necessarily hold it against him—in part because (as Lee Metcalf was quoted) he was "at the forefront of agricultural policy making." Journalists commonly remarked on his B-24 exploits, Food for Peace, and his uncanny success in a Republican state, as well as his friendship with both Humphrey and Bobby Kennedy. Whereas they saw little chance of his nomination, they accorded his candidacy legitimacy and accepted the motive behind it—to guarantee the inclusion of an authentic peace plank in the party platform. With 1,312 needed for nomination, the latest AP poll of delegates (August 12) showed Humphrey with 792, McCarthy with 423, and 1,408 uncommitted or pledged to favorites sons. Should the Humphrey-McCarthy contest prove "at all close," reported the *Times*, it was "likely McGovern will command a bloc of delegates sufficient to put him in a bargaining position at the convention." *Time* magazine asserted that he would "strengthen the anti-Administration forces by engaging . . . inactive Kennedy supporters and bringing added pressure to bear against the Vice President."[49]

During his first week in the arena McGovern appeared on major network TV programs—*Meet the Press* on Sunday, the *Today Show* on Monday, Johnny Carson's *Tonight Show* on Tuesday, and the *Dick Cavett Show* on Thursday. He did interviews with the editorial boards of *Life*, *Time*, and the *New York Times*, accompanied by Gloria Steinem and Salinger. Any Vietnam plank, he told the *Times*, must call for a bombing halt in the North and a coalition government in the South. At the end of his *Time* interview, editor Headley Donovan raised another matter: People said he was "too nice" to be president. "Are you a son of a bitch?" he inquired, as if that was what it took to be a good one. "I don't know whether it takes a son-of-a-bitch to be President," McGovern reckoned, "but it does seem to me that we've given that thesis a generous test in recent years."[50]

At Steinem's behest, he later spoke at a rally of United Farm Workers picketing a Greenwich Village supermarket. He also appealed to African American clergy in Brooklyn's Bedford-Stuyvesant district who unanimously endorsed him because of his "compassion for the plight of the disadvantaged" and "concern for the problems of the cities." That evening in New Jersey he solicited delegates at a memorial dinner for RFK and said he could not accept a platform that endorsed Johnson's Vietnam policy and that search-and-destroy missions must be ended. The next day he commented on Humphrey at the National Press Club: "I don't think he can win the election unless he moves away from the position he's been following." Yet he did not insist that the vice president repudiate LBJ, and he was hopeful that language for a Vietnam plank reflecting "the McCarthy-McGovern position" could be hammered out to satisfy all three candidates. The day after that, Humphrey Democrats "warmly welcomed" McGovern in Detroit. "He was very impressive and candid," said state party chairman Sander Levin, and hundreds "cheered him heartily" after his impassioned talk on the war. Some district chairs predicted he would win a decent share of Michigan's ninety-six delegates on "the promise of being a strong president." An African American audience cheered him as well when he attacked as veiled racism Nixon's pandering about urban unrest. "Law and order without justice," McGovern declared, "is a dangerous and meaningless phrase." In all, the *Times* reported, Michigan Democrats perceived him as "a bridge between factions."[51]

The opening week also rudely wrenched McGovern's family and staff out of their routines. Moments after George's announcement, the press descended on Eleanor and the children, shouting questions about his candidacy and Terry's arrest: "Why is your husband running?" "Why did your daughter turn to drugs?" When they returned home to Coquelin Terrace, local TV stations were setting up cameras for interviews in the front yard. By Monday, Eleanor had her own Secret Service detail and had acquired a press secretary to advise her on interviews and scheduling. Next came reporters from the *Washington Post*, the *New York Times*, and *Women's Wear Daily*. Some asked serious questions, but one reporter wanted to know if George snored and another wanted photos of the family pets. Then there was the task of getting the family ready for Chicago.[52] Meanwhile, several Kennedy hands had moved into George's office and had a bank of phones installed. With veterans of Bobby's organization, Bill Dougherty had begun a delegate-counting operation in Chicago in a suite at the Sheraton Blackstone, where the campaign would soon occupy forty rooms. Their aim was to contact every one of the delegates across the country. Amid his other engagements, McGovern phoned as many as possible himself. He spent the weekend in South Dakota running for the Senate. To crowds in Huron and Sioux Falls he hardly mentioned his national bid, emphasizing instead how an expansion of Food for Peace and Food for Wages could advance farm prosperity and a better foreign policy. On Sunday he was back in Washington to address the Democratic Platform Committee hearings, the only presidential candidate to do so.[53]

Then, on the night before that, LBJ made a defiant speech to the VFW in Detroit, deploring the "foolhardy gestures" of his critics. Thus McGovern decided he had to stake out a position to the committee that went beyond his previous statements. He began by stressing the waste of American resources on Saigon's dictatorial regime and the need to stop the killing overseas in order to start the reconstruction of city and rural life at home. "Face-saving must give way now to life-saving and to ending the pursuit of illusory goals that were not attainable in 1954, 1961, or 1965—and that are not attainable now," he said. Paraphrasing his mentor's great civil rights speech in 1948, he prayed Humphrey was "seeking a way to walk out into the bright light of peace." Then he said that the plank should call for the withdrawal of 250,000 US troops, to begin immediately. Along with a complete halt to the bombing of the North, he demanded a curtailment of it in the South as well—the quickest way "to end this fruitless genocide" and to move to a negotiated peace. "Ending the war and redeeming our own society are not divisible issues." They were one issue, "and they go to the heart of our historic ideals."[54]

Forty or so of the 110 committee members applauded several times during his speech, but the majority backed the administration. Fulbright and Gaylord Nelson followed with more moderate commentaries. Then came Dean Rusk, opposing a bombing halt and attempts to be wiser than the president. All that was required, Rusk said, was a platform statement that the United States sought "an early but honorable peace that will enable the free peoples of Asia to live together in freedom." The *New York Times* juxtaposed photos of the secretary of state and McGovern on the front page, facing each other like debaters. This impasse prompted the counselors of McGovern and McCarthy to start new drafts of the plank that more people could accept before the convention opened. The trick was finding language critical of the war that was not critical of LBJ.[55]

An unforeseen event was about to skew the dynamics of the platform fight in favor of the administration, however. On August 20, during Rusk's testimony, Soviet troops suddenly invaded Czechoslovakia. Within hours, tanks and machines guns had extinguished hopes born of the "Prague Spring" for liberalizing the country's politics and economic policies. As antiwar Democrats parleyed over a unity plank, the committee's majority hardened its opposition. On August 22, governor John Connally of Texas seized the moment to attack McGovern and McCarthy for advocating "appeasement and surrender." Connally, a Johnson protégé, implored the platform committee to write "a plank denouncing not our actions but denouncing Communist aggression in South Vietnam, Czechoslovakia and anywhere else in the world." The majority gave him a standing ovation. McGovern was unfazed. Condemning the Soviet takeover as "a blatant disregard for international order," he asserted that the United States bore "a considerable part of the blame." For it had helped "to establish the claim of large nations to intervene in small nations." How could Americans rebuke the Russians for intervening against a perceived security threat on their border when, on the same grounds, the United States justified intervention in Vietnam 10,000 miles away? Two days later he urged the youth of both Europe and America to hold peaceful protests "to bring the full force of world opinion against this intervention."[56]

Despite this distraction, on Friday, August 23, McGovern's and McCarthy's advisers yielded up a Vietnam plank they both could endorse. That evening, as the first candidate to arrive in Chicago, McGovern announced the breakthrough. The new draft still called for an unconditional bombing halt in the North but omitted his demand for a curtailment in the South. To conciliate Humphrey, the plank no longer insisted on Saigon's having a "coalition government." Rather, it would "encourage" the regime "to negotiate a political reconciliation" with the NLF and other elements in South Vietnam. Finally, in place of McGovern's plan to start bringing troops home, the plank proposed a phased mutual withdrawal of American and North Vietnamese troops, and a tapering off of search-and-destroy missions rather than a cessation. In all, it was a reasonable, nonincendiary compromise.[57]

Developments on Saturday were just as encouraging. Senator Abraham Ribicoff of Connecticut gave McGovern's candidacy a boost when he endorsed him as the "best man" to unite the party and the nation. A former member of JFK's cabinet, Ribicoff believed that McGovern would win the nomination if Humphrey failed on the first ballot and agreed to be his floor manager at the convention, as he had done for Kennedy in 1960. He also accompanied McGovern and Richard Wade, the eminent urban historian, on a courtesy call to Mayor Richard J. Daley. There would be no voice at the convention more powerful than this old-style political boss and loyal Kennedy man. But the mayor was unhappy with the party's straits and uncommitted. He deemed Humphrey "a lousy candidate" and disliked McCarthy for "running against the party." He considered McGovern a reformer in the RFK mold. Moreover, Wade, who chaired Daley's "Model Cities," vouched for the senator. According to Wade, "the chemistry was there," and McGovern made a "compelling, elegant presentation." As they left, the mayor aired his doubts about Hubert and remarked that he had promised to poll his delegation after the candidates made their pitches the next day; now he decided to wait until Wednesday. "You go out and do what you can," he said. It was not an endorsement, but Frank Mankiewicz rejoiced. As he put it, "We just got ourselves a three-day hunting license."[58]

Sunday turned out well for McGovern, if terribly for Humphrey. The senator began the day as the guest on ABC's *Issues and Answers*. The vice president began his with a flight to O'Hare Airport where Daley failed to show up to greet him. Then, after the 118 Illinois delegates caucused and heard all the candidates, the mayor spoke to the press: in order to foster "an open convention," the delegation was postponing its vote for three days. Yet a third slap stung Humphrey when William Clark, a member of the platform committee and Daley's candidate for the US Senate, endorsed McGovern that evening as the only Democrat who could "bring peace both to Vietnam and at home."[59]

In the hours before the convention began on Monday evening, the twenty-sixth, George, accompanied by Eleanor, deployed from caucus to caucus telling delegates that Hubert could not beat Nixon and that Gene believed in a "a passive and inactive Presidency." He sounded tougher than before, the *New York Times* opined, though he was "warmly received" everywhere. "McGovern was the friendliest man in Chicago," Norman Mailer wrote in his account; he impressed one with "a sincerity of presentation, a youthfulness of intent, no matter his age, which was reminiscent of Henry Fonda." Moments after the opening gavel, mayor Jerome Cavanaugh of Detroit endorsed him for his "courage" and "capacity to reconcile and unify us." McGovern was claiming 150 "absolutely hard, personal commitments."[60]

His headquarters at the Blackstone now swarmed with volunteers from across the country as well as with staff and delegates from South Dakota, not to mention Eleanor and the children, most of them on the phones courting delegates. Gloria Steinem reported for duty with a purse stuffed with $7,000 in cash she had raised among friends. A fair share of RFK's brain trust also had assembled—Fred Dutton, William vanden Heuvel, Adam Walinsky, and, of course, Schlesinger, Salinger, and Mankiewicz—to draft speeches and statements and solicit delegates. "I am impressed by George's easy competence—by his capacity to understand and meet all the conventional political demands," Schlesinger wrote from the helm of this campaign built from scratch in two weeks. "He really has done terribly well and would obviously be a better president than Humphrey or McCarthy."[61]

The keynote address of Senator Daniel Inouye of Hawaii should have been the opening night's big story. But three others eclipsed it. First, there was the boomlet for a Ted Kennedy candidacy, which the networks chased doggedly. Floated by former Ohio governor Michael DiSalle and abetted by Jesse Unruh, the notion had been bruited about for a week—a sign of the foreboding of many Democrats. Indeed, the purpose behind Daley's Sunday hedging, it turned out, was to buy time to talk Kennedy into running. To Humphrey, this was a major presentiment. McGovern, too, was discomfited; for a couple of days some of his own people wore both a Kennedy and a McGovern button. Yet as he suspected and verified personally, his thirty-six-year-old Senate seatmate had rebuffed all draft overtures. "I have a gut feeling that this is not the year," Ted told Schlesinger.[62]

A more important issue—about credentials and the seating of delegates—erupted no sooner than the convention came to order. The situation in part revealed the divisions within the party and held implications for its commitment to civil rights and grassroots politics. For starters, over the opposition of the Texans, the convention by voice vote jettisoned the "unit rule" whereby a delegation's majority vote became a winner-take-all unanimity. But Humphrey vacillated on this crucial reform, and the conventioneers were inconsistent. They upheld the credentials of the boss-picked, nearly all-white Texas delegation against a challenge by underrepresented African and Hispanic Americans. Then, in protest of the similar Georgia delegation, the young Julian Bond led an alternate delegation, half white and half black, onto the floor to demand recognition. Amid the commotion, one regular delegate berated Bond for his views on Vietnam, but the hall gave the group a friendly welcome. The next day, the convention made the Georgia regulars share the state's forty-one votes with the Bond delegates, each one getting half a vote.[63]

This outcome was a mark of progress. But it also evidenced the failure of the upholders of the old system to anticipate change at its most elemental level—the demand for authentic participatory democracy. RFK and McCarthy had won all the presidential primaries while the Humphrey-Johnson ticket had won not a single contest. Yet out of a total of 2,622 delegate votes, by Kennedy's count on the night he was shot, Humphrey had amassed 994 to McCarthy's 204 and his own 524. Less than a third of the delegates were chosen through primaries, despite the clamor surrounding them. Humphrey was going to prevail because he enjoyed the support of tightly controlled state organizations. In some states, bosses like Daley appointed the delegates. At least six hundred had been chosen in secret a full two years before. Most state organizations had no established rules for selection or even provisions for public notice of the time and place of their meetings. Nor did these methods respect women, blacks, or young people. Of the delegates at the Chicago convention, women composed 14 percent, African Americans 5 percent, and those under the age of thirty, 2 percent. In the circumstances, insurgents had ample grounds for feeling that Humphrey's impending nomination was born of a process that flaunted the very name of their party.[64]

An equally important matter on this first night was the off-stage struggle for the Vietnam plank. Over the weekend, Humphrey finally had seen the wisdom of meeting his rivals halfway. His men worked out an almost ideal compromise draft. For instance, even though it sidestepped the issue of coalition government in Saigon and deleted the references to "civil war," McGovern and McCarthy said they could live with it and, even with the bombing halt intact, Dean Rusk and Walt Rostow said they could, too. LBJ, however, could not. The sticking point was the bombing halt. The president insisted on conditions that would thwart the prospect indefinitely. "That plank undercuts my whole policy and, by God, the Democratic Party ought not to be doing this to me, and you ought not to be doing it—you've been part of this policy," he bawled over the phone to Hubert on Monday afternoon. Hale Boggs, chair of the Platform Committee, told Humphrey that if the plank was unacceptable to LBJ, it was to him also. Harassed on every front and unsettled by the Kennedy boomlet, the vice president did not have the fortitude to brave the threat of executive repudiation. Thus he permitted Johnson to dictate it. The Vietnam plank would abide a bombing halt only "when [it] would not endanger the lives of our troops in the field"—which critics interpreted as rejecting it "as long as their lives *might* be endangered"—and not until Hanoi showed some reciprocity. Boggs presiding, the committee adopted it 62 to 35. Humphrey, as his biographer has written, had devolved into "the candidate offering no change." McGovern and McCarthy vowed to take the minority version to the convention floor.[65]

McGovern considered the collapse of the compromise a "political tragedy." Yet it set the stage for the convention's one edifying moment—a Tuesday morning debate among the three candidates before the California delegation, arranged by Unruh. Nearly a thousand people crowded into the LaSalle Hotel's ballroom, and all three networks carried the event. The *Times* called it a "civilized and often good-humored exchange." But McCarthy was moody. Despite his own tardiness, he complained that Humphrey was late arriving. In his opening statement he sniped at McGovern for accusing him of passivity the day before. When his turn came, McGovern cited reasons why he admired both of his rivals, noting the coincidence that the three of them were all midwesterners and former college professors in the social sciences. He reflected on Vietnam mainly by emphasizing its human costs at home. Nixon's cries for law and order, he said, could not stand "on a foundation of injustice and neglect and despair." For his opener, Humphrey talked about his civil rights record and the dangers of nuclear war.

Questions from the audience obliged fuller discussion of Vietnam. "Specifically, in what ways . . . do you disagree with . . . Johnson's position," Humphrey was asked. "I did not come here to repudiate the President of the United States," he replied sharply. But he pleaded that three presidents had bequeathed the war to LBJ and that "No one sought to escalate it on our side." Those recent elections in Saigon "stand up pretty well," he also asserted; they produced "a broader-based government." As for peace, the roadblock was in Hanoi, not Washington. Applause was moderate. McCarthy's chance to win over the audience had come, but his response was merely frustrating. "The people know my position," he sniffed, and then sat down. McGovern stepped forward.

He sought the presidency, he said, in order "to end the war . . . and to be about the business of reconstructing our own country." Certainly many could share the blame for it, but "we Democrats bear a special burden before the American people in 1968 in that four years ago we sought their votes . . . on the rallying cry of 'No wider war.'" Heavy applause interrupted him. Regarding the course of other presidents, he paraphrased JFK's statement about the Diem regime in September 1963: "we can assist them, we can send our advisers, but in the last analysis this is their war, they are the ones that must win the issues." That earned McGovern a standing ovation. "The people of this great country of ours poured out the blood of our young men," he continued. "25,000 of them died, another 175,000 are maimed or wounded. We have poured out $100 billion." He demolished Humphrey's construal of South Vietnam's election. It was all well and good, "but let's remember that one of the most honorable candidates was recently [sentenced to] five years at hard labor for the simple crime of advocating . . . a negotiated end of the war." The audience gave him another standing ovation.

Answering questions about delegates' credentials, he shone once more. To begin, he esteemed Julian Bond. And he pointed out—after Humphrey had sided with its regular delegation and McCarthy defended the unit rule—that in Texas "45 percent of the people are in minority groups," yet they made up only 16 percent of the delegation that the convention recognized. "How can one call for a broader base and a more representative government . . . in South Vietnam and then deny it to the delegations here in our country?" he asked, and again a thousand people were on their feet cheering.[66]

In James Reston's opinion, this was "the most honest and illuminating debate of the entire campaign of 1968." From the British journalist who dubbed McGovern "clearly the hero of the hour" to the *Times*, which declared him the runaway winner "for the clarity of his remarks," there was no variance among the accounts of the showdown. "Magically, McGovern had become a Presidential candidate," Gloria Steinem wrote. "It was one of those electric moments when you know a person or an idea is being born." Eleanor called it his "triumph." At an afternoon tea that the actress Shirley MacLaine hosted for the California delegation and the McGoverns, everyone was still exhilarated. In the evening, Pennsylvania senator Joe Clark, stirred by his "fantastic performance," endorsed McGovern as the candidate "with the best chance . . . of saving the country from . . . Richard Nixon." Senators

Gore, Vance Hartke of Indiana, and Joe Tydings of Maryland followed suit. The racially mixed Mississippi delegation accorded him his fourth standing ovation that day for pledging to pursue the goals of Dr. King and John and Robert Kennedy. McGovern thought he might capture three hundred delegate votes.[67]

At this juncture, however, because of his loyalty to Johnson, four sizable southern delegations now moved firmly over to Humphrey. Larry O'Brien, his manager, claimed 1,654 delegates (with no help from California or Illinois). Then McCarthy, who had seven hundred pledged to him, all but conceded the nomination in an ABC News interview on Tuesday—with no thought of its impact on the convention's imminent clash over Vietnam.[68]

Chicago's "day of infamy" ensued on Wednesday afternoon. It started with an acrimonious floor debate over the McGovern-McCarthy minority plank, which a full 40 percent of the delegates to the convention supported. The deliberations were coiled around the unconditional bombing halt. That proposal would "jeopardize the lives of American servicemen in Vietnam," asserted the governor of Minnesota to jeers and boos. Then Pierre Salinger stood up and declared, "If Robert Kennedy were alive today, he would be . . . speaking for the minority plank." That set off a big demonstration and chants of "Stop the War!" by the delegates from California and New York and young people in the gallery. After three hours, on a motion to adopt, the McGovern-McCarthy plank was rejected, 1,042 votes to 1,567.[69] Emotions surged among peace delegates. Hundreds of them began to sing "We Shall Overcome" and sway to the song's rhythm. Watching the television coverage in her suite at the Blackstone and feeling "crushed and bitter," Eleanor wept over the plank's fate. "But there are still people with hope," George said as he held her closely a few moments, "and we cannot let them down."[70]

A little while later she noticed that two of their young volunteers, Paul and Tom, had changed into jeans, tie-dyed shirts, and black armbands. They were heading to Grant Park for some sort of vigil. She did not know then, but Terry and Steve had gone across the way also, though they returned to get dressed for their father's formal nomination at the convention hall. (That morning on the *Today Show*, Barbara Walters had asked her and George, "Where did your son, Steve, spend the night?" It turned out that he had spent it in Grant Park with friends.) When Secret Service men escorted Eleanor and the children to their motorcade in front of the hotel, the crowd in the park was huge, police were everywhere, and tear gas hung in the air. Chicago, Ann thought, had turned into "an armed camp."[71]

It was not illogical, given the fact that the Democrats bore greater responsibility for Vietnam than the Republicans, that antiwar demonstrations would engulf Chicago. These would not be as ecumenical, orderly, or as well attended as the ones mounted by SANE and SDS in Washington in 1965 and by the Spring Mobilization Committee in New York in 1967 (which had drawn 200,000 marchers). By August 1968 the movement was less cohesive than it had ever been, and its base and leadership were narrower. This was due partly to the absence of a sizable number of activists co-opted by alternatives in the liberal establishment—RFK, McCarthy, and McGovern who believed the system could still be changed for the better. As the convention loomed, militant leftists grew more contemptuous of liberals and prone to factionalism as they tried to create what Tom Hayden of the now-splintered SDS described as a "vast, decentralized people's movement."[72]

Some 5,000 to 10,000 protesters answered the call—hippies, yippies, and radicals from around the country, although the majority were college students from the adjoining tristate area. To greet them, Richard Daley deployed his entire police force of 12,000, assisted by 6,000 national guardsmen and 5,000 federal troops. The mayor showed poor judgment in refusing them permits to demonstrate, imposing curfews, and prohibiting sleeping in public parks overnight. Downtown hotels were very heavily guarded and four miles to the south the convention met in the International Amphitheater, encircled by barbed wire and a chain-link fence seven feet high. Security inside was so tight that playwright/delegate Arthur Miller compared it "to a session of the All-Union Soviet."[73]

The first incidents occurred on Sunday and Monday nights when police used tear gas and nightsticks to clear out protesters camping in Lincoln Park, bordering Lake Michigan. On Tuesday, August 27, large numbers returned to hold an "unbirthday party" to mock President Johnson—until 150 police broke it up and attacked journalists covering the event as well. On Wednesday, the imminence of Humphrey's first-ballot victory and the results of the struggle over the Vietnam plank were a fitting prelude to the evening's explosive climax downtown. This time TV cameras and spectators were more evident. In Grant Park, across the street from the Hilton Hotel, upwards of 5,000 demonstrators had gathered by 7:00 p.m. ostensibly to march to the Amphitheater just as the nominating speeches commenced. Earlier in the day there had been a skirmish with the police when someone hauled down the American flag. Everyone was on edge. To try to prevent the assemblage from leaving the park, the police formed phalanxes and fired fusillades of tear gas. "The whole world is watching!" the crowd chanted. Around 8:00 p.m. they moved onto Michigan Avenue in clusters, some intending to march on the convention. On signal, hundreds of truncheon-wielding policemen charged and began battering not only the protesters but onlookers too—women and the elderly along with men. Officers of the law in one mindless frenzy set upon dozens of sidewalk bystanders, including children, and pushed them up against the Hilton restaurant's plate glass window until it failed and the victims fell backward into the shattered glass screaming.[74]

What Winston Churchill's journalist-grandson reported from the street as "horrifying scenes of police violence," the wives and families of the delegates beheld from hotel windows as the tear gas wafted into their rooms. The fourth floor suite of the Blackstone afforded a better view of the battleground than McGovern's entourage might have desired. His family doctor, who accompanied him, was disturbed by how two or three police would pin down a single protester and beat him in a deliberate way. "Dr. Thompson would say, 'Look, they're hitting him in the kidneys!'" Pat Donovan recalled. "We were just in horror up there." McGovern had never witnessed police brutality. Gloria Steinem later wrote that his staff was shocked to hear him shouting obscenities out the window "at teams of policeman ganging up on individuals." George Cunningham (no defender of protesters) would never forget how one of their volunteers was taking some files "across the street to the Hilton . . . [and] got hit right in the mouth with a billy club." Her front teeth were knocked out "and she was just a bloody mess." McGovern had "seen nothing like it since the films of Nazi Germany," he told Tom Wicker of the *Times*—a "blood bath" that "made me sick to my stomach."[75]

Meanwhile, at the Amphitheater, speeches were under way. Delegates were unaware of the street fighting because technical problems had delayed the network broadcasts. By 8:30, however, McGovern's and McCarthy's staffers had gotten the news through to their delegates by phone. Susan and Jim Rowen, who had friends in the fray, were nearly in tears when reports reached the family in their box overlooking the packed hall. Then, around 9:30, the networks were ready to go. Cleveland mayor Carl Stokes was seconding Humphrey's nomination when they switched over to the videotapes. For the next seventeen minutes eighty-nine million Americans watched the shocking scenes. When the television coverage returned to the Amphitheater, Abe Ribicoff stood at the podium to nominate McGovern. In the wings he had asked Frank Mankiewicz what he thought he should do. "Why don't you throw away the speech and talk about what's going on here on the floor and in the city?" Mankiewicz replied.[76]

Taking note of "the confusion in this hall and the turmoil and violence that is competing with this great convention for the attention of the American people," Ribicoff told the delegates, "I'm here to nominate George McGovern just for that reason." George was "a man who has peace in his soul," he said, "a man without guile" who could "bring a sense of wholeness to a divided nation that so desperately needs its parts put together." He reviewed McGovern's leadership of Food for Peace and his unique record of warning against sending thousands of soldiers to Vietnam since 1963. George's "concept for underdeveloped countries," he said, "is shelter, education, health, opportunity, and to bring a sense of brotherhood to submerged millions of people wherever they may be." And he was "not satisfied that 10 million Americans go to bed hungry every night . . . [or] that four and a half million American families live in rat-infested houses" either. "The youth of America rally to the standards of men like George McGovern like they did to the standards of John Kennedy and Robert Kennedy," the senator observed, reflecting on the riots downtown. And then: "And with George McGovern as President of the United States we wouldn't have those Gestapo tactics in the streets of Chicago." For a moment the hall fell silent, then erupted in a roar of approval from most of the delegates. That ratcheted the enraged Mayer Daley and the entire Illinois delegation out of their seats, shaking their fists and shouting unquotable expletives at Ribicoff. "How hard it is to accept the truth," he said, facing them down and igniting, in the *Christian Science Monitor*'s words, "a wild, reverberating torrent of sound . . . explosive in its force." It was the convention's most dramatic moment.[77]

By midnight all the speeches were over and the roll was called. Humphrey received 1,761 votes; McCarthy, 601; McGovern, 146; and Channing Phillips, 67. McGovern was disappointed with his numbers, especially from California.[78] But he did not complain or make excuses; he sought to be a healing influence. The next morning he gave McCarthy credit for entering the race and opening the way for a major debate on the war. He also prevailed on his followers to get behind Humphrey despite his position on the peace plank—on "faith that, now that he is his own man, he is going to move in a different direction on Vietnam." In contrast, McCarthy told his supporters they should "forget the Vice President." He spurned Humphrey's invitation to him and McGovern and their wives to sit in his guest box for his acceptance speech. George and Eleanor accepted and afterward stood beside Hubert and Muriel at the rostrum. For some fleeting moments the two former rivals joined hands and smiled broadly, and the hall quaked with thunderous approval. As they left the stage, Humphrey's youngest son, Doug (Terry's pal from the early times), stopped the McGoverns and, as his eyes welled with tears, said, "Thanks for standing with my dad tonight."[79]

Such forgiveness initially dismayed some of McGovern's supporters. Although she understood the show of unity, Gloria Steinem wrote that he "finished on an equivocal note" in standing "arm-in-arm with Humphrey." Yet he was serious about rationing his support according to Humphrey's flexibility and good faith. ("I cannot accept this plank as my view on how to end this war," he said, but maintained that it provided enough leeway for a candidate like himself to run on.) Moreover, Humphrey had vowed in his acceptance speech to do "everything in my power" to end the war, noting, "the policies of today need not be limited by the policies of yesterday." If one worried about Nixon becoming president, McGovern's was both the practical and the principled thing to do. He had observed to the press on Thursday morning, "we have made some progress in 1968." The convention had had "a full dress debate" on Vietnam, and he expected it "would continue . . . all across the country." A year earlier he could not have guessed that over 40 percent of the delegates would adopt his position on the war against LBJ's policy and that they would constitute as powerful a wing of the Democratic Party as they now did. Out of 2,609 delegate votes, the journalist David Broder later remarked, the insurgents had come within 263 of having their way.[80] That perspective on American foreign policy had been regarded as comparatively radical until recently.

McGovern also was certain the party's structural dysfunctions called for hardheaded measures. At his press conference he referred to the convention manager's "repressive procedures" almost in the same breath with the "naked example of brutality" of Chicago's police. He was happy to congratulate Hubert, but he was convinced "that our political system must be restructured and revitalized if it is to command the respect and meet the needs of our society." Their convention, he added, "may well mark the end of the old back-room politics and the first birth pangs of the new politics centered on people and principle." That, Broder in retrospect pointed out as well, "was to become the convention's most important by-product—the mandate for reform of the procedures for selecting future delegates."[81] Based on his new stature coming out of Chicago, McGovern soon would be chosen to chair such a historic reform commission.

It was no exaggeration to propose, as the *New York Times* did, that "Senator McGovern made more impact on the . . . convention than his delegate votes indicated" and "undoubtedly contributed to the growing sentiment within the party against the war and for democratization of the party machinery." An "articulate and humble spokesman for the dissidents," he was even "applauded . . . by delegations that did not share his views." Another national publication designated him an "overnight star . . . who, in less than three weeks, has become a major force in American politics." *Time* magazine predicted that "his restrained performance as a presidential candidate will enhance his reputation . . . [and] gain him consideration for a spot on some future national ticket." With enthusiasm, *Life*'s editorial tribute to the "high-minded intellectual" concurred but offered a sobering caveat: his "last-minute campaign enhanced his prestige in 49 states and damaged it in one—his own."[82]

There was some difference of opinion about whether or not that was really so. But on Friday night, as his family returned to Washington, the new star of the Democratic Party was flying home to resume his campaign for the Senate. He would be there in the morning, at the South Dakota state fair.

17 THE KIND OF MAN THE FUTURE MUST HAVE

Ten thousand fairgoers filled the grandstand in Huron to hear McGovern speak on his first day back from Chicago. They welcomed him with the loudest applause he could ever remember getting in the state. He stayed at the fair for three days, shaking thousands of hands and listening to what people had to say. They encouraged his hope, as he put it, that they were "realistic enough to know I will be a better senator" because of his pursuit of the presidential nomination, which he believed had made him "a stronger and more effective voice to serve the interests of South Dakota and the nation."[1] But his lead had dwindled. On July 17, in the last statewide poll before he announced for the nomination, he held a two-to-one lead over Archie Gubbrud, 65 percent to 31. Then, just before the convention, on August 21, he had dropped to 56 and his opponent climbed to 40 percent. By mid-September the gap between them would nearly close. "You were the most sane voice at the convention," folks at the state fair had told him. Yet events in Chicago, if not his presidential bid, had worked against him.[2]

Since the campaign had gotten under way in the spring, McGovern had conceded little to political expediency. In mid-March, to the Mitchell Chamber of Commerce, he had remarked of Vietnam, "It's staggering to consider the fantastic amount of money being funneled into that tiny country," the "real reason" behind the allies' loss of confidence in America's capacity to resolve the war.[3] At Brown University in May, he said there was not much incentive for North Vietnam to welcome negotiations when the United States was "supporting a military dictatorship." He also told the students that the Vietcong knew that US troops could not "root them out" among the southern populace without killing innocent civilians. "Frankly, there are times when I think the only way we are ever going to end the war is simply to get out," he admitted while expressing hope for negotiations. Still, in his May newsletter to constituents, he wondered whether the United States would ever "end the war and begin dealing with the squeeze on our farmers and small businessmen, disorder in our cities, and the need for better educational and job opportunities."[4]

As for agriculture, the Republicans had a hard time belittling his record. "If farmers could bale the thousands of press releases McGovern has put out and sell them at a decent price, farm income might go up," the state chairman jabbed. But the National Farmers Union honored him for "Outstanding Service to Agriculture" in 1967—for his authorship of the voluntary wheat certificate program, for a bill in 1964 to limit the importation of beef, and for his part in the passage of the Food and Agricultural Act of 1965. The NFU's president believed there was not a "more effective champion of family farm agriculture in America" than McGovern. Few among peers would have denied it, given his role in improving price supports and controls on output through local balloting. And per capita farm income had doubled since 1961, though by the end of 1967 it had declined 11 percent as the war ate into supports.[5]

From winter to summer 1968, to address that problem, McGovern introduced bills to enable farmers to bargain collectively for better prices, to restrain corporate farming undertaken simply to avoid income tax, and to enlarge emergency food stocks and programs like Food for Peace—all initiatives that aimed "to preserve and expand family farm opportunities." In April in the Senate he presented a treatise on the 25 percent decline in the number of farms in the previous decade while corporate agriculture expanded. Family farms and the towns supporting them were being squeezed out as a consequence. As these communities failed, the displaced populations, "untrained in urban employment," often moved into the ghettos of such cities as Detroit and South Chicago. Thus the farm problem was a national problem—in the relationship between rural and urban poverty. That month he also authored a proposal to investigate the scope of hunger and malnutrition in America—because the school lunch program was "reaching only one-third of the 6 million children who need free or low-cost lunches" and "only 18 percent of the 30 million poorest Americans are receiving

Federal food aid." The problem was rife in the South, but schools in Philadelphia and St. Louis provided a free lunch to only 8 and 4 percent of their poor children, and many urban schools had no cafeterias at all. Related problems such as the effects of dietary deficiencies on two million children were disturbing but soluble. It was possible, he explained, "to help close both the farm income and the nutrition gap in the Nation." Within the week he had thirty-eight cosponsors.[6]

Thus Democrats made short work of attacks on McGovern for "selling out the farmers." Jim Magness quoted praise from the National Cattlemen's Association and touted Food for Peace, in both a market and a humanitarian context for putting "hundreds of millions of dollars in the pockets of American farmers while strengthening the cause of peace abroad." And all the South Dakota polls showed that farmers and ranchers regarded George as "their true friend." In the August 21 poll they supplied his best numbers, over two-thirds of them holding steady in their support. One week after the convention, the thirteen members of the Senate's new bipartisan Select Committee on Nutrition and Human Needs honored him by unanimously picking him as their chair.[7]

So Republicans had to find another angle. Partly taking a cue from Richard Nixon, their theme became "law and order" and "South Dakota thinking." Candidate Gubbrud offered a preview before Chicago. On July 24, he cited a recent riot in a Cleveland ghetto as an example of "the lawlessness and disorder that has arisen from the spirit fostered by such people as Johnson, Humphrey, and McGovern." Subsequently he exploited the remarks that McGovern had made about the Chicago police "going berserk." Whereas the senator voiced his sympathy for the frustrations they faced, he stressed the need for upgrading "police standards all across this land" and a "searching investigation" of the violence in Chicago. He also had defended the right of students to "peacefully protest policies they deplore and . . . over which they have had no voice." In November a commission, chaired by Dr. Milton Eisenhower, would declare the incident "a police riot," confirming "indiscriminate police violence . . . often inflicted upon persons who had broken no law, disobeyed no order, made no threat." Yet a majority of Americans (and South Dakota editorial pages) believed the demonstrators, not the police, were at fault, and that television coverage had distorted what had happened.[8] On September 3, the *Mitchell Daily Republic* ran a front-page story in which Republican officials predicted "tough sledding" for McGovern. Karl Mundt cautioned that in pursuing the presidential nomination, he had had to solicit delegates "from the ghettos, city bosses, labor, and hippies." Gubbrud's campaign manager was downright pleased about some of McGovern's comments in Chicago "that he has to live with for two months in South Dakota." The campaign began to run ads featuring a silhouette of the Democrat retouched to make him resemble the devil, with the headline, "Does This Man Represent South Dakota Thinking?" Bullet points included: "Encourages Demonstrators and Hippies," "Proponent of the Permissive Society," and "Supports Court Decisions that Hamstring Police." Some ads attacked him for accepting several contributions from labor unions as well as financial help from other out-of-state sources. (They overlooked the $4,223 raised by a "Historians' Committee for McGovern.") Most of the ads ended with, "He is the acknowledged spokesman of the ultra-liberal fringe."[9]

For a while these appeals had the desired effect. In early September, in the first survey since Chicago, McGovern skidded to 48 percent and Gubbrud leaped to 46. (For president, South Dakotans preferred Nixon to Humphrey by 58 to 17 percent; 9 percent supported George Wallace of Alabama.) But then, two days before that poll was published, a new ad warned, "Would Ship Unemployed Negroes to South Dakota," in an absurd distortion of statements McGovern had made on ways to fight poverty. America's first domestic priority, he had said in Chicago, should be to help poor African Americans find better jobs and better housing in less urban areas beyond the inner-city, which could help to bring about "the dispersal of the ghetto."[10]

The attack backfired. Repelled by the "dehumanization element," one letter to the *Argus Leader* said the GOP was trying to stir up "deeply seated racist fears." Another compared it to the kind of "mistrust" that George Wallace "has built his whole campaign on." Yet another accused Gubbrud of "reckless abandon" and of insulting "every thinking voter in this state." McGovern himself found the ad "disgusting to read" and deplored other "cheap falsehoods" in which his opponent indulged. "Let us have an end to silly charges of this kind and get on with a discussion of the real problems . . . that face us in 1968, including . . . war and peace, the plight of the farmer, and the disorder in our cities."[11] By October 2 his position in the polls had recovered to 51 percent; Gubbrud had fallen to 42. On the sixteenth the numbers stood at 53 to 41, and over 30 percent of Republicans said they planned to vote for McGovern.[12]

All of this revealed a serious problem for Gubbrud. He was waging a strictly negative campaign. Even his ad for a television documentary about his life took a swipe at Charles Guggenheim's "Hollywood" effort "to slick-sell George McGovern." At the same time he had no ideas about what he actually might do as senator, except to establish a "hot line" between the state capitol and the White House and assure voters "there will be no question of my support for J. Edgar Hoover."[13] The former two-term governor was a decent man. A life-long farmer, he had served ten years in the state legislature before unseating incumbent Democratic governor Ralph Herseth in 1960 by a margin of 1 percent out of 304,000 votes. Local journalists regarded his victory as "accidental," owing mostly to Nixon's winning the state by 16 points over JFK. Gubbrud governed creditably, and he and his successor, Nils Boe, managed to double state aid to education. But he was such a weak candidate that McGovern was reluctant to join him on a stage. As Gloria Steinem explained, he was "so unimpressive a speaker and so poorly prepared on the issues that to debate him would only create sympathy." In John Holum's opinion, Gubbrud was a sacrificial candidate; until Chicago, "nobody seriously thought that McGovern was vulnerable." Yet two-thirds of the state's newspapers endorsed him, albeit stretching to make their case. The *Argus Leader* invoked generalities about his honesty and character; it also ran its endorsement on the front page and moved it up to coincide with the arrival of 8,000 teachers for a convention in Sioux Falls. The state's GOP would pour most of its resources into Gubbrud's campaign.[14]

In contrast, in every aspect of his campaign, McGovern accentuated the positive. His advertising, often topped with the banner, "Courageous Prairie Statesman," quoted reviews of his performance in Chicago—the "display of courage" and the "voice of logic and reason" he brought to bear at the convention and how it advanced South Dakota's interests now that "he is regarded as a national statesman." Large ads highlighted Food for Peace and the tens of millions of dollars that his acreage diversion and voluntary wheat certificate programs had brought the state's farmers, along with other programs. As for substantive editorial endorsements, it surprised no one when the *Daily Republic* called him "the most effective voice this state ever has had in the U.S. Senate." But the Republican *Daily Plainsman* of Huron and *Public Opinion* of Watertown struck the same chord. The former played up his role in securing the Oahe irrigation project on the Missouri River, his "exemplary" conduct in Chicago, and his "thoughtful, considered" opposition to the war. The *Public Opinion* praised his achievements in agriculture and his courage in standing up to the White House; and his presidential bid had reaped "new respect for South Dakota." It ended with, "He is the kind of man the future must have."[15]

A group called "Republicans for McGovern" pitched in, too. "When You are Selling South Dakota You Need Influence," said one of its ads, emphasizing his seniority. The headline of a more startling one read, "His Leadership on Vietnam Is One Reason Why We South Dakota Republicans Will Vote for George McGovern." Its text observed, "He has been among the most respected voices on this complex issue, and the country is coming to realize that he was right." In October they published half-page ads to explain the two-step voting machine process for casting a straight Republican ballot with the exception of the Senate race. Bipartisan groups such as "Veterans for McGovern" and "Ministers for McGovern" played comparable roles without untoward references to Gubbrud. One of these broadsides featured Republican Clifford Hope of Kansas, former chair of the House Ag Committee, declaring McGovern "the most articulate spokesman for agriculture who has ever sat in the Senate."[16] McGovern often argued that it was "important for rural states to have representation that can draw national attention to the programs and projects we require for economic progress." He entreated voters to reject his opponents' attempts to discredit him on the basis of his concern for the problems of the cities. America's problems were interconnected, he said. "I believe I can influence senators in other parts of the nation to support agricultural and resource development for South Dakota because I have not turned my back on the rest of the nation."[17]

Nonetheless he left nothing to chance. As he told a reporter in late October, he had "never fought a harder battle." And it certainly showed in the number of billboards he rented and the amount of newspaper and television advertising he marshaled. Then, too, throughout the campaign busloads of college students arrived to canvass door to door, just as they had done for McCarthy in New Hampshire; thus, for the first time, McGovern benefited from a bona-fide national political following. Respected senators such as Stuart Symington and Walter Mondale also came to give major endorsements. (Mondale called him "a triple threat who writes, speaks, and passes bills.") With his son Christopher, Frank Mankiewicz crisscrossed South Dakota by car. And Gloria Steinem visited twice for several days to tour with the McGoverns. She was especially struck by the role Eleanor played, traveling and speaking on her own as often as with George. Steinem was also impressed by how well she fielded questions ("as most political wives do not") and how reporters expected her to comment on issues as readily as her husband did. The McGovern children were involved more than ever. Susan and

Jim Rowen campaigned full time and, like all the student volunteers, got "Clean for Gene" for George. "We were antiwar radicals moving to South Dakota," as Jim recalled. "So I wore a coat and tie and Susan wore a dress." Together they drove thousands of miles in their red car decorated with psychedelic flower stick-ons, doing voter registration work mainly with senior citizens, who seemed not to be put off by the senator's antiwar position.[18]

This was also the campaign in which the years of excellent constituent work and forthright relations with local journalists paid off. By now McGovern had built a cordial relationship with every major newspaper editor in the state, and he knew thousands upon thousands of South Dakotans on a first-name basis. More than one reporter commented on how people came up to him on the street to shake hands and say, "I feel I know you well enough to call you George." Over the long haul he had gone "to every single town in South Dakota" and spoken with probably every person old enough to vote, his daughter Ann later remarked; they might "not necessarily agree with everything," but they were won over by his "gift for making complex issues understandable" and by his decency. By 1968, she added, there also was a significant core of South Dakota Democrats "deeply committed to working very hard to get Dad elected."[19]

If, at midway point, he was on his way to victory, his old friend and fellow South Dakotan was not. In the state poll of September 18 (the one that showed McGovern and Gubbrud almost tied) Hubert trailed Richard Nixon by more than 40 points, or 17 percent to 58; "undecided" placed second at 19 and George Wallace last, at 9 percent. With the party divided 60–40 over the war and still reeling after Chicago, every indicator suggested a landslide defeat for Humphrey. McCarthy's refusal to endorse him and Johnson's indifference did not help.

More than anything else Nixon and Wallace talked about law and order. Having been a big factor in the backlash against Democrats in the 1966 midterms, the issue now eclipsed the war as the major concern of most Americans. The militant segregationist Wallace, whose third-party candidacy worried Republicans as well as Democrats, ran away with it. To the cheers of impassioned white working-class audiences, he vented his spleen over crime in the streets, ghetto riots, antiwar protesters, and civil rights activists. "Let the police run this country for a year or two and there wouldn't be any riots," he liked to say as he blamed big government, the liberal Supreme Court, and "pointy-headed professors" for the nation's woes. To counteract Wallace in the South (no longer solidly Democratic), Nixon spoke of "the forgotten Americans . . . the non-shooters, the non-demonstrators" in his acceptance speech. "The first civil right of every American is to be free from domestic violence," he averred. These applause lines formed the basis of his "southern strategy" to woo Wallace supporters and disaffected Democrats elsewhere in the country. Nixon's less strident version of demagoguery aimed in particular to assure any would-be Republican voters in the border states and the South that he would refrain from pressing school desegregation and open housing laws.

Their positions on Vietnam were fairly similar, too. The two hawks had come to see the war as a costly mistake and publicly favored a negotiated settlement and "peace with honor." But in early October, Wallace's running mate, the retired air force general Curtis LeMay, severely compromised the ticket's credibility when he advocated bombing North Vietnam "back into the Stone Age" with nuclear weapons. Nixon, unlike Wallace, was a serious student of foreign policy. Despite his claim to have some sort of plan to end the war, however, he refused to offer specifics. While avoiding criticism of LBJ, the frontrunner favored "neither peace at any price nor camouflaged surrender." Incredibly, he won his party's nomination then campaigned nationally without ever having to discuss his views on the war in any greater detail.[20]

In the circumstances, Humphrey's only chance to reverse the tide lay in breaking with the administration on Vietnam (as McGovern kept urging him to do). Still, he floundered in indecision and fear of LBJ. In September, antiwar protesters heckled the vice president in Philadelphia when he claimed the mantle of social justice, and the president publicly repudiated his statement after he hinted that units of GIs might begin to come home from the war in early 1969. Two weeks later, in Boston, Humphrey and Ted Kennedy gamely persevered over hundreds of antiwar protesters determined to disrupt a midday rally. The candidate then flew to Sioux Falls. With McGovern beside him, he showed more backbone in a speech to an audience of farmers and townspeople. Upon accusing Nixon of "evasion" on civil rights and agricultural policy, he pledged that he would make it "the top item on my agenda to find a way to end this war. I'm going to seek peace in every way possible, but only the President can do that now. Come January . . . I will make peace." Thereupon the South Dakotans gave him a rousing standing ovation. In Springfield, Illinois, and Louisville that week he met with the same reward when he borrowed a McGovern phrase, that the war must be ended "so we can get on with business here at home." Max Frankel of the *New York Times* attributed this "new spirit" to "the remarkable day" Humphrey had spent with Kennedy and McGovern.[21]

On September 30, in Salt Lake City, the new spirit moved him finally to make a formal speech about Vietnam, which was televised nationally. "As President I would be willing to stop the bombing of the North as an acceptable risk for peace," he vowed, "because I believe it could lead to success in the negotiations and thereby shorten the war." McCarthy and McGovern supporters responded positively. At the White House LBJ grumbled but said nothing to undermine Humphrey. On the campaign trail, protests tapered off and students began to carry signs that said, "We're For You, Hubert." The North Vietnamese soon appeared to be more open to compromise in the deadlocked Paris peace talks. By mid-October Humphrey started moving up in the polls. The AFL-CIO launched a campaign to expose Wallace's hostility to unions and the minimum wage and helped to pull a sizable bloc of northern blue-collar workers (whose sons served in Vietnam) back into the Democratic fold. Nixon was no longer as complacent as he had been.[22]

The final weeks of the campaign did not go well for Gubbrud either. Sticking close to Nixon, he enjoined South Dakotans to vote a straight ticket in a series of ads quoting Nixon's endorsement at Sioux Falls: "I need this man. He will stand with me, not against me." He also promised that Nixon offered "the best hope of a real peace" and would "lead this nation back to law and order." About Vietnam, he usually uttered words of support for "our fighting men" and criticized the administration for its ineptitude in handling the war. Gubbrud's broadsides called for "a *fast, honorable, & lasting peace* . . . not a gradual surrender to the Communist will" and said McGovern's peace proposals "endanger[ed] the lives of American young men." His campaign also publicly accused McGovern of supplying the Vietcong with anti-American propaganda. Karl Mundt, "the whip master," lent a hand to admonish Republicans against "cross-voting" and praised Nixon for "setting forth ideas on good government which he will implement."[23]

Then, a week before the election, Gubbrud blundered. He began to parrot the remarks of a retired air force general, Neil Van Sickle, who told Republicans in Rapid City they could lose Ellsworth Air Force Base if McGovern was reelected. The Pentagon might punish the state for his opponent's views on Vietnam, Gubbrud warned. Senator Symington, former secretary of the air force, came to McGovern's aid. He vouchsafed that his friend always had worked to "assure this country's defense was second to none" and wanted to expand the facilities at Ellsworth. The *Minneapolis Tribune* called Van Sickle and Gubbrud's assault "a threat to democratic processes." South Dakotans, its editorial observed, had "an added reason to return McGovern to the Senate."[24]

Although "shocked" by Gubbrud's latest tactic, McGovern never broke his stride, especially on the war. "The full energy of this government ought to be used to end the Vietnam war at the earliest possible date," he said in Madison, Karl Mundt's hometown. "We owe this to our men fighting there." On October 12, during their big convention in Sioux Falls, teachers gave him sustained applause when he argued that it was "not in the national interest to use our blood and treasure trying to rescue a regime that is so corrupt it doesn't command the confidence of its own people." Ten days later he was calling for the start of a "systematic reduction" of US troops in Vietnam.[25]

Meanwhile, since Humphrey's speech, LBJ had endorsed the Democratic ticket and inched closer toward a bombing halt to catalyze a major peace initiative; on October 16, he called all three candidates to tell them about it. The Saigon regime was panicked now because its existence could be threatened if such a breakthrough involved a coalition government. Nixon was no less unnerved because peace might mean his defeat in the election; in an appalling act of treachery he conspired through back channels to advise Thieu and Ky to obstruct the process (though they hardly needed convincing). On October 31, a complete bombing halt of North Vietnam went into effect after General Creighton Abrams, Westmoreland's successor, reassured Johnson, "It is the proper thing to do." The president's action all but rendered the Humphrey-Nixon race too close to call. McGovern continued to speak about "the death of 30,000 young Americans and the expenditure of $100,000 billion" and condemned Saigon for flinching at "talks designed to stop the killing of our men." Amid all the commentary on the bombing halt and the election, South Dakota Democratic chair Peder Ecker said of Johnson's momentous decision, "This must be Senator George McGovern's finest hour."[26]

Snow flurries settled over much of South Dakota on Election Day. The McGoverns watched the returns on television at home in Mitchell. Before long, the expected Republican sweep began to unfold, except for "the big one that got away." McGovern's margin of victory surprised everyone—the largest of any Democrat in the state's history since FDR in 1932. In the final count, he won a second term by 158,961 votes to 120,951, or 56.8 percent to 43.2. He carried fifty-one of sixty-seven counties, including such major GOP strongholds as Sioux Falls and Rapid City, and even Gubbrud's home county by 54 percent. In the presidential race, Nixon defeated Humphrey, 149,841 to 118,023, or 53.3 to 42 percent. Wallace, with 13,400 votes, took 4.8 percent. It did not go unnoticed that McGovern outstripped Nixon as the state's far bigger vote getter.[27] When they finally made it to campaign headquarters in Sioux Falls over icy roads at 1:00 a.m., George and Eleanor were greeted by the tumult of cheers of the young supporters packed inside the building and spilling out into the street. He was good-humored and heartfelt in his thanks to them and to South Dakotans for "thinking independently."[28]

As to how he won so decisively in a state where three out of five voters were registered Republicans, some commentators would underscore "his record in Washington and his developing seniority in the Senate" as the overriding factor. To explain his carrying cities as well as rural areas, one analysis alluded to McGovern's proposition that "an effective senator must see the urban problem" in order to persuade his colleagues to attend to agricultural problems; another credited his Washington staff's quick-response policy to various requests from the Sioux Falls business community. At least one journalist cited, as Ann McGovern did, the work of a new generation of South Dakota Democrats, such as Bill Dougherty and Peder Ecker, who gravitated naturally to candidates like her father and Bobby Kennedy. Others believed he had won simply because a majority "appreciate the stands he has taken and that he has been willing to hold to his convictions." The *Los Angeles Times*, after seeing how his opponents invoked "ancient fears of rural people about cities, distant regions, educated men, and central government," marveled at the voters' rejection of such ploys "as an awesome feat of imagination and courage."[29]

With twelve years' productive incumbency in the House and Senate and at Food for Peace, McGovern had become a highly skillful politician; he greatly benefited also from having the courage of his convictions, a dedicated state organization, a national standing, and a pleasing personality. But South Dakota Republicans ran basically the same campaign against him that they had always run. They argued that he was not an effective spokesperson for agricultural interests and cast aspersions on his patriotism for voicing doubts about significant aspects of America's anticommunist foreign policy. In 1956 their focus was Red China; in 1968, it was Vietnam.

McGovern ran for reelection to the Senate on parallel issues and principles that characterized all of his campaigns; with one or two exceptions, they fit his circumstances in 1968 like a second skin. As he had done since 1956, he emphasized how he had advanced the cause of agriculture and the family farm, and he made people in both South Dakota and Washington see that the farmers' abundance was not a curse, and that their commodities could help secure the promise of the Great Society at home and alleviate the worst kinds of human suffering that spawned tyranny abroad. As before, his deeds and diligence afforded the political space for his decided tilt to the left of the Vital Center, which was further mitigated this time by the fact that he had been right about Vietnam all along. (Just before Chicago he had written of his constituents, "Few of them agreed with me on this issue five years ago; today, I suspect most of them do.") Likewise, McGovern had repeatedly called for "union with urban society" and told South Dakotans they "must understand the problems of urban America" in order to solve their own. According to the *Argus Leader*, his electoral triumph indicated that they were receptive and "in the mood for change," and that they were catching up with him on the war. Given the source, that was a gracious admission about an amazing personal achievement. Indeed, if some had been dubious about his presidential candidacy, the majority as of November 5 no longer seemed to favor "hiding a national light under a South Dakota bushel," as Gloria Steinem put it. In October the public opinion analyst Elmo Roper ranked McGovern second (after Fulbright) in a list of twelve current senators of "distinguished intellectual stature who fully measure up to the great senators of a century ago" such as Clay and Webster. And, in December, *Time* magazine would list him, Ted Kennedy, and Edmund Muskie as the three most likely prospects for the Democratic nomination for president in 1972.[30]

It was, then, no doubt for all kinds of reasons, fitting that he should end his victory speech on election night with an invocation of Ecclesiastes, 3:1–8: "To everything there is a season, a time to every purpose under heaven . . . a time to kill, and a time to heal . . . a time to love, a time to hate; a time of war, and a time of peace."[31]

EPILOGUE
COME HOME, AMERICA

Although 1968 turned out to be George McGovern's best year in politics so far, that could not be said for his party, despite the closeness of the presidential race and the fact that the Democrats would still control Congress (the Senate by 58 to 42 and the House by 243 to 192, a net loss of five and four, respectively). Scarcely 520,000 votes separated Nixon and Humphrey out of the seventy-three million votes cast. Nixon won 31,785,000 votes (43.4 percent) to Humphrey's 31,275,000 (42.7 percent) and Wallace's 9,906,000 (13.5 percent). Humphrey did well in the Northeast and among African Americans and blue-collar union voters; more importantly, he did poorly in the Midwest and the Far West and won less than 10 percent of the white vote in the South. Overall he garnered twelve million fewer votes than Johnson in 1964. Nixon did well where Humphrey faltered and split the southern and border-state vote with Wallace, who carried five Deep South states. Together, the Nixon and Wallace vote constituted undeniable evidence that the liberal consensus and the New Deal coalition had unraveled. If the meaning of the 1964 election had been "that the American people had overwhelmingly affirmed their allegiance to the progressive tradition," as Arthur Link had written, then the significance of 1968 was the 59 percent preference for more conservative policies.[1]

No one would assess the Democrats' dilemma—or, rather, half of it—more succinctly than LBJ himself. "The average voter thought we had pushed too far and too fast in social reform," he wrote in his memoirs two years later. The "blue collar worker felt that the . . . party had traded his welfare for the welfare of the black man . . . [who] began demanding his rightful share of the American promise faster than most of the nation was willing to let him have it."[2] The other half of the problem was the war—the work of Cold War liberals led by Johnson—undertaken in the name of liberal democracy but which had done so much to afflict liberalism. The critiques and reproach came from within the liberal establishment as well as from New Left radicals and, of course, from the conservative reaction to the entire antiwar movement. Rendered indistinguishable in the eyes of the large numbers on the sidelines, liberals and radicals had been discredited along with the war. As the activist Todd Gitlin later reflected on Chicago in his book, *The Sixties*: "New Left radicalism was a vine that had grown up around liberalism; they had sprung from the same energy and soil of possibility, and although by now the two represented different cultures, different styles, different ideologies, like it or not they were going to stand or fall together."[3]

In the weeks and months after the election George McGovern did not see any of that as cause for despair. He was ambitious, idealistic, self-assured, and successful enough to think that he might succeed where the others failed. His reelection demonstrated the possibilities in larger spheres, and he intended to pursue a progressive agenda in the coming two or three years and gradually turn the negatives into positives.

At a victory dinner in December the forty-six-year-old outlined his most ambitious legislative goal—to eradicate hunger and malnutrition in America. "It is unacceptable that we have millions of youngsters who cannot even afford a school lunch," he said. "It makes no sense for some Americans to be suffering from protein deficiency while we permit our farmers to suffer from 18 cent eggs and generally low farm prices." Since the election, he had secured an expansion of the insufficient food stamp program to cover an additional 235 counties across the country, including twenty-nine in South Dakota (up from six). And his committee was about to undertake the first serious investigation in US history of the nation's nutritional health. The results of this quest would become his greatest domestic achievement and legacy of his second term.[4]

Then there was the matter of election reform. The obsolete system that rendered the Democratic convention "pretty well locked up before it was held" had to be fixed, he said. It provided for too few direct primaries in choosing presidential candidates and it permitted too many bosses to select delegates and in secret. In the election's aftermath, McGovern would become the indispensible man, the only prominent party leader acceptable to Johnson-Humphrey Democrats and McCarthy-McGovern antiwar insurgents alike. The results of his chairing the crucial Commission on Party Structure and Delegate Selection ultimately would have a profound impact on both the Democratic and Republican Parties and would compose the second most important achievement and legacy of his second term. Yet there were other things. He was hammering out a new initiative to create more job opportunities in rural areas; he hoped to revive economic conversion as events might allow; and he questioned the merits of military spending for a costly missile defense system that Johnson thought could protect the United States against China. (McGovern considered it a "blunder of major proportions" that "would actually decrease our national security.") He also wanted to replace the draft with an all-volunteer army.[5]

Obviously, none of this or the party's recovery could happen unless the war was shut down. It was the spawning disaster behind the broader national crisis. The ADA fully mirrored McGovern's overarching concern when it had resolved in February 1968: "We have opposed the Vietnam War not because we are preoccupied with one issue, but because it has blighted every liberal and progressive program here at home."[6] But his optimism about an early end to the war began to wane by Thanksgiving when the Pentagon reported that, since the preliminary peace parleys had commenced in May, 6,399 American soldiers had been killed and 22,161 wounded in Vietnam. Then, a week before Christmas, after LBJ's bombing halt had resuscitated the Paris talks, Saigon's chief negotiator, Vice President Ky, stymied them, owing to the shape of the negotiating table. McGovern made headlines by denouncing Ky as "a little tinhorn dictator," a "Benedict Arnold" who had "sold out to the French" in the first Indochina war of 1946–54. "There is no military objective in Vietnam now that is worth the sacrifice of one additional soldier or pilot," he said upon calling for a prisoner exchange with North Vietnam and the start of a pullout of American troops. Clark Clifford was then pressing for the same thing; the South Vietnamese had been "coddled and cuddled beyond belief," the secretary of defense protested to LBJ. "They're making all the decisions, but we pay, we die, we fight." Ky advised his two critics, McGovern and Clifford, to "shut their mouths."[7]

Even though he had decided to run for president by this time, McGovern did not, perhaps, absolutely need to do so in order to establish his most significant legacy, for which he had already established the foundations. His greatest priority was to get his country out of Vietnam as quickly as possible and to help Americans figure out how they got there—the better to avoid repeating that tragic mistake. "If I have any special asset for national leadership," he had said in August, "it is a sense of history—an understanding of the forces that have brought this country to a position of power and influence and an appreciation of what is important in our own time." Vietnam clarified for him the larger issue—the cumulative perversions of Containment—and brought him to an alternative to it, a conception of an authentic internationalist foreign policy. "The day of unilateral intervention is over; the need for more effective international peacekeeping machinery is clear," he had written in July. "No single nation has the power, the wisdom or the mission to be the world's policeman, banker or judge. These are the functions of the United Nations, the World Bank, the World Court, and other agencies of the international community." Then he asked: "*What would have happened if, instead of sending 500,000 troops to Vietnam, we had sent 10,000 Peace Corpsmen armed with medical ability, agricultural know-how, sanitation and nutrition skills, and dedicated teaching talent, and had left the Vietnamese to develop their political and economic institutions in their own way?*" It was a breathtaking question.[8]

Just before entering upon his second term, McGovern contemplated what the future might hold, in an address at the American Historical Association convention in New York, appropriately so on Woodrow Wilson's birthday, December 28. As "a practicing politician increasingly grateful for his own historical education," he said, he believed "that the quest for a more peaceful international community is the most crucial task of our age." It was also his conviction that "the only potential gain" that could come of Vietnam was "the humility and wisdom that may guide us toward a more rational view of our future role in the international community." Vietnam "should have taught us a new respect for caution and restraint in the exercise of military power abroad." Some of his remarks were devoted to misleading historical analogies and Walt Rostow and Dean Rusk's belief that Southeast Asia presented "the same challenge that Hitler posed to the West at Munich," which, along with the myth of monolithic communism, he demolished. The real issue was "whether the United States shall continue to intervene unilaterally in the affairs of other states as we have done during the 1960s . . . [or] will we seek to move away from this go-it-alone approach toward a greater measure of international cooperation based on a respect for the world's diversity." That was the proper question, rather than whether Americans were going to revert to isolationism, as Rusk had recently suggested. The secretary of state apparently measured isolation and internationalism "according to the number of military ventures we are willing to undertake," he continued, and "American influence in the world by the number of troops we send abroad." Would not the better measure, he asked, be "the quality and health of our own society and the intelligence and compassion that we manifest in responding to the needs and aspirations of our fellow human beings around the globe?"[9]

These questions, of course, McGovern had raised before—as a graduate student, as a professor, as a member of both houses of Congress. "Do we intend to rush into every revolutionary situation in the world on the theory that we have a mandate to impose an American solution?" he had asked his colleagues on June 17, 1965, as escalation in Vietnam impended. "Do we intend to work with or against the powerful nationalistic and social forces now convulsing Asia, Africa, and Latin America?" The broader challenge was "to avoid unilateral intervention and to work for multilateral support for our efforts," he proposed. "If it is impossible to get effective multilateral backing, I think that should be a clue to us that our policies and objectives may need reevaluation." He could not have guessed it, but he had put his finger on the core problem of American foreign policy that would endure into the twenty-first century.[10]

And so, from the start of his second Senate term, he would carry on in his reliance on first principles and his understanding of America's past in defense of its future, just as he had done since his first days in the House. His next campaign, for the presidency, would become the unique highlight of a life's work driven by a relentless sense of duty to explore alternatives to the ideas and institutions that forged the American Century and Cold War globalism. As before, the propositions he would ask his fellow citizens to consider would hold implications not only for interventionism in the Third World but also for the armaments race and the use of force in international relations, the political economy of the United States relative to other industrial powers, and, not the least, for the very nature of their country's political and social institutions. With an enduring faith in the possibilities for national redemption through authentic internationalism, education, and humanitarian endeavor, George McGovern would beckon, "Come home, America."

ACKNOWLEDGMENTS

Anyone who reads this book will understand why I begin my acknowl-edgments with George McGovern himself, for his cooperation was essential to the project. Through the scores of hours of our recorded interviews between the 1990s and 2010, he was consistently gracious and generous with his time. In his commentaries—about the events in which he played a major part, his concerns and goals as a politician, and family and personal matters—he was forthcoming, incisive, and revealing. From time to time his memory of certain things understanda-bly went astray. Yet his capacity to reconstruct important conversations with colleagues and to view events objectively and capture their larger historical significance was unfailing, while he also evinced remarkable critical detachment in weighing his own motives and performance. He died on October 21, 2012, at the age of ninety. It pains me deeply that I will never have the pleasure of putting a copy of this book into his hands.

My second most important debt is to the late Arthur S. Link, the eminent biographer of Woodrow Wilson and an inspiring mentor, who supervised my dissertation on Wilson and the League of Nations at Princeton University in the 1980s. Three decades earlier, Link performed the same role for McGovern at Northwestern University; to the end of his career he delighted in telling his graduate students stories about the former presidential candidate, his life-long friend. By the time he had facilitated the donation of McGovern's papers to Princeton, I had

ACKNOWLEDGMENTS

begun to develop a keen interest in the subject, and he encouraged me to take on the challenge of a McGovern biography.

I am happy also to acknowledge the archivists and librarians at numerous institutions who provided indispensible service to me over the course of several years. I am especially grateful to the staff at Princeton's Mudd Library, where I did most of my manuscript research; in particular, my sincere thanks go to Ben Primer and Daniel J. Linke for their cooperation and expert advice, and to Gene Pope and Nanci Young for their good turns on my behalf in the reading room. At the Lyndon B. Johnson Presidential Library I benefited from the guidance of T. Michael Parrish (now a historian at Baylor University) and Ted Gittinger. I owe a debt of gratitude to university archivist Linda Doezema at Houghton College who located for me important materials on Joseph McGovern's studies there; to Bonnie Olsen who counseled me on the ins and outs of research in the Papers of Karl Mundt at Dakota State University; and to Peter Blodgett of the Huntington Library who assisted me in gaining access to the Ray Allen Billington Papers. At Southern Methodist University, my home institution, I came to depend on the assistance and good cheer of Billie Stovall of interlibrary loan and the resourcefulness of Rebecca Graff at the reference desk at Fondren Library; my thanks also go to James Kessenides, Tyson Seale, Jane Wong, and (at Dedman Law Library) Greg Ivy.

At Dakota Wesleyan University, Laurie Langland, the university archivist and a valued friend, since the early 2000s has shared with me her impressive knowledge of both the institution's history and its McGovern Collection and directed my attention to crucial documents; she was an extraordinary curator in suggesting various photographs for this book as well. I thank the University Archives at the George and Eleanor McGovern Library for permission to publish the images. Robert Duffett, DWU's former president, also has been a good friend.

For generous financial support for my writing and research (including oral history interviews and their transcription), I am beholden to several entities at Southern Methodist University: the University Research Council, the Stanton Sharp Endowment and William P. Clements Endowment, the Dean of Dedman College for the Humanities and Sciences for three one-semester sabbatical leaves since 1998, and SMU's Center for Presidential History for awarding me its semester-long Writing Fellowship in 2014. I am likewise obliged to the Charles Warren Center for the Study of American History at Harvard University for a year-long fellowship in 1995–96 as my project was getting under way.

Among those who read and commented on portions of my manuscript, I very much appreciated the friendship and input of my cofellows at the Warren Center—Petra Goedde, Tim Naftali, Phillip Nash, Daniela Rossini, and Rafia Zafar—and Professors Akira Iriye and Ernest May. Elsewhere, while I worked on George McGovern, other scholars worked on his Senate colleagues, J. William Fulbright, Ernest Gruening, and Frank Church; thereon, my conversations and friendship with Randall Woods, Robert ("Casey") Johnson, and David F. Schmitz meant a great deal to me. John Milton Cooper Jr., whose knowledge of twentieth-century American political history is unsurpassed, read the manuscript in its entirety; the time and effort he put into his commentary far exceeded any reasonable expectations I might have anticipated, even from a close friend. Through Princeton University Press I was honored to have Michael Kazin and Julian Zelizer as readers, and I cannot thank them enough for their incisive criticisms and kind remarks. Also at the Press, I will always appreciate the thoughtful response of Brigitta van Rheinberg, editor in chief, to the first several chapters, as well as the good offices and support of Gary Gerstle. Since our first meeting Eric Crahan, senior editor, has been an excellent guide and supportive counselor and a pleasure to work with. I am also thankful to Deborah Tegarden, senior production editor, for the consideration and enthusiasm she has shown for the project. Dawn Hall copyedited the manuscript with exceptional care and intelligence; Barbara Sellers expertly read the page proofs for me; and Martin White crafted a fine index.

I am fortunate in having been a member of SMU's Clements Department of History since completing graduate school. Over the years I have felt especially fortified by the encouragement and comradeship of the late David J. Weber, Daniel T. Orlovsky, and James K. Hopkins (all three former departmental chairs) as well as of Jeremy Adams, Edward Countryman, Crista DeLuzio, Ling Shiao, Melissa Dowling, Sherry Smith, Alexis McCrossen, Kenneth Hamilton, Sabri Ates, and, most of all, Kathleen Wellman. For much the same reasons, I am also grateful to my colleagues Jeffrey Engel, director of the Center for Presidential History, and to Andrew Graybill, our current chair. Like all of us, I feel lucky to have had the wonderful day-to-day support and friendship of Mildred Pinkston and Sharron Pierson, our administrative staff. Within the university community, for their companionship and good humor and helping me to keep a balanced perspective on things, I would like to thank Rick Cogley, Bruce Levy, Beth Newman, Scott Arey,

ACKNOWLEDGMENTS

and Barbara Hill-Moore and Bonnie Wheeler. Among friends elsewhere I remain grateful to Valerie Hotchkiss, David Price, Ronn Cummings, Tony Smith, Justin Hart, Jim Amelang, Louis Rose, Chris Lunardini, Catherine Clinton, Paul Miles, James E. Reynolds, Ronald Kalin, David Martin, Gregg Asher, Jeffrey Wells, Jonathan Rosenberg, Fred Foster, and Alan Corcoran.

As for my family, I would like to express my gratitude and love to my mother and father, my stepmother Bobby, my siblings Joe and Tammy, my nieces Olivia Mori and Adele Mori, and their father, Ken. A little over ten years ago the Sellers family, to whom I am equally appreciative, came into my life—my mother-in-law and father-in-law, Meda and Eldean, and their three daughters, Melissa, Fran, and my dear friend, Barbara.

The dedication is to my partner in life, George D. Sellers, and my sister, Betty Jane Mori; without them it is all unimaginable.

434

A NOTE ON SOURCES

This work in grounded primarily in research in the Papers of George McGovern, housed in the Mudd Manuscript Library at Princeton University and measuring some 838 linear feet in 943 boxes. McGovern donated this main corpus of his papers in 1977, 1981, and 1987. Arthur S. Link, his former dissertation adviser at Northwestern who had moved to Princeton in 1960, arranged the donation. (Mudd Library also holds Link's papers, which contain correspondence with McGovern dating from the early 1950s to the 1980s.) Other essential sources for this study include the papers of Hubert Humphrey, Frank Church, and J. William Fulbright; and collections at the John F. Kennedy Presidential Library, the Lyndon Johnson Presidential Library, and Richard Nixon's papers held at the National Archives prior to NARA's certification of the Nixon Presidential Library. (Detailed records of thirty-three of the thirty-five combat missions that McGovern flew as a bomber pilot over Germany and Austria during World War II are in the National Archives as well.) On many trips to South Dakota, I did research in the George and Eleanor McGovern Library at Dakota Wesleyan University in its collections on McGovern, his brother-in-law Robert Pennington, and Francis Case; and in the Karl Mundt Papers at Dakota State University in Madison. In addition to such publications as the *Congressional Record*, the *New York Times*, and the *Washington Post*, I became well acquainted with a number of excellent South Dakota newspapers from the 1940s through the 1960s. Myriad books and scholarly articles can be found in the endnotes.

A NOTE ON SOURCES

I would also like to say something about the oral history base of my study. The recorded interviews I have done number over one hundred (including twenty-three sessions with McGovern and multiples with others). The process afforded me a once-in-a-lifetime opportunity to do a comprehensive oral history project that has deeply enriched my understanding of the subject. Along with his wife, Eleanor Stegeberg McGovern, interviewees among McGovern's family include Ila Stegeberg Pennington, Robert Pennington, Mildred McGovern Brady, Harold Brady, and McGovern's children—Ann McGovern, Susan Rowen McGovern, Steven McGovern, and Mary McGovern—and his son-in-law, James Rowen. (His daughter Terry died before my project was under way.) In South Dakota I interviewed various school chums, local politicians, and former students of McGovern; they include Dean Tanner, Bill Timmins, Gordon Rollins, John Solberg, Barbara Rollins Nemer, and William Dougherty. Several of McGovern's academic colleagues—including Link, William H. Harbaugh, Alfred Young, Lefton Stavrianos, and Richard Leopold—provided insights into their experiences with McGovern at Northwestern and after. Likewise, in their fields of interaction with him, several of his Senate colleagues and other politicians, advisers, and close friends who played important roles in his career generously offered accounts of fundamental importance. They include Gary Hart, Mark Hatfield, James Abourezk, Bob Dole, Alan Simpson, and Gaylord Nelson; Bob Shrum, Frank Mankiewicz, Pierre Salinger, and Richard Stearns; John Kenneth Galbraith, Gloria Steinem, Arthur Schlesinger, Jr., and Richard Wade; Bethine Church, Robert Strauss, Sargent Shriver, and Sissy Farenthold; Charles Guggenheim, the documentarian; John Holum, McGovern's on-staff foreign policy adviser; George Cunningham and Patricia Donovan, his administrative assistant and secretary for over 20 years; Jeff Smith, his aide during the 1972 campaign; Kenneth Higgins of the Dakota Queen; Judy Harrington, formerly of the Peace Corps; Margaret Douglas Link, Peter Stavrianos, and David Kranz, a brilliant South Dakota journalist who covered McGovern for thirty years. I am extremely grateful to them all.

ABBREVIATIONS

The following is a list of abbreviations employed in the endnotes for important manuscript collections, libraries, and publications and the like that are cited repeatedly throughout the volume. Also, the titles of the numerous newspaper articles cited in the notes have been reduced to two or three words each.

LIBRARIES AND MANUSCRIPT COLLECTIONS

ASLP   Arthur S. Link Papers, Seeley Mudd Library, Princeton University

DNA   National Archives, Washington, DC

GEML   George and Eleanor McGovern Library, Dakota Wesleyan University

GSMP   George McGovern Papers, Seeley Mudd Library, Princeton University

JFKL   John F. Kennedy Presidential Library

JWFP   J. William Fulbright Papers, Special Collections, University of Arkansas Libraries

KMP   Karl E. Mundt Papers, Karl E. Mundt Library, Dakota State University

LBJL   Lyndon Baines Johnson Presidential Library

RABP   Ray Allen Billington Papers, Huntington Library and Art Gallery, Pasadena, CA

RPC   Robert Pennington Collection, McGovern Library

PUBLICATIONS

AAN   *Aberdeen American News*

BR   *Brookings Register*

CR   *Congressional Record*

HDP   *Huron Daily Plainsman*

LAT   *Los Angeles Times*

MDR   *Mitchell Daily Republic*

NYT   *New York Times*

RCJ   *Rapid City Journal*

SFAL   *Sioux Falls Argus Leader*

WP   *Washington Post*

WPO   *Watertown Public Opinion*

NOTES

PROLOGUE

1. Jacqueline L. Salmon, "The President's Honor Role," *Washington Post* (hereinafter *WP*), August 10, 2000.

2. "The President Presents the Medal of Freedom to Senator George McGovern," copy of citation, in possession of the author.

3. Clinton in *Mitchell Daily Republic* (hereinafter *MDR*), October 7 and 8, 2006. To date, the main biographical sources are Robert Sam Anson, *McGovern: A Biography* (New York: Holt, Rinehart, and Winston, 1972); George McGovern's *Grassroots: The Autobiography of George McGovern* (New York: Random House, 1977); and Robert P. Watson, ed., *George McGovern: A Political Life, A Political Legacy* (Pierre: South Dakota State Historical Society Press, 2004); see also Bruce Miroff, *The Liberal's Moment: The McGovern Insurgency and the Identity Crisis of the Democratic Party* (Lawrence: University Press of Kansas, 2007), and my own scholarly articles on McGovern cited in the endnotes.

4. Billington to McGovern, July 17, 1972, in the Ray Allen Billington Papers, Henry E. Huntington Library and Art Gallery, Pasadena, California (hereinafter RABP).

5. George McGovern, *A Time of War, A Time of Peace* (New York: Random House, 1968), 99.

6. *Congressional Record* (hereinafter *CR*), September 24, 1963, 17884, and April 25, 1967, 10611; author's interview with Robert Dole, November 27, 2001.

7. Johnson quoted in G. McGovern, *Grassroots*, 228.

CHAPTER 1   YOURS, FOR FIXING UP THIS WORLD

1. "Thomas Henry McGovern," genealogical data; Andy Kirby to George McGovern, November 24, 1990; and Robert Pennington to Kirby, January 12,

1991, all in Robert Pennington Collection (hereinafter RPC) in the George and Eleanor McGovern Library, Dakota Wesleyan University.

2. Ibid; see also Melvyn Dubovsky, *Industrialism and the American Worker, 1865–1920* (Arlington Heights, IL: AHM Publishers, 1975), 19–20.

3. McGovern on his father, *Life* magazine, July 7, 1972, 33; G. McGovern, *Grassroots: The Autobiography of George McGovern*, 3.

4. Quoted in Dubovsky, *Industrialism and the American Worker*, 18.

5. McGovern Family history, by Marguerite King Carlson (daughter of George McGovern King), March 31, 1984, held by Mildred McGovern Brady, copy in RPC.

6. Anson, *McGovern: A Biography*, 15–16, and G. McGovern, *Grassroots*, 6; for the social milieu in which Joe McGovern played baseball, Allen Guttmann, *A Whole New Ball Game: An Interpretation of American Sports* (Chapel Hill: University of North Carolina Press, 1988) and Charles Alexander, *Our Game: An American Baseball History* (New York: Henry Holt, 1991). On these points I am also indebted to Richard Cogley.

7. Author's interviews with Ann McGovern, December 29, 1995; Susan McGovern Rowen, December 29, 1995; and Steven McGovern, December 29, 1995.

8. "Thomas Henry McGovern" and McGovern Family history by Carlson, RPC; Registrar's Records, 1893–95, Willard J. Houghton Library, Houghton College, Houghton, New York (information provided by Linda A. Doezema, University Archivist); Doezema to Knock, September 2, 1999 (letter).

9. Frieda Gillette and Katherine Lindley, *And You Shall Remember: A Pictorial History of Houghton College* (Houghton, NY: Houghton College, 1982), 19, 24–25, and 29–39; author's telephone interview with Doezema, September 2, 1999.

10. Registrar's Records, in Doezema to Knock, September 2, 1999; *Houghton Seminary Annual Catalogue* (Syracuse, NY, 1887); Gillette and Lindley, *And You Shall Remember*, 49–51 and 58–61.

11. Gillette and Lindley, *And You Shall Remember*, 80–81.

12. José Ortega y Gassett, in Kathleen Norris, *Dakota: A Spiritual Geography* (New York: Ticknor and Fields, 1993), iii.

13. Linda Hasselstrom, *Roadside History of South Dakota* (Missoula, MT: Mountain Press, 1994), 123.

14. John Steinbeck, *Travels with Charlie* (New York: Bantam, 1963), 153–54.

15. Herbert S. Schell, *History of South Dakota*, 3rd ed., rev. (Lincoln: University of Nebraska Press, 1975), 3–7 and 11–13; Hasselstrom, *Roadside History*, 2–6.

16. Schell, *History of South Dakota*, 140–44 and 158–65.

17. Ibid., 168–70, and Robert Ostergren, "European Settlement and Ethnicity Patterns on the Agricultural Frontiers of South Dakota," *South Dakota History* (Spring–Summer 1983): 49–82.

18. Schell, *History of South Dakota*, 180–81 and 244–45; Hasselstrom, *Roadside History*, xxi.

19. Schell, *History of South Dakota*, 119–21 and 182–83; Hasselstrom, *Roadside History*, xx and 20–23.

20. Schell, *History of South Dakota*, 389–91; Pennington to Knock, April 1, 1996, with enclosures.

21. Pennington to Knock, April 1, 1996, with enclosures.

22. Ibid., and author's interview with George Cunningham, May 21, 1994; *Life*, July 7, 1972, 33.

23. Carlson notes, March 31, 1984, and Kirby to George McGovern, November 24, 1990, RPC.

CHAPTER 2 A BOY NEVER GETS OVER HIS BOYHOOD

1. Author's interview with McGovern (unrecorded), September 14, 1999; G. McGovern, *Grassroots*, 7.

2. Alan Clem, *Prairie State Politics: Popular Democracy in South Dakota* (Washington, DC: Public Affairs Press, 1967); author's interviews with McGovern's children, Ann McGovern, December 28, 1995; Susan McGovern Rowan, December 29, 1995; Steven McGovern, December 29, 1995; Mary McGovern, December 29, 1995; and George McGovern (unrecorded telephone), March 28, 1996.

3. G. McGovern, *Grassroots*, 7; interviews with Susan McGovern Rowan, December 29, 1995, and George McGovern, September 14, 1999.

4. Interview with George McGovern, September 14, 1999; interview with Olive McGovern Briles, in *MDR*, August 31, 1972; author's interview with Susan McGovern Rowen; G. McGovern, *Grassroots*, 15.

5. Interview with Mildred McGovern Brady, in *MDR*, August 31, 1972.

6. Author's interview with Mildred McGovern Brady, May 26, 1995; and with Susan McGovern Rowen; G. McGovern, *Grassroots*, 15–16.

7. G. McGovern, *Grassroots*, 11–12; Susan Rowen McGovern; Ann McGovern, December 29, 1995.

8. G. McGovern, *Grassroots*, 13–14; Anson, *McGovern*, 20.

9. Author's interviews with George McGovern, August 9, 1991, and October 8, 1994; Eleanor McGovern, October 27, 1995; Mildred McGovern Brady, May 26, 1995; Robert Pennington, March 27, 1996; Steven McGovern, December 29, 1995; and Lefton Stavrianos to author, June 5, 1995, with enclosure; G. McGovern, *Grassroots*, 5–6, and Anson, *McGovern*, 20–21.

10. Author's interview with McGovern, September 14, 1999, and Steven McGovern, December 29, 1995.

11. G. McGovern, *Grassroots*, 4–6.

12. Ibid., 4, 8, and 14.

13. *MDR*, July 10, 1981; G. McGovern, *Grassroots*, 13; Hasselstrom, *Roadside History*, 56–62; interviews with Eleanor McGovern and Steven McGovern.

14. Hasselstrom, *Roadside History*, 58–61.

15. Author's interview with McGovern (unrecorded), October 25, 1998; G. McGovern, *Grassroots*, 7; *Life*, July 7, 1972, 39.

16. Author's interview with Bill Timmins, October 24, 1998; G. McGovern, *Grassroots*, 7 and 13.

17. Schell, *History of South Dakota*, 282–95 and 350–52; among the best studies are William E. Leuchtenburg, *Franklin D. Roosevelt and the New Deal, 1932–1940* (New York: Harper and Row, 1963), Robert McElvaine, *The Great Depression: America, 1929–1941* (New York: Times Books, 1984), and David M. Kennedy's

Freedom from Fear: The American People in Depression and War (New York: Oxford University Press, 1999); Wilson, in Arthur S. Link et al., eds., *The Papers of Woodrow Wilson*, 69 vols. (Princeton, NJ: Princeton University Press, 1966–94), 18: 631.

18. McGovern, quoted in Anson, *McGovern*, 25.

19. McGovern, *The Third Freedom, Ending Hunger in Our Time* (New York: Simon and Schuster, 2001), 19–23; author's interview with Mary McGovern, December 29, 1995, and with Bill Timmins, October 24, 1998.

20. McGovern interview, October 1, 1991.

21. See Schell, *History of South Dakota*, 223–41, and Clem, *Prairie State Politics*, 21–30.

22. See Arthur S. Link and Richard L. McCormick, *Progressivism* (Arlington Heights, IL: Harlan Davidson, 1983); Howard Lamar, "Perspectives on Statehood: South Dakota's First Quarter Century, 1889–1914," *South Dakota History* (Spring 1989): 13.

23. See William H. Harbaugh, *The Life and Times of Theodore Roosevelt* (New York: Collier, 1963) and H. W. Brands, *T. R.: The Last Romantic* (New York: Basic Books, 1997); Wilson, in Link, *Papers of Woodrow Wilson*, 6: 304, and 5: 562.

24. Schell, *History of South Dakota*, 258–69, and Clem, *Prairie State Politics*, 31–33 (quote, 32). See also, Gilbert Fite, *Peter Norbeck: Prairie Statesman* (Columbia: University of Missouri, 1948), and Richard L. Clow, "In Search of the People's Voice: Richard Olsen Richards and Progressive Reform," *South Dakota History* (Winter 1979): 39–58.

25. Schell, *History of South Dakota*, 289 and 295–97, and Clem *Prairie State Politics*, 31–38 and 125–26 (quote, 31). See also, John E. Miller, "McCarthyism before McCarthy: The 1938 Election in South Dakota," *Heritage of the Great Plains* (Summer 1982): 1–21.

26. For details, see Schell, *History of South Dakota*, 283 and 296–97, and Clem, *Prairie State Politics*, 13, 36–37, 58–60, and 80–81.

27. For two weeks in August 1936, FDR toured the drought-stricken states; he spent three days in South Dakota, with stops in Aberdeen, Huron, Pierre, and Rapid City. "What I have seen . . . convinces me we are on the right track," he said in Huron. "We are trying to restore this country out through here to a position where we can go ahead in South Dakota to better times, not only in the cities, but on the farms." John E. Miller, "The Failure to Realign: The 1936 Election in South Dakota," *Journal of the West* (Fall 2002): 22–29, especially 24–25.

28. Author's interview with McGovern, August 9, 1991; G. McGovern, *Grassroots*, 10–11; Joseph McGovern remarks recreated by his son in the *New Zion's Herald*, March 31, 2004.

29. Transcript of grades, Registrar's Office, Dakota Wesleyan University; author's interviews with Timmins and Ann McGovern.

30. G. McGovern, *Grassroots*, 12; Anson, *McGovern*, 28.

31. Author's interviews with Dean Tanner, October 23, 1998, and Timmins.

32. G. McGovern, *Grassroots*, 12; Anson, *McGovern*, 27–30; Timmins interview.

33. G. McGovern, *Grassroots*, 16–17.

34. Timmins interview; McGovern tells of his graduation in *Grassroots*, 16.

35. Author's interviews with McGovern, May 15, 2004, and March 22, 2008; unpublished draft pages of *Grassroots*, McGovern Collection, Box 7, George and Eleanor McGovern Library, Dakota Wesleyan University.

CHAPTER 3 A CLASPING OF HANDS MEANT EVERYTHING

1. Author's interview with Eleanor McGovern, October 27, 1995; and Eleanor McGovern, with Mary Finch Hoyt, *Uphill, A Personal Story* (Boston: Houghton Mifflin, 1974), 13–14, 21, and 25.

2. E. McGovern, *Uphill*, 19–20 (quote), 21, and 25; Eleanor McGovern interview.

3. Eleanor McGovern interview and E. McGovern, *Uphill*, 17, 22–23, 26–27, 31–33, and 41 (quote).

4. E. McGovern, *Uphill*, 28–29, 34–36, and 47–48; author's interviews with Eleanor McGovern, Ann McGovern, and Mary McGovern.

5. E. McGovern, *Uphill*, 45–47; Eleanor McGovern interview.

6. Eleanor McGovern interview; interviews with Susan McGovern Rowen and Mary McGovern; E. McGovern, *Uphill*, 35–36, 41, 47–52.

7. E. McGovern, *Uphill*, 52–53.

8. Eleanor McGovern interview; E. McGovern, *Uphill*, 53–54.

9. E. McGovern, *Uphill*, 55–56, and Eleanor McGovern interview.

10. Violet Miller Goering, *Dakota Wesleyan University, Century I* (Freeman, SD: Pine Hill Press, 1996), vii and 1–2.

11. Ibid., 7–11, 31–36, 51, and 127.

12. Ibid., 47 and 49–51.

13. Ibid., 16, 17–19, 40, 41, 44, 56, 57–58, and 60–61.

14. Ibid., 16–17, 42–43, 57, and 125.

15. *Phreno Cosmian*, November 12, 1940; February 4 and 11, April 1, and December 16, 1941; and February 24, 1942, George and Eleanor McGovern Library (GMEL), DWU; see also, Anson, *McGovern*, 35.

16. *Phreno Cosmian*, November 12 and December 3, 1940; January 14, April 8, May 20, June 3, September 23, October 29, and November 11, 1941; and March 10 and April 20, 1942; *The Tumbleweed* (Yearbook) for 1942, GMEL; and Goering, *Dakota Wesleyan University, Century I*, 57.

17. See Justus Doenecke, *From Isolation to War, 1931–1941*, 3rd ed. (Arlington Heights, IL: Harlan Davidson, 2006); for South Dakota's isolationism, see Schell, *History of South Dakota*, 298.

18. *Phreno Cosmian*, December 18, 1940, and May 13 and 30, 1941. See also, Ronald Radosh, *Prophets on the Right: Profiles of Conservative Critics of American Globalism* (New York: Simon and Schuster, 1975), 222–24.

19. G. McGovern, *Grassroots*, 31; author's interview with McGovern, August 9, 1991.

20. Author's interview with McGovern, August 9, 1991; *Phreno Cosmian*, December 16, 1941; and G. McGovern, *Grassroots*, 19.

21. "As I See It," *Phreno Cosmian*, February 10 and March 24, 1942.

22. Ibid., December 16, 1941.

23. G. McGovern, *Grassroots*, 20; and Stephen E. Ambrose, *The Wild Blue: The Men and Boys Who Flew the B-24s over Germany* (New York: Simon and Schuster, 2001), 43; Schell, *History of South Dakota*, 316.

24. *Phreno Cosmian*, January 20, 1942.

25. Ibid., January 27, 1941.

26. For other examples see ibid., March 10 and April 20, 1942.

27. Eleanor McGovern interview; E. McGovern, *Uphill*, 57; and G. McGovern, *Grassroots*, 21.

28. G. McGovern, *Grassroots*, 21, and Eleanor McGovern interview.

29. Ila McGovern Pennington, quoted in Eleanor McGovern interview; Anson, *McGovern*, 33.

30. Anson, *McGovern*, 33, and Goering, *Dakota Wesleyan University, Century I*, 51–52, and 58.

31. E. McGovern, *Uphill*, 57–58; G. McGovern, *Grassroots*, 21; Eleanor McGovern interview.

32. Eleanor McGovern interview, and E. McGovern, *Uphill*, 70.

33. McGovern to Robert Pennington, January 31, 1943, RPC; Eleanor McGovern interview; E. McGovern, *Uphill*, 60; and G. McGovern, *Grassroots*, 21–22.

34. E. McGovern, *Uphill*, 60–61; Eleanor McGovern interview; and author's interview with Robert and Ila Pennington, March 27, 1996.

35. McGovern to Pennington, October 14, 1942, RPC.

36. McGovern to Pennington, October 14 and November 3, 1942; and November 15, 1943, RPC.

37. McGovern to Pennington, November 25, 1942, RPC.

38. McGovern interview, August 9, 1991; G. McGovern, *Grassroots*, 19–20; Anson, *McGovern*, 35; Ambrose, *Wild Blue*, 46.

39. Frances McGovern, quoted in McGovern interview, August 9, 1991; Ambrose, *Wild Blue*, 46–47; Anson, *McGovern*, 36 and 49–50 (Mildred McGovern Brady; Joseph McGovern letter).

CHAPTER 4   THE BEST B-24 PILOT IN THE WORLD

1. *Phreno Cosmian*, April 20, 1942.

2. McGovern quote in G. McGovern, *Grassroots*, 19; Daryl Lembke, "Sen. McGovern and War Years—I," *Daily Democrat*, Woodland, California, October 9, 1972 (first of a six-part series for the *Los Angeles Times* (hereinafter *LAT*); Ambrose, *Wild Blue*, 32–33.

3. G. McGovern, *Grassroots*, 20; Joseph McGovern quote in Anson, *McGovern*, 36; E. McGovern, *Uphill*, 66–67.

4. Anson, *McGovern*, 36 (quote); Ambrose, *Wild Blue*, 33.

5. McGovern to Pennington, February 25, 1943, RPC; Ambrose, *Wild Blue*, 49–50.

6. McGovern to Pennington, February 25, 1943, RPC.

7. McGovern to Pennington, March 19, 1943, RPC; Ambrose, *Wild Blue*, 50–51; Toscanini in Marian Anderson, *My Lord, What a Morning* (Urbana: University of Illinois Press, 2002), 157–58.

8. Lembke, "Sen. McGovern and War Years—II," *Daily Democrat*, October 10, 1972; Ambrose, *Wild Blue*, 52–57.

9. McGovern to Pennington, June 27 and August 2, and September 5, 1943, RPC.

10. Eleanor McGovern interview, October 27, 1995; E. McGovern, *Uphill*, 59–63; and McGovern to Pennington, November 8, 1943, RPC; and Lembke, "McGovern War Years II," October 10, 1972.

11. Lembke, "McGovern War Years II," October 10, 1972, and Ambrose, *Wild Blue*, 66–68.

12. Anson, *McGovern*, 38; Eleanor McGovern interview; E. McGovern, *Uphill*, 64–65; Lembke, "McGovern War Years II," October 10, 1972; McGovern to Pennington, November 8 and 15, 1943, RPC.

13. McGovern to Pennington, December 28, 1943, and May 2, 1944; E. McGovern, *Uphill*, 65, 68; Ambrose, *Wild Blue*, 68–69.

14. Ambrose, *Wild Blue*, 52 and 70–71; Lembke, "McGovern War Years II," October 10, 1972; McGovern to Pennington, December 28, 1943, and February 8 and 13, 1944, RPC.

15. E. McGovern, *Uphill*, 65–66.

16. Robert Dorr, *US Bombers of World War Two* (London: Arms and Armour, 1989), 57–58 and 66; Roger A. Freeman, *B-24 Liberator at War* (London: Ian Allan, 1983), 6, 16, and 124–26; William Green, *Famous Bombers of the Second World War* 2nd ed., rev. (London: Macdonald and Jane's, 1975), 170–71.

17. Freeman, *Liberator at War*, 11–12 and 78; Green, *Famous Bombers*, 165–66 and 170–71; Larry Davis, *B-24 Liberator in Action* (Carrollton, TX: Signal Publications, 1987), 19–21; Lindbergh in Kennedy, *Freedom from Fear*, 654.

18. Dorr, *US Bombers*, 58 and 64; Green, *Famous Bombers*, 178.

19. G. McGovern, *Grassroots*, 23; and author's interview with McGovern, August 9, 1991.

20. Freeman, *Liberator at War*, 90 and 95; Lembke, "McGovern War Years II," October 10, 1972; McGovern to Pennington, May 2, 1944; and Ambrose, *Wild Blue*, 80–81.

21. Author's interview with Kenneth Higgins, July 17, 1995; Lembke, "McGovern War Years II" and "McGovern in the War," *Daily Democrat*, October 10 and October 11, 1972; G. McGovern, *Grassroots*, 23–28; and Anson, *McGovern*, 40–41.

22. Lembke, "McGovern War Years I and II," October 9 and 10, 1972; Higgins interview; McGovern to Pennington, July 29, 1944, RPC; G. McGovern, *Grassroots*, 23; and Christian Appy, *Working-Class War: American Combat Soldiers and Vietnam* (Chapel Hill: University of North Carolina Press, 1993), 27.

23. Michael Sherry, *The Rise of American Air Power: The Creation of Armageddon* (New Haven, CT: Yale University Press, 1987), 204–5; McGovern quote in Ambrose, *Wild Blue*, 100–101; and E. McGovern, *Uphill*, 68.

24. McGovern to Pennington, December 28, 1943, and July 29 and August 25, 1944, RPC.

25. E. McGovern, *Uphill*, 67.

26. McGovern to Pennington, August 25, 1944, and December 28, 1943; E. McGovern, *Uphill*, 67.

27. Lembke, "McGovern in the War," October 11, 1972; McGovern quote in Ambrose, *Wild Blue*, 128; author's interview with Robert Pennington, March 27, 1996.

28. Higgins interview; Rounds diary, quote in Lembke, "McGovern in the War," October 11, 1972; McGovern to Pennington, November 2, 1944, RPC; G. McGovern, *Grassroots*, 24; Ambrose, *Wild Blue*, 127–42. Pyle in John Morton Blum, *V Was for Victory: Politics and Culture during World War II* (New York: Harcourt Brace Jovanovich, 1976), 67.

29. Ambrose, *Wild Blue*, 160–61 and 165–66.

30. Freeman, *Liberator at War*, 89; Ambrose, *Wild Blue*, 144–45.

31. Ambrose, *Wild Blue*, 144–45, 153–59, 165–66, and 175–77; G. McGovern, *Grassroots*, 25; Higgins interview.

32. Higgins interview; Ambrose, *Wild Blue*, 159; Freeman, *Liberator at War*, 90.

33. Ambrose, *Wild Blue*, 178 and 183–84; Sherry, *Rise of American Air Power*, 212.

34. McGovern interview, August 9, 1991; McGovern to Pennington, February 3, 1945, RPC; G. McGovern, *Grassroots*, 28–29.

35. For flak boxes, see Ambrose, *Wild Blue*, 161 and passim.

36. G. McGovern, *Grassroots*, 26; Lembke, "McGovern in War," October 11, 1972; Higgins interview and flight diary, December 15, 1944, copy in author's possession; Freeman, *Liberator at War*, 100.

37. Lembke, "McGovern War Years" and "Sen. McGovern and War Years," *Daily Democrat*, October 12 and 9, 1972; G. McGovern, *Grassroots*, 26; Ambrose, *Wild Blue*, 181–82. Ambrose and McGovern date the incident incorrectly (*Wild Blue*, 179–80, and *Grassroots*, 26); it occurred on the seventh mission (Higgins flight diary, December 26, 1944).

38. See 455th Bomb Group Field Orders 70/ 172, Odertal Oil Refinery, December 17, 1944, Record Group 18, Box 1762, Records of the Army Air Forces, in National Archives, College Park, Maryland (hereinafter AAF Records, DNA); Higgins interview; Lembke, "McGovern War Years," *Daily Democrat*, October 12, 1972; and G. McGovern, *Grassroots*, 26 (McGovern mistakenly refers to this mission as the crew's second).

39. See 455th Bomb Group Field Orders 70/ 174, Pilsen, Czechoslovakia, and Brüx, Germany, December 20, 1944, Record Group 18, Box 1762, AAF Records, DNA; Higgins interview and flight diary, December 20, 1944; McGovern to Pennington, February 3, 1945, RPC; Lembke, "McGovern War Years," *Daily Democrat*, October 12, 1972; G. McGovern, *Grassroots*, 27; Ambrose, *Wild Blue*, 192–96.

40. For statistics on the Strategic Air Offensive, see John Keegan, ed., *The Oxford Companion to World War II* (Oxford and New York: Oxford University Press, 2001), 836–39.

41. McGovern to "Mr. and Mrs. Rounds," September 1, 1944, in Lembke, "McGovern War Years," October 9, 1972; McGovern to "Mrs. Adams," April 14, 1945 (copy in possession of the author); G. McGovern, *Grassroots*, 25; Anson, *McGovern*, 40 and 46.

42. Eleanor McGovern interview; E. McGovern, *Uphill*, 67–69; and Lembke, "McGovern War Years—67 Holes on Mission," *Daily Democrat*, October 13, 1972.

43. E. McGovern, *Uphill*, 71–72.

44. G. McGovern, *Grassroots*, 29.

45. Higgins interview; Ambrose, *Wild Blue*, 230–31.

46. Quoted in Ambrose, *Wild Blue*, 233.

47. Paul Fussell, *Wartime: Understanding and Behavior in the Second World War* (New York: Oxford University Press, 1989), 17–18 and 283–84.

48. Sherry, *Rise of American Air Power*, 260, 272–77, and 413n43.

49. Ibid., 197, 251–55, 260–64, and 286–87; Richard Overy, *Why the Allies Won* (New York: W. W. Norton, 1995), 104–18 and 122–33; Ambrose, *Wild Blue*, 107–11, 117–25, and 247–51.

50. Sherry, *Rise of American Air Power*, 204–5.

51. Ibid., 205–11.

52. Ibid., 209–18.

53. Lembke, "McGovern War Years—67 Holes on Mission," October 13, 1972.

54. Quoted in Ambrose, *Wild Blue*, 231 and 233.

55. McGovern to Pennington, September 5, 1943, RPC.

56. Quotes in Blum, *V Was for Victory*, 66–68; see also Fussell, *Wartime*, 129–43.

57. Mauldin in Blum, *V Was for Victory*, 69; McGovern interview, August 9, 1991 (FDR and Churchill quote); and Lembke, "McGovern War Years—67 Holes on Mission."

58. McGovern to Pennington, January 31 and March 19, 1943, and February 3, 1945, RPC.

59. McGovern to Pennington, February 3, 1945; McGovern interview, August 9, 1991. Charles Beard and Mary Beard, *The Rise of American Civilization* (New York: Macmillan, 1927; and 1936—new ed., rev., and enl.). Richard Hofstadter, *The Progressive Historians: Turner, Beard, Parrington* (New York: Knopf, 1970), 298–304 and 477; for a full appreciation, 167–346. For Beard on foreign policy, see Radosh, *Prophets on the Right*, 17–65.

60. Beard and Beard, *Rise of American Civilization*, 2: quotes 53–54; Hofstadter, *Progressive Historians*, 302–4.

61. Beard and Beard, *Rise of American Civilization*, 1: vii and ix; G. McGovern, *Grassroots*, 31–32; McGovern interview, August 9, 1991.

62. "Farm" in Ambrose, *Wild Blue*, 233; McGovern to Pennington, May 30, 1945. Citation for DFC, Air Medals, and three oak leaf clusters in McGovern Collection, Box 15, GEML.

63. For official pre- and postmission reports in a typical week see 455th Bomber Group, Field Orders 70/221, Newburg, Germany, March 21; FO 222, Kraulupy, Czechoslovakia, March 22; and FO 225, Liben, Czechoslovakia, March 25, 1945, in Record Group 18, Box 1765, AAF Records, DNA. For its tactical missions, see FO 239, Ghedi/Bologna, April 15, and FO 245, Padua, April 23, 1945, Record Group 18, Box 1766 and 1767. See also Higgins flight diary, March through April 1945.

64. See 455th BG, FO 247, Linz, Austria, April 25, 1945, Record Group 18, Box 1767, AAF Records, DNA; and "Ex-Navigator Defends McGovern," *Fort Worth Star-Telegram,* June 22, 1972.

65. See 455th BG, FO 247, Linz, Austria, April 25, 1945, Record Group 18, Box 1767, AAF Records, DNA; and Lembke, "McGovern War Years—67 Holes on Mission."

66. Lembke, ibid., and October 9, 1972; Higgins interview; G. McGovern, *Grassroots,* 27–28; Ambrose, *Wild Blue,* 242–43.

67. Higgins interview; Lembke, "McGovern War Years—67 Holes on Mission"; McGovern to Knock, May 21, 2004.

68. Ambrose, *Wild Blue,* 254–55; Lembke, "McGovern War Years," October 13, 1972.

69. Lembke, "McGovern War Years," October 13, 1972, and Ambrose, *Wild Blue,* 254 and 258.

70. Based on author's interview with McGovern, August 9, 1991, and G. McGovern, *Grassroots,* 28–29; Cooper quoted in Ambrose, *Wild Blue,* 226; Nimitz quoted in Kennedy, *Freedom from Fear,* 831.

71. McGovern interview, August 9, 1991.

CHAPTER 5   I WOULD HAVE TO CALL HIM A PROGRESSIVE AGRARIAN

1. G. McGovern, *Grassroots,* 30–31; Ambrose, *Wild Blue,* 259–60.

2. G. McGovern, *Grassroots,* 30; unrecorded remarks to author, June 15, 2004.

3. Author's interview with Eleanor McGovern, October 27, 1995; E. McGovern, *Uphill,* 73–75.

4. Tom Brokaw, *The Greatest Generation* (New York: Random House, 1998), xxx.

5. McGovern to Pennington, December 28, 1943, RPC; statistics in Arthur S. Link and William B. Catton, *American Epoch: A History of the United States since 1900,* 5th ed. (New York: Alfred A. Knopf, 1980), 2: 654–55.

6. G. McGovern, *Grassroots,* 30; McGovern interview, August 9, 1991; Kennedy, *Freedom from Fear,* 849–50.

7. The articles are quoted in Sherry, *Rise of American Airpower,* 351–53, as is Leslie Groves ("a thousand suns," 343); see also 327–29, 333–41, 344–55, and 414–19. The controversy centers partly on whether the bombs were necessary to bring about Japan's surrender, and whether one attack would have sufficed. See Martin Sherwin, *A World Destroyed: The Atomic Bomb and the Grand Alliance* (New York: Knopf, 1975), and Gar Alperovitz, *Atomic Diplomacy: Hiroshima and Potsdam* (New York: Penguin, 1985); special issue of *Diplomatic History* (Spring 1995); and Rufus Miles Jr., "Hiroshima, The Strange Myth of Half a Million American Lives Saved," *International Security* (Fall 1985): 121–40.

8. Quotes in G. McGovern, *Grassroots,* 30–31, and Anson, *McGovern,* 51.

9. See Goering, *Dakota Wesleyan University, Century I,* 53–54, and the 1944 edition of the *Tumbleweed* (DWU's yearbook), 19, 26, 63, 64, and 72–74; G. McGovern, *Grassroots,* 32.

10. G. McGovern, *Grassroots,* 32–34; Charles Howard Hopkins, *The Rise of the Social Gospel in American Protestantism, 1865–1915* (New Haven, CT: Yale

University Press, 1940), and Donald K. Gorrell, *The Age of Social Responsibility: The Social Gospel in the Progressive Era, 1900–1920* (Macon, GA: Mercer University Press, 1988).

11. Quotes from Walter Rauschenbusch, *Christianity and the Social Crisis* (New York: Macmillan, 1907), xxxv and 342; and Link and Catton, *American Epoch*, 1: 23–25; G. McGovern, *Grassroots*, 35.

12. Rauschenbusch, *Christianity and the Social Crisis*, 35; G. McGovern, *Grassroots*, 35–36; McGovern interview in the *New Zion's Herald*, March 31, 2004 (quote); McGovern interview, August 9, 1991.

13. "From Cave to Cave," copy in McGovern Collection, Box 4, GEML.

14. Eleanor McGovern and Pennington interviews; E. McGovern, *Uphill*, 76; G. McGovern, *Grassroots*, 36 and 38.

15. G. McGovern, *Grassroots*, 38.

16. Ibid.; Pennington interview.

17. G. McGovern, *Grassroots*, 38; McGovern interview, August 9, 1991.

18. McGovern interview, August 9, 1991, and McGovern to Billington, July 15, 1950, RABP.

19. Author's interviews with William H. Harbaugh, October 23, 1995, and Alfred F. Young, January 9, 2000; Alfred F. Young, "An Outsider and the Progress of a Career in History," *William and Mary Quarterly* (July 1995): 499–512; and the introduction in Robert Karrow Jr., and Alfred F. Young, eds., *Past Imperfect: Essays on History, Libraries, and the Humanities—Lawrence W. Towner* (Chicago: University of Chicago Press, 1993), xv–xxxviii.

20. See Richard H. Leopold, "Arthur Link at Northwestern, the Maturing of a Scholar," in *The Wilson Era: Essays in Honor of Arthur S. Link*, ed. John Milton Cooper Jr. and Charles E. Neu (Arlington Heights, IL: Harlan Davidson, 1991).

21. Pennington interview; G. McGovern, *Grassroots*, 39; Anson, *McGovern*, 56.

22. Harbaugh and Young interviews and unrecorded interview with Arthur and Margaret Link, ca. June 1993; G. McGovern, *Grassroots*, 40; E. McGovern, *Uphill*, 78.

23. See Allan G. Bogue, *Frederick Jackson Turner: Strange Roads Going Down* (Norman: University of Oklahoma Press, 1998). This discussion is indebted to Richard Hofstadter, *The Progressive Historians: Turner, Beard, Parrington* (New York: Knopf, 1968), 47–163; but, for the frontier thesis, see 47–54 and 125–29 (quote, 127).

24. For Beard, see chapter 4's citations to Hofstadter, *Progressive Historians*; for Parrington, Hofstadter, *Progressive Historians*, 349–434; Kazin and Parrington quotes, 352, 370 and 438; Young, "An Outsider and the Progress of a Career in History," 503; Harbaugh interview.

25. Hofstadter, *Progressive Historians*, 60–61, 70, 82, and 107; for Turner and Roosevelt, 56 and 106–7 (quote). Beard preferred TR to Wilson.

26. See William H. Harbaugh, *Power and Responsibility: The Life and Times of Theodore Roosevelt*, rev. ed. (New York: Octagon Books, 1975) 123–24, 155–56, 165–79, 227–36, and 248–51; and Arthur S. Link, *Woodrow Wilson and the Progressive Era, 1910–1917* (New York: Harper, 1954), 54–80 and 223–51. See also Eric F. Goldman, *Rendezvous with Destiny: A History of Modern Reform* (New York: Knopf, 1952); Richard Hofstadter, *The Age of Reform: From Bryan to*

F.D.R. (New York: Knopf, 1955); Gabriel Kolko, *The Triumph of Conservatism: A Re-interpretation of American History, 1900–1916* (Chicago: Quadrangle Books, 1963); and Robert H. Wiebe, *The Search for Order, 1877–1920* (New York: Hill and Wang, 1967). Progressivism had more variety than these reforms suggest; it operated at all levels of civic society and embraced activists who often worked at cross-purposes.

27. Author's interview with McGovern, October 1, 1991.

28. Ibid.

29. McGovern to Link, May 25 and June 22, 1950, in the Arthur S. Link Papers, Seeley Mudd Library, Princeton University (hereinafter ASLP).

30. McGovern to Billington, July 15, 1950, RABP.

31. McGovern interview, October 1, 1991; McGovern to Link, June 22 and August 19, 1950, ASLP.

32. George McGovern, "The Colorado Coal Strike, 1913–1914" (PhD diss., Northwestern University, 1953), 1–8 (quotes, 51 and 8). The following story is derived from this source as well as an expanded version, George McGovern and Leonard F. Guttridge, *The Great Coalfield War* (Boston: Houghton Mifflin, 1972).

33. McGovern, "Colorado Coal Strike," 12–17 (quotation, 17); McGovern and Guttridge, *Great Coalfield War*, 23–25.

34. McGovern and Guttridge, *Great Coalfield War*, 25–27; McGovern, "Colorado Coal Strike," 18–22.

35. McGovern, "Colorado Coal Strike," 23–33; see also McGovern and Guttridge, *Great Coalfield War*, 32–35.

36. McGovern, "Colorado Coal Strike,", 34–37 and 41–42.

37. Ibid., 52–57, 60–66, and 70–77.

38. Ibid., 79–81, 115–19, 137–51, and 223–24.

39. Ibid., 152–59, 161–65, 183–89, 191–95, 238, and 364–87; McGovern and Guttridge, *Great Coalfield War*, 208–14 and 221–22.

40. Harbaugh, *Power and Responsibility*, 165–79.

41. McGovern, "Colorado Coal Strike," 221–25, 234–36, and 264–67; Bowers quotes, 179 and 236, and Stewart, 223–24.

42. McGovern and Guttridge, *Great Coalfield War*, 203–4.

43. Ibid., 211–15; McGovern, "Colorado Coal Strike," 270–79.

44. McGovern, "Colorado Coal Strike," 280–95; McGovern and Guttridge, *Great Coalfield War*, 216–31.

45. McGovern and Guttridge, *Great Coalfield War*, 239–42 and 263–67; McGovern, "Colorado Coal Strike," 297–98 and 303–6 (quote, 307).

46. McGovern, "Colorado Coal Strike," 308–25 (quote, 359); McGovern and Guttridge, *Great Coalfield War*, 263 (secretary of war quote) and 266–68.

47. McGovern, "Colorado Coal Strike," 327–32 and 348–59 (quote, 330).

48. Ibid., 428–46; McGovern and Guttridge, *Great Coalfield War*, 279–80, 334–36, and 341–42; McGovern quote in *Dissertation Abstracts International*, vol. 13-06, 1166.

49. See Thomas Andrews, *Killing for Coal: America's Deadliest Labor War* (Cambridge, MA: Harvard University Press, 2008). See also Link to McGovern, October 2 and November 28, 1951, and March 12, 1952, ASLP.

50. Turner in Hofstadter, *Progressive Historians*, 101; TR in Harbaugh, *Power and Responsibility*, 165 and 367–68.

51. Link, *Papers of Woodrow Wilson*, 27: 148–52.

52. McGovern interview, October 1, 1991.

53. Harbaugh and Young interviews.

CHAPTER 6   AMERICA WAS BORN IN REVOLUTION AGAINST THE ESTABLISHED ORDER

1. Towner quoted in Anson, *McGovern*, 58.

2. John C. Culver and John Hyde, *American Dreamer: The Life and Times of Henry A. Wallace* (New York, 2000), 419–31; David McCullough, *Truman* (New York: Norton, 1992), 513–18; Thomas W. Devine, *Henry Wallace's 1948 Presidential Campaign and the Future of Postwar Liberalism* (Chapel Hill: University of North Carolina Press, 2013), 16–18.

3. Along with the foregoing see Alonzo L. Hamby, *Beyond the New Deal: Harry S. Truman and American Liberalism* (New York: Columbia University Press, 1973), 127–34; and Robert J. Donovan, *Conflict and Crisis: The Presidency of Harry S. Truman, 1945–1948* (New York: Norton, 1977), 219–28.

4. Culver and Hyde, *American Dreamer*, 438–59; Hamby, *Beyond the New Deal*, 147–61.

5. Author's interview with Al Young, January 9, 2000, and with McGovern, August 9 and October 1, 1991; Anson, *McGovern*, 58; and McCullough, *Truman*, 551–53.

6. Culver and Hyde, *American Dreamer*, 28–29, 67–73, 82–83, 89–91, 148–50, 249–51. Norman Borlaug, who in 1970 won the Nobel Peace Prize for developing high yield wheat strains, credited Wallace for this revolution.

7. Culver and Hyde, *American Dreamer*, 57, 102–8, 113–29, 159–63, 178–79, 199, 204–5, and 229; Miller, "The Failure to Realign" (cited in chapter 2), 24–25.

8. Culver and Hyde, *American Dreamer*, 227–30; Truman quote in James Chace, *Acheson: The Secretary of State Who Created the American World* (New York: Simon and Schuster, 1998), 158.

9. Culver and Hyde, *American Dreamer*, 191–95, 275–80 (Wallace quote, 277), and 304–25.

10. Quotes from first of several essays on it, *Life*, February 17, 1941; see Alan Brinkley, *The Publisher: Henry Luce and His American Century* (New York: Knopf, 2010), 265–73.

11. Culver and Hyde, *American Dreamer*, 191–95, 304–84, 343; quotes, 347 and 271.

12. Humphrey to Wallace, April 12, 1945, in the Hubert H. Humphrey Papers, 148A.2.4F, Box 2, VIP Correspondence, Minnesota Historical Society.

13. McGovern to Link, August 19 and September 30, 1950, ASLP.

14. In his infamous "percentages" arrangement Churchill proposed that the Russians should have 90 percent control in Romania and 75 percent in Bulgaria, and the British should have 90 percent control in Greece; in Yugoslavia and Hungary, a 50–50 split. See Warren Kimball, *The Juggler: Franklin*

Roosevelt as Wartime Statesman (Princeton, NJ: Princeton University Press, 1991), 159–84.

15. See John Lewis Gaddis, *The United States and the Origins of the Cold War, 1941–1947* (New York: Columbia University Press, 1972), 201–6, 217–20, 222–24, and 238–41; Truman quote, Thomas Paterson, *Meeting the Communist Threat: Truman to Reagan* (New York: Oxford University Press, 1988), 37; Hopkins quote, Hamby, *Beyond the New Deal*, 99.

16. Paterson, *Meeting the Communist Threat*, 38–41; I. C. B. Deer, ed., *The Oxford Companion to World War II*, (Oxford: Oxford University Press, 2001), 321, 609, 886, and 898.

17. Paterson, *Meeting the Communist Threat*, 21–23 and 42.

18. See John Lewis Gaddis, *Strategies of Containment: A Critical Appraisal of Postwar American National Security Policy* (New York: Oxford University Press, 1982), 25–88, and his *George F. Kennan: An American Life* (New York: Penguin, 2011), passim; David L. Mayers, *George Kennan and the Dilemmas of US Foreign Policy* (New York: Oxford University Press, 1988), 105–88 and 219–44; Anders Stephanson, *Kennan and the Art of Foreign Policy* (Cambridge, MA: Harvard University Press, 1989), 51–103, 111–49, and 168–9; and Kennan's *Memoirs, 1925–1950* (Boston: Little, Brown, 1967), 216–367.

19. Gaddis, *Strategies of Containment*, 22–23, 59, 64–65; and Walter LaFeber, *America, Russia, and the Cold War, 1945–2006*, 10th ed. (Boston: McGraw-Hill, 2008), 57–70; Paterson, *Meeting the Communist Threat*, 76–94.

20. Hamby, *Beyond the New Deal*, 175–79 and 197–98 (quote); LaFeber, *America, Russia, and the Cold War*, 61 (quote) and 63.

21. LaFeber, *America, Russia, and the Cold War*, 65–73 and 76–80; Paterson, *Meeting the Communist Threat*, 21–32; see also Melvin Leffler, "The American Conception of National Security and the Beginnings of the Cold War, 1945–1948," *American Historical Review* (April 1984): 346–81.

22. *Argus Leader* (of Sioux Falls and South Dakota's largest daily), March 11, 1984 (hereinafter *SFAL*).

23. Stavrianos to Knock, June 5, 1995, and April 8, 1996; notes on telephone interview with Stavrianos, ca. June 1995, author's collection.

24. McGovern interview, August 9, 1991.

25. Gaddis emphasizes this in *The United States and the Origins of the Cold War, 1941–1947*, 63–94; see also Steven E. Ambrose and Douglas Brinkley, *Rise to Globalism: American Foreign Policy since 1938*, 8th rev. ed. (New York: Penguin, 1997), 15–34.

26. McGovern interview, August 9, 1991.

27. Howard K. Smith, *The State of Europe* (New York: Knopf, 1949), 287–93, 372–73, 401, (quote, 289).

28. Ibid., 77, 89–91, and 236.

29. Ibid., 98–100, 272–73, 403–4, and 406.

30. McGovern in *SFAL*, March 11, 1984; Towner in Anson, *McGovern*, 58; G. McGovern, *Grassroots*, 43–44; Al Young interview.

31. Al Young interview; Anson, *McGovern*, 59. See also Richard M. Fried, *Nightmare in Red: The McCarthy Era in Perspective* (New York: Oxford University Press, 1991), 73 and 109.

32. Culver and Hyde, *American Dreamer*, 478–80; Hamby, *Beyond the New Deal*, 209–12, 232–33, and 269–70. Zachary Karabell's *The Last Campaign: How Harry Truman Won the 1948 Election* (New York: Knopf, 2007) maintains that Wallace made the campaign "more dynamic and more ideologically diverse than anyone of political age in 1948 would experience in their lifetimes" (185).

33. G. McGovern, *Grassroots*, 31–32; Robert W. Karrow and Alfred Young, eds., *Past Imperfect: Essays on History, Libraries, and the Humanities—Lawrence W. Towner* (Chicago: University of Chicago Press, 1993), xviii–xix; Young interview.

34. Clifford memo and Wallace quoted in Culver and Hyde, *American Dreamer*, 466–67; Truman in Hamby, *Beyond the New Deal*, 222–23; on the question of communist influence in the Progressive Party, see Devine, *Henry Wallace's 1948 Presidential Campaign*, 15–28 and 154–71; see also Fried, *Nightmare in Red*, 9, 82, and 84; and David Caute, *The Great Fear: The Anti-Communist Purge under Truman and Eisenhower* (New York: Simon and Schuster, 1978), 33–35.

35. Quotes in Culver and Hyde, *American Dreamer*, 403 and 478, and Hamby, *Beyond the New Deal*, 231.

36. Pennington interview, March 27, 1996.

37. Quoted in Arthur M. Schlesinger Jr., *A Life in the Twentieth Century: Innocent Beginnings, 1917–1950* (Boston: Houghton Mifflin, 2000), 399–400; see also, 394–417.

38. Quotes in Hamby, *Beyond the New Deal*, 162 and 164; see also 159–68. The leading study is Steve Gillon, *Politics and Vision: The ADA and American Liberalism, 1947–1985* (New York: Oxford University Press, 1987), see 23–39.

39. McGovern, "Three Illusions," *MDR*, April 20, 1948; microfilm edition of J. Edgar Hoover Official and Confidential Files, No. 106, memorandum compiled by M. A. Jones, March 9, 1971, pp. 2, 8, and 9 (University Publications of America, 1990) edited by Athan Theoharis.

40. Among the more famous attendees were FDR's economic adviser, Rexford Tugwell; congressman Vito Marcantonio of New York; the historian and civil rights activist W.E.B. Du Bois; the historian F. O. Matthiesen of Harvard; Frederick Schuman, the Woodrow Wilson Professor of Government at Williams College; Paul Robeson, the actor and singer; the sculptor Jo Davidson; and novelist Norman Mailer.

41. See Culver and Hyde, *American Dreamer*, 484–86; Karabell, *Last Campaign*, 177 and 183; McCullough, *Truman*, 645–46.

42. See the foregoing sources, 485, 178, and 645, respectively, and G. McGovern, *Grassroots*, 43.

43. Culver and Hyde, *American Dreamer*, 488–89, and Devine, *Henry Wallace's 1948 Presidential Campaign*, 165–70.

44. Culver and Hyde, *American Dreamer*, 480–81 and 487; Hamby, *Beyond the New Deal*, 245–46; McCullough, *Truman*, 645–46; Karabell, *Last Campaign*, 179–80; Graham White and John Maze, *Henry A. Wallace: His Search for a New World Order* (Chapel Hill: University of North Carolina Press 1995), 275–76; and Devine, *Henry Wallace's 1948 Presidential Campaign*, 172–79.

45. *Mitchell Daily Republic* carried the Alsops' piece, July 26, 1948.

46. Culver and Hyde, *American Dreamer*, 487 (first quote); see also, Hamby, *Beyond the New Deal*, 245; Devine, *Henry Wallace's 1948 Presidential Campaign*,

173–77; McCullough, *Truman*, 646; Karabell, *Last Campaign*, 179–80; White and Maze, *Henry A. Wallace*, 276, none of which agrees entirely with the others. Hamby states, "delegates voted it down by an overwhelming margin," whereas White and Maze state, "the amendment was narrowly rejected on a voice vote." McGovern quotes from October 1, 1991 interview; he does not mention the controversy in *Grassroots* (43–45) but see Anson, *McGovern*, 58–61.

47. Caute, *Great Fear*, 161 and 163; Culver and Hyde, *American Dreamer*, 493–99.

48. McCullough, *Truman*, 638–45; Gillon, *Politics and Vision*, 47–50; and Karabell, *Last Campaign*, 164–65.

49. LaFeber, *America, Russia, and the Cold War*, 78–80 and 83–87; Hamby, *Beyond the New Deal*, 221–23, 239, and 253–55; Chace, *Acheson*, 186–89; and McCullough, *Truman*, 630–31, and 647–49.

50. Hamby, *Beyond the New Deal*, 183–85 and 204–5, and 189–90, 243–44, and 247; "pitchfork" in Schlesinger, *A Life in the Twentieth Century*, 479; Ohio and Illinois vote in McCullough, *Truman*, 713.

51. Donovan, *Conflict and Crisis*, 415; Culver and Hyde, *American Dreamer*, 491–93.

52. Culver and Hyde, *American Dreamer*, 498–503; McCullough, *Truman*, 704 and 710–19; Donovan, *Conflict and Crisis*, 430–39; and Karabell, *Last Campaign*, 254–66 and 293–94.

53. Quotes in Pennington, Harbaugh, and Young interviews. Gallup in Culver and Hyde, *American Dreamer*, 500.

54. McGovern states (October 1, 1991) that Wallace was not on the ballot in South Dakota, but, in fact, he was, and he received about 2,000 votes; Dewey carried the state with 129,000 to Truman's 117,000. Wallace was not on the ballot in Illinois; had he been, he might have easily thrown the state to Dewey; instead, Truman took it by barely 33,000 out of nearly four million votes (Culver and Hyde, *American Dreamer*, 498 and 500–501).

55. *MDR*, September 22, 1948.

56. McGovern to Pennington, November 4, 1944, RPC.

57. McGovern interview, October 1, 1991.

58. Ibid., and G. McGovern, *Grassroots*, 43 and 45.

59. McGovern interview, August 1, 1991.

60. Ibid.

CHAPTER 7   THE CONFUSED AND FEAR-RIDDEN TEMPER OF THE TIMES

1. E. McGovern, *Uphill*, 76.

2. Harbaugh interview, October 23, 1995; interview with Margaret Douglas Link, June 1993.

3. E. McGovern, *Uphill*, 79.

4. Ibid., 78–79, and G. McGovern, *Grassroots*, 31 and 37.

5. E. McGovern, *Uphill*, 79 and 81–83; Eleanor McGovern interview, October 27, 1995; George McGovern, *Terry: My Daughter's Life-and-Death Struggle with Alcoholism* (New York: Villard Books, 1996), 44–45.

6. G. McGovern, *Terry*, ix and 45; McGovern to Link, December 13, 1950; April 26, July 9, and August 14, 1951, ASLP.

7. McGovern to Link, February 24, April 26 (quote), July 9, 1951, and December 13, 1950, ASLP.

8. Goering, *Dakota Wesleyan University: Century I*, 54–55.

9. McGovern to Link, July 9 and August 14, 1951, ASLP; Goering, *Dakota Wesleyan University: Century I*, 55; and James D. McLaird, *The Dakota Wesleyan Memory Book, 1885–2010* (Mitchell, SD: Dakota Wesleyan University, 2010), 71–73.

10. Fried, *Nightmare in Red*, 101–3 and 106–9; R. Alton Lee, "McCarthyism at the University of South Dakota," *South Dakota History* (Fall 1989): 424–38; see also Ellen Schrecker, *No Ivory Tower: McCarthyism and the Universities* (New York: Oxford University Press, 1986).

11. Pennington interview.

12. McGovern to Link, December 13, 1950; April 26 and July 9, 1951; and September 15, 1952, ASLP. J. Edgar Hoover Official and Confidential Files (as cited in chapter 6, note 39), No. 106, memo compiled by M. A. Jones, March 9, 1971, 6, 7, 8, and 9.

13. Robert Griffith, *The Politics of Fear: Joseph R. McCarthy and the Senate* (Lexington: Published for the Organization of American Historians by the University Press of Kentucky, 1970), 48–51; see also, 27–114.

14. Ibid., 48.

15. Michael Schaller, *The U.S. Crusade in China, 1938–1945* (New York: Columbia University Press, 1979), 14.

16. Robert Dallek, *The American Style of Foreign Policy: Cultural Politics and Foreign Affairs* (New York: Knopf, 1983), 143.

17. T. Christopher Jespersen, " 'Spreading the American Dream' of China: United China Relief, the Luce Family, and the Creation of American Conceptions of China before Pearl Harbor," *Journal of American–East Asian Relations* (Fall 1992): 273–88; Fussell, "Hoax," in *Wartime*, 161–63.

18. Schaller, *U.S. Crusade in China*, 3–9, 109–10, and 126–27.

19. Ibid., 53–54, 104–6, 111, and 138; Barbara Tuchman, *Stilwell and the American Experience in China, 1941–1945* (New York: Macmillan, 1971), 322.

20. Schaller, *U.S. Crusade in China*, 130–31, 141, 159–61, 164, and 184–85.

21. Ibid., 295–300.

22. Ibid., 301–3; Lattimore quote, in Owen Lattimore, *The Situation in Asia* (Boston: Little, Brown, 1949), 42. See also Thomas J. Christensen, *Useful Adversaries: Grand Strategy, Domestic Mobilization, and Sino-American Conflict* (Princeton, NJ: Princeton University Press, 1996); Jian Chen, "The Myth of American 'Lost Chance' in China: A Chinese Perspective in Light of New Evidence," *Diplomatic History* (Winter 1997): 77–86; Nancy B. Tucker, "China's Place in the Cold War: The Acheson Plan," in *Dean Acheson and the Making of American Foreign Policy*, ed. Douglas Brinkley (New York: St. Martin's Press, 1993), 109–24.

23. Griffith, *Politics of Fear*, 74–80 and 84–90 (quote, 77).

24. For NSC-68, see Gaddis, *Strategies of Containment*, 68–71, 83–87, and 89–126; LaFeber, *America, Russia, and the Cold War*, 74–98 (Acheson, 98); and Schaller, *U.S. Crusade in China*, 302–5.

25. *Phreno Cosmian*, December 16, 1941; G. McGovern, *Grassroots*, 19; McGovern interview, August 9, 1991. Chiang's Methodism in Jonathan Spence, *The Search for Modern China* (New York: Norton, 1990), 385–86; described scenes in John Wayne's *The Flying Tigers* (1942).

26. Related by Young, interview, January 9, 2000.

27. Akira Iriye, *Across the Pacific: An Inner History of American–East Asian Relations* (New York: Harcourt, Brace and World, 1967), 257–58, for its impact in the United States.

28. Theodore H. White and Annalee Jacoby, *Thunder Out of China* (New York: William Sloane Associates, 1946), xiii, xv–xvi, 256, and 268.

29. Ibid., 228–29, 314, 235–37, and 280.

30. Ibid., 287–89, 290–92, 312, 317, 320, and 324.

31. John K. Fairbank, *The United States and China* (Cambridge, MA: Harvard University Press, 1948), 294–95 and 299–302, and 350. See also Paul M. Evans, *John Fairbank and the American Understanding of China* (New York: B. Blackwell, 1988).

32. Fairbank, *United States and China*, 3, 16, 272, and 310–11.

33. Ibid., 331–32 and 334.

34. Ibid., 310, 335, 337, 337–38, 339–40, and 341.

35. The invasion was the culmination of a struggle between the right-wing dictatorship of Syngman Rhee and the communist dictatorship of Kim Il-sung after the United States and the Soviet Union had arbitrarily divided Korea in 1945. Each hoped to reunify the country under his own rule. The ongoing civil war had already cost the lives of 100,000 Koreans.

36. McGovern to Billington, July 15, 1950, RABP.

37. McGovern to Link, August 19, 1950, ASLP.

38. McGovern to Link, September 30 and August 19, 1950. For McCarran Act, see Fried, *Nightmare in Red*, 116–19, and Griffith, *Politics of Fear*, 117–22.

39. See Christensen, *Useful Adversaries*; Bruce Cumings, *Korea's Place in the Sun: A Modern History* (New York: W. W. Norton, 1997); Michael H. Hunt, "Beijing and the Korean Crisis, June 1950–June 1951," *Political Science Quarterly* (Fall 1992): 457–74; and James I. Matray, "Truman's Plan for Victory: National Self-Determination and the 38th Parallel Decision in Korea," *Journal of American History* (September 1979): 314–33.

40. McGovern to Link, April 26, 1951, ASLP.

41. McGovern to Link, December 13, 1950, ibid.

42. J. Edgar Hoover Official and Confidential Files, No. 106, March 9, 1971, 7–8 and 6.

43. *MDR*, June 18, 1951; McGovern to Link, July 9, 1951, ASLP.

44. See Francis C. Goodell to the editor, *MDR*, June 15, 1951.

45. McGovern to the editor, ibid., June 18, 1951.

46. McGovern to Link, April 26, 1951, ASLP.

47. Author's interview with Barbara Rollins Nemer, October 27, 1998.

48. *Tumbleweed* Yearbook 1951, 93–94; for 1952, 67–69 and 70–72; for 1953, forensics section of yearbook.

49. Nemer interview; *Tumbleweed* (1955), 45; *Phreno Cosmian*, September 16, 1955 (story and editorial on McGovern); McLaird, *Dakota Wesleyan Memory Book*, 177 (quote); McGovern to Link, April 27, 1955, ASLP.

50. *Tumbleweed* (1952), 6; forensics section in 1953 yearbook; and *Phreno Cosmian* editorial, September 16, 1955.

51. McGovern to Link, July 21, 1952; February 24, 1951; and January 12, 1952, ASLP.

52. Ibid., and Goodell to editor, *MDR*, June 15, 1951.

53. Clem, *Prairie State Politics*, 39–40.

54. McGovern to Link, July 21, 1952 (quote); Link to McGovern, October 2 and November 28, 1951, and March 12, 1952; McGovern to Link, March 27, 1952, ASLP.

55. Link to Caldwell, January 12, 1952; Link to Gilmore, June 25, 1952, ASLP; and Billington to Aydelotte, November 2, 1952, RABP.

56. McGovern to Billington, August 30, 1952, and Aydelotte to Billington, March 4, 1953; and McGovern to Link, March 8, 1953.

57. The foregoing paragraphs are based on McGovern interview, October 1, 1991; Griffith, *Politics of Fear*, 143–46 and 191–94; Herbert S. Parmet, *Eisenhower and the American Crusades* (New York: Macmillan, 1972), 131–32; and James T. Patterson, *Grand Expectations: The United States, 1945–1974* (New York: Oxford University Press, 1996), 253–55.

58. Patterson, *Grand Expectations*, 254; Arthur S. Link et al., *The American People: A History*, 2nd ed. (Arlington Heights, IL: Harlan Davidson, 1987), 2: 777; McGovern interview, October 1, 1991; G. McGovern, *Grassroots*, 50.

59. Stevenson quoted in G. McGovern, *Grassroots*, 50; McGovern to Link, July 21, 1952 ASLP; McGovern interview, October 1, 1991.

60. G. McGovern, *Grassroots*, 50; E. McGovern, *Uphill*, 85–86; and G. McGovern, *Terry*, 41 and 49–50.

61. McGovern to Link, January 12 and July 21, 1952, ASLP.

CHAPTER 8   WHAT A LOSS TO HISTORY!

1. On his article see Schlesinger, *A Life in the Twentieth Century* (Boston: Houghton Mifflin, 2000), 509; for "The Vital Center," 504–23. See also *The Vital Center: The Politics of Freedom* (Boston: Houghton Mifflin, 1949), in particular, 38 and 40–46; 120–21 and 189–91; 47–49, 168–69, and 187–88; 213–17; 220–33.

2. If he were writing the book today, he confessed in *A Life in the Twentieth Century* (2000), "I would tone down the rhetoric." He also refers to the federal loyalty program as "hopelessly inadequate" and wishes he had "written more about the dangers of nuclear war" (514, 493–94, and 519–520).

3. G. McGovern, *Grassroots*, 47.

4. *MDR*, October 10, 1952; G. McGovern, *Grassroots*, 50–51.

5. *MDR*, August 13, 1952; G. McGovern, *Grassroots*, 50–51; see also, "W. R. Ronald, Prairie Editor and AAA Architect," *South Dakota History* (Summer 1971): 272–92.

6. *MDR*, August 30, 1952 (emphasis added).

7. Ibid., September 12, 1952.

8. Ibid., September 23, 1952.

9. Ibid.

10. Ibid., October 2, 1952.

11. Ibid.

12. Ibid., October 10, 1952.

13. Ibid.

14. McGovern to Billington, October 18, 1952, RABP.

15. Stevenson quote, *American Heritage Pictorial History of the Presidents of the United States* (New York: American Heritage Publishing, 1968), 2: 922.

16. Adam L. Clem, *South Dakota Political Almanac: A Presentation and Analysis of Election Statistics, 1880–1960* (Governmental Research Bureau, State University of South Dakota, 1962, Report No. 47), 21 and 66–67; Clem, *Prairie State Politics*, 13, 40, and 38–45; McGovern quoted in *SFAL*, November 15, 1956.

17. McGovern to Link, January 12, 1952, ASLP, and G. McGovern, *Grassroots*, 50–51 (quotes). Both McGovern and Anson (*McGovern*, 66–67) incorrectly state that the articles brought him to Clark's attention; Clark had initiated contact long before.

18. Pennington interview; G. McGovern, *Grassroots*, 52–53; and Anson, *McGovern*, 67.

19. E. McGovern, *Uphill*, 86; McGovern to Billington, March 2 and 22, June 8 (quote), 1953, RABP; McGovern to Link, January 6, March 8, July 27, 1953, ASLP; G. McGovern, *Grassroots*, 53; Harbaugh interview.

20. Author's interview with David Kranz, July 28, 1995; McGovern to Billington, June 8, 1953, RABP; and G. McGovern, *Grassroots*, 53.

21. By 1960, South Dakota's population was 680,500. One-third, or 220,500, lived in twelve cities with populations of 5,000 or more: Sioux Falls, 66,500; Rapid City, 42,400; Aberdeen, 23,100; Huron, 14,200; Watertown, 14,100; Mitchell, 12,600; Brookings, 10,500; Pierre, 10,100; Yankton, 9,300; Lead, 6,200; Vermillion, 6,100; and Madison, 5,400. (All but Rapid City were in the East River district.) About 8.5 percent, or 56,800 people, lived in eighteen towns of populations from 2,000 to 4,900. Another 44,300 (6.5 percent) lived in thirty-three towns of 1,000 to 2,000. Fifty-four percent of all South Dakotans—some 368,000—lived in or near towns of under 1,000 people.

22. McGovern to Link, July 27, 1953; G. McGovern, *Grassroots*, 54.

23. G. McGovern, *Grassroots*, 53–54; interviews with George Cunningham, May 21, 1994, and Eleanor McGovern.

24. Cunningham interview; Ecker quoted in Anson, *McGovern*, 69; McGovern to Billington, December 10, 1954.

25. Cunningham interview; Pennington interview; and G. McGovern, *Grassroots*, 57.

26. G. McGovern, *Grassroots*, 57–58.

27. Ibid., 55–56.

28. John E. Miller, "The Failure to Realign: The 1936 Election in South Dakota," *Journal of the West* (Fall 2002): 22–29, and Miller's "McCarthyism before McCarthy: The 1938 Election in South Dakota," *Heritage of the Great Plains* (Summer 1982): 1–21; and Clem, *Prairie State Politics*, 35–39.

29. See Miller, "Failure to Realign," 22 and 28, and Miller's "A Cyclical Model of South Dakota Politics, 1889 to the Present," in the Proceedings of the

Center for Western Studies, *Papers of the 33rd Annual Dakota Conference on History, Literature, and Archaeology*, 482–504 (esp., 490–91).

30. Miller, "Failure to Realign," 25, and "McCarthyism before McCarthy," 12, 13, and 2; see also *SFAL*, September 25 and October 7, 1938.

31. Miller, "Failure to Realign," 25–26.

32. See Miller, "McCarthyism before McCarthy," 2, 4–8, and 13 (quotations); for Mundt on Loriks, see Scott N. Heidepriem, *A Fair Chance for a Free People: Biography of Karl E. Mundt, United States Senator* (Madison, SD: Leader Print, 1988), 22–28. See also Elizabeth E. Williams, *Emil Loriks: Builder of a New Economic Order* (Sioux Falls, SD: Center for Western Studies, 1987).

33. See Fried, *Nightmare in Red*, 131–35 and 141–42, and Griffith, *Politics of Fear*, 243–69 and 270–320; for Mundt travails, see 250–51, 255, 261–62; and for Case's, 295, 308–10, and 316. See also Heidepriem, *A Fair Chance for a Free People*, 171–75, 179–81, 185, and 190–92. McGovern quote on Mundt, in Keynote Address, May 12, 1954, to the North Dakota Democratic State Convention, in the Papers of George S. McGovern, Box 3, Seeley G. Mudd Library, Princeton University, hereinafter cited as GSMP; for Case's resignation, see McGovern to Link, December 28, 1954, ASLP.

34. See Jon E. Lauck, "George S. McGovern and the Farmer: South Dakota Politics, 1953–1962," *South Dakota History* (Winter 2003): 331–53; Allen J. Matusow, *Farm Policies and Politics in the Truman Years* (Cambridge, MA: Harvard University Press, 1967); and Thomas G. Ryan, "Farm Prices and the Farm Vote in 1948," *Agricultural History* (July 1980): 389.

35. Lauck, "McGovern and the Farmer," 336–37; Link and Catton, *American Epoch*, 744–45.

36. Address to the North Dakota Democratic Convention, May 12, 1954, cited above; Lauck, "McGovern and the Farmer," 337 and 337n12 and 13.

37. McGovern to Billington, December 20, 1954, RABP; McGovern to William Blair, August 18, 1954, Box 54, Papers of Adlai E. Stevenson, Seeley G. Mudd Library, Princeton University (hereinafter Stevenson Papers); and Heidepriem, *A Fair Chance for a Free People*, 192–94.

38. Heidepriem, *A Fair Chance for a Free People*, 117 and 194; G. McGovern, *Grassroots*, 58–59; McGovern to Blair, cited above.

39. McGovern to Billington, December 20, 1954, RABP; and McGovern to Link, December 28, 1954 and April 27, 1955, ASLP; Cunningham interview; McGovern interview, October 1, 1991.

40. See *SFAL*, October 14 (League of Women Voters survey); November 4, 5 (Lovre advertisement), and "The Voters Speak," November 7, 1956.

41. Lovre quoted in Anson, *McGovern*, 76; *Brookings Register* (hereinafter *BR*) and *SFAL* quoted in campaign brochure ("What the Editors Say about George McGovern"); and *SFAL*, October 21, 1956.

42. G. McGovern, *Grassroots*, 63–65.

43. Anson, *McGovern*, 74; Cunningham interview; *Watertown Public Opinion*, in McGovern campaign brochure cited above.

44. G. McGovern, *Grassroots*, 66–67.

45. Ibid., 67–68.

46. Author's interview with Peter Stavrianos, March 27, 1996; Cunningham interview; Anson, *McGovern*, 79–80.

47. G. McGovern, *Grassroots*, 69; and "Peace and Politics," script of television address by McGovern, August 26, 1956, copy in private collection of Judge Richard Maranos of Hartford, Connecticut.

48. "Peace and Politics," script; *SFAL*, September 4, 1956.

49. *SFAL*, August 10 and 14, 1956.

50. *SFAL*, August 14 and 16, and October 21, 1956.

51. See *SFAL* for: Truman's remarks, August 16; Stevenson speech, September 14; Nixon and Mundt on Truman's defense of Hiss, September 6, 18, and 23, 1956; *MDR* editorial, September 15, 1956; Link and Catton, *American Epoch*, 735.

52. *SFAL*, September 4 and 15, 1956, quotes, respectively; and Aug. 19, 1956.

53. *SFAL*, August 19 and 29, and September 12, 1956.

54. *SFAL*, September 5, 6, and 11, 1956.

55. *MDR*, September 7; *SFAL*, September 23 and 26, 1956. The meaning of parity was ably summed up in an *Argus Leader* editorial (September 24) on the Soil Bank: "What the farmer wants is a farm dollar that is in harmony with the city dollar. Whatever the outcome, let's not forget for one minute that cities are dependent upon farm income. If the farmers do well, the towns and cities do well. If the farmers don't do well, they don't."

56. Letters in the *SFAL*, October 2 and 23; *MDR*, September 15, 1956.

57. *SFAL*, September 30, and October 2, 1956.

58. *SFAL*, September 26, 1956.

59. *SFAL* and *MDR*, both September 29, 1956.

60. *MDR*, October 3, 6, 8, 9, and 10, 1956.

61. *MDR*, October 10, 15, and 17, and November 2; letters to the editor, October 9, 15, 17, 18, 1956.

62. Eleanor McGovern interview, October 27, 1995; E. McGovern, *Uphill*, 90–91.

63. Cunningham interview, May 21, 1994; *SFAL*, October 16, 1956.

64. *SFAL*, October 21, 1956.

65. *SFAL*, October 11, 15, 17, and 30, and November 3, 1956.

66. *SFAL*, September 21 and October 17 and 31, 1956.

67. *SFAL*, September 27 and 30, 1956.

68. *SFAL*, October 31 and November 1, 1956.

69. *SFAL*, October 23 and 29, 1956.

70. *SFAL*, October 23; letters to editor, October 24, 29, and 22, 1956.

71. *SFAL*, November 1, 1956.

72. Letter to editor, *SFAL*, November 1; and for polls, November 3 and 4, 1956; Robert J. Donovan, *Eisenhower: The Inside Story* (New York: Harper, 1956), 132. Based on interviews with cabinet members and White House staff, *The Inside Story* is probably the best contemporary account of Eisenhower's first term. In the 1980s Donovan would write a well-regarded two-volume study of Truman's presidency.

73. *MDR*, November 6 and 7, 1956.

74. *MDR*, November 7 and 8, 1956; final results in Clem, *South Dakota Political Almanac*, 30 and 70–71; see also Clem, *Prairie State Politics*, 41; in the national

election, Ike trounced Adlai by 35,582,000 popular votes to 26,028,000 (a margin of 57 percent) and by 457 to 73 in the Electoral College, but never before had the Republican Party won the White House while losing both houses of Congress. The 85th Congress would have forty-nine Democrats and forty-seven Republicans in the Senate and 234 Democrats and 201 Republicans in the House. Link and Catton, *American Epoch*, 735–37.

75. Interviews with Eleanor McGovern, Pennington, and Cunningham; McGovern and editorial in *SFAL*, November 7, 1956.

76. *SFAL*, November 7 and 16, 1956; see also John Mark Hansen, *Gaining Access: Congress and the Farm Lobby, 1919–1981* (Chicago: University of Chicago Press, 1991), 138–40.

77. Eleanor McGovern interview.

78. McGovern to Link, November 26, 1956, ASLP; G. McGovern, *Grassroots*, 31; Alfred Young interview; *MDR*, March 26, 1957, and Raymond, *SFAL*, November 15, 1956.

79. Raymond, *SFAL*, November 15, 1956, quote.

80. E. McGovern, *Uphill*, 91.

CHAPTER 9   WASHINGTON, DC

1. G. McGovern, *Grassroots*, 71; Howard Gillette Jr., *Between Beauty and Justice: Race, Planning, and the Failure of Urban Policy in Washington, D.C.* (Baltimore: Johns Hopkins University Press, 1995), 127–48; John Thompson, *Washington, D.C.*, 3rd ed. (Washington, DC: National Geographic Society, 2008); *Washington Post and Times Herald* entertainment section, December 20–23 and 25–27, 1956; January 5 and 20–22 and February 7–11 and 18, 1957; G. McGovern, *Terry*, 57 and 59.

2. Dan Cohen, *Undefeated: The Life of Hubert H. Humphrey* (Minneapolis: Lerner Publications, 1978), 141–44.

3. *Time*, January 17, 1949, 16, quoted in Cohen, *Undefeated*, 149 and 158; Griffith, *Politics of Fear*, 119–21 and 291–94; Carl Solberg, *Hubert Humphrey: A Biography* (New York: Norton, 1984), 115–23 and 157–59; Robert A. Caro, *The Years of Lyndon Johnson: Master of the Senate* (New York: Alfred Knopf, 2002), 453–62.

4. Interviews with Eleanor and Ann McGovern; G. McGovern, *Terry*, 54–55; Link to author, unrecorded conversation; Arthur M. Schlesinger Jr., *Journals, 1952–2000*, ed. Andrew Schlesinger and Steven Schlesinger (New York: Penguin Press, 2007), 136; Mary McGovern interview; HHH to McGovern, November 8, 1956, and McGovern to HHH, November 27, 1956, Box 501, George S. McGovern Papers, Seeley Mudd Library, Princeton University (hereinafter GSMP); "Good Neighbors," *WP*, September 2, 1964.

5. G. McGovern, *Grassroots*, 75; author's interview with Patricia J. Donovan, April 9, 1997.

6. Author's interview with Patricia J. Donovan; Donovan obituary, *WP*, January 28, 2008; and G. McGovern, *Grassroots*, 76.

7. The Committee on Education and Labor, chaired by Graham Barden of North Carolina, had a membership of thirty, including Adam Clayton Powell of

New York, the first African American congressman since Reconstruction; Stewart Udall of Arizona, the future secretary of the interior; and James Roosevelt of California, FDR's son who had also served as his aide.

8. "Education Post," *MDR*, January 19, 1957; Caro, *Master of the Senate*, 124, 157–58; Nancy Beck Young, *Wright Patman: Populism, Liberalism, and the American Dream* (Dallas: Southern Methodist University Press, 2000), 104–6; Robert V. Remini, *The House: The History of the House of Representatives* (New York: Smithsonian Books in association with HarperCollins, 2006), 341 (Powell quote); and D. B. Hardeman, *Rayburn: A Biography* (Austin: Texas Monthly Press, 1987), 389–91 (LBJ).

9. See Link and Catton, *American Epoch*, 744–45.

10. Ibid., and "Corn Support" and "90% Parity," *MDR*, January 26 and 30, 1957; see also Jon E. Lauck, "George S. McGovern and the Farmer: South Dakota Politics, 1953–1962," *South Dakota History* (Winter 2003): 341–42.

11. See *CR*, February 21, 1957, 2438–49 (quotations, 2438). McGovern's HR 3987, ibid., January 29, 1957, 1223; see also "Cover Up," *MDR*, February 21, 1957.

12. *CR*, February 21, 1957, 2439.

13. Ibid., 2440.

14. Ibid., 2440, 2443, 2444–45, and 2449; Carroll Kilpatrick, *Washington Post and Times Herald*, March 11, 1957; Yeager, "McGovern," *SFAL*, February 27, 1957.

15. John Mark Hansen, *Gaining Access: Congress and the Farm Lobby, 1919–1981* (Chicago: University of Chicago Press, 1991), 129–35; and "Leaders Battle," *MDR*, January 26, 1957.

16. *CR*, March 5, 1957, 3266–93 (Knutson, 3287–88).

17. Ibid., 3267–81 and 3290–91.

18. Ibid.

19. Ibid., 3284 and 3287; McGovern's amendment, 3287; and "Corn Support," *MDR*, March 6, 1957.

20. *CR*, March 5, 1957, 3287.

21. Ibid., 3287–90; McGovern to Clark, March 18, 1957, GSMP, Box 40; Kilpatrick, "Corn and the '58 Vote," *WP*, March 11, 1957; and "McGovern Impressing" and "Frustrated Man," *MDR*, March 26 and April 11, 1957; *MDR*, "Farm Compromise" and Benson editorial, March 8 and 9, 1957; *Minneapolis Tribune* quoted in campaign brochure, "One Good Term Deserves Another," author's private collection; McGovern interview, October 1, 1991; and "House Votes Down" and "Corn Bill," *SFAL*, March 16 and 25, 1957.

22. All in *MDR*: "Corn Support," January 26; "90% Parity," January 30; "Audit Soil Bank," February 9; "Probe of Prices," March 6; "Durum Signup," March 6; "Farmer on Spot," May 10; and "Egg Supports," June 6; "L'Affair Benson" and "Egg-Thrower," November 1 and 6, 1957.

23. "Farm Plan," *MDR*, February 25, 1958; Lauck, "George S. McGovern and the Farmer," 343n37; *CR*, February 27, 1958, 3063–69, especially 3066. McGovern's resembled the plan of Secretary of Agriculture Charles Brannan in 1949; see Reo M. Christenson, *The Brannan Plan: Farm Politics and Policy* (Ann Arbor: University of Michigan Press, 1959); and Hamby, *Beyond the New Deal*, 303–10.

24. *CR*, March 20, 1958, 4916–17; "McGovern Cites," *MDR*, March 22, 1958.

25. McGovern quotes, "Ag Bill 'Poor,' " in *MDR*, July 28, 1958, and *CR*, February 27, 1958, 3064; "Bill 'Bad, Dangerous' " (HHH), *MDR*, July 15, 1958. For final bill, see *MDR*, July 15 and 28, August 9, 11, 14 and 28, 1958; Link and Catton, *American Epoch*, 745.

26. "Ike's Mideast" and "Demo Revision," in *MDR*, January 30 and February 14, 1957; McGovern interview, October 1 1991, and G. McGovern, *Grassroots*, 92 (HHH and GSM quotes). See also George C. Herring, *From Colony to Superpower: U.S. Foreign Relations since 1776* (New York: Oxford University Press, 2008), 677–78; and Douglas Little, *American Orientalism: The United States and the Middle East since 1945* (Chapel Hill: University of North Carolina Press, 2004), 127–36. See also Stephen Kinzer, *All the Shah's Men: An American Coup and the Roots of Middle Eastern Terrorism* (Hoboken, NJ: J. Wiley and Sons, 2003); for the New Look, Gaddis, *Strategies of Containment*, 127–97.

27. *CR*, January 31, 1957, 1368, including piece on Saud in *Aberdeen American News* (hereinafter *AAN*), January 20, 1957; see also, "To See Ike," *MDR*, January 21, 1957.

28. "McGovern's Stand," *MDR*, February 2, 1957; LaFeber, *America, Russia, and the Cold War*, 195 (public opinion); "Little Hope," "Proper Question," "Mideast Resolution," and "Foreign Aid," *SFAL*, February 22 and 25, March 7, and April 1, 1957; G. McGovern, *Grassroots*, 92.

29. "Honor for McGovern," *MDR*, April 9, 1957.

30. See LaFeber, *America, Russia, and the Cold War*, Herring, *From Colony to Superpower*, and Little, *American Orientalism*; and "U.S. to Bolster," "McGovern Ends Tour," and "Meets Malik," *MDR*, April 25 and May 2 and 8, 1957; Drew Pearson and "Food for Peace," *MDR*, May 24 and September 4, 1957; *CR*, January 27, 1958, 1101.

31. McGovern to Link, August 19, 1950, ASLP.

32. "Cut in Budget," "Military Waste," and "Farm Problem," *MDR*, June 1 and 7 and July 15, 1957.

33. See "Ike Scales Down," "Ike Pleads," "House Bill," "McGovern Vote," *MDR*, May 9 and 21, July 21, and August 15, 1957. The original $3.9 billion request earmarked all but $1 billion for military aid.

34. "Food for Peace," "Farm-Labor," "McGovern at REA," *MDR*, September 4, 9, and 11, 1957.

35. *CR*, January 27, 1958, 1101.

36. Ibid., March 29, 1957, 4815–16.

37. Ibid., 4816–17.

38. Ibid., April 3, 1957, 5022–23 and 5026–27.

39. Dixon of Utah, ibid., July 24, 1957, 12602–06; Gallup report, *WP*, February 10, 1957; Link and Catton, *American Epoch*, 749.

40. *CR*, July 24, 1957, 12587–89 and 12594–95.

41. Ibid., 12614–17; see also 12618–25 and 12634–37.

42. Ibid., 12595–96 and 12602; "School Construction," *MDR*, February 1, 1957; Link and Catton, *American Epoch*, 749–51.

43. *CR*, July 25, 1957, 12722–23 and 12751–54; July 24, 12,615; "School Aid," *MDR*, July 27, 1957; Drew Pearson, *MDR*, July 29 and August 15, 1957.

44. LaFeber, *America, Russia, and the Cold War*, 201–3, and Stephen E. Ambrose, *Eisenhower: Soldier and President* (New York: Simon and Schuster, 1990), 449–54 and 459–63.

45. "National Policies," "SD Teachers," and "Satellite Lag," *MDR*, November 5, 8, and 13, 1957, and other reports, October 10, 23, and 26 and November 6 and 9, 1957; "Humphrey Calls," November 30, 1957; and "Missiles," January 4, 1958.

46. *New York Times* (hereinafter *NYT*), November 14 and 30 and December 30, 1957 on Ike; and "Solons Say," *MDR*, January 2, 1958.

47. See materials in GSMP, Box 39; in *CR*: McGovern's remarks, March 6 and August 8, 1958, 3622 and 16690–99; Fulbright's, March 20, 1958, 4955–56; Elliott's, August 5, 1958, 16301; and "Scholarships," *MDR*, June 25, 1958; McGovern interview, October 1, 1991.

48. *CR*, August 8, 1958, 16690–92, 16713–15, and 16744.

49. Ibid., 16689–91; Wells quote, 16689.

50. Ibid., 16691, 16694–95, and 16698.

51. Ibid., 16744–47, 16702, and 16715–17.

52. Ibid., August 23, 1958, 19595–97, 19607, and 19614 (quotes, 19597).

53. Ibid., 19615–16 and 19617–18.

54. See materials in GSMP, Box 39; "Indians" and "Benefit Deaf," *MDR*, July 25 and August 16, 1958; H.R. 12670 (Indians), and H.R. 13678 (Deaf), *CR*, 9413 and 16288, May 23 and August 5, 1958; Hasselstrom, *Roadside History of South Dakota*, 130–31; Schell, *History of South Dakota*, 305–7.

55. See H.R. 13252, 13290, and 13757, *CR*, July 1, July 3, and August 13, 1958, 12872, 13019, and 17479; and "McGovern's Efforts," *MDR*, August 23, 1958.

56. Link and Catton, *American Epoch*, 593–95; "Labor Bill," *MDR*, June 25, 1958; *CR*, August 6, 1958, 16462–69. The bill required public disclosure of union finances, criminal sanctions for embezzlement of union funds, and secret ballots for the election of officers. It also required employers to report to the secretary of labor expenditures over $5,000 intended to influence employees regarding their right to bargain collectively and prohibited them from bribing employees regarding that right.

57. "Reform Legislation," "McGovern Fights," and "Snowstorm," *MDR*, July 15 and August 12 and 15, 1958; "McGovern and Udall," *MDR*, August 16, 1958; and Doris Fleeson, *MDR*, June 26, 1958. McGovern quote in interview, April 24, 1964, for the Oral History Project, John F. Kennedy Library and Museum (hereinafter JFKL); see also, McGovern interview, July 16, 1970, Robert F. Kennedy Oral History Project, JFKL. Clare Hoffman in *CR*, August 18, 1958, 18267.

58. *CR*, August 6, 1958, 16463–64 and 16468–69; and August 18, 1958, 18266–88, in particular, 18266–67, 18270–71, and 18285–88. "Sorry Show," *Washington Evening Star*, and "Labor Reform," *Christian Science Monitor*, both August 20, 1958; "Compromise," "McGovern Mundt," and "Good Fight," *MDR*, July 15 and August 19 and 20, 1958; McGovern interview, April 24, 1964, JFKL.

59. "Bright Young Men in Politics," *Esquire*, September 1958, 35–37. The other Democrats were Frank Church, Bobby Baker, Robert Kennedy, and Jim Wright.

CHAPTER 10 THE APOSTLE OF AGRICULTURE, EDUCATION, AND PEACE

1. Anson, *McGovern*, 87; Joe Foss with Donna Wild Foss, *A Proud American: The Autobiography of Joe Foss* (New York: Simon and Shuster, 1992), 108–204; "Foss Won't Run" and "Foss to Run," *MDR*, September 3, 1957, and January 3 1958; *Current Biography Yearbook 1955* (New York: H. W. Wilson, 1955), 211–12.

2. Foss and Foss, *Proud American*, 219–57; "Profile of Foss," in Louis Harris Associates, *A Study of the Race for United States Senator in South Dakota*, December 1961, p. 14, GSMP, Box 59; "Budgets to Blame," "Answers Foss," and "The Story Told," *SFAL*, October 23 and November 2 and 8, 1956.

3. See *MDR*: "Trade Political Blows," "McCormack," "Rhodes, Morrell," "Rhodes Charges," "Headline Hunting," June 12 and 25 and July 2, 15, and 20, 1957.

4. Martz files in Box 40 and 915, GSMP; "McGovern Files Suit," "Running Scared," "Mundt Denies," and "Rhodes against 2-Party," *MDR*, August 14 and September 3, 5, and 13, 1958; and Moulder in *CR*, July 2, 1958, 12988; "Attacks Smear," "More Ethics," "Martz Counters," and "McGovern Welcomes," *MDR*, August 22 and 27 and September 12 and 16, 1958; Hoover Confidential File, No. 106, memo by Jones, March 9, 1971, 9.

5. McGovern to Link, September 10, 1958, ASLP; "Rhodes Willing," "Foss: McGovern Backed," and "Share Platform," *MDR*, September 11 (2) and 12, 1958.

6. See Heidepriem, *A Fair Chance for a Free People*, 210–20 (quote, 219); Christopherson, *SFAL*, April 8, 1958. See also Nelson Lichtenstein, *The Most Dangerous Man in Detroit: Walter Reuther and the Fate of American Labor* (New York: Basic Books, 1995).

7. See Heidepriem, *A Fair Chance for a Free People*, 213.

8. "Ludlow Massacre of 1914," *CR*, April 11, 1957, 5539; interaction with labor, see GSMP, Box 39, 40, and 47; and McGovern interview, April 24, 1964, JFKL.

9. See materials in GSMP, Box 39; see also *MDR* editorials, "Unjustified Implications" and "Campaign Spending," September 13 and 15, 1958; and "Mundt Switched," "Foss Crusade," "McGovern, Foss," "Foss Opposed," and "Not Sympathetic," *MDR*, September 12, 16, 18, and 20 and October 10, 1958; "McGovern Says," *SFAL*, October 14, 1958; and "McGovern Not Indebted," *Watertown Public Opinion*, October 10, 1958.

10. "Foss For Benson," *MDR*, September 19, 1958; and "McGovern Says Ag," *SFAL*, October 2, 1958.

11. "Hurl Charges," *SFAL*, October 7, 1958; and "Fire Salvos," "To Harm Economy," and "McGovern, Foss Stand," *MDR*, October 7, 11, and 25, 1958.

12. "Foss Opposed," "Joint Appearance," and "Foss Indifferent," *MDR*, August 22, September 18 and 22, 1958; "McGovern Takes Issue," *SFAL*, October 3, 1958.

13. SD Poll, *SFAL*, October 15, 1958 (cosponsored by *AAN* and *WPO*); Eleanor McGovern interview, October 27, 1995; G. McGovern, *Grassroots*, 80, and Anson, *McGovern*, 88.

14. "Foss Says Labor," *MDR*, October 26, 1958; see letters to the editor in October and "Labor Argument" and "McGovern Says Foss," *MDR*, October 23, 25, and 28, 1958.

15. "McGovern: GOP" and "GOP Conducting," *MDR*, October 14 and 15, 1958; "Beware of Spooks" and "GOP Repeating," *SFAL*, November 1 and 2, 1958; "Foss as Front," *AAN*, October 17, 1958.

16. "Foss Critical" and "Not Security Expert," *MDR*, October 23 and 29, 1958; "Foss Says Return," *AAN*, October 23, 1958; October 26, 1958; "Crowd Hears Nixon" and "Ike Endorses," *SFAL*, October 26 and 30, 1958. Pearson, "Plotter Mundt," and "Nixon Calling Demos 'Radicals,'" *MDR*, October 26 and 27, 1958.

17. "Humphrey Says," "Praises McGovern," and "Business for McGovern," *MDR*, September 22 and October 17, and October 25, 1958; "Sen. Church," *SFAL*, October 26, 1958.

18. "A Second Term," *MDR*, October 31, 1958.

19. Examples in *MDR*, October 30 and November 1, 1958.

20. "Herseth, McGovern," *SFAL*, November 2, 1958; Anson, *McGovern*, 89, Foss, *Proud American*, 256.

21. McGovern to Link, November 16, 1958, ASLP.

22. Clem, *South Dakota Political Almanac*, 72–73, and Clem, *Prairie State Politics*, 41 and 109; "Democrat Sweep" and "Demos Win Senate," *MDR*, November 5 and 6, 1958; "Demos Control" and "Democrat Victory," *SFAL*, November 6 and December 15, 1958; and "McGovern Sees Chance," *MDR*, December 18, 1957. Fite to McGovern, December 5, 1958, GSMP, Box 40.

23. "Turnout Heavy" and "Demos Grab," *SFAL*, November 4 and 5, 1958; "McGovern Tops," "Smears Repudiated," and "Mundt a Loser," *MDR*, November 5, 6, and 11, 1958.

24. See, all in *MDR*, "McGovern Thanks," November 5; and "Farmers' Group" and "GOP Bosses," both November 3; and "Drive Chairman," letter to editor, December 9, 1958.

25. See Link and Catton, *American Epoch*, 737–38; Hansen, *Gaining Access: Congress and the Farm Lobby, 1919–1981*, 141–43; and "Sharp Gains" and "Senate Control," *MDR*, both November 5, 1958; "Demos Gain," *SFAL*, November 6, 1958. Fite to McGovern, December 5, 1958, GSMP, Box 40.

26. Ambrose, *Eisenhower*, 471–74; "Ike Says," *MDR*, November 5, 1958; in *U.S. News and World Report*, "Eisenhower vs. Congress," January 2, 1959, 26–27, and "'Conservatives' on Top," January 23, 1959, 62 and 64.

27. Remini, *The House: The History of the House*, 374–75 and 366–82. Leaders of the group included Lee Metcalf of Montana; George Rhodes of Pennsylvania; Frank Thompson Jr., of New Jersey; and Henry Reuss of Wisconsin. See their letter to Melvin Price, November 14, and to "Dear Colleague," December 2, 1958, outlining their concerns and plans; a fourteen-page memo, "A New Liberalism" (undated, ca. January 1959); and Robert Kastenmeier to McGovern, July 25, and McGovern to Kastenmeier, July 27, 1959, with *Time* clipping, all in McGovern Papers, Box 40. See also "Demo Liberals" and Doris Fleeson's column, "Liberalization," in *MDR*, both on December 9, 1958; "Interview Rayburn," *U.S. News*, December 19, 1958, 41–43; "Fight in Congress," *U.S. News*,

January 16, 1959, 33–35; and "Conservatives on Top," *U.S. News*, January 23, 1959, 62 and 64.

28. See Robert Griffith's "Dwight D. Eisenhower and the Corporate Commonwealth," *American Historical Review* (February 1982): 87–122.

29. "NATO Meet," "175 Attend," and "Farmers Views," *MDR*, November 10 and December 11 and 13, 1958; "McGovern," *SFAL*, September 4, 1956.

30. "McGovern Offers," "McGovern Wins," and editorial, "SD Farm," *MDR*, January 7, 16, and 17, 1959; Hansen, *Gaining Access*, 143n.71.

31. Gilbert C. Fite, *American Farmers: The New Minority* (Bloomington: Indiana University Press, 1981), 87, 88, 110–12, 115–16, and 126–27.

32. Ibid., 103, 107, 109, and 133; "Family Farm," *CR*, February 10, 1960, 2379.

33. "Washington Report," February 21, 1919, *CR*, April 10, 1959, 5707; McGovern in *CR*, March 4, 9, and 24, 1959, 3252, 3601, and 5104; "Farm Program," "Benson Reversal," and "Measure by McGovern," *SFAL*, March 2, 15, and 24, 1959; and "McGovern Sees," *MDR*, February 24, 1959.

34. "Agriculture," *CR*, May 25, 1959, 9046, and "McGovern Criticism," *MDR*, August 1, 1959.

35. See in *MDR*, "McGovern Asks," "Ike's Veto," "Case and Mundt," and "Government by Veto" (quote), March 9 and April 23, 29 and 30, 1959.

36. Fite, *American Farmers*, 1, 130–31 and 133–34.

37. *NYT*, March 9, 1960; "Little Hope," *MDR*, January 6, 1959; *CR*, March 9, 1960, 4805; floor debate, "Family Farm," *CR*, February 10, 1960, 2378–80 and February 18, 1960, 2928–41; and Box 54, GSMP.

38. See Thomas J. Knock, "Feeding the World and Thwarting the Communists: George McGovern and Food for Peace," in *Architects of the American Century: Individuals and Institutions in Twentieth Century U.S. Foreign Policymaking*, ed. David F. Schmitz and T. Christopher Jespersen (Chicago: Imprint Publications, 2000), 98–120; Peter A. Toma, *The Politics of Food for Peace: Executive-Legislative Interaction* (Tucson: University of Arizona Press, 1967), 39–42; and Vernon W. Ruttan, *United States Development Assistance Policy: The Domestic Politics of Foreign Economic Aid* (Baltimore: Johns Hopkins University Press, 1996), 55, 70–72, 152–56.

39. "FFP Resolution," *CR*, January 29, 1959, 1410–12; "FFP," *MDR*, January 29, 1959.

40. "FFP Act," *CR*, April 20, 1959, 6324–27; "Washington Report," May 25, 1959, *CR*, June 9, 1959, 10353–54. Humphrey's bill (S. 1711) and speech, in *CR*, April 16, 1959, 6119–31, as well as Ruttan, *United States Development Assistance Policy*, 156–59, and Toma, *Politics of Food for Peace*, 41–43. House PL 480 debate, *CR*, August 19 and 20, 1959, 16404–33 and 16552–88; McGovern interview, October 1, 1991.

41. *MDR*, "FFP Plan" and "Surplus Disposal," February 4 and September 25, 1959.

42. Sorensen to McGovern, November 17, and McGovern to Sorensen, December 9, 1958; and McGovern to Humphrey, January 30, 1959, all in GSMP, Box 40. "McGovern Strongly," *MDR*, June 24, 1959; McGovern interview, October 1, 1991; McGovern's interview, April 24, 1964, JFKL; author's interview with John

Kenneth Galbraith, May 7, 1996; "Kennedy May Risk," *Huron Daily Plainsman* (hereinafter *HDP*), July 26, 1959; Roosevelt in Solberg, *Hubert Humphrey*, 195.

43. Food Administration Act, *CR*, April 20, 1959, 9492; McGovern's "Farm Program," *CR*, September 9, 1959, 18,857–59.

44. McGovern interview, October 1, 1991; "Labor Reform," *MDR*, January 14, 1959.

45. "Senate Labor," *SFAL*, March 26, 1959; "McGovern Is Sponsor" and "McGovern Again," *MDR*, April 29 and July 20, 1959; *CR*, July 16, 1959, 13635–57 (quote, 13636).

46. "Labor-Management Reporting and Disclosure Act," *CR*, August 13, 1959, 15824–70 (vote and quotes, 15859–61); "Ike Calls" and "McGovern/ Berry," *MDR*, April 28 and August 14, 1959.

47. *CR*, August 13, 1959, 15866–67; "McGovern/Berry Labor," *MDR*, September 5, 1959.

48. "How McGovern," *SFAL*, August 25, 1959, and "McGovern on Side," *AAN*, August 27, 1959.

49. "Labor Reform," "Editor Denies," "Rhodes," and "McGovern Blast," *MDR*, August 26, 27, 28, and 29, 1959.

50. "Aid to Education," in *MDR*, March 16, 1959; "Appropriations Bill, 1959," *CR*, March 24, 1959, 5086–92.

51. *CR*, March 24, 1959, 5091–92.

52. McGovern's remarks in *CR*, April 30, 1959, 7222; "McGovern Asks," *MDR*, April 17, 1959; and press release on Library Services, GSMP, Box 54.

53. The fourteen were Denmark, Norway, France, Italy, Spain, Greece, Turkey, Iran, Pakistan, Japan, South Korea, the Republic of China, the Philippines, and South Vietnam.

54. "$3.9 Billion," *SFAL*, and "Ike Requests," *MDR*, both March 13, 1959; Randall Woods, *Fulbright: A Biography* (New York: Cambridge University Press, 1995), 237–39; Mutual Security Act, *CR*, June 17, 1959, 11119–20, 1122–23, and 11127.

55. *CR*, 11126; see also "Inside Story of Iraq," *U.S. News and World Report*, December 26, 1958, 46.

56. *CR*, June 17, 1959, 11126–27. George Meador, Michigan Democrat, then cited a report that showed "overspending actually harmed our objectives in Laos." The United States had forced more assistance on Laos "than its economy could absorb," and communists had exploited scandals about the "nefarious activities" of the wealthy few (11128).

57. *CR*, June 17, 1959, 11129; "Foreign Military Aid," "McGovern For," and "President Signs," *MDR*, June 22 and July 23 and 24, 1959.

58. "Dangers of Nuclear Conflict," *CR*, July 2, 1959, 12630. The other recipients were Great Britain, France, Germany, Holland, Greece, and Canada.

59. "Top Demos Say," *MDR*, January 5, 1959; Ambrose, *Eisenhower*, 470–71 and 478–79.

60. *CR*, July 2, 1959, 12630; Herring, *From Colony to Superpower*, 696–97 and 700; and Gaddis, *Strategies of Containment*, 181–87.

61. "Head Start" and "Busy Week," *MDR*, July 14 and October 13, 1959; "Poll Predicts," *HDP*, October 13, 1959.

62. Alexandr Fursenko and Timothy Naftali, *Khrushchev's Cold War: The Inside Story of an American Adversary* (New York: Norton, 2006), 214–40; for Garst story, 236–39.

63. "Cold War Shifting," *MDR*, October 10, 1959; "Addresses PTA," *BR*, October 18, 1959; "McGovern Stresses," *Centerville Journal*, October 22, 1959.

64. "Food for Peace," *Centerville Journal*, October 22, 1959; "McGovern Sees," *HDP*, October 21, 1959; "McGovern Surplus," *Edgemont News*, October 15, 1959; and "Can Aid Peace," *MDR*, October 27, 1959.

65. "Demo Chairmen," *MDR*, November 5, 1959.

66. "McGovern Bid," *MDR*, January 6, 1960; see also *SFAL, AAN, Salem Special*, and Vermillion *Plain Talk*, all on January 7, 1960.

67. *MDR* and others reprinted Shannon's "Into the Badlands" on January 8, 1960; see also Yeager, "With Whom Does the Tide Turn," *SFAL*, January 10, 1960; "McGovern and Mundt," *Mobridge Tribune*, January 7, 1960.

CHAPTER 11 THE QUEST FOR THE SENATE

1. Eleanor McGovern interview.

2. E. McGovern, *Uphill*, 91–95.

3. E. McGovern, *Uphill*, 97–99 and 100–101; Eleanor McGovern interview; Ann McGovern interview; McGovern to Link, June 12 and July 23, 1957, and Link to McGovern, June 17 and July 23 and 29, 1957, ASLP.

4. E. McGovern, *Uphill*, 97–99 and 100–101; Eleanor McGovern interview; Ann McGovern interview; McGovern to Link, June 12 and July 23, 1957, and Link to McGovern, June 17 and July 23, 1957, ASLP.

5. E. McGovern, *Uphill*, 98, 99, 101, and 102; Ann McGovern and Susan McGovern Rowen interviews; and G. McGovern, *Grassroots*, 72 (see also, 71–74).

6. E. McGovern, *Uphill*, 102; Eleanor McGovern interview.

7. In February 1958, Mundt wrote privately that if Joe Foss lost, "McGovern will then probably decide to take a shot at me in '60, so we have been watching the records and writing down the facts accordingly." Mundt to Foss, February 4, 1958, quoted in Heidepriem, *A Fair Chance for a Free People*, 228.

8. G. McGovern, *Grassroots*, 80; "Editorially Speaking," *Lake Preston Times*, January 7, 1960; "McGovern Mundt," *Milbank Review*, and *SFAL* editorial, both quoted in "Political Talk" in *AAN*, January 10, 1960; "McGovern and Mundt," *Mobridge Tribune*, January 7, 1960; "Political Pie," *Lemmon Leader*, January 7, 1960; "The Courageous McGovern," *BR*, January 10, 1960; "Exciting Contest" and "State Could Lose," *HDP*, January 17 and 24, 1960. The foregoing stories can be found in Scrapbook 99 in the Papers of Karl Mundt, Dakota State University (hereinafter KMP).

9. See Jon K. Lauck, "Binding Assumptions: Karl E. Mundt and the Vietnam War, 1953–1969," *Mid-America* (Fall 1994): 279–309; R. Alton Lee, " 'New Dealers, Fair Dealers, Misdealers and Hiss Dealers': Karl Mundt and the Internal Security Act of 1950," *South Dakota History* (Fall 1980): 277–90, and Lee's "McCarthyism at the University of South Dakota," *South Dakota History* (Fall 1989): 424–38. See also "Mundt Distrusts," in *MDR*, January 16, 1960; letter

to editor, "Loyalty Oath," *MDR*, January 28, 1960. In his *The Budget, 1961*, p. M57, Eisenhower states that the "requirement is unwarranted and justifiably resented by a large part of our educational community." McGovern commends him for recognizing "oaths of this kind have no place in the American tradition," GSMP, Box 54; McGovern to Link, September 30, 1950, ASLP.

10. Author's interviews with David Kranz, May 1995; Pat Donovan, April 9, 1997; and George Cunningham, May 21, 1994.

11. Cunningham interview; *MDR* reprinted Shannon's "Into the Badlands" on January 8, 1960.

12. For analysis of McGovern-Mundt poll (conducted by the *SFAL*, *AAN*, and *WPO*), see *MDR* editorial, January 15, 1960; "Farm Issue," *MDR*, January 20, 1960.

13. Heidepriem, *A Fair Chance for a Free People*, 131–35; Jon Lauck, "Prairie Roots: Francis Case, George McGovern, Karl Mundt, and the Food for Peace Initiative," *Papers of the Twenty-Sixth Annual Dakota History Conference* (Center for Western Studies and the South Dakota Humanities Council," 1994), 395–406.

14. *SFAL*, January 12, 1960 (examples of reprints in *Milbank Herald Advance*, January 14; and *Britton Journal*, January 21, 1960). "McGovern . . . Union Bosses," *De Smet News*, January 14, 1960; "Hoffa Will Be Happy," *Lemmon Leader*, undated clipping, Scrapbook 99, KMP; "Labor's Blacklist," *AAN*, January 28, 1960.

15. "McGovern's Attitude" and "Editor's Note," *SFAL*, January 28, 1960. McGovern urged Dave Beck's expulsion from the AFL board in 1957 (Box 47, GSMP). Christopherson wrote to McGovern privately: "Though I found abundant evidence in the publications of the Teamsters Union of a dislike for Senator Mundt, I found no specific listing of you as a member of Congress to be supported" (Christopherson to McGovern, January 26, 1960, Box 40, GSMP)

16. "That Fish," *MDR*, January 14, 1960; "Wrong Man" and "Campaign by Myth," *Salem Special*, January 14, 1960. For Mundt vs. Kennedy, see Heidepriem, *A Fair Chance for a Free People*, 213 and 221; Evan Thomas, *Robert Kennedy: His Life* (New York: Simon and Schuster, 2000), 85–86; Arthur M. Schlesinger Jr., *Robert Kennedy and His Times* (New York: Ballantine, 1979), 167–70; and "Senators Row" and "Kennedys Close," *MDR*, January 15 and February 19, 1960. Mundt became embroiled in the broader dispute with Democrats on the rackets committee in February. He charged Robert F. Kennedy, the committee's counsel, with thwarting an investigation of the United Auto Workers, to cover up "a clear pattern of crime and violence." He believed Kennedy had shielded Reuther (Mundt's chief target until the campaign began) because he supported Democratic candidates. Kennedy abhorred the attacks on Reuther, whose honesty and life-style were impeccable. But Mundt's assault on Hoffa did not impress RFK after they had been so friendly during the hearings, highlighting their common ground on the free enterprise system, as distinct from the "socialist" Reuther. Mundt had "no guts," Kennedy said. "I did not respect him for the way he played up to Hoffa . . . and other witnesses when they were on the stand, yet attacked them viciously when they were not present."

17. *Herald Tribune* ran three Hoffa stories on March 15, 1960. See in Scrapbook 99, KMP: "Hoffa Purge List," *Sioux City Journal*, March 16, 1960; "Not in South Dakota," *BR*, March 23; "Dog House," *Selby Record*, March 24; "Hoffa

Threatens," *Lennox Independent*, March 24; "Union Boss," *De Smet News*, March 24; "McGovern Snaps," *WPO*, March 21, 1960; letters to the editor in *SFAL* and *Rapid City Journal* (hereinafter *RCJ*), April 13; and *HDP*, April 14, 1960. McGovern to Schrader, April 5, and Schrader to McGovern, April 8, 1960, Box 40, GSMP. McGovern was mindful of the potential of the labor vote, despite its small size. On April 5 he wrote to Cliff Schrader of the Sioux Falls Trade and Labor Assembly, who was organizing precinct workers: "In my opinion, the 1960 election between Mundt and myself may turn on the vote that you people are able to turn out in Sioux Falls. Rapid City and Aberdeen are . . . of great importance, too."

18. Carlson to *MDR*, March 30, 1960; "Mundt Denies," in *MDR* and the *HDP*, April 6, 1960; "McGovern Answers," *MDR*, April 9, 1960, and Carlson letter to *MDR*, April 19, 1960. See also Anson, *McGovern*, 82, and Heidepriem, *A Fair Chance for a Free People*, 234–35; *WPO*, April 26, 1960. For a paid political ad, *Alexandria Herald*, May 19, 1960 (Scrapbook 99, KMP); for a student's defense of McGovern, see Royce Jones to *MDR*, October 3, 1960.

19. On Motley, see *MDR*, April 9, 11, 12, 14, and 23, 1960; and "Mundt Lauded," *SFAL*, May 9, 1960; "McGovern Hits," *RDJ*, May 13, 1960; and "McGovern Blasted," *BR*, May 15, 1960.

20. Ambrose, *Eisenhower*, 508–15; Aleksandr Fursenko and Timothy Naftali, *Khrushchev's Cold War* (New York: Norton, 2006), 263–87 (quote, 281).

21. "Incident Serious Blunder," *RCJ*, March 14, 1960, Scrapbook 99, KMP.

22. In KMP, "McGovern's Attack," *AAN*, May 17, and *Selby Record*, May 19 and 26, 1960.

23. "Mundt Talks," *Collegian*, May 26, 1960, KMP; "Mundt Says," *SFAL*, May 23, 1960.

24. Press release, May 13, 1960, Box 55, GSMP; LBJ introduction at Big Bend Dam, May 29, 1960, in *CR*, June 2, 1960, 11782; G. McGovern, *Grassroots*, 82; McGovern interview, October 1, 1991.

25. McGovern speech, May 13, 1960, cited above; appeal from Mrs. Franklin D. Roosevelt, June 10, 1960, and McGovern to Roosevelt, June 16, 1960, Box 471 and 58, GSMP; "Kennedy, Johnson," *RCJ*, June 10, 1960; Tom Donnelly, "SD New Leaf," *Washington Daily News*, ca. June 10, 1960 (Scrapbook 99, KMP).

26. McGovern introduction, June 18, 1960, Box 40, GSMP; advertisement, *MDR*, June 11; "Kennedy's Visit," *AAN*, June 17; "Kennedy Courts," *RCJ*, June 19; "Kennedy Given" and "Des Moines," *MDR*, June 20 and August 20, 1960.

27. See, in *CR*, floor debate, "Farm Surplus," June 21, 1960, 13628–68, and June 23, 1960, 14055–56; "Stockgrowers," *Lennox Independent*, May 12; "Cattlemen Oppose," *WPO*, May 17, 1960, in Scrapbook 99, KMP; "McGovern Says," *MDR*, June 21, 1960.

28. "Not Allied" ca. May 1960, and "Poll Shows," *Yankton Press*, July 8, 1960, Scrapbook 99, KMP. Poll data in *SFAL*, July 6, 1960. In *MDR*: "Following Benson," June 21; "REA," August 23, 24, 25, and 31; "Farmers for McGovern" August 24; and "McGovern Would Debate," April 25, 1960; and Heidepriem, *A Fair Chance for a Free People*, 226–27.

29. Mundt staff member Jim Smith arranged the endorsement through an official close to Hoffa. In 1972 Smith told an interviewer it was "a masterpiece"

they "fully anticipated McGovern would try to reject," but designed to make that almost impossible (Heidepriem, *A Fair Chance for a Free People*, 230–31).

30. "Hoffa Fights," *Omaha World Herald*, August 17, 1960; "Governor Says," August 18, 1960, and "Four Speak," *Lemmon Leader*, August 25, 1960, Scrapbook 99, KMP; Pearson's "Washington Merry-Go-Round," *MDR*, October 14, 1960, portions of which were deleted in *SFAL*'s October 14 edition. See also, "Hoffa Interest in SD," *AAN*, August 24, 1960.

31. Edna Lonigan, "Mundt vs. McGovern," *Human Events* (July 1960), reprint in Box 1140, KMP. "Charges Tactics," *AAN*, September 7, and "Mundt Asks," *Madison Leader*, September 9, 1960; *Sturgis Tribune* clipping, March 17, and "How Liberal is SD," May 9, 1960, in Scrapbook 99, KMP; "Slaps Back," *HDP*, September 11, 1960; in *MDR*: "McGovern Lashes," August 26, and "Charges by Mundt," October 29, 1960.

32. See *MDR* and *HDP* for September 16 and *SFAL*, September 17, 1960.

33. "McGovern and Mundt," *MDR*, September 19, 1960.

34. Mundt had a report that said McGovern received from labor a total of $7,150 (Box 1140, KMP). See Boxes 55 and 56, GSMP, correspondence from Kenneth Peterson of the International Union of Electrical Radio and Machine Workers, September 28; George Agree of the National Committee for an Effective Congress, October 22; and I. W. Abel of the Political Action Fund of the United Steelworkers of America, November 2, 1960, which together account for contributions totaling $5,000. For "Historians for McGovern," see McGovern to Billington, October 12 and 25, and Billington to McGovern, October 20 and November 19, 1960, RABP. (About three hundred historians from across the United States made contributions, mostly in the $5 to $10 range.)

35. "Flag Incident," "Candidates Learn," and letter, *MDR*, September 21 and 29 and October 3, 1960.

36. Kennedy and Nixon in Sioux Falls, *MDR*, September 23 and 29, 1960; G. McGovern, *Grassroots*, 82; McGovern interview, April 24, 1964, JFKL.

37. McGovern interview, April 24, 1964, JFKL, and *The Speeches of Senator John F. Kennedy, August 1 to November 7, 1960* (Washington, DC: Government Printing Office, 1961), 325–28. "Food Is Strength," "Rain Falling," and photos, *MDR*, September 23, 1960; Magness to editor, *MDR*, October 3, 1960; G. McGovern, *Grassroots*, 82–83. See also JFK press release, "Food for Peace," Box 470, GSMP.

38. Data for all races, *SFAL*, October 12, 1960; *HDP*, August 19, 1960.

39. G. McGovern, *Grassroots*, 83; author's interview with McGovern, August 9, 1991; McGovern interview, August 24, 1964, JFKL; McGovern to Billington, September 23, 1960, RABP.

40. See John Lauck, " 'You Can't Mix Beans and Potatoes in the Same Bin': Anti-Catholicism in Early Dakota," *South Dakota History* (Spring 2008): 1–46 (2, 6, and 37–45); Eleanor McGovern interview; author's interview with William Dougherty, May 25, 1995. (Anson, *McGovern*, 95–96, states that Herseth and other Democrats "pointedly refused to share the platform" with Kennedy; this was not the case according to news reports.) See also George Gallup, "Religious Issue Cuts," *SFAL*, October 30, 1960.

41. Anson, *McGovern*, 96–97; "Mundt Challenges," *Pierre State News*, and "Big 'M' Debate," *RCJ*, both September 27, 1960, Scrapbook 99, KMP.

42. That is, the McCarran Internal Security Act of 1950, based on the Mundt-Nixon bill of 1948 and often referred to locally by the latter name.

43. "Hit Warpath," *SFAL*, October 5, 1960; "McGovern, Mundt" and "How a Man Talks," *MDR*, October 5 and 8, 1960. See also "Mundt, McGovern Agree," *SFAL* September 17, 1960.

44. The Democrats were John McCormack of Massachusetts and John J. Rooney of New York; the other Republican was Styles Bridges of New Hampshire.

45. "Hoover Lauds" and Christopherson to Hoover, September 30, 1960, and Hoover to Christopherson, October 4, 1960, in *SFAL*, October 9, 1960; Heidepriem, *A Fair Chance for a Free People*, 84–85, 108–9, and 230–33; and G. McGovern, *Grassroots*, 81.

46. Editorial and letters, *SFAL*, October 11, 12, and 14, 1960.

47. Ibid., October 17, 1960.

48. See in ibid., "Mundt Should" and letters, October 20; and "Hoover for Mundt," October 27, 1960.

49. Letters to *MDR*, October 5 and November 4, 1960; Anson, *McGovern*, 93; Dougherty interview.

50. See in the *MDR*: "Moore Questions" and "Bottum Charges," both October 11; editorial, October 12; "New Clashes," October 13; "Used as Decoy" and "SF Man Attacks," both October 25; and "Mundt Counters" and "Magness Raps," November 4 and 7, 1960. See *SFAL*, October to early November, and November 3 editorial and letters. See also, Anson, *McGovern*, 93–94, and Heidepriem, *A Fair Chance for a Free People*, 232–33.

51. Polls and analyses in *SFAL*, October 12 and 26; and *HDP*, October 27, 1960. All of the numbers on October 12 disappointed Democrats. Herseth had fallen to 41 percent, from his lead of 57 percent in July. In the race for McGovern's seat, Ray Fitzgerald had always trailed Ben Reifel, but he had dropped to 33. By October 26, Herseth had recovered with 47.8 percent to Archie Gubbrud's 49. Nixon and Kennedy held steady in South Dakota at 60 to 36 percent. Nationally, the Gallup poll put Kennedy at 49 and Nixon at 45, with 6 percent undecided.

52. *SFAL*, November 6; *WPO* and *MDR* both November 7; Milner, "Demos Defeat," *WPO* and *MDR* both November 10, 1960.

53. *SFAL*, October 25, and *MDR*, November 1, 2, and 7, 1960.

54. *SFAL*, October 25 and 28; *MDR*, November 1; *HDP*, November 5, 1960.

55. Stories in *HDP*, November 8; see also November 5 and 7, 1960.

56. *HDP*, November 9, 1960.

57. "Turnout in SD," *HDP*, November 19, 1960; Clem, *South Dakota Political Almanac*, 19, 21, 30, 41–42, and 74–75.

58. "McGovern Concedes," *MDR*, November 9, 1960.

59. "Nixon Helps" and Milner, "Demo Defeat," both *MDR*, November 10, 1960; Les Helgeland, "Who's Going," *MDR*, November 10, 1960; "The Voice," *SFAL*, November 11, 1960; "Wise Choice," *HDP*, November 14, 1960; and

"Something for Everybody," *Sturgis Press*, and "Election Analysis, *Pierre State News*, undated clippings, Scrapbook 99, KMP.

60. "Emotional Factor," *MDR*, November 14, 1960; Arthur M. Schlesinger Jr., *A Thousand Days: John F. Kennedy in the White House* (Boston: Houghton Mifflin, 1965), 118.

61. Letters from George A. Bangs, November 11; Ross Horning Jr., November 17; and James Shaeffer, November 19, 1960; McGovern letters to Nathan, Symington, Link, Young, and Stahl all on November 18, in Box 56, GSMP; Anson, *McGovern*, 93.

62. See letters to McGovern from Yarborough, November 14; Link, November 13; Gruening, November 11; McCarthy, November 15; Burns, November 11; Hughes, November 18, 1960, Box 56, GSMP; and Billington, November 19, 1960, RABP; and *SFAL* editorial, November 11, 1960; from Stevenson, November 7, 1960, Box 54, Stevenson Papers.

63. Schlesinger, *A Thousand Days*, 118–19; author's interview with Arthur Schlesinger Jr., July 10, 1996; McGovern interview, August 24, 1964, JFKL; Anson, *McGovern*, 98–99; G. McGovern, *Grassroots*, 83.

CHAPTER 12   FOOD FOR PEACE

1. "McGovern Flattered," *MDR*, September 27, 1960; Patton to McGovern, November 14, 1960, Box 56, GSMP. "Cabinet Speculation," *Pierre Daily Journal*, November 18, 1960, Scrapbook 99, KMP; "McGovern Top Prospect," *Des Moines Register*, in *MDR*, November 30; and "Kennedy Calls" and "Food for Peace," *MDR*, November 14 and 30, 1960.

2. McGovern interview, July 16, 1970, RFK Oral History, JFKL; "Bob Kennedy," *MDR*, November 2, 1960.

3. Author's interviews with Schlesinger, July 10, 1996, and John Kenneth Galbraith, May 3, 1996; Anson, *McGovern*, 101; Arthur M. Schlesinger Jr., *Robert F. Kennedy and His Times* (Boston: Houghton Mifflin, 1978), 226–27; and Schlesinger, *A Thousand Days*, 144.

4. Al Young to McGovern, November 14, 1960, GSMP, Box 56; McGovern interview, April 24, 1964, JFKL; see FFP committee report, January 19, 1961, President's Office Files (POF), Box 78, JFKL. JFK inaugural, *Public Papers of the Presidents* (Washington, DC: US Government Printing Office, 1961), 1–3.

5. McGovern interview, July 16, 1970, JFKL. Both Orville Freeman and Dean Rusk coveted Food for Peace, each believing that it should belong in his respective department. Two months into the job he had to enlist Kennedy personally to thwart a State Department scheme to take over the program (McGovern to JFK, March 15, 1961, POF, Box 78, JFKL). See also McGovern to JFK, April 27, 1962, POF, Box 79, JFKL; and Schlesinger to JFK, April 30, 1962, and McGovern to RFK, June 4, 1962, Box 471, GSMP. See also Schlesinger, *A Thousand Days*, 169–70.

6. E. O. 10915 and Memorandum for Heads of Executive Departments, January 24, 1961, in the Papers of Richard Reuter (McGovern's successor), Box 13, JFKL. His first E. O. (No. 109140), January 21, 1961, expanded the food dis-

tribution program for about one million needy American families, doubling the volume available previously.

7. See McGovern, *War against Want: America's Food for Peace Program* (New York: Walker, 1964), 12–15, and Mitchell Wallerstein, *Food for War—Food for Peace, United States Food Aid in Global Context* (Cambridge, MA: MIT Press), 26–28.

8. Wallerstein, *Food for War*, 27–32, and Walter Cohen, "Herbert Hoover Feeds the World," in *The Trojan Horse—A Radical Look at Foreign Aid*, ed. Steve Weissman (San Francisco: Ramparts Press, 1974).

9. See the study by the CRS for the House Committee on International Relations, *Use of U.S. Food Resources for Diplomatic Purposes—An Examination of the Issues*, House, 95th Cong., 2nd sess., January 1977, 23.

10. Senate Committee on Foreign Relations, Hearings: Mutual Security Act of 1954, Senate, 83rd Cong., 2nd sess., 1954. See also Toma, *Politics of Food for Peace*, 39–42; and McGovern, *War against Want*, 17–21.

11. Ruttan, *United States Development Assistance Policy*, 70–72 and 152–59; "International Food for Peace Act of 1959," and Humphrey speech, *CR*, April 16, 1959.

12. Meanwhile, McGovern put together his staff—Nelson Post, a former dairy lobbyist, as special assistant; James Symington, as deputy and liaison to the State Department; and Pat Donovan as executive secretary. McGovern found a suite of offices in the best location possible—the Old Executive Office Building, the grandiose late nineteenth-century structure next door to the White House. Squatter's rights were involved. Vice President Johnson, in search of office space, admired their quarters, and McGovern had to fend him off.

13. G. McGovern, *Grassroots*, 297; "Three Fold," *MDR*, December 19, 1960; McGovern interview, April 24, 1964, and McGovern to JFK, January 26 and February 2, 1961, POF, Box 78, JFKL; McGovern interview, August 9, 1991.

14. JFK to McGovern and the secretaries of state and agriculture, January 31, 1961, Reuter Papers, Box 15, JFKL; Schlesinger, *A Thousand Days*, 168 and 170.

15. Schlesinger, *A Thousand Days*, 175–76.

16. Schlesinger interview (quote), July 10, 1996; Schlesinger, *A Thousand Days*, 157–80.

17. See Stephen G. Rabe, "Controlling Revolutions: Latin America, the Alliance for Progress, and Cold War Anti-Communism," in *Kennedy's Quest for Victory: American Foreign Policy, 1961–1963*, ed. Thomas G. Paterson (New York: Oxford University Press, 1989), 105–122.

18. Kyle Longley, *In the Eagle's Shadow: The United States and Latin America* (Wheeling, IL: Harlan Davidson, 2002), 167–70 and 176–77; Rabe, *Eisenhower and Latin America: The Foreign Policy of Anticommunism* (Chapel Hill: University of North Carolina Press, 1988), 6–9.

19. Rabe, *Eisenhower and Latin America*, 7–9 and 16–17.

20. Ibid., 31–33, 38–39, and 87 (Dulles); for Árbenz, 42–63; Langley, *Eagle's Shadow*, 215–20.

21. Rabe, *Eisenhower and Latin America*, 85–87, 101–6, 112–16, and 162–73; LaFeber, *America, Russia, and the Cold War*, 157–65 and 212–22.

22. McGovern quotes, floor debates in January 1957 and 1958 and June 1959 (see chapters 9 and 10).

23. Schlesinger, *A Thousand Days*, 176–78; Schlesinger memo for JFK, "Current Crisis in Latin America," POF, Countries, Latin America, General, 1960–61, Box 121a, JFKL.

24. See James W. Symington to McGovern, March 15, 1961, POF, Box 78, and Symington interview, 25–31, both in JFKL.

25. "Food for Peace Mission," February 14–20, 1961," McGovern memo to JFK, February 27, 1961, POF, Box 78, JFKL; Frondizi to JFK, January 1, and JFK to Frondizi, January 10, 1962, and WH press release, February 25, 1962, in POF, Countries, Argentina, General, 1962, Box 111, JFKL.

26. McGovern, *War against Want*, 1; Schlesinger, *A Thousand Days*, 178; McGovern speech, the National Farmers Union, Washington, DC, March 16, 1961, Box 766, GSMP; G. McGovern, *Grassroots*, 87.

27. Memo to JFK on FFP Mission, February 27, 1961, POF, Box 78, JFKL; Anson, *McGovern*, 108.

28. See J. M. Cabot interview, Oral History, JFKL; Rusk to JFK, March 21, 1961, Dulles to JFK, undated, in POF, Box 112, Countries, Brazil, Security, 1961, JFKL; Anson, *McGovern*, 109.

29. See McGovern to JFK, February 27, 1961, POF, Box 78; and WH Press Releases, March 29, 1961, POF, Box 121a, Countries, Latin American, Security 1960–13, and May 19, 1962, POF, Box 78, all in JFKL; Anson, *McGovern*, 109; Symington to McGovern, March 15, 1961 and McGovern to JFK, March 30, 1961, both memos in POF, BOX 78

30. McGovern to JFK, Memo and Report on FFP (quote, 20), March 10, 1961, POF, BOX 78, JFKL.

31. See ibid., and Walt W. Rostow, *The Stages of Economic Growth: A Non-Communist Manifesto* (Cambridge: Cambridge University Press, 1960); see also David Milne, *America's Rasputin: Walt Rostow and the Vietnam War* (New York: Hill and Wang, 2008), 76–81 and 111–13.

32. WH Press Release, July 22, 1961, and "1961 Report to the President: FFP," both in POF, Box 78, JFKL; and Symington to Chester Bowles, October 31, 1961, Box 15, Reuter Papers, JFKL. See in GSMP: press release, June 15, 1961, and address at DOA, January 10, 1962, Box 766; and McGovern report to President, July 10, 1962, on commodities shipped for Food for Work Program, Box 472 (file 1962 reports).

33. McGovern to JFK, Memo on FFP, March 10, 1961, cited above and McGovern press release, December 20, 1961, Box 766, GSMP.

34. See McGovern to JFK, "1961 Report to the President," POF, Box 78; McGovern to JFK, March 29 and July 18, 1962, POF Box 79, JFKL; and McGovern, *War against Want*, 32–42 (Galbraith, 37).

35. McGovern, *War against Want*, 100–112; author's interview with McGovern, December 30, 1997; Wallerstein, *Food for Peace*, 93–95 and 169–171; McGovern interview, April 24, 1964, JFKL.

36. Editorial compilation in Jim Symington to Anson Yeager of *SFAL*, April 27, 1962, quoted in Knock, "Feeding the World and Thwarting the Communists," 107–8 and 118n47; Humphrey quoted in Anson, *McGovern*, 112; "Food

for Foreigners," *Wall Street Journal*, April 5, 1961; *The Progressive*, March 1962; "The Coming War on Hunger," in *Sunday Empire* magazine in *Denver Post*, August 29, 1965; and transcript of *Issues and Answers*, February 12, 1961, in 1961 Speeches and Statements File, GSMP. See also, McGovern to JFK, May 3 and October 26, 1961, and WH press release, May 6, 1961, POF, Box 78; McGovern to JFK, March 26, 1962, with enclosure, Murrow to McGovern, March 12, 1962, POF, Box 79; and McGovern to Ken O'Donnell, January 4, 1962, Reuter Papers, all in JFKL; and McGovern/FFP Press Release, June 23, 1961, Box 739, GSMP.

37. JFK remarks, Conference on International Economic and Social Development, Washington, DC, June 16, 1961, Box 35, POF Speech File, JFKL. See also Robert A. Pastor, *Congress and the Politics of U.S. Foreign Economic Policy, 1929–1976* (Berkeley: University of California Press, 1980), 268–73; Burton Kaufman, "Foreign and the Balance of Payments Problem: Vietnam and Johnson's Foreign Economic Policy," in *The Johnson Years*, vol. 2, ed. Robert A. Divine (Lawrence: University Press of Kansas, 1987), 79–81.

38. Foregoing paragraph based on these addresses and memoranda: 59th Convention of the National Farmers Union, Washington, DC, March 16, 1961; Food and Nutrition Conference, 1961, New London, NH, August 24, 1961; the Conference on Food and People, DOA, January 10, 1962, all in Box 766, GSMP; Memo to JFK, August 3, 1961, POF, Box 78, JFKL. McGovern interview, April 24, 1964, JFKL; McGovern, *War against Want*, 113–20 (Rostow quote, 115).

39. McGovern interview, August 9, 1991.

40. Ibid., and McGovern interview, December 29, 1991; McGovern to Rostow, May 24, 1961, and Rostow to JFK, "A Memo for the Thanksgiving Weekend," November 22, 1961, National Security File, China, Box 22, JFKL. George Ball ("Secret") to McGovern, December 6, 1961; a CIA analysis, "Food Shortages in the Communist Bloc," July 15, 1961; Roger Hilsman, "Peiping's 'Interest' in Purchasing US Grain," February 28, 1962, all in Box 472, GSMP, and McGovern, *War against Want*, 124.

41. McGovern, *War against Want*, 89; McGovern to JFK, October 26, 1961, POF, Box 78, JFKL.

42. McGovern, *War against Want*, 85–99; McGovern to JFK, March 29, 1962, POF, Box 79, JFKL; and Galbraith interview, May 3, 1996; see also materials in Box 473 and 474, GSMP. For India's "Five-Year Plan" see Dennis Merrill, *Bread and the Ballot: The United States and India's Economic Development, 1947–1963* (Chapel Hill: University of North Carolina Press, 1990), 169–203; and Robert J. McMahon, "Food as a Diplomatic Weapon: The India Wheat Loan of 1951," *Pacific Historical Review* (August 1987): 349–77.

43. JFK to McGovern, July 18, 1962, in compilation, "Comments on Food for Peace from the Public Papers of the President—John F. Kennedy, 1962," in Reuter Papers, Box 13, JFKL; Kennedy/McGovern "Exchange of Letters," Box 472, GSMP.

44. McGovern interview, July 16, 1970, RFK Oral History Project; "McGovern Remarks," January 9, 1962, Box 766, GSMP; McGovern to Link, May 10, 1962, ASLP; G. McGovern, *Grassroots*, 88–89.

45. McGovern to JFK, April 27, 1962, POF, Departments and Agencies, Box 79, and McGovern interview, RFK Oral History, both in JFKL; Schlesinger

memo to JFK, April 30, 1962, and McGovern to RFK, June 4, 1962, copies in Box 471, GSMP. For his resignation, McGovern to JFK and JFK to McGovern, both July 18, 1962, POF, Box 79, JFKL.

46. Author's interview with William Dougherty, May 25, 1995; Anson, *McGovern*, 117–18.

47. "GOP Unimpressed" and "McGovern's Candidacy" (summary of editorial opinions), *HDP*, April 19 and 22, 1962; McGovern statement, April 18, 1962, Box 766, GSMP.

48. For Case's life and death, see *NYT*, June 23, 1962, and "Case's Sudden Death," *HDP*, June 24, 1962; and Richard Chenoworth, *Francis H. Case: A Political Biography* (South Dakota Historical Collections 39, 1978), 288–433; Cunningham interview.

49. "Conservatives Bid," *HDP*, June 25; "Knotty Problem," *SFAL*, June 29, and several reports in *MDR*, July 10, 1962. See also Alan L. Clem, *The Nomination of Joe Bottum* (Vermillion, SD: Governmental Research Bureau, 1963).

50. In *MDR*, "G.O.P. Picks," July 11, 1962; "SD Editors," July 31, 1962; committeeman quote, July 10, 1962; "Bottum," *SFAL*, October 26, 1962; Cunningham and Dougherty interviews.

51. "GOP Convention" and "Keynote Speaker," *MDR*, both July 16, "SD Republicans," ibid., July 17, 1962; "GOP Rolls," *HDP*, July 16, 1962; Anson, *McGovern*, 120.

52. McGovern's "New Opportunities," July 2, 1962, Box 62, GSMP; "Demos Urge," *MDR*, July 2, 1962; "SD Senatorial," October 3, 1962, *HDP*; polling data in *SFAL*, July 25 and October 24, 1962.

53. See James N. Giglio, *The Presidency of John F. Kennedy*, 2nd ed. (Lawrence: University Press of Kansas, 2006), 99–108.

54. Ibid., and 109–115 for agriculture. See "Defeat of Farm Bill" and "Congress Adjourns," *HDP*, June 22 and October 14, 1962; "Vote Hurt Farmers," *MDR*, July 17, 1962; "Medicare," "Senate Votes," and "GOP Leaders," *MDR*, July 16 and 17 and August 8, 1962.

55. "McGovern Says," *MDR*, August 7, 1962; "Bottum Included," *HDP*, July 20, 1962.

56. Lusk, "JFK Shows," *HDP*, August 12, 1962.

57. "McGovern Gets," *MDR*, August 17, 1962; and "Udall Drew," "Bottum Defeat," and "Jamie Damon," all in *HDP*, August 19, 1962.

58. For Bottum's ads, *HDP* for September 6 and 30 and October 5 and 21; and "McGovern Defends," *HDP*, September 23, 1962.

59. "McGovern Bottum Debate" and "GOP Confident," *HDP*, September 21 and October 14, 1962.

60. "SD Demos," *SFAL*, October 2, 1962; "Senate Rivals" and "McGovern Seeks," *HDP*, October 4 and 5, 1962; "One Will Be," *SFAL*, October 21, 1962.

61. "McGovern Ill," *SFAL*, October 9, 1962; G. McGovern, *Grassroots*, 89–90.

62. E. McGovern, *Uphill*, 108–10; Anson, *McGovern*, 125 (quote); "Humphrey Appears," *HDP*, October 17, 1962; author's interview with Charles Guggenheim, May 30, 1996.

63. Quotes from video tape at JFKL.

64. Pat Donovan interview; Guggenheim's opinion was far more modest; see also Anson, *McGovern*, 126.

65. The fiasco was not solely the result of inept planning and execution. The CIA had failed to appreciate that within two years the new regime had made life better for most Cuban peasants compared to life under Batista. Improvements in education and literacy, housing, and public health, as well as the termination of the Mafia's rule in Havana inspired great loyalty to Fidel during the invasion.

66. Essential works include Graham T. Allison, *The Essence of a Decision: Explaining the Cuban Missile Crisis* (Boston: Little, Brown, 1971); Robert F. Kennedy, *Thirteen Days: A Memoir of the Cuban Missile Crisis* (New York: Norton, 1971); Ernest R. May and Phillip Zelikow, eds., *The Kennedy Tapes: Inside the White House during the Cuban Missile Crisis* (Cambridge, MA: Belknap Press of Harvard University Press, 1997); James Nathan, ed., *The Cuban Missile Crisis Revisited* (New York: St. Martin's Press, 1992); Philip Nash, *The Other Missiles of October: Eisenhower, Kennedy, and the Jupiters* (Chapel Hill: University of North Carolina Press, 1997); Thomas G. Paterson, *Contesting Castro: The United States and the Triumph of the Cuban Revolution* (New York: Oxford University Press); Fursenko and Naftali, *One Hell of a Gamble*, 77–256; and Schlesinger, *A Thousand Days*, 233–97 and 794–841.

67. See Thomas G. Paterson and William J. Brophy, "October Missiles and November Elections: The Cuban Missile Crisis and American Politics, 1962," *Journal of American History* 73 (1986): 87–119 (94–98); "McGovern Defends," *HDP*, September 23, 1962; Samuel Lubell, "The People Speak," *HDP*, October 5, 1962.

68. See all in *HDP*, "Four Weeks," "Bottum Best Man." October 8 and 14; "Bottum Wants" and "Kennedy Lashes," October 11 and 14, 1962; McGovern press releases, October 12, 22, 23, and 24, 1962, Box 766, and Cuban Crisis file, Box 61, GSMP.

69. Thomas G. Paterson, "Fixation with Cuba: The Bay of Pigs, Missile Crisis, and Covert War against Castro," in Paterson, *Kennedy's Quest for Victory*, 123–55 (142–45).

70. LaFeber, *America, Russia, and the Cold War*, 231–37 (quote, 234; 1990s revelations, 235–36); see also, Giglio, *John F. Kennedy*, 223–30; Paterson, "Fixation with Cuba," 144–52. Not for thirty years would Americans learn that missiles in Turkey were part of the deal, or that Kennedy's noninvasion pledge was conditioned on the removal of the Soviet missiles and on Castro's good behavior thereafter. More disturbing was the plan to invade Cuba on October 30 if Khrushchev did not accept these terms. In 1992 the Russians revealed that JFK and the ExCom were unaware of the fact that forty-two intermediate-range missiles had been readied with warheads well before the crisis had ended, thus (according to McNamara) virtually assuring a nuclear war if the United States had launched its attack.

71. "SD Political Heads," "Mundt Criticizes," and "End of Tensions," *HDP*, October 23, 28, and 29, 1962; "Mundt Says," *SFAL*, October 28, 1962; Paterson and Brophy, "October Missiles," 106–112.

72. "Citizens Endorse," *SFAL*, October 23, 1962; Lubell in *HDP*, October 29, 1962.

73. "McGovern Takes," *SFAL*, November 2, and "Both Camps," *HDP*, November 4, 1962. Stories on Ethel Kennedy in *HDP*, October 26, and *SFAL*, October 25 and 26, 1962; McGovern interview, July 16, 1970, RFK Oral History Project, JFKL.

74. "McGovern Calls" and "Effort for Bottum," *SFAL*, October 31 and November 3, 1962; in *HDP*: "Kefauver," October 29; "Senatorial Candidates" and "Crisis Proves" (ad), November 2; "Both Camps" and "Bottum Hits," November 4, 1962.

75. Schlesinger, *A Thousand Days*, 756–58 and 832–33, has an interesting analysis.

76. "Razor-Thin Lead," "McGovern's Thin," and "Investigators," *SFAL*, November 7, 8, and 10, 1962.

77. Cunningham interview; and "Keeps Boiling," "McGovern Lead," "Vote Canvass Ends," and "Gains 51," *SFAL*, November 11, 16, 21, and 28, 1962; and "Lead Grows" and "Lead Safe," *HDP*, November 28 and 30, 1962.

78. *SFAL* stories, November 2 and 3, 1962; Paterson and Brophy, "October Missiles," 112–19; McGovern interview, RFK Oral History, JFKL; Eleanor McGovern interview.

79. "McGovern 516" and "McGovern to Leave," *SFAL*, December 5 and 6, 1962; Cunningham interview.

CHAPTER 13 WE ARE DETERMINING THE PRIORITIES OF OUR NATIONAL LIFE

1. Don Oberdorfer, *Senator Mansfield: The Extraordinary Life of a Great American Statesman and Diplomat* (Washington, DC: Smithsonian Books, 2003), 170–77 (quote, 176); "McGovern to Seek" and "Not a Rubber Stamp," *HDP*, January 4 and 15, 1963; Ted Kennedy joke in "The New Senate and the New Senators," January 31, 1963, Box 769, GSMP.

2. "The New Senate and the New Senators," January 31, 1963, Box 769, GSMP.

3. McGovern was by no means unique in this regard. Among senators who had bridged the gap between academics and politics, Hubert Humphrey, Mike Mansfield, Gene McCarthy, Gale McGee, and (later) Mark Hatfield all had done comparable graduate work in history and politics and had taught as well.

4. *CR*, March 15, 1963, 4344–46; also in G. McGovern, *A Time of War, A Time of Peace*, 95–102.

5. Sorensen and Mansfield quoted by McGovern, interview, August 9, 1991; Schlesinger to McGovern, May 1, 1963, Box 767, GSMP; "The Cuban Fixation," *WP*, in *HDP*, March 31, 1963; Morse in *CR*, July 9, 1963, 11603; "Is Castro an Obsession with Us," *NYT Magazine*, May 19, 1963, 9 and 106–9.

6. "Neither War Nor Peace," *CR*, June 27, 1963; colloquy on Cuba, ibid., July 9, 1963, 11603. See also Rabe, "Controlling Revolutions: Latin America," in Paterson, *Kennedy's Quest for Victory*, 116–22; and Giglio, *John F. Kennedy*, 248–52.

7. State of the Union message, January 14, 1963, JFKL website.

8. American University address, June 10, 1963; Khrushchev in Giglio, *John F. Kennedy*, 231.

9. The foregoing is based on McGovern's "New Perspectives on American Security," August 2, 1963, and "A Proposal to Reverse the Arms Race," September 24, 1963, in his *A Time of War, A Time of Peace*, 5–22 and 24–35; see also materials in Box 767, GSMP.

10. *CR*, August 2, 1963, 13990–95.

11. Ibid., August 15, 1963, 14421–22 (Morgan); *NYT*, August 16, 1963.

12. *WSJ*, August 17, 1963; *WP*, September 19, 1963; collection of editorials, *CR*, October 31, 1963, 20771–86.

13. For McGovern's test ban speech, see *CR*, September 16, 1963, 17051–54; for the Senate's vote, ibid., September 24, 1963, 17832; and Giglio, *John F. Kennedy*, 230–33.

14. Chalmers Roberts, *WP*, September 29, 1963; the Economic Conversion Act, printed in G. McGovern, *A Time of War, A Time of Peace*, 48–60, but see also *CR*, October 31, 1963, 20768–86 (and ibid., November 6, 7, 8, and 13, and December 4, 13, and 30, 1963); for the appropriation, *CR*, September 24, 1963, 17865–93 (McGovern, 17881–85).

15. G. McGovern, *Grassroots*, 41–42, and McGovern interview, December 29, 1992.

16. See Patrick J. Hearden, *The Tragedy of Vietnam* (New York: HarperCollins, 1991), 24–43 (FDR, 28); Robert J. McMahon, "Harry Truman and Roots of U.S. Involvement in Indochina, 1945–53," in *Shadow on the White House: Presidents and the Vietnam War, 1945–1975*, ed. David L. Anderson (Lawrence: University Press of Kansas, 1993), 19–42; George C. Herring, *America's Longest War: The United States and Vietnam, 1950–1975*, 4th ed. (New York: McGraw-Hill, 2002), 3–13; Lattimore, *Situation in Asia*, 194 and 195 (also 9–13 and 42–27).

17. See Stephen E. Ambrose, *Eisenhower*, 2 vols. (New York: Simon and Shuster, 1983–84), 2: 173–84. Among leading works is David L. Anderson, *Trapped by Success: The Eisenhower Administration and Vietnam* (New York: Columbia University Press, 1991), but see his "Dwight D. Eisenhower and Whole-Hearted Support for Ngo Dinh Diem," in *Shadow on the White House*, 43–62. Fredrik Logevall's *Embers of War: The Fall of an Empire and the Making of America's Vietnam* (New York: Random House, 2013) is a sweeping account of this crucial period to 1960.

18. For Geneva, see works cited above; evaluation of Ho in *Foreign Relations of the United States* (Far East China), 1948 (Washington, DC: State Department, 1948), 6: 43–49; Lattimore, *Situation in Asia*, 217.

19. To provide Saigon added security, in September 1954 the United States created the Southeast Asia Treaty Organization. Its members included Great Britain, France, Australia, Pakistan, New Zealand, the Philippines, and Thailand.

20. Herring, *America's Longest War*, 48–61; Anderson, "Dwight D. Eisenhower and Whole-Hearted Support for Ngo Dinh Diem," 51–55; George McT. Kahin, *Intervention* (New York: Alfred Knopf, 1986), 66–95; and Bernard B. Fall, *The Two Vietnams: A Political and Military Analysis* (New York: Praeger, 1964), 234–46, 254–59; Logevall, *Embers of War*, 674–82.

21. Anderson, "Dwight D. Eisenhower and Whole-Hearted Support for Ngo Dinh Diem," 48–59; Logevall, *Embers of War*, 695–99; Ronald H. Spector, *Advice and Support: The Early Years of the United States Army in Vietnam, 1941–1960* (New York: Free Press, 1985), 308–10 and 315–16, and 323–27; Eric Bergerud, *The Dynamics of Defeat: The Vietnam War in Hau Nghia Province* (Boulder, CO: Westview, 1991), 15–21.

22. "Works of Peace," *CR*, January 27, 1958, 1101.

23. See CIA analysis, "Food Shortages in the Communist Bloc," July 15, 1961, Box 474, GSMP; and Lansdale to Reuter, May 7, 1964, and "Vietnam Nutrition Survey—October 1959" (January 1965), in Reuter Papers, Box 13, and McGovern to Kennedy, October 26, 1961, POF, Box 78, JFKL; McGovern, *War against Want*, 55–56.

24. "The War in Indochina," *CR*, April 6, 1954, 4678, 4673, and 4674; Lawrence J. Bassett and Stephen E. Pelz, "The Failed Search for Victory: Vietnam and the Politics of War," in Paterson, *Kennedy's Quest for Victory*, 225–26; and Schlesinger, *A Thousand Days*, 320–23.

25. Bergerud, *Dynamics of Defeat*, 33–38; Bassett and Pelz, "Failed Search," 227, 231–33, and 239–40.

26. Bassett and Pelz, "Failed Search," 229–43; Giglio, *John F. Kennedy*, 256–61; Fall, *Two Vietnams*, 323–25; and Herring, *America's Longest War*, 89–102 and 109–13.

27. Herring, *America's Longest War*, 114–22.

28. Ibid., 103 and 107–9; Fall, *Two Vietnams*, 367–79; Bergerud, *Dynamics of Defeat*, 54–59 (quote, 55); and Bassett and Pelz, "Failed Search," 223–24 (Galbraith), 227–29, and 239–43.

29. Trueheart to McGovern, August 16, 1963, Box 474, GSM; U. Alexis Johnson to McGeorge Bundy, November 28, 1961, POF, Box 128, Countries, Vietnam, Security, JFKL; and Wallerstein, *Food for War*, 134–35 (notes 16–19).

30. Fall, *Two Vietnams*, 336; Herring, *America's Longest War*, 116–18; Bassett and Pelz, "Failed Search," 243–48; and *Public Papers of the Presidents of the United States: John F. Kennedy* (Washington, DC: US Government Printing Office, 1962–64), 3: 651–52 and 658–59. For senatorial reaction, etc., *CR*, August 23 and September 4, 10–12, 16, 18, 20, 23, and 26, 1963.

31. For the Church resolution, see *CR*, September 12, 16, 18, and 26, 1963, 16824–25, 17019–20, 17353–54, and 18183, respectively; McGovern, "The Vietnam Mess," September 26, 1963, 18205.

32. Kahin, *Intervention*, 146–81; Herring, *America's Longest War*, 123–29; Giglio, *John F. Kennedy*, 267–70; McGovern interview, December 29, 1992; Robert S. McNamara, with Brian VanDeMark, *In Retrospect: The Tragedy and Lessons of Vietnam* (New York: Random House, 1995), 55–61 and 75–87; and Andrew Preston, *The War Council: McGeorge Bundy, the NSC, and Vietnam* (Cambridge, MA: Harvard University Press, 2006), 125–28.

33. McGovern interview, December 29, 1992; Ann McGovern interview, December 29, 1995; E. McGovern, *Uphill*, 105–6; and G. McGovern, *Grassroots*, 102.

34. McGovern interviews, October 1, 1991, and December 29, 1992; Herring, *America's Longest War*, 119; Bassett and Pelz, "Failed Search," JFK quote,

249. Scholarly exonerations include David Kaiser, *American Tragedy: Kennedy, Johnson, and the Origins of the Vietnam War* (Cambridge, MA: Harvard University Press, 2000); and Fredrik Logevall, *Choosing War: The Last Chance for Peace and the Escalation of the Vietnam War* (Berkeley: University of California Press, 1999).

35. *Public Papers of the Presidents of the United States: Lyndon B. Johnson, 1963–64*, vol. 1 (Washington, DC: US Government Printing Office, 1965), 8–10; and Doris Kearns Goodwin, *Lyndon Johnson and the American Dream* (1976; New York: St Martin's Press, 1991), 178.

36. For his boyhood and parental relationships see, in addition to Goodwin (esp., 19–45), Robert Dallek, *Lone Star Rising: Lyndon Johnson and His Times, 1908–1960* (New York: Oxford University Press, 1991), and Randall Woods's *LBJ: Architect of American Ambition* (Cambridge, MA: Harvard University Press, 2006).

37. *Public Papers, LBJ, 1965* (1966), 1: 412–14.

38. Quoted in William E. Leuchtenburg, *In the Shadow of FDR: From Harry Truman to Ronald Reagan* (Ithaca, NY: Cornell University Press, 1983), 127 and 136.

39. Quotes in Goodwin, *Lyndon Johnson*, 176 and 178.

40. G. McGovern, *Grassroots*, 102–3; "Plug McGovern," *RCJ*, June 10, 1960; "South Dakota," *Washington Daily News*, ca. June 10, 1960, Scrapbook 99, KMP; McGovern to LBJ, June 3, 1960, with *CR*, June 2, 1960, (Append, 4693–94); LBJ to McGovern, June 8, 1960; McGovern to LBJ, May 27, 1960, and LBJ to McGovern, November 19, 1960, in U.S. Senate, 1949–61, Papers of Democratic Leader, Box 373, Lyndon B. Johnson Library (hereinafter LBJL); McGovern to LBJ, May 10, 1962, and LBJ to McGovern, September 29 and December 14, 1962, Vice President's files, Box 33, LBJL.

41. Address to Congress, November 27, 1963, cited above.

42. G. McGovern, *Grassroots*, 103, quotes; *WP*, December 2, 1963.

43. The members of the Committee on the Economic Impact of Defense and Disarmament included the chairman of the Council of Economic Advisers and the secretaries of Defense, Labor, and Commerce; the directors of the Atomic Energy Commission, the Bureau of the Budget, NASA, the Office of Emergency Planning, and the US Arms Control and Disarmament Agency.

44. *CR*, December 30, 1963, 25644–47; *NYT*, December 22 and 23, 1963; Myer Feldman to McGovern, June 2, 1964, WHCF, Box 270, LBJL.

45. *CR*, January 8, 1964, 22; LBJ speeches, January 8 and May 22, 1964, *Public Papers, LBJ, 1963–64*, 1: 112–18 and 704–7.

46. Harris poll in *NYT*, January 6, 1964; LBJ, in Woods, *LBJ*, 444; McGovern floor remarks, *CR*, March 20, 1963 (including "Poverty and Arms Reduction," *NYT*, February 22, 1964), 5781–82.

47. Woods, *LBJ*, 443–47, and Allen J. Matusow, *The Unraveling of America: The History of Liberalism in the 1960s* (New York: Harper and Row, 1984), 51–59; see also Maurice Isserman and Michael Kazin, *America Divided: The Civil War of the 1960s*, 2nd ed. (New York: Oxford University Press, 2004), 113 and 131–32.

48. Woods, *LBJ*, 449–58; Matusow, *Unraveling of America*, 119–26; Isserman and Kazin, *America Divided*, 111–15. For Thurmond, Pell, and McGovern, *CR*, July 23, 1963, 16704–9.

49. G. McGovern, *Grassroots*, 92–93; Steven McGovern interview, December 29, 1995.

50. Arthur Link illustrated the contradictions by telling students about his friendship with John Hope Franklin, the eminent African American scholar, who taught at Fisk University in Washington in the 1950s when Link did his research at the Library of Congress. Occasionally the two historians and their wives dined out together, but they were usually restricted to restaurants at Union Station, one of the few places where a black and a white couple could do so unharassed. Link had told McGovern the story as well.

51. Richard Reeves, *President Kennedy, Profile of Power* (New York: Simon and Shuster, 1993), 485–89, 492–96, and 517–27; see also Giglio, *John F. Kennedy*, 173–202.

52. "The Continuing American Revolution and the American Negro," in G. McGovern, *A Time of War, A Time of Peace*, 149–55.

53. See letters to McGovern, Box 478 and 767, GSMP, and "Civil Rights Act" and "Civil Rights and SD," *CR*, March 20, 1963, 5829–37 and May 22, 1963, 11767–68.

54. *CR*, June 4, 1963, 12669–71.

55. See McGovern addresses in Detroit (February 8), Chapel Hill (April 4), and Madison (May 30), and New York, July 9, 1964, and other examples in Box 768, GSMP.

56. G. McGovern, *Grassroots*, 102; Ronald Steel, *Walter Lippmann and the American Century* (Boston: Little, Brown, 1980), 556; speech in Madison, May 30 (cited above).

CHAPTER 14 THE RIGHT SONG FOR THE WRONG SEASON

1. McNamara, *In Retrospect*, 85, 100–101, and 105; Logevall, *Choosing War*, 89–90; and Herring, *America's Longest War*, 131–41.

2. Schulman, *Johnson and American Liberalism*, 135; *JFK Pubic Papers*, 3: 658–59; McNamara, *In Retrospect*, 106–7, 113, and 117–19; Logevall, *Choosing War*, 92; Michael R. Beschloss, *Taking Charge: The Johnson White House Tapes, 1963–64* (New York: Simon and Schuster, 1997), 371; and Robert Mann, *Grand Illusion: America's Decent into Vietnam* (New York: Basic Books, 2001), 305–14.

3. McNamara to Johnson, March 16, 1964, *Foreign Relations of the United States*, 1964–68, 1: 154–56 and 166–67; Beschloss, *Taking Charge* 293; Woods, *Fulbright: A Biography*, 334–39; McGovern interview, April 30, 1969, Oral History Collection, LBJL.

4. G. McGovern, *Grassroots*, 102; Logevall, *Choosing War*, 135 and 195; Rick Perlstein, *Before the Storm: Barry Goldwater and the Unmaking of the American Consensus* (New York: Hill and Wang, 2001), 347, 352, and 373; Russell and LBJ in Beschloss, *Taking Charge*, 365.

5. McNamara to Johnson, March 16, 1964; Beschloss, *Taking Charge*, 370–73; Herring, *America's Longest War*, 139–41.

6. Woods, *Fulbright*, 345–50; Robert Mann, *A Grand Delusion: America's Descent into Vietnam* (New York: Basic Books, 2001), 345–55; Logevall, *Choosing War*, 193–203.

7. Woods, *LBJ*, 515–17; Logevall, *Choosing War*, 197–99; Mann, *Grand Delusion*, 349–51 and 359–61; and McNamara, *In Retrospect*, 132–35.

8. See, for example, McGovern to Fulbright, July 11, 1961, and Fulbright to McGovern, April 9, 1963, Series 48.1, Box 5, J. William Fulbright Papers, Special Collections, University of Arkansas Libraries (hereinafter JWFP); on opposition to Eisenhower Doctrine, see Woods, *Fulbright*, 353.

9. *CR*, August 6, 1964, 18399–421; Mann, *Grand Delusion*, 361–67; Robert David Johnson, *Ernest Gruening and the American Dissenting Tradition* (Cambridge, MA: Harvard University Press), 253.

10. McGovern interview, December 29, 1992; see also G. McGovern, *Grassroots*, 102–4; Woods, *Fulbright*, 353–55; Herring, *America's Longest War*, 137.

11. See *CR*, August 8, 1964, 18668–70.

12. *WP*, September 2, 1964 and *HDP*, September 9, 1964.

13. *HDP*, September 4 ("Businessmen"), 20, and October 1, 13, and 16, 1964; *CR*, September 8, 21690; *WP*, September 8, 1964 (poll).

14. Perlstein, *Before the Storm*, 512–14; "LBJ, Humphrey" and "SD Voters' Favorite," *HDP*, November 4 and December 6, 1964; Link and Catton, *American Epoch*, 851; Clem, *Prairie State Politics*, 42–43. In South Dakota, Republican incumbents in the House won easily, but their candidate for governor won by only 10,000 out of 190,000 votes, and for lieutenant governor by 330 out 182,000 ballots. The GOP would control the legislature by 64 to 46.

15. McGovern interview, LBJL, April 30, 1969; Mann, *Grand Delusion*, 376–78; and Lloyd C. Gardner, *Pay Any Price: Lyndon Johnson and the Wars for Vietnam* (Chicago: Ivan Dee, 1995), 129–31, 142, 144, and 149–50.

16. Gardner, *Pay Any Price*, 147 and 149 (Bundy and Ball quotes); Logevall, *Choosing War*, 269–71 and 273; Woods, *LBJ*, 597–99; and Herring, *America's Longest War*, 147–51.

17. Gardner, *Pay Any Price*, 157 (quote); Woods, *LBJ*, 597; Goodwin, *Lyndon Johnson*, 259–60 (quote); and Logevall, *Choosing War*, 272–73 (288 for Alsop).

18. Herring, *America's Longest War*, 151.

19. Logevall, *Choosing War*, 273–74, 285–87 and 300–309; Jim Lehrer, "Fulbright Sees Way," *Dallas Times Herald*, December 8, 1964; SMU *Daily Campus*, December 9, 1964; and stories in *U.S. News and World Report*, January 11, and *Newsweek*, January 4. 1965.

20. Fall, *The Two Vietnams*, 343–46; 381, 390 and 406; see also Fall, *Street without Joy* (Harrisburg, PA: Stackpole, 1961; 4th ed., 1967); obituary on Fall, *The Nation*, March 13, 1967 (McGovern quote). See Box 567, GSMP, for correspondence with George McT. Kahin of Cornell.

21. Conversation reconstructed by McGovern in interview, December 29, 1992.

22. *CR*, January 15, 1965, 784–86.

23. See the *NYT* and the *WP*, both January 16, 1965, and "McGovern vs. Nixon," *The Nation*, February 8, 1965. See also LeRoy Ashby and Rod Gramer, *Fighting the Odds: The Life of Senator Frank Church* (Pullman: Washington State University Press, 1994), 183–86 and 190–99; and David F. Schmitz and Natalie Fousekis, "Senator Frank Church, the Senate, and the Emergence of Dissent on the Vietnam War, 1963–1966," *Pacific Historical Review* (August 1995): 561–81; Gallup in *WP*, January 31, 1965.

24. Logevall, *Choosing War*, 324–26 and 329–31, and 349; Mann, *Grand Delusion*, 393–97; Reston, *NYT*, February 14, 1965; and *Newsweek*, February 22, 1965, 32–36.

25. *CR*, February 17, 1965, 2869–78; Mann, *Grand Delusion*, 409–11; and Ashby and Gramer, *Fighting the Odds*, 192–93.

26. *CR*, February 17, 1965, 2878–81; memo to Senator from Phyllis, ca. February 15, 1965, Box 567, GSMP.

27. Transcript in Michael Beschloss, *Reaching for Glory: Lyndon Johnson's Secret White House Tapes, 1964–1965* (New York: Simon and Shuster, 2001), 181–82 and 184–85.

28. McGovern interview, April 30, 1969, LBJL; Ashby and Gramer, *Fighting the Odds*, 193–93; Preston, *War Council*, 181–85.

29. *CR*, February 18, 1965, 3146–51 and 3188–90.

30. *CR*, February 23, 1965, 3346–58; colloquy 3375–81.

31. White, "Viet-Nam Policy," ca. January and February 8, 1965, attached to McGovern to White, February 9, 1965, Box 567, GSMP.

32. "Vietnam: Debate," *NYT*, February 28, 1965.

33. See transcript, "Vietnam: The Hawks and the Doves," March 8, 1965, Box 730, GSMP.

34. Woods, *LBJ*, 579–87, and McGovern to LBJ, March 23, 1965, GSMP; and Jack Valenti to McGovern, March 25, 1965, WHCF, Box 270, LBJL. See also, Matusow, *Unraveling of America*, 181–85, and Schulman, *Lyndon Johnson*, 114–18.

35. Mann, *Grand Delusion*, 417–19; Woods, *LBJ*, 603–5; Valenti to LBJ, March 24, 1965, WHCF, Box 270, McGovern interview, April 30, 1969, LBJL; McGovern interview, December 29, 1992.

36. Reconstructed by McGovern, McGovern interview, December 29, 1992; McGovern memo for LBJ, March 26, 1965, Box 567, GSMP, and Horace Busby files, Box 6, LBJL.

37. McGovern interview, December 29, 1992; Bucknell speech, April 1, Box 769, GSMP; G. McGovern, *Grassroots*, 104–5; McGovern to LBJ, April 1, 1965, copy in Humphrey Papers, 150.E.9.8.F, Box 841; *WPO*, April 19, 1965 (speech).

38. Charles DeBenedetti and Charles Chatfield, *An American Ordeal: The Antiwar Movement of the Vietnam Era* (Syracuse, NY: Syracuse University Press, 1990), 107–11.

39. Ibid., 21–22 and 31–33; G. McGovern, *Grassroots*, 108; Isserman and Kazin, *America Divided*, 175–79.

40. Joseph Kraft, "Johnson Has the Right," *Chicago Daily News*, March 1, 1965.

41. Woods, *LBJ*, 606–7; Melvin Small, *Johnson, Nixon, and the Doves* (New Brunswick, NJ: Rutgers University Press, 1988), 36–41; Robert Dallek, *Flawed Giant: Lyndon Johnson and His Times, 1961–1973* (New York: Oxford University Press, 1998), 260–62.

42. JHU Address, April 7, 1965, *The Public Papers of the Presidents of the United States: Lyndon B. Johnson, 1965* (Washington, DC: 1966), 1: 394–99. McGovern interview, April 30, 1969, LBJL. Two weeks earlier assistant secretary of defense John McNaughton had drawn up for LBJ a rationalization for expanding the war. Seventy percent of the motive was to "avoid a humiliating U.S. defeat (to our reputation as a guarantor)." Twenty percent was to keep "SVN [out of] . . . Chinese hands," and 10 percent was to "permit the people of SVN to enjoy a

better freer way of life." McNaughton to McNamara, March 24, 1965, in George Herring, ed., *The Pentagon Papers* (New York: McGraw Hill, 1993), 115–16.

43. McGovern quoted in Anson, *McGovern*, 159; Ashby and Gramer, *Fighting the Odds*, 200–202; "The Work of Peace," February 8, 1965, Box 769, GSMP.

44. Lippmann in *Newsweek*, April 12, 1965; Gardner, *Pay Any Price*, 197–98; McGovern in *CR*, May 14, 1965, 10504–6; DeBenedetti and Chatfield, *An American Ordeal*, 111–13; Small, *Johnson, Nixon, and the Doves*, 41–42; McGovern quote, *CR*, July 27, 1965, 18306.

45. *MDR*, March 5, 1965; *SFAL*, April 25, 1965; and *WPO*, April 19, 1965.

46. "Joe Thorne and the Vietnam War," with news accounts, *CR*, April 28, 1965, 8764–66, and materials in Box 770, GSMP; Herring, *America's Longest War*, 157.

47. Mann, *Grand Delusion*, 431–37; McNamara, *In Retrospect*, 183–89; Gardner, *Pay Any Price*, 213; *CR*, June 24, 1965, 14631.

48. Schlesinger to Moyers, May 17, 1965, WHCF, Box 270, LBJL; Humphrey to McGovern, June 7, 1965, Series 150.E.47B, Cont. File 1965, Box 846, Humphrey Papers, Minnesota Historical Society Library; and Humphrey to McGovern, August 11, 1967, Box 914, GSMP; DeBenedetti and Chatfield, *An American Ordeal*, 115; Lewis Chester, Godfrey Hodgson, and Bruce Page, *An American Melodrama: The Presidential Campaign of 1968* (New York: Viking Press, 1969), 58; author's interviews with Schlesinger, July 10,1996, and with Steinem, July 5, 1996; Gloria Steinem, *Outrageous Acts and Everyday Rebellions* (New York: Henry Holt, 1983; 1993 ed.), 76–80; see also Andrew Schlesinger and Stephen Schlesinger, eds., *The Letters of Arthur Schlesinger, Jr.* (New York: Random House, 2013), 416–18.

49. *CR*, June 24, 1965, 14631–21.

50. *CR*, June 17, 1965, 14038–39; Herring, *America's Longest War*, 164.

51. Beschloss, *Reaching for Glory*, 358–59 and 403 (Lady Bird); McNamara, *In Retrospect*, 192; *Newsweek*, August 2, 1965, 16, quoted in Woods, *LBJ*, 615.

52. Press Conference, July 28, 1965, *Public Papers*, Johnson, 1965, 2: 794–803; Herring, *America's Longest War*, 164–69; Woods, *LBJ*, 615–20.

53. See *CR*, July 27, 1965, 18308–12. Church, Clark, Morse, and Gruening also spoke.

54. *CR*, August 17, 1965, 20627–28, and *RCJ*, August 11, 1965; Woods, *LBJ*, 563–67.

55. Woods, *LBJ*, 567–68, and *CR*, September 2, 1965, 22703–11, colloquy, McGovern and other senators.

56. *CR*, January 6, 1965, for remarks by McGovern, Anderson, and Javits; Matusow, *Unraveling of America*, 226–29; Woods, *LBJ*, 569–74.

57. Harris poll, *CR*, August 10, 1965, 19753; tribute, *CR*, September 2, 1965, 22772–73; see also *CR*, February 1, 1693–95; May 26, 11750; and August 18 and 19, 1965, 20876–78 and 21133–34.

58. *CR*, July 27, 1965, 18308–12.

59. McGovern UAW speech, San Diego, February 26, 1965, Box 769 and 740, GSMP.

60. FFP Act of 1965, *CR*, June 17, 1965, 13998–14005; "The Most Important War," September 23, 1965, G. McGovern, *A Time of War, A Time of Peace*, 165–76 (quote, 171); LBJ in *War against Want*, viii; Joseph Califano to LBJ, October

18, 1965, WHCF, Box 270, LBJL; Rusk to FFP Council, October 20, 1965, Reuter Papers, Box 13, JFKL; Ruttan, *U.S. Development Assistance*, 162n32; Wallerstein, *Food for War*, 134–35 and 275n19; McGovern interview, August 9, 1991; Schlesinger to JFK, April 30, 1962, Box 471, GSMP.

61. McGovern interview, August 7, 1993; Anson, *McGovern*, 161–62.

62. G. McGovern, *Grassroots*, 107.

63. *SFAL*, December 17, 1965. See also *Newsweek*, December 13, 1965, and *NYT*, December 3, 1965 and January 25, 1966 (McGovern letter); and December 1965 Newsletter, Box 740, GSMP.

64. *CR*, July 27, 1965, 18309–12; "Sincere Dissenter," *WPO*, April 19, 1965.

65. McNamara, *In Retrospect*, 107 and 113–14; Logevall, *Choosing War*, 23–25 and 85–93; *The Nation*, February 8, 1965; *SFAL*, April 25, 1965.

66. McGovern interview, LBJL, April 30, 1969.

67. Goodwin, *Lyndon Johnson*, 282–85; Logevall, *Choosing War*, 377 and 381; LBJ in Beschloss, *Reaching for Glory*, 345; Woods, *LBJ*, 620; McNamara, *In Retrospect*, 190.

68. Russell in Beschloss, *Taking Charge*, 363–70; Logevall, *Choosing War*, 273–81; 345–47; 377–82; Solberg, *Hubert Humphrey*, 271–77; Woods, *LBJ*, 684; Ball memo to LBJ, March 1, 1966, State Dept., A/CDC, copy in LBJL.

69. McGovern interview, LBJL.

CHAPTER 15 THE CUP OF PERIL IS FULL

1. G. McGovern, *Terry*, 57–59 and 19–20; E. McGovern, *Uphill*, 115–16.

2. Eleanor McGovern interview; E. McGovern, *Uphill*, 114; and G. McGovern, *Terry*, 50–51.

3. Interviews with Ann McGovern and Susan McGovern Rowen; E. McGovern, *Uphill*, 117.

4. Eleanor McGovern interview.

5. G. McGovern, *Terry*, 63–69.

6. Interviews with Susan Rowen, Eleanor, and Steve McGovern.

7. *LBJ Public Papers*, 1966, 1: 3–12; see also Woods, *LBJ*, 684–87.

8. McNamara, *In Retrospect*, 219–20 and 225–27; Young, *Vietnam Wars*, 180; Pearson, "McGovern Inspired Vietnam Truce," *SFAL*, December 29, 1965.

9. McGovern to Moyers, January 14, 1966, WHCF, Box 270, LBJL; *Newsweek*, January 17, 1966, 16; *NYT*, January 6, 1966; *Today* show transcript, January 5, and press release, January 5, 1966, Box 567, GSMP.

10. "McNamara and Rusk were excellent advocates of a weak case," McGovern once said. At off-the-record briefings they presented quantitative measurements of each side's war effort, stressing the rate the enemy was exhausting its resources while the United States increased its strength. On a chart McNamara showed a convergence beyond which the enemy "should quit fighting and recognize they were defeated, that their losses would reach a point where the war would make no sense."

11. McGovern interview, August 7, 1993; *CR*, January 20, 1966, 775–80, and Box 567, GSMP; Valenti to McNamara and to Rusk, January 22, 1966, WHCF,

Box 270, LBJL; DeBenedetti and Chatfield, *An American Ordeal*, 142; *CR*, March 13, 1967, 6459, McNaughton to McNamara, January 19, 1966, Herring, *Pentagon Papers*, 138–39.

12. Cousins to McGovern, February 16, 1966, and Reston to McGovern February 14, 1966, Box 771, GSMP.

13. See *CR*, January 31, 1966, 1577, 1583, and 1584 (1576–86 for the entire colloquy).

14. Ibid., 1581–83; 1587–89 (CBS transcript).

15. Ibid., February 8, 1966, 2560–61; *Today* transcript, February 24, 1966, Box 567, GSMP; McPherson to Califano, February 23, 1966, WHCF, Box 270, LBJL; Woods, *Fulbright*, 400.

16. Woods, *Fulbright*, 402–10; Gardner, *Pay Any Price*, 281–93; Mann, *Grand Delusion*, 491–98; DeBenedetti and Chatfield, *An American Ordeal*, 143.

17. *CR*, March 1, 1966, 4404–11 (quotes, 4408, 4409, and 4410), and McGovern interview, April 30, 1969, LBJL.

18. "Committee of One Million," Box 770, GSMP; Goldwater, *WP*, April 28, 1965; McGovern, *CR*, April 28, 1965, 8826–28; McGovern at US/China conference, April 29, *CR* May 10, 1965, 10054–55; and McGovern remarks, *CR*, May 26, 1965, 11836–37.

19. See Woods, *Fulbright*, 412–13; *Commentary* discussion, February 14, 1966, Box 770; letters to McGovern from Kennan, April 19, and from Fairbank, April 21; Schlesinger to McGovern, with enclosures, April 20, 1966; McGovern to Fred Dutton, March 28, 1966, all in China speech file, Box 771, GSMP.

20. "Ignorance Curtain," *CR*, May 3, 1966, 9609–14; G. McGovern, *A Time of War, A Time of Peace*, 105–10. "If we had had more Asia experts" McNamara wrote in *In Retrospect*, "perhaps we would not have been so simpleminded about China and Vietnam." He admitted he "misread China's . . . rhetoric[,] . . . underestimated the nationalist aspect of Ho Chi Minh's movement," and "took no account of the centuries-old hostility [with] China (117, 32–33, and 219).

21. G. McGovern, *A Time of War, A Time of Peace*, 111–15.

22. Ibid., 116–18.

23. Ibid., 119–22.

24. Ibid., 122–23.

25. *CR*, May 3, 1966, 9614–17, for Fulbright; ibid., 9605–07, and *CR*, July 20, 1966, 16420, for Kennedy; letters to McGovern from Shriver, May 12; Dutton, April 20 and May 6; and Billington, May 13, 1966, Box 771, GSMP.

26. *CR*, May 3, 1966, 9617–18; AP story, Humphrey and China, *HDP*, May 3, 1966; LBJ speech, July 12, 1966, *LBJ Public Papers, 1966*, 2: 718–22.

27. The Russians did not relish involvement, but rivalry with the PRC forced it. Through 1967 they had sent tanks, planes, and antiaircraft batteries as well as 3,000 personnel to operate them. But by 1967 the Chinese had provided Hanoi with thirty-two fighter jets (and trained the North Vietnamese to fly them), 90,000 rifles, and ammunition, and had sent 170,000 troops to operate artillery and to construct roads so Hanoi could project maximum numbers of its own soldiers into the South.

28. Herring, *America's Longest War*, 176–79; Qiang Zhai, "An Uneasy Relationship: China and the DVR during the Vietnam War," in *International Perspectives on Vietnam*, ed. Lloyd Gardner and Ted Gittinger (College Station: Texas A&M University Press, 2000), 109–13, 116–18, and 137–39.

29. Legion text, Box 913; Metromedia letters to McGovern, August 12 (program transcript, September 8), and from Lefton Stavrianos, September 10, 1966, Box 730, GSMP; "Vietnam, A Proposal," *NYRB*, July 7, 1966.

30. Colloquy, *CR*, June 30, 1966, 14863–72.

31. Isserman and Kazan, *America Divided*, 143–45. John Morton Blum, *Years of Decision: American Politics and Society, 1961–1974* (New York: Norton, 1991), 252–60; Harvard Sitkoff, *The Struggle for Black Equality, 1954–1980* (New York: Hill and Wang, 1981), 200–202.

32. Dallek, *Flawed Giant*, 337, 340, and 375–76; Woods, *LBJ*, 742 and 751.

33. South Dakota's returns reversed the trend toward two-party politics in the 1964 election. Karl Mundt and Representatives Berry and Reifel retained their seats with an average of 64 percent of the vote. Governor Nils Boe won reelection with 57 percent. In the legislature, Democrats lost 26 of the 46 seats they had held; Republicans would now control it by 90 to 20.

34. Woods, *LBJ*, 741–45 (quote, 743); Dallek, *Flawed Giant*, 335–39; Huntley in *SFAL* editorial, ca. December 1966, in Lindley to Califano, January 19, 1967, FG/RS/PR/18, Box 16, LBJL; and Tom Wicker, *One of Us: Richard Nixon and the American Dream* (New York: Random House, 1991), 279–87 (quote, 283); Clem, "The 1966 Election in South Dakota," *Public Affairs* (Government Research Bureau, University of South Dakota), February 15, 1967, 1–6.

35. McGovern interview, July 16, 1970, RFK Oral History, JFKL; Schlesinger, *Journals*, 249–53.

36. Evan Thomas, *Robert Kennedy* (New York: Simon and Shuster, 2000), 96–99, 277–79, 306, and 313–16; Goodwin, *Lyndon Johnson*, 199–202 and 253 (quote); McGovern interview, RFK Oral History.

37. McGovern interview, RFK Oral History; Thomas, *Robert Kennedy*, 302; interviews with McGovern, December 29, 1992 and August 7, 1993, and Pat Donovan; RFK remarks in Mitchell, May 10, 1968, Box 450, GSMP.

38. McGovern interview, LBJL.

39. Ibid.; author's interview with Mankiewicz, May 29, 1996; Schlesinger, *Robert Kennedy and His Times* (Boston: Houghton Mifflin, 1978), 769–71.

40. *CR*, March 2, 1967, 5279–96; *WP*, March 3, 1967; Mann, *Grand Delusion*, 533–35; Schlesinger, *Robert Kennedy*, 771–75.

41. Schlesinger, *Robert Kennedy*, 771–75, and McGovern, "Why Don't You," *New Republic*, March 18, 1967, 10–11; Thomas, *Robert Kennedy*, 334–35; McGovern interview, LBJL.

42. Herring, *America's Longest War*, 182 and 267.

43. Ibid., 179, 181, and 186–88.

44. Ibid., 171–73, 181, 183, and 195–97; Young, *Vietnam Wars*, 186–88 and 190–91; *CR*, April 25, 1967, 10611.

45. DeBenedetti and Chatfield, *An American Ordeal*, 128–29 and 131–32.

46. Ibid., 142–45, 151–53, 163, and 173–77; Isserman and Kazin, *America Divided*, 191; Young, *Vietnam Wars*, 197–200; Woods, *LBJ*, 764.

47. *CR*, June 30, 1966, 14872–84 and August 25, 1966, 20564, *New Republic*, March 18, 1967, 11; *NYT*, February 26, 1967 (King); Carey McWilliams (editor of *The Nation*) to McGovern, October 18, 1966, Box 442, GSMP; and DeBenedetti and Chatfield, *An American Ordeal*, 172–73; author's interview with James Rowen, December 28, 1996. The war was "supporting a new form of colonialism," Dr. King said; in light of domestic cutbacks, it was "making the poor, white and Negro, bear the heaviest burdens both at the front and at home." By February 1967 there were "twice as many Negroes in combat in Vietnam . . . and twice as many died in action—20.6 percent—in proportion to their numbers in the population as whites." It was on this occasion, five weeks before his celebrated address at the Riverside Church in New York, that King first called for American withdrawal from Vietnam.

48. *NYT* and *WP*, April 25 and 26, 1967; *MDR*, April 27, 1967; *SFAL*, April 25, 1967; McGovern interview, LBJL; Schlesinger, *Journals*, 260; William Westmoreland, *A Soldier Reports* (Garden City, NY: Doubleday, 1976), 272–75.

49. "Lessons of Vietnam," and colloquy, *CR*, April 25, 1967, 10610–22 (10610–11).

50. Ibid., 10611.

51. Ibid., 10614–15.

52. Ibid., 10616.

53. *WP*, April 26; *NYT*, April 26, 27, and 30; *The Nation*, May 8; *The Progressive*, April 1967; *MDR*, April 29 and May 1 (*Post-Dispatch* editorial), 1967.

54. *CR*, April 25, 1967, 10613–18; *NYT*, April 26 and 27; *HDP*, April 27 and 28; *MDR*, April 29; *The Nation*, May 22, 1967, 642; *New Republic*, May 27, 1967; Pearson in *SFAL*, April 30, 1967.

55. *NYT*, April 30, 1967; McNamara, *In Retrospect*, 264–66; Woods, *LBJ*, 763–65; Dallek, *Flawed Giant*, 473–76; Westmoreland, *A Soldier Reports*, 275–77; Milne, *America's Rasputin*, 189–91.

56. *MDR*, April 27 and 28; *HDP*, April 25, 1967; see *SFAL*, April 27, 28, and 29, 1967 ("McGovern's Statement"); UPI wheat story, December 5, 1966, WHCF, Box 270, LBJL.

57. Blum, *Years of Decision*, 261–64; Sitkoff, *Struggle for Black Equality*, 202–4.

58. Thomas, *Robert Kennedy*, 348–49; Woods, *LBJ*, 790–95; Chester Bowles to McGovern, with enclosure, and McGovern to Bowles, April 14 and May 27, 1967, Box 443, GSMP.

59. Dallek, *Flawed Giant*, 391–405 and 533–36; Woods, *LBJ*, 795–97.

60. "McGovern Reports," August 1967, Senator's Personal Amendment file 1970, GSMP. For the election, Herring, *America's Longest War*, 195–96, and Young, *Vietnam Wars*, 184–86.

61. Memo, "Personal and Confidential," September 22, 1967, Box 691, GSMP. The guests were Mike Mansfield, Russell Long, Carl Hayden, Gaylord Nelson, Joe Clark, Frank Church, Warren Magnuson, Mike Monroney, Wayne Morse, and Rostow and Humphrey.

62. John F. Lindley to Califano, enclosing *SFAL* editorial ("Subtle Campaign"), January 19, 1967, Confidential File FG/RS/PR 18; Califano to LBJ, August 27, enclosing Lindley to Humphrey, July 25, 1967; and William Connell to Marvin Watson, December 19, 1967, with enclosure from Lindley; memo on

ADA to LBJ, August 3, 1967, WHCF, Box 270, LBJL; and McGovern interview, July 16, 1970, RFK Oral History, JFKL.

63. McGovern interview, LBJL; William Chafe, *Never Stop Running: Allard Lowenstein and the Struggle to Save American Liberalism* (New York: Basic Books, 1993), 262–75; and Chester, Hodgson, and Page, *American Melodrama*, 61–66.

64. Author's interviews with McGovern, April 4, 1994 and December 29, 1992, and with Schlesinger.

65. McGovern interviews, RFK Oral History, JFKL, and LBJL (Lowenstein quote); author's interview with Dougherty; Chafe, *Never Stop Running* (Lowenstein), 271; Anson, *McGovern*, 8; Chester, Hodgson, and Page, *American Melodrama*, 66–67.

66. DeBenedetti and Chatfield, *An American Ordeal*, 195–97; Isserman and Kazin, *America Divided*, 192–94; author's interviews with Susan McGovern, December 29, 1995, and James Rowen, December 28, 1996.

67. DeBenedetti and Chatfield, *An American Ordeal*, 196–98 (Brinkley, 198) and 203–5; Mailer in *American Divided*, 192; McNamara, *In Retrospect*, 303–5; Dallek, *Flawed Giant*, 487–89; Tom Wells, *The War Within: America's Battle over Vietnam* (Berkeley: University of California Press, 1994), 195–203.

68. Wells, *War Within*, 109–11, 198–99, and 203–5; DeBenedetti and Chatfield, *An American Ordeal*, 198–200; McNamara, *In Retrospect*, 311–17; Dallek, *Flawed Giant*, 486.

69. See McGovern's interviews, April 30, 1969, LBJL; and July 16, 1970, RFK Oral History, JFKL; Schlesinger, *Journals*, 263–75.

70. Schlesinger, *Journals*, 263–64; Steinem interview, July 5, 1996; Chester, Hodgson, and Page, *American Melodrama*, 70 and 74–75; Dominic Sandbrook, *Eugene McCarthy and the Rise and Fall of Postwar American Liberalism* (New York: Random House, Anchor Books, 2004), 110–16, 125–27, 161 (quote), and 191; Wells, *War Within*, 120; DeBenedetti and Chatfield, *An American Ordeal*, 201–2.

71. Sandbrook, *Eugene McCarthy*, 149–51, 175–77, and 182–83; DeBenedetti and Chatfield, *An American Ordeal*, 201 and 209; *NYT*, March 10, 1968; McGovern, *CR*, March 11, 1968, 5963; Steinem, *Outrageous Acts*, 87; Chester, Hodgson, and Page, *American Melodrama*, 79, 83 (quote), and 84–87.

72. Thomas, *Robert Kennedy*, 351–55 (Dutton quote, 354); McGovern interview, RFK Oral History, JFKL; Schlesinger, *Journals*, December 10, 1967, 268–70, and January 19 and 25, 1968, 275 (quotes); see also, Schlesinger, *Robert Kennedy*, 836–41.

73. McGovern to M. B. Hart, November 30, and to Donald Bogue, December 13, 1967, cited in Ben Young, "A Magnificent Obsession and an Impossible Dream: George McGovern and the Electoral Politics of 1968" (Princeton University Senior Thesis, 2006), 19; and Memo for the President, October 12, 1967, Box 691, GSMP.

74. Herring, *America's Longest War*, 221; Woods, *LBJ*, 809–11; and McGovern to LBJ, October 24, 1967, with *St. Louis Post-Dispatch*, Box 443, GSMP.

75. Mann, *Grand Delusion*, 569–71; Young, *Vietnam Wars*, 210; Westmoreland, *A Soldier Reports*, 284–85; Wells, *War Within*, 241.

76. Westmoreland, *A Soldier Reports*, 283–84; Dallek, *Flawed Giant*, 521–27.

77. "Democrats Face," *NYT*, May 29, 1967; White, "Test for Doves," *WP*, April 8; 1967; Marquis Childs, "McGovern and Nelson," in *MDR*, April 6, 1967; "Speaking Out," *The Nation*, May 8, 1967.

78. *HDP*, April 16, 1967; *WP*, July 5, 1967; *MDR*, July 8 and 26 (editorial), 1967; Harold Spitznagel to McGovern, June 20; McGovern to Spitznagel, June 23, and George to Eleanor, November 16, 1967, all in Box 443, GSMP; *Village Voice*, June 15, 1967.

79. *SFAL*, May 31 and December 20, 1967; *HDP*, December 21 and 27, 1967. *SFAL*, *WPO*, and *AAN* conducted the polls.

CHAPTER 16 BUT THERE ARE STILL PEOPLE WITH HOPE

1. Mann, *Grand Delusion*, 570–72; Herring, *America's Longest War*, 225–29.

2. Herring, *America's Longest War*, 231–32; Young, *Vietnam Wars*, 216–25; DeBenedetti and Chatfield, *An American Ordeal*, 209–10; casualties, Dallek, *Flawed Giant*, 504.

3. Wells, *War Within*, 240–41; Dallek, *Flawed Giant*, 503–4 and 527; Lewis Gould, "Never a Deep Partisan: Lyndon Johnson and the Democratic Party, 1963–1969," in *The Johnson Years*, ed. Robert A. Divine, vol. 3, *LBJ at Home and Abroad* (Lawrence: University Press of Kansas, 1994), 39; Mann, *Grand Delusion*, 573–74 and 576; Milne, *America's Rasputin*, 212–16.

4. Dallek, *Flawed Giant*, 505–10; Walter LaFeber, *The Deadly Bet: LBJ, Vietnam, and the1968 Election* (Lanham, MD: Rowman and Littlefield, 2005), 28 and 30–31; Wells, *War Within*, 241–43; McGovern remarks in *CR*, March 7, 1968, 5662.

5. Dallek, *Flawed Giant*, 506; for the Fulbright speech and colloquy, *CR*, March 7, 1968, 5644–67; AP on the Tonkin incident, in newspapers February 22, 1968.

6. Chester, Hodgson, and Page, *American Melodrama*, 93 and 96–99; De-Benedetti and Chatfield, *An American Ordeal*, 211; and Sandbrook, *Eugene McCarthy*, 177–79 and 184–85; and Steinem, *Outrageous Acts and Other Rebellions*, 87; LaFeber, *Deadly Bet*, 44–45; McCarthy and ADA in Gillon, *Politics and Vision*, 211–14.

7. Thomas, *Robert Kennedy*, 357–58 (quote); Schlesinger, *Robert Kennedy and His Times*, 840–41 and 845–51, and *Journals*, 280 (quote); McGovern interview, LBJL.

8. McGovern interview, RFK Oral History, JFKL; Pat Donovan interview; Schlesinger, *Robert Kennedy*, 853 (for Udall) and 859–61, and *Journals* (March 13 and 17), 279–84.

9. Herring, *America's Longest War*, 245–47; Robert Buzzanco, *Masters of War: Military Dissent and Politics in the Vietnam Era* (New York: Cambridge University Press, 1996), 321–31; McGovern in *CR*, March 12, 1968, 6162–63.

10. Wells, *War Within*, 243–46 and 250–53; Herring, *America's Longest War*, 248–50.

11. McGovern, KELO-TX News, April 1, 1968, Box 450, GSMP; Schlesinger, *Journals* (April 3), 285; Dallek, *Flawed Giant*, 529–31 (Fulbright).

12. Dallek, *Flawed Giant*, 533–34; Sitkoff, *Struggle for Black Equality*, 221; Woods, *LBJ*, 838–40; Schlesinger, *Robert Kennedy*, 873–75.

13. See LaFeber, *Deadly Bet*, 75–79; Isserman and Kazin, *America Divided*, 209–11; Woods, *LBJ*, 818–19; Dallek, *Flawed Giant*, 515–17; Solberg, *Humphrey*, 332–33; 1968 State of the Union, LBJL website.

14. Thomas, *Robert Kennedy*, 371; Sandbrook, *Eugene McCarthy*, 193 and 197–98.

15. Sandbrook, *Eugene McCarthy*, 195–96; Chester, Hodgson, and Page, *American Melodrama*, 339–41; Schlesinger, *Journals* (April 24), 287.

16. Thomas, *Robert Kennedy*, 371–73 and 376–77; Sandbrook, *Eugene McCarthy*, 198–200; Schlesinger, *Robert Kennedy*, 889–94; see also, LaFeber, *Deadly Bet*, 91–95.

17. *MDR*, March 19 and May 16, and *HDP*, March 22 and 24 (editorial), May 10, 14, and 16 1968; *CR*, March 11, 1968, 5963–64; Anson, *McGovern*, 189–90; Box 774, GSMP.

18. *MDR*, April 27 (quote) and May 10; *HDP*, May 12, 1968; McGovern interview, December 29, 1992 (quote); McGovern to Humphrey, January 4 (quote) and March 30, 1966, Box 841, Humphrey Papers; E. McGovern, *Uphill*, 133, and Eleanor McGovern interview for her quotes; Schlesinger, *Journals* (March 11, 1966), 246; see also Solberg, *Hubert Humphrey*, 159 and 468–69; see also Box 774, GSMP.

19. Dougherty interview; John Herbers, "RFK in South Dakota," *NYT*, April 17, 1968; "RFK Bids for SD," *MDR*, April 16, 1968; McGovern introduction in Box 774, GSMP; *CR*, July 31, 1968, 24478; "Crowds Greet," *SFAL*, April 16, 1968.

20. See, in *MDR*, "RFK to Eye," April 16, and "Kennedy Visits," April 17, 1968; in *HDP*, "Kennedy Enters," April 16, and "RFK Gets Bleak" (quote), April 17, 1968; and "Kennedy Hearing, *SFAL*, April 17, 1968; Thomas, *Robert Kennedy*, 352–53 and 371.

21. "Mobbed By" and "Kennedy Talks" (quote), *HDP*, May 12, 1968; "Kennedy Favors," *MDR*, May 11, 1968 (on McGovern).

22. Richard Reeves, "Making of a Candidate," *NYT Sunday Magazine*, March 31, 1968, 133; McGovern in Schlesinger, *Robert Kennedy*, 903.

23. "McGovern Swamps," *SFAL*, February 27, 1968; "McGovern Still," "Poll Prompts," and "Republican Drifting," *MDR*, February 22 and 26 and April 4, 1968; "Boe Not," "Boe's Announcement," and "Aspirants for Senate," *HDP*, March 22, 24, and 29, 1968.

24. "Dakota Poll," *SFAL*, May 1; "Demos Favor" and "Gubbrud Pleased," *HDP*, May 2 and 5, 1968.

25. "Give Humphrey" and "Kennedy Leads," *SFAL*, April 17 and May 1, 1968; "Demos Favor," *HDP*, May 2 1968; Thomas, *Robert Kennedy*, 375–82.

26. See "Kennedy Leads," *SFAL*, May 29, 1968; in *HDP*: "Humphrey Aides," May 26, and "Kennedy Tops," "Big Names," and "Brother Sees," all on May 31, 1968; in *MDR*: "Primary Campaigns," "Spotlight," and "Strong Demo," May 22 and June 1 and 3, 1968.

27. The numbers were 32,157 to 19,304 to 13,215. Nixon, unopposed in the Republican primary, won 71,042 votes. About 121,000 Democrats and 176,000 Republicans were registered to vote.

28. "RFK Scores," *MDR*, June 5, 1968; "Kennedy's Victory" and "Democrat Votes," *MDR*, June 5 and 6, 1968.

29. G. McGovern, *Grassroots*, 117; McGovern interview, December 29, 1992; "RJK: People," *HDP*, June 5, 1968; "Kennedy's Visits," *SFAL*, June 6, 1968; Thomas, *Robert Kennedy*, 386–90.

30. Thomas, *Robert Kennedy*, 390–94; Schlesinger, *Journals*, 290; Eleanor McGovern interview; McGovern interview, December 29, 1992; reflections in *SFAL* and *MDR*, June 6, 1968; for funeral, Theodore White, *Making of the President 1968* (New York: Atheneum, 1969), 213–15.

31. McGovern interview, December 29, 1992; E. McGovern, *Uphill*, 129–30; "Honor Guard" and "Details of Funeral," *SFAL*, June 7 and 16, 1968.

32. Dougherty interview; G. McGovern, *Grassroots*, 117–18; Anson, *McGovern*, 192; and Chester, Hodgson, and Page, *American Melodrama*, 414.

33. Interviews with Dougherty, Donovan, and John Holum (November 18, 1994).

34. Interviews with Schlesinger and Mankiewicz; G. McGovern, *Grassroots*, 113; and "McGovern Widens," *SFAL*, June 26, 1968.

35. Proxmire colloquy, *CR*, June 25, 1968, 18542–51 (quote, 18,550); Herring, *America's Longest War*, 252–61; Woods, *LBJ*, 855–59; DeBenedetti and Chatfield, *An American Ordeal*, 218–23; Isserman and Kazin, *America Divided*, 236–38.

36. G. McGovern, *Grassroots*, 118.

37. Steinem interview and "Notes from a Political Diary," *Ms.*, October 1972, 41–42.

38. Steinem interview and "Notes," ibid.

39. "Likes McGovern" (Ecker quote), "Factions Will Seek," and "Favorite Son," *SFAL*, July 6, 8, and 12, 1968.

40. "Discord Grows" and "McGovern to Allow," *SFAL*, July 14 and 25, 1968; and "RFK's Ideals" and "Delegates Endorsement," *HDP*, July 14, 1968.

41. "McGovern Urges," *LAT*, July 28, 1968; text in Box 774, GSMP.

42. See G. McGovern, *Grassroots*, 119–20, and G. McGovern, *Terry*, 70–71.

43. "McGoverns," *SFAL*, July 30, 1968; "Continuance," *MDR*, July 29, 1968.

44. "Hearing to Continue" and "Drops Narcotics," *HDP*, August 4 and 7, 1968; and "Miss McGovern" and "Some Evidence," *SFAL*, October 8 and December 7, 1968.

45. "McGovern's Daughter," *HDP*, July 28, 1968; see letter files, Box 443, GSMP.

46. "McGovern Emerging," *MDR*, July 31; "SD Dark Horse," *Newsday* and *Oakland Tribune*, August 1 and 8, 1969; "NY Citizens—McGovern," August 1, 1968, Box 774, GSMP.

47. Text in *SFAL* and *NYT*, August 11, 1968.

48. "Dove," *NYT*, and Schlesinger, AP story in *SFAL*, August 11 (several stories); *Washington Evening Star*, August 12; and Childs, *WP*, August 16, 1968; Salinger, August 9, in Box 774, GSMP.

49. Quotes from *Time*, August 16, 22; *U.S. News*, August 26, 14; and from Herbers, "McGovern's Motives," *NYT*, August 12; see also Marjorie Hunter, "McGovern Opens," and Steven Roberts, "McGovern's Race," *NYT*, August 11; "McGovern's Bid, *Washington Evening Star*, August 12, 1968.

50. "McGovern Joined," *SFAL*, August 11; "McGovern Urges," *NYT*, August 13, 1968; G. McGovern, *Grassroots*, 122; Steinem, "Notes," *Ms.*, October 1972, 43 and 97; "Meet the Press" transcript, August 11, 1968, Box 915, GSMP.

51. "McGovern Meets Clergy," *SFAL*, August 13; "McGovern to Oppose" and "McGovern Sees Viet," *WP*, August 15 and 17; "McGovern Hopes" and "McGovern Draws," *NYT*, August 17 and 18, 1968; and materials in Box 774, GSMP.

52. E. McGovern, *Uphill*, 132–35; see also, "Favors Pets," *WP*, August 20; "Secret Service," *SFAL*, August 22; and "Campaign Novices," *NYT*, August 26, 1968.

53. "McGovern Urges" and "Twin Appeal," *SFAL*, August 17 and 18, 1968.

54. See Materials in Box 774, GSMP; Chester, Hodgson, and Page, *American Melodrama*, 529–30; "Johnson Bars" and "McGovern Urges," *NYT*, August 20, and "McGovern Urges End," *SFAL*, August 20, 1968.

55. *SFAL*, August 20, 1968; "Kennedy Backers," "Proposed Plan," and "Rusk Excerpts," *NYT*, August 21, 1968.

56. Herring, *From Colony to Superpower*, 755–57; Chester, Hodgson, and Page, *American Melodrama*, 532; "Antiwar Forces," "Connolly Scores," and "Senator Decries," *NYT*, August 22, 23, and 24,1968; press release in Cleveland (on youth), August 23, Box August 78, GSMP.

57. "At Convention Early," *SFAL*, August 24; "Plank on Vietnam," "Senators' Vietnam," and "Senator Decries," *NYT*, August 24, 1968; draft proposal, DNC platform, August 23, 1968, Box 79, GSMP; see also, Chester, Hodgson, and Page, *American Melodrama*, 331–37.

58. Ribicoff statement, August 24, Box 774, GSMP; "Ribicoff Endorses McGovern," *NYT*, August 25, 1968; Solberg, *Humphrey*, 358; author's interview with Richard Wade, January 1997; Mankiewicz in Anson, *McGovern*, 203; "McGovern Meets," *NYT*, August 26, 1968.

59. "Daley Withholds" and "Ex-Kennedy Aides," *NYT*, August 26, 1968; Solberg, *Humphrey*, 357–59.

60. "Tough McGovern," *NYT*, August 27, 1968; Norman Mailer, *Miami and the Siege at Chicago: An Informal Account of the Republican and Democratic National Conventions of 1968* (New York: New American Library, 1968), 122; Cavanaugh in Box 450, GSMP.

61. Steinem interview; "South Dakotans," *SFAL*, August 26, and "Ex-Kennedy Aides," *NYT*, August 26, 1968; Schlesinger, *Journals* (August 24), 297.

62. Schlesinger, *Journals* (August 24), 298; files, Box 450, GSMP; "Kennedy Rebuffs" and "New Harris Poll," *NYT*, August 27 and 28, 1968; Chester, Hodgson, and Page, *American Melodrama*, 544, 550, and 564–76; Solberg, *Humphrey*, 358–59; Anson, *McGovern*, 207–8.

63. See files, Box 78, GSMP; "Unit Rule" and "Delegate Fights," *NYT*, August 27 and 28, 1968; Chester, Hodgson, and Page, *American Melodrama*, 555–59.

64. G. McGovern, *Grassroots*, 129–30 and 141–43; Sandbrook, *McCarthy*, 201–3.

65. McGovern interview, August 7, 1993; Solberg, *Humphrey*, 352–54 and 359–62 (quotes, 353 and 360); "Plank Supports" and "Planks Compared," *NYT*, August 27, 1968.

66. "Rivals in Debate" and "Debate Excerpts," *NYT*, August 28, 1968; transcript, Box 774, GSMP; Mailer, *Miami and the Siege*, 118–27.

67. Steinem, "Notes," *Ms.*, October 1972, 97; Chester, Hodgson, and Page, *American Melodrama*, 562; E. McGovern, *Uphill*, 143–44; "California Gets 3,"

"McGovern Bid Buoyed," and Reston, "Chicago," *NYT*, August 28, 1968; Clark in Box 450, GSMP.

68. "Humphrey Gains" and "Right Issues," *NYT*, August 28, 1968; Solberg, *Humphrey*, 360.

69. Thirteen states and the District of Columbia voted overwhelmingly in favor. California voted 166 to 6; New York, 148 to 42; Massachusetts, 56 to 16; Wisconsin, 52 to 7; Oregon, 29 to 6; and South Dakota, 26 to 0.

70. "Defeat for Doves" and "Roll on War," *NYT*, August 29, 1968; E. McGovern, *Uphill*, 146; Chester, Hodgson, and Page, *American Melodrama*, 579–81; Holum interview.

71. E. McGovern, *Uphill*, 142 and 146–47; Ann McGovern interview.

72. DeBenedetti and Chatfield, *An American Ordeal*, 221–25 (Hayden, 225); Isserman and Kazin, *America Divided*, 239–41.

73. DeBenedetti and Chatfield, *An American Ordeal*, 225–27 (Miller, 227); *Time*, September 6, 1968, 21–22; and *U.S. News*, August 26, 1968, 24–25.

74. DeBenedetti and Chatfield, *An American Ordeal*, 227; "Police Battle" *NYT*, August 29, 1968; *Time*, September 6, 1968, 22 and 24.

75. Interviews with Donovan, Cunningham, and McGovern (August 7, 1993); Steinem, "Notes," *Ms.*, October 1972, 97; "Humphrey Nominated," *NYT*, August 29, 1968.

76. E. McGovern, *Uphill*, 147–49; Mankiewicz interview; Chester, Hodgson, and Page, *American Melodrama*, 583.

77. "Raging Protest," *Christian Science Monitor*, August 30; "Nominating Speeches" and "Humphrey Nominated," *NYT*, August 29, 1968.

78. McCarthy remained fairly popular despite his performance in Tuesday's debate and won 91 delegate votes to McGovern's 51. Unruh did not endorse McGovern because he planned to run for governor in 1970 and could not afford to alienate McCarthy's supporters. McGovern also lost scores of votes to Phillips, RFK's manager in the District of Columbia, who entered at the last minute, the first African American to compete for the party's presidential nomination.

79. "How Delegates," *NYT*, August 29; "McGovern Urges," and Wicker, "Humphrey Bars," *NYT*, August 30, 1968; and G. McGovern, *Grassroots*, 125.

80. Steinem interview and *Ms.*, 97; "McGovern to Resume," *SFAL*, August 29; "McGovern Urges Unity" and "Humphrey Bars," *NYT*, August 29 and 30, 1968; press conference transcript, August 29, 1968, Box 774, GSMP; Sandbrook, *Eugene McCarthy*, 213 (Broder).

81. Sandbrook, *Eugene McCarthy*, 213; Herbers and Wicker's stories, *NYT*, August 30, 1968; "McGovern Vote Change," *SFAL*, September 4, 1968.

82. "McGovern Must Resume," *NYT*, August 29, 1968, in Young, "Magnificent Obsession," 59; *Time*, September 6, 1968, 26; "Some Choices," *Life*, November 1, 1968, 32.

CHAPTER 17   THE KIND OF MAN THE FUTURE MUST HAVE

1. "McGovern Sees," *HDP*, September 1, 1968.

2. *SFAL*, July 17, August 21, and September 18, 1968; McGovern interview, August 7, 1993.

3. "Who's at the Wheel" (*WPO* editorial) and "Only U.S. Can," *HDP*, February 21 and 25, 1968; "Vietnam Underlies," *MDR*, March 19, 1968.

4. Brown University address, May 2, 1968, and "George McGovern Reports," April–May 1968, Box 774, GSMP.

5. "Administration Leaders" and "McGovern's Farm," *HDP*, April 16 and May 24, 1968; "Cites McGovern," *SFAL*, May 26, 1968; NFU Press release, March 16, 1967, Box 743, GSMP; Woods, *LBJ*, 813.

6. "Ag Crisis," *MDR*, May 21, 1968 and *CR*, February 1, 1968, 1802–8; "Farm Bill," "$400 Million," and "McGovern Asks," *HDP*, February 16 and March 20 and 24, 1968; *CR*, April 22, 1968, 10181–84 (quotes 10181 and 10183); *CR*, April 24, 1968, 10498–99, April 26, 1968, 10789 (resolution); Box 774, GSMP. See also, Susan Levine, *School Lunch Politics: The Surprising History of America's Favorite Welfare Program* (Princeton, NJ: Princeton University Press, 2009), 127–41.

7. "Magness," *MDR*, May 22, 1968; Bruce Stoner, "A Dove in the Dakotas: Can McGovern be Reelected?" *The Progressive* (April 1968): 16–19; "Nutrition Committee," *SFAL*, September 7, 1968.

8. Press conference transcript, August 29, 1968, Box 774, GSMP; Herbers, "McGovern Urges Aid," *NYT*, August 30, 1968; "Probers Blame," *SFAL*, December 2, 1968; DeBenedetti and Chatfield, *An American Ordeal*, 229. See also *SFAL* editorials, September 1 and 2, 1968.

9. "Republicans Offer," *SFAL*, September 1, and "May Have Trouble," *MDR*, September 3, 1968; quotes from ads in *SFAL* on September 16 and October 7, 1968. Schlesinger and Billington organized the Historians' Committee; correspondence in RABP.

10. See in *SFAL*, SD poll, September 18; Gubbrud ad, September 16; "Ghetto Dispersal," September 17, 1968; and *Christian Science Monitor*, August 19, 1968.

11. "Voice of the People," *SFAL*, September 19, 20, 22, and 23; "Scare Tactics," September 20, 1968.

12. *SFAL*, October 2 and 16, 1968.

13. "Gubbrud Stresses," "New Proposal," and "TV Special," *SFAL*, October 15 and 26 and November 2, 1968.

14. Interviews with David Krantz, George Cunningham, and John Holum; Steinem, "Notes from a Political Diary," *Ms.*, October 1972, 98; "Why Archie," "Teachers Meet," and "Senatorial Hopefuls," *SFAL*, October 9, 10, and 18, 1968; Clem, "The 1968 Election in South Dakota," *Public Affairs*, February 15, 1969 (Vermillion, SD, Government Research), 5.

15. McGovern ads, *SFAL*, September 20 and 24, 1968; *HDP*, October 18, and *WPO*, October 25, 1968.

16. See *SFAL*, September 3 and October 15, 20, 29, and 31, 1968.

17. "Senator and Opponent" and "McGovern Lists," *SFAL*, October 27 and 19, 1968.

18. "Mondale Lauds," "Older Citizens," "McGovern Says," and "Symington Backs," *SFAL*, October 16, 28, and 31 (2); author's interviews with Mankiewicz, Steinem, and Rowen; Steinem, "Notes," *Ms.*, October 1972, 98–99.

19. Interviews with Ann McGovern, George Cunningham, and John Holum; "McGovern Says," *SFAL*, October 31, 1968.

20. Isserman and Kazin, *America Divided*, 245–47; Lewis Gould, *1968: The Election That Changed America* (Chicago: Ivan Dee, 1993), 135–41 and 147–78; Link and Catton, *American Epoch*, 887–89; LaFeber, *Deadly Bet*, 139–45 and 171–75.

21. "Vietnam Remarks," *SFAL*, September 20; *NYT*, September 20 and 21, 1968; and Solberg, *Hubert Humphrey*, 375–79.

22. Solberg, *Hubert Humphrey*, 381–85; Woods, *LBJ*, 865–70; Gould, *1968*, 141–53; LaFeber, *Deadly Bet*, 145–47.

23. In *SFAL*: "Nixon-Gubbrud," "Gubbrud Stresses," "Urban Vote," "Needs Nixon," October 5, 16, 23, and 26; "Mundt Joins," "Mundt Censures," "Campaign Funds," "Wide Range," and "Battle to Wire," October 21, 24, 29; November 2 and 3; ads, October 20 and 31, November 1, 1968.

24. "Varied Issues," "Symington Backs," and "Minneapolis Editorial," in *SFAL*, October 28 and 31 and November 1, 1968; "Needs Nixon" and "Supporters Take," *SFAL*, October 26 and 30, 1968.

25. "War, Farm," "Candidates Offer," and "Urban Vote," *SFAL*, October 8, 12, and 23, 1968.

26. See Gould, *1968*, 153–61; LaFeber, *Deadly Bet*, 159–63; and Woods, *LBJ*, 870–75; "Politicians Cover" and "McGovern Says," *SFAL*, November 2 and 4, 1968.

27. Clem, "The 1968 Election," 1–5; "McGovern Shocks" and multiple stories in *SFAL*, *MDR*, and *HDP*, November 6, 1968.

28. "Tired but Happy," *SFAL*, November 6, 1968.

29. "Keeps Seat," *SFAL*, and "Rural Areas," *HDP*, both November 6, 1968; "Despite Misgivings," *LAT*, November 20, 1968.

30. Steinem, "Notes," *Ms.*, October 1972, 43; McGovern, "The New American," in *A Time of War, A Time of Peace*, 199; Roper, "A Tale of Two Senates" excerpts, *SFAL*, November 1, 1968; "George McGovern," *WPO*, October 25, 1968; *Time*, December 20, 1968, 19.

31. "Tired but Happy," *SFAL*, November 6, 1968.

EPILOGUE   COME HOME, AMERICA

1. Link and Catton, *American Epoch*, 889 and 851.

2. LBJ, *Vantage Point: Perspectives of the Presidency, 1963–1969* (New York: Holt, Rinehart and Winston, 1971), 549; LaFeber, *Deadly Bet*, 165 and 174–76.

3. Todd Gitlin, *The Sixties: Years of Hope, Days of Rage* (New York: Bantam, 1987), 334, and DeBenedetti and Chatfield, *An American Ordeal*, 229–31 and 235–37.

4. "Food Program," "Goals Outlined," and "Changes Had Influence," *SFAL*, November 18 and December 10 and 24; and "End Malnutrition," *MDR*, December 12, 1968.

5. "Vote Change," *SFAL*, September 4; "Missile System " and "Goals Outlined," *SFAL*, November 21 and December 10; and; see also Stephen K. Ward, "George McGovern and the Promise of a New Democrat: Reform and Electoral Politics in the Democratic Party, 1969–1970," in Watson, *George McGovern: A Political Life, a Political Legacy*, 92–117.

6. Quoted in Ward, "Promise of a New Democrat," in Watson, ed., *George McGovern: A Political Life, a Political Legacy*, 95.

7. "6400 Americans Killed" and "Withdrawal Urged," *SFAL*, November 17 and December 17, 1968; Herring, *America's Longest War*, 265; *NYT*, December 17 and 18, 1968.

8. "The New American," in G. McGovern, *A Time of War, A Time of Peace*, 201 (emphasis added).

9. "History, Policy, and Peace Research," December 28, 1968, Box 915, GSMP.

10. *CR*, June 17, 1965, 14,038–39.

INDEX

Abernathy, Tom, 216
Abrams, Creighton, 421
Acheson, Dean, 131, 143, 383
ADA. *See* Americans for Democratic Action (ADA)
Adams, John, 149
Adams, Sam, 56, 59, 64–65, 66, 67
Addams, Jane, 82
AFL-CIO (American Federation of Labor-Congress of Industrial Organizations): on antiwar activity, 365; Kennedy-Ives Act supported, 200–201; McGovern seen as hired hand of, 239, 249; merger, 200; Reuther purges communists from CIO, 205; Teamsters contrasted with, 237–38; George Wallace opposed by, 420
African Americans: Birmingham, Alabama, attacks on, 311–12; *Brown v. Board of Education*, 194, 311, 318; Civil Rights Act of 1964, 311, 312–13, 314, 316, 318; conditions of black urban neighborhoods, 359; as delegates at 1968 Democratic convention, 403; Humphrey supported by, 425; as issue in McGovern's Senate campaign of 1968, 415; in 1968 Democratic convention credential and delegate seating controversy, 402–3; Phillips as first to compete for Democratic presidential nomination, 497n78; prefer Kennedy over McCarthy, 385; at Progressive Party convention of 1948, 117; public opinion on treatment of, 340; race relations become key issue in 1968, 384; race riots of 1960s, 359–60, 369, 384, 414, 418; in South Dakota, 156; support for McGovern in 1968, 398; Voting Rights Act of 1965, 311, 331, 359. *See also* civil rights movement; racism; segregation
Agent Orange, 300, 316, 363
Age of Jackson, The (Schlesinger), 146
Agricultural Act of 1949, 158
Agricultural Act of 1958, 186
Agricultural Adjustment Acts, 79, 103
Agricultural Trade Development and Assistance Act (Public Law 480): as bureaucratic shuttlecock, 257–58; coordinating body for, 259; on exports to be carried in American ships, 270; India as largest

on war as consequence of failed US China policy, 355; on war in late 1950s, 298–99; on what John Kennedy would have done had he lived, 304–5

in World War II, 48–76; accidental bombing of Austrian farmhouse, 67–68, 72, 80; advanced flight training in Pampa, Texas, 53–54; Marian Anderson heard, 50; basic flight training at Coffeyville, Kansas, 52–53; basic training, 49–50; B-24 training in Liberal, Kansas, 54; on civilian casualties, 69–70; in civilian pilot training program, 48–49; correspondence with Bob Pennington, 45–46, 50, 51, 52, 53, 57, 58, 61, 70, 71, 72, 122; crew, 56–57; delivers surplus rations to European populations, 75; Distinguished Flying Cross, x, 72, 76, 85, 137, 171, 201; enlists in Army Air Corps, 40; fifth combat mission with blown tire, 63–64; first combat mission with his crew, 59–61; five missions as copilot, 59; flak nearly decapitates, 62–63; flies B-24 back to US, 75; grounded during January 1945, 65–66; ground training at Southern Illinois University, 50; gunnery and bombing practice at Mountain Home, Idaho, 56–58; homecoming from war, 77–78; impatience to get into the war, 46; joins 741 Squadron, 455 Bombardment Group, Fifteenth Air Force, 58; journey to Cerignola, Italy, 58–59; military career and public career of, 72; missions in tactical support of Fifth Army, 73; navigator Sam Adams killed on catch up mission, 66; nightmares about the war, 78, 80; ordered to report for duty,

46–47; primary flight training at Muskogee, Oklahoma, 51, 52; quarters in Cerignola, 59; on the reason for fighting the war, 40; reads American history during, 71–72; in San Antonio, Texas, in "the grind to the wings," 50–51; second mission, 61–62; as self-conscious about his youth, 57; send-off for duty, 46–47; sixth combat mission with two engines out, 64–65, 66; on Soviet Union in World War II, 71, 73; thirty-fifth and last mission, 73–75; on US having done right thing, 76

McGovern, George and Eleanor, Library, x

McGovern, Joseph (father): age difference with wife Frances, 12; approach to religion of, 15; attempts to keep family together after mother's death, 2–3; baseball career, 3, 15, 16; birth, 1; as building minister, 9; charisma, 9; child labor by, 2, 22, 99; children with Frances, 11; in *A Dakota Story* documentary, 279; death, 61; first wife's death, 9–10; at George and Eleanor's wedding, 51, 52; on George being called up, 47; George contrasts Social Gospel with, 83; on higher education for his children, 13; and his children's movie attendance, 18; hoboes fed by, 20; hopes for son George, 26; at Houghton Wesleyan Methodist Seminary, 3–5; on making the best use of one's time, 49; marries Frances McLean, 11; meets Eleanor, 44; musical evenings with family, 15; ordination, 5; personality, 12; relationship with his children, 12; relationship with son George, 12, 16, 47, 61; on religious education of his children, 14–15; relocates to Avon, 11; relocates to

377, 388, 391; McGovern v. Foss, 208, 210; McGovern v. Gubbrud, 377, 388, 391, 412, 415; on McGovern v. Lovre, 164, 169; McGovern v. Mundt, 236, 247, 250–51; on McGovern's Vietnam stand, 377; South Dakota 1968 Democratic presidential primary, 388; South Dakota presidential preference, 246–47 (1960), 414 (1968); on Vietnam, 326, 344, 353–54, 360, 373, 380–81
public works projects, 79–80, 276, 320
Pullman strike, 94
Pure Food and Drug Act, 22
Pyle, Ernie, 59, 70

Quadros, Jânio, 264, 265
Quiet American, The (Greene), 342

race riots of 1960s, 359–60, 369, 384, 414, 418
racism: Great Society for ameliorating, 311; McGovern attributes to Nixon, 398; Students for a Democratic Society call for action on, 333. *See also* segregation
radicalism. *See* political radicalism
railway strike of 1877, 94
Randolph, Jennings, 292, 294
Raskin, Marcus, 371
Rauh, Joseph, 371, 374
Rauschenbusch, Walter, 82, 83, 84, 93, 97
Rayburn, Sam: former First Ladies at banquet for, 160; on getting along by going along, 188; Johnson gotten New Deal position by, 306; and Kennedy-Ives Act, 200; McGovern endorsed in 1958, 209; on McGovern in agricultural price support debate, 185; as middle-of-the-road, 213–14, 306; as Speaker of the House, 180
REA (Rural Electrification Administration), 79, 160, 168, 217, 242–43, 278, 320
red-baiting: McGovern fears experiencing in Mitchell, 122; in McGov-

ern's Senate campaign of 1960, 242; by Mundt, 157; by Truman campaign, 113, 128; Vermont Resolution seen as accommodation with, 118
Red Scare: purge of East Asia specialists from State Department, 356, 489n20; warps American politics and foreign policy, 110, 116. *See also* McCarthyism
Reeves, Richard, 387
Reifel, Ben, 252, 473n51
Republican Party: antagonism toward Franklin Roosevelt, 23, 149; "communists in government" issue, 120, 128–29; congressional victories in 1946, 106; congressional victories in 1952, 152; contending wings of, 213; convention of 1968, 396; election results of 1958, 211–12; election results of 1966, 360; election results of 1968, 421–22; Federalists as forerunner of, 148; and Greek civil war, 109; isolationism in, 38; on Johnson's Vietnam policy, 316; Lend-Lease supported in, 39; McGovern complains of their monopoly in South Dakota, 275; McGovern on history of, 149–51; McGovern reaches out to Republicans in 1956 congressional election, 161–62, 173, 174, 205; on McGovern's "Christianity and the Challenge of Communism" speech, 138–39; missteps of 80th Congress, 120; on New Deal, 147, 150, 157; oil industry support for, 206; progressive wing, 21, 22; Roosevelt and Wilson's progressive policies dismantled by, 150; sectional and ideological shift after 1964 election, 321; in South Dakota 1952 presidential primaries, 142; South Dakota victories in 1962, 283–84; strategy for defeating McGovern, 422–23; takes conservative path, 23; on Yalta agreements, 106

POLITICS AND SOCIETY IN TWENTIETH-CENTURY AMERICA

Series Editors
William Chafe, Gary Gerstle, Linda Gordon, and Julian Zelizer

For a full list of books in this series see:
http://press.princeton.edu/catalogs/series/pstcaa.html

RECENT TITLES IN THE SERIES

The Rise of a Prairie Statesman: The Life and Times of George McGovern
by Thomas Knock

The Great Exception: The New Deal and the Limits of American Politics
by Jefferson Cowie

The Good Immigrants: How the Yellow Peril Became the Model Minority
by Madeline Y. Hsu

A Class by Herself: Protective Laws for Women Workers, 1890s–1990s
by Nancy Woloch

*The Loneliness of the Black Republican: Pragmatic Politics and the Pursuit
of Power* by Leah Wright Rigueur

*Don't Blame Us: Suburban Liberals and the Transformation of the
Democratic Party* by Lily Geismer

*Relentless Reformer: Josephine Roche and Progressivism in Twentieth-
Century America* by Robyn Muncy

Power Lines: Phoenix and the Making of the Modern Southwest
by Andrew Needham

Lobbying America: The Politics of Business from Nixon to NAFTA
by Benjamin C. Waterhouse

*The Color of Success: Asian Americans and the Origins of the Model
Minority* by Ellen D. Wu

The Second Red Scare and the Unmaking of the New Deal Left
by Landon Storrs

Mothers of Conservatism: Women and the Postwar Right
by Michelle M. Nickerson

*Between Citizens and the State: The Politics of American Higher Education
in the 20th Century* by Christopher P. Loss